D1712977

PUBLICATIONS OF THE NEW CHAUCER SOCIETY

THE NEW CHAUCER SOCIETY

Studies in the Age of Chaucer, the yearbook of The New Chaucer Society, is published annually. Each issue contains substantial articles on all aspects of Chaucer and his age, book reviews, and an annotated Chaucer bibliography. Manuscripts, in duplicate, accompanied by return postage, should follow the *Chicago Manual of Style,* 14th edition. Unsolicited reviews are not accepted. Authors receive free twenty offprints of articles and ten of reviews. All correspondence regarding manuscript submissions should be directed to the Editor, Frank Grady, Department of English, University of Missouri-St. Louis, 8001 Natural Bridge Road, St. Louis, MO 63121. Subscriptions to The New Chaucer Society and information about the Society's activities should be directed to David Lawton, Department of English, Washington University, CB 1122, One Brookings Drive, St. Louis, MO 63130. Back issues of the journal may be ordered from The University of Notre Dame Press, Chicago Distribution Center, 11030 South Langley Avenue, Chicago, IL 60628; phone: 800-621-2736; fax: 800-621-8476, from outside the United States: phone: 773-702-7000; fax: 773-702-7212.

Studies in the Age of Chaucer

Studies in the Age of Chaucer

Volume 25
2003

EDITOR

FRANK GRADY

PUBLISHED ANNUALLY BY THE NEW CHAUCER SOCIETY
WASHINGTON UNIVERSITY IN ST. LOUIS

PER
BR
1901
.58

The frontispiece design, showing the Pilgrims at the Tabard Inn, is adapted from the woodcut in Caxton's second edition of *The Canterbury Tales.*

ISBN 0-933784-27-9
ISSN 0190-2407

CONTENTS

CONTENTS

REVIEWS

CONTENTS

CONTENTS

Studies in the Age of Chaucer

PRESIDENTIAL ADDRESS
The New Chaucer Society
Thirteenth International Congress
July 18–21, 2002
University of Colorado at Boulder

The Presidential Address

After Chaucer

Helen Cooper
University College, Oxford

NEW CHAUCERIANS may have begun to notice a pattern about recent conferences—or at least about the three most recent, three being the minimum number for showing patterns at all. When we met in Paris in 1998, we focused on one major aspect of Chaucer's background culture, the French connection: the Francophone culture that dominated most of Europe, and which had included England in that domination since the time of the Norman Conquest. The year 2000 was the six hundredth anniversary of his death, and so we chose to meet in London, his home territory, the city where he was born and lived and died. There, we finished by, so to speak, killing him: or at least by assembling beside his tomb in Westminster Abbey in an event that testified not so much to his death as to his enduring appeal. As those of you who were there will recall, there was a huge audience for our readings. It filled the nave to capacity. Since his tomb became the center of Poets' Corner, our meeting there was a testimony not only to Chaucer himself but implicitly to his continuing influence on later writers; so it seemed only logical that we should continue that implied progression in this congress. Its theme of "Chaucer and After" was chosen to give us a chance to look at his reception and his influence.

The sheer power of Chaucer's text has been astonishing: he is creative dynamite. C. S. Lewis suggested that the whole core tradition of English

The following Presidential Address to the thirteenth New Chaucer Society congress at Boulder, Colorado, in July 2002, was designed as an introduction to the theme given to the conference, of "Chaucer and After." It is reproduced here as it was given, except for minor clarifications; and some small cuts made for reasons of time have been restored, most particularly in the text of *The Wanton Wife of Bath*.

poetry, what he called the "golden" tradition, lay in a line from *Anelida and Arcite*, from the invocation to Polyhymnia who

Singest with vois memorial in the shade[1]

—a line that one could argue to be central not only because of its sheer lyricism, but for its claims about poetry as fusing speech and memory, the contemporary and the traditional, the private voice of the poet given a public function. Borges, speaking from outside the English tradition, made an even greater claim for Chaucer: that the foundation of the whole genre of the novel lay in single line from the *Knight's Tale*,

The smylere with the knyf under the cloke.[2]

They are both claims such as one could base an entire conference on; and what better kind of conference to do it in than a Chaucer conference? So although there isn't the same tight connection with our place of meeting as there was for Paris or London, it is still appropriate that we should be meeting in the New World. Now, we are not looking back—or not only looking back—to Chaucer's background and place and history, but looking around at what is going on now; maybe even looking into the future.

As New Chaucerians, we have been translated, in the best medieval sense: *carried across* from one place to another, like a bishop transferring his see, or like the *translatio studii*, the westward transfer of learning. That movement was traditionally from Greece to Rome, then to France and the western edge of Europe, and now it has moved still further, over the Atlantic to the United States. And Chaucer is part of that body of learning, that canon of knowledge, that has been carried across. Chaucer was recognized as a canonical writer within a very few years of his death—as the best that English poetry could produce. Two hundred years after that, Robert Greene cast Chaucer as the patron saint of English poetry, seeing him not just as a canonical author, but as positively canonized.[3] Like the followers of the cult of a saint, we have brought his

---

[1] *Anelida* 18; C. S. Lewis, *The Allegory of Love* (Oxford: Oxford University Press, 1936), p. 201.

[2] *CT* I.1999; Jorge Luis Borges, "From Allegories to Novels," in *Other Inquisitions 1937–52*, trans. Ruth L. Simms (Austin: University of Texas Press, 1964), p. 157.

[3] *Greenes Vision* (?1592), in *The Life and Complete Works in Prose and Verse of Robert Greene*, ed. A. B. Grosart (1881–86; repr. New York: Russell and Russell, 1964), 12.201–81 (p. 215). The claim is put in Chaucer's own mouth within the fiction: "Who hath bin more canonised for his workes, than Sir Geffrey Chaucer?"

relics with us—translated them; not in the form of a body believed to hold perpetually living powers (our meeting close to his tomb in Westminster Abbey represented that kind of act of veneration), but in the form of a body of work, which unquestionably does hold such continuing power. In an age that has rejected the traditional canon of great writing, Chaucer is still indispensable.

Translation is perhaps the best image for what this congress is about. You will recall that the medieval Latin term for metaphor is itself "translation," *translatio*, the transfer of one meaning into a different vehicle. Our metaphor, our *translatio*, is translation itself.[4] In the first instance, that involves the transferring of Chaucer and his text into the alien vehicle of a conference (alien, because he would have found the idea so bizarre). It is a conference, moreover, in which we are considering a multitude of other translations of Chaucer—not just in the sense of verbal translation, though that comes into it: we even have a translation competition under way, which is currently in the process of being judged. One of the oddities of the English language is that a written text is translated by a translator, but spoken words are interpreted by an interpreter. Interpretation is, in that sense, the act of producing meaning; and we shall be doing plenty of that. But we shall be working with an abundance of other medieval senses of translation too: with translation as movement, for instance, whether movement between places, or from one period to another, or from one culture to another. That cultural change in turn points to translation as ideological supersession; "translation" was a term used for the replacement of the Old Law by the New. The reception of Chaucer over time shows a succession of such translations—something more than just appropriation, since each step includes a re-interpretation, a change of meaning. So Chaucer is translated in the Reformation, or the Enlightenment, or by the Romantics, or with the rise of the novel, as one reading of him supersedes another. Translation can also mean a radical alteration of state or condition, such as occurs between media, whether in the shift from manuscript to print, or print to hypertext, or into animation and film. Connected with that is translation in the sense of the transfer of domin-

---

[4] The various meanings of *translacioun* and *translaten* in Middle English are ably covered in the *Middle English Dictionary*. For a representative discussion of *translatio* as metaphor, see for instance Geoffroi de Vinsauf, *Documentum de modo et arte dictandi et versificandi* II.3.7–22, in *Les Arts poétiques du XIIe et du XIIIe Siècle*, ed. Edmond Faral (Paris: Champion, 1962), pp. 286–89.

ion or power or ownership (as in the *translatio imperii*): in the rivalry between the scholars' implicit claim to own Chaucer and the popularizing assumption that ownership doesn't come into it, that he is an inheritance common to everyone.

Conveniently, we have a little iconic example to hand of translation in most of those senses: namely, the cover design of the conference program you were sent in advance.[5] It shows a delightful illustration of the translation of Chaucer over place: Chaucer in the Rockies, with the mountains in the background. We know that it concerns Chaucer, because there are his works, in the shape of a fat clasp-bound, and therefore by implication manuscript, Complete Works. Yet such an image of Chaucer's works is of course a modern one—by which I mean an image that has existed only since the sixteenth century, when Chaucer's complete works were first assembled into one volume, as a *printed* book. The very title on the spine of the book in the picture, *Chaucer*, implies a unified authoritative and canonical author; and that too was a sixteenth-century invention, as shown in the title they gave to that printed volume, *The Works of Geoffrey Chaucer*. *Works* is a translation of the Latin *Opera*, the term reserved for canonical classical authors, and it was scarcely used again for any other English writer until the late seventeenth century.[6] Chaucer in his own lifetime, by contrast, was not canonical. He rejected all overt claims to any authority of his own, and he left his works incomplete, unfixed and scattered. That book on the program cover is a *constructed* Chaucer—though we are so used to it that we scarcely recognize it as such. Look too at the castle in the picture: it is not the kind of thing that was ever built in fourteenth-century England. This is late-medieval continental European architecture, from the

[5] An updated program with a different cover picture, of medieval aristocrats riding across a computer chip, was issued at registration: a substitution that gave the President a few anxious moments. The original cover was drawn by Dan Christoffel.

[6] The apparent exceptions are instructive. *The Workes of Sir T. More . . . wrytten by him in the Englysh tonge* (1557) implicitly derives its title from an author who writes predominantly in Latin. Skelton's *Pithy pleasaunt and profitable workes* (1568) offers a qualification of its authority by its very wording. Ben Jonson, who chose *Works* as the title for his collected plays in 1616, was greeted with derision. There are just two writers who come close to the Chaucerian model: Lindsay, whose works were collected as *The warkis of the famous and varthie knicht Schir Dauid Lyndesay* in 1568, a title which may perhaps represent the promotion of Lindsay as a Scots counterpart to Chaucer; and George Gascoigne, whose collected works appeared with the variant titles *Whole Woorkes* and, apparently as a correction, *Pleasauntest Workes* in 1587. All these editions except for Jonson's were posthumous collections. Spenser was first accorded a *Works* in 1679, Milton and Dryden in 1695, and Shakespeare in 1709.

Rhineland or the Loire, as popularized by Walt Disney. It's the kind of castle in which the prince lives in *Snow White*. This is a modern, media-derived, Disneyfied image of the Middle Ages, and so one that we feel at home with: there is no alterity of the Middle Ages here, because we have made it ours.

Maybe least obvious, look at the label—the ribbon with writing on it twisting around the castle. The underlying design of that, of an upright column with a label curling around it, formed half of the emblem of the Emperor Charles V, Holy Roman Emperor at the time of the great Spanish expansion into the New World. Doubled, it represented the Pillars of Hercules, as identified with the Straits of Gibraltar, the gateway to the Atlantic. The labels curling around the pillars in his emblem were inscribed with his motto for that westward expansion: "Plus Ultra," dog-Latin for "Yet Further." "Yet Further" is an appropriate motto for our own research too, for what we hope these congresses will achieve; but there is more to the emblem too. Those Pillars of Hercules were represented on some of the coins of the early Spanish settlers in the Americas, with the value of the coin sometimes replacing the motto on the labels. Hence, according to one theory, they came to be used as a monetary symbol, the one we now know as the $ sign.[7] It was probably not intentional on the part of the program illustrator to use that sign as his basic pattern, though if he made an initial doodle of the structure of his design he may well have noticed it, and it therefore makes a nice little exemplum of the limits of intentionality. Intentional or not, however, we can read it as a mini-allegory (a metaphor, a *translatio*), about the things that concern us, just as medieval scholars read allegories into Ovid: concerns that include the incorporation of the medieval, of knowledge and teaching and research (and indeed film-making), within modern economic structures, and the opportunities and the strains that that creates for all of us. It invites questions about globalization: not only about the *translatio studii*, studying Chaucer in the Rockies, but about how it is that a man who was writing before he or his readers knew that this continent existed, and writing moreover in

---

[7] See Marina Warner, "The Pillars of Hercules: *Plus Ultra*, Or the Limits to 'Virtù e Canoscenza'," forthcoming in *Raritan*; I gratefully acknowledge her assistance here. First minted in Milan in 1527 after Charles V's conquest of Italy, coins showing the device of the Pillars of Hercules were struck in New World silver after the colonial expansion of the 1530s, and continued to appear into the eighteenth century. The pieces of eight, the "8" of which has sometimes also been linked to the $, were among those to display the emblem.

what was then the most marginal of languages—one on the very edge, like Welsh today (only far more fragile than Welsh, since fourteenth-century English was subject to significant change every generation in time and in every county in space)—how it is that the whole anglophone world and beyond has now adopted this marginal and alien figure, and found him both central and oddly recognizable: someone in whom they can claim ownership. To put it another way: you can, if you want to be pedantic, read that design as wrong, unscholarly, and inauthentic; or you can read it as a central and genuine expression of Chaucer in the modern world, something that is rightly and properly a subject of analysis in itself, and an emblem for thinking about both the conscious and the unconscious degree of translation that we bring to Chaucer.

That program cover is therefore an emblem too for the kinds of things we have to keep in mind in a conference that identifies itself as being concerned with "Chaucer and After." There have been innumerable different perspectives and creative misreadings, entirely valid in themselves, that have been brought to his work by readers over the six hundred years since he died, and not least by ourselves, the modern academic community. These perspectives may show a greater or lesser degree of scholarship or authenticity, but they all have ways of telling us about how Chaucer can be read, and how we can read him. For scholarship alone will not keep Chaucer alive. None of us, I guess, became Chaucerians because we were fascinated by the textual differences between Hengwrt and Ellesmere,[8] nor even because of any of the theories you can apply to him. I was a committed medievalist by the age of four, and that was all to do with dragons and knights in armor: hopelessly unscholarly, and endlessly enthralling, and therefore in a way more authentic than scholarship. The Middle Ages simply had all the best stories; and, as I soon found out, Chaucer has the very best of the best stories. That is why it is so important that we have the filmmakers here at this congress: the people who are translating the Middle Ages into new media, into contemporary culture, for popular audiences of the twenty-first century. It's their work, not ours, that is likely to provide us with the Chaucerian enthusiasts of the future.

The filmmakers whom we have invited to the conference moreover show a remarkable creative intelligence in the various ways they mediate

---

[8] I was wrong; I was introduced to one such Chaucerian later in the conference.

(translate) the Middle Ages to such audiences. Brian Helgeland has had to withdraw because of production schedules, but his *Knight's Tale*, which appears at first glance to aim to portray a complete (though rather cleaned-up) medieval world, makes a generous and overt use of anachronism to appeal to modern adolescents. It was given a five-star top rating by the *Guardian* newspaper just a couple of weeks ago, on the grounds that its sheer enjoyability ought to override critical sniffiness (not least about its presentation of Chaucer as a very unstreetwise and stark-naked loser, even if one with a genius for words); and the *Guardian* got it right. Its plot, moreover, is a good conventional medieval "squire of low degree" story, poor boy wins the heart of disdainful noblewoman; and if the initial low degree is democratized downwards from the medieval analogues, that is compensated for by a good king-in-disguise (or prince-in-disguise) intervention to ensure the happy ending—one doesn't want to carry democracy too far, even for a modern audience. Anything I might say about *Monty Python and the Holy Grail* could only be superfluous; it is perhaps the most outrageously anachronistic of all such films, because of, rather than in spite of, its attention to authentic detail, and yet at least half the jokes are twice as funny if you are a medievalist than if you are not. Jonathan Myerson's remarkable animated *Canterbury Tales* was made with two soundtracks for separate broadcasts, one in modern English, one in Middle English. There, the basis of the animation is to find different visual equivalents for the stylistic and generic and thematic contrasts of the various tales, even a narrative equivalent for the parallelism of the Miller's and Reeve's tales; and so it foregrounds things that are sometimes, in these days of theory, pushed too far to the edge of our consciousness. Then there is the film that will be shown later in the conference, the Powell-Pressburger *A Canterbury Tale* of 1944: a grainy black-and-white film made with amateur actors, and the most complete translation of Chaucer of any of these, since after the first two minutes it seems to have nothing to do with him whatsoever. Yet it is astonishingly and impressively faithful to a vision that it believes to be his, and which we can recognize as such even though some of us may not agree with it: of disparate people from different and potentially hostile groups, rich and poor, male and female, upper and lower class, adult and child, military and civilian, from the old world and the New, who discover their common ground and unexpected sympathies. They are plausible people, like Chaucer's tellers, caught up in an implausible story, like the tales Chaucer had them tell; and each of those people has a love, an *entente*, a direction of the will, that can find its culmination in Canterbury. Its very obliqueness to Chaucer suggests that it assumes a much more sophisticated knowledge of him on the part of its audience than the modern films can.

That assumption of knowledge is an acknowledgment of the fact that Chaucer has been not just an object of study but an unbroken living tradition of reading since his own time, in a way that makes him unique in Europe. No other medieval vernacular author has been so consistently read. Even Dante and Petrarch went through many decades of obscurity in the seventeenth century (the worst period for Chaucer too, but in his case it seems to have been both briefer and less deep). That very continuity of tradition assumes a re-interpretation, a translation, as he is passed from one culture to another;[9] and it makes our own scholarly attempts to recover a kind of Chaucerian authenticity exceptionally complex, since our responses are colored, inflected, by that tradition, and it has itself created some ideas of Chaucer that we accept not as constructs but as fact—such as that Complete Works. We come at the end—though an end that's still moving forward—of six centuries of perpetual translation, which has its roots and its inspiration in Chaucer himself, for translation is central to his own writings too.

The first reference we have to Chaucer as a writer is that designation of him by Deschamps as a *grant translateur*.[10] We tend to take it as derogatory, to think of translators as not being poets in their own right; they are second-hand, enslaved to what their source authors have written. In those wider medieval meanings of *translatio*, however, Chaucer left his source authors far behind. He was one of the greatest translators of all time. He put anglophone culture—Middle English literature—in *living* touch with continental movements. By the fourteenth century, French and Latin literatures tended to exist alongside English, rather than interbreeding with it. Chaucer radically changed that. He brought into English the dominant French form of the *dit*. He transformed the universally popular continental form of the *fabliau*. He opened a channel to the greatest work of European vernacular literature, Dante's *Divine Comedy*. He took England's first step into Petrarchism. He reworked Boccaccio's genre-defying classical narratives. He traced the steps that

---

[9] See Stephanie Trigg's *Congenial Souls: Reading Chaucer from Medieval to Postmodern*, Medieval Cultures 30 (Minneapolis: University of Minnesota Press, 2002).

[10] In *Chaucer: The Critical Heritage*, ed. Derek Brewer (London and Boston: Routledge and Kegan Paul, 1978), 1.40.

Petrarch and Boccaccio had made in early humanist Latin; and he thought hard and seriously about Virgil and Ovid. He doesn't so much translate texts into Middle English as translate entire cultures over into England; and he changes them radically in the process, turns them into something different. It is therefore not just a carrying over, but a conversion from one thing into another, in the sense that Shakespeare used the term in *A Midsummer Night's Dream*: "O Bottom, thou art translated!"[11]

That radicalism of Chaucer's translation—acts of transformation rather than just transference—is nonetheless most clearly demonstrable at the level of the individual text.[12] Just how extreme the transformation can be is indicated by comparing what Lydgate called Chaucer's "Dante in Inglissh"[13] with Dante in Italian. "Dante in English" suggests an English translation of Dante; yet the only possible claimant to such a description, the *House of Fame*, is so different that it has sometimes been queried whether that is what Lydgate was referring to at all. If you think of it as a translation in those broader terms of interpretation and refashioning, however, then it makes much more sense. The *House of Fame* is, I believe, powered by two massively strong responses to Dante on Chaucer's part: first, that he was awesomely, mind-blowingly great as a poet; and second, that he was *wrong*. Second-guessing, or indeed first-guessing, the judgments of God was theologically inadmissible and close to heresy; and passing off your own opinions as eternal divine judgment was not the task of the poet, who had more than enough to do with coming to terms with the judgements offered by the unverifiable record of history. I have argued that case elsewhere[14] so I shall not re-argue it now; let me just offer it as an example of translation at its most extreme. "Dante in English"—in *Chaucer's* English—is Dante turned inside out and upside down, not because Chaucer misunderstood

[11] Chaucer's own most famous use of the word in this sense occurs in the *Clerk's Tale*, when Griselda is reclothed: "Unnethe the peple hir knew for hire fairnesse / Whan she translated was in swich richesse" (*CT* IV.384–85).

[12] The scholarship on this area of Chaucer studies is vast; Paul Beekman Taylor's *Chaucer Translator* (Lanham: University Press of America, 1988) is one that examines Chaucer's translation as a widely varying "hermeneutic procedure" that "mediates distinct and divergent zones of time, space and cultural perspectives" across a broad range of texts.

[13] *Lydgate's Fall of Princes* vol. 1, ed. Henry Bergen, EETS E.S. 121 (1918), Prologue 302–3; quoted in *Chaucer*, ed. Brewer, 1.53.

[14] "The Four Last Things in Dante and Chaucer: Ugolino in the House of Rumour," *New Medieval Literatures* 3 (1999): 39–66.

Dante—because he translates the *Comedy* inaccurately—but because he understands it all too well, in ways that we have been habituated into overlooking.

Now when you talk about Dante and Chaucer to Dantists, or even to many Chaucerians, you get a very patronizing response: not that Chaucer thought Dante was wrong, but that Chaucer got Dante wrong—that he was a weak follower, a bit thick, incapable of seeing Dante's glories, and so on. If that is true of views of the *House of Fame*, it is even more true of a much closer adaptation Chaucer made from the *Comedy*, his retelling of the story of Ugolino in the *Monk's Tale*, which is regularly charged with losing the terror and majesty of the original. That may be so; but it is also a very accurate and considered *response* to what is there in the *Inferno*. For Chaucer notices what Dante puts at the very end of his account, that there is no evidence for Ugolino's treachery except rumor, and he moves that to the very beginning.[15] If Dante will assume Ugolino's guilt, and back that up by claiming that God knows it too, Chaucer will insist on the inadequacy of human knowledge both of men's actions and of God's judgments, and offer a rival interpretation in which Ugolino may well be innocent. Dante starts from the premise that he as author is omniscient—as omniscient as God. Chaucer rewrites that as a premise that authorial omniscience is itself a fiction.

The point of that very briefly worked example of translation is not just to illuminate the *Monk's Tale*. I offer it rather as an exemplum of what translation in this broader sense can mean. Adaptation (such as happens for Ugolino) or influence (which is a better word for what is going on in the *House of Fame*) can too easily look like inadequacy—not least because Dante repeatedly tells us that he is a great poet, and we take his word for it. Chaucer perpetually tells us that he is quite hopeless, and we buy into that a surprising amount too. It's easy to forget that Chaucer is likely to have had an IQ the equal of Dante's, and a great deal more wiliness—streetwiseness. Matthew Arnold declared, famously, that Chaucer lacked high seriousness, that being another angle on the same reluctance to see the fullness of what is there in Chaucer.[16] The notion of a Chaucer who is *essentially* a poet of low frivolity, which I take it is the opposite of high seriousness, goes back to

[15] Dante, *Inferno*, 33.85; *CT* VII.2417.
[16] First appearing in the General Introduction to T. H. Ward's "English Poets" of 1880, the remark was reprinted in his 1888 *Essays in Criticism*; the passage is quoted in *Chaucer*, ed. Brewer, 2.219–20.

the 1590s: the decade when Robert Greene wrote a prose dream vision consisting of a story-competition between moral Gower and (by natural extension) immoral Chaucer, in what is explicitly a debate over the value and function of literature, in which "solaas" is pitted against "sentence." Chaucer tells a low and frivolous variant on the *Miller's Tale*, a fabliau with a university setting; but it is Gower's didactic tale that wins. Everyone whose first association of Chaucer is with the *Miller's Tale* is still thinking within that tradition. It was enlarged later, by an age that valued politeness, into the notion of "genial Chaucer"[17]—an image first put forward by Dryden, boosted by Arnold, and still widely repeated now. It may or may not be an accurate image of him, but even if it were, it is certainly not enough. As one of the great Chaucerian critics remarked, who ever heard of a genial customs officer?[18]

Chaucer's immediate followers, however, did not read him through the filter of Dryden or Arnold, and they did not compare him unfavourably with Dante (who was still very little known outside Italian-speaking areas).[19] They saw the comedy and the lightness, but the first thing they saw was the high seriousness: the Chaucer of the first of the Canterbury tales, not the Miller's, but the Knight's, with its questioning of the gap between deserving and reward—an anti-providential tale, about the arbitrary nature of cosmic justice. We have a habit of looking at Lydgate's *Destruction of Thebes* (a much more telling title than the mere *Siege of Thebes*, as James Simpson has pointed out),[20] and seeing an inadequate follower of Chaucer. We tend to forget that he wrote the Nun's Priest–influenced *Fables* and the Wife of Bath–influenced *Mumming at Hertford* too. Lydgate's sense of humor may be a bit elephantine,

[17] That Chaucer's geniality and bawdiness were connected is indicated by the popularity of his fabliaux as texts for modernization in the early years of the eighteenth century: see *Eighteenth-Century Modernizations from the Canterbury Tales*, ed. Betsy Bowden (Cambridge: D. S. Brewer, 1991), pp. 10–72.

[18] This paraphrases E. Talbot Donaldson's discussion (*Speaking of Chaucer* [London: Athlone Press, 1970], p. 2) of G. Lyman Kittredge's remark that "a naïf Collector of Customs would be a paradoxical monster."

[19] Two English bishops commissioned a Latin translation of the *Commedia* from the Franciscan Giovanni Bertoldi de Serravalle in the course of their attendance at the Council of Constance in 1415–16, in order to make it accessible to non-Italian readers in England, but it did not achieve wide circulation. See further David Wallace, "Dante in Somerset: Ghosts, Historiography, Periodization," *New Medieval Literatures* 3 (1999): 9–38.

[20] " 'Dysemol daies and fatal houres': Lydgate's *Destruction of Thebes* and Chaucer's *Knight's Tale*," in *The Long Fifteenth Century: Essays for Douglas Gray*, ed. Helen Cooper and Sally Mapstone (Oxford: Oxford University Press, 1997), pp. 15–33.

but it is simply leaping to conclusions on our part to imagine that he could not recognize those other qualities in Chaucer; and it is sheer arrogance on our part to assume that Lydgate himself did not know what he was doing. It is true that closeness to an author or an event does not necessarily guarantee accuracy of response; but neither does distance—our own distance from Chaucer, or from Lydgate. We tend to assume that Lydgate was trying to be a clone of Chaucer, and failing. We need to start from a different assumption, that he was translating Chaucer in that sense of *carrying him across* to something different. Neither Lydgate's voice nor his time was Chaucer's. He was writing two decades or more into that troubled fifteenth century, when the certainties of both Church and state were being called into question: when for the first time heretics were being burned in England, and when God seemed to have reneged on endorsing the lineal descent of the Crown.

That process of change should be obvious, especially in these days of "Only historicize!"; but the early Chaucerian poets are regularly damned to a man (with, just possibly, the occasional woman among them).[21] Within the last ten years, a major book was published that calls them, on its first page, "inept, dull or useless," writers who "share in the shadows of the secondary" and are "unworthy of [Chaucer's] mantle," and it repeats those assertions on almost every one of its over two hundred pages.[22] Take those as your premises, however, and they will simply be self-fulfilling. Accuse those writers of not being Chaucer, or not doing what Chaucer does, and of course you find that it is true. But if you take them rather as translators of Chaucer, as writers who are re-interpreting his work for their own culture, then they look very different. Fifteenth-century poetry has for too long been the Cinderella—even the ugly sister—of medieval studies. This conference, I hope, will give Cinderella a chance to go to her ball.

When we are looking at what happens After Chaucer, therefore, what is most interesting is not whether or not later writers got him wrong (which assumes that we know how to get him right), but that process of translation itself, of lifting him into another culture—whether it was a culture that valued most highly his rhetoric, as in the fifteenth cen-

[21] Two of the fifteenth-century Chaucerian poems, *The Floure and the Leafe* and *The Assembly of Ladies*, have first-person female narrators; they are anonymous, but there is no particular reason why they (and possibly some other poems in this tradition) should not have been female-authored, and in the case of *The Floure and the Leafe* it seems likely.

[22] Seth Lerer, *Chaucer and His Readers* (Princeton: Princeton University Press, 1993).

tury; or his anti-clericalism, which Reformation readers could interpret as proto-Protestantism; or his bawdiness, first signalled as his *dominant* quality in the 1590s; or his geniality, that social ease of the urbane but broad-minded gentleman, of the Enlightenment; or his naturalism, so prized in the era of the naturalistic novel; or his unwavering religious orthodoxy, which dominated the radical 1960s; or, now, his capacity to be mined for dissent, his resistance to the orthodoxies of Church and state, or for postcolonialism, or feminism, or queer theory, or new historicism, or any of our other current agendas. It is a long list of possibilities; and that too has its roots in a very odd feature of Chaucer's text—or rather, of its reception: which is, that despite the universal and consistent recognition of his greatness, there is almost no consensus whatsoever as to what that greatness consists of. Chaucer has been and is, I think, subject to more radical disagreements over meaning—over what he's saying, how we interpret or translate him—than any other major author, English or worldwide. Was he orthodox Catholic, or Lollard? misogynist or "womanis frend"?[23] a teacher of ethics, or a corrupter of the morals of youth,[24] or someone who regarded ideals as mere delusions, or as mystification by the political elite? a shrewd political commentator, or someone who kept his head on by keeping it down?

Those disagreements are not just the result of changes in culture: we typically find them co-existing. They are made possible by Chaucer's own refusal to give himself a stable identity. One moment he is claiming to follow, however humbly, in the steps of Virgil, Ovid, Homer, Lucan, and Statius (as he claims at the end of *Troilus*), and indeed of Dante, since he cribbed the idea from him. The next, he casts himself as the most feeble of poets, who, when called on for a tale, can only produce the *Melibee* (a translation in the most literal sense) or *Sir Thopas*. *Sir Thopas* is itself a different kind of translation—a single text that needs to be read, interpreted, in two opposing and exclusive ways at the same time, rather as Chaucer himself does. As the Host and the fictional listeners take both text and poet, it is quite dreadful; as Chaucer's real listeners and readers take it, it is a virtuoso performance by a brilliant poet. (Could Dante have done that? He certainly never did.) Chaucer translates the whole corpus of Middle English romance into something

[23] Gavin Douglas's famous epithet from the Prologue to his 1513 *Eneados* (line 448); see *Chaucer*, ed. Brewer, 1.86.

[24] This was William Tyndale's view, as expressed in 1528: see *Chaucer*, ed. Brewer, 1.87.

16

asinine—he gives it ass's ears, like Bottom. And yet he translates, reinvents, those ass's ears as a silk purse.

It is worth remembering that the interlude in which Bottom plays, "Pyramus and Thisbe", is the nearest thing we have in later literature to *Sir Thopas*, in which a virtuoso author writes something of quite breathtaking and brilliant awfulness. It is set within a play about a duke of Athens named Theseus, who has a Master of Ceremonies named Philostrate—the name taken by Arcite when he returns to Theseus's court in disguise. It is a play in which two young men in love with the same woman escape to the woods outside Athens, and in which human affairs are disrupted by a quarrelling fairy king and queen. Insofar as it has a source, the *Knight's Tale* is it, helped out by the *Merchant's Tale*, and by *Sir Thopas* too.[25] *A Midsummer Night's Dream* is, in other words, a translation of Chaucer, in one of those larger senses: a translation from one form into another—a reconceptualization of Chaucer, so radical as scarcely to be recognizable at all (as the *House of Fame* is scarcely recognizable as Dante), but which could not exist without him. O Chaucer, thou art translated!

A Midsummer Night's Dream was written in the middle of the 1590s: one of the most remarkable decades in whole history of English literature, and remarkable too for the abundance and variety of its translations of Chaucer, its ability to see half a dozen different Chaucers at once. So let me end with a quick Chaucerian tour of that decade, to show how densely rich and varied writing After Chaucer could be.

It opened with the publication of a story-collection entitled *The Cobbler of Canterbury*: a series of stories (mostly bawdy) told in imitation of "old father Chaucer" by a group of passengers in a boat going down the Thames.[26] They include an "old wife" who combines the coarser qualities of the Wife of Bath with the looks of her loathly lady; and the tale she tells was in turn incorporated as the subplot into a Jacobean

---

[25] For further discussion, see in particular E. Talbot Donaldson, *The Swan at the Well: Shakespeare Reading Chaucer* (New Haven and London: Yale University Press, 1985), pp. 7–49 (especially valuable on *Sir Thopas*, which Renaissance scholars have only recently begun to recognize as influential: see Peter Holland's edition of *A Midsummer Night's Dream* [Oxford: Oxford University Press, 1994], p. 88).
[26] *The Cobbler of Canterburie and Tarltons Newes out of Purgatory*, ed. Geoffrey Creigh and Jane Belfield, Medieval and Renaissance Texts 3 (Leiden, 1987). It was reprinted in 1598, and reworked (without the old wife) under the title *The Tinker of Turvey* in 1630.

dramatization of the Wife of Bath's own tale.[27] It was in response to the *Cobbler* that Robert Greene (who had been accused of writing it) commented on Chaucer's canonization, and wrote his own contestation of it in that dream-vision story-competition in which Chaucer represents a whole approach to literature, literature as pleasure. The year 1590 was also when Sir Thopas was given his apotheosis, when Spenser translated his dream of an elf-queen into Arthur's vision of his very different Faerie Queene, Gloriana.[28] That same first half of the *Faerie Queene* also contains Spenser's most direct translation from Chaucer, in the sense, that is, of lifting a chunk out of his text and carrying it over into his own poem. The very first speech put in the mouth of Spenser's exemplar of faithful married love, Britomart, incorporates three lines from the *Franklin's Tale*:

> Ne may love be compeld by maisterie;
> For soone as maisterie comes, sweet love anon
> Taketh his nimble wings, and soone away is gone. (III.i.25)

The passage has the potential to change meaning in the course of translation, as the elf-queen does; but here, importantly, it carries meanings over with it as well as words. The length and precision of the quotation show that the allusion is meant to be recognized, and so it invokes the original context of the lines as part of Spenser's initial definition of good love. Given how intensely contested the meaning of the *Franklin's Tale* now is, we should take Spenser's evidence into account as we read that tale; for again, translation can tell us not only about itself but about the original. Later in the decade Spenser wrote a completion of a kind to the *Squire's Tale*,[29] and Drayton wrote a whole little narrative poem

---

[27] John Fletcher's *Women Pleased*, in vol. 5 of *The Dramatic Works of the Beaumont and Fletcher Canon*, ed. Fredson Bowers (Cambridge: Cambridge University Press, 1982); and see Helen Cooper, "The Shape-Shiftings of the Wife of Bath," in *Chaucer Traditions: Studies in Honour of Derek Brewer*, ed. Ruth Morse and Barry Windeatt (Cambridge: Cambridge University Press, 1990), pp. 168–84.

[28] Edmund Spenser, *The Faerie Queene*, ed. A. C. Hamilton (2d edition, London and New York: Longman, 2000), I.ix.12–14.

[29] *Faerie Queene*, IV.ii.30–iii.52 (Books IV–VI were first published in 1596, together with a reprint of I–III). A completion that takes rather more of the original into account was written in the early seventeenth century by John Lane, a friend of Milton's father; one wonders if his fondness for the tale infected Milton, who gives it a special mention in *Il Penseroso* ("call up him who left half told / The story of Cambuskan bold"). Lane's version, which adds ten further cantos to Chaucer's two books, was not printed until it was edited by F. J. Furnivall, *John Lane's Continuation of Chaucer's Squire's Tale* (London: Chaucer Society, 1888, 1890).

modelled on *Sir Thopas*.[30] Then in 1598, Speght's great edition of Chaucer's works appeared: the first edition to be provided with a full scholarly paratext, such as our own editions still have, and which marked the start of the academic tradition of the study of Chaucer. Yet it was also that decade that made him most freely available even to the illiterate, by retelling some of the tales in broadside ballads[31] and by putting him on the public stage. Quite apart from the submerged Chaucerianism of *A Midsummer Night's Dream*, three of the tales were dramatized: two of them, eponymously titled after Palamon and Arcite and Constance, are now lost, and just one survives, *Patient Grissil*.[32] Were there people in the 1590s, I wonder, who watched those plays, or later Shakespeare's own much darker *Troilus and Cressida* or *The Two Noble Kinsmen*, and complained that they got Chaucer wrong?

Let me finish, however, with a work that offers a translation in another sense as well: the sense of rapture into another world, translation to heaven. This is the broadside ballad called *The Wanton Wife of Bath*. The first record of its existence dates from 1600, the very end of that great decade; and that comes in the form of an order for the burning of all copies. We know of its continuing existence over the succeeding years since in 1632 a publisher was imprisoned for reprinting it—specifically, for "scurrilously abusing holy scripture": the worst of charges in an age that privileged the Word over the Incarnation.[33] Not surprisingly, in view of this history, the earliest surviving copy dates only from 1670,

[30] "Dowsabell," in *The Works of Michael Drayton*, ed. William Hebel (Oxford: Blackwell, 1961), 1.88–91. See also John Burrow, "Sir Thopas in the Sixteenth Century," in *Middle English Studies Presented to Norman Davis*, ed. Douglas Gray and E. G. Stanley (Oxford: Clarendon Press, 1983), pp. 69–91.

[31] A broadside ballad of the Griselda story dates from this decade; in addition to the *Wanton Wife of Bath*, given below, a ballad version of the *Wife's Tale* appeared in 1612. For details, see Helen Cooper, *The Oxford Guides to Chaucer: The Canterbury Tales* (2d ed., Oxford: Clarendon Press, 1966), pp. 423, 427. *Troilus* had been put into ballad form as early as 1566.

[32] The anonymous *Palamon and Arcite* is recorded in Henslowe's diary as performed in 1594; it was almost certainly different from the version by Richard Edwardes played before the Queen at Christ Church when she visited Oxford in 1566. The *Dream* probably dates from 1595, so may well have been influenced by the 1594 play, though Shakespeare's admixture of other tales strongly suggests that he went back to Chaucer too. *Patient Grissil*, by Dekker, Chettle and Haughton, is edited in Fredson Bowers's *The Dramatic Works of Thomas Dekker* (Cambridge: Cambridge University Press, i.207–98). On the Renaissance dramatizations of Chaucer, including *Fair Constance of Rome* by Dekker and others (1600), see Ann Thompson, *Shakespeare's Chaucer: A Study in Literary Origins* (Liverpool: Liverpool Texts and Studies, 1978), Chap. 2.

[33] See Caroline Spurgeon, *Five Hundred Years of Chaucer Criticism and Allusion, 1357–1900*, Chaucer Society (1914–25), IV.54 (Appendix A).

but once its publication was freely allowed, it became widely popular.[34] The *Cobbler of Canterbury* had imitated the obvious things about the Wife in its own Old Wife; but the original Alison has the ability to *surprise* in ways that you recognize as right, as in some sense authentic. The Prologue to the fifteenth-century *Tale of Beryn*, having brought her to Canterbury, shows her not husband-hunting, but inviting the Prioress and the hostess of the inn where the pilgrims take lodging into the tavern garden for a good female gossip, of the kind the original Wife tells us she enjoys.[35] The broadside takes up another feature of her Prologue, her familiarity with Scripture—though here, the Bible is given more of a sinner's reading than a woman's reading.[36] So here is the translation into another world of the Wife of Bath: one of the most delightful translations ever made After Chaucer.[37]

> In Bath a wanton wife did dwell,
>   as Chaucer he doth write,
> Who did in pleasure spend her days,
>   in many a fond delight.
>
> Upon a time sore sick she was,
>   and at the length did dye:
> Her soul at last at Heavens gate
>   did knock most mightily.

[34] On its history from its first appearance to the nineteenth century, including its parallel appearance after 1700 in a longer and more religious version, see Betsy Bowden, "The Oral Life of the Written Ballad of *The Wanton Wife of Bath*," *North Carolina Folklore Journal* 35.1 (Winter-Spring 1988): 40–77. She has traced 23 different prints of the shorter version and 20 of the long.

[35] See her Prologue, *CT* III.544–47.

[36] The idea underlying the ballad, of an altercation between a soul and the keepers of either Heaven or Hell, appears in a number of texts across Europe, and seems to have been widespread in folk currency. The closest analogue is perhaps the fabliau *Le Vilain qui conquist Paradis par plait* (in *Nouveau Recueil complet des fabliaux*, ed. Willem Noomen and Nico van den Boogard, vol. 5 [Assen/Maastricht: Gorcum, 1990], no. 39 [pp. 1–38]), in which the protagonist verbally attacks Peter, Thomas and Paul; God allows him entry after he claims the right to Paradise on the basis of his good works towards the poor. There had been a manuscript in England since the early fifteenth century (Nottingham University Library MS Mi.LM.6), but it is highly unlikely to have been a source for the ballad.

[37] The reading was dedicated to the memory of Beverley Kennedy, that great supporter of the Wife of Bath, who died in 2001. The text is transcribed from what is probably the earliest surviving copy, as contained in *The Pepys Ballads*, facsimile with introduction by W. G. Day (Cambridge: D. S. Brewer, 1978), II.39. Bowden provides a facsimile of a copy of the same print held in the Bodleian Library, Oxford, "Oral Life," pp. 44–45. Obvious misprints, such as incorrect pronouns, are silently emended, and punctuation lightly modernized where it might be confusing.

Then Adam came unto the gate,
   who knocketh there? quoth he.
I am the wife of Bath, she said,
   and fain would come to thee.

Thou art a sinner, Adam said,
   and here no place shall have.
[And so art thou, I trowe,][38] she said,
   now gip, you doting Knave.

I will come in, in spight, she said,
   of all such churles as thee;
Thou wast the causer of our woe,
   our pain and misery;

And first broke Gods Commandements,
   in pleasure of thy wife.
When Adam heard her tell this tale,
   he ran away for life.

Then down came Iacob to the gate,
   and bids her pack to Hell:
Thou false deceiver, why? said she,
   thou maist be there full well.

For thou deceiv[d]st[39] thy father dear,
   and thine own brother too.
Away went Iacob presently
   and made no more ado.

She knocks again with might and main:
   and Lot he chides her straight.
Why then, quoth she, thou drunken ass,
   who bids thee here to [prate]?[40]

With thy two Daughters thou didst lye,
   on them two Bastards got:

---

[38] This is a variant (for the Pepys "Alas for you, good sir") given by Thomas Percy in the first edition of his *Reliques of Ancient Poetry* (London, 1767, 3.145–51; the ballad was censored from the third, standard, edition). Percy used the Pepys copy as his own copy-text, but incorporates a few variants that make better sense, and which may well be drawn from other versions since they are not indicated as being his own substantive "improvements" (which he often marks by inverted commas; he also silently archaizes the spelling and smoothes the meter, in ways not adopted here).

[39] Percy; Pepys "deceivest."

[40] Percy; Pepys "wait."

And thus most tauntingly she chast
   against poor silly Lot.

Who knocketh there, quoth Iudith then,
   with such shrill sounding notes?
Alas fine Minks, you ca[me] not he[re],[41]
   quoth she, for cutting throats.

Good Lord, how Iudith blusht for shame,
   when she heard her say so:
King David hearing of the same,
   he to the gate did go.

Quoth David, Who knockes there so loud,
   and maketh all this strife?
You were more kind, good Sir, she said,
   unto Vriahs Wife.

And when thou caused thy Servant
   in battel to be slain;
Thou caused then more strife than I,
   who would come here so fain.

The Womans mad, said Solomon,
   that thus doth taunt a King.
Not half so mad as you, she said,
   I know, in many a thing.

Thou hadst seven hundred wives at once,
   for whom thou didst provide;
For all this, three hundred whores
   thou didst maintain beside:

And those made thee forsake thy God,
   and worship stocks and stones;
Besides the charge they put thee to
   in breeding of young bones.

Hadst thou not been beside thy wits,
   thou wouldst not [thus][42] have ventred;
And therefore I do marvel much,
   how thou this place have entred.

[41] For Pepys "cannot hear"; Percy "This fine minkes surely came not here."
[42] Supplied from Percy.

I never heard, quoth Ionas then,
   so vile a scold as this.
Thou whoreson Run-away, quoth she,
   thou diddest more amiss.

I think, quoth Thomas, womens tongues
   of Aspen leaves be made.
Thou unbelieving wretch, quoth she,
   all is not true that's said.

When Mary Magdalen heard [her][43] then,
   did come unto the gate:
Quoth she, good woman, you must think
   upon your former state.

No sinner enters in this place
   quoth Mary Magdalen, then
Twere ill for you, fair Mistris mine,
   she answered her again.

You for your Honesty, quoth she,
   should have been stoned to death:
Had not our Saviour Christ come by,
   and written on the earth.

It is not by your occupation
   you are become Divine:
I hope my soul in Christs passion,
   shall be as safe as thine.

Then rose the good Apostle Paul,
   unto this wife he [cried],[44]
Except thou shake thy sins away,
   thou here shall be denied.

Remember, Paul, what thou hast done,
   all th[r]ough[45] a lew'd desire,
How thou didst persecute Gods Church,
   with wrath as hot as fire.

Then up starts Peter at the last,
   and to the gate he hies:
Fond fool, quoth he, knock not so fast,
   thou weariest Christ with cries.

[43] Supplied from Percy.
[44] Percy, completing the rhyme; Pepys "said."
[45] Percy; Pepys "although."

Peter, said she, content thy self,
    for mercy may be won,
I never did deny my Christ,
    as thou thy self hath done.

When as our Saviour Christ heard this,
    with heavenly Angels bright,
He comes unto [t]his[46] sinful soul;
    who trembled at his sight.

Of him for mercy she did crave.
    quoth he, thou hast refused
My proffer, grace, and mercy both,
    and much my name abused.

Sore have I sinned, O Lord, said she,
    and spent my time in vain,
But bring me like a wandring sheep
    unto thy flock again.

O Lord my God, I will amend
    my former wicked vice;
The thief [for one] poor silly word[47]
    past into Paradise.

My Laws and my Commandements
    saith Christ, were known to thee;
But of the same in any wise
    not yet one word did ye.

I grant the same, O Lord, quoth she,
    most lewdly did I live;
But yet the loving Father did
    his Prodigal Son forgive.

And I forgive thy soul, he said,
    through thy repenting cry;
Come therefore enter into my joys,
    I will thee not deny.

---

[46] Percy; Pepys "his."
[47] Percy; Pepys "at the poor silly words."

THE BIENNIAL CHAUCER LECTURE
The New Chaucer Society
Thirteenth International Congress
July 18–21, 2002
University of Colorado at Boulder

The Biennial Chaucer Lecture

Changing Chaucer

Richard Firth Green
Ohio State University

L ET ME BEGIN BY APOLOGIZING for the somewhat gnomic quality of my title. It's the result of a scholarly subterfuge I suppose most of us have practiced at one time or another: the trick of being noncommittal when asked to provide the title for a paper we're still months away from writing. If, last January, I was pretty sure I wanted to talk to you today about forms of metamorphosis in Chaucer, I was still unsure whether to choose *The Franklin's Tale* or *The Canon's Yeoman's Tale* as my primary text. The first, with its shapeshifting black rocks, would, I felt, be an appropriate choice for a talk in Boulder, Colorado, though I discovered to my chagrin not only that Chaucer himself never uses the word "boulder," but that in Middle English it invariably denotes something we would probably refer to as a cobblestone, certainly nothing that could possibly be construed as a potential hazard to coastal shipping. The alchemical transformations of *The Canon's Yeoman's Tale*, then, were looking like the better bet as the subject for a talk in a city that was, after all, founded on a gold rush, when I was struck by line 751. It offered me, I suddenly realized, the opportunity to move beyond alchemy itself into a wider consideration of Chaucerian metamorphosis. Let me read it to you in its immediate context:

> Whan we been there as we shul exercise
> Oure elvysshe craft, we semen wonder wise,
> Oure termes been so clergial and so queynte. (VIII [G]:750–52)[1]

I might equally well have stumbled across line 842 from the same tale:

> Nay, nay, God woot, al be he monk or frere,
> Preest or chanoun, or any oother wyght,

[1] All Chaucer references are to *The Riverside Chaucer*, 3d ed., ed. L. D. Benson et al. (Boston: Houghton Mifflin, 1987).

> Though he sitte at his book bothe day and nyght
> In lernying of this elvysshe nyce loore,
> Al is in veyn, and parde, muchel moore. (VIII [G]:839–43)

The key word shared by both these passages is, of course, *elvysshe*: alchemy is an elvish calling and the alchemist's expertise is elvish. Now Chaucer famously describes himself as elvish in the prologue to *Sir Thopas*, and that passage has garnered a certain amount of critical attention (from John Burrow among others),[2] but these two appearances of the word have excited far less comment. Beth Robertson, for instance, in her recent piece on Constance's "elvyssh" power, alludes to the Thopas prologue but not the *Canon's Yeoman's Tale*.[3] Most critics, if they notice the lines at all, seem to believe that *elvysshe* is merely a synonym for "devilish,"[4] though Lee Patterson and Lisa Kiser are notable exceptions. Patterson calls *elvysshe* a "loaded" term that draws attention to "the analogy between the poet and his alchemical yeoman" (an important insight, though not one I shall be exploring this afternoon);[5] for Kiser, it suggests "the ease with which people can be led to believe in illusion as if it were truth" (for my immediate purposes, a more promising line of thought).[6]

Now, for some reason modern editors have been uncomfortable with the Canon's Yeoman's unequivocal statement that the alchemist's expertise is an elvish one. They evidently don't want to believe that he says what he quite patently does say. Skeat, substituting connotation for denotation, glosses both occurrences of *elvysshe* as "mysterious (but used in the sense of foolish)";[7] Robinson glosses the second only as "strange

---

[2] "Elvish Chaucer," in *The Endless Knot: Essays in Old and Middle English in Honor of Marie Borroff*, ed. M. Teresa Tavoramina and R. F. Yeager (Cambridge: D. S. Brewer, 1995): 105–11.

[3] "The 'Elvysshe' Power of Constance," *SAC* 23 (2001): p. 178.

[4] I.e., Bruce A. Rosenberg, "Swindling Alchemist, Antichrist," *Centennial Review* 6 (1962): p. 577.

[5] "Perpetual Motion: Alchemy and the Technology of the Self," *SAC* 15 (1993): p. 55; see also David Raybin, "'And pave it al of silver and of gold': the Humane Artistry of the Canon's Yeoman's Tale," in *Rebels and Rivals: The Contestive Spirit in the Canterbury Tales*, ed. Susanna Greer Fein, David Raybin, and Peter Braeger (Kalamazoo: Medieval Institute, 1991), pp. 189–212, and Mark Bruhn, "Art, Anxiety, and Alchemy in the Canon's Yeoman's Tale," *ChauR* 33 (1999): 288–315.

[6] *Truth and Textuality in Chaucer's Poetry* (Hanover, N.H.: University Press of New England, 1991), p. 145.

[7] The sense of "foolishness" evidently became attached to *elvysshe* from its juxtaposition with *nyce* at line 842.

[and foolish]"; Baugh gives "weird, strange" for the first, and "mysterious [(and) foolish]" for the second; Pratt gives "mysterious, weird," and Benson, "strange, mysterious" for both; while Schmidt offers "strange, weird" for the first and simply "strange" for the second. Finally, the Oxford *Chaucer Glossary* offers "mysterious" for both occurrences, though its definition *is* graced with a question mark. The *Middle English Dictionary* (never one to stick its neck out in such matters), despite having found six citations to justify its rendering the word elsewhere as "belonging or pertaining to the elves; possessing supernatural skill or powers" dutifully glosses both the Canon's Yeoman's uses of the word as "mysterious, strange." I have found only three exceptions to this intimidating scholarly consensus: both Maurice Hussey and John Fisher remain in the realm of connotation, but at least in the right corner of that realm, it seems to me: the first glossing both instances of the word as "supernatural" and the second (glossing the first only) as "mysterious, magical." Finally, while A. C. Cawley glosses the *elvysshe* of line 751 as "mysterious," the *elvysshe nyce* of line 842 he renders somewhat tautologously as "[silly] elvish." Here, then, is a useful demonstration of the limitations of statistical proof in the humanities: *elvysshe* in these passages is glossed as "mysterious" a total of thirteen times, as "strange" eight times, and as "weird" four times, but only once each as "supernatural" and "magical," and once (correctly, if redundantly) as "elvish." This final gloss, though it may well be a slip on Cawley's part, is, I believe, the only adequate one: *elvysshe* does mean "elvish," or, in other words, the craft of alchemy, says the Canon's Yeoman, is a fairy craft. In fact, "faery-like, fantastick" is precisely the gloss given these passages by Thomas Tyrwhitt in 1778, and this, or some variant of it, was standard in all the major Victorian editions except Skeat's: Edward Moxon (1843), Thomas Wright (1853), Robert Bell (1854), Richard Morris (1872) and Alfred Pollard (1898).[8] I shall return later to the interesting question of why this simple proposition seems to have been so difficult for Skeat and his successors to accept, but first I must try to show why I believe Chaucer means what he says here.

The word *fairy* in Middle English regularly refers to a place or region,

---

[8] Wright's Percy Society edition (1847–51) was printed without a glossary but, following Moxon's example, subsequent reprintings simply appended Tyrwhitt's glossary (see E. P. Hammond, *Chaucer: A Bibliographical Manual* [London: Macmillan, 1908], pp. 138, 212, 509); Bell glosses "like a fairy," Morris, "fairy-like, supernatural," and Pollard, "elflike" (though a 1919 reprint has "aerial").

the abode of those creatures known to the French as *fées* (Latin, *fata*): *fées*, in other words, live in *fé-erie*.[9] Though *fairy*, influenced perhaps by the native word *ferli*,[10] might also be used as a synonym for a "marvel" or "wonder" (and indeed is so used, at least twice, by Chaucer himself),[11] and sometimes in a more generalized sense as "magic," it does not seem to be used to denote an actual creature, a fairy, much before the middle of the fifteenth century.[12] Nor, as far as I can see, is it used unambiguously an as adjective: in Middle English one referred to a "fairy knight" much as we now refer to a "New York policeman," that is to say *fairy* in such phrases was primarily appositional not adjectival. The standard word in Chaucer, as in most other Middle English writers, for what we generally call a fairy was *elf*, and, if he felt himself in need of an adjective, the one Chaucer would have found nearest to hand was *elvish*. The denotative meanings of "elvysshe craft" and "elvysshe loore," then, are "a skill, or knowledge, exercised by (or resembling one exercised by) the fairies." But to say this is merely to beg a further question: "Why is an alchemist like a fairy?" But before I attempt an answer I want us to be quite clear about the kind of fairy we are talking about here.

What Chaucer calls elves were what C. S. Lewis, sounding very like his friend J. R. R. Tolkein, called "high fairies"—though in actuality many medieval commentators would have thought of these beings as the lowest (in the hierarchical sense) of the fallen angels.[13] Keith Thomas has pointed to a common tendency among those who discuss fairies to assign them to the past, and in order to show that this has always been the case he cites the opening lines of *The Wife of Bath's Tale*,[14] yet we don't have to go back "manye hundred yeres" before

[9] Cf. "Gawain . . . / Though he were comen ayeyn out of Fairye" (*SqT* 95–96).

[10] Cf. "Me befel a ferly, of fairie me þouȝte" (Pr. 6); *Piers Plowman: The A Version*, ed. George Kane (London: Athlone Press, 1960), p. 175.

[11] I.e., *MerchT* 1743, *SqT* 201 (cf. *SGGK* 240).

[12] *The Chaucer Glossary* glosses *fayerye* (at *WBT* 872 and 859, and *MerchT* 2039) as "magic creatures," though in none of these instances is this meaning unavoidable. The English prose translation of *Melusine* (ca. 1500), however, clearly uses the word to denote a creature: "the whiche somme called Gobelyns / the other ffayrees, and the other 'bonnes dames' or good ladyes" (7–9); ed. A. K. Donald, EETS ES 68 (London, 1895), p. 4.

[13] *The Discarded Image: An Introduction to Medieval and Renaissance Literature* (Cambridge: Cambridge University Press, 1964), p.130. For a more recent study of these "high fairies," see Laurence Harf-Lancner, *Les Fées au moyen âge* (Paris: Champion, 1984).

[14] *Religion and the Decline of Magic: Studies in Popular Beliefs in Sixteenth- and Seventeenth-Century England* (1971; Harmondsworth: Penguin Books, 1973), p. 726.

Chaucer's time to find a writer willing to acknowlege fairies as his contemporaries. Gervase of Tilbury writing at the beginning of the thirteenth century has left us a succinct account of them in his *Otia Imperialia*;[15] after paraphrasing a passage from Augustine's *City of God* (15:23) on *incubi* (which he breaks off when Augustine begins to express skepticism), he writes:

For, indeed, we know that this has been daily proved by men of unimpeachable reputation, because we have heard of certain lovers of these kinds of spirit (which are called *fada*), and how, when they committed themselves in marriage to other women, they died before they intermingled themselves in carnal coupling with their consorts. And we have observed that most enjoyed the highest state of worldly fortune, but when they extricated themselves from the embraces of this kind of fairy, or spoke of them in public, they lost not only worldly prosperity but even the paltry comfort of life itself.[16]

Such fairies in other words were human in appearance and scale, and were capable of engaging in social and sexual intercourse with human beings. Originally they seem to have been regarded as beneficent or at least admirable creatures, though they were early demonized in Christian tradition.[17] But when Shakespeare paired Oberon with the mischievous Puck or had Titania send her diminutive servants to steal honey bags from the humble bee he unfortunately promulgated a confusion between these high fairies and other very different kinds of spirit that has lasted down to our own day.

There is no question that, unlike Shakespeare, Gervase regarded his *fata* as quite distinct from the kind of household spirits that Shakespeare's probable informant, Reginald Scot, calls *virunculi terrei*, "such as was Robin good fellowe, that would supplie the office of seruants."[18] The more benevolent of such spirits Gervase calls *portuni* (ed. Banks and Binns, pp. 674–77). Though of diminutive stature, they are capable, like Robin Goodfellow, of assisting with household chores, but, while generally harmless, they do seem to find some amusement in leading

[15] On Gervase himself, see H. G. Richardson, "Gervase of Tilbury," *History* 46 (1961): 483–86.
[16] Ed. and trans. S.E. Banks and J.W. Binns (Oxford: Clarendon Press, 2002), p. 730.
[17] H. Stuart, "The Anglo-Saxon Elf," *Studia Neophilologica* 48 (1976): 313–19.
[18] *The Discouerie of Witchraft* [STC 21864] (London, 1584), p. 521.

benighted travelers astray.[19] The more mischievous, on the other hand, he calls *folletti* (English *foliots*). These "inhabit the houses of simple rustics" and are given to throwing sticks, stones, and domestic utensils about; though capable of human speech, their appearance is nonhuman (ed. Banks and Binns, pp. 98–9). Beliefs of this kind were certainly common enough in Chaucer's day, but though there were a number of English terms for such spirits (the most common seems to have been *gobelyn*),[20] *elf* was not one of them.

Though an Englishman, Gervase of Tilbury himself nowhere employs a latinized form of the Germanic word *elf*,[21] but in an earlier discussion of *incubi* (which, following Geoffrey of Monmouth, he describes as "impure spirits dwelling between the moon and the earth, . . . their nature partly that of humans and partly of angels"), he adds that "when they wish, they assume human shape and lie with women. Of these Merlin, who (as the *Historia Britonnorum* tells us) had a mother, but no human father, is said to have been conceived." He then adds, "we know that many such things are seen daily."[22] A very late thirteenth-century writer Robert of Gloucester gives us much the same account of Merlin's origins, but he, significantly, does use the word *elf*:

> He [Vortigern] esste at is clerkes . were it to leue were.
> Þe clerkes sede þat it is . in philosofie yfounde .
> Þat þer beþ in þe eyr an hey . ver fram þe grounde .
> As a maner gostes . wiȝtes as it be .
> And me[n] may ȝem ofte an erþe . in wilde studes yse .
> & ofte in mannes forme . wommen hii comeþ to .
> & ofte in wimmen fourme . hii comeþ to men al so .
> Þat men clupeþ eluene (lines 2747–54)[23]

---

[19] Cf. *Les Évangilles des quenouilles*, ed. Madeleine Jeay (Montréal: Les Presses de l'Université de Montréal, 1985), p. 141 (lines 2296 ff.).

[20] Cf. *Dives and Pauper*'s attack on such superstitions "as settynge of mete or drynke be nyȝt on þe benche to fedyn Al-holde [eiþer gobelyn]," ed. Priscilla H. Barnum, 2 vols., EETS, 275, 280 (London, 1976–80), I: 157; and a Middle English sermon's mention of "alle suche [that] been led al nyȝt with gobelyn, and erreth hider and thider," cited in G. R. Owst, *Literature and Pulpit in Medieval England*, 2d ed. [Oxford, Blackwell: 1966], p. 113).

[21] For the etymology of *elf*, see Claude Lecouteaux, *Les Nains et les elfes au moyen âge*, 2d ed. (Paris: Imago, 1997), pp. 121–23.

[22] Ed. Banks and Binns, p. 96.

[23] *The Metrical Chronicle of Robert of Gloucester*. ed. W. A. Wright, 2 vols., Rolls Series (London, 1887), 1:196.

So, too, does the *South English Legendary*, a closely related text.[24] In a description of the ranks of the fallen angels, it gives a similar account of these creatures, but adds some intriguing details:

And ofte in forme of womman . in moni deorne weie
Me sicþ of hom gret companie . boþe hoppe & pleie
Þat eleuene beoþ icluped . þat ofte comeþ to toune
And bi daie muche in wode beoþ . & biniȝte upe heie doune
Þat beoþ of þe wrecche gostes . þat of heuene were inome
And many of hom a Domesday : ssolleþ ȝute to reste come (lines 253–58)[25]

That Chaucer himself associated elves with *incubi* is proved by his juxtaposition of the two terms in the opening lines of *The Wife of Bath's Tale*. The author of *Dives and Pauper*, writing in the early fifteenth century, shows that this was a common association: "And þe fendis þat temptyn folc to lecherie ben mest besy for to aperyn in mannys lycnesse & wommanys to don lecherye with folc & so bryngyn hem to lecherie, & in speche of þe peple it arn clepyd eluys. But in Latyn whan þei aperyn in þo lycnesse of man it arn clepyd *incubi*, and whan þei aperyn in þo lycnesse of woman it arn clepyd *succuby*."[26]

Now that we have some idea of what kind of creature is denoted by the phrase *elvysshe loore*, it is time finally to return to the question "why is an alchemist like a fairy?" Actually this riddle turns out to be considerably simpler than "why is a raven like a writing desk?" and when we ask ourselves how what Alan Fletcher has recently called "the discourse of fairyland"[27] resembles "the discourse of alchemy," the similarities appear really quite striking. For one thing, alchemists, like fairies, are liminal figures, both geographically and culturally, hovering around the edges of established communities and established beliefs. In a well-known passage, Chaucer describes his Canon's natural habitat as "the suburbes of a toun":

Lurkynge in hernes and in lanes blynde,
Whereas thise robbours and thise theves by kynde

[24] O. S. Pickering, "*South English Legendary* Style in Robert of Gloucester's *Chronicle*," *Medium Ævum* 70 (2001): 1–18.
[25] Ed. Charlotte D'Evelyn and Anna J. Mill, 3 vols., EETS OS 235, 236, and 244 (London, 1956 and 1959), 2:410.
[26] Ed. Barnum, 2:118
[27] "*Sir Orfeo* and the Flight from the Enchanters," *SAC* 22 (2000): 158–62.

> Holden hir pryvee fereful residence,
> As they that dar not shewen hir presence. (VIII (G). 658–61)

Like his master, the Canon's Yeoman also belongs, in Judith Herz's words, "to no particular place," a Protean man "who must shift about the world seeking an identity."[28] Finally, the second alchemist is equally rootless:

> On his falshede fayn wolde I me wreke,
> If I wiste how, but he is heere and there;
> He is so variaunt, he abit nowhere. (VIII (G). 1173–75)[29]

Culturally, too, alchemists were outsiders, even potential proto-revolutionaries. As John Reidy pointed out in 1972, "no alchemist ever seems to have been a genuine member of the establishment."[30] Some, indeed, like Chaucer's "Arnold of the Newe Toun," a follower of Joachim of Flora, were even involved in revolutionary movements that brought them to the notice of the Inquisition (Reidy, p. 46), though by and large, as Sheila Delany points out, alchemy was an even more marginal social phenomenon than heresy. Still there is no mistaking, as Delany puts it, "the subversive orientation" of alchemical practice in general nor of Chaucer's alchemists in particular.[31] For John Scattergood, the "suburban tenements of those who were by choice and necessity outsiders" represents "the potential for growth and change and the energy to turn the world upside-down."

The cultural liminality of *fairies* scarcely needs elaborating—indeed, for Diane Purkiss in a recent book this becomes one of their defining characteristics: "a fairy is someone who . . . presides over the borders of our lives, the seams between one phase of life and another,"[32] but in a geographical sense, too, fairies are marginal figures, appearing suddenly (rather as Chaucer's Canon and his Yeoman do) in "wilde studes," "in

---

[28] "The Canon's Yeoman's Prologue and Tale," *Modern Philology* 58 (1961): 231.

[29] Cf. Senior's injunction to his fellow alchemists to "shun the society of men" [*abhorre conventum hominum*]; quoted in Joseph E. Grennen, "Chaucer and the Commonplaces of Alchemy," *Classica et Mediaevalia* 26 (1965): 311.

[30] "Alchemy as Counter-Culture," *Indiana Social Studies Quarterly* 24 (1971–72): 49.

[31] "Run Silent, Run Deep: Heresy and Alchemy as Medieval Versions of Utopia," in *Medieval Literary Politics: Shapes of Ideology* (Manchester: Manchester University Press, 1990), p. 11.

[32] *At the Bottom of the Garden: A Dark History of Fairies, Hobgoblins, and Other Troublesome Things* (New York: New York University Press, 2001), p. 4.

wode," and "upe heie doune," though also capable of making clandestine visits to human habitations: "þat ofte comeþ to toune." Their own dwelling places lie beyond the pale of the civilized world (though, for all that, they are not uncivilized in themselves). Almost always one must cross water to reach them, and sometimes, as in the romances of *Huon of Bourdeux*, *Partenope of Blois*, or *Reinbrun*, they lie at the very margins of Christendom itself, in far-off Asia Minor or even Africa. In French romance *fées* generally inhabit splendid castles buried deep in the woods (Bercilak's castle in *Sir Gawain and the Green Knight* conforms to this type). In the insular tradition, however, fairies are quite as likely to live, as in *Orfeo*, *Reinbrun*, *Thomas of Ercledoune*, and Marie de France's *Yonec*,[33] in underground kingdoms entered through a cave, and such a locus is confirmed in non-romance English sources. The normally skeptical William of Newburgh, for instance, has left us a vivid account of a local countryman (a *rusticus*), returning late and slightly drunk from visiting a friend, who stumbles upon "a large well-lit dwelling crowded with men and women reclining at table, as at a formal feast" located inside a nearby hillock (*proximo tumulo*).[34] This subterranean dimension to elvish lore may well have deepened its alchemical associations in Chaucer's mind.

Fairy beliefs, like alchemy, hovered at the very edge of orthodox thought. Unwilling to reject them outright, most churchmen rationalized fairies into minor devils (rather as, we might remember, the Yeoman demonizes his alchemists),[35] a position that even a Wycliffite preacher might be prepared to contemplate:

And summe dremen of þes feendis [of the loweste rank] þat summe ben elues and summe gobelynes, and haue not but litil power to tempte men in harme

---

[33] *Sir Orfeo*, ed. A. J. Bliss, 2d ed. (Oxford: Clarendon Press, 1966), lines 347–54; for *Reinbrun*, see *The Romance of Guy of Warwick*, ed. Julius Jupitza, EETS ES 42, 49, and 59 (London, 1883–91), 3:657 (st. 78); *Thomas of Erceldoune*, ed. Ingeborg Nixon (Copenhagen: Akademisk Forlag, 1980), 1:38–39 (lines 169–72); for *Yonec*, see Marie de France, *Lais*, ed. Alfred Ewert (Oxford: Blackwell, 1963), pp. 90–91 (lines 345–56).

[34] *The History of English Affairs, Book I*, ed. and trans. P. G. Walsh and M. J. Kennedy (Warminster: Aris and Phillips, 1988), pp. 118–21 (chap. 28). Cf. Ralph of Coggeshall's account of the green children of Woolfpits in his *Chronicon Anglicanum*, ed. J. Stevenson, Rolls Series (London, 1875), pp. 118–20; Gerald of Wales on the adventures of Eliodor in his *Itinerarium Kambriae*, ed. James F. Dimock, *Opera Omnia VI*, Rolls Series (London, 1868), pp. 75–78; and Gervase of Tilbury on the antipodeans (ed. Banks and Binns, pp. 242–45). For seventeenth-century survivals of this tradition, see John Aubrey, *Remaines of Gentilisme and Judaisme*, ed. James Britten, Folklore Society 4 (London, 1881), pp. 30 and 123.

[35] See John Gardner, "*The Canon's Yeoman's Prologue and Tale*: An Interpretation," *Philological Quarterly* 46 (1967): 1–17.

of soule; but siþ we kunne not proue þis ne disproue þis spedili, holde we vs in þe boundis þat God telliþ vs in his lawe. But it is licli þat þes feendis haue power to make boþe wynd and reyn, þundir and lyȝttyng and oþir wedrus.[36]

Far more radical is the *South English Legendary*'s speculation that many of these "wrecche gostes . þat of heuene were inome . . . a Domesday ssolleþ ȝute to reste come."[37] The romances are sometimes eager to enfold fairies within the bosom of the church. The hero of Marie de France's *Yonec*, for example, despite living in an underground kingdom and being able to turn himself at will into a hawk, protests to his lady that he is a true Christian.[38] Melusine (p. 31) and *Desiré*'s fairy mistress[39] are similarly insistent on their own religious orthodoxy, while Sir Partenope is reassured to hear his invisible lady, whose bed he happens to be sharing at the time, swear by the Virgin Mary.[40] In much the same vein, Oberon presents Huon of Bordeaux with a magic cup, whose powers are activated by making the sign of the cross over it.[41] However, such passages smack strongly of rationalization, and the popular view is probably better represented by *Thomas of Erceldoune* (lines 201–20) and its descendant, the ballad *Thomas Rymer*:[42]

> O see not ye yon narrow road,
>> So thick beset wi thorns and briers
> That is the path of righteousness,
>> Tho after it but few enquires.
>
> And see not ye that braid braid road
>> That lies across yon lillie leven?
> That is the path of wickedness,
>> Tho some call it the road to heaven.

[36] *English Wycliffite Sermons, 1*, ed. Anne Hudson (Oxford: Clarendon Press, 1983), p. 686. Chaucer himself might have been prepared to concede this much; cf. his association of "ayerissh bestes" with bad weather in the *House of Fame* (lines 964–69).
[37] See W. P. Ker, "The Craven Angels," *MLR* 6 (1911): 85–87.
[38] *Lais*, p. 85 (lines 149–52).
[39] *Lais féeriques des XIIᵉ et XIIIᵉ siècles*, ed. Alexandre Micha (Paris: Flammarion, 1992), p. 128 (lines 386–90).
[40] *The Middle English Versions of Sir Partenope of Blois*, ed. A. Trampe Bödtker, EETS ES 109 (London, 1912), p. 36 (lines 1341–47; cf. lines 1883–93).
[41] *The Boke of Duke Huon of Burdeux*, ed. S. L. Lee, EETS ES 40 and 41 (London: 1884–1883), p. 76.
[42] *The English and Scottish Popular Ballads*, ed. Francis James Child, 5 vols. (Boston: Houghton Mifflin, 1882–98), 1:317–29.

And see not ye that bonny road
    Which winds about the fernie brae?
That is the road to fair Elfland,
    Whe[re] you and I this night maun gae. (Child 37A: 12–14)

I know of no text that so vividly exemplifies the marginal status of elvish lore, approached only by way of this third path unmapped in orthodox Christian cartography.[43] Whether dabbling in such lore implied a "subversive orientation," analogous to that we have noted in connection with alchemical practice, is rather more difficult to determine, but a riot that occurred in Kent in 1451 suggests that this might not be an altogether preposterous speculation: in a curious precursor of the events leading to Robert Walpole's notorious Black Act, a hundred men invaded the deer park of Humphrey Stafford, Duke of Buckingham, at Penshurst, and disguised with long beards and blackened faces, stole 82 beasts, "*nuncupantes se esse servientes Regine del Faire* [proclaiming themselves to be the servants of the Queen of Fairy]."[44] It is amusing to imagine these poachers as precursors of another set of dissidents as well: modern British environmental protesters apparently refer to their acts of sabotage against construction equipment as "pixieing."[45]

Closely related to the sense of marginality shared by these two discourses is their common concern with secrecy. Again, Chaucer's Yeoman cites Arnold of Villanova: "'For this science and this konnyng,' quod he, / 'Is of the secree of the secretes, parde.'" (VIII (G). 1446–47). Thomas Norton tells us that the alchemist must jealousy protect this secret of secrets from all but a single trusted pupil:

> When age shal greve hym to ride or go,
> One he may teche but then nevir no mo,
> For this science most evir secrete be. (lines 235–37)[46]

If (as William Thynne and Elias Ashmole suppose) Norton learned his craft from George Ripley, his master was a poor role model, for only a few years later Ripley was offering the same secret to Edward IV:

[43] Cf. Thomas D. Hill, "'The Green Path to Paradise' in Nineteenth-Century Ballad Tradition," *Neuphilologische Mitteilungen* 91 (1990): 483–86

[44] *Documents Illustrative of Medieval Kentish Society*, ed. F. R. H. Du Boulay (Ashford: Kent Archaeological Society, 1964), p. 255.

[45] Andy Letcher, "The Scouring of the Shires: Fairies, Trolls, and Pixies in Eco-Protest Culture," *Folklore* 112 (2001): 151.

[46] *Ordinal of Alchemy*, ed. John Reidy, EETS 272 (London, 1975), pp. 11–12.

For like it you to trust that truly I have found,
The perfect way of most secret Alchymie,
Which I will never truly for marke nor for pound
Make common but to you, and that conditionally,
That to your selfe you shall keepe it full secretly.[47]

The irony of proclaiming occult knowledge in so public a place seems
lost on both these authors,[48] though, as Joseph Grennen pointed out in
1965, the empty admonition to secrecy is so widespread in alchemical
treatises as to constitute something of, in Ernst Curtius's sense of the
term, a *topos* (lines 309–11);[49] it is certainly one Chaucer himself employs in the *Canon's Yeoman's Tale*.[50]

A similar epistemological paradox occurs in Gervase of Tilbury's account of fairies, for those who spoke of their fairy mistresses in public,
he tells us, lost "even the paltry comfort of life itself." But in that case,
we might wonder what they had been doing telling Gervase's infor-
mants about them. In fact a proscription against revealing the name or
the existence of a fairy lover is a commonplace in the romances, though,
like Helen Cooper's "magic that does not work,"[51] such prohibitions
rarely seem to be rigidly enforced in practice. English readers will be
most familiar with this motif from Thomas of Chestre's retelling of
Marie de France's *Lanval*,[52] but it also appears in a French analogue to
Lanval called *Graelent* (lines 311–12), in another Breton lai called *Ty-
dorel*, in which a fairy lover who has been making regular nocturnal
visits to the hero's mother disappears for ever after he has been acciden-
tally glimpsed by a knight of the court (l. 214), and in yet a third, *Desiré*,

[47] "The Epistle . . . written to King Edward the 4," st. 5, from *The Compound of Alchymy (1591)*, ed. Stanton J. Linden (Aldershot: Ashgate, 2002), p. 90.
[48] There are six fifteenth-century manuscripts of Ripley's *Compound* and two of Nor-ton's *Ordinal*; see, *A Manual of the Writings of Middle English*, gen. ed. Albert Hartung, Vol. 10, Pt. 25 (*Works of Science and Information*), ed. George R. Keiser (New Haven: Connecticut Academy of Arts and Sciences, 1998), pp. 3793 and 3797.
[49] "Chaucer's 'Secree of Secrees': An Alchemical 'Topic'," *Philological Quarterly* 42 (1963): 562–66; also the same author's "Chaucer and the Commonplaces of Alchemy," *Classica et Mediaevalia* 26 (1965): 309–11.
[50] The Yeoman himself makes a similar admonition even as he offers to betray al-chemical secrets to the pilgrims (line 643), the first canon berates him for this breach of confidence (line 696), and the second prepares to gull the chantry priest by dangling before him the prospect of initiation into arcane mysteries (lines 1136–39).
[51] Helen Cooper, "Magic That Does Not Work," *Medievalia et Humanistica: Studies in Medieval and Renaissance Culture* ns. 7 (1976): 131–46.
[52] *Sir Launfal*, ed. A. J. Bliss (London and Edinburgh: Nelson, 1960), lines 361–65.

where even the hero's revelation of his fairy mistress in the privacy of the confessional endangers their future happiness together (lines 371–72).[53] Among the longer romances, *Partenope of Blois* makes particular use of this motif; Partenope's mother's inquisitiveness leads him to break his mistress's command ("þys loue be-twyn vs shall be kepte preve" [l. 1826]), and almost destroys the relationship.

If alchemy might easily be imagined as elvish in both its cultural situation and its epistemological status, it was also akin to the fairy world in the elusive nature of the rewards it promised.

> The philosophres stoon,
> Elixer clept, we sechen faste echoon;
> For hadde we hym, thanne were we siker ynow.
> But unto God of hevene I make avow,
>
> . . . .
>
> For al oure sleighte, he wol nat come us to. (VIII (G).862–67)

Two of these rewards are almost identical in both the discourse of alchemy and the discourse of fairyland: unlimited wealth and the prolongation of life. Though the power to turn base metal into gold might be the most celebrated of the philosopher's stone's properties, for Thomas Norton it is was rather the prospect of its extending his life that made it most desirable:

> For above all erthlye thynge
> I mooste desire & love connynge;
> And for the red stone is preseruatife,
> Moost precious thynge to length my life,
> The rede stone, saide I, is levire to me
> Then all were Golde that I wolde so to be. (lines 2595–600)

George Ripley expresses a similar disdain for filthy lucre, but evidently still found comforting the notion that the stone would support him into an extreme old age:

> And if thou had not at the beginning to fill a spoon,
> Yet maist thou them so multiply both white and red.
> That if thou live a 1000. yeres, they shall stand thee in sted.[54]

[53] See *Lais féeriques*, ed. Micha, pp. 36, 164, and 126.
[54] "Recapulatio totius operis praedicti," st. 9; ed. Linden, p. 84.

Like Norton, Ripley seems to have lived a good long life, though still far short of the millennium he'd apparently been hoping for.

It is not difficult to show that the elusiveness of the philosopher's stone was matched in the middle ages by a similar belief in evanescent fairy gold. The worldly prosperity of those who enjoyed the embraces of fairies is mentioned by Gervase of Tilbury, as is its propensity to vanish as soon as its source was revealed.[55] Again, Thomas of Chestre's *Launfal* offers the example that will be most familiar to readers of Middle English: Triamour gives Launfal a magic purse, but as soon as he reveals her existence to Guivevere it loses its power (lines 733–36). Similarly a gold ring given to Desiré by his lover vanishes from his finger when he mentions her to his confessor. The lavish munificence of the fairies is almost a commonplace in the romances we have been discussing, as is its conditional nature and its association with danger, but these motifs can also turn up in some rather unexpected places: in Sir John Mandeville's account of the Castle of the Sparrowhawk in Armenia, for example,[56] or in Adam de la Halle's thirteenth-century farce, the *Jeu de la Feuillée*.[57] They even make an appearance in the fabliau *Le chevalier qui fist parler les cons*, where one of three grateful fairies endows the knight with inexhaustible wealth.[58] Perhaps the oddest manifestation of these motifs is in a set of Latin exercises, composed for use in Exeter Grammar School around 1450. One of these reads:

A general rumour is spreading among the people that the spirits of the air, invoked by necromantic art to find mines of gold, silver, azure, and other treasures hidden in the ground, have appeared in bodily form, stirring up great tempests in the air which are not yet calmed, it is believed, nor allayed.[59]

Of course, this should no more be regarded as the record of an actual event than the sentence from the Victorian traveler's phrase-book, "our

[55] For seventeenth-century survivals of this tradition, see Aubrey, *Remaines of Gentilisme*, ed. Britten, pp. 29 and 102.

[56] *Mandeville's Travels*, ed. M. C. Seymour (Oxford: Clarendon Press, 1967), p. 108 (lines 17–21)

[57] Ed. Jean Dufournet (Gand: Éditions scientifiques, 1977), p. 74 (lines 659–63 and 667–69).

[58] *Nouveau recueil complet des fabliaux*, ed. Willem Noomen and Nico Van Den Boogaard, 10 vols. (Assen/Maastricht: Van Gorcum, 1983–98), 3:163 (lines 206–13).

[59] Nicholas Orme, "An English Grammar School ca. 1450: Latin Exercises from Exeter (Caius College MS 417/447, Folios 16v–24v)," *Traditio* 50 (1995): 280 (C20).

postillion has been struck by lightning," but it does presumably represent the kind of thing that someone might credibly have said.

If the philosopher's stone prolonged human life, so too did contact with the fairies. The fairies themselves were, of course, famously long-lived, as C. S. Lewis recognizes when he calls them the *longaevi* (pp. 122 ff.), a term he found in Martianus Capella (echoed later by Bernardus Silvestris). Oberon, a son of Julius Caesar, tells Huon of Bordeaux that "I shall never seme elder than thou seest me now" (p. 74), and whenever fairies appear in romance they seem to enjoy this gift of eternal youth.[60] It is perhaps less often recognized that they also have the power to bestow this gift on their mortal companions. After what he believes to have been only a three-day stay with his fairy mistress, Guingamour returns home to discover that more than three hundred years have passed, that the king, his uncle, is long dead, and his castle lies in ruins.[61] Similarly, in *Thomas of Ercledoune*, when the hero complains about being sent home after what he, too, thinks has been only three days, he learns that the truth is rather different:

> "Lufly lady, now late me bee,
> ffor certis, lady, I hafe bene here
> Noghte bot þe space of dayes three."
> "ffor sothe, Thomas, als I þe telle,
> Þou hase bene here thre ȝere and more;
> Bot langere here þou may noghte dwelle." (lines 282–87)

Where a disillusioned Guingamour had returned to his fairy refuge, True Thomas, after this briefer temporal disruption, lives out the rest of his life among humankind.

If the discourse of alchemy and the discourse of fairyland resemble one another in their shared marginality, their obsession with secrecy, and the nature of the rewards they dangle before their initiates, their most obvious point of resemblance, of course, is their common concern

---

[60] Despite religious hostility, the beauty and nobility of the elves remained proverbial throughout the middle ages; see, e.g., the description of Candace in *The Wars of Alexander* (ed. Walter W. Skeat, EETS ES 47 (London, 1886), p. 263): "Scho was so faire & so fresche . as faucon hire semed, / An elfe oute of an-othire erde / or ellis an Aungell" (lines 5257–59); or the goddesses who vie for the judgment of Paris in *The Seege or Batayle of Troye* (ed. Mary Elizabeth Barnicle, EETS OS 172 (London, 1927), p. 40): "In þat forest weore gangand / ffoure ladies of eluene land" (lines 507–8).

[61] *Lais féeriques*, ed. Micha, pp. 96–97 (lines 596–608)

with transformation. In the case of alchemy this hardly needs to be demonstrated: the transmutation of metals to which the alchemical enterprise was directed arose from a profound engagement with the fact of mutability; to appreciate what the alchemists were doing, says Sherwood Taylor, "we must think ourselves back to the position of the intelligent man [or woman] viewing changes in things and changes in himself and focusing his mind not so much on the details of the individual changes as on the idea of change."[62] With fairyland, however, the proposition may need little more elaboration. Paradoxically, for creatures that enjoy a state of perpetual youthfulness, the very substance of fairies seems inherently unstable: as John Gower writes of Medea as she is cursing Jason: "In sondri wise hir forme changeth, / She semeth *faie* and no womman."[63] Thus it is that the old can appear young, as in *The Wife of Bath's Tale*, for instance, and the young old, as in *Thomas of Erceldoune* (or vice versa). Even more striking, in view of the oft remarked changes in the Canon's Yeoman's complexion,[64] is the frequency with which fairies also undergo shifts of colour. Bercilak in *Sir Gawain and the Green Knight* is an obvious instance, but so typical is such chromatic instability that when the narrator encounters the protean figure of "Prevy Thought" in the late-fifteenth-century allegory *The Court of Love* he is immediately reminded of fairyland:

> "Yon is," thought [I], "som spirit or som elf,
> His sotill image is so curious:
> How is," quod I "that he is shaded thus
> With yonder cloth, I not of what colour?" (lines 1270–73)

Petitcrû, the dog from Elfland that Tristram sends as a present to Ysolt, is similarly polychrome: no one "could relate or record its shape or appearance, for however one looked at the dog it displayed so many colours that no one could discern or fix them,"[65] and in Malory the ring that Lyones lends to Sir Gareth for the Tournament at the Castel Peryl-

---

[62] F. Sherwood Taylor, *The Alchemists* (1952; St Albans: Granada, 1976), p. 16.

[63] *Confessio Amantis*, 5:4104–05, in *The English Works of John Gower*, ed. G. C. Macaulay, 2 vols. EETS ES 81 and 82 (London, 1900–1901), 2:58.

[64] See Joseph E. Grennen, "Chaucer's Characterization of the Canon and His Yeoman," *Journal of the History of Ideas* 25 (1964): 279–81.

[65] *The Saga of Tristram and Ísönd*, trans. Paul Schach (Lincoln: University of Nebraska Press, 1973), p. 95. Cf. *Le Roman de Tristan par Thomas*, ed. Joseph Bédier (Paris: SATF, 1902), 1:218–19.

lous endows him with a similar quality: "at one tyme [he] semed grene, and another tyme at his ageynecomyng he semed blewe. And thus at every cours that he rode to and fro he chaunged his colour, so that there myght neyther kynge neyther knyghte haue redy congnyssaunce of hym."[66]

A further aspect of fairy lore that may resonate with *The Canon's Yeoman's Tale* is the belief, in George Puttenham's words, "that the Fayries vse to steale the fairest children out of their cradles, and put other ill fauoured in their places, which they called *changelings*, or *Elfs*."[67] Latham claims that this belief was peculiar to late-sixteenth-century England,[68] but Jean-Claude Schmitt has found traces of it throughout Europe from the thirteenth century onward,[69] and has used it brilliantly to explicate Etienne de Bourbon's curious description of the cult of Saint Guinefort, the Holy Greyhound; evidently, this cult fed on a popular conviction that the canine saint was able to restore stolen babies to their heartbroken parents. Though there appear to be no direct references to changelings in England before the mid sixteenth century, indirect evidence for such a belief is provided by the use of the Middle English noun *conjoun*, cognate with a rare French word *chanjon*, meaning "changeling."[70] Although it often seems to be little more than a vague term of abuse (the *Middle English Dictionary* offers "fool, nincompoop, worthless person, rascal . . . a lunatic, . . . a brat"), there are enough places where it is used of children, particularly in contexts where there might be a question about their parentage, to suggest that its original sense still clung to it. Thus in the Auchinlech *Of Arthour and of Merlin*, the young Merlin is twice called *conioun* (lines 1071, 1217),[71] and in the *Chester Plays*[72] it is used by Cain of his brother Abel (2:601) and by Herod of the infant Christ. This last example is especially pertinent:

[66] *Caxton's Malory*, ed. James W. Spisak, 2 vols. (Berkeley and Los Angeles: University of California Press, 1982), 1:189 (Bk.7, Chap. 29). Cf. "The Boy and the Mantle" (Child 29: sts. 11 and 12).

[67] *The Arte of English Poesie*, ed. Gladys Doidge Willcock and Allice Walker (Cambridge: Cambridge University Press, 1936), p. 173.

[68] Minor White Latham, *The Elizabethan Fairies* (New York: Columbia University Press, 1930), p. 150.

[69] *The Holy Greyhound: Guinefort, Healer of Children Since the Thirteenth Century*, trans. Martin Thom (1979; Cambridge: Cambridge University Press, 1983), pp. 74–82.

[70] See P. M[eyer], "*Chanjon*, enfant changé en nourrice," *Romania* 32 (1902): 452–53.

[71] *Of Arthour and of Merlin, I*, ed. O. D. Macrae-Gibson, EETS 268 (London, 1973), pp. 83 and 93 (cf. l. 1110, p. 87).

[72] *The Chester Mystery Cycle, I*, ed. R. M. Lumiansky and David Mills, EETS. SS3 (London, 1974).

Alas, what presumption should move that peevish page
or any elvish godlinge to take from me my crowne?
But, by Mahound, that boye for all his greate outrage
shall die under my hand, that elfe and vile [congion]. (8:325–28)

It may seem farfetched to associate this particular aspect of elvish lore
with the clever substitutions by which the second Canon gulls the chantry priest, but we might recall that alchemical theory envisaged the
engendering of minerals by processes closely analagous to human and
animal procreation: after all, the philosopher's stone was imagined to be
the progeny of a quite literal "chemical wedding" between sulfur and
mercury. As Del Kolve has shown, in visual representations of this wedding the image of sexual congress could scarcely be more explicit.[73]

A final aspect of transmutation in the discourse of fairyland is the
belief that fairies have the ability to change human beings into animals
and even inanimate objects. Again, direct evidence for this belief is
scanty but its existence can be inferred from a number of sources. The
early-fourteenth-century *Fasciculus Morum* reproves "those superstitious
wretches who claim that at night they see the most beautiful queens
and other girls dancing in the ring with Lady Diana, the goddess of the
heathens, who in our native tongue are called *elves*" (p. 579).[74] It then
continues: "and they believe that these can change both men and
women into other beings [*in alias naturas transformare*] and carry them
with them to *elvenland*." John Gower (*Confessio Amantis*, 5:4937–5162)
tells the story of a peasant who tries to rescue a man that had fallen into
a pit by lowering down a rope to him, but who at his first attempt
rescues instead an ape that had also been trapped in the pit:

But whan he sih it was an Ape,
He wende al hadde ben a jape
Of fairie, and sore him drad. (lines 5001–03)

Evidently the simple peasant thinks he has rescued a man who has been
transformed into an ape. Similarly, in the *Second Shepherd's Play* Mak tries

[73] "Chaucer's *Second Nun's Tale* and the Iconography of Saint Cecilia," *New Perspectives in Chaucer Criticism*, ed. Donald M. Rose (Norman: Pilgrim Books, 1981), pp. 155–56.
[74] *Fasciculus Morum: A Fourteenth-Century Preacher's Handbook*, ed. and trans. Siegfried Wenzel (University Park: Pennsylvania State University Press, 1989).

to pass off the stolen sheep that has just been discovered by its rightful owners as a baby transformed by the fairies:

> He was takyn with an elfe,
> I saw it myself;
> When the clok stroke twelf
> Was he forshapyn. (4:616–20)

Finally, in the ballad of *Tam Lin*, Janet's lover gives her detailed instructions on how to win him back from the fairies and warns her about the transformations that they will employ to try and frustrate her:

> They'll turn me in your arms, lady,
>   Into an esk and adder;
> But hold me fast, and fear me not,
>   I am your bairn's father.
>
> 'They'll turn me into a bear sae grim,
>   And into a lion bold;
> But hold me fast, and fear me not,
>   As ye shall love your child.
>
> .   .   .   .
> .   .   .   .
>
> And last they'll turn me in your arms
>   Into the burning gleed;
> Then throw me into well water,
>   O throw me in wi speed
>
> And then I'll be your ain true-love,
>   I'll turn a naked knight;
> Then cover me wi your green mantle,
>   And cover me out o sight. (Child, 39A: sts. 31–35)

At root, the alleged power to transform (minerals, in the case of the alchemists, and living creatures, in the case of the fairies) is, I believe, what linked these two discourses for Chaucer, so that *The Canon's Yeoman's Tale* may be read as a late manifestation of what Carolyn Walker Bynum has recently called "the facination with rules of change that permeate[d] twelfth- and thirteenth-century discussions of the natural world."[75] If Gerald of Wales could discuss werewolves in terms of sacramental transubstantiation (Bynum, p. 107), Chaucer can certainly consider alchemy in the light of fairyland. Many of the epiphenomena these discourses share (their liminality, their subversiveness, their secrecy) can be traced to a common concern with metamorphosis, and clearly that was what linked them in the mind of the sixteenth-century skeptic Reginald Scot, who treats both in his *Discouerie of Witchcraft*. (Incidentally, Scot evidently regarded Chaucer as a kindred spirit: he quotes both the Wife of Bath and the Canon's Yeoman with approval.) Here, for instance, is Scot on alchemical transmutation:

Let the dealers in Alcumystrie vnderstand, that the *verie* nature and kind of things cannot be changed, but rather made by art to resemble the same in shew and likenesse: so that they are not the *verie* things indeed, but seeme so to be in appearance: as castels and towers doo seeme to be built in the clouds. (pp. 368–69)

And here are his views on a story about a man turned into an ass:

But where was the yoong mans owne shape all these three yeares, wherin he was made as asse; It is a certeine and a generall rule, that two substantiall formes cannot be in one subiect *simul & semel*, both at once. . . . The forme of the beast occupied some place in the aire, and so I thinke should a man doo also. For to bringe the bodie of a man, without feeling, into a thin airie nature, as that it can neither be seene nor felt, it may well be vnlikelie, but it is *verie* impossible. (p. 98)

Scot's views on alchemical transformation would have been perfectly orthodox in the middle ages; they were held by Avicenna (as he acknowledges), but also by such authorities as Thomas Aquinas and Giles of Rome.[76] His views on biological transformation are more radical in that he denies even the possibility of an airy simulacrum,[77] but in essence his claim that anything like genuine material transformation is impossible would have been shared by such doctrinal heavyweights as

---

[75] *Metamorphosis and Identity* (New York: Zone Books, 2001), p. 90.

[76] See William R. Newman, ed., *The Summa Perfectionis of Pseudo-Gerber* (Leiden: Brill, 1991), pp. 30–35.

[77] Cf. *Discouerie*, p. 516. Also Stuart Clark, "The Scientific Status of Demonology," in *Occult and Scientific Mentalities in the Renaissance*, ed. Brian Vickers (Cambridge: Cambridge University Press, 1984), p. 368.

Gratian and Aquinas.[78] Aquinas, indeed, in his Commentary on the Sentences draws an explicit comparison between the impotence of both alchemists and devils to "induce substantial forms."[79]

I hope that by now enough has been said to show that in the late middle ages the discourse of alchemy and the discourse of fairyland shared a considerable amount of common ground and that there is every reason to take the Canon's Yeoman literally when he describes alchemy as an "elvysshe craft" and as "elvysshe lore." I would like to conclude by considering briefly why this simple proposition appears to have been so difficult for recent editors to accept. What qualities might seem to divide these discourses in the minds of modern readers, and what are the implications of such a division? Well, in the first place we tend to see alchemy as belonging squarely with learned, literate discourse (as the coda to the *Canon's Yeoman's Tale* itself, with its references to Arnold and Senior makes clear), while the discourse of fairyland appears largely popular and oral, and can now be only painstakingly reconstructed from scraps of information culled from romances, ballads, sermons, tracts, and anecdotes. As a corollary to this, while most will recognize an element of magic in alchemy, such magic may well seem different in kind to the magic of fairyland, the natural, scientific magic that Richard Kieckheffer distinguishes from popular, demonic magic.[80] (We might notice in passing, however, that if Langland associates alchemy with learned necromancy,[81] our Exeter schoolroom text makes a similar connection between necromancy and fairies.)[82] This contrast might also take on a gendered aspect, so that Susan Crane's useful distinction between "uncanny women" and "subtle clerks" may similarly serve to separate for us the Wife of Bath's nostalgia for a "land fulfild of fayerye" from the Canon's Yeoman's "clergial" talk of "citrinacioun / . . . cementyng and fermentacioun" (lines 816–17). A distinction might equally be

[78] *Decretum Magistri Gratiani*, ed. Emil Friedberg, *Corpus Iuris Canonici* 1 (Leipzig: Tauschnitz, 1879), pp. 1032–36 (2nd pt. cause 26, question 5. c. 14); *Summa theologiae*, gen. ed. Thomas Gilby and T. C. O'Brien, 60 vols. (London: Eyre and Spottiswoode; New York: McGraw-Hill, 1964–76), 9:31–41 (1a, 51, 1–3).

[79] Newman, ed., *Pseudo-Gerber*, pp. 30–31.

[80] *Magic in the Middle Ages* (Cambridge: Cambridge University Press, 1989), pp. 8–10.

[81] *A Text* (ed. Kane), XI: 159–61.

[82] Michael D. Bailey ("From Sorcery to Witchraft," *Speculum* 78 [2001]: 960–90) has recently argued that the common and elite traditions were gradually coming together in the fourteenth century and that this coalescence lies behind the European witchhunts of the later fifteenth and sixteenth centuries.

drawn in terms of Marxist analysis, the fairy magic of the Wife of Bath and the Canon's Yeoman's alchemy forming opposite sides of the same historical coin—the first, in Louise Fradenburg's words "a vision of everything lost under capitalism,"[83] the second, as Peggy Knapp has recently written, "gesturing towards a capitalism yet to come."[84] However, as soon as we seek to situate these two discourses in history (as the Marxist critic must inevitably do), an even more fundamental disjunction raises its head.

One of the earliest, and in many ways still the most challenging, of modern critics of *The Canon's Yeoman's Tale* is Charles Muscatine. For Muscatine (as for Lynn Thorndike), alchemy was a precursor of modern chemistry and Chaucer's rejection of alchemy as "blind materialism" contains "a germ of wry prophesy in it."[85] In other words, where the discourse of fairyland might have looked to the past the discourse of alchemy is speaking the language of the future:

The dogged refusal to admit the intractability of matter, one of the virtues to which we owe so much of our civilization, is here represented by a group of sooty figures sifting and picking for salvage in a pile of refuse. He who cheers them on is a fool. In the light of later history, indeed, the poem is reactionary. This kind of alchemy gave us chemistry (p. 221).

Muscatine's phrase *"this kind of* alchemy" is intended to set the practice of Chaucer's canons against the kind of philosophical alchemy that regarded matter as hylozoic (p. 218). But does such a distinction really hold? For me, the yeoman's breathless inventory of technical terms suggests something quite different: the futility of his master's attempts to contain and control matter that was, indeed, "instinct with life":

> Thise metals been of so greet violence
> Oure walles mowe nat make hem resistence,
> But if they weren wroght of lym and stoon;
> They percen so and thurgh the wal they goon.
> And somme of hem synken into the ground—

[83] "The Wife of Bath's Passing Fancy," *SAC* 8 (1986): p. 51.

[84] "The Work of Alchemy," *Journal of Medieval and Early Modern Studies* 30 (2000): 576. See also Britton J. Harwood, "Chaucer and the Silence of History: Situating the Canon's Yeoman's Tale," *PMLA* 102 (1987): 338–50.

[85] *Chaucer and the French Tradition* (Berkeley and Los Angeles: University of California Press, 1960), pp. 217 and 221.

> Thus han we lost by tymes many a pound—
> And somme are scaterd al the floor aboute;
> Somme lepe into the roof. (lines 908–14)

If the descendant of medieval alchemy (applied, as well as theoretical) must be sought among the modern sciences, it was conceptually far closer to genetic engineering than inorganic chemistry. But, in fact, the immense gulf dividing the mentality of the alchemist from the scientist cannot be papered over by any such superficial resemblances.

Lee Patterson, to whose 1992 Biennial Chaucer Lecture this one is in many ways but a footnote, recognizes the difficulty of treating alchemy as simply a "prelude to chemistry," but he still wants read it as "a site where modernizing values could take root," and Chaucer's own interest in it as thus anything but "reactionary." With this last point I am wholeheartedly in agreement, but I still have difficulty accepting even Patterson's more muted account of the alchemical project: "the non-existence of the philosopher's stone," he writes, "lured alchemy into a quest without a goal" (p. 47), and, a little later, "if alchemy is progressive, then, its dynamism cannot be understood in the usual terms by which scientific progress is measured" (p. 49). Patterson recognizes that alchemical knowledge was not, like modern science, aggregative, but, like Scattergood, he still finds in its commitment to technology the potential to transform society. On the contrary, I suggest, the alchemical project was studiously regressive, not progressive, and its goal, at least in terms of its own discourse, seemed far from unattainable.

Most will naturally assume that medieval alchemists saw themselves as building upon knowledge gained by their predecessors and advancing the project step by step toward a distant goal. But, as Sherwood Taylor puts it, "on the whole {alchemy} looked backward where modern science looks forward. The alchemist believed that the 'ancients' knew the secrets of the work and could perform it, and his principal endeavour was to understand the meaning of their books" (p. 12). Nothing could better exemplify such an attitude than John Gower's discussion of alchemy in Book IV of the *Confessio Amantis*:

> This Ston hath pouer to profite.
> It makth multiplicacioun
> Of gold, and the fixacioun
> It causeth, and of his habit

> He doth the work to be parfit
> Of thilke Elixer which men calle
> Alconomie, as is befalle
> To hem that *whilom* weren wise.
> By *now* it stant al otherwise;
> Thei speken faste of thilke Ston.
> Bot hou to make it, *nou* wot non,
> After the sothe experience. (4:2572–83)

By contrast, modern science, as Taylor says, "looks forward to the time when her efforts will make known the things that have never been known. To those who made her she looks back with respect, with honour, but not with any belief that their works contain hidden secrets to be unraveled for her enlightenment" (p. 12).

Moreover, it is a mistake to suppose that the medieval alchemist, like the modern scientist, was striving for an imaginable but as yet unrealizable goal—that the philosopher's stone, in other words, was the medieval equivalent of nuclear fusion, or a cure for HIV/AIDS. Though we may now know that this particular goal was unattainable, or at least hugely impractical, the striving, we might suppose, was the same, then as now. But this is emphatically not how the alchemists themselves saw it: many among them had, they believed, achieved the stone, and not just in the distant past. Chaucer's French contemporaries, Nicholas and Peronelle Flamel, were alleged to have succeeded; so, too, were two fifteenth-century Englishmen, Thomas Norton and George Ripley. In fact, Norton's great-grandson Samuel tells us that in Edward IV's time, no less than seven men, including his great-grandfather and Ripley, possessed the secret of alchemy.[86] Sherwood Taylor regards it as "the central problem" of alchemy that "apparently sincere alchemical writers do claim success and describe in detailed and pretty consistent language how they obtained the white and the red stone and carried out transmutations" (Taylor, pp. 90–91). In other words, to imagine that medieval alchemists saw themselves as using practical experiments to test an as yet unproven hypothesis is to view them in the distorting mirror of modern empirical science.

On this reading, medieval alchemy can lay claim no particularly privileged status as "a site where modernizing values could take root"; there

---

[86] Ed. Reidy, p. xxxviii.

is no obvious reason why the discourse of fairyland, for instance, should not offer an equally hospitable (or inhospitable) site, and indeed, judging by his two uses of the word "elvysshe" in *The Canon's Yeoman's Tale*, for Chaucer himself it functioned in precisely this way. Chaucer's skeptical attitude to "elvysshe lore" is widely recognized: the satirical opening lines of *The Wife of Bath's Tale*, the all-too-human deities in *The Merchant's Tale*, the onlookers' various attempts to explain the steed of brass in *The Squire's Tale*, the naturalistic explanation for the vanishing rocks in *The Franklin's Tale*, and the absurd quest for an elf-queen in *Sir Thopas*, all suggest that Chaucer was deeply suspicious of such popular beliefs, but that he should have regarded alchemy in the same way appears on the surface rather more surprising. A man who could write a technical manual on the astrolabe and who evinces, as Scott Lightsey has recently shown, a fascination with "the mechanical marvels that were part of late medieval court life,"[87] might be expected to have shown a similar fascination with alchemy. In fact, he must at one time have done so. The weight of detailed technical information in *The Canon's Yeoman's Tale* can only have been acquired by someone who felt a genuine intellectual curiosity about alchemy. At the time that he borrowed from Jean de Meun the image of turning ferns into glass as a parallel to the one of the marvels of *The Squire's Tale* (V (F).253–57), he may well have shared the Frenchman's confidence in the alchemist's ability to understand and harness the principles of change: "arquemie est ars veritable," Jean de Meun had declared flatly.[88] If so, by the time he came to write *The Canon's Yeoman's Tale* disenchantment had clearly set in. To suggest this is certainly not to espouse ten Brink's old conjecture that Chaucer himself had once been gulled by a crooked alchemist,[89] merely to speculate that he felt he could no longer sustain an old enthusiasm—a speculation for which Donald Howard's reading of the poem offers some support.[90] Viewed in this way, the bitterness of *The Canon's Yeoman's Tale* is not the mark of a reactionary who thinks he glimpses in the alchemist's furnace a nightmare future consecrated to a technologized materialism, it is the

[87] "Chaucer's Secular Marvels and the Medieval Economy of Wonder," *SAC* 23 (2001): 289.
[88] *Le Roman de la rose*, ed. Daniel Poirion (Paris: Garnier-Flammarion, 1974), p. 433 (l. 16084).
[89] *History of English Literature (Wyclif, Chaucer, Earliest Drama, Renaissance), Vol. 2, Pt. 1*, trans. W. C. Robinson (New York: H. Holt, 1893), p. 181.
[90] See Donald R. Howard, *The Idea of the Canterbury Tales* (Berkeley and Los Angeles: University of California Press, 1978), pp. 292–98.

disillusionment of a genuine inquirer who has come to recognize the discourse of alchemy as no less "slidynge" a science than the illusory discourse of fairyland. However it may have looked to Walter Skeat, alchemical transformation for Chaucer was neither "mysterious" and "strange" nor "weird"; it was a mere figment of the imagination. It was, in a word, all-too-literally, "elvysshe."

Chaucer the Heretic

Alan J. Fletcher
University College, Dublin

DEAD AUTHORS refuse to lie quietly in their graves. They keep returning to haunt us, and perhaps this is as it should be. Tall among these literary revenants lately summoned into critical consciousness walks the ghost of Geoffrey Chaucer, for in the last thirty years or so, the writing of scholarly assessments of Chaucer the man and of the nature of his relation to his contingent history has, if anything, accelerated, acquiring defiant momentum in the face of the theory that would insist that he ought not matter.[1] Even when mindful of the skepticism of the theorists, commentators on Chaucer have finally shown themselves undeterred by it, and continue to harbor a conviction that something solid ought still to be salvageable even after theory has done its problematizing worst. Doubtless, the stiffening of their resolve results in part for highly problematical reasons, from Chaucer's ability to sustain so convincing an illusion of an empirically available authorial presence that some readers, even as technically they confess the illusion, have been emboldened to parry the objections of theoretically driven skepticism with increasingly sophisticated attempts at determining whether the illusion anywhere accesses reality. They have tried to winnow authorial fact from fiction, finding things to say about the historical Chaucer that might be thought to sediment out from the artifice of his various self-representations, and from the slippery rhetoric of his writing in general, things whose palpability can be defended against many theoretically invigorated forms of objection.[2] Arguably, even that very slipperiness

---

[1] See Roland Barthes, *Image, Music, Text*, trans. Stephen Heath (London: Fontana, 1977), pp. 142–48. The decentered author is also familiar from the 1969 essay by Michel Foucault, "What Is an Author?" (ed. and trans. in Josué Harari, *Textual Strategies: Perspectives in Post-Structuralist Criticism* (Ithaca, N.Y.: Cornell University Press, 1979), pp. 141–60).

[2] Though not, of course, of all forms; the insistence of some theorists (Louis Althusser, for example) upon the unanalyzability of historical totalities is liable to undermine the medievalist's usual endeavour. The present essay, similarly threatened by such insistence, attempts the compromise of the *petit récit* (see note 6 below).

might be susceptible to an historicized understanding and an explanation in terms of historically real considerations and of demonstrable discourses within whose terms Chaucer lived, moved, and had his being.[3]

Of course, traditionally recognized sites exist for transacting the business of recuperating dead authors, the most obvious being the literary biography, a site tenanted most recently in Chaucer's case by Derek Pearsall. In writing a literary biography, he accordingly consorts with the values of an old and resiliently self-perpetuating biographical genre predicated on equally old and often, unreconstructed notions about why the author as subject should matter. Pearsall's *Life*, notwithstanding its nod at theory's skepticism, might thus represent a turning back of the clock in more senses than one.[4] Yet as I began by saying, the return of the dead author is perhaps as it should be, for it will probably happen, even if by a back door, in any historicist enterprise; historicisms will ensure that the author as subject continues to matter, though not for some of the reasons after which literary biography still hankers. The big-picture dash and seductively broad brushstrokes of Pearsall's *Life* can beguile readers into forgetting its astute preliminary disclaimer that what it compasses is a form of scholarly impressionism.[5] In this essay, I will be more interested in a matter of pointillist detail because, if impressionism is what we are inevitably going to be put to even as we try to

---

[3] There are several excellent recent examples of this, but to take two with which I will later engage: David Aers, in David Wallace, ed., *The Cambridge History of Medieval English Literature* (Cambridge: Cambridge University Press, 1999), p. 444, reflects on Chaucer's apparent relative aloofness from the rebellion of 1381 thus: "what seems absent may, in its very absence, be a present force in shaping a work . . . even the most dazzling complexities may be replete with significant social implications which are themselves part of a distinct political response to a determinate situation." His thinking in this respect agrees with that of Lynn Staley, his co-author for *The Powers of the Holy: Religion, Politics, and Gender in Late Medieval English Culture* (Pennsylvania State University Press: University Park, 1996); compare, for example, Staley's characterization of *The Canterbury Tales'* relation to its political moment (p. 180): "If we can find very few explicit references to contemporary events in Chaucer, we can nonetheless find the issues that fueled contemporary conflicts refigured in the fiction of the tales."

[4] For example, when Derek Pearsall, *The Life of Geoffrey Chaucer: A Critical Biography* (Oxford: Blackwell, 1992), p. 5, says, "although [Chaucer] tells us little about himself, or about his attitudes to the great events of his day, *the quality of his poetic presence is such that he stimulates in us an unusually powerful desire to know what he was 'really' like*" (my italics), his rhetorical "us" here enjoins upon his readers a universally uniform response. Should it? The sentence would position us all as members of a like-minded community, one accustomed to satisfying the traditional curiosities that traditional biographies cater for. The present essay, however, even as it teases that community's curiosity, will finally disavow allegiance to it.

[5] Pearsall, *Life*, p. 7.

reckon with the author as subject, it will be out of the quality of their pointillism that compelling impressionist works emerge.

The detail in question, the *petit récit* of my enquiry, is made up of neglected aspects of Chaucer's relation to contemporary religious radicalism, if not outright heresy.[6] The essay has flagged its interest under a broad banner heading, "Chaucer the Heretic," intended to be as eye-catching and duplicitous, in its way, as is the illusion of Chaucer's presence in his writing, the elvish presence that has beckoned so invitingly to the biographers.[7] The gambit has served its turn. Time for its replacement with something more exact: what this essay precisely seeks to unfold are the two principal ways in which Chaucer enlisted what will be called "the culture of heresy" in his writing, and to illustrate their nature and purpose. On the one hand, we must consider his invention of poetic personae which are to be seen as poetic alter-egos, and in whose construction heresy, or its lesser harbinger, error, constitute overt and important figures; and on the other, there are his allusions to sentiments and turns of phrase characteristically current in the chief radical/heretical discourse of his day, whose presence makes some of his writings arenas in which that radical/heretical discourse may be thought to contend.[8] The range of these allusions, despite recent investigations, has

[6] I lift the idea of the priority of the *petit récit*, the micronarrative, for any viable form of history writing from Jean-François Lyotard, *The Postmodern Condition*, trans. G. Bennington and B. Massumi (Manchester: Manchester University Press, 1984); see p. 60. In Peter Brown, ed., *A Companion to Chaucer* (Oxford: Blackwell, 2000), p. 140, Alcuin Blamires notes the "interesting signs that [Chaucer's] writing breathes the wider 'crisis of dissent' of the 1380s and 1390s," and invites further reflection on this topic. The present article is partly intended to respond to that invitation.

[7] The title also calques that used by Alcuin Blamires, "Chaucer the Reactionary: Ideology and the General Prologue to *The Canterbury Tales*," *RES* 51 (2000): 523–39, the difference being that Blamires's title takes itself a little more seriously as a summary of what he writes about. Robert Meyer-Lee's award-winning essay, "The Allure of the Phantom Poppet," *The Chaucer Newsletter* 22, no. 2 (2000): 6, focuses the appeal of the illusory presence with neat concision.

[8] The compound "radical/heretical" here is used advisedly. It attempts to contain the complex and shifting status of reformist ideology c. 1380–1420, a period during which many positions within that ideology, though originally orthodox, increasingly lost their orthodox respectability as they became characteristically colonized by the heretics. Thus, broadly speaking, orthodoxy during these years may have gradually distanced itself from some of its own earlier reformist impulses. Steven Justice, *Writing and Rebellion: England in 1381* (Berkeley and Los Angeles: University of California Press, 1994), p. 233, identifies this shift well when he speaks of "the transformation of 'reform' into 'heresy' after Wyclif's abortive trial in London before Bishop Courtenay in 1377"; or again, when in commenting upon ecclesiastical disendowment, he ventures that when William Langland wrote the B-text of *Piers Plowman*, "disendowment was an indistinct lump of reformist ideology not yet the property of anyone," but "by the time [Langland] wrote C, it belonged so completely to Wyclif that no one else wanted it." Some recent critics,

still not been sufficiently appreciated.[9] Overt heretical figures appear in *An ABC* and in the *Prologue* to *The Legend of Good Women*; while serial allusions to heresy's contemporary discourse (or to an earlier theological radicalism that contemporary heresy came characteristically to espouse and thus either to absorb or to court confusion with) appear throughout certain of *The Canterbury Tales*. Illustration of these two manifestations of the culture of heresy in Chaucer's work will comprise the first part of my brief; the second part will be to speculate, on the back of them, about what his personal investment in the culture of heresy may have been. Thus I will be interested in amplifying into present-day audibility an original radical/heretical resonance in certain of his writings that, notwithstanding recent advances, we disadvantaged modern readers are no longer capable of hearing, and also in considering how we may be tempted to read back from that resonance, back from the oeuvre into the actual life of the author (though not so as to worship at the altar of the author god, nor to provide so gratifyingly total a package as a cradle-to-grave *Life* promises). In short, I will try first to see whether anything new in this respect can be detected in Chaucer's work and, following on from that, whether the historical Chaucer can be thought to have divulged any new personal secrets. Anticipating the destination, fresh knowledge there may be, but it will finally succeed only in stimulating fresh speculation.

---

however, are increasingly tending to apply the term "reformist" to texts hitherto referred to as "Lollard" or "Wycliffite" (for example, Lee Patterson, "Chaucer's Pardoner on the Couch: Psyche and Clio in Medieval Literary Studies," *Speculum* 76 (2001): 638–80; see p. 644). While understandable, this application is problematic. Although it is true that the shifting espousals of reformist ideology during this period may create grey areas in which distinctions between the radical orthodox and the conservative Lollard may now be difficult for us to perceive, originally there *were* distinctions, or at least, distinctions were *felt* to exist, irrespective of whether everyone would have agreed on where precisely the lines of a distinction were to be drawn. Therefore, as increasing use of the word "reformist" blankets out the words "Lollard" or "Wycliffite," it practices its own form of effacement of distinctions now difficult enough for us to distinguish, thus helping ensure that they remain irretrieveable. In this essay, notwithstanding their limitations, I retain the more traditional terms "Lollard" and "Wycliffite."

[9] The assertion of Nicholas Watson that Chaucer had a "detailed interest" in the theological, social and linguistic contours of Lollardy (Jocelyn Wogan-Browne, Nicholas Watson, Andrew Taylor, and Ruth Evans, ed., *The Idea of the Vernacular: An Anthology of Middle English Literary Theory 1280–1520* (Pennsylvania and Exeter: Pennsylvania State University Press and Exeter University Press, 1999), p. 346) is surely right, but needs fuller demonstration (though very recently Watson seems to have become more cautious about this in Brown, *Companion to Chaucer*, p. 81: "Chaucer may or may not have been interested in all the ideas associated with Lollardy"). Certain aspects of that familiarity and the sophisticated literary uses to which Chaucer put them are well explored by Alcuin Blamires, "The Wife of Bath and Lollardy," *MÆ* 58 (1989): 224–42.

Heretical Types and Conditions

The heretic, in being so vibrantly transgressive a character, was assured of an enduring textualized existence, often less in terms of his own making than in those made for him by his orthodox detractors. His various incarnations had long preoccupied Church writings—indeed, had served orthodoxy as a convenient means whereby it could define its own boundaries—where the precise terms of his heresy could be isolated, exposed, and, the orthodox hoped, quarantined. We should first be clear, however, about where the later Middle Ages thought heresy resided. Aquinas's definition would have held good for Chaucer's contemporaries. This maintained that the heretic was someone who not only believed something contrary to standard Church teaching, but who perversely willed to remain in the error of his contrary belief. Heresy's distinguishing condition lay in this, that it was *error voluntarius*.[10] Theological error, though dangerous enough, was not in itself heresy. It became so if the erroneous believer contumaciously persisted in the face of orthodoxy. Once that kind of believer also expressed his heresy externally, by words or signs, he might expect to incur an automatic, public ecclesiastical sanction, the standard one being excommunication. So we have to reckon in the first instance with error and then with heresy, the former developing into the latter by dint of a stubborn act of will.

What, then, of the penitent narrator of *An ABC*, who invokes the idea of *error* twice, its first occurrence being in the very opening stanza of the poem:

> Almighty and al merciable queene,
> To whom that al this world fleeth for socour,
> To have relees of sinne, of sorwe, and teene,
> Glorious virgine, of alle floures flour,
> To thee I flee, confounded in errour.[11]

There is nothing in the poem's immediate source, an ABC poem forming a section of *Le pèlerinage de la vie humaine* of Guillaume de Deguile-

---

[10] P. Caramello, ed., *S. Thomae Aquinatis Doctoris Angelici Summa Theologiae*, 3 vols. (Marietti Editori: 1952–56), II, 64–65 (II–II, q. 11, a. 1).

[11] Larry D. Benson, gen. ed., *The Riverside Chaucer*, 3d ed. (Boston: Houghton Mifflin, 1987), p. 637, lines 1–5; all subsequent references to Chaucer's writing are to this edition, with line numbers cited parenthetically in the text.

ville, that could have suggested an exact match to this, nor in the wider context of the *Pèlerinage* either. Deguileville simply says:

> A toy du monde le refui,
> Vierge glorieuse, m'en fui
> Tout confus, ne puis miex faire;
> A toy me tien, a toy m'apuy,
> Relieve moy, abatu suy.[12]

Even after invoking Helen Phillips's valuable principle of "redistributive" translation, it is not possible fully to explain the appearance of error here in "redistributive" terms.[13] To be sure, there is a personification of error's endgame, Heresy, elsewhere in the *Pèlerinage* outside its ABC section, but Deguileville's penitent pilgrim, though hard pressed, managed to *avoid* falling into Heresy's snares. And although the penitent pilgrim saw himself as one who "erre par (la) voie torte" ("strays by the wrong path") when seven thieves (the Seven Deadly Sins) give him chase, this is not an exact fit against Chaucer either. Evidently, then, the detail of the error-confounded penitent was Chaucer's emphasis, not Deguileville's.[14] The same can be said of its second appearance. Here, the penitent generalizes away from himself to embrace all who, like him, have been guilty of error. For such people Mary is a sovereign recourse (lines 67–70):

> For whan a soule falleth in errour
> Thi pitee goth and haleth him ayein.
> Thanne makest thou his pees with his sovereyn
> And bringest him out of the crooked strete.

---

[12] W. W. Skeat, ed., *The Complete Works of Geoffrey Chaucer: Romaunt of the Rose; Minor Poems*, 2d ed., 7 vols. (Oxford: Clarendon Press, 1899), vol. 1, p. 261. Skeat's edition conveniently includes the Deguileville source along with Chaucer's text. The standard edition of Deguileville's poem is J. J. Stürzinger, ed., *Le pèlerinage de la vie humaine de Guillaume de Deguileville* (London: Nichols and Sons, 1893); see p. 338 for the corresponding stanza.

[13] Helen Phillips, "Chaucer and Deguileville: The *ABC* in Context," *MÆ* 62 (1993): 1–19.

[14] Interestingly, Chaucer has come closer to retrieving the emphasis of the earlier work that Deguileville used, a homily on Luke by St. Bernard of Clairvaux; see Patrologia Latina 183 (Paris, 1854), cols 55–88, especially cols 70–71: "Ipsam sequens non devias . . . ipsam cogitans non erras" ("Following her, you will not deviate . . . thinking upon her, you will not err").

Deguileville has nothing exactly matching this either, even though Chaucer's "crooked strete" metaphor has been redistributed from an earlier Deguileville stanza:

> Quar quant aucun se desvoie,
> A ce que tost se ravoie,
> De ta pitié li fais convoy.[15]

But what could Chaucer's penitent have meant by saying that he was error-confounded? Had his condition specific theological significance, or was it some vague expression of general moral malaise? Certainly, Chaucer elsewhere appears to have understood this technical theological meaning of the word *errour*, as is clear, for example, from its use in a stanza of the *Troilus* where Pandarus expects that Troilus, now converted to Love, will prosecute Love's cause all the more zealously (lines 1002–08):

> Ensample why, se now thise wise clerkes,
> That erren aldermost ayeyn a lawe,
> And ben converted from hire wikked werkes
> Thorugh grace of God that list hem to hym drawe,
> Thanne arn thise folk that han moost God in awe,
> And strengest feythed ben, I undirstonde,
> And konne an errowr alderbest withstonde.

The wise clerk who has erred, and afterwards renounced his wicked work, will henceforth be God's most loyal servant and best placed to detect *errour* in future. Moreover, this technical theological meaning was well established in Middle English generally, as a glance at its entry in both the *Oxford English Dictionary* and the *Middle English Dictionary* (*MED*) will show.[16] In fact, it is this meaning that the lemmata cited under *MED*'s first definition of the word attest.[17] Yet *MED*, under its third definition of *errour*, records another meaning which, although also

---

[15] Skeat, *Complete Works*, p. 265 (Stürzinger, *Pèlerinage*, p. 342, has the corresponding stanza). Phillips, "*ABC* in Context," p. 7, acknowledges the difficulty of matching the idea of falling into error with anything in Deguileville.

[16] J. A. Simpson and E. S. C. Weiner, eds., *The Oxford English Dictionary*, 2d ed., 20 vols. (Oxford: Clarendon Press, 1989); Hans Kurath and Sherman M. Kuhn, et al., eds., *Middle English Dictionary* (Ann Arbor: University of Michigan Press, 1952–2001).

[17] The equivalent meaning in the *Oxford English Dictionary* is listed there under subsense 3 of *error*.

bearing theological weight, does so far less specifically. Here, *errour* is defined in a much more general way as an "Offense against morality or justice; transgression, wrong-doing, sin".[18] It is under this third definition that *MED* has chosen to locate the *errour* of *An ABC*, and subsequent authoritative Chaucer glossaries have followed suit, defining *errour* in *An ABC* as "sin" in this wider, less particularized sense.[19]

However, we should reconsider whether *MED* (and all later glossaries) are justified in making quite so crisp a distinction. To begin with, the grounds for denying *errour* in *An ABC* one of its commonest meanings—theological error—are not firm. In fact, the five other lemmata taken from texts earlier than or contemporary with Chaucer that *MED* cites in support of its more generalized third sense either fail to support it or are at best equivocal. The earliest, an *errour* that appears in the Auchinleck manuscript version of the romance *Of Arthour and of Merlin*, is uttered in the context of a recrimination by the burgesses of Winchester and the people of England against the usurping King Fortiger at the turning point of his fortunes and when he is nearing his overthrow: "Wicke traytour / Þou schald abigge þine errour!"[20] But the romance has made it clear that the *errour* that Fortiger was guilty of was not merely his traitorous usurpation, a "sin" in the sense of a treasonable transgression against legitimate royal descent, but the *errour* of perverting the Christian faith. This he did by consorting with those archetypal infidels of the Middle Ages, the Saracens. He had married one, "And was cursed in al his liue / For he lete Cristen wedde haþen / And meynt our blod as flesche and maþen." As a result, "Þer was wel neiȝe al þis lond / To þe Deuel gon an hond".[21] And finally, when Fortiger and his

---

[18] The *Oxford English Dictionary* records a near equivalent sense to this under subsense 5 of *error*, where it offers the meaning "departure from moral rectitude; a transgression, wrong-doing," citing its sole instance earlier than Chaucer from Robert Mannyng of Brunne's *Chronicle* of *c.* 1338: "William the Conquerour changis his wikked wille, / Out of his first errour, repentis of his ille" (T. Hearne, ed., *Peter Langtoft's Chronicle, (as illustrated and improv'd by Robert of Brunne)*, 2 vols. (London: Mercler and Chervet, 1810), vol. 1, p. 78). Yet this too is equivocal: it is perfectly clear from its context that the error in question is specifically a transgression against God and the Church, for William had allowed his men to burn churches and relics; though he later relented and restored Church temporalities, no penance was done for his original sacrilege.

[19] For example, Norman Davis, Douglas Gray, Patricia Ingham and Andrew Wallace-Hadrill, eds., *A Chaucer Glossary* (Oxford: Oxford University Press, 1979), p. 48; or Benson, *Riverside Chaucer*, p. 1244.

[20] O. D. Macrae-Gibson, ed., *Of Arthour and of Merlin*, EETS, os 268 (London: Oxford University Press, 1973), p. 133, lines 1811–12.

[21] Macrae-Gibson, *Of Arthour and of Merlin*, p. 37, lines 482–84 and 487–88.

family got their comeuppance (being burnt in a siege), the narrator summed up his career thus: "Þus ended sir Fortiger / Þat misbileued a fewe ȝer".[22] The important word here is *misbileued*. Whatever else it was, Fortiger's *errour* was misbelief, the lapse defined by Aquinas as one of the gravest of sins in being a sin against God himself, and one classifiable as error in the technical theological sense.[23] So *MED*'s earliest citation in support of its third generalized meaning actually sits better under its first meaning of theological error. Exactly the same can be said of *MED*'s next citation, again antedating Chaucer. The author of *The Seven Sages of Rome* relates a tale of seven masters in Rome who have grown rich on the proceeds of charging people for dream augury: "So longe þai vsed þis errour / Þai were richcher þan þemperour".[24] They also consult books—dreambooks of arcane lore, we should doubtless infer—from which they spin their divination. The author of *The Seven Sages* has sided with the orthodox view categorically expressed in Gratian's *Decretum* on the question of dream divination, and has used *errour* with technical theological accuracy for what the seven masters were doing: they were not committing a "sin" or "transgression" in *MED*'s third generalized sense at all but, like pagans and apostates, were committing a very particular kind of sin, one against the faith itself and against God.[25] Their sin was of the sort that might lead to heresy. Thus, like the misbelieving Fortiger, the dream interpreters of *The Seven Sages* too were in *errour* in *MED*'s first sense.

MED's next two citations in support of the third generalized sense are contemporary with Chaucer. The problem with these lies in the nature of the source from which they both derive. Their value as witnesses to the state of current idiomatic English usage is compromised for the

---

[22] Macrae-Gibson, *Of Arthour and of Merlin*, p. 139, lines 1899–1900. Also, note the fact that Fortiger died by *burning*, which might have been considered a singularly appropriate purge for his particular sin; the burning of heretics was originally provided for by Pope Gregory IX in his constitution *Excommunicamus et anathematisamus* of 1231 (and see F. Pollock and F. W. Maitland, *The History of English Law Before the Time of Edward I*, 2d ed. with new intro. and select bibliography by S. F. C. Milsom, 2 vols. (Cambridge: Cambridge University Press, 1968), vol. 2, pp. 549–50, 556–57).

[23] Caramello, *Summa Theologiae*, I, 331–32 (I–II, q. 73, a. 3); II, 37–38 (II–II, q. 5, a. 3).

[24] Karl Brunner, ed., *The Seven Sages of Rome*, EETS, os 191 (London: Oxford University Press, 1933), p. 107, ll. 2343–44.

[25] F. Friedberg and Emilius L. Richter, eds., *Corpus Iuris Canonici*, 2d ed., 2 vols. (Leipzig, 1879; rpt., Graz, 1955), Pars 2, causa 26, quaestio 7, capitulum 16; see also Steven F. Kruger, *Dreaming in the Middle Ages* (Cambridge: Cambridge University Press, 1992), pp. 7–16.

simple reason that they come from the English Wycliffite Bible (Early Version).[26] As is well known, the Early Version's translation of the Vulgate was notoriously literal and unidiomatic, prone to render the Latin in whatever English words were of nearest resemblance. Thus the Latin word *error* in the Vulgate would be liable to appear in Middle English as *errour*, as indeed it does, irrespective of whether *errour*'s semantic field in English might be inappropriate in any way, and therefore not strictly the best translation choice. Most lexicographical citation from the English Wycliffite Bible must confess this intrinsic limitation.

The fifth lemma cited by the *MED* in support of *errour*'s third sense is drawn from Book 7 of Gower's *Confessio Amantis*, and here the lemma may be thought to lay rather better claim to illustrate the sense that *MED* seeks to define. However, even this citation is not without difficulty. A philosopher warns a king against flatterers at court, distinguishing for him three *errours* of which flatterers are guilty. The first of these is an *errour* "toward the goddes hihe."[27] That is, the first clause of the philosopher's ternary distinction on flattery maintains that court flatterers assail the gods themselves. This proposition is given a sharper, Christian edge in the accompanying Latin marginal gloss, which asserts that the first party whom court flatterers offend is God himself. That is, Gower presents court flattery in the worst possible light when he uses *errour* to name it; it is not simply a generalized "sin," but a sin *contra Deum*, as the gloss makes clear, and to that extent, of a piece with *errour* in the technical theological sense. Certainly, Gower may have taken a theological liberty here in choosing to stigmatize court flattery in such resounding terms, but the point is that, as Gower uses it, *errour* may be retaining the gravity of its technical theological charge without being technically theologically correct. Therefore, although this time *MED* justifiably cites *errour* here as an illustration of the third generalized sense, it may simultaneously be missing the nuance that Gower's semantic license seems to be introducing as he damns court flatterers all the more deeply in branding their sin as error *contra Deum*, error resonating with the danger of incipient heresy.

Having exhausted *MED*'s antecedent and contemporary attestations,

[26] Romans 1:27; James 5:20. The word *error* is also allowed to carry over into the more idiomatic Later Version.
[27] G. C. Macaulay, ed., *The Complete Works of John Gower*, 4 vols. (Oxford: Clarendon Press, 1899–1902), vol. 3, p. 292, line 2181. The passage on the three distinctions of flattery runs between ll. 2177–206.

we return to Chaucer and *An ABC*. As has been seen, it seems that the grounds are unsound for reading *An ABC*'s *errour* in the "diluted" third sense that *MED* and subsequent Chaucer glossaries propose. But there is another reason for suspecting that *An ABC* preserves something of the technical theological sense of *errour* so amply illustrated in *MED*'s first definition: this lies precisely in the poem's configuration of erring, penitent sinner, and Virgin Mary. Increasingly from the twelfth century Mary was promoted as heresy's sovereign antidote. She was at the forefront of the reconciliation of those in error, and of those whose contumacious error had toppled them into heresy proper.[28] Thus when Chaucer specified from the outset of his poem that his penitent was in error, not only is there no good lexicological reason for denying *errour* here any trace of its technical theological sense, but also, following the source, since his penitent is placed in relation to theological error's traditional remedy, the Virgin Mary, the case for regarding the penitent as someone guilty of technical theological error is strengthened.

If a case needs to be made for Chaucer's having evoked the culture of heresy in the terms in which he has presented the penitent of *An ABC*, no such case needs to be made for his presentation of his own persona in *The Legend of Good Women*, for there the evocation is explicit. Chaucer uses the word "heresy" but once in his extant works, in the *Prologue* to the *Legend*. The heresy of the *Legend*, of course, is less a representation of an actual spiritual sickness requiring a recognized antidote than a playfully rhetorical, literary conceit that Chaucer the author causes the God of Love to project onto Chaucer's persona. Through that projection, as we will shortly see, the God of Love becomes himself implicated in a particular social dialectic that mirrors the terms in which the discourse of heresy is being conducted in the real world. Playful though its final effect may be, the terms from which the *Legend*'s heretical conceit is fabricated originate in the language of heresy's real-life discourse.

In order to illustrate this, let us consider those terms a little more

---

[28] Compare the commentary of St. Bernard of Clairvaux on the Marian liturgical apostrophe: "Tu cunctas haereses sola interemisti [You alone have confounded all heresies]"; Jean Leclercq, Charles H. Talbot and Henri M. Rochais, eds., *Opera Sancti Bernardi*, 8 vols. (Rome: Editiones Cistercienses, 1957–77), vol. 5, p. 265, lines 4–8. And on the early-thirteenth century tradition, see Beverly Kienzle, "Mary Speaks against Heresy: An Unedited Sermon of Hélinand for the Purification, Paris, B. N. MS lat. 14591," *Sacris Erudiri* 32 (1991), 291–308; also, J. Szövérffy, "Maria und die Haretiker—Ein Zisterzienserhymnus zum Albigenserkrieg," *Analecta Cisterciensia* 43 (1987): 223–32.

carefully, beginning at that moment in the text when they are most vocal. The God of Love's opening words frame Chaucer's persona in an accusation: he has no business, claims the God of Love, approaching the daisy (F, lines 320–31):

> "For thow," quod he, "art therto nothing able.
> Yt is my relyke, digne and delytable,
> And thow my foo, and al my folk werreyest,
> And of myn olde servauntes thow mysseyest,
> And hynderest hem with thy translacioun,
> And lettest folk from hire devocioun
> To serve me, and holdest it folye
> To serve Love. Thou maist yt nat denye,
> For in pleyn text, withouten nede of glose,
> Thou hast translated the Romaunce of the Rose,
> That is an heresye ayeins my lawe,
> And makest wise folk from me withdrawe."

If it is true, as the notes in the *Riverside* edition maintain, that the heresy motif here was instilled in Chaucer's head by virtue of its appearance in his French sources, then it must also be confessed that in those sources the motif was at best embryonic:[29] Guillaume de Machaut's *Jugement dou Roy de Behaingne* has nothing obviously suggestive of it,[30] and that poem's subsequent companion piece, the *Jugement dou Roy de Navarre*, contains only the idea, alleged by the Lady Bonneürté against the poet, that he has held and previously expressed in writing a "descouvenue" (an "impropriety") against women for which he must do penance.[31] That is all. Nor is there much in the *Roman de la Rose*, other than the announcement by Jean de Meun to the "leal amant" that if he ends up confused about the meaning of the dream narrated, he will have it all explained "quant le texte m'orrez gloser" ("once you hear me gloss the

---

[29] The notes in *Riverside Chaucer* risk suggesting that heresy was transparently present in Chaucer's sources (Benson, *Riverside Chaucer*, p. 1060). It was not.

[30] R. Barton Palmer, ed. and trans., *Guillaume de Machaut, The Judgment of the King of Bohemia*, Garland Library of Medieval Literature 9, Series A (New York and London: Garland, 1984).

[31] R. Barton Palmer, ed. and trans., *Guillaume de Machaut, The Judgment of the King of Navarre*, Garland Library of Medieval Literature 45, Series A (New York and London: Garland, 1988), p. 42, line 918; Lady Bonneürté accuses Machaut of writing his opinions earlier (ibid., p. 38, lines 866–68, where she refers to the opinions expressed in the earlier *Jugement dou Roy de Behaingne*).

text").[32] In its own time, the third quarter of the thirteenth century, this business of explanatory textual glossing invoked by de Meun had little specifically heretical implication clinging to it, but not by Chaucer's day, when glossing had come to acquire a peculiar sensitivity to which we will return in a moment; the glossing that might be neutral for de Meun would subsequently serve Chaucer with a more tendentious point of departure.[33] These earlier precedents, then, are the most fleeting of hints that Chaucer for some reason picked up and ran with.[34]

We should appreciate how consistently Chaucer contoured the *Prologue* passage quoted above in accordance with a real-life discourse of contemporary heresy, for it contains a remarkably coherent network of ideas echoing that discourse. Some earlier medieval *accessus* to Ovid's *Heroides* may have suggested to Chaucer this interview between his persona and the God of Love. For example, one such twelfth-century *accessus* prologue provides a striking parallel in explaining that Ovid wrote the *Heroides* as an act of reparation after he had been arraigned by Caesar for corrupting the morals of matrons through discussing in his earlier writing illicit love affairs. However, it is not in terms of heresy that the *accessus* constructs Ovid's offence.[35] Whether or not Chaucer derived his idea for the interview from some *accessus* to the *Heroides*, the God of Love begins his accusation against Chaucer's persona with a charge that finds its analogue, rather, in contemporary (and also in established) orthodox writings on heresy, that the enemies of holy things—as all heretics are— are not to approach those things (indeed, in some cases will not even have the power to do so).[36] Thus, from the very first, the God of Love

---

[32] Félix Lecoy, ed., *Le Roman de la Rose*, 3 vols., Classiques Français du Moyen Âge, 92, 95 and 98 (Paris: Champion, 1966–70), vol. 2, p. 210, line 15120.

[33] For some notes on the history of glossing and its catachresis, see Beryl Smalley, "The Gospels in the Paris Schools in the Late Twelfth and Early Thirteenth Centuries: Peter the Chanter, Hugh of St. Cher, Alexander of Hales, John of La Rochelle," *Franciscan Studies* 39 (1979): 230–54; *Franciscan Studies* 40 (1980): 298–369 (see pp. 366–68); rpt. in her *The Gospels in the Schools, c. 1100–c. 1280* (London: Hambledon, 1985), pp. 99–196 (see pp. 193–95).

[34] Benson, *Riverside Chaucer*, p. 1060. As there expressed (for the "underlying fiction of Chaucer's heresy against love, there are various literary parallels, in addition to Machaut's *Jugement dou Roy de Navarre* and *Jugement dou Roy de Behaingne* . . . including Jean de Meun's excuses"), the impression is perhaps conveyed that the motif was common.

[35] See the excellent account by Rita Copeland, *Rhetoric, Hermeneutics, and Translation in the Middle Ages* (Cambridge: Cambridge University Press, 1991), pp. 188–89.

[36] The motif of the impious being supernaturally disabled from approaching holy things features elsewhere in Chaucer in *The Pardoner's Prologue*, where the Pardoner turns it to unscrupulous ends (Benson, *Riverside Chaucer*, p. 195, lines 377–84). Compare the idea found, for example, in John Mirk's *Festial*, that the reason why heretics/Lollards

projects onto Chaucer's persona a characterization whose terms are already steeped in heretical potentiality. That potentiality actually crystalizes in the word "heresye" proper a few lines later: heretics, the orthodox maintained, were traditionally defined through their malevolent opposition to the established order, its representatives and its icons.[37]

The heretical discourse ramifies as the God of Love goes on to say that the weapon used by Chaucer's inimical persona in waging war against the God of Love and his folk is "translacioun": by its means, the God of Love's "olde servauntes," that is, his devotees in times past whom Chaucer has written about in English, have been reviled and vilified. The net result, he says, is that folk are impeded in and deterred from their devotion to him. The literary and cultural politics of translation in *The Legend of Good Women* have recently attracted searching critical commentary.[38] For the sake of the present argument, some additional points need to be made. Translation had been recognized by the orthodox as an activity to which heretics were vocationally drawn (preeminently in their case, of course, to translation of the Bible) long before it ever became a hallmark issue of the prime popular heretical movement of Chaucer's day, Lollardy.[39] So the God of Love's hostility to translation, or at least, to the sort of translation that he claims Chaucer's persona had been practicing, also complements the heretical complexion of Chaucer's persona achieved in this passage. Yet it complements it not only in a traditional way—as earlier remarked, canon law had long since identified the inclination of heretics to translate—but also contempora-

---

attacked churchmen was because they were out of charity (Theodor Erbe, ed., *Mirk's Festial*, EETS, es 96 (London: Kegan Paul, Trench, Trübner, 1905; rpt., New York: Kraus, 1973), p. 164, lines 23–29; for "Lombards" in this passage read "Lollards"); and since charity was traditionally regarded as one of the prerequisites of the good Bible translator and exegete, the heretic, being out of charity, could not therefore be a sound translator. For a discussion of medieval conceptions of what made a good translator, see Ian Johnson, "Vernacular Valorizing: Functions and Fashionings of Literary Theory in Middle English Translation of Authority," in Jeanette Beer, ed., *Translation Theory and Practice in the Middle Ages*, Studies in Medieval Culture 38 (Kalamazoo: Western Michigan University, 1997), pp. 239–54.

[37] The idea of the heretic as militant aggressor, as uncharitable enemy of the sacred, is implicit here and found widely elsewhere in contemporary characterizations of the heretic's temperament (compare, for example, John Mirk's characterization of the heretic cited in the previous note). The heretic therefore becomes recognizable, inter alia, by his lack of charity.

[38] See Copeland, *Rhetoric, Hermeneutics, and Translation*; also, her "Rhetoric and Vernacular Translation in the Middle Ages," *SAC* 9 (1987): 41–75.

[39] For example, the *Decretum* observes the fondness of heretics for Bible translation (Friedberg and Richter, *Corpus Iuris Canonici*, II, 785).

neously, when under the stimulus of the Wycliffite heresy the traditional issue of heretical translation was acquiring a new immediacy and a controversial edge. While Anne Hudson has been at pains to emphasize that it was not until 1407 that translation of the Bible into English was banned outright, being before that time an open issue,[40] this should not deter us from hearing a note of reactionary anxiety in the God of Love's use of the word "translacioun" here that finds its reflection in the anxiety felt by orthodox churchmen at precisely the time when Chaucer was writing the *Legend*, some twenty years earlier than the ban of 1407, at the prospect of mass, unmediated lay access to the key texts of clerical culture.[41] Just as Chaucer's persona is both implicitly and overtly characterized as a heretic, so too the God of Love projects that heretical characterization from a position which is itself freshly recognizable within the politics of current heretical discourse of the mid-1380's, from the position of the aggrieved and defensive authority of orthodoxy. Translation for the God of Love has amounted to lèse-majesté; he complains of losing control on account of it. This complaint essentially compares with the political analysis offered by Wyclif himself, a couple of years before the *Legend*'s composition, of the real motives lurking behind orthodox churchmen's objections to the making available of the Bible and other clerical writing in English.[42]

[40] Anne Hudson, "The Debate on Bible Translation, Oxford 1401," *EHR* 90 (1975): 1–18; rpt. in her collection, *Lollards and Their Books* (London and Ronceverte: Hambledon Press, 1985), pp. 67–84.

[41] The topicality of the issue of translation at the time the *Legend* was being written (Robert W. Frank, Jr., *Chaucer and the Legend of Good Women* [Cambridge, Mass.: Harvard University Press, 1972], pp. 1–10, makes a good case for the *Legend*'s inception in 1386) is clearly witnessed, for example, in the defense of translation mounted in 1387 by John Trevisa in his *Dialogue Between the Lord and the Clerk on Translation*. It is not important that this work has nothing overtly Wycliffite about it (though without question, Trevisa shared a cultural formation in Oxford similar to the Lollard Nicholas Hereford, whose possible involvement in the project of vernacular Bible translation can be more confidently credited); it participates in a wider, associated vernacularizing movement to empower the laity with knowledge not exclusively theological. Valuable investigation of this aspect of late-fourteenth century culture has been undertaken by Fiona E. Somerset, "Vernacular Argumentation in *The Testimony of William Thorpe*," *MS* 58 (1996): 207–42. See also by her, "'As just as is a squyre': The Politics of 'Lewed Translacion' in Chaucer's *Summoner's Tale*," *SAC* 21 (1999): 187–207.

[42] For example, in Wyclif's *De triplici vinculo amoris* (Rudolf Buddensieg, ed., *John Wiclif's Polemical Works in Latin*, 2 vols (London: Trübner and Co., 1883), vol. 1, p. 168, lines 6–9): "ex eodem patet eorum stulticia, qui volunt dampnare scripta tamquam heretica propter hoc, quod scribuntur in anglico et acute tangunt peccata, que conturbant illam provinciam" ("from that is the foolishness evident of those who want to condemn writings as heretical for this reason, because they are written in English and teach sharply on the sins that throw that province into disarray"). The *De triplici vinculo*

In one sense, Alastair Minnis is quite right to arbitrate that "there is nothing specifically Lollard about the discourse of translation which we find reflected in the *Legend*," but in another sense, this arbitration may be misleading, for reasons that will shortly be made clear, if it also results in the effacement of a certain contemporary political immanence in the *Legend*'s translation discourse. Minnis's statement would be unhelpful were it to lead to divorcing translation's contested enterprise from the culture of contemporary heresy: after all, the God of Love himself did not seem to think that anyone should dissociate the two when he cited "pleyn text" translation of the *Roman de la Rose*, "withouten nede of glose," as a heresy against his law. Minnis perceives here commonplaces about translation that amount to this: that Chaucer was in touch with an earlier exegetical tradition which prized the literal sense of Scripture and which warned that the literal sense was in danger of suffocating beneath the higher levels of exegesis. This return to the literal sense was orthodox before the Lollards, following Wyclif's example, ever chose to champion it. When Wyclif declared the *sensus litteralis* to be the one that must be afforded priority as "dulcissimus, sapientissimus et tanquam preciosissimus amplectandus" ("the sweetest, wisest and, as it were, the most precious to embrace"),[43] he was not, on this occasion at least, saying anything particularly radical. All this is true. But let us consider a little more carefully what the God of Love appears to be accusing Chaucer's persona of doing, and the wider valence of that accusation in Chaucer's own time.

What is really being said here? There seem to be three distinct possibilities, though finally, whichever one we opt for, the net consequences of each tend in a similar direction. Minnis explains "For in pleyn text,

---

amoris is dated mid to late 1383 by Williell R. Thomson, *The Latin Writings of John Wyclyf*, Subsidia Mediævalia 14 (Toronto: Pontifical Institute of Mediæval Studies, 1983), pp. 294–95. Also compare Wyclif's view in his *Opus evangelicum*, composed between 1383 and the end of 1384 (Thomson, *Latin Writings*, p. 220), that "fratres, episcopi et sui complices abhorrent quod evangelium in Anglico cognoscatur" ("friars, bishops and their accomplices deplore that the gospel be known in English"); Johann Loserth, ed., *Iohannis Wyclif Operis Evangelici Liber Tertius et Quartus sive De Antichristo Liber Primus et Secundus* (London: Trübner, 1896), p. 115, lines 7–9).

[43] Johann Loserth, ed., *Iohannis Wyclif Sermones*, 4 vols (London: Trübner, 1887–90), vol. 1, p. 83, line 17; compare also Loserth, *Sermones*, vol. 3, p. 170, line 34, where Wyclif maintained that the most important thing was that the literal sense be clear; or Loserth, *Sermones*, vol. 3, p. 140, line 13, that it is wrong to explain away the *sensus litteralis*. For some recent commentary on Wyclif's theory of exegesis, see Kantik Ghosh, *The Wycliffite Heresy: Authority and the Interpretation of Texts* (Cambridge: Cambridge University Press, 2002), pp. 22–66.

withouten nede of glose" as meaning that Chaucer's persona is being credited with having produced a translation of the *Roman de la Rose* so transparent that no further apparatus of explanatory glossing is called for.[44] Perhaps this is so. The fact remains, however, that the God of Love is threatened by the existence of such a translation. Is it being said that the *Roman de la Rose* itself contains heresy against the God of Love's law? If it is, as some of the skeptical content of de Meun's continuation of the *Roman* might reasonably incline us to suppose, then Chaucer's persona aids and abets the heresy in that, having translated the *Roman* in so perfectly pellucid a way, its heretical tenets are communicated fluently and thus served up unchecked for general consumption. Or is it that the production of a translation "in pleyn text, withouten nede of glose" is where the problem lies, an irresponsibly dangerous undertaking of its very nature since, in that case, the volatility of textual meaning goes undisciplined? Moreover, when such translation is afforded to a text as potentially subversive in its meanings as the *Roman*, when text of this sort is left to speak for itself, with no sanitizing gloss to help protect the unwitting reader against infection by senses inconvenient to the established sovereignty—one might say, in recognition of his aura of quasi-clerical authority, the magisterium—of the God of Love, then "pleyn text" translation "withouten nede of glose" may become a strategy of opposition. Or is it rather that it is a translation driven by ill will, rather than charity, that Chaucer's persona is accused of having produced, its lack of gloss serving only to highlight its malice aforethought? He has slandered the God of Love's "olde servauntes" through his translation, and by so alleging, the God of Love reinvents in poetic guise an idea which, though of ancient lineage, was currently being rejuvenated: that the heretic is a slanderer, and that the heretic's translation, since it does not proceed from charity, is a malpractice.[45] Hardly surprising, then, in view of these terms, that the God of Love experiences a slanderous lèse-majesté, when the love/charity that he presumes to embody is assailed by such translation.[46]

Whichever explanations we choose, Chaucer's persona is charged

---

[44] Alastair J. Minnis, with V. J. Scattergood and Jeremy J. Smith, *The Shorter Poems* (Oxford: Clarendon Press, 1995), p. 334. Sheila Delany, *The Naked Text: Chaucer's Legend of Good Women* (Berkeley and Los Angeles: University of California Press, 1994), pp. 122–23, had also canvassed this possibility as one among others.

[45] See Johnson, "Vernacular Valorizing."

[46] I wish to thank Dr. Anne Marie D'Arcy for helpful discussion on this point.

with having engaged in a translation that, knowingly or unknowingly, furthers heresy. Either he is a heretic, or is heresy's accomplice. Certainly, the God of Love considers him a wilful heretic by the time he reaches the end of his accusation.[47] And while Minnis may be distantly right to maintain that commonplaces circulating in the general exegetical tradition have prompted the detail about the translation's lack of "glose," it should also not be forgotten that the question of whether textual glossing is provided or withheld is one raised sharply in contemporary consciousness by the debates surrounding Wycliffism, and that such debates constituted part of the immediate intellectual context in which the *Legend* was received.[48] To be sure, Wycliffites did not object to glossing per se. Yet whatever traditional reservations may already have existed about a potential obfuscation of the *sensus litteralis* that glossing might entail, Wycliffites were quick to further any such unease by castigating glossing specifically as practiced by those who regarded themselves as the guardians of orthodoxy, a glossing of the perverted sort that, in the Lollard view, deliberately traduced and disabled the literal meaning of texts that otherwise might expose the baselessness of the clerical status quo.[49]

Indeed, an antipathy generally to glossing seems to have become a trademark of at least some quarters of the Lollard movement. Thus while this antipathy cannot be considered exclusively theirs, it is nevertheless theirs characteristically.[50] Bishop Reginald Pecock, a mid–

[47] Benson, *Riverside Chaucer*, p. 598, F336, 339–40: "For thogh thou reneyed has my lay, / . . . If that thou lyve, thou shalt repenten this / So cruelly that it shal wel be sene!" The God of Love states that the fierceness of the penance will be plainly evident; conceivably, Chaucer's early readers would have understood the God of Love to intend the spectacle of public penance, an appropriately plainly evident penance if heresy was really what was at issue.

[48] Minnis seems to be reacting to Delany, *Naked Text*, p. 120. While Delany's account oversimplifies, I believe it to be essentially correct.

[49] We need to distinguish two views of glossing from the Wycliffite perspective. There was legitimate glossing; compare the Wycliffite Glossed Gospels, for example, an argument-in-action for legitimate glossing, and perhaps also what the accusation leveled at the Parson by the Shipman may imply ("He schal no gospel glosen here ne teche"; Benson, *Riverside Chaucer*, p. 104, line 1180), for this conceivably refers to a characteristic, line-by-line exposition practiced in some Wycliffite exegesis. (I retract as premature and incomplete my earlier explanation of the meaning of the accusation that the Parson might "glosen the gospel," published in *Preaching, Politics, and Poetry in Late-Medieval England* [Dublin: Four Courts Press, 1998], p. 206.) There was also illegitimate glossing, conventionally attributed by Wycliffites to their opponents, especially to the friars. For some examples of their accusations of illegitimate glossing, see note 53 below.

[50] An instance of comparable antipathy to glossing earlier than Lollardy is found in *Piers Plowman*, where friars glossed the gospel "as hem good likide"; A. V. C. Schmidt, ed., *William Langland Piers Plowman A Parallel-Text Edition of the A, B, C and Z Versions*,

fifteenth century opponent of the Lollards, may not have been representing them altogether fairly in claiming that they maintained "that alle expowners and glose ȝeuers to Holi Scripture ben cursid"[51]— some Lollards did, after all, practise glossing—but the spirit of his observation was essentially sound. And another witness well placed to gain acquaintance of how Lollardy's habits of thought might typically find expression, Thomas Gascoigne, on various occasions chancellor of Oxford University and Pecock's contemporary, associated with *diversi heretici*" their characteristic exploitation of a particular vernacular word play, the purpose of which was to denigrate glossing. (Evidently the "diverse heretics" that Gascoigne had in mind were the Lollards.) The wordplay in question turned upon the fact that since "gloss" and "gloze" were homonyms in Middle English, their ready confuseability could be diverted by heretics to polemical ends: " 'Glosa' enim, si dicatur in vulgo, aliquo putatur 'falsitas'. Dicunt enim diversi heretici quod doctores sancti putative 'glosant' evangelium secundum voluntatem propriam" ("For if [the word] 'gloss' is uttered in the vernacular, it may be interpreted as 'falseness' by anyone [i.e., as 'gloze']. For diverse heretics say that holy doctors 'gloss/gloze' the gospel by supposition, according to their own will").[52] *False* glossing (or glozing, as modern English might now distinguish it) had evidently been one of the more insistent charges leveled at the exegesis of the orthodox clergy in Lollard polemic.[53] It is

---

2 vols (London and New York: Longman, 1995–), vol. 1, p. 9, line 57 (further references to *Piers Plowman* are to this edition, unless otherwise stated). The equivalent sentiment also appears in the Z-text (possibly a little earlier than the A-text just cited, if A. G. Rigg and Charlotte Brewer, eds., *Piers Plowman: The Z Version*, Pontifical Institute of Mediæval Studies, Studies and Texts 59 (Toronto: Pontifical Institute of Mediæval Studies, 1983), pp. 12–20, are correct; though as A. V. C. Schmidt, ed., *William Langland, The Vision of Piers Plowman* [London and Rutland, Vermont: J. M. Dent and Charles E. Tuttle, 1995], p. xxiv maintains, the Z-text cannot be before 1362). The hostility to glossing in the early Z- and A-text is carried over into the later B- and C-text versions, as B.XIII.70, 73–74 witnesses: "Periculum est in falsis fratribus! . . . Ac I wiste neuere freke þat as a frere ȝede bifore men on Englissh / Taken it for hir teme, and telle it wiþouten glosyng!" (Schmidt, *Piers Plowman*, I. 516). Indeed, even St. Francis, ironically enough, had worried about the application of sense-distorting glosses to his own words (rendered faithfully from the original in the Wycliffite translation of St. Francis' Rule; see Matthew, *English Works*, p. 47).

[51] Churchill Babbington, ed., *The Repressor of Over Much Blaming of the Clergy*, Rolls Series 19, 2 vols (London: Longman, Green, Longmans and Roberts, 1860), I, 65. The *Repressor* is dated to c. 1449 (ibid., p. xxii).

[52] Oxford, MS Lincoln College 118, fol. 111v (J. E. Thorold Rogers, ed., *Loci e Libro Veritatis* [Oxford: Clarendon Press, 1881], pp. 142–43, has misread the Lincoln College manuscript's *falsitas* here as *felicitas*).

[53] A preoccupation consistent with Wyclif's; compare, for example, his *Opus evangelicum*: "Et sic scriptitant super legem Domini ut super evangelium et partes alias trahentes per suas glossas sinistras ad suum propositum totam sentenciam legis Dei" ("And thus do they often write upon God's law as [they do] upon the gospel and other parts,

easy to see how the orthodox clergy had walked into the trap of this accusation because, distrusting as they generally did the capacity of anyone beyond the pale of clerical privilege to interpret the plain text of Scripture accurately and safely,[54] they valued the way that their glossing might forestall any interpretation which they were liable to consider "perilous". Thus, for example, we find an orthodox vernacular preacher, composing his sermon sometime between 1389 and 1404 and fully conscious of the threat that Wycliffism posed, revealing tellingly his heightened (orthodox) awareness of the value of prophylactic glossing when commenting on a passage of St Paul: "Þe comen glose declariþ þis texst o þis wyse, & I pray ʒhe takis good hede, vor it is a perlus texst but a

---

hauling the whole meaning of God's law by evil glosses into line with their intention"; Loserth, *Iohannis Wyclif Operis Evangelici Liber Tertius et Quartus*, p. 15, lines 8–11). Among the many vernacular examples, compare these in *Pierce the Ploughman's Crede*: "That folweth fulliche þe feith and none other fables, / With-outen gabbynge of glose as the godspelles telleth"; "Lere me to som man my Crede for to lerne, / That . . . loueth no synne, / And gloseth nought the godspell"; "Swiche a gome godes wordes grysliche gloseth; / Y trowe he toucheth nought the text, but taketh it for a tale" (Helen Barr, ed., *The Piers Plowman Tradition: A Critical Edition of Pierce the Ploughman's Crede, Richard the Redeless, Mum and the Sothsegger and The Crowned King* [London and Rutland, Vermont: J. M. Dent and Charles E. Tuttle, 1993]; see respectively p. 73, lines 274–75, p. 75, lines 343–45, and p. 85, lines 585–86); or this in the tract *De pontificum Romanorum schismate*: "in oure dayes seiþ Antecristis clerkis, þat among alle lawes þat evere God suffride, beþ boþe his testamentis falseste of alle oþere; and herfore men schulde glose hem aftir her owne wille, and þe wordis of þes glosatouris passiþ Goddis lawe" (Thomas Arnold, ed., *Select English Works of John Wyclif*, 3 vols. [Oxford: Clarendon Press, 1867–71], III.258, lines 15–19). (A few other vernacular examples are given in Anne Hudson, "A Lollard Sect Vocabulary?," in Michael Benskin and M. L. Samuels, eds., *So meny people longages and tonges: Philological Essays in Scots and Medieval English presented to Angus McIntosh* [Edinburgh, 1981], pp. 15–30; rpt. in *Lollards and Their Books*, pp. 165–80; see p. 178, note 27.)

[54] Wyclif accused the orthodox of monopolizing the right of interpretation. For example, in his letter, given under the heading *De condemnatione xix conclusionum* in the *Fasciculi Zizaniorum*, he remonstrates: "Et sic papa potest quemlibet librum de canone scripturae subtrahere et novum addere, et per consequens potest totum bibliam innovare, et per consequens totam scripturam sacram haereticare, et oppositum christianae fidei catholicare" ("And thus the pope can remove any book from the canon of Scripture and add a new one, and consequently he can make the Bible anew, and thus hereticate the whole of sacred Scripture, and make Catholic what is opposed to the Christian faith"; Walter Waddington Shirley, ed., *Fasciculi Zizaniorum Magistri Johannis Wyclif cum Tritico*, Rolls Series 5 [London: Longman, Brown, Green, Longmans, and Roberts, 1858], p. 481); or again in his Latin sermons: "Pervertunt enim sensum scripture suis simulacionibus, impediunt simplices Christi a predicacione evangelii suis fictis machinacionibus et trahunt ad se totam interpretacionem scripture suis subdolis cavillacionibus" ("For they [i.e., the evil sects within the Church] pervert the sense of Scripture with their fictions, they impede Christ's simple [folk] from the preaching of the gospel by their invented machinations, and they appropriate unto themselves the whole interpretation of Scripture with their cunning quibbles"; Loserth, *Sermones*, p. 404, lines 4–8).

man take þe glose þerwith".[55] This was the sort of hermeneutic that Wycliffites held in the greatest suspicion, accusing the orthodox of premeditated textual hijacking and claiming that such glossing/glozing was being used to coerce the meaning of a text in directions supportive of vested interests. Thus Chaucer's persona, in producing a "pleyn text" translation "withouten nede of glose," has produced the kind of text that, in the real world, we have evidence that many a Wycliffite would have been thought to have approved (notwithstanding any actual glossing that certain Wycliffites may themselves have generated around the canonical texts).

To sum up so far: outside *The Canterbury Tales* (and in addition to the *Troilus* passage noted above), Chaucer dealt at least twice with heretical types and conditions. First, we need to introduce into our reading of *An ABC* an awareness of how Chaucer may have constructed his penitent in terms of the culture of heresy, situating him within *errour*. (Incidentally, were it to prove that this construction stemmed from Chaucer's acquaintance with newly urgent heresy, it follows that *An ABC* was written sometime after 1381–82, the time after which heresy became an increasingly alarming issue for the English Church.)[56] And second, we also need to introduce to our reading of the *Prologue* to *The Legend of Good Women* a fuller awareness of how Chaucer caused the God of Love to cast Chaucer's persona in an oppositional role, that of heretical challenger to his authority. While in *An ABC* heresy's real-life discourse seems to be inscried in "pleyn text," in the *Legend* that discourse is sophisticated into the playful literary "glose" through which Chaucer's persona, and his relation to the God of Love, is to be understood; in this poem, the culture of heresy is transmuted into a trope that endows the God of Love's pronouncements, and the transgressions of Chaucer's

---

[55] The text is found in the great Benedictine sermon anthology preserved in Worcester, Cathedral Library, MS F.10, fol. 44 (D. M. Grisdale, ed., *Three Middle English Sermons from the Worcester Chapter Manuscript F.10*, Leeds School of English Language Texts and Monographs 5 [Kendal: Titus Wilson, 1939], p. 33, lines 369–71).

[56] Fourteenth-century England was not noticeably agitated by heresy before the arrival of Wycliffism. Gregory XI's bull listing Wyclif's errors was issued in May 1377 (see Shirley, *Fasciculi Zizaniorum*, pp. 242–44, and see David Wilkins, ed., *Concilia Magnae Britanniae et Hiberniae*, 4 vols. [London: Gosling, Gyles, Woodward and Davis, 1737; rpt., Brussels, 1964], vol. 3, p. 123, for the list of errors there condemned; the condemnation is studied by Joseph H. Dahmus, *The Prosecution of John Wyclyf* [New Haven: Yale University Press, 1952], pp. 25, 49–51), but it was not until 1382 that Wyclif's Eucharistic doctrine was hereticated at the Blackfriars Council in Oxford (the Blackfriars proceedings are outlined in H. B. Workman, *John Wyclif: A Study of the Medieval Church*, 2 vols. [Oxford: Clarendon Press, 1926], vol. 2, pp. 140–48).

persona, with their own peculiar pseudo-solemnity. A fresher resonance is audible in this passage, and then again in Alceste's later defense of Chaucer's persona,[57] once it is acknowledged that we have to reckon here not just with traditional ideas about translation and exegesis, but also with their status as contested practices in a current and increasingly polemicized debate. How all this may open a window into Chaucer's biography is a question that the last part of this essay will explore.

Intertextual heresy

From *An ABC* and *The Legend of Good Women*, we turn now to *The Canterbury Tales*, and so from poetic personae framed in relation to the culture of heresy to a series of intertextual allusions to sentiments and turns of phrase characteristically current in Wycliffism. Recent work on this particular Chaucerian intertextuality has yielded impressive results, notably in the case of the Wife of Bath.[58] However, much more remains to be said. We will begin by revisiting the pilgrim in *The Canterbury Tales* whom many have found the most contemptible, the Pardoner, before moving to some of the other Canterbury culpables. Finally, we will consider their moral antithesis as represented by the paragon Parson; for if the culpables illustrate between them things wrong in the Church, the paragon illustrates something right in it. The paragon and the culpables counterpoint and help to define each other, legitimating in the process a grid of ecclesiological norms. But many of the terms that Chaucer chose for expressing the poles of clerical right and clerical wrong were not neutral, as we shall see; on the contrary, they carried with them a radical, if not factional, charge that would have sounded increasingly alarming the further on the right wing of orthodoxy early readers positioned themselves. Which means that in this aspect of his

---

[57] Essentially, Alceste argues four points in support of Chaucer's persona: 1) there is much malice at court, so he may stand falsely accused; 2) he may have acted in innocence, not out of malice, "for he useth thynges to make"; 3) he may have acted in response to a command that could not be gainsaid (compare John Trevisa's claim that he was responding to the express request of Lord Berkeley in translating Ranulf Higden's *Polychronicon*; Wogan-Browne, Watson, Taylor and Evans, *Idea of the Vernacular*, pp. 134–35, lines 132–60); and 4) he has certainly written material supportive of the God of Love in the past. Also, Chaucer's persona maintains his innocence, since his *intention* had been "To forthren trouthe in love and yt cheryce" (Benson, *Riverside Chaucer*, p. 601, F472); on the intention of the translator, see the references in notes 35 and 37 above.

[58] Blamires, "Wife of Bath."

writing, Chaucer would have sounded rather more topical to early readers than has generally been allowed, and to some of them even provocative. In short, in this aspect of his work as in so many others, Chaucer
laid the basis for a range of possible reader responses, all of which were
nevertheless refreshed in common with contemporary relevance, not left
dustily bookish and remote.

The Pardoner

Orthodox believers within the Church were as troubled as Lollards were
by a grass-roots malpractice that had grown up around the Church's
theology of pardon and indulgence (though Lollard objections extended
even further, to defy the orthodox theology of pardon and indulgence
itself). Well before the 1390s, ecclesiastical legislation had been put in
place to curb embezzling pardoners. By Chaucer's day, as is well known,
they had scandalous reputations.[59] (Their first recorded appearance in
English known to date is in the earliest versions of *Piers Plowman*, the
Z- and A-texts, composed by William Langland probably sometime in
the early 1360s.)[60] Yet while the Church was well aware of its delinquent
pardoners and was making some effort to police the ranks, it was not
Church policy to publicize at large shortcomings uncovered so uncomfortably close to home. This ecclesiastical habit of not washing dirty
linen in public, and certainly not in the vernacular, where the "lewd"
laity would get to hear of scandalizing clerical crimes that would breed
resentment between the estates, had a long history. And the policy was
widely advertised: compare, for example, the advice given to clerics in
various preaching manuals, that castigation of clerical vice should be
strictly reserved for clerical audiences and occasions.[61] So while criticism

[59] See A. L. Kellogg and L. A. Haselmayer, "Chaucer's Satire of the Pardoner,"
PMLA 66 (1951): 251–77.

[60] It has been argued by Jill Mann, *Chaucer and Medieval Estates Satire: The Literature
of Social Classes and the General Prologue to the Canterbury Tales* (Cambridge: Cambridge
University Press, 1973), pp. 149, 208–12, that Chaucer's inclusion of the Pardoner in
the *General Prologue* was influenced by Langland, and her view is endorsed by Patterson,
"Chaucer's Pardoner on the Couch," p. 671. However, the fact that pardoners have a
substantial existence in the vernacular Wycliffite derivatives could as easily be used to
argue Chaucer's proximity to Lollard writing as much as to Langland's, and thus renders
the proposed Langlandian influence here much less compelling; connections between
Langland and Chaucer are better argued on other grounds than this.

[61] Compare, for example, the fourteenth-century *De modo componendi sermones* of the
Dominican preacher Thomas Waleys: "ubi solum est populus, non invehatur contra
clerum aut vitia quae solum clericis consueverunt inesse, quia hoc est exhortari populum
ut clerum contemnat" ("where there is laity only present, do not inveigh against the
clergy or against vices which the clergy alone are wont to display, because this is to

of pardoners, or of any other "noble ecclesiaste," for that matter, was perfectly legitimate (and certainly traditional), there were strong (ortho-dox) views on what the appropriate forum for that criticism might be. Chaucer, like Langland, had implicitly flouted those views.[62] So, of course, had the followers of John Wyclif, but this on principle.[63] The fourteenth-century citations given for the word "pardoner" in the *Oxford English Dictionary* and the *MED* reveal a suggestive fact. Apart from Langland, who already held a mandate for social reform earlier than anything that the subsequent arrival of Wycliffism might have put into his head,[64] the only vernacular (and therefore necessarily public) in-stances of the word "pardoner" appear in Chaucer and in various English writings of Wycliffite sympathy.[65] Is this coincidence between Chaucer and the Lollards solely the result of the randomness of record survival? More may be at stake than that. In the context of what the orthodox considered fit matter for public discussion, to assert that Chaucer's Par-doner was merely a traditional reprobate misses a political dimension to his presentation that is accessed by the very fact of his public airing in *English*.[66]

---

encourage the laity to scorn the clergy"; Th.-M. Charland, ed., *Artes Praedicandi: Contri-bution à l'histoire de la rhétorique au moyen âge*, Publications de l'Institut d'Études Médié-vales d'Ottawa 7 (Paris and Montréal: Vrin; Institut d'études médiévales, 1936), p. 338).

[62] It would seem to matter little, as far as the spirit of the Church's advice was concerned, that Chaucer was of lay status: he would still have risked appearing to have been out of charity. Langland's case, of course, if he really was in minor Orders, was much more sensitive.

[63] Note the blunt Wycliffite contempt for the Church's policy of discretion in not openly mentioning sinners by name: "anticristis prelatis & veyn religious seyn þat it is aȝenst charite to nemne hem bi name in open sermon & in here absence" (Matthew, *English Works*, p. 273, in the tract *How Satan and His Priests*).

[64] See generally Wendy Scase, *Piers Plowman and the New Anticlericalism* (Cambridge: Cambridge University Press, 1989). The question of the relation between Langland and Lollardy is complex. For some recent commentary, see Alan J. Fletcher, *Preaching, Politics and Poetry in Late Medieval England* (Dublin: Four Courts Press, 1998), pp. 201–14.

[65] The vernacular Wycliffite tracts and polemics, many of which have been published in the collections edited by Arnold, *Select English Works*, and by F. D. Matthew, ed., *The English Works of Wyclif hitherto unprinted*, EETS, os 74 (London: Trübner, 1880), are, for the greater part, notoriously difficult to date with precision. Nevertheless, it is likely that the majority were produced within a period of approximately thirty years, between c. 1390 and c. 1420; and further, that the bulk of them appeared earlier, rather than later, in this period.

[66] On the traditional literary aspects of the Pardoner, see Mann, *Medieval Estates Sat-ire*, pp. 145–52. Yet as she rightly observes (ibid., p. 277, note 14), there is often some "topical situation in which Chaucer conceives of his estates stereotypes." Indeed, the topicality of the Rouncival reference in Chaucer's portrait of the Pardoner was early noticed by S. Moore, "Chaucer's Pardoner of Rouncival," *MP* 25 (1927): 59–66.

This dimension is probed further. There are several other pungent details of Chaucer's presentation that the anticlerical lobby of the 1390's, whether its members would have consciously regarded themselves as followers of Wyclif or not, would have soon sniffed out and relished. The unholy alliance between the Pardoner and the Summoner, for example, opens up the vista of a corrupt chain of collusions which in Wyclif's writings and those of his even more stridently partisan followers was conceived as reaching throughout the orthodox Church and right up to Rome itself.[67] Why did Chaucer pair the Pardoner and the Summoner in the way he has, if not to capitalize on a familiar, dangerous liaison that some radicals were already minded to detect between such dubious Church functionaries?[68]

Work on *The Pardoner's Prologue* and *Tale* has thrown light on the extent to which this text is in touch with the terms of the contempory Lollard-versus-orthodox controversy.[69] A case already made need not be

[67] Compare Wyclif's polemical figure of "the twelve daughters of the leech." These "daughters" ranged from popes and cardinals at the top of the Church hierarchy down to pardoners at the bottom. Loserth, *Sermones*, vol. 3, p. 453: "sunt duodecim filie sanguissuge in brachio clericali, quos quidam sic nominant: pape, cardinales, episcopi, archidiaconi, officiales et decani, rectores, presbyteri seculares, religiosi possessionati et mendici, clerici et questores. Isti autem duodecim post dotacionem ecclesie et postquam clerus sit ad *cupiditatem* temporalium *que est radix omnium malorum* secundum Apostolorum inclinatus, sunt tortores temporalium et ad onus ecclesie, non profectum." ("In the clerical arm are twelve daughters of the leech, that some men name as follows: popes, cardinals, bishops, archdeacons, officials and deans, rectors, secular priests, the religious (possessioners and mendicants), clerks and pardoners. However, these twelve, following the endowment of the Church and, after the clergy, inclined towards greed for temporalities [which according to the Apostle is the root of all evils], are [become] extorters of temporalities and a burden on, not a profit to, the Church.")

[68] For example, they fraternize in one of the stanzas of *The Plowman's Tale* (W. W. Skeat, ed., *Chaucerian and Other Pieces* [Oxford: Clarendon Press, 1897], pp. 147–90; see p. 157, lines 325–28). This Lollard poem may have been written in the early fifteenth century (Andrew Wawn, "The Genesis of The Plowman's Tale," *YES* 2 [1972]: 21–40; see p. 39), though it is extant only from the sixteenth century. (I make this point without intending to exclude other suggestive areas opened up by Chaucer's pairing; for example, Paul A. Olson, *The Canterbury Tales and the Good Society* [Princeton, N.J.: Princeton University Press, 1986], pp. 184–85, makes an interesting case for seeing the Summoner and Pardoner as inversions of the keys of binding and loosing.)

[69] Fletcher, *Preaching, Politics and Poetry*, pp. 266–80; see also now the sensitive reading of Carolyn Dinshaw, *Getting Medieval: Sexualities and Communities, Pre- and Postmodern* (Durham: Duke University Press, 1999), pp. 55–99. The frame of reference argued in the present article for reading the Pardoner (that is, for reading him morally within terms established by a field of orthodox versus radical/heretical texts), is given additional nuance by Patterson, "Chaucer's Pardoner on the Couch," pp. 664–71. For commentary specifically on the substance/accident issue to which *The Pardoner's Prologue* alludes (Benson, *Riverside Chaucer*, p. 197, lines 538–40), see Paul Strohm, "Chaucer's Lollard Joke: History and the Textual Unconscious," *SAC* 17 (1995): 23–42.

repeated, but it seems worth noting that more can be said for it than has been, and this in at least three departments. One is the question of the position that *The Pardoner's Prologue* and *Tale* takes on the theology of pardon and indulgence itself. As is well known, the orthodox rationale for pardon, and the theological mechanisms by which pardon was thought to operate, were commonly considered indefensible by the Lollards.[70] It is also true that, well before Lollardy, the operation of pardon had already occasioned debates within orthodoxy. Indeed, some of this antecedent (orthodox) anxiety about pardon's praxis may be refracted in the controversial scene in the A- and B-texts of *Piers Plowman* where Piers tears up the pardon sent from Truth.[71] Yet, while orthodoxy fully recognized some of the theological danger inherent in its own praxis, it never rejected that praxis per se, as would the Lollards later. Even as Piers tore up Truth's pardon, Langland never allowed things progress as far as that.[72] One could thus regard the Lollard position on pardon as having exploited the fissure of anxiety already running through pardon's orthodox praxis, though now in Lollardy widened to the point of collapsing that praxis. But did Chaucer through his Pardoner do something similar? This is far more difficult to decide, but what seems of interest is that disquiet resides in the very fact of its undecideability. To illustrate how provocative what the Pardoner says about pardon may have sounded, we need to set it carefully within its contemporary context, and remark what emerges.

The Pardoner's verdict on pardon constitutes the momentary "paroxysm of agonized sincerity" that George Kittredge famously perceived the Pardoner to lapse into towards the end of the *Tale* (lines 916–18):

> And Jhesu Crist, that is oure soules leche,
> So graunte yow his pardoun to receyve,
> For that is best; I wol yow nat deceyve.[73]

[70] For the orthodox theology of pardon and indulgence, see *quaestiones* 25 to 27 of Thomas Aquinas on the *Sentences* of Peter the Lombard (Caramello, *Summa Theologiae*, vol. 3, pp. 75–83). Lollard objection to pardon and indulgence is well attested; compare, for example, the ninth of the *Twelve Conclusions* of the Lollards posted in 1395 (Anne Hudson, ed., *Selections from English Wycliffite Writings* [Cambridge: Cambridge University Press, 1978; rpt., Toronto: Toronto University Press, 1997], pp. 27–28, lines 114–34), and the further discussion below here.

[71] Schmidt, *Piers Plowman*, vol. 1, p. 345, lines 101–7 (A text), p. 344, lines 115–21 (B text).

[72] Langland stresses his orthodoxy on the question of the validity of pardon and indulgence (Schmidt, *Piers Plowman*, vol. 1, lines 158–64 [A-text], p. 350, lines 174–9 [B-text], and 351, lines 324–29 [C-text]).

[73] See George L. Kittredge, *Chaucer and His Poetry* (Cambridge, Mass.: Harvard University Press, 1946), p. 217.

Let us try to estimate how this "paroxysm" would have been received by Chaucer's orthodox contemporaries. Before we can properly do that, it will be helpful first to compare what another text, one of impeccable orthodoxy, says about pardon, and use it as a benchmark. The text in question is extracted from a sermon written by Chaucer's contemporary, the Augustinian canon John Mirk, probably during the decade in which Chaucer started work on *The Canterbury Tales*.[74] On the face of it, it would seem that Mirk has done something similar to what the Pardoner has done in suggesting that there is a *hierarchy* of pardon. Commenting on the papal indulgence that granted a full pardon every fifth year to pilgrims to Rome, Mirk reasonably observed that not everyone could manage to get there to avail of it. So, what of them?

Bot for alle mowe not come þidur and haue þis pardon, þe Pope of Heuen, Ihesu Criste, of hys special grace graunteth alle men and wommen ful pardon of hure synnus in here deth-day, so þat þei wol kepon be here lyve [*during their life*] þre thyngus þat ben nedeful to hem. Þe wheche ben þese: fful contricion wyth schryuing, hol charite wythoute feynyng, and stabul fayth wythowtyn flottering. Sothly, wythowtyn þese þre, þer may no man haue pardon at Rome ne ellyswhere.[75]

Here, the "Pope of Heuen," Jesus Christ, implicitly supersedes the earthly pope. But in that may lie the precise distinction between Mirk and Chaucer. Such supersession in Mirk is present only implicitly; it is not overtly exploited. Chaucer, by contrast, allows his Pardoner to say bluntly that Christ's pardon is best. Since the best pardon is Christ's pardon—even John Mirk, had that proposition been put to him, could not have disagreed—any other form is necessarily inferior. (Also, since any other form appears so regrettably prone to unscrupulous manipulation—witness the Pardoner's corrupt *modus vivendi*—readers unconcerned about nice distinctions may have found pardon's demonstrated vulnerability the next best thing to an attack on the theology behind it.) The sheer absoluteness of the Pardoner's words thus enables a judgment on the orthodox praxis of pardon: his moment of "agonized sincerity" could be interpreted as working to undermine both him and the institution that fosters him by nudging orthodox readers into contem-

---

[74] On the date of Mirk's *Festial* (probably c. 1382–90), see Alan J. Fletcher, "John Mirk and the Lollards," *MÆ* 55 (1987): 59–66.

[75] London, British Library, MS Cotton Claudius A.ii, fol. 42v (given from this manuscript, a text of the *Festial* generally superior to that edited by Erbe, *Festial*, p. 74, lines 21–28).

plating a position that they would not ordinarily contemplate. When this corrupt deceiver expresses a truth—Christ's pardon is best—it is an unmediated truth that, in the moment of its utterance, has also laid the foundation for a critique both of the Pardoner's profession and, whether intentionally or not on Chaucer's part, of the orthodox institution of pardon. Thus Chaucer's text makes *explicitly* clear something that is only latent in Mirk, and in so doing, it has manoeuvered readers into considering the final step in a logical sequence: if Christ's pardon is best, why bother with any other? The *explicit* supersession in the Pardoner's words gestures now toward the contemplation of an actual suppression of the praxis. And suppression, of course, is the Lollard position: "þer comeþ no pardon but of God for good lyuynge & endynge in charite, & þis schal not be bouȝt ne solde as prelatis chafferen [*buy and sell*] þes dayes".[76] There is no pardon but God's, claims this Wycliffite tract, so let all the rest be done away with. Has the Pardoner, then, announced an orthodox position on pardon and indulgence, or has he broached a Wycliffite one? The answer seems undecideable. Yet that very undecideability leaves reader response teetering on an edge between orthodox and heterodox possibilities.[77] Through the Pardoner and his words, the standard, orthodox theology of pardon and indulgence is left looking sickly. Whether rightly or wrongly, some could have guessed Wycliffism here at the time this tale was written.

As if this troubled take on orthodox pardon and indulgence would not have sounded suspicious enough in some quarters, tinier details of the Pardoner's portraiture are also likely to have sounded similar. We come now to a second group of instances. To be told, for example, in *The General Prologue* that the Pardoner's wallet was "Bretful of pardoun comen from Rome al hoot" is mischievous when we recall what people's sensitivities currently were: "But of þo pardoun þat men use to day fro þe Court of Rome, þei have no sikernesse [*warrant*] by holy writte ne resoun, ne ensaumple of Crist or his apostlis,"[78] says the Lollard tract *Fifty Errors and Heresies of Friars*, and another (related) Lollard argument against pardon and indulgence was that one of the chief beneficiaries of swindling pardoners was the Roman curia itself. Through their agency,

---

[76] Matthew, *English Works*, p. 238 (in the tract *Of Servants and Lords*).

[77] And compare the indeterminacy identified in *The Monk's Tale* by Olson, *Good Society*, p. 161, where he finds Chaucer situating the *Tale* "between the Wycliffites and their monastic opponents".

[78] Arnold, *Select English Works*, vol. 3, p. 385.

good English money was hemorrhaging Romewards.[79] So Chaucer's naming of the source of the Pardoner's walletful of pardons, Rome, catches at a topical, nationalist resentment that Lollards were capitalizing on and thus becoming identified with. In addition to this, the Pardoner's sprightly indifference to what happened to the souls of those he fleeced (lines 405–6)—"I rekke nevere, whan that they been beryed, / Though that hir soules goon a-blakeberyed!"—sounds like Chaucer's poetic reworking of another motif commonly found in Lollard writing, namely, that mercenaries like him do not care about what happens to the souls they traffic in: "ȝif mennus soulis gon to helle bi brekynge of goddis comaundementis no warde [*no matter*], so þat þe peny come faste to fille here hondis & coffris," observes one Wycliffite author, and another, "ȝif þei han money & gold at here lykynge bi extorsion & robberie, þei recken not of cristene soulis [*they do not care about Christian souls*] hou foul deuelis deuouren hem".[80] And a precisely dated instance of this Lollard preoccupation with men of the Church whose *cura* is of Mammon, not of souls, appears in a sermon by Chaucer's contemporary, the Lollard Robert Lychlade, which he preached in Oxford on the vigil of the Ascension in 1395: "Videte igitur quomodo pastores, qui populis preesse debent, temporibus modernis sequentes mammona iniquitatis et non querentes vitam eternam animas perdunt gregis Christi, modicum aut nullum zelum habentes pro animabus set pro pecuniis"[81] ("See, therefore, how pastors nowadays, who ought to set an example to people, pursuing the Mammon of iniquity and not caring for eternal life, bring the souls of Christ's flock to perdition, barely or not at all having zeal for [their] souls, but for [their] money"). The likes of the uncaring Pardoner, then, for whom souls are as milch cows, inhabit the pages of contemporary Lollard polemic in terms that come very close to Chaucer's own, even were his detail about post-mortem rambles to pick blackberries his own unique touch. More of Chaucer's construction of

[79] Benson, *Riverside Chaucer*, p. 34, line 687. To reference but two Lollard complaints on the export of currency, see, for example, Matthew, *English Works*, p. 82 (in the tract *Of Prelates*) and p. 154 (in the tract *The Office of Curates*).

[80] Matthew, *English Works*, p. 72 (in the tract *Of Prelates*) and p. 266 (in the tract *How Satan and his Priests*), respectively. Compare also *The Plowman's Tale* (Skeat, *Chaucerian and Other Pieces*, p. 170, lines 729–32): "A cure of soule[s] they care nat for, / So they mowe money take; / Whether hir soules be wonne or lore, / Hir profits they woll nat forsake."

[81] Siegfried Wenzel, "Robert Lychlade's Oxford Sermon of 1395," *Traditio* 53 (1998): 203–30; see p. 212.

the Pardoner than has been recognized may have been suggested by radical, indeed heterodox, models such as these. Certainly, in their company, the Pardoner's opinions sound strangely familiar.

The third department in which Chaucer's invention of the Pardoner connects with current controversy requires a return to the famous "gelding or mare" equivocation of *The General Prologue*. More remains to be said about this. In Chaucer's time as today, society's objects of polemical attack might find themselves tarred with some infraction of those gender normativities through which society customarily articulated its sense of selfhood. The Pardoner has without question been conscripted to the margins where the representations authorized by dominant ideology typically oblige such abjected objects to exist. The mapping of the particular marginal terrain that the Pardoner inhabits has recently been undertaken by Carolyn Dinshaw.[82] While much has been made of the Pardoner as "eunuch," in various senses of that word, rather less has been made of the Pardoner as "hermaphrodite."[83] Yet this latter status deserves greater attention. For whatever else it may be, the Pardoner's polemical sexual projection is also hermaphroditic, and what seems to call for fuller appreciation is the way in which this hermaphroditic projection writes and literalizes in the Pardoner's flesh a polemical metaphor—conspicuous less in terms of formally attested frequency than of

---

[82] Carolyn Dinshaw, *Chaucer's Sexual Poetics* (Madison: University of Wisconsin Press, 1989); also, her *Getting Medieval: Sexualities and Communities, Pre- and Postmodern*. Both studies are invaluable.

[83] The category "hermaphrodite" in the Pardoner's case is highly complex, however. The medieval hermaphrodite was generally understood as a simultaneous combination (though not necessarily a simultaneous plenitude, complete in every last detail) of male and female genital equipment, however that combination was precisely registered and achieved physiologically. In the portrait of the Pardoner in *The General Prologue*, his hare's eyes suggest an hermaphroditic condition directly and positively, but in the "gelding or mare" equivocation, he is also characterized as hermaphrodite negatively, in terms of *absences*, not of simultaneous male and female genital presences: according to the equivocation, either he is a gelding (penis, no testicles, so a "not-man," as Dinshaw, *Sexual Poetics*, p. 158, notes, but not a woman either); or he is a mare (no male genitals, or their displacement by female genitals, and thus their absence by displacement, but again a "not-woman," as Dinshaw, ibid., notes, because he is still a "he"). However, could it be that the ground of the Pardoner's equivocal definition, in its second term, "mare," is being allowed to shift, and that he is now starting to be defined less in terms of varying degrees of absence of male genitals than in terms of his taking the "mare's" role in heteronormative (and hence gender-defining) sex acts (that is, in terms of an absence of the male penetrative role)? If so, this would leave him as "not-woman" in actual genital terms, but as not-man in sex-act terms, thus preserving the suggestion of hermaphroditism around him while shifting the duality that constitutes hermaphroditism onto a different level.

high public profile—mobilized in a famous moment of Lollard versus orthodox dispute. The either/or equivocation that summarizes the impression that Chaucer the pilgrim has formed of the Pardoner in *The General Prologue*—"I couldn't say whether he was one thing (a castrated male [horse]) or another (a female [horse])"—mimes in its syntax of indecision the radical undecideability with which hermaphroditism similarly plays in its unhinging, see-saw balance between (usually and normatively distinct) genders.[84] And should this reading seem too subtle, the hermaphroditic intimation that I argue the syntactic equivocation figures is figured less controversially in the Pardoner's eyes, eyes that glare with a hare's intensity, an animal long recognized as hermaphrodite in bestiary lore.[85] But in 1395, it was for the polemically derogatory, neither-this-nor-that muddle of hermaphroditism that the Lollards reached when they sought an appropriate figure for churchmen who perversely, in their view, mixed spirituality with temporality.[86] Lollards maximized the circulation of this figure, moreover, when they posted their *Twelve Conclusions* on the doors of Westminster Hall (also of St Paul's Cathedral, according to the chronicler Walsingham) during the time of the parliament that sat between 27 January and 15 February.[87] Thus an intimation of hermaphroditism, in this context, may become not simply one of a strangely unmeasurable sexuality, but also a contemporary partisan construction, one in which Chaucer's Pardoner, a confounder of the material and spiritual, just as his body seems to confound the traditional exclusivities of gender, might also be reckoned to have participated.

[84] Critics have often sought to resolve the tense ambivalence here that threatens intelligibility, sometimes doing so by foregrounding one aspect of the equivocation at the expense of the other (as, for example, does the fine article by Monica McAlpine, "The Pardoner's Homosexuality and How It Matters," *PMLA* 95 (1980): 8–22).

[85] Benson, *Riverside Chaucer*, pp. 824–25, note to line 684.

[86] The English text of the *Twelve Conclusions* is edited in Hudson, *Selections*, pp. 24–29; see p. 26, lines 62–72, for the sixth conclusion in which the slur is made. The conclusion also calls men "of duble astate" ambidexters, a term whose significance Hudson's commentary neglects (as does her essay "*Hermofrodita or Ambidexter*: Wycliffite Views on Clerks in Secular Office," in Margaret Aston and Colin Richmond, eds., *Lollardy and Gentry in the Later Middle Ages* [New York; St Martin's Press; Stroud, U.K.: Alan Sutton, 1997], pp. 41–51), but as Dinshaw, *Getting Medieval*, pp. 79–80, has perceived, it is a traditional one (and see the further material in note 125 below).

[87] Shirley, *Fasciculi Zizaniorum*, pp. 360–69; H. S. Cronin, ed., *Liber contra duodecim errores et hereses Lollardorum* (London: Wyclif Society, 1922). See also Henry T. Riley, ed., *Thomæ Walsingham, quondam Monachi S. Albani, Historia Anglicana*, Rolls Series 28, 2 vols. (London: Eyre and Spottiswoode, 1863–64), II. 216.

The Friar

When looking for material from which to manufacture his Friar, Chaucer had a huge legacy of antimendicant writing and sentiment to hand. Criticism of the friars had been piling up now for the best part of a century and a half.[88] Consequently, it comes as no surprise to find that each of the four principal attributes of the Friar in *The General Prologue*—an insinuation of lechery, his cultivation of the well-to-do, the disputed question of his claims against parish curates to be able to hear the confessions of their parishioners, and his general venality in the matter of imposing penance—is plentifully in evidence well before the 1390s.[89] Attributes like these were musty antimendicant stereotypes. But what requires notice is the way in which Chaucer appears to have spring-cleaned them, bringing them up to date and so making them seem less stereotypical than they actually were. While certain aspects of the Friar's presentation, therefore, have a traditional ring to them, others have been couched in terms that may be more recent. These renovated aspects would have given a varnish of contemporary relevance to what otherwise might have seemed a stale and familiar matter (and stale familiarity would have been a depressing prospect to any poet entertaining ambitions approaching Chaucer's). So we should not be surprised to find that even some of the most traditional failings attributed to the Friar appear to have been refurbished in a contemporary style.

Three can be considered here. First, there is the detail that the Friar's "semycope," a short cloak comprising part of his habit, was luxurious. (Luxury can be inferred from the fact (line 262) that it was made "Of double worstede.")[90] It was therefore contrary to the spirit of holy poverty officially cherished by his Order. This question of luxuriously hab-

<hr/>

[88] For a general survey, see Penn R. Szittya, *The Antifraternal Tradition in Medieval Literature* (Princeton: Princeton University Press, 1986).

[89] See Janette Richardson's headnote to *The Friar's Tale* in Benson, *Riverside Chaucer*, pp. 807–8.

[90] "Double worsted" is a favourite target in other Lollard contexts. Compare *Pierce the Ploughman's Crede*: "His cope that biclypped him wel clene was it folden, / Of double worstede y-dyght doun to the hele" (Barr, *Piers Plowman Tradition*, p. 71, lines 227–28); and *The Plowman's Tale* (Skeat, *Chaucerian and Other Pieces*, p. 179, line 1002) where the monk is said to be "With double worsted well y-dight." In *Friar Daw's Reply*, Daw turns the tables, using Lollard-sounding accusations against his accuser Jack Upland (P. L. Heyworth, ed., *Jack Upland, Friar Daw's Reply and Upland's Rejoinder* [Oxford: Oxford University Press, 1968], p. 84, lines 364–65): "Why is þi gowne, Iakke, widder þan þi cote, / And þi cloke al aboue as round as a belle."

ited friars was one of the issues raised in the attack launched against the mendicant Orders by John Ashwardby, a vicar of the University Church of St Mary the Virgin in Oxford in the late 1380s. Ashwardby, as his more famous opponent, the Carmelite friar Richard Maidstone, insinuated, was a follower of Wyclif.[91] Ashwardby's attacks, delivered publicly from the pulpit in English, urged the laity not to give alms to friars vested in *capae* ("cloaks") that were expensive. These texts do not survive, but their substance can be deduced from Maidstone's rebuttals of them.[92] The date of the Maidstone versus Ashwardby controversy is hard to pinpoint, though it is likely to have developed over a period of time, after 1384 and probably a little before 1390.[93] Thus it occurred close to Chaucer's writing of *The General Prologue*, generally thought to date between c. 1388–92.[94] This is not to suggest that the dispute between Ashwardby and Maidstone was the source of Chaucer's "semycope" detail, and that he had somehow got to hear of it. But what it does show is how topical the detail was and this in the heated atmosphere of a debate that was not simply anticlerical, but associated with the current war of polemic being waged between orthodoxy and Wycliffite heterodoxy. In fact, other Wycliffite sources that are also closely contemporary single out for censure the richness of the cloth used for friars' "cloaks" in a similar way.[95] The Lollard tract *Jack Upland*, for example, composed c. 1390,[96] poses the accusing question:

[91] Benson, *Riverside Chaucer*, pp. 808–9; see Valerie Edden, "The Debate between Richard Maidstone and the Lollard Ashwardby (ca. 1390)," *Carmelus* 34 (1987): 113–34 (another account of the dispute, convenient but less detailed, is found in Anne Hudson, *The Premature Reformation: Wycliffite Texts and Lollard History* [Oxford: Clarendon Press, 1988], pp. 95–97).

[92] Edden, "Debate," p. 123: "expresse docuit quod nullus daret elemosinam fratri qui forte haberet meliorem capam quam essent omnia bona sua" ("he openly taught that no one should give alms to a friar who perhaps might have a *capa* worth more than all his possessions").

[93] J. Crompton, "*Fasciculi Zizaniorum*," *JEH* 12 (1961): 35–45 and 155–66, has suggested a date c. 1392 (see p. 157). However, Edden, "Debate," pp. 114–15, argues strongly for a date between 1384 and 1390, perhaps a little before 1390. She notes that Ashwardby was vicar of St. Mary's from 26 November 1384 to January 1395, so Maidstone's rejoinder must fall between those dates. Ashwardby is referred to as "meus doctor" by Maidstone, a degree Ashwardby received some time before 1391.

[94] Benson, *Riverside Chaucer*, p. xxix.

[95] The Latin word for "cloak" in these sources is *capa* and the English word is "cope." (It should be understood, of course, that the *capa* / "cope" here refers to the cloak which formed part of the mendicant habit, not the liturgical vestment.)

[96] Heyworth's dating of *Jack Upland* to between c. 1390 and 1420, perhaps to rather later than earlier in this period, needs revision. A composition anytime between the death of Wyclif at the end of 1384 and the year 1401 is possible (Eric Doyle, "William

Frere, what bitokeneþ ʒoure greet hood, ʒoure scapalarie [*scapular*], & ʒoure knottid girdel, and ʒoure side & wide copis þat ʒe maken ʒou of so dere cloþe [*your ample and wide cloaks that you make of such expensive cloth for yourselves*], siþ lesse cloþis & of lesse prijs is more token of pouert [*since meaner and less costly clothes are a greater token of poverty*]?[97]

The Latin source from which this question seems ultimately to derive speaks simply of *cape* ("cloaks"),[98] doubtless to be understood in their context as luxurious ones, but the English text has left nothing to chance in explicitly describing the "cloaks" as "ample and wide" and made of "expensive cloth."[99]

A counterargument should be considered, that Chaucer, the Lollard suspect Ashwardby and the radical author of *Jack Upland* all *coinciden-*

Woodford, O.F.M. (c.1330–c.1400), his Life and Works, together with a Study and Edition of his 'Responsiones contra Wiclevum et Lollardos'," *FranS* 43 (1983): 17–187; see pp. 90–91, and also Szittya, *Antifraternal Tradition*, pp. 196–97, note 44). Further careful consideration of *Jack Upland*'s dating by Fiona E. Somerset, *Clerical Discourse and Lay Audience in Late Medieval England* (Cambridge: Cambridge University Press, 1998), pp. 216–20, concludes that "the versions of *Jack Upland* available to us were produced or revised in the early 1380s to early 1390s" (ibid., p. 217). The questions found in *Jack Upland* appear in Latin in the *Responsiones ad questiones LXV* of the Franciscan friar William Woodford, written some time between 1389 and 1396 (Jeremy I. Catto, "William Woodford, O.F.M. (*c.* 1330-*c.* 1397)," unpubl. D.Phil. thesis [Oxford, 1969], pp. 31–6). They are found uniquely in Oxford, Bodleian Library, MS Bodley 703, fols 41–57.

[97] Heyworth, *Jack Upland*, p. 60, lines 140–43. Note that the friar whom Jack Upland attacks seems a generic composite, not identifiably a member of any one mendicant Order. *Friar Daw's Reply* similarly implies a generically representative friar (Heyworth, *Jack Upland*, p. 8).

[98] Oxford, Bodleian Library, MS Bodley 703, fol. 42v col. a: "Dvodecima questio. Quid signant capucia fratrum lata, vel cape, scapularia et corde nodose?" ("The twelfth *quaestio*: what do the wide capuces, or cloaks, of the friars signify, their scapulars and knotted cords?"). It is interesting to note how in his response, Friar Woodford turned the tables on the accusers in a way reminiscent of the table-turning of Friar Daw in *Friar Daw's Reply* (MS Bodley 703, fol. 42v col. a): "Item dico quod similiter potest queri a Lollardis: quid signant eorum lata capucia furrata extensa vsque ad scapulas, et subter eas eorum camicie de tela subtili et tenui lino, similiter eorum zone ornate argento et pendente longo; et similiter eorum toge siue clocule furrate extense vsque ad pedes." ("Likewise I say that the same can be asked of the Lollards: what do their wide, furred hoods, extended as far as their scapulars, signify? And under their scapulars [are] shirts of fine cloth and delicate linen; similarly, their belts adorned with silver and long pendants; and similarly, their gowns or little cloaks [are] furred and hanging to their feet.")

[99] The quality and costliness of the mendicant habit is a refrain of Lollard polemic. Compare, for example, these lines from the late-fourteenth or early-fifteenth century poem "The Friar's Answer": "Þan þei loken on my nabete, / & sein, 'forsoþe, withoutton oþes, / Wheþer it be russet, black, or white, / It is worþe alle oure werynge cloþes.'" (Rossell Hope Robbins, ed., *Historical Poems of the XIVth and XVth Centuries* [New York: Columbia University Press, 1959], p. 167, lines 21–24).

tally gave greater local color and particularity to an old idea that went back a long way in the tradition of antimendicant thinking.[100] One Latin poem, for example, composed probably not long after 1382, points out, though in terms vaguer than those used by Chaucer, Ashwardby and *Jack Upland*, that friars' habits are luxurious and that these habits have substituted for appropriate "shame" inappropriate "great honor": "Non tamen dedecoris, sed magni honoris, / Habitu se protegunt panni melioris, / Tunicis, pelliciis frigus claudunt foris."[101] ("They [i.e., the friars] clothe themselves in a habit of superior cloth, not, however, out of shame, but for the sake of great honor, and they keep out the cold with tunics and furs"). Yet the fact that these more general terms seem to contain the germ of an idea that appears more colorfully developed in Chaucer, Ashwardby, and *Jack Upland* is not a wholly adequate explanation. Irrespective of whether Chaucer, Ashwardby, and *Jack Upland* had recycled an inherited motif and expressed it with richer particularity, the precise terms of that particularity do not appear to be as old as the idea itself may have been.[102]

So while it is true that the seed of the criticism of friars' luxurious habits could have been sown more than a century earlier in William of St. Amour, the first major opponent of the friars who was active in thirteenth-century Paris and who had spoken out about the false outer show that friars made "in their habit" (*in habitu*),[103] and while that seed was later more widely scattered in a field of antimendicant writing pro-

[100] Even though this counterargument still might be thought not entirely to explain the (otherwise fortuitous) degree of coincidence between Chaucer, Ashwardby, and *Jack Upland*.

[101] Thomas Wright, ed., *Political Poems and Songs*, 2 vols. (London: Eyre and Spottiswoode, 1859), vol. 1, p. 256. This poem, entitled *Heu! quanta desolatio Angliae praestatur*, is evidently Lollard, and introduces a roll call of Lollard greats (John Wyclif, Nicholas Hereford, Philip Repingdon and Richard FitzRalph are all extolled; Wright, *Poems and Songs*, vol. 1, pp. 259–60 and 262–63).

[102] It is worth noting that even the more generalized description of the Latin poem *Heu! quanta desolatio Angliae praestatur* appears in a text that once again is staunchly Wycliffite. (I have not noticed the detail, incidentally, in any of the writings of two of the earlier seminal antimendicant authors, William of St. Amour and Richard FitzRalph.) Arnold Williams, "Two Notes on Chaucer's Friars," *MP* 54 (1956): 117–20, ventured that the motif may have been "a commonplace, well known to Chaucer and his readers" (p. 118). But if it was, to date I know of no cases of it other than Lollard ones.

[103] He drafted into his argument Matthew 23:5 ("All their works they do in order that they might be seen by men; for they widen their phylacteries and enlarge their tassels"). This gospel lemma provided antimendicant critics with convenient amunition, given that the mendicant Rule itself forbade luxurious dress. Also, see Szittya, *Antifraternal Tradition*, p. 39.

duced both in England and on the Continent,[104] it remains the case that
its particular flowering in Chaucer, as far as Chaucer's contemporaries
would have recognized it, corresponds most nearly to that found in Ashwardby (a Wycliffite, if Maidstone was right), and in the Wycliffite tract
Jack Upland. The significance of this shared similarity for an informed
reader of the 1390s is easy to imagine. It would have extended beyond
any putative origin of the idea in earlier tradition. Thus merely to identify an early prototype for the idea is not enough to account for the
likely response that Chaucer's particular treatment of it in the 1390s
would have triggered.

The second *General Prologue* detail concerns the small knives and pins
that the Friar had stuffed into his tippet, gifts for the women that he
was angling to seduce (lines 233–34):

> His typet was ay farsed ful of knyves
> And pynnes, for to yeven faire wyves.

This motif is more striking still in that it does not seem current before
the fourteenth century.[105] However, once invented, it proved popular,
and by the fifteenth century had been appropriated for utterly scurrilous
uses. One of the most outrageous runs:

> Fratres Carmeli navigant in a bothe apud Eli.
> Non sunt in celi, quia *gxddbov xxkxzt pg ifmk*.

[104] Notably, in the tract *Filios enutrivi* of Jean d'Anneux, composed in 1328 (Oxford,
Bodleian Library, MS Bodley 52, fol. 195v) and in a *quaestio* of Thomas de Wilton, who
was also active in the 1320s (Oxford, Bodleian Library, MS Rawlinson A. 273, fol. 100v;
de Wilton's *quaestiones* are headed on fol. 99v, "Auctoritates contra ualidos mendicantes"
["Arguments against able-bodied mendicants"]). On d'Anneux and de Wilton, see Szittya, *Antifraternal Tradition*, pp. 82–84 and 94–95 respectively. Note also that the treatise *Omne bonum* of James le Palmer absorbs both d'Anneux and de Wilton, along with
other works, in its article on "Fratres" (Szittya, *Antifraternal Tradition*, Appendix B).
The fringes/phylacteries motif was also entering Lollard sources, for example the *De
perfectione statuum* written by Wyclif in 1383 (Rudolf Buddensieg, ed., *John Wiclif's Polemical Works in Latin*, 2 vols. [London: Trübner, 1883], vol. 2, p. 473, lines 6–10), but
there the motif appears in its (parallel) guise, closer to its guise in the thirteenth century
where it originated, than in the guise developed by Chaucer, Ashwardby or *Jack Upland*.
(As Szittya, *Antifraternal Tradition*, pp. 204–7, notes, the motif also entered secular
literature in the *Roman de la Rose*.)

[105] The earliest and closest case of which I am aware occurs in Richard FitzRalph's
Defensio curatorum (completed in 1357) where FitzRalph refers to the "little gifts" (*munus-
cula*) that friars give to youths to lure them into their Order (London, British Library,
MS Lansdowne 393, fol. 253): "iuuenes fratrum fraudibus et munusculis datis allecti"
("youths enticed by the deceits of the friars and by the small gifts given to them").

Omnes drencherunt, quia sterisman non habuerunt.
Fratres cum knyvys goth about and *txxkxzv nfookt xxzxkt*.[106]

[Carmelite friars sail in a boat at Ely.
They are not heavenly/miserable[107]
because *they fuck the women of Ely*.
They all drowned, because they had no steersman.
Friars with knives go about and *screw men's wives*.]

The translation above in brackets renders in italics the words that the original gives in cipher. The encrypted words contain a text in English and dog Latin necessary to complete these bawdy macaronic verses. The verses are not noticeably Lollard, and feature in a late-fifteenth century manuscript whose contents, for the rest, are not noticeably Lollard either.[108] They demonstrate how long-lived and widely used the motif was to be. But in the 1390s, it is only in Lollard texts and contexts that it seems to be recorded, and here with some frequency. The Lollard tract *Of the Leaven of Pharisees*, for example, says:

ʒif þei [*friars*] becomen pedderis [*pedlars*] berynge knyues, pursis, pynnys and girdlis and spices and sylk and precious pellure and forrouris [*furs*] for wymmen, and þerto smale gentil hondis [*dogs*], to gete loue of hem and to haue

---

[106] London, British Library, MS Harley 3362, fol. 47.

[107] Two different translations seem possible. If "in celi" is to be understood as Latin, it is ungrammatical, for were the Latin correct, "in celis" ("in heaven" or "heavenly") is what the line should have read. But alternatively, "in celi" could be understood as playful English (for "unseli," meaning "wretched" or "miserable"). Thus "in celi" could be taken in two senses, depending upon whether it is read as barbarous Latin (the friars are not heavenly because they fuck the women of Ely) or as skittish English (the friars are not miserable, for the same reason).

[108] The motif may have passed from characteristically Lollard contexts into more general antimendicant ones, where it may also have been preferred for its potential value as a double-entendre (since "knife" may connote "penis"). The first editors of these verses, Wright and Halliwell, observed that a version of them was still popular among schoolboys (though in a considerably more sanitized form as quoted in Wright and Halliwell; see Thomas Wright and J. O. Halliwell, eds., *Reliquiæ Antiquæ. Scraps from Ancient Manuscripts, illustrating chiefly Early English Literature and the English Language*, 2 vols. [London: John Russell Smith, 1845], vol. 1, p. 91). Another fifteenth-century example of the motif, again without Lollard affiliation, appears in Benedict Burgh's rendition of the *Disticha Catonis* (M. Förster, "Die Burghsche Cato-Paraphrase," *Archiv* 115 [1905]: 298–323; see p. 310, lines 289–93: "The lymytour, that visiteth the wyues, / Is wise inouh. Of hym a man may leer / To yiuen girdiles, pynnes and knyues. / This craft is good; thus dothe the celi freere: / Yiueth thynges smale for thynges that been deer.") On Benedict Burgh (†1483), see A. B. Emden, *A Biographical Register of the University of Oxford to A.D. 1500*, 3 vols. (Oxford: Clarendon Press, 1957–59), vol. 1, p. 309.

many grete ʒiftis for litil good ore nouȝt [*in exchange for little or nothing*]; þei coueiten euyle here neiȝeboris goodis [*they wickedly covet their neighbors' goods*].[109]

And friars were presented in Lollard sources not only as bearers of fine knacks for ladies; the motif of the ingratiating gift also gelled with that of the friars' devices for procuring children to swell their Orders: "þei [*i.e., friars*] feeston hem [*i.e., they regale children*] and ʒyuon hem ʒiftus as applus, pursos and oþre iapes [*purses and other trifles*]".[110] Rumors of child abduction had been doing the rounds much earlier than this; Archbishop Richard FitzRalph, for example, perhaps the most strenuous opponent of the friars in the mid fourteenth century who took his case against them as far as the papal curia in Avignon until his death halted

[109] Matthew, *English Works*, p. 12. Another example, from London, British Library, MS Cotton Cleopatra B.ii, fol. 62v, is as follows: "Þai [*i.e., friars*] dele with purses, pynnes, & knyves, / With gyrdles, gloues for wenches & wyues" (Robbins, *Historical Poems*, p. 158, lines 37–8). This poem betrays its Lollard affiliation by using the CAIM anagram; this anagram appears often and only in Lollard contexts, as Szittya, *Antifraternal Tradition*, p. 196, notes, and see especially Margaret Aston, " 'Caim's Castles': Poverty, Politics, and Disendowment," in R. B. Dobson, ed., *The Church, Politics and Patronage in the Fifteenth Century* (New York: St Martin's Press; Gloucester: Alan Sutton, 1984), pp. 45–81, rpt. in her book *Faith and Fire: Popular and Unpopular Religion, 1350–1600* (London and Rio Grande: Hambledon Press, 1993), pp. 95–131. The poem also occurs in its manuscript immediately after the Lollard *Heu! quanta desolatio Angliae praestatur* poem excerpted above.

[110] Thus the *Vae octuplex* (Anne Hudson and Pamela Gradon, eds., *English Wycliffite Sermons*, 5 vols. [Oxford: Clarendon Press, 1983–96], vol. 2, p. 368, lines 66–67; compare in the sermon for the Vigil of St. Andrew in *English Wycliffite Sermons*, vol. 2, p. 182, lines 101–2: how friars "wiþ dyuerse and luytule ʒiftus, and false wordus, dysseyuon chyldron"). The precise mechanics of their coercion seem not recorded in Wyclif himself (compare Johann Loserth, ed., *Johannis Wyclif Opera Minora* (London: C. K. Paul, 1913), pp. 339, line 3–340, line 22), nor in Richard FitzRalph, though the latter levels at friars the accusation of child theft, to be sure (see note 111 following and compare note 105 above where *iuuenes* ["youths"], are in question). Even so, this is not quite the "knives" motif. Hudson and Gradon, *English Wycliffite Sermons*, vol. 5, pp. 203–5, neglect in their commentary to consider whether FitzRalph's *Defensio curatorum* may have any bearing on this Vigil of St Andrew sermon. The wording of the *Defensio* is in places strikingly similar. Compare, too, FitzRalph's point in the *Defensio* (London, British Library, MS Lansdowne 393, fol. 253) that, if the theft of a cow or a sheep is punishable, even more so is the theft of children, with Arnold, *Select English Works*, vol. 3, p. 348: "And here men noten many harmes þat freris don in þe Chirche. . . . Þei stelen pore mennis children, þat is werse þen stele an oxe . . ."; and with III, 374: "And siþ he þat steelis an oxe or a kow is dampnable by Gods lawe, and monnis also, myche more he þat steelis a monnis childe, þat is bettere þen ben stele erthely godis, and drawes hym to þo lesse perfit ordir" (in the tracts *The Church and Her Members* and *Fifty Heresies and Errors of Friars* respectively). But such similarities cannot be further pursued here. (An edition of the *Defensio curatorum* by Terence P. Dolan is due to be published by the Pontifical Institute of Mediaeval Studies; I am grateful to him for allowing me to consult parts of his edition in advance of its appearance.)

90

it in 1360, wove variations on this theme into his own campaign, though there he relied not merely on hearsay, but cited a case known to him personally of "an honest Englishman" who had complained that friars at Oxford had poached his son, a lad not yet thirteen years old.[111] But once again the point is that the precise circumstantial details in which the theme is here couched do not appear to have been recorded before the late fourteenth century. Thus another of the nuances in the way Chaucer presented his Friar could have been construed by an ultra-orthodox reader as evidence that he had been culling his material from infected sources.

The third and last *General Prologue* detail is the matter of the Friar's venal "*In principio*" (lines 253–55):

> For thogh a wydwe hadde noght a sho,
> So plesaunt was his "*In principio*,"
> Yet wolde he have a ferthyng, er he wente.

From an early date, these two words, which open the gospel of St. John, were used for para-liturgical, sometimes magical, purposes, so by the time Chaucer was writing, people may have been used to hearing them bandied about.[112] But what has not been appreciated is that by the late fourteenth century, the friars' use of *In principio* was characteristically being sneered at by Lollards and turned by them into antimendicant ammunition. The spin Lollards put on *In principio* was that friars had bastardized it for conning cash out of the unsuspecting. Criticism of *In principio* appears in the radical tract *Jack Upland*, where friars "winnen more wiþ *In principio* þan Crist & hise apostlis & all þe seintis of heuene".[113] It also appears in two poems both entered in a fifteenth-century hand onto the flyleaf of a late–fourteenth century copy of the

---

[111] "vnus probus homo de Anglia"; London, British Library, MS Lansdowne 393, fol. 253. Also see Szittya, *Antifraternal Tradition*, p. 205, note 62, for a discussion of the Oxford statute of 1358 against underage recruitment by friars. The statute noted that people were afraid to send their sons to Oxford lest mendicants snaffle them. Compare too the cases cited by C. M. Erickson, "The Fourteenth-Century Franciscans and Their Critics," *FranS* 35 (1975): 107–35; see pp. 112–13 and 116–18.

[112] Morton W. Bloomfield, "The Magic of *In Principio*," *MLN* 70 (1955): 559–65. Bloomfield did not observe that any of his sources connected *In principio* typically with the friars.

[113] Heyworth, *Jack Upland*, p. 64, lines 240–42. As Bloomfield, "Magic," noted, but he did not develop the possible implication of this.

Middle English prose treatise known as *Pore Caitif*.[114] The first poem, which betrays its dissident origin through using typically Lollard catch-phrases, contains the accusation: "In principio erat verbum / Is þe worde of god, all & sum, / þat þou sellest, lewed frere."[115] Here, the friar is presented as a simoniac selling sacred Scripture. And the second poem pictures a beleaguered friar complaining: "When I come into a schope / for to say "in principio," / Þei bidine me [*bid me*], "goo forþ, lewed poppe!" [*get out, lewd little fop*] / & worche & win my siluer so! [*work and earn my money that way*]"[116] Here, In principio is not connected to a specific abuse, but is the unwelcome herald of the friar's sidling arrival. Advertising the abuse of *In principio* by the mendicants, then, may have had a familiar Lollard ring to it.

Moving on from Friar Hubert of *The General Prologue*, the next major portrayal of friars (of whom Friar Hubert is in any event a generic representative) is to be found in *The Summoner's Prologue* and *Tale*.[117] Recent research has shown that several antimendicant themes of the *Prologue* and *Tale*, like those we have been considering in connection with Friar Hubert, were not wearily traditional but topical or based on current topicalities—for example, the friars' infestation of the arse of the devil—so there is no need to cover that ground again.[118] One further supporting detail is worth noticing, however, whose innocence is very doubtful indeed. Friar John of *The Summoner's Tale* had with him a "fel-awe" (friars customarily traveled in pairs) who carried:

A peyre of tables al of yvory,
And a poyntel polysshed fetisly,

[114] Anne Hudson, ed., *The Works of a Lollard Preacher*, EETS, os 317 (Oxford: Oxford University Press, 2001), p. xix, incorrectly says of these poems that "one [is] against the friars and the other [is] in their defence." In fact, both disparage the friars. *Pore Caitif* has itself been thought to have a Lollard connection, though Margaret T. Brady, "The Pore Caitif: An Introductory Study," *Traditio* 10 (1954): 529–48 concludes (pp. 542–48) that the Lollard connection is no stronger than the tract's circulation with other writings of more obviously Wycliffite temper.

[115] Robbins, *Historical Poems*, p. 166, lines 4–6 ("The Layman's Complaint"). Its antimendicant accusation "Goddis law ȝe reuerson" (Robbins, *Historical Poems*, p. 166, line 13) registers typical Lollard turns of phrase (on Lollard discourse and sect language, see the references in note 53 above).

[116] The poem is called "The Friar's Answer" by Robbins, *Historical Poems*, p. 167, lines 13–16. It is probably also a Lollard product by association.

[117] I pass over the satirical reference to them at the beginning of *The Wife of Bath's Tale* (lines 865–81).

[118] For this and other themes, see Fletcher, *Preaching, Politics and Poetry*, pp. 281–303.

And wroot the names alwey, as he stood,
Of alle folk that yaf hym any good,
Ascaunces that he wolde for hem preye.

Much is made of these elegantly manufactured "tables" on which the names of the friars' benefactors were inscribed with a beautifully polished stylus. Ostensibly, they were to serve the friars as aides-mémoires from which to recall their benefactors' names in their prayers. The "tables" are alluded to again a few lines later in Friar John's mendicant sales patter (line 1752): "lo! Heere I write youre name"—provided, that is, that in return for writing the name he gets alms in cash or in kind. Evidently the trick worked, for when the "tables" make their third and final appearance five lines later (lines 1757–9), Friar John is seen rubbing out the names inscribed once he has secured his donation and made his getaway.

In view of all this, it is interesting to note that one of the Lollard arguments against perceived mendicant abuses against which a vigorous opponent of the Lollards, Friar William Woodford, took up arms, similarly fastened on this practice of entering the names of benefactors on *tabellae* ("tables"): "Frater, quare scribis tu nomina illorum qui tibi conferunt elemosinam in tabellis tuis ex quo Deus omnia nouit? Apparet namque ex scriptura quod aliter Deus non reminiscaret illis nisi tu scriberes hic."[119] ("Friar, since God knows all things, why do you write the names of those who give you alms on *tabellae*? For it seems by your writing that God would not otherwise remember them if you did not write them here.") Chaucer's "tables," doubtless because he is writing poetry and not a spare polemic, are treated in a more richly particularized way. They are sumptuously made of ivory—like habits of double worsted, hardly compatible with the friars' profession of holy poverty—and into the bargain he has dramatized their use in an actual scam. To that extent, the *tabellae* of the Lollard argument have assumed a singularly more elaborate guise in Chaucer's version of them. Yet the essential issue is similar: the Lollard argument disapproves of *tabellae*, while Chaucer similarly enlists them into the paraphernalia of mendicant de-

---

[119] Oxford, Bodleian Library, MS Bodley 703, fol. 47v cols a–b. The English equivalent in *Jack Upland* reads: "Frere, whi writist þou mennes names in þi tablis? Wenest þou þat God is suche a fool þat he wot not of mennes dedis but if þou telle hym bi þi tablis?" (Heyworth, *Jack Upland*, p. 66, lines 282–84).

ceit. If attacks on the *tabellae* of the friars had been an old commonplace of antimendicant writing, it might have gone some way toward accounting for the "tables" that Chaucer put into his *Tale*. But such attacks seem to have been rather more recently introduced into the growing antimendicant tradition. A growing tradition is, after all, an evolving tradition, and to my knowledge, Chaucer's satire on the friars' "tables" is parallelled only in Lollard contexts.

The Summoner

Next, the Summoner. The mutual hatred between Summoner and Friar would have seemed to many of Chaucer's contemporaries not simply a device for propelling the narratives of their tales along, but also another link in an ominous chain of associations. Lollards had been prompt to point out that the orthodox clergy—in their view, clerks of Antichrist— when they were not in collusion, were habitually at loggerheads. Their animosity, as much as their collusion, was a sign of Antichrist's dominion within the Church: "membra Antichristi reciproce se conculcant" ("the members of Antichrist tread upon each other"), observed Wyclif.[120] The Summoner and the Friar's mutual hatred, conventionally read by literary critics as another operation of Chaucer's "quiting" motif, also gave Chaucer's contemporaries the option of viewing that mutual hatred from the vantage point of current Lollard opinion: to echo Wyclif again, within the Church, "the members of Antichrist tread upon each other." Furthermore, the Summoner's alliance with the Pardoner implicates him in the rhetoric of Lollard polemic in a similar way.[121] A par-

---

[120] Johann Loserth, ed., *Iohannis Wyclif Opus Evangelicum* (London: Trübner, 1895), p. 75, lines 4–5. The ominous view that emerges of the Church from such clerical strife (and that John V. Fleming, "The Antifraternalism of the Summoner's Tale," *JEGP* 65 [1966]: 688–700, had observed purely on the basis of astute literary analysis) had already been identified by Wyclif as a sign of Antichrist's dominion within the Church.

[121] They are paired too in terms of comparable descriptive techniques that inscribe in their flesh their underlying spiritual perversions. Of the Summoner's physical blemishes, Helen Cooper, *The Canterbury Tales*, 2d ed. (Oxford: Clarendon Press, 1997), p. 57, says, "Both the disease and its resistance to the more violent remedies suggest inner corruption"; similarly, Laurel Braswell-Means, "A New Look at an Old Patient: Chaucer's Summoner and Medieval Physiognomic," *ChauR* 25 (1990): 266–75, says (p. 273) that the Summoner's facial traits "can be seen as real indicators of the moral corruption of his soul and the corrosion of his profession." Thus both Cooper and Braswell-Means avoid closing on a specific spiritual diagnosis. But if the Summoner's physical symptoms would have been diagnosed as leprosy (as Cooper thinks, though Braswell-Means is unsure), the Summoner's inner corruption may have been interpreted as heresy, since leprosy was often thought heresy's physical symptom. An addition of Nicholas of Lyra to the *Glossa ordinaria* makes this tradition clear (*Biblia sacra cum glossis, interlineari, et ordinaria, Nicolai Lyrani Postillae* [Venice, 1588], fol. 236v): "Secundum doctores cathol-

doner and a summoner make a brief joint appearance in one of the stanzas of *The Plowman's Tale*, a Lollard poem written possibly in the early fifteenth century, though arguably here, the Lollard author has been prompted by their association in Chaucer rather than by some specifically Lollard tradition.[122] Be that as it may, of all the people that the Pardoner could have taken up with, Chaucer has selected as his "compeer" another corrupt official of the Church. The choice hardly seems accidental once located within the network of anticlerical writing circulating in the 1390s; on the contrary, it begins to look provocative, or at least, as if it could so have appeared to people familiar with the current controversies. So the net effect of Chaucer's unholy pairing of Summoner and Pardoner is to contribute towards *The Canterbury Tales'* wider projection of a canker riddling the Church and this, of course, was the comparable, if more emphatic, projection of the Lollard reformers at the time *The Canterbury Tales* were being composed. Lollards did not have a monopoly on calls for ecclesiastical reform, to be sure, but the terms in which they characteristically dressed their reformist sentiments seem to single them out, binding them in a group solidarity, and probably helping to corrall those reformist sentiments, whatever their first point of origin, into the Lollard camp.

By contrast with that of the Friar, it must nevertheless be admitted that Chaucer's portrait of the Summoner contains rather less that is likely to have alarmed orthodox sensibilities. Summoners came with nothing near the amount of polemical baggage as did friars, nor were they widely lambasted as corrupt agents of orthodoxy in Lollard writings.[123] Yet such appearances as they make there agree with Chaucer's

---

icos per lepram intelligitur falsa doctrina hereticorum in moribus vel in fide, & ideo secundum ipsos leprosi dicuntur qui de numero sunt ecclesiae, sed varias sequuntur maculas erroris" ("According to catholic doctors, by leprosy is understood the false doctrine of heretics in their customs or in their faith, and therefore according to those [doctors] they are called heretics who are numbered in the Church, but who follow the blemishes of error"; I am grateful to Dr. Anne Marie D'Arcy for drawing my attention to Lyra's gloss). And a sermon for the fourteenth Sunday after Trinity from the influential *Sermones dominicales* cycle composed by the early-fourteenth century Franciscan, Nicholas de Aquevilla, makes a similar identification: "Ista lepra occupati sunt heretici et quodammodo homines et mulieres in sortilegiis et terminibus credentes" ("Heretics, and certain men and women believing in witchcraft and [astrological?] terms, are implicated in that leprosy"; Oxford, Bodlein Library, MS 857, fol. 67). Thus yet again the Summoner would match the Pardoner, whose religious hypocrisy similarly suggested heresy as his underlying spiritual disease (Fletcher, *Preaching, Politics and Poetry*, pp. 266–80).

[122] Skeat, *Chaucerian and Other Pieces*, p. 157, lines 325–28.

[123] Modest evidence for corrupt summoners in English historical documents was gathered by Louis A. Haselmayer, "The Apparitor and Chaucer's Summoner," *Speculum*

essential presentation, namely, that summoners cite people on false pretences to the ecclesiastical courts in order to extort their money.[124] That, in a nutshell, is the main narrative thrust of *The Friar's Tale*. And Lollard writings make the further point, again not unlike the point that Chaucer makes about the summoner of *The Friar's Tale*, that such Church minions are thoroughly familiar with the sexual misdemeanours of the working classes, and that they exploit that familiarity to summon lechers to "chapiters" (that is, to sessions of the archdeacon's court) where they can be robbed.[125] Though the summoners appearing in *Piers Plowman*, a work whose earliest version antedates Wyclif's papal condemnation of 1377, were also slaves to money, and though Langland presented them as fraternizing with peculating clerics of the kind that Wycliffites too later complained about, in no other respects do Langland's summoners quite compare with those of Chaucer and of the Wycliffites, for these summoners have their besetting sins more fully and consistently laid

---

12 (1937): 43–57; see p. 55 for vernacular examples, though evidently Haselmayer did not include Wycliffite sources. A useful supplement on the historical malpractices of summoners is Thomas Hahn and Richard W. Kaeuper, "Text and Context in Chaucer's Friar's Tale," *SAC* 5 (1983): 67–101. Mann, *Estates Satire*, p. 274, note 60, observes that summoners do not appear in estates satire much before Langland.

[124] The tract entitled *The Grete Sentence of Curs Expouned* says: "Also somenors bailies and servauntis, and oþere men of lawe, kitten [*cut*] perelously mennus purses, for þei somenen and aresten men wrongfully to gete þe money out of his purse" (Arnold, *Select English Works*, vol. 3, p. 320).

[125] Compare *The Friar's Tale*, line 1361. Also, the Wycliffite theme that Church minions (summoners qualified as such) are familiar with the sexual incontinence of the laboring classes and that they prey upon it, is reminiscent of the (more elaborate) presentation of this theme in Chaucer's summoner of *The Friar's Tale*, a man whose network of spies ensured his successful detection of lechers. Compare with *The Friar's Tale*, lines 1310–26 and 1338–74, the kernel of a similar idea in the Wycliffite tract *On the Seven Deadly Sins*: "Þo þridde part of þo Chirche [i.e., the estate of those who labour] is not clene of lecchorie, for þei gone togedir as bestis. And þis is knowen to bischop clerkis, for þei spoylen hom in chapiters, as who wolde spoyle a thef" (Arnold, *Select English Works*, vol. 3, p. 166). However, the idea that diocesan administrators might "eat and drink the sins of the people" predates the Wycliffites, and as in so many other respects, so here, Wycliffites may have been embroidering in their own characteristic ways an idea already traditional. John of Salisbury, for example, warned an archdeacon of his acquaintance in a letter of *c*. 1160–61 not to let the archidiaconal office become a sort of business. John feared that deans and archdeacons might live off the misery of the poor, reckoning their discomfiture good sport, and he called such clerics *ambilaevi* ("ambisinistrous"; see W. J. Millor and Harold E. Butler, eds., *The Letters of John of Salisbury, I: The Early Letters (1153–1161)*, rev. Christopher N. L. Brooke [London: Nelson, 1955; corr. rpt., Oxford: Clarendon Press, 1986], p. 194. Compare the corrupt ambidexters of the Lollard *Twelve Conclusions* and see also note 86 above). Chaucer's hinted collusion between archdeacon and summoner in *The Friar's Tale* is another example, in small, of those corrupt ecclesiastical collusions introduced in several places in *The Canterbury Tales*.

out.[126] Even so, it would be wrong to press the similarities between the treatments of Chaucer and the Wycliffites to the point of identity. We find ourselves on more clearly dangerous ground in the person of the final flawed "ecclesiaste" to be considered here, the Monk.

The Monk

The Monk, says Chaucer the narrator, was a handsome man. The very next thing we hear about him (line 166) is that he was an "outridere," that is, his business took him outside his monastery. His dealings outside the cloister, focused and then justified (from his point of view, if not necessarily from the narrator's) in the rhetorical question "How shal the world be served?," become a key issue in his portrait.[127] The traditional monastic antidote for worldly preoccupations of the sort the Monk is busied with was withdrawal from the world into a quiet and regular life of contemplation, labor, and prayer. Structured retreat of this sort was a founding principle of monasticism, but here in *The General Prologue*'s description of the Monk (lines 173–88) it is branded as "old and somdel streit" and shelved.

In broaching this issue of the acceptability of the monk out of his cloister, Chaucer accessed a current controversy about monastic (and indeed general clerical) involvement in worldly affairs.[128] Prominent among those arguing the case for such involvement when Chaucer was writing was the Benedictine monk Uthred of Boldon (†1397), who had tried to justify the participation of clergy in secular government and

---

[126] Most of Langland's summoners collocate with *sisours*, the latter being members of sworn assizes of inquest (the B-text instances are representative: B.II.59; B.III.134; B.IV.167; and B.XIX.373). At B.II.170, summoners have a line of verse to themselves, but follow on in the company of Simony and Civil from the previous line; and at B.XV.132, summoners collocate with executers and sub-deans. Langland's summoners are generally drafted to exemplify the corrupt interface between the Church and the law.

[127] "How shal the world be served?" (line 187), posed ostensibly in rhetorical justification of the Monk's worldly involvement, in effect entices the reader to ponder what underlying legitimacy a justification merely rhetorically made may have. Olson, *Good Society*, p. 165, shrewdly comments, "Chaucer was, by virtue of his friendships, in a position to ponder Wyclif's arguments from favourable and unfavourable perspectives and probably was reflecting this position when he had his Monk ask, 'How shall the world be served?'"

[128] Already in 1371, Parliament had been presented with a petition that the king no longer employ clerics in posts dischargeable by laymen (see *Rotuli Parliamentorum*, vol. 2, p. 304).

administration.[129] The case against, which argued that all churchmen should hold themselves aloof from compromising worldly activities, was being urged by Wycliffites, to be sure (in Wycliffite writing, as noted earlier, men who juggled with clerical and secular careers might even be stigmatized as hermaphrodites),[130] but also by the friars. In fact, it is not clear whether it was the protests of Wycliffites or mendicants (or both) that galvanized Uthred of Boldon into writing.[131] We know that John of Gaunt, Chaucer's patron, was conservative on this issue, being opposed in principle to clerics occupying high secular positions (even though he did not object to clerics helping run his household).[132] So too was Chaucer's friend, the poet John Gower.[133] In view of this, Chaucer's fellow-feeling may have lain first with his patron and with his friend, and with the Wycliffites and mendicants only coincidentally. But the matter does not end there. Certain other vivid touches in the Monk's description, when their characteristic field of use is borne in mind, could have encouraged contemporaries to veer toward a more radical reading of this issue of the permissibility of churchmen following secular occupations. Of one of these touches Chaucer was fond, for he used it twice, once in *The General Prologue* description of the Monk and again in the allusion to the Monk made in the *Prologue* to *The Nun's Priest's Tale*: this

[129] In his treatise *De dotacione ecclesie sponse Christi*; Durham, Cathedral Library, MS A.IV.33, fols 69–99v.

[130] And also ambidexters; see the aforegoing discussion, and notes 86 and 125 above. Compare also, for example, Wyclif's *De officio regis* (Alfred W. Pollard and Charles Sayle, eds., *Iohannis Wyclif Tractatus de Officio Regis* [London: Trübner, 1887], p. 142, line 17 ff). *The Grete Sentence of Curs Expouned* tract opposes the secular employment of bishops as follows: "þei may not wel togidre do her gostly office and worldly, for Crist and alle his postlis, wiþalle here witt, kouden not and wolden not entermete wiþ worldly office, but fledden it as venym" (Arnold, *Select English Works*, vol. 3, p. 335). Of course, opposition to clerical involvement in secular affairs was mounted well before Wyclif and his sect; see Robert N. Swanson, *Church and Society in Late Medieval England* (Oxford: Blackwell, 1989), pp. 103–10.

[131] William A. Pantin, *The English Church in the Fourteenth Century* (Cambridge: Cambridge University Press, 1955; rpt., Toronto: Toronto University Press, 1980), p. 170, suggests that the *De dotacione ecclesie* may have been provoked by attacks from friars rather than from Wycliffites.

[132] On John of Gaunt's position, see Olson, *Good Society*, pp. 162–63; also, L. M. Bisson, *Chaucer and the Late Medieval World* (Basingstoke and London: Macmillan, 1998), p. 81. This position did not go as far as blanket disapproval, however; Gaunt's own household affairs were substantially run by clerics (see Robert Somerville, *History of the Duchy of Lancaster* [London: Chancellor and Council of the Duchy of Lancaster, 1953], vol. 1, pp. 115, 364–69). It should also be recalled that until Wyclif incurred condemnation for heresy, Gaunt had been his protector.

[133] For example in his *Mirour de l'Omme* (Macaulay, *John Gower*, vol. 1, p. 228, lines 20245–56).

is the seemingly innocuous and colorful little detail that bells decorated and jingled on the bridle of the Monk's horse.[134]

The detail as Chaucer introduces it is, as we might expect, highly picturesque. To be sure, there also existed a widespread, earlier tradition that keeping plushly caparisoned horses was evidence of pride, and so seasoned moralists in Chaucer's audience would have been able to make the connection between the Monk and this earlier tradition. For example, the influential *Summa vitiorum* of the French Dominican William Peraldus, issued in 1236, declared that equestrian pride betrayed itself in four guises: first, the keeping of too many horses; second, the use of horses in unnecessary circumstances; third, the keeping of fine horses for vanity's sake; and finally, the bedecking of horses in trappings of gold and silver while Christ, in the persons of poor folk, was sent naked and empty away.[135] It is well known that Peraldus's *Summa* provided Chaucer with one of the principal sources for *The Parson's Tale*, and here, the four topics of Peraldus just paraphrased may ultimately lie behind the following lines of the *Tale* (lines 431–32 and 434):

Also the synne of aornement [*adornment*] or of apparaille is in thynges that apertenen to ridynge, as in to manye delicat horses that been hoolden [*maintained*] for delit, that been so faire, fatte, and costelewe [*costly*]; and also in many a vicious knave that is sustened by cause of hem; and in to curious harneys [*excessively elaborate harness*], as in sadeles, in crouperes [*cruppers*], peytrels [*poitrels*], and bridles covered with precious clothyng, and riche barres and plates of gold and of silver. . . . This folk taken litel reward of [*give little heed to*] the ridynge of Goddes sone of hevene, and of his harneys whan he rood upon the asse, and ne hadde noon oother harneys but the povre clothes of his disciples; ne we ne rede nat that evere he rood on oother beest.[136]

---

[134] Benson, *Riverside Chaucer*, p. 26, lines 169–72 and p. 252, lines 2794–97. Derek Pearsall, ed., *The Nun's Priest's Tale*, A Variorum Edition of the Works of Geoffrey Chaucer, Vol. 2 (Norman: University of Oklahoma Press, 1984), p. 133, note to line 3984, "nere clynkyng of youre bellis," omits mention of the Lollard analogues discussed below.

[135] *Svmmae Virtvtvm ac Vitiorvm* (Lyons, 1585), p. 405. On the *Summa vitiorum* and its date, see A. Dondaine, "Guillaume Peyraut, vie et oeuvres," *AFP* 18 (1948): 162–236, esp. pp. 184–97.

[136] The question of the sources of *The Parson's Tale* is complex, and to date has been most satisfactorily addressed by Siegfried Wenzel, ed., *Summa virtutum de remediis anime* (Athens: University of Georgia Press, 1984). While Wenzel's case that Chaucer used a redacted Peraldine source is conceivable, the possibility nevertheless remains that what he actually used was some further version intermediary between himself and the Peraldine redaction.

The moral contrast pointed up by the introduction into this passage of Christ's humble ass, while not in Peraldus, is certainly also found in other writings before Chaucer. (For example, one anecdote used by medieval preachers for enlivening their sermons told of an old woman who seized the bridle of a preacher's horse and then pointedly asked him whether Christ ever rode on the like.) It is also probable that when Peraldus penned his passage on equestrian pride he was himself recalling an earlier, twelfth-century authority, though he did not cite the authority by name. This was St. Bernard of Clairvaux, who in a work on the manners and office of bishops drew a picture in stark contrasts between the pomp of riding bishops and the plight of walking poor men: "Jumenta grandiuntur onusta gemmis, et nostra non curatis crura nuda caligulis. Annuli, catenulae, tintinnabula, et clavatae quaedam corrigiae, multaque talia, tam speciosa coloribus, quam ponderibus pretiosa, mulorum dependent cervicibus."[137] ("The horses [of bishops] are aggrandised and loaded with jewels, while our naked legs are unprotected by shoes. Little rings, chains, bells, and certain studded reins, and many suchlike things, both splendid in their colours and precious in their weight, hang from the necks of their mules.")

Yet, more can be said than this, that the Monk's proud horse with its jingling bridle bells and its (implicit) contrast with Christ's humble ass may simply have come to Chaucer from a medley of ancient and traditional motifs.[138] There is evidence that Lollards had embraced the "proud horse" theme afresh, so much so that it had become something of a hallmark of Lollard invective. This is revealed by the author of the Lollard tract *On the Twenty-Five Articles*, who maintained that orthodox churchmen—bishops and friars in this case—were conscious of how "pore men" (an expression which probably encoded a reference to members of the Lollard sect)[139] not only used the "proud horse" theme, but were inclined to harp upon it:

[137] Patrologia Latina 182 (Paris, 1859), col. 816. The work is the *De moribus et officio episcoporum*. Compare also St Bernard's condemnation of "proud horses" expressed in his *Apologia ad Guillelmum* (Leclercq, Talbot and Rochais, *Opera Sancti Bernardi*, vol. 3, p. 103, lines 13–16) which the Lollard Robert Lychlade recycled in his sermon of 1395 and which is quoted below.

[138] Mann, *Estates Satire*, p. 23, notes that Chaucer may not have been original "in giving his Monk a taste for fine horses." She cites the case of the mid-fourteenth century Belgian poet Gilles li Muisis who discanted on monastics keeping fine horses and entourages. Mann's analysis of the literary potential of the jingling bells (pp. 26–27) omits the motif's Lollard currency, however.

[139] See Hudson, "Sect Vocabulary?," rpt. in *Lollards and Their Books*, pp. 170–71.

Also bischops and freris putten to pore men þat þai sayne [*bishops and friars put it to poor men that they say*] þat men of þo Chirche schulden not ride on so stronge horsys, ne use so mony jewelis, ne precius cloþis, or delicate metys, but renounce alle þingus and ȝyve hem to pore men, goynge on fote, and takynge stavys in hondis . . . Here Cristen men thynken no grete heresie, þowe worldly prelatis [*think it no great heresy if worldly prelates*] . . . renounce alle vanitees and waste godis, and selle þer fatte horsis and all þer waste jewelis and waste clothis, delynge hem to [*sharing them with*] pore men.[140]

Note the claim in the first sentence, that bishops and friars had a habit of charging "pore men" with blaming the clergy for their vain equestrian tastes. Nor was this awareness of orthodox churchmen that the "proud horse" theme was common in Lollard discourse unfounded: the *Twenty-Five Articles* author himself used it earlier in his tract, on that occasion with no evident self-consciousness.[141] And because the theme also made its way into Lollard sermons, it found an even wider audience and circulation than it would had it remained confined solely to the written page. It is often impossible to tell whether a medieval sermon surviving in manuscript was ever actually preached—and thus potentially capable of reaching a large number of people—or whether its existence was primarily literary and consultative, hence more limited and private. But of the sermon preached by a disciple of Wyclif in Oxford on 15 May 1382 (Ascension Day) there can be no doubt. The sermon survives in note form, and was jotted down by an orthodox spy who had been sent along to listen and report back to the Church authorities about what had been said. The preacher, the notorious Lollard Nicholas Hereford, included in a wide-ranging attack on clerical abuses a swipe at the monastic possessioners (the "possessionati"), of whose ranks was Chaucer's Monk. These men, said Hereford, "volunt vocari 'domini' et equitare in magnis equis et apparatu sollempni" ("want to be called 'Lord' and to ride about on fine horses and in solemn array").[142] Simi-

---

[140] Arnold, *Select English Works*, vol. 3, pp. 494–95.

[141] Arnold, *Select English Works*, vol. 3, p. 473: "And efte Bernarde sais, Seye, ȝee bischoppis, what dos golde in ȝoure bridel? hit dryves not away cold; ȝoure bestis gone honourid wiþ gemmys, precius stonys, and jewelis, ande oure sidis bene nakid, seyne pore men." The reference to St. Bernard here is specifically to the question "Dicite, pontifices, in freno quid facit aurum?" appearing in chapter 2 of his *De moribus et officio episcoporum* (Patrologia Latina 182, col. 815).

[142] Simon N. Forde, "Nicholas Hereford's Ascension Day Sermon, 1382," *MS* 51 (1989): 205–41; see p. 239, line 66. Compare Schmidt, *Piers Plowman A Parallel-Text Edition*, I, 181–83 (C.V.156–62). There is some historical justification for the perception that monastics had a weakness for equestrian pomp, and that it was not merely a literary topos (see the notes by Susan H. Cavanaugh on the Monk's portrait in Benson,

larly, in a sermon delivered in Oxford on 19 May 1395 (the date of the vigil of the feast of the Ascension in that year), the Lollard preacher Robert Lychlade recruited another of St. Bernard of Clairvaux's works to similar effect: "Quid enim, ut cetera taceam, specimen humilitatis est, cum tanta pompa et equitatu incedere, tantis hominum seruitorum stipari obsequiis, quatenus duobus episcopis vnius abbatis sufficiat multitudo? Mencior si non vidi abbatem sexaginta equos et eo amplius in suo ducere comitatu"[143] ("For what sort of humility is it—to bypass others—when such a one proceeds in great pomp or on horseback and is surrounded by so many servants that the retinue of one abbot would suffice two bishops? I would lie if I said that I had never seen one abbot lead sixty horses and more in his entourage.") By expressing themselves like this, Hereford and Lychlade fanned the orthodox expectation, identified so clearly by the *Twenty-Five Articles* author, of the sort of anticlerical accusation that Lollards might typically be heard coming out with. In fact, the "proud horse" theme appears in yet other Lollard sermons (though their status as preached texts, unlike the 1382 and 1395 sermons of Hereford and Lychlade, is not definitively known). For example, in a sermon for the first Sunday in Advent that was collected into a Lollard sermon anthology, possibly in the 1390s, we hear the following:

And heere auȝten [*ought*] proude men of þis world, but principalli prelatus and prestis, be sore aschamed to see her Lord and her Mayster, whom þey schulden principalli suen [*emulate*], ride in þus pore aray, as is bifore seide and þey to ride so proudeli in gai gult [*gay, gilded*] sadeles wiþ gingelinge brideles and v score or vi score hors of prout arayid men, as þouȝ hit were a kynge rydinge toward a reuel, and her chariottis wiþ her jeweles goynge tofore ful of grete fatte hors fed for the nones [*for the nonce*]. But fer beþ þe true disciplis of Crist from þis arai.[144]

Riverside Chaucer, p. 806). Stephen Knight, " 'My Lord, the Monk'," *SAC* 22 (2000): 381–86, reads the Monk as embodying "estate false consciousness" (p. 382) in having such tastes, seeing him as "a bogus knight" (p. 383).

[143] Wenzel, "Robert Lychlade," pp. 214–16. Compare Leclercq, Talbot and Rochais, *Opera Sancti Bernardi*, III. 103, lines 13–16. The work is the *Apologia ad Guillelmum*.

[144] Gloria Cigman, ed., *Lollard Sermons*, EETS, os 294 (Oxford: Oxford University Press, 1989), pp. 1–2, lines 26–34. Compare also in the second Sunday in Advent sermon in the same collection another attack on proud prelates who keep "gret multitude of fatte horses and proude, wiþ gai gult sadeles and schynynge brideles, wiþ miche wast and proude meyne" (Cigman, *Lollard Sermons*, p. 23, lines 423–24). For a hypothesis that this sermon collection dates to the last decade of the fourteenth century, see Alan J. Fletcher, "The Essential (Ephemeral) William Langland: Textual Revision as Ethical Process in *Piers Plowman*," *YLS* 15 (2001): 61–84, especially pp. 83–84.

The gospel reading for the first Sunday of Advent was the account of Christ's triumphal entry into Jerusalem (Matthew 21:1–9). This gave the anonymous Lollard preacher his chance. It was an ass that Christ rode on, he said, and in doing so he challenged prelates and priests nowadays to consider how wide of the moral mark was their preferred means of transport.

The favourite topics of Lollard discourse could prove resilient and that of the "proud horse" was no exception: in Lollard texts, simply to mention a cleric on horseback was to sound a note of disapproval. Taking their cue from St. Bernard, Lollards elaborated the theme further, exploiting a damning contrast between clerics who rode and clerics who walked. A simple but obvious moral opposition, they claimed, could be seen within the ranks of the clergy in this regard: riders were proud, walkers humble. Another Lollard Ascension Day sermon promoted this distinction when it observed how Christ had said to his disciples:

"Euntes in mundum vniuersum predicate euangelium omni creature." Ad denotandum quod essent vere humiles pedestres et non equestres superbi. Ideo dicit "euntes" et non "equitantes."[145]

("Going into all the world, preach the gospel to every creature." In signification that they might truly be humble and going on foot, not proud and going on horseback. For that reason he says "going," and not "riding.")

In the light of this Lollard emphasis on the moral pedestrian cleric as opposed to the immoral equestrian one, the detail in *The General Prologue* (lines 491–95) that Chaucer's Parson went around his wide parish *on foot* to visit his parishioners may not be a mere fleck of local color, a small brushstroke in the general picture of a good pastor striding out staunchly in all weathers to tend his flock. While it does help to do that, it also has precedents, and these most notably in Lollard writings: the detail is therefore entirely consistent with the many other hints of Wycliffism that critics have long recognized to cluster around the Parson.[146] In moral and in factional terms, the walking Parson and the

---

[145] Oxford, Bodleian Library, MS Laud Misc. 200, fols 134v-5. On this sermon collection, see Christina von Nolcken, "An Unremarked Group of Wycliffite Sermons in Latin," *MP* 83 (1986): 233–49.

[146] Robert N. Swanson, "Chaucer's Parson and Other Priests," *SAC* 13 (1991): 41–80, provides a valuable historical contextualization of the Parson, but the literalism of his reading strategies (p. 80) causes him to miss the polemical nuance contained in the detail that Chaucer's Parson *walked* around his parish (whatever about his riding as part

riding Monk define each other by opposition. The most noticeable equivalents to this, at the time Chaucer was writing, were Wycliffite. Encountered both in the "mass medium" of preaching, as well as more privately on the written page, the sheer frequency of the "proud horse" theme in Lollard writing suggests that the author of the *Twenty-Five Articles* tract was certainly not exaggerating. The theme had indeed been commandeered by Lollards. And this necessarily means that Chaucer's own application of it to the Monk (especially in the context of how the Parson, by contrast, normally got about) could have been interpreted by anyone with ears to hear not only as another moment of anticlericalism, but a tendentious one into the bargain.[147]

A final example of the "proud horse" theme may be cited in illustra-

---

of a troupe of pilgrims): "After all, there is an obvious, though generally ignored, paradox in this depiction of a paragon who does not abuse his benefice and walks around his parish to minister to his flock: here is he, on pilgrimage to Canterbury. Simply to be in that position he must have accumulated a surplus from his revenues; even if only for a short time, he must have abandoned his parish to the charge of a stand-in. Nor is he walking." For a historical application of this particular Lollard polemic, note how the notorious Leicester Lollard John Belgrave twitted Philip Repingdon, bishop of Lincoln and one-time follower of Wyclif, on the bishop's visitation in 1413: "dicensque episcopo moderno quod contravenit predicacionibus per ipsum olim factis, quia si faceret secundum quod olim in minoribus constitutus predicavit, circuiret per patrias pedibus eundo et more apostolorum predicaret" ("saying of the current bishop that he contradicts sermons that he formerly preached, because if he did what he preached when he was young, he would go around the country on foot and preach in the manner of the apostles"; James Crompton, "Leicestershire Lollards," *Transactions of the Leicestershire Archæological and Historical Society* 44 [1968–69]: 11–44; see p. 40).

[147] A few examples of the motif in Lollard discourse are: Matthew, *English Works*, p. 60 (in the tract *Of Prelates*): "O lord! what tokene of mekenesse & forsakynge of worldly richesses is þis; a prelat as an abott or a priour, þat is ded to þe world & pride & vanyte þer-of, to ride wiþ foure score hors, wiþ harneis of siluer & gold, & many raggid & fittrid squyers & oþere men swerynge herte & bonys & nailis & oþere membris of crist"; Matthew, *English Works*, p. 92 (in the tract *Of Prelates*): worldly prelates "leuen not as pore prestis aftir crist & his apostlis, but as lordis, ȝe kingis or emperours, in shynynge vessel & delicat metis & wynes, in fatte hors & precious pellure & ryche cloþ & proude & leccherous squyeris & meyne"; Matthew, *English Works*, p. 149 (in the tract *The Office of Curates*): "hou euyl it is to suffre pore men perische for hungire & þriste & cold, & here curatis han fatte hors with gaye sadlis & bridelis"; Matthew, *English Works*, p. 210 (in the tract *How Satan and his Children*): "ȝe, prelatis & men of singuler religion, þat taken þe charge to ben procuratouris & dispenderis of pore mennus liflode, cloþen fatte horsis & gaie sadlis & bridlis & mytris & croceris wiþ gold & siluer & precious stonys & suffren pore men & children perische for cold"; Arnold, *Select English Works*, vol. 3, p. 520: a petition to king and parliament, that poor men should not be coerced into paying tithes to worldly clerics who go about "wiþ fatte hors, and jolye and gaye sadeles, and bridelis ryngynge be þe weye, and himself in costy cloþes and pelure, and to suffre here wyues and children and here pore neyȝboures perische for hunger and þrist and cold."; Hudson and Gradon, *English Wycliffite Sermons*, vol. 3, p. 128, lines 16–17: bishops are arrayed "in hors and meyne" and are great in their household.

tion of the resilient adaptability of some of the characteristic themes of Lollard thought. These were often supple enough to recombine with other favored motifs. Proof of the Lollard outlook of William Thorpe is available at many turns of the interview that he reported taking place between himself and Archbishop Thomas Arundel. Thus one need not depend on Thorpe's scorn of "þe gingelynge . . . Cantirbirie bellis" (on the horse bridles of Canterbury pilgrims) as evidence of it.[148] Yet his choice of this detail, as should by now be clear, is once again consistent with the Lollard emphasis earlier identified. In Thorpe's case, however, the motif has mutated. This time it is not proud clerics who are guilty, but worldly pilgrims vainly indulging in pilgrimage (another reprehensible pursuit, according to Lollard belief). It does not seem accidental that Thorpe the Lollard should siphon off parts of the "proud horse" motif for instilling into his general disapproval of pilgrimage. To Archbishop Arundel he reputedly said:

Also, sire, I knowe wel þat whanne dyuerse men and wymmen wolen goen þus aftir her owne willis and fyndingis [wish to go thus following their own devices and desires] out on pilgrimageyngis, þei wolen ordeyne biforehonde to haue wiþ hem boþe men and wymmen þat kunnen wel synge rowtinge songis [who well know how to sing bellowing songs], and also summe of þese pilgrimes wolen haue wiþ hem baggepipis so þat in eche toun þat þei comen þoruȝ, what wiþ noyse of her syngynge, and wiþ þe soun of her pipinge, and wiþ þe gingelynge of her Cantirbirie bellis, and wiþ þe berkynge out of dogges aftir hem, þese maken more noyse þan if þe king came þere awey wiþ his clarioneris and manye oþer mynystrals.[149]

And notice, too, the comparison that Thorpe annexed to his reworking of the "proud horse" theme in the last sentence: pilgrim entourages made such a noise that one might suspect the king himself to be riding by with all the ceremonial music of state. That exact comparison was heard before, in the vernacular Lollard sermon for Advent Sunday quoted earlier.[150]

So this celebrated vignette of a late-medieval pilgrims' progress may have been painted with more than simply scenic touches: it is dressed in rhetorical tropes customized by Lollards to convey their moral disap-

---

[148] Anne Hudson, ed., *Two Wycliffite Texts*, EETS, os 301 (Oxford: Oxford University Press, 1993), p. 64, line 1326.

[149] Hudson, *Two Wycliffite Texts*, p. 64, lines 1320–29 (italics mine).

[150] And compare the inappropriate "kingliness" of clerics criticized in the tract *Of Prelates* cited in note 147 above.

proval. These are tropes which other Lollards would promptly recognize, as would their enemies. And would those Lollards or their enemies have been any the less capable of recognizing a comparable trope within Chaucer's use of the detail, *whatever* the original motive may have been that led him to introduce it, twice over, into his portrait of the Monk?

To sum this section up: we have seen new ways in which Chaucer's presentation of the Pardoner, Friar, Summoner, Monk, and Parson have networked intertextually with the contemporary culture of heresy, thus enmeshing Chaucer ever more closely than already appreciated within that particular cultural formation. That much would seem incontrovert-ible. The consequent questions of biographical interest lie largely ahead in the final part of this essay, and grow naturally from the attempt to grasp as fully as possible Chaucer's personal relation to the culture of heresy.

Chaucer the heretic?

To conclude, where does all this leave the historical Geoffrey Chaucer, quarry of the biographers? Various questions arise. An obvious one—it has dogged Chaucer criticism for many years—is that of his own relation to Lollardy. What, exactly, was this? And related to it is a wider question of what cultural work he accomplished by yoking his writing to radical/heretical discourse.

To take the first question first. It admits various responses along a sliding scale: at one end, the sense in which it has been most frequently asked in the past, would Chaucer have regarded himself as a Lollard; or at the other, was he simply an interested though neutral observer of the ideals of a group of people who were increasingly being identified and disparaged as "Lollards" by reactionaries within the Church? Some ear-lier critics supposed Chaucer was committed to Lollardy, and it is easy to see why.[151] Indeed, we have seen here further Chaucerian motifs chiming with typically Lollard ones, apparently being matched in some cases only in texts that adopt a pronounced pro-Wycliffite stance. (Nor would the fact of the availability of prototypes of certain of those motifs in anticlericalisms predating Lollardy seem sufficient wholly to explain

---

[151] See F. N. Robinson, ed., *The Works of Geoffrey Chaucer*, 2d ed. (London: Oxford University Press, 1957), pp. 663–64, for references to early studies of Chaucer as Wycliffite. Indeed, the earliest critics on record to regard Chaucer as a crypto-Lollard were his sixteenth-century editors.

the coincidence, for reasons earlier explained.) Nevertheless, what can be categorically claimed about the complexion of the historical Chaucer's confessional allegiance on the basis of this new evidence may be modest, for reasons soon to be made clear. The historical bottom line, as earlier observed, must be that Chaucer emerges as yet further conversant with the culture of heresy, with radical/heretical sentiment and the turns of phrase in which that sentiment was characteristically couched.

Any venturing beyond this bottom line must necessarily be tentative, and at this juncture must also engage with some other recent opinions on the nature of Chaucer's relation to Lollardy. Anne Hudson seems to believe that Chaucer may indeed have had Wycliffite sympathies, if only in the minimal and coincidental sense that, since several Wycliffite themes also coincided with general intellectual interests of the time, Chaucer would have been similarly (and coincidentally) interested in what Wycliffites were saying; yet while putting this view forward, she also acknowledges that Chaucer *deliberately* clothed his Parson, a pilgrim whom most critics would agree was meant to be regarded as a paragon, in "a suggestion of Wycliffism."[152] (Here in her analysis, coincidence now yields to deliberateness.) This second point, that elements in the Parson's depiction would have corresponded to a recognizably Wycliffite ideal for the priesthood, is surely correct and has been given fresh support in the present essay although, of course, it is not new: well before Hudson and this essay, the Parson's Wycliffite coloring was something that critics had already perceived, if with less finesse and sometimes for reasons not always fully reliable. However, Hudson's first point concern-

---

[152] Hudson, *Premature Reformation*, p. 392. In fact, there is more evidence of the Parson's Wycliffite coloring than Hudson has acknowledged, though earlier critics had laid the ground for its recognition: Doris V. Ines, "'A Man of Religion'," *MLR* 27 (1932): 144–48, seems to have been the first to notice the frequency of the appeal to "Christ and his apostles" in Lollard writing as one of its typical collocations (see p. 145; an identification of the collocation as characteristically Lollard was made more forcefully by Roger Sherman Loomis, "Was Chaucer a Laodicean?," in *Essays and Studies in Honor of Carleton Brown* [New York and London: New York University Press and Oxford University Press, 1940], pp. 129–48; see pp. 142–43). Katherine Little, "Chaucer's Parson and the Specter of Wycliffism," *SAC* 23 (2001): 225–53, claims of the Parson (p. 238) that "Chaucer does not seem to be at all concerned about whether or not his ideal is viewed as Wycliffite; instead he simply gives us a portrait of a reformed priest." Not only do I disagree with this, Little's argument verges on internal inconsistency when she goes on to speak of the "Wycliffite undertones" of the Parson, and of how "Chaucer does not include anything in his description to distance the Parson's portrait from Lollardy" (pp. 239–40). If Little is saying that Chaucer facilitates his Parson's identification with Lollardy, then she has contradicted herself.

ing Chaucer's possible coincidentally "Lollard" interests is more difficult to arbitrate: how may we effectively discriminate between coincidental correspondences and deliberate ones? Since normally we may not, the value of the distinction is theoretical and of limited practical consequence. If we reflect on Hudson's minimal and coincidental sense, that common concerns pervading Chaucer's culture would have caused his interests to converge coincidentally with Lollard ones, nothing particularly remarkable or surprising has been said. Nor does such a view, unless more carefully articulated, amount to much when we can demonstrate that Chaucer has deliberately skewed his presentation of some of those supposed common-property interests in ways that appear to have been characteristically, if not distinctively, Lollard (as in the Parson's case just referred to or in many of the other cases opened in this essay). Presumably he did so because he was for some reason content that they should also register a factionally Lollard, rather than vaguely general, topicality.[153] If, alternatively, we pursue the maximal sense—nowhere apparently ruled out by Hudson and certainly ruled in by some earlier critics—that Chaucer's "Lollard" correspondences may signal an active Lollard sympathy in Chaucer himself, we run into difficulty again for a different set of reasons. To anticipate part of my conclusion, in spite of his familiarity with the culture of heresy—evidently closer than hitherto suspected—and his implicit willingness that this familiarity should resonate in some of his writing, it seems to me impossible finally to decide whether Chaucer was even as moderately committed in reality to certain of the ideals of the Lollard radicals as the word "sympathy" might suggest.[154] But in any event, there is room to move beyond Hudson's digest of Chaucer's relation to Lollardy.

More carefully nuanced and strongly argued are the analyses of Lynn Staley and David Aers, who both propose specific detailed correspondences of *theme* and *idea* between Chaucer and the culture of heresy, and who in the light of them incidentally gauge his position vis-à-vis heretical discourse. To that extent, their projects resemble my own.[155] My

[153] And Chaucer demonstrated the fact of his awareness of Lollardy as a factional possibility when he had the Host "smelle a Lollere in the wynd" in respect of the Parson (Benson, *Riverside Chaucer*, p. 104, line 1173).
[154] Though this may not necessarily mean that we should stop trying. David Lawton, "Chaucer's Two Ways: The Frame of *The Canterbury Tales*," *SAC* 9 (1987): 3–40, sees "uncertainty" as much as "sympathy" in Chaucer's attitude to Lollardy (p. 36).
[155] Aers and Staley, *Powers of the Holy*; David Aers, *Faith, Ethics and Church: Writing in England, 1360–1409* (Cambridge: D. S. Brewer, 2000). I must also note the excellent

aim, by contrast, has been to highlight unremarked *intertextual* affiliations, ones that by that very token seem to me more empirically palpa-
ble.[156] Yet for all that, the Chaucer that can be derived from them is less
consolingly determinate than the Chaucer emergent from the analyses
of Staley and Aers. This is a Chaucer who, while not personally aligned
with Lollardy, nevertheless used his poetry to ask questions with which
Lollards were similarly concerned;[157] who also made some of it a site for
critical meditation on specific Wycliffite positions, such as the heresi-
arch's faith in the expansion of kingly power as a possible solution to
current ecclesiastical ills.[158] This Chaucer was evidently well acquainted
with various Wycliffite issues and through his poetry engaged in their
searching interrogation. He also resisted their final determination, and,
analytical and cool, maintained his own independent attitude. That attitude insulated him from unreflecting adherence either to Wycliffism or
to the reactionary Catholic orthodoxy currently being formulated by the
likes of the Canterbury archbishops Courtenay and Arundel and their
theological fellow travellers.

Were the truth known, these analyses, attractively stable and coherent, are perhaps historically correct.[159] But the fact is that the range of
Chaucer's writing eligible for the sort of critical investigation in hand in
this article is extensive and its exact chronology, though unknown, is at
least known to have spanned a period of a few years. Therefore, any *a
priori* assumption that it should sustain a fixed picture through time of
his relation to the culture of heresy has no sound logical basis. As a
result, the best we may hope for from the analyses of Staley and Aers,
grounded as they are on detailed, though selective, samplings, are fo-

---

article by Lawrence Besserman, " 'Priest' and 'Pope,' 'Sire' and 'Madame': Anachronistic
Diction and Social Conflict in Chaucer's *Troilus*," *SAC* 23 (2001): 181–224; see pp.
221–22 for a judicious assessment of Chaucer's relation to Lollardy.

[156] Aers also cites approvingly what seems to me a dangerous procedure that he has
discovered in Hudson (*Premature Reformation*, p. 391) of mounting arguments *ex silencio*.
This procedure is logically a risky one.

[157] Staley, in Aers and Staley, *Powers of the Holy*, p. 216. This Chaucer sounds a little
like one of Hudson's mooted Chaucers, someone coincidentally interested in issues also
of interest to Lollards.

[158] Aers, *Faith, Ethics and Church*, p. 37.

[159] To this extent, the indeterminate stance of Chaucer would resemble the indeterminacy that Arnulf of Orléans, for example, observed as the characteristic of the poet: "in
the manner of the philosopher he [Lucan] puts forward three opinions, but in the manner of the poet he neither resolves nor affirms any of them" (Alastair J. Minnis and
A. B. Scott, with David Wallace, ed., *Medieval Literary Theory and Criticism c. 1100–c.
1375* [Oxford: Clarendon Press, 1988], p. 115).

cused snapshots of particular Chaucerian moments. As such, while certainly valuable stimulants to debate, their analyses are also necessarily contingent. In illustration of this, let me introduce to their (relatively steady) picture of Chaucer's relation to the culture of heresy a teasing and complicating possibility, and allow its unproveability also to flag the uncertainty that complicates attempts to read back from the oeuvre into the life. We know that Chaucer, eventually left exposed to the scrutiny of the new regime after 1399 on account of his former loyalty to the circle of Richard II, seems to have attempted a damage limitation exercise by addressing a soothing poem, the *Complaint to his Purse*, to the usurping Henry IV.[160] In this poem, which echoes with Lancastrian arguments in favour of the usurpation, Chaucer strove to signal his allegiance to the new regime and to underwrite Henry's claim to the throne.[161] Since he was evidently capable of using poetry to give himself a secular political make-over, may he not also have given himself a theological make-over in *An ABC*? One recent investigation of *An ABC* declares that "this is not autobiography."[162] Perhaps. Yet why sever it from its author's own self-interest quite so categorically? After all, as we saw, precisely in its manner of introducing theologically transgressive *error* into the penitent's persona, this poem is not quite an exact replica of Deguileville's pieties. Instead, the penitent's presentation was customized in a way unmatched in Deguileville, which Chaucer was personally responsible for, and which would have been an increasingly familiar and significant penitential pose (his own included?) after 1381–82, when the Wycliffite heresy took a new turn in notoriety following the condemnations issued at the Blackfriars Council.[163] It seems safer to say that the question of whether Chaucer was also using the penitent of *An ABC* for his own mouthpiece as much as for a universal, penitential

[160] Conceivably, the poem's ostensible annuity-wheedling disguises something more material to Chaucer's interests: it might serve as a pretext for a blanketing flattery of the new king and a reassurance of where Chaucer's loyalties now lay.

[161] Paul Strohm, *Hochon's Arrow: The Social Imagination of Fourteenth-Century Texts* (Princeton: Princeton University Press, 1992), pp. 75–94.

[162] Georgia Ronan Crampton, "Chaucer's Singular Prayer," *MÆ* 59 (1990): 191–213; see p. 202.

[163] Crampton, "Chaucer's Singular Prayer," p. 203, also observes that "the speaker [of *An ABC*] leaves his spiritual *vita* fastidiously general." But the penitent's emphatic *error*, discussed above, damages the categorical clarity of this view. (While no substantial argument about the date of *An ABC* can be based on the date of its surviving manuscripts, it is nevertheless interesting that none of these is as early as the earliest surviving *Canterbury Tales* manuscripts. May *An ABC* have been written very late after the 1381–82 suggested above?)

voice, is one better left open, not closed by the declaration that "this is not autobiography."[164] Supposing, for argument's sake, that it *were* somehow proveable that Chaucer intended that *An ABC* should launder him in orthodoxy. He would then emerge, if obliquely, as publicly backing off from a former personal commitment to positions that the Church had decreed erroneous, and thus potentially heretical. Such a Chaucer would, of course, be different from Staley and Aers's, though reconcileable with theirs once the possibility, elided in their analyses, had been acknowledged that the nature of his relation to the culture of heresy might alter through time. Such a putative, formerly erroneous Chaucer might also be thought compatible with the man prepared to valorize within *The Canterbury Tales* certain salient aspects of Wycliffite ecclesiology—though far less obviously any salient Wycliffite theology—for undisputably, this is what a cluster of his tales appears to have done.[165]

So the contribution of the evidence gathered in the present essay to solving the Chaucer-the-heretic conundrum puzzling the biographers summarizes as follows: in certain writings, Chaucer deployed his appropriations of the culture of heresy with versatility, now using them either to maneuver his audience into a scandalizing apprehension of the state of the Church, or to remind that audience of what the ecclesiological opinions it already held were (and this within some of *The Canterbury Tales* where, as previously noted, a broadly sketched ecclesiology is valorized in whose outline certain Wycliffite precedents would have been clearly recognizable); or now using them as the raw material for his rhetorical self-fashioning, either for the sake of game (*The Legend of Good Women*) or conceivably, though unproveably, even in personal earnest (*An ABC*).[166] In brief, Chaucer diverted matter originally of ecclesiastical sensitivity into the domain of a courtly practice and conversation, where

[164] More moderate is William A. Quinn, "Chaucer's Problematic *Priere*: *An ABC* as Artifact and Critical Issue," *SAC* 23 (2001): 109–41; see pp. 136–37 for his delicate balancing of the communal and personal voices in *An ABC*.

[165] While an ecclesiology is necessarily the practical expression of a particular theology, it might nevertheless be thought to express that theology far less directly. It seems to me that in *The Canterbury Tales*, it is not so much contested theological issues that are foregrounded than the ecclesiological ones to which the theological issues, to be sure, have given rise. Broadly speaking, the "new sects" of the Church (to use the Lollard parlance) come off badly in *The Canterbury Tales*, but not the seculars, the only wing of the clergy having members evangelically sanctioned and of whom Wyclif therefore approved.

[166] Their use as analyzed by Besserman, "Anachronistic Diction and Social Conflict," pp. 220–21, should also be added to my compound assessment.

theological concerns and topicalities (ones becoming dangerously volatile as the 1390's advanced) were aired to differing effect according to the work in question; in *The Canterbury Tales*, if the political turbulence attending those concerns and topicalities was not entirely dispersed by their being cast in a fictive guise—and it is difficult to imagine how it could have been—then perhaps that guise might still have been thought enough to veil their author from seeming too closely identified with the issues he was raising.[167] In terms of its wider cultural work, Chaucer's activity in relocating matter from one arena to another also resembles a democratizing of access to the intellectual property of clerical culture that the 1380s and 1390s were generally witnessing (partly as a consequence of pressure exerted from the orthodox-versus-heterodox debate to air in English questions hitherto reserved for discussion in Latin).[168] In this larger cultural movement certain of Chaucer's writings participated.

This, then, is what Chaucer has done, but why did he do it? Motives have been conjectured in the case of *An ABC* and *The Legend of Good Women*; conjecturing them in the case of *The Canterbury Tales* breeds possibilities beyond those raised in Hudson's account, or even in the more considered analyses of Staley and Aers. Two that seem not to have been broached but that may usefully extend the range currently available are as follows.

Conceivably, the Lollard rapprochement in some of Chaucer's *Canterbury Tales* anticlericalism, a rapprochement that as I have observed registers less obviously in theological than in ecclesiological positions, could have amounted to a literary version of what behavioral psychologists

---

[167] The opinion that Chaucer may have used his fiction to screen himself from unwelcome attention is persistent among critics; both Staley and Aers express it, and similarly Sherry L. Reames, "Artistry, Decorum, and Purpose in Three Middle English Retellings of the Cecilia Legend," in M. Teresa Tavormina and R. F. Yeager, eds., *The Endless Knot: Essays in Honor of Marie Borroff* (Cambridge: D. S. Brewer, 1995), pp. 177–99; see p. 199, where after an account of how the *Second Nun's Tale* may allude to contemporary political persecutions, she ventures that "Chaucer's exceptional caution in the [*Second Nun's Tale*] is significant because it suggests that the persecuting authorities he had in mind were so powerful and so near at hand that he did not dare write openly against them."

[168] Valuable work in this area has been undertaken by Margaret Aston, "Lollardy and Literacy," *History* 62 (1977): 347–71, rpt. in her book *Lollards and Reformers: Images and Literacy in Late Medieval Religion* (London: Hambledon Press, 1984), pp. 193–217; also her "Wycliffe and the Vernacular," in Anne Hudson and Michael Wilks, eds., *From Ockham to Wyclif*, Studies in Church History, Subsidia 5 (Oxford: Clarendon Press, 1987), pp. 281–330, rpt. in her book *Faith and Fire*, pp. 27–72. See also generally Somerset, *Clerical Discourse and Lay Audience*.

might now call "postural echo," a sign simply of his inclination to play to the anticlerical gallery at court, mimicking its characteristic poses and by a display of kinship signals bonding with its group; after all, given the existence in certain court circles of sympathy to the values of the radicals, such moves in Chaucer's writing would doubtless have been well received.[169] Perhaps, then, his writing, like a defining mirror, reassured and gratified the target community before which it was placed by reflecting some of that community's cherished ecclesiological postures. Indeed, rather than conceive his echoes of Lollard ecclesiology as indicating any sincere adherence on his part, or even, after the school of Staley and Aers, as indicating any sincere personal commitment to exploring issues that nevertheless avoided any final determinate resolution, this sort of Chaucer could simply be a club member for whom the belonging was what mattered. The need simply to belong might supersede worrying about the letter of the club rules. And here we might additionally ponder how meaningful any mooted "sympathy" on Chaucer's part could be that tolerated at other places within the Canterbury sequence matter that Lollards characteristically despised, or that sometimes collapsed in helpless laughter at issues that they took very seriously.[170] (Their writings, unlike many of Chaucer's, are normally written in dogged earnest and are not noted for their sense of humor.) Such "sympathy" in Chaucer, if we finally choose to believe in it, is at best intermittent or partial, making him an *à la carte* Lollard who selected most noticeably from the Wycliffite ecclesiological menu; looked at from another angle—for example, as a sort of literary anthropology—it

---

[169] On the question of court Lollardy, see J. Anthony Tuck, "Carthusian Monks and Lollard Knights: Religious Attitude at the Court of Richard II," *SAC Proceedings* 1 (1984): 149–61. Olson, *Good Society*, p. 127, persuasively imagines "the royal court" as "almost a second convocation for ecclesiological dispute". Thus Chaucer's stances in this respect further the dialogue at court in which he was well placed to participate and which he encourages elsewhere in his work (and compare again Olson, *Good Society*, p. 26: "*The Canterbury Tales* are a simulated conversation designed to promote court conversation").

[170] The dependence, for example, of *The Second Nun's Prologue* and *Tale* (originally a pre-*Canterbury Tales* composition) upon the *Legenda aurea* of the Dominican friar Jacobus de Voragine and upon other Franciscan-inspired material, was upon precisely the sort of fabulation that staunch Lollards would have deplored. See Sherry L. Reames, "A Recent Discovery Concerning the Sources of Chaucer's 'Second Nun's Tale'," *MP* 87 (1990): 337–61, and David Raybin, "Chaucer's Creation and Recreation of the *Lyf of Seynt Cecile*," *ChauR* 32 (1997): 196–212. And in *The Nun's Priest's Tale*, predestination, an issue of grave importance to Wyclif a few years earlier, becomes the stuff of jest, as Hudson, *Premature Reformation*, p. 393, has noticed.

might be thought shallow to the point of evaporation. May Chaucer really be considered "sympathetic" more than he may be considered consciously calculating, if not ultimately indifferent? Of course, this sort of Chaucer, unlike the man on the brink of a committed integrity such as the appealing account of Aers, especially, seems to figure, risks becoming less congenial for idealists to believe in. He may even seem a time-server, someone resistant to the consoling myth that would incline to make great poets also into great people.

Alternatively, or perhaps complementarily, what if Chaucer's primary loyalties were to the momentum of writing itself, to an aesthetic excitement pure and simple that fed luxuriously on the political excitement aroused by the culture of heresy but that finally floated free from any determinate moral commitment either to it or to the cultural stakes it played for? Indeed, such exploitative artistic ingestion might be thought well exemplified in the exchange between the Host and the Monk that prefaces *The Monk's Tale*. There is good reason not to find out-and-out Lollardy in the Host, but even he is permitted to voice radical (if not ultimately Lollard-inspired) opinion. This time what is at stake is the question of clerical celibacy.[171] It is conceivable that Chaucer has served

---

[171] Comedic interest in the prospect of a married clergy was already in the air, as the continued manuscript copying in the fourteenth century of earlier Goliardic works such as the *Convocacio sacerdotum* testifies (for example, in London, British Library, MS Titus A.xx). The *Convocacio* was itself a jesting response to a decree of the Fourth Lateran Council of 1215 mandating clerical celibacy (Thomas Wright, ed., *The Latin Poems Commonly Attributed to Walter Mapes*, Camden Society [London: Nichols and Son, 1841], pp. 180–82). The Lollards held a more serious view of the matter, however. Wyclif himself opposed the obligation of clerical celibacy, though he seems not strenuously to have advocated a married clergy (see Henry Hargreaves, "Sir John Oldcastle and Wycliffite Views on Clerical Marriage," *MÆ* 42 [1973]: 141–46). Others, however, did (see the references in Hudson, *Premature Reformation*, pp. 114, 292 and 357–58). One such, the chamber knight Sir Lewis Clifford, had been a member of the "Chaucer circle" (Pearsall, *Life*, p. 181). In 1402, Clifford recanted his Lollard beliefs before Archbishop Arundel, and informed on certain *Lollardi* whom he knew, passing their names on to the archbishop. The second of these beliefs recalls, albeit in a more extreme form, the position jokingly entertained by the Host: "quod virginitas et presbyteratus non sunt status approbati a Deo, sed status conjugii optimus est, et ordinatus a Deo. Quapropter omnino virgines et presbyteri, religiosique populi, si salvari desiderant, debent conjugari, vel esse in voluntate et proposito conjugandi" ("that virginity and priesthood are not states approved by God, but that the married state is best, and ordained by God. Wherefore virgins and priests and religious people ought to get married, or be of a mind and disposition to marry, if they want to be saved"; Riley, *Historia Anglicana*, vol. 2, p. 252). Blamires, "Wife of Bath," p. 241, note 41, believes that the Host's view of the Monk as a potential "tredefowel" illustrates that such views were not exclusively Lollard, but this avoids the more interesting question of from where the Host may be supposed to have derived his view. The Host is fond of celebrating the sexual potency

us in this exchange with a momentary slice of life, a glimpse into the kind of grass-roots support that at least certain aspects of radical theology had come to enjoy in late-fourteenth-century London, becoming now naturalized to the extent of turning into the stuff of secular, working-class banter.[172] However, we should also reflect on the place occupied by such momentary radicalism in the larger web of rhetorical strategies that consititute the Host's intervention.

The Host's speech is full of imagined role reversals and role projections. His first reaction on hearing *The Tale of Melibee* is to recall his virago wife Goodelief, and wish that she had been present to take note of the patience of Melibee's wife, Prudence. He then ventriloquizes one of the typical role reversals that Goodelief projects onto him. He has not, she would remonstrate, sufficiently taken her part (lines 1905–57):

> False coward, wrek thy wyf!
> By corpus bones, I wol have thy knyf,
> And thou shalt have my distaf and go spynne!

Cut off from his "knyf" and man's work, he must handle a distaff instead. This rich rhetorical emasculation is imaged as a moment of comic transvestism, a momentary picturing of an alternative, carnivalesque reality where such reversals and inversions might just happen to come true. And once set in motion, notice the rollicking gamut of role changes to which the Host proceeds to submit himself as the passage progresses. He becomes in Goodelief's view (though we remember that he is the one who takes credit for reporting it) by turns a "milksop," a "coward ape"; to satisfy her appetite for retribution he must become a "wilde leoun"; then, in self-deprecating appreciation of the Monk's impressive physicality, he pictures himself and all laymen by contrast as

---

of clerics; compare his attitude to the Nun's Priest (Benson, *Riverside Chaucer*, p. 261, lines 3447–61). In 1402, Clifford also recanted the view that religious celibates, by refusing to marry and procreate, were murderers of potential offspring in their seed. Again, this is somewhat similar to the Host's view of why the Monk should beget children. In the light of the view of Clifford and his associate *Lollardi*, F. N. Robinson's note, recycled in Benson, *Riverside Chaucer*, p. 929, that the Host's argument was seldom used and that there was little reference to the effect on the population of celibate clergy, needs revision.

[172] Certainly, by the time Chaucer was working on *The Canterbury Tales*, a theological radicalizing of the general London populace had already been underway from at least the year 1377, when according to the chronicler Thomas Walsingham, Wyclif ran from church to church preaching and causing a stir (see E. Maunde Thompson, ed., *Chronicon Angliae*, Rolls Series 64 [London: Eyre and Spottiswoode, 1874], pp. 116–17).

"shrympes" or "fieble trees" that produce weedy offspring; religion has claimed the best breeding stock, he says. And his moment of radical/ heretical imagining—abandonment of clerical celibacy—is tucked effortlessly into this series of rhetorical transformations and alternative picturings: imaging himself now back in the human world where he holds sway as "pope," his fiat would allow all such mannish men of religion to take wives.[173] Since it falls within imaginative literature's remit to license the site of "What if?," opening up a realm of alternatives where the discourses and metanarratives by which people actually live in the real world put in an appearance, but are nevertheless allowed to clash and combine in ways that, in the real world, would seem outlandish, then in this unbordered terrain of literary free space, heresy becomes a trope that readily lends itself for acquisition, and perhaps simply for this reason: it is of heresy's essence that, in common with the practice of literary fiction, it too dares to imagine and celebrate alternatives. This being so, the heretical impulse is necessarily partly commensurate with the creative one, and may provide the creative artist with additional impetus. As the heretical impulse redimensions itself, emptying into artistic action, its final achieved value in the (plurivocal) art work may inhere less in any authentic testimony that it bears to prior ideological commitment in the artist from whom it sprang than in its power to help stir literary life into the art work being undertaken. That literary life animates a discourse that may fasten the real-life discourses sustaining it into an allegiance to nothing other than itself, and in that supervening allegiance, the historical reality of the author, although it may not be utterly lost, and hence still in principle be worthy of speculation, will be variously refracted.

Yet if the question of Chaucer's personal relation to the culture of heresy may ultimately prove undeterminable (not least because it may have vacillated through time), the range of hypothetical answers to the question may contain somewhere within its boundaries a variegated truth, and for that reason the range continues to remain worth exploring. To be sure, the curiosity of the traditional biographers may have to go unsatisfied for the time being. But even though decisive answers to

---

[173] It might also be noted that the prospect of the Host as a lay pope packs a rum Lollard joke, given that according to Wyclif, the real pope was the most just man alive, and thus anyone, whether clerical or lay, was a potential papal candidate, the Host included (see Wyclif's views, for example, in Loserth, *Sermones*, vol. 2, p. 352, lines 35–36 and 353, lines 11–13).

all these questions—whether or not Chaucer really was in any meaningful way Lollardy's sympathizer, or simply a committed scrutineer of Lollardy, or a social opportunist who made the right "noises," or a literary
opportunist whose writing the culture of heresy helped galvanize—may
be beyond our present reach, just as interesting historically is the answer
to a question less frequently asked. Disregarding his own religious inclination through time, whether conservative, radical, or drifting over the
years along a continuum between both extremes, could Chaucer have
been *viewed* as a Lollard by his contemporaries, however much it might
be supposed that the loophole of fiction let him slip a personal identification with certain issues to which his writing alluded? Notwithstanding
fiction's veil, could any of Chaucer's contemporaries have *perceived* him
as having been sympathetic to Lollardy? Or indeed, as having been partisan, since in the eyes of the beholder, the line between sympathizer
and paid up club member is likely to have been exceedingly fine? This
is a question that also has every reason to pique the biographers, and its
answer, self-evidently, is yes. Whatever the reality, he could have been
so perceived.[174] And it is conceivable that as Chaucer neared his death,
this perception worked toward his disadvantage. But to support this
concluding suggestion, we need to return to some ground already tilled
by Anne Hudson.

Hudson's attempt to situate and understand Chaucer's stance and the
nature of his relation to Lollardy is evidently also conditioned by her
prior assumption of a more temperate climate prevailing before 1401
(the year of the draconian *De heretico comburendo*, when the Church successfully petitioned the secular arm for legislation enacting death by
burning for recidivist heretics). In this pre-1401 period, she says, "there
were many questions on which it was possible to write or speak without
commitment—questions that later divided the 'orthodox' from the 'heretic' ".[175] Again, Hudson's position is not new; in fact, it sounds remarkably similar to Paul Olson's, advanced two years earlier.[176] Hudson's
implication seems to be that issues characteristic of Lollardy could have

[174] Although were we to discover that Chaucer had indeed been a known Lollard
sympathizer, his sympathy could have done little to commend him after Arundel's return from exile.

[175] Hudson, *Premature Reformation*, p. 394.

[176] Olson, *Good Society*, pp. 128–29; the only material difference between him and
Hudson is his choice of 1407–9 (the years of the draft and issue of Arundel's Oxford
Constitutions), as opposed to hers of 1401, for marking the decisive turning point in
policy.

been explored, even promoted, quite safely during this (relatively tranquil) period without much attendant fear of personal taint or danger to life and limb. Without question, party lines are likely to have hardened after the passing of the capital legislation of 1401; *De heretico comburendo* upped the stakes dramatically, and to that extent, Hudson's view is justified. But on the one hand, it fails to consider whether any perceived Lollard sympathy in one as socially well placed as Chaucer would have been regarded by the new regime in quite the same way as in someone outside court circles whose views, because they were held beyond the pale of political power, were far less likely to matter; and on the other, her "before-and-after" chronology is not without its difficulties. It risks conveying too black and white an impression of a (pre-1401) calm before a (post-1401) storm. For how comparatively balmy were the months immediately before the time when, according to Hudson's pivotal 1401 chronology, everything changed and attitudes polarized? The question needs asking.

The Lollards themselves would not have thought that they were. Their writings are often haunted by the specter of persecutions, some imagined, some real. And Lollards had every reason to be concerned.[177] Two years earlier, in 1399 when Chaucer was still alive, Archbishop Thomas Arundel had swept back into power, now vindicated and massively supported by the usurping king whom he necessarily supported in return; the uprooting of heresy was now newly urgent since it was coextensive with the uprooting of treason against an incoming king who was nervously aware that he appeared an arriviste.[178] Two years earlier than that, in 1397, the orthodox authorities had made their first push to secure a statutory death penalty for heresy. Two years earlier again, in 1395, the twelve outspoken Lollard conclusions calling on the king to move against a corrupt Church had been publicly posted in London, as earlier noted, during a sitting of the parliament; and as Margaret Aston has plausibly suggested, it may have been the alarm generated by this incident that prompted the prosecution of certain notable Lollards later in that year.[179] Thus whatever the life-and-death proportion

---

[177] On orthodox efforts to suppress Lollardy in the 1380's and 1390's, see H. G. Richardson, "Heresy and the Lay Power under Richard II," *EHR* 51 (1936): 1–28.

[178] And see Peter McNiven, *Heresy and Politics in the Reign of Henry IV: The Burning of John Badby* (Woodbridge, Suffolk: Boydell, 1987), p. 92.

[179] Margaret Aston, "Lollardy and Sedition, 1381–1431," *Past and Present* 17 (1960): 1–44; see pp. 22–23.

into which issues would inflate in and after 1401, events like these not very long before suggest that the period immediately before *De heretico comburendo* was not a time of comparative nonchalance when "there were many questions on which it was possible to write or speak without commitment." On the contrary, already as Chaucer approached his death—if the traditional death date of late autumn, 1400, is correct, *De heretico comburendo* was enacted but a couple of months after—some of the things that he had written earlier in the decade may have come back to plague him. Paul Strohm has argued strongly for a perceived "commensurability between Lollardy and anti-Lancastrian activity"; Chaucer, if perceived as a Lollard, would also have been perceived as anti-Lancastrian.[180] But that is no more than his Ricardian affinity might already have prompted some of the new ascendancy to suspect. Even if we go as far as conceding that Chaucer may originally have been unperturbed about making allusions to certain issues, even ones becoming increasingly contentious and alarming for the orthodox party when he was penning them, we should less quickly assume that nothing had changed immediately before his death.[181]

So a good case can be made that, even if Chaucer foresaw no damaging consequences for himself in what he wrote precisely at the time he wrote it,[182] he may with the benefit of hindsight have been playing with fire. If we wish to persist in seeking a pivotal year when all things changed, then as far as Chaucer was concerned, 1399 seems a worthy candidate. Even if Chaucer had found it possible at court to valorize aspects of Lollard ecclesiology within *The Canterbury Tales* without risk-

---

[180] Paul Strohm, *England's Empty Throne: Usurpation and the Language of Legitimation, 1399–1422* (New Haven: Yale University Press, 1998), p. 59.

[181] Traditionally, 25 October 1400 (Pearsall, *Life*, p. 276). Other critics have seen the 1390's as a dangerous time for being frank about certain religious views: David Lawton, "Lollardy and the 'Piers Plowman' Tradition," *MLR* 76 (1981): 780–93, says (p. 780) that by the later 1380's and 1390's, "Lollard sympathizers would have had to make a choice whether to accept or reject an increasingly dangerous label"; and Blamires, "Wife of Bath," p. 235, says "however much Chaucer wished to gain a hearing for Lollard views via the Wife, he would not have deemed it prudent to advertise this too explicitly (even in the case of a speaker for whose words he pretends to admit no responsibility). He was writing at a time when the risk attaching to lay polemic founded upon 'express' scriptural warrant, if difficult to quantify, could not have been minimal."

[182] For some discussion of the constraints placed upon writing theological statements between 1378 and 1406, see James Simpson, "The Constraints of Satire in 'Piers Plowman' and 'Mum and the Sothsegger'," in Helen Phillips, ed., *Langland, the Mystics and the Medieval English Religious Tradition: Essays in Honour of S. S. Hussey* (Cambridge: D. S. Brewer, 1990), pp. 11–30.

ing threat to career or personal safety, by the time of Archbishop Arundel's return in 1399, that valorization may in retrospect have seemed foolhardy, commensurable as it may now have appeared, to repeat Strohm, with the anti-Lancastrian camp. Times had changed already before Chaucer's death in a way that would reveal much of the anticlericalism in *The Canterbury Tales* as something that, if weighed in Archbishop Arundel's strict scales, would have been found wanting.[183] It may not have been "worldly vanitees" alone that Chaucer was revoking in his Retractions; when it came to "the tales of Caunterbury," conceivably "thilke that sownen into synne" included ones tinged with a guilty anticlericalism and ecclesiology of the sort that the orthodoxy fanfared in the Retractions, had it admitted interrogation on the point, would have turned its face against.

So to end where we began, dead authors refuse to lie quietly in their graves. Even as it began by professing its avoidance of the grand project of the biographical *Life*, the *petit récit* of this essay nevertheless recognizes how liable to assimilation into such a project it may be, for its findings are haunted not only by the idea of a certain sort of dead author, but

[183] In 1464 in Amersham, Buckinghamshire, ownership of a copy of *The Canterbury Tales* was cited as evidence in a Lollard heresy trial. (On this group of Chiltern Lollards, see C. Cross, *Church and People: England 1450–1660*, 2d ed. [Oxford: Blackwell, 1999], pp. 22–25.) Anne Hudson, "Lollardy: The English Heresy?," rpt. in *Lollards and their Books*, pp. 141–64, has dismissed the Amersham authorities as knee-jerk reactionaries who simply fastened on the possession of anything written in English as a basis for incrimination. But perhaps they had greater cause for alarm than Hudson allows. In the company of certain other texts, whose orthodoxy is far from clear, the temper of the anticlericalism of *The Canterbury Tales* may have looked amiss at that time and in those circumstances. (And we might recall that radical Protestant reformers in the century just ahead had no difficulty in perceiving in Chaucer opinions that coincided with their own, and praised him for his covert opposition to Rome and all her evils; Linda Georgiana, "The Protestant Chaucer," in C. David Benson and E. Robertson, eds. *Chaucer's Religious Tales* [Cambridge: D. S. Brewer, 1990], pp. 55–70.] The other texts owned by these Chiltern Lollards included "a play of seint Dionise," a "Myrrour of Synners," a "Myrrour of Matrimony," a "lyff of oure Lady," "Adam and Eve," "sermones," biblical translations and other religious works. (See J. A. F. Thomson, *The Later Lollards 1414–1520*, 2d ed. [Oxford: Clarendon Press, 1967], pp. 243–44.) The saint play of its very nature is not likely to have been Lollard, since Lollards were not notable advocates of religious drama (and see Nick Davis, "The Tretise of Myraclis Pleyinge: On Milieu and Authorship," *Medieval English Theatre* 12 [1990]: 124–51); also, there existed an orthodox tract known as the "Mirror of Sinners" (P. S. Jolliffe, *A Check-List of Middle English Prose Writings of Spiritual Guidance* [Toronto: Pontifical Institute of Mediæval Studies, 1974], p. 81), which perhaps corresponds to the "Myrrour of Synners" in the cited list. But certain other cited texts are less clearly likely to have been orthodox: the biblical translations, for example, and perhaps even the "Myrrour of Matrimony"; could the latter have been a copy of the Lollard tract *Of weddid men and wifis* (Arnold, *Select English Works*, vol. 3, pp. 188–201)?

also by the idea of his place in a certain sort of historical narrative: a ghostly scenario unfolds of an historical Chaucer at the end of his life, watching his world convulse, keeping his head down, suing for favor, reinventing himself in a realignment of loyalties, and doing so, given the momentary unorthodoxies that *The Canterbury Tales* might be seen to underwrite, with a greater cause for alarm than we have customarily fancied.[184]

[184] I would like to thank the editor of *SAC*, Frank Grady, the previous editor, Larry Scanlon, and an anonymous reader, for their helpful suggestions on this article.

Gower's "bokes of Latin": Language, Politics, and Poetry

Siân Echard
University of British Columbia

T HE HEAD of John Gower's effigy in Southwark Cathedral rests on three books, their titles presented to the viewer as *Speculum Meditantis*, *Vox Clamantis*, and *Confessio Amantis*. While Gower's three major works are in three different languages—French, Latin, and English—Latin here inflects the final presentation of John Gower's oeuvre. Many would argue that Gower would approve; a more bookish poet could not be imagined, and to be *litteratus* in Gower's day still meant to be Latinate. But Gower himself was highly conscious of his trilinguality. In the colophon *Quia vnusquisque*, which appears at the end of over twenty *Confessio* manuscripts, as well as at the end of five manuscripts of the *Vox*,[1] the account of Gower's books stresses the language in which each was composed. While there are some variations in the descriptions of the contents of each work, the sequence and emphasis are always the same: "First he published a book in French" (the *Speculum*, or *Mirour de l'Omme*); "The second book was written in Latin verses" (the *Vox*); and "This third book, which was made up in English . . ."[2] The structure of the *Quia vnusquisque* suggests two ideas. One is that Gower is a master of three tongues; the second, that he was evolving toward the use of English.

[1] And possibly in more—there are quite a few manuscripts which now lack final folios. For a complete discussion of the treatment of the end matter, see my "Last Words: Latin at the End of the *Confessio Amantis*," in *Interstices: Studies in Late Middle English and Anglo-Latin Texts in Honour of A. G. Rigg*, ed. Linne R. Mooney and Richard Firth Green (Toronto: University of Toronto Press, 2003).

[2] John Gower, *The English Works of John Gower*, ed. G. C. Macaulay (Oxford: Early English Text Society, 1901), 2 vols.: "Primus liber Gallico sermone editus . . ."; "Secundus enim liber sermone latino metrice compositus . . ."; "Tercius iste liber . . . Anglico sermone conficitur . . . ," ii. 479–80. This is the third recension version of the colophon. For more on the differences between the different recensions with respect to the colophon, see below.

123

This medieval version of Gower's progress through the languages offers no overt evaluation, but I will argue that when Gower's practice
and his politics become tangled up with the assumptions underlying
current discussions of vernacularity,[3] we become limited in our ability
to understand how he works through his own relationship to language
throughout his poetic career. In particular, the politicization of the vernaculars—the casting of vernacular languages as challengers to the hegemonic authority of Latin—[4] characterizes Latin in such a way as to
predetermine our response to Gower's Latin writing. Sarah Stanbury has
described this trend in recent Middle English criticism as a tendency to
"romance the vernacular,"[5] arguing that the association commonly

[3] There is a wealth of recent scholarship on the relationship between Latin and the
vernacular in medieval England. Some of this work appears in the notes below. I take
the opportunity here to refer to some important critics who are not directly addressed
later: these would include Christopher Baswell, *Virgil in Medieval England: Figuring the
"Aeneid" from the Twelfth Century to Chaucer* (Cambridge: Cambridge University Press,
1995); Rita Copeland, *Rhetoric, Hermeneutics, and Translation in the Middle Ages: Academic
Traditions and Vernacular Texts* (Cambridge: Cambridge University Press, 1991), and the
edited collection *Criticism and Dissent in the Middle Ages* (Cambridge: Cambridge University Press, 1996); John H. Fisher, "A Language Policy for Lancastrian England," *PMLA*
107.5 (1992): 1168–80; David Wallace, *Chaucerian Polity: Absolutist Lineages and Associational Forms in England and Italy* (Stanford: Stanford University Press, 1997). Two collections are also central to current views on these relationships: *The Idea of the Vernacular:
An Anthology of Middle English Literary Theory, 1280–1520*, ed. Jocelyn Wogan-Browne,
Nicholas Watson, Andrew Taylor, and Ruth Evans (University Park: Pennsylvania State
University Press, 1999), and David Wallace, ed., *Cambridge History of Medieval English
Literature* (Cambridge: Cambridge University Press, 1999). Particularly relevant in the
latter are Christopher Baswell, "Latinitas," pp. 122–51; Christopher Cannon, "Monastic
productions," pp. 316–48; John V. Fleming, "The friars and medieval English literature," pp. 349–75; David Aers, "*Vox populi* and the literature of 1381," pp. 432–53;
David Lawton, "Englishing the Bible, 1066–1549," pp. 454–82; Steven Justice, "Lollardy," 662–89; as well as David Wallace's introductions to each section, with their
frequent emphasis on the changing nature of "Englishing." See the references to Stanbury, below, for a discussion of the implications of *CHMEL*'s focus on "Englishing."
[4] I am thinking of arguments such as Ruth Evans's when she points out that English,
today "a language of world domination," in the Middle Ages had to confront Latin as
"the chief instrument of political power." "Like their modern postcolonial counterparts," Evans writes, "medieval vernacular writers found ways to evade the all-encom-
passing authority of the colonial language"; "Historicizing Postcolonial Criticism," in
The Idea of the Vernacular, pp. 366 and 368. This essay is part of a collection which seeks
to lay out the medieval evidence for the "changing, uneasy, and complex status of
vernacular writing" (p. xiv); my point is that this attempt to create "a literary history
centred on the theme of the vernacular" (p. xvi), when travelling in tandem with the
characterization of Latin as an authoritative monolith, tends to imply that Latin does
not have its own complexities, an implication which makes it difficult to read Latin as
subtly—or indeed as politically—as we might read other languages.
[5] Sarah Stanbury, "Vernacular Nostalgia and *The Cambridge History of Medieval English
Literature*," *Texas Studies in Literature and Language* 44.1 (2002): 99. It should be noted
(as Stanbury recognizes) that a major innovation in *CHMEL* is its insistence on Britain's

made between English and various forms of resistance is at least in part a fiction born of our own nostalgic desire, a wish to see the medieval English vernacular as "a democratizing and rebellious *vox populi*."[6] Yet in the *Vox clamantis*, a work whose language and subject matter have both tended to relegate it to the periphery in assessments of Gower's work, Gower claims to speak for the *vox populi* even as he decries the 1381 rebellion—and he makes that claim in Latin. In what follows, I explore Gower's stance toward language in the *Vox*, and I touch as well on another of Gower's Latin political pieces, the *Cronica tripertita*. Throughout this essay, I map Gower's deployment of his Latinity in these texts over a landscape of the poet's persistent attention to tongues throughout his works. I intend to show that common concerns about speech in all three of Gower's languages both challenge the idea that Gower finds Latin an easy refuge from political or poetic uncertainty,[7]

---

multilingual nature, however the relationship between those languages is portrayed. I admire *CHMEL* very much—agreeing with Stanbury's remark that the romantic "fiction" of the vernacular in the collection is "compelling and often persuasive," 102.

[6] Stanbury, "Vernacular Nostalgia," 97. It is important to note that there are readers of the rise of the vernacular who have been careful to recognize the complex political and social affiliations of the vernacular. Alison Cornish points out that while translation from Latin to vernacular (in this case Italian), broadens access and valorizes the vernacular, it is nevertheless the case that "The ocean of translations produced in Italy and France in the thirteenth and fourteenth centuries was no democratic initiative to educate the masses; they were intended, rather, to accommodate a linguistic handicap of the prominent and well-to-do"; her analysis of Guido Cavalcanti's "Donna me prega" points out that "putting Latin thought into the vernacular does not necessarily make things easier" ("A Lady Asks: The Gender of Vulgarization in Late Medieval Italy," *PMLA* 115.2 (2000): 166, 174). In the English context, Fiona Somerset notes that "the legitimation of some kinds and contexts of written English tended to suppress or delegitimate others," *Clerical Discourse and Lay Audience in Late Medieval England* (Cambridge: Cambridge University Press, 1998), p. 10; she cites Nicholas Watson's seminal piece on Arundel's Constitutions: "Censorship and Cultural Change in Late-Medieval England: Vernacular Theology, the Oxford Translation Debate, and Arundel's 'Constitutions' of 1409," *Speculum* 70.4 (1995): 822–64.

[7] Many sympathetic readers of Gower argue that Latin is understood by the poet as a more stable language than the vernaculars. Derek Pearsall, for example, writes of the Latin in the *Confessio* that it may be intended to "contain or encase the potentially volatile nature of the English"; "Gower's Latin in the *Confessio Amantis*," in *Latin and Vernacular: Studies in Late-Medieval Texts and Manuscripts*, ed. A. J. Minnis (Cambridge: D.S. Brewer, 1989), p. 22. In "Learning to Speak in Tongues: Writing Poetry for a Trilingual Culture," in *Chaucer and Gower: Difference, Mutuality, Exchange*, ed. R. F. Yeager (Victoria, B.C.: University of Victoria, 1991), Yeager argues that Latin, the "higher" tongue for Gower, is present in the *Confessio* as part of an attempt to "lend authority and sophistication" to the English poetry, p. 122. Winthrop Wetherbee's "Latin Structure and Vernacular Space: Gower, Chaucer and the Boethian Tradition," however, argues that Gower's complex use of Latin in the *Confessio Amantis* "[makes] explicit and central the confrontation between traditional Latin *auctoritas* and a vernacular with its own claims to meaning"; *Chaucer and Gower*, p. 10. I discuss the elusiveness of the Latin

and militate against the conclusion that Gower finally found his poetic voice in English.[8] He found *a* voice in that language—his strongest and most enduring voice—but all tongues remained for him simultaneously tantalizing and suspect, to the very end of his poetic career.

The evolutionary narrative that is often generated about Gower's English is more a partial one than completely unreasonable, however. The *Quia vnusquisque* is not the only part of the manuscript apparatus to suggest the idea that French and Latin were stepping-stones on the way towards Gower's fulfilment of his poetic destiny through the English vernacular—and it is not merely a modern preoccupation with vernacularity that has crowned Gower's English efforts as his supreme work. Two *Confessio* manuscripts and four manuscripts of the *Vox*[9] include a poem apparently sent to Gower in praise of his work by "a certain philosopher," the *Eneidos Bucolis*:

> To Virgil, for his Georgic lays,
> Bucolics, *Eneidos*, the praise

---

in the *Confessio* at more length in "With Carmen's Help: Latin Authorities in Gower's *Confessio Amantis*," *SP* 95.1 (1998): 1–40.

[8] Gower's critical reception is traced in the first chapter of John H. Fisher's *John Gower: Moral Philosopher and Friend of Chaucer* (New York: New York University Press, 1964), and by Derek Pearsall in "The Gower Tradition," in *Gower's Confessio Amantis: Responses and Reassessments* (Woodbridge, Suffolk: Boydell and Brewer, 1983), pp. 179–97; both conclude that Gower's Chaucerian epithet—"moral Gower"—is largely responsible for his critical neglect from the eighteenth century on. The reception both Fisher and Pearsall trace is almost exclusively of Gower's English work, doubtless because the linking of Gower with Chaucer which took place almost immediately after the poet's death firmly entrenched Gower in the developing story of the founding of the *English* literary tradition. While Fisher stresses the "singlemindedness" of Gower's interests and even argues that "In a very real sense, Gower's three major poems are one continuous work," he nevertheless casts that connection in evolutionary terms: "The three works progress from the description of the origin of sin and the nature of the vices and virtues at the beginning of the *Mirour de l'omme*, through consideration of social law and order in the discussion of the estates in the *Mirour* and *Vox clamantis*, to a final synthesis of royal responsibility and Empedoclean love in the *Confessio Amantis*," *John Gower*, pp. 135, 136–37. More recently, R. F. Yeager sees Gower figuring himself as a new, English Arion: "The goal of universal peace can be furthered by a poetry of appropriately convincing characters and fictions, expressed in a vernacular of increasing stature and availability for presenting serious subjects"; the evolution implied here is not necessarily aesthetic, however, as Gower's choice of English is characterized as a political one—"Targeting the court of the young King Richard . . . the aging moralist may very well have felt he had a final opportunity to strike a righteous blow"; *John Gower's Poetic: The Search for a New Arion* (Woodbridge, Suffolk: Boydell and Brewer, 1990), pp. 241, 262.

[9] These are Oxford, Bodleian Library MS Fairfax 3 and London, British Library MS Harley 3869; and Oxford, All Soul's College MS 98; Glasgow, Glasgow University

Of schools is due; and the wreath
That poets' tribe his works bequeath.
So Virgil's honour's claimed at Rome,
While, Gower, you weave gifts at home
Of little books for Englishmen—
Your threefold song within the ken
Of all. Virgil's Latin verse
Italic letters must rehearse;
But French, then Latin stirred your tongue,
That, last and best, in English sung.
He pipes vain things to Roman ears—
A pagan muse is his—but here
Your work illumines Christendom:
In heaven's realm your praise is won.[10]

This paradoxical piece asserts in Latin that the key aspect of Gower's poetic identity is his mastery of English. This poem is evidently contemporary with Gower, but it shares with modern readings of the poet's progress a triumphalist appraisal of Gower's adoption of English verse.

Library MS Hunter 59 (T. 2.17); and London, British Library MSS Cotton Tiberius A.iv, and Harley 6291.

[10]   Eneidos Bucolis que Georgica metra perhennis
           Virgilio laudis serta dedere scolis;
           Hiis tribus ille libris prefertur honore poetis,
           Romaque precipuis laudibus instat eis.
           Gower, sicque tuis tribus est dotata libellis
           Anglia, morigeris quo tua scripta seris.
           Illeque Latinis tantum sua metra loquelis
           Scripsit, vt Italicis sint recolenda notis;
           Te tua set trinis tria scribere carmina linguis
           Constat, vt inde viris sit scola lata magis:
           Gallica lingua prius, Latina secunda, set ortus
           Lingua tui pocius Anglica complet opus.
           Ille quidem vanis Romanas obstupet aures,
           Ludit et in studiis musa pagana suis;
           Set tua Cristicolis fulget scriptura renatis,
           Quo tibi celicolis laud sit habenda locis.

The Complete Works of John Gower, ed. G. C. Macaulay (Oxford: Clarendon Press, 1899–1902), vol. 4, p. 361. Macaulay suggests, vol. 4, p. 419, that the author might have been Ralph Strode—the same "philosophical Strode" to whom Chaucer directed the *Troilus*. This and all translations of Latin and French are my own; my goal throughout has been to suggest something of the flavor of Gower's metre and rhyme, and there are times when I have chosen to sacrifice strict literalness in this pursuit. I am most grateful to Claire Fanger, whose advice on both the translations and the argument of this essay have been, as usual, invaluable.

The poet of the *Eneidos Bucolis* manages to have his cake and eat it too, as he compares Gower to Virgil—a comparison any medieval poet would desire—while also managing to denigrate the medieval school-men for whom Virgil was still the poetic touchstone. Gower's English-ness becomes even more important in the next few generations after his death, as can be seen, for example, in Thomas Berthelette's address to Henry VIII at the opening of his 1532 edition of Gower's *Confessio Amantis*. Berthelette commends Gower for avoiding those excesses of foreign coining which were fashionable at the time,[11] and urges readers to have recourse instead to Gower's (English) language:

yet that ought not to be a president to vs / to heape them in / where as nedeth not / and where as we haue all redy wordes approued and receyued / of the same effecte and strength. The whiche if any man wante / let hym resorte to this worthy olde wryter John Gower / that shall as a lanterne gyue hym lyghte to wryte counnyngly / and to garnysshe his sentencis in our vulgar tonge.[12]

For medieval, early modern, and modern readers alike, then, Latin (or Latinate learning) is seen as elite and limited. Thus far it seems possible to agree that Gower's English poetry is understood to represent a broad-ening, an evolution, but in fact arguments based in language are easily tangled, and our own assumptions about the status of Latin and English tend, in the case of a poet such as Gower, to produce overlapping and confused narratives about the relationship between poetry and politics.

While the author of the *Eneidos Bucolis* may see the progression through the tongues to English as unproblematic, my purpose in this essay is rather to read Gower's deployment of Latinity in his earlier work as part of his anxiety about his poetic voice and its political dimen-sions—an anxiety he kept throughout his poetic career. In order to ex-plore that anxiety, I focus on one of Gower's most overtly political poems, the *Vox clamantis*, concentrating on the political uses of Latin and of the vernacular in Gower's depiction of the turmoil of the Peas-ants' Revolt of 1381. Berthelette's praise of Gower opposes the poet to then-current fashion, so that in his presentation Gower's English is en-listed in the service of cultural conservatism. Modern criticism of the

---

[11] See Tim William Machan, "Thomas Berthelette and Gower's *Confessio*," *SAC* 18 (1996): 149.

[12] Thomas Berthelette, *Jo. Gower de confessione Amantis* (London, 1532), aa.iii.

Vox, however, shows that Gower's own political position is often signalled for modern readers not by his Englishness, but rather by his Latinity—because Latin is both the language of Gower's poetry against the Peasants' Revolt, and the means by which, whatever his subject, Gower asserts his own *auctoritas*, his right to speak. Thus Latin is understood to be socially and poetically conservative.[13] Yet Latin is the language in which Gower's political commentary is most pointed—and that commentary is directed against social elites as well as against the peasantry.[14] Latin is also, I have argued elsewhere, an element that complicates rather than simplifies the poet's presentation of his own authority in the *Confessio*.[15] For Gower, language itself is a means by which he effects a mimesis of the political uncertainties of his age. It is also potentially, *but always uncertainly*, a means by which he might influence the

[13] For versions of this kind of reading of the *Vox*, see the notes to Aers and Justice below, as well as the comments about current views of the vernacular above. Aers has also argued that the tensions, contradictions, and conflicting political and philosophical positions in the *Vox* and in the *Confessio Amantis* are not manifestations of a subtle and coherent moral / political vision; he describes Gower's methods in these works as "a paratactic mode which seals off units from each other and facilitates the propagation of conflicting positions whose conflicts are left unattended, unnoticed." (David Aers, "Reflections on Gower as *'Sapiens* in Ethics and Politics', in *Re-Visioning Gower*, ed. R. F. Yeager [Asheville, NC: Pegasus Press, 1998], p. 199. Aers is challenging such recent readings of Gower as those found in James Simpson, *Sciences and the Self in Medieval Poetry: Alan of Lille's* Anticlaudianus *and John Gower's* Confessio Amantis (Cambridge: Cambridge University Press, 1995) and Larry Scanlon, *Narrative, Authority, and Power: The Medieval Exemplum and the Chaucerian Tradition* (Cambridge: Cambridge University Press, 1994); his title is of course also a reference to Alastair Minnis's "John Gower, *Sapiens* in Ethics and Politics," *MÆ* 49:2 (1980): 207–29, and perhaps by implication as well "'Moral Gower' and Medieval Literary Theory," in *Gower's Confessio Amantis*, pp. 50–78.

[14] Judith Ferster, for example, remarks that Gower is bolder in his criticisms of the king in Latin than he is in English; see *Fictions of Advice: The Literature and Politics of Counsel in Late Medieval England* (Philadelphia: University of Pennsylvania Press, 1996), pp. 111–12. There is a long tradition of discussing Gower in terms of the mirror-for-princes tradition, a genre whose roots are in Latin; George R. Coffman made the link in 1945, seeing the poet as a conservative moralist concerned to advise the ruler; see "John Gower in His Most Significant Role," *Elizabethan Studies and Other Essays in Honor of George F. Reynolds, University of Colorado Studies*, Series B, II (Boulder: University of Colorado Press, 1945), pp. 52–61 and "John Gower, Mentor for Royalty: Richard II" *PMLA* 69.4 (1954): 953–64. See also Maria Wickert, *Studien Zu John Gower* (Cologne: Cologne University Press, 1953; translated by Robert J. Meindl as *Studies in John Gower* [Washington: University Press of America, 1981]); Russell H. Peck, *Kingship and Common Profit in Gower's Confessio Amantis* (Carbondale and Edwardsville: Southern Illinois University Press, 1978; Elizabeth Porter, "Gower's Ethical Microcosm and Political Macrocosm," in *Gower's Confessio Amantis*, pp. 134–62.

[15] In "With Carmen's Help."

political realm.[16] This inextricable linkage of language with politics means that Gower's politics and his poetry are, in a very real sense, the same thing—and neither is a simple thing. In what follows, then, I want to suggest that the alignment of Latinity with Gower's conservative reaction to the Peasants' Revolt is far more complex, and more fraught with *poetic* uncertainties, than it has traditionally been understood to be.

The first book of the *Vox*—the nightmarish dream vision of the peasants turned beasts marching on an allegorized London—is the part of the work which attracts most critical attention today, but the poem as a whole consists of over 10,000 lines of Latin verse (in unrhymed elegiac couplets), arranged now into seven books.[17] The work begins by juxtaposing the incoherent, animalistic speech of the rabble of the 1381 revolt with the vatic Latin voice of "the one crying" (John Gower as John the Baptist and also John of Patmos)—a move that seems clearly to be, and has been read to be, the deployment of Latinity against the social and political insurgencies which are also colored as vernacular.[18] Cer-

[16] The uncertainty is crucial here. Frank Grady has recently suggested that we have rather a lot invested in "the neat binary that counterposes a Gower directly involved with the court, first gratefully receiving the king's commission and then passionately rejecting Richard in the 1390s, with an amusedly detached and apolitical Chaucer, tactfully skirting and deflecting the urgent political issues of the day"; Grady is quite right to urge suspicion of the "neatness" of the contrast (and of our desire for it); "Gower's Boat, Richard's Barge, and the True Story of the *Confessio Amantis*: Text and Gloss," *Texas Studies in Literature and Language* 44.1 (2002): 11.

[17] The last six books contain an estates satire and related material, and these Gower evidently completed first, before the Revolt. For further discussion of the changes made to the form of the *Vox*, see below.

[18] In his discussion of the first book of the *Vox*, Steven Justice argues that Gower, fashioning himself as a public poet, feared the English-speaking rabble's apparent usurpation of the ground of political contest; *Writing and Rebellion: England in 1381* (Berkeley: University of California Press, 1994), p. 209. The Latinate Gower sought to regain his ground by enclosing the English gruntings of the peasants in his own Latin verse, reasserting his own right to speak for the people—a people who are not the rebels. David Aers makes a similar argument: Gower's problem in the *Vox*, he says, is that the common voice needs to be rendered in Latin and freed from the mother tongue before it becomes possible to transmit safely what it has to say; "*Vox populi* and the Literature of 1381," in *The Cambridge History of Medieval English Literature*, ed. David Wallace (Cambridge: Cambridge University Press, 1999), p. 440. See also Andrew Galloway, "Gower in his Most Learned Role and the Peasants' Revolt of 1381," *Mediaevalia* 16 (1993 for 1990). I would point out that the people rehearse many of the same complaints about the various estates in Gower's Anglo-Norman *Mirour de l'Omme*, as well; for example, Gower prefaces his remarks about bishops in this way: "What's spread around in common's what / I say, and nothing else but that" [Sicomme l'en dist communement, / Ensi dis et noun autrement]; *Mirour de l'Omme*, *Works*, vol. 1, lines 19057–58. That is, this is not merely a contest between Latin and English. One could preserve the tenor of Aers's and Justice's arguments by recognizing that the "people" who speak French are not the peasants of the Revolt—they are the rulers and not the

tainly language is at issue from the outset: in the *Prologue* to the *Vox*, Gower introduces the idea of tongues almost immediately:[19]

> If my frail breast but held a stronger voice—
> And had I many mouths with many tongues—
> The evils of this time are yet too much:
> I still could not tell out the whole of them.[20]

The idea of multiple mouths with multiple tongues almost begs to be read as a nod to Gower's own sense of the linguistic variety of his age—one which is not necessarily desirable, as the image of the Tower of Babel, a foundational image in both the *Vox* and the *Confessio*, suggests.[21]

---

mob. It will become clear, however, that I see Gower exploring the dangers inherent in *all* tongues.

[19] Tongues, literal and figurative, are a source of anxiety for Gower throughout his career. In the opening Latin verse to the *Confessio Amantis*, Gower manifests, in short space, many of the elements of his complex view of language:

> . . . Let me, in Hengist's tongue, in Brut's isle sung,
> With Carmen's help, tell forth my English verse.
> Far hence the boneless one whose speech grinds bones,
> Far hence be he who reads my verses ill.

> [Qua tamen Engisti lingua canit Insula Bruti
> Anglica Carmente metra iuuante loquar.
> Ossibus ergo carens que conterit ossa loquelis
> Absit, et interpres stet procul oro malus.]

Text and translation from Siân Echard and Claire Fanger, *The Latin Verses in John Gower's Confessio Amantis: An Annotated Translation* (East Lansing, Mich.: Colleagues Books, 1991), p. 3. In these lines Gower both asserts the value and antiquity of the English language and nation—linked to both Saxons and Trojans—while also calling on the help of Carmen, originator of the Latin alphabet, for the writing of his work. The final couplet, with its image of the malevolent tongue of a critic, speaks to the anxiety over uncontrolled speech (vulgar or learned) which dominates the *Vox* as well.

[20] *Vox*, *Prol.* 43–46:

> Si vox in fragili michi pectore firmior esset,
> Pluraque cum linguis pluribus ora forent,
> Hec tamen ad presens mala, que sunt temporis huius,
> Non michi possibile dicere cuncta foret.

Gower is drawing on Ovid's *Tristia* and *Ex Ponto*. See the notes in Eric W. Stockton, *The Major Latin Works of John Gower: The Voice of One Crying and The Tripartite Chronicle: An Annotated Translation into English With an Introductory Essay on the Author's Non-English Works* (Seattle: University of Washington Press, 1962), p. 343.

[21] It occurs in the *Vox* as one of many unfortunate towers: "Turris diuisa linguis Babilonis ad instar" (I.xviii.1763); in the *Confessio*, it is part of the *Prologue*'s account of the entry of division into the world, lines 1017–25:

But I want first to take up the declaration of impotence in these lines. The narrative voice declares its inability to speak more than once in the *Prologue* and first book of the *Vox*. This is not merely a conventional modesty topos. Instead, it is the speaker's response to the horrors of the revolt to fall silent, to lose his ability to communicate at all (while paradoxically retaining the ability to write about it, at least after the fact, in impeccable Latin . . .) With Steven Justice, I think that the *Vox* is in part about finding out how to be, not just the Voice of One Crying, but also the Voice of the People: but this is a fraught, uncomfortable, and ultimately uncertain search.

The speaker tells us that, like others, he fled to the forest from the rabble. There he loses the possibility of authentic speech, as words become a trap:

> And when at times I almost dared to speak,
> I'd fear the traps that always laid in wait;
> And looking at the ground, I'd speak few words.
> And when my fate compelled me talk to one
> I met, I'd pass vain time in fawning speech.
> A soft response would often turn back wrath,
> And safety then was found in pleasing words;
> And often when I tried to speak my will,
> My tongue lay dormant, chilled with icy fear.
> In order that my speech should not complain,
> I kept my tongue restrained from daily ills;

> And over that thurgh Senne it com
> That Nembrot such emprise nom,
> Whan he the Tour Babel on heihte
> Let make, as he that wolde feihte
> Ayein the hihe goddes myht,
> Wherof divided anon ryht
> Was the langage in such entente,
> Ther wiste non what other mente,
> So that thei myhten noght procede.

The Latin gloss to these lines reads: "Qualiter in edificacione turris Babel, quam in dei contemptum Nembrot erexit, lingua prius hebraica in varias linguas celica vindicta diuidebatur." [How, when Nimrod was raising the tower of Babel, in contempt of God, the originary Hebrew language was divided, through heavenly vengeance, into various tongues]. The designation of Hebrew as "prius" suggests that all other languages since—and this would include Latin—are debased versions of a lost original.

> And often though I longed to speak my mind,
> I feared my foes, and stilled my tongue again.[22]

This frozen tongue is all that is available to the speaker, in face of the deceptive and bestial tongues all around him. Later, he says "I would have made my plaint in words, but bowels / Filled with grief, refused, and then allowed no words."[23] This is one of many passages in the *Vox* that is a pastiche of Ovidian reference. R. F. Yeager has shown that what Macaulay unkindly called "schoolboy plagiarism"[24] is in fact a deliberate

---

[22] *Vox* I.xvi.1505–16:

> Memet in insidiis semper locuturus habebam,
> Verbaque sum spectans pauca locutus humum:
> Tempora cum blandis absumpsi vanaque verbis,
> Dum mea sors cuiquam cogerat vlla loqui.
> Iram multociens frangit responsio mollis,
> Dulcibus ex verbis tunc fuit ipsa salus;
> Sepeque cum volui conatus verba proferre,
> Torpuerat gelido lingua retenta metu.
> Non meus vt querat noua sermo quosque fatigat,
> Obstitit auspiciis lingua retenta malis;
> Sepe meam mentem volui dixisse, set hosti
> Prodere me timui, linguaque tardat ibi.

The Ovidian references are to the *Fasti* and *Heroides* (and from *Tristia* both before and after the cited lines; see Stockton, *The Major Latin Works*, p. 364). A similar, though less overwrought, picture of dumbness in the face of political calamity is repeated at the opening of the second book of the *Cronica tripertita*:

> O dolor in mente, set prothdolor ore loquente!
> Heuque mee penne, scribam quia facta gehenne!
> Obice singultu, lacrimis pallenteque vultu,
> Vix mea lingua* sonat hec que michi Cronica donat. (*Cronica* II:1–4)

*Macaulay gives *penna* as the primary reading, but *lingua* occurs in three manuscripts, and seems to make more sense here.

> Oh anguish in mind—and yet more I find
> For my speaking mouth;
> And alas for my pen, for deeds of Gehenna
> Are what I must write.
> Choked off by sobs, and with face pale with tears,
> My tongue scarce can sound those things that are found
> In this Chronicle.

[23] *Vox* I.xvi.1579–80: "Verbis planxissem, set viscera plena dolore / Obsistunt, nec eo tempore verba sinunt."

[24] Macaulay, vol. 4, p. xxxii. Macaulay's disapproval of Gower's practice includes a complete dismissal of the poet's Latin style: "Most of the good Latin lines for which

reworking of such references, perhaps using the technique of *cento* verse,[25] and one might argue that the speaker's recourse to such resources of style and reference here simultaneously illustrates his personal muteness and his position of privileged access to words. This kind of doubleness—genuine anxiety with an equal conviction of access to authority—is what complicates for me the picture of Gower's stance toward his own poetic language.

The speaker's representation of his inability to speak of the ills of his time is presented in marked contrast to the speech which is not speech of the peasants. In the first part of the dream vision, the speaker recounts seeing the mobs in the forms of various animals, converging on the city. The mob is characterized over and over again as a source of noise without sense, without true speech. Here, for example, is the description of that part of the crowd which the speaker sees as dogs:

> If anyone might hear them then, or feel
> The trembling world, by voices there amazed,
> Then he might say that no realm ever heard
> With ears an ululating howl like theirs.
> And when the baying of the hounds went down
> To Satan's ears, then hell in this new sound
> Rejoiced; and Cerberus, Gehenna's cur,
> Gave ear, and raged with joy at what he heard.[26]

When the mobs reach London, the famous passages follow in which Wat Tyler is portrayed as a jackdaw—"Graculus vnus erat edoctus in

---

Gower has got credit with critics are plagiarisms. . . . the perpetual borrowing of isolated lines or couplets from Ovid, often without regard to their appropriateness or their original meaning, often makes the style, of the first book especially, nearly as bad as it can be" (vol. 4, p. xxxiii).

[25] R. F. Yeager, "Did Gower Write *Cento*?" in *John Gower: Recent Readings*, ed. R. F. Yeager (Kalamazoo, Mich.: The Medieval Institute, 1989), pp. 114–15.

[26] *Vox* I.v.425–32:

> O tunc si quis eos audisset, quomodo mundus
> Vocibus attonitus hic et vbique fremit,
> Dicere tunc posset similes quod eis vlulatus
> Auribus audiuit nullus ab ante status.
> Cumque canum strepitus Sathane descendit in aures,
> Gaudet et infernus de nouitate soni,
> Cerberus ecce canis baratri custosque gehenne
> Prebuit auditum letus et inde furit.

arte loquendi";[27] that is, educated in the art of public speaking. John Ball, too, is shown to be (mis)applying a certain kind of learning: "Ball the prophet teaches them, himself / Malignant spirit's pupil; he's their school."[28] The mob is reduced to bestial grunting, and Gower vents a great deal of poetic spleen in representing their noise. He first associates them with monstrosity: "Often they cried out with monstrous voice / And thundered different sounds in different ways."[29] A series of animal comparisons follow immediately, beginning with the domestic beasts (to whom the agrarian peasants might seem naturally to be linked):

> Some bray in bestial tones, like asses do,
> And some with bovine mooing fill the air.
> Some let forth the horrid grunts of swine,
> And all the earth must shudder at the sound.[30]

Next comes a mix of animals wild and domestic, a bewildering hodge-podge which includes as well the insect world:

> The foaming boar, enraged, makes great tumult,
> The boar-pig shrieks its own part of the din;
> The city's air's oppressed by savage barks,
> And frantic voice of dogs, discordant, flies.
> The fox yelps, hungry; the sly wolf on high
> Keeps shouting loud and calling to its mates.
> No less does garrulous gander strike the ear
> With sound; with sudden sorrow trenches shake:
> Wasps buzz and buzz, their noise is horrible,
> And none can count their swarms; and all as one

[27] *Vox* I.ix.681.

[28] *Vox* I.xi.793–94: Balle propheta docet, quem spiritus ante malignus / Edocuit, que sua tunc fuit alta scola.

[29] *Vox* I.xi.797–98: Sepius exclamant monstrorum vocibus altis, / Atque modis variis dant variare tonos.

[30] *Vox* I.xi.799–802:

> Quidam sternutant asinorum more ferino,
> Mugitus quidam personuere boum;
> Quidam porcorum grunnitus horridiores
> Emittunt, que suo murmure terra tremit:

> They raise a cry that's like to lion's roar,
> That hairy beast, and all that's bad, grows worse.[31]

The frightful sound fills the world, threatening the spread of cacophony and chaos to other realms:

> Rude clang, reverberate sound, and savage brawl—
> No voice before was terrible as this.
> The rocks resound with murmur and the air
> Repeats; and Echo takes up the reply.
> The heavy uproar with its din afrights
> The neighbouring lands, which fear the ills to come.[32]

The striking thing about this passage is not, I would argue, the admittedly heavy-handed comparison of the rabble to animal. Rather, it is the astonishing variety of the vocabulary of sound. These twenty-three lines contain a dozen different words for sound, and a dozen different verbs for making sound. Justice suggests that in enclosing the rabble's speech in Latin, Gower "erases any trace of verbal performance on the part of the rebels,"[33] thus showing the inappropriateness of their entry into po-

[31] *Vox* I.xi.803–14:

> Frendet aper spumans, magnos facit atque tumultus,
> Et quiritat verres auget et ipse sonos;
> Latratusque ferus vrbis compresserat auras,
> Dumque canum discors vox furibunda volat.
> Vulpis egens vlulat, lupus et versutus in altum
> Conclamat, que suos conuocat ipse pares;
> Nec minus in sonitu concussit garrulus ancer
> Aures, que subito fossa dolore pauent:
> Bombizant vaspe, sonus est horrendus eorum,
> Nullus et examen dinumerare potest:
> Conclamant pariter hirsuti more leonis,
> Omneque fit peius quod fuit ante malum.

[32] *Vox* I.xi.815–20:

> Ecce rudis clangor, sonus altus, fedaque rixa,
> Vox ita terribilis non fuit vlla prius:
> Murmure saxa sonant, sonitum que reuerberat aer,
> Responsumque soni vendicat Eccho sibi:
> Inde fragore grauis strepitus loca proxima terret,
> Quo timet euentum quisquis adire malum.

[33] Justice, *Writing and Rebellion*, p. 213. The general critical opinion as to Gower's *aesthetic* success in shifting from English to Latin may be measured in part by Justice's argument that Chaucer's *Nun's Priest's Tale* is a devastating parody of Gower's desperate

litical discourse. That may well be what Gower is trying to do; and the varied diction to which I have referred is of course in part a matter of poetic pyrotechnics, pyrotechnics which are part of Gower's staking his claim to the public air (another word that is repeated several times in the descriptions of the peasants). But when the varied noise of the rebels is placed in the context of the fear that even many tongues are not enough to speak the ills of the time (the *Prologue*), and in the context of the speaker's own loss of voice in the forest, and in the context of the references to the deceptiveness of the *taught* oratorical words of Tyler and Ball, then it seems clear there are tensions here which are not readily assimilated by being wrapped in the master tongue. Aers points out that in Gower's rendition of Tyler and Ball, it is clear that they have learned their (limited) verbal performances from the structures with which Gower is identified[34]—but that is precisely the problem for Gower. The jangling jay may be a pet of the elite, but it has acquired an ability to speak, and that ability cannot, as Gower points out, be kept in a cage.[35] Indeed, the anxieties about misapplied speech lead me to the rest of the *Vox*, and to an awareness of the pitfalls inherent in Latin as well as in the vernacular. Anne Hudson quotes a Lollard tract which argues against the idea that English books are necessarily heretical:

many men wolen seie that ther is moche eresie in Englische bookis, and therfore no man schulde haue Goddis lawe in Englische. And I seie be the same skile ther schulde no man haue Goddis lawe in bookis of Latyn, for ther is moche heresie in bookis of Latyn, more than in Englisch bookis.[36]

Heresy is not the issue for Gower in the *Vox*, but the analogy demonstrates that Latin as well as the vernaculars could be suspect, whether

---

poetic crowings in passages such as these, pp. 214–18 (Ann W. Astell has also argued that Chaucer was responding directly to Gower; see "The Peasants' Revolt: Cock-Crow in Gower and Chaucer," *Essays in Medieval Studies* 10 (1993): 53–64). In a recent article, however, Joanna Summers has argued that another poet appropriated the *visio* section of the *Vox* in order to bolster his own position, arguing that Thomas Usk's *Testament of Love* consciously alludes to the *Vox* in its pro-royalist version: "Usk therefore appropriates the discourse of censure from a work clear in its political stance and affiliations"; "Gower's *Vox clamantis* and Usk's *Testament of Love*," *MÆ* 68.1 (1999): 58.

[34] Aers, "*Vox populi*," p. 442.

[35] After introducing the *graculus* that is Tyler, the poetic voice remarks that "There's no cage can keep it locked at home [Quem retinere domi nulla catasta potest]"; *Vox* I.ix.682.

[36] Anne Hudson, *Lollards and Their Books* (London: Hambledon Press, 1985), p. 158.

in the religious, political, or poetic spheres. For his part, Gower both defends and undermines his "bokes of Latyn" in the rest of the *Vox*, and the love-hate relationship with words—all words—is a prime link between the work's two parts.

The second book of the *Vox*, it has often been pointed out,[37] has the appearance of a new beginning: the speaker invokes aid, refers to his illness, warns off ill-intentioned readers, and makes other moves repeated later in the opening of the *Confessio Amantis*. The last lines of the invocation refer specifically to the speaker's textuality:

> The words hereafter speak not my own cares,
> I carry them as herald, one well-taught.
> From varied blooms the honey's gathered in,
> And shells are caught from many varied shores—
> So thus this work's the work of many mouths,
> And many visions too produce this book.
> My songs are fortified by men of old,
> I wrote my words to their examples' form.
> This volume shall be called the Voice of One
> Crying: for it brings news of grievous things.[38]

Familiar medieval images of reading and writing are used here—the bees, the shells—and what the English translation does not show is that Gower uses *lego* for "collect," well aware of its specifically textual valence. There are oral images here, too: the multiple mouths that the voice of Book I feared would be insufficient to the task; the image of the messenger (*nuncius*) and his news (*noui*); the characteristic combination of the textual *volumen* with the *carmina* of verse. I am particularly

---

[37] By, among others, Macaulay, *Works*, vol. 4, p. xxxi; Fisher, *John Gower*, p. 103, and most recently, by Rigg, *A History of Anglo-Latin Literature*, pp. 287–88.

[38] *Vox* II. *Prol.* 75–84:

> Non tamen ex propriis dicam que verba sequntur,
> Set velut instructus nuncius illa fero.
> Lectus vt est variis florum de germine fauus,
> Lectaque diuerso litore concha venit,
> Sic michi diuersa tribuerunt hoc opus ora,
> Et visus varii sunt michi causa libri:
> Doctorum veterum mea carmina fortificando
> Pluribus exemplis scripta fuisse reor.
> Vox clamantis erit nomenque voluminis huius,
> Quod sibi scripta noui verba doloris habet.

interested in the repetition of ideas of learning: the speaker presents himself as well-taught, and he is taught both by the voices of the people and by the well-taught men of old.

For all the original disjunction between Book I and the rest of the *Vox*, this cluster of ideas shows how well the first part, even if composed later, fits both the anxieties and the sense of mission expressed in the rest of the work. For Gower points many of the criticisms in the estates satire section of the *Vox* in terms of the misuse and misapplication of both language and learning, and the ease with which people can be misled by educated abusers of both the spoken and the written word. The negative effects include a mixing of rank and form, as for example in Book VII, where "The clerks are turned to rabble, and the mob / Disputes the things of God in clerkly form."[39] This remark sounds like Gower's later concerns about Lollardy, characteristically expressed in classed terms in the *Prologue* to the *Confessio*:

> And so to speke upon this branche,
> Which proud Envie hath mad to springe,
> Of Scisme, causeth forto bringe
> This new Secte of Lollardie,
> And also many an heresie
> Among the clerkes in hemselve.
> It were betre dike and delve
> And stonde upon the ryhte feith,
> Than knowe al that the bible seith
> And erre as somme clerkes do.[40]

But part of the point is here that *clerks* are getting it wrong, are misbehaving; and the concern in the *Vox*, too, is as much with those faulty

---

[39] *Vox* VII.iv.233–34: "In vulgum clerus conuertitur, et modo vulgus / In forma cleri disputat acta dei." The inappropriateness of disputation over the things of God is a concern of the time, as is suggested by Dame Studie's remarks in *passus* X of the B-version of *Piers Plowman*: "For alle that wilneth to wite the whyes of God almyghty, / I wolde his eighe were in his ers and his fynger after . . ."; William Langland, *The Vision of Piers Plowman: A Complete Edition of the B-Text*, ed. A. V. C. Schmidt (London: Dent, 1978), X.124–25. However, while Dame Studie is concerned with the inappropriate application of learning among clerks, she does not seem to fear any social upheaval, instead praising the contrasting simplicity of the unlearned, and expressing more fear about the souls of learned clerks than of peasants: "lewed men and of litel knowyng, / Selden falle thei so foule and so fer in synne / As clerkes of Holy Kirke" X.469–71. I would like to thank an anonymous reader for suggesting the relevance of this passage.

[40] *Confessio Amantis*, Prol. 346–55.

doctors as it is with peasants who refuse to concentrate on "diking and delving."[41]

To be sure, the same kind of undisciplined vernacular tongues represented in Book I recur in the description of urban characters such as Fraud and Susurrus (Whisperer, Tale-Bearer), and a contempt for oral, vernacular gabbling is clear—Whisperer, for example, is the cause for another excursus on that troublesome tongue:

> While Whisper roams the city, gossiping,
> He spreads out scandals, harming many men.
> The man who talks too much harms others, like
> A second plague, and strikes like whirlwind strikes.
> But since a wicked tongue brings every ill,
> I'll try to speak of what its powers are.
> The tongue stirs strife, strife wars, and wars stir men;
> Men stir swords, swords schisms, schisms, death;
> The tongue roots rulers from their realms, burns down
> Estates; the tongue sends people from their homes.
> The tongue dissolves the marriage bond, and makes
> Of one, as made by God, unhappy two.[42]

Similarities between this passage and anti-feminist commonplaces about gossiping women help to explain what is going on here, but the real

---

[41] Gower's conservative political attitude towards the peasantry can easily lead modern readers to overlook the condemnation of other classes, including the privileged ones, and easy caricatures of his attitude can lead to an inevitable simplification of the project of the *Vox*. See, for example, David Aers's remarks on Gower on the ploughmen: "this is a persuasion to perceive the world in a certain way, to classify large numbers of fellow human beings in a particular way which in turn legitimates particular ways of treating them, of seeking to control and punish them. In the light of this outlook, the poet's response to the great rising of 1381 is predictable"; *Community, Gender, and Individual Identity: English Writing 1360–1430* (London: Routledge, 1988), p. 32.

[42] *Vox* V.xvi.883–94:

> Dum Susurro manet et vir linguosus in vrbe,
> Plebis in obprobrium scandala plura mouet;
> Nam linguosus homo reliquos velut altera pestis
> Ledit, et vt turbo sepe repente nocet.
> Set quia lingua mala mundo scelus omne ministrat,
> Que sibi sunt vires dicere tendo graues.
> Lingua mouet lites, lis prelia, prelia plebem,
> Plebs gladios, gladii scismata, scisma necem;
> Extirpat regnis, dat flammis, depopulatur
> Lingua duces, lingua predia, lingua domos:
> Lingua maritorum nexus dissoluet, et vnum
> Quod deus instituit, efficit esse duo.

concern for much of the estates satire of the *Vox* seems to be in the misapplication of *learned* speech, and the terms are such as not only to rebuke the clergy (and lawyers and judges and rich men and Richard's advisers), but also to complicate considerably Gower's own sense of his poetic mission. The clergy ought to speak the word of God—a divine speech whose effects are wholesome—but in chapter after chapter, the speaker reproves clergy (including in this category all learned men) who do not speak when or as they should.

Gower's friars, like Chaucer's, can "glose" to get what they want (though they do it in Latin), and at first their faults are spoken in that *vox populi* which Gower claims for his own and which is, it turns out, also God's:

> The people's voice is harmony with God's,
> And must in doubtful times be heard with awe;
> Thus common parlance teaches me to speak,
> There's no newfangledness in what I say.
> The Pharisees now climb to Moses' seat,
> And scribes scribe dogmas: actions take they none.[43]

The repeated claim, here and elsewhere in the *Vox*, to speak with the voice of the people, seems to me to be more than a reclaiming of the right to speak (for or instead of the people) in the political sphere. While the proverb from which Gower borrows this idea is in Latin rather than in a vernacular, this is nevertheless the realm of traditional wisdom rather than classical reference.[44] The insistence in the passage above that there is nothing new in what the speaker says, and the avoidance of, for instance, Ovid *at this point*, needs to be heard in the context of frequently repeated concerns about the ill effects of misapplied learning, and even

---

[43] *Vox* III.xv.1267–72:

> Vox populi cum voce dei concordat, vt ipsa
> In rebus dubiis sit metuenda magis:
> Hec ego que dicam dictum commune docebat,
> Nec mea verba sibi quid nouitatis habent.
> In cathedram Moysi nunc ascendunt Pharisei,
> Et scribe scribunt dogma, nec illud agunt.

[44] Aers, "*Vox populi*," p. 440. The proverb *Vox populi, vox dei* is also referred to in the *Mirour de l'Omme* 12725–26: "Au vois commune est acordant / La vois de dieu . . ." Ferster notes Gower's apparently shifting attitudes toward the voice of the people in *Fictions of Advice*, pp. 130–32; her concern is with contemporary ideas about royal government, rather than with the issues of poetic language that I am discussing here.

more particularly, of misused *poetic* words. Consider, for example, this section on the Hypocrite, from Book IV:

> Many such there are who color words;
> Who stuff our ears with aureate-sounding speech,
> Their words burst forth with leaves, but there's no fruit;
> Sweet talk is all, to move the innocent.
> God's temple shuts them out, for it abhors
> The ornaments of words, and flees such gauds.
> The texts of poets, overgilt with paint,
> Are spoke with golden tongue; but yet beware:
> It is the simple word which merits trust,
> But duplex word, *sans* God, attempts the mind.
> God despises eloquence, when polished
> Wrappings—honey'd words—hide bile.
> Who makes good words, but acts for ill, does sin;
> For moral deeds should follow moral words.
> Who frequents learning, he, with polished words,
> Sows subtle scandals under colored speech.[45]

Here we do not simply have false orators or deceitful lawyers or self-interested counsellors or undisciplined peasants; here we have untrustworthy poets or, at best, unscrupulous people who take advantage of

---

[45] *Vox* IV.xxii.1065–80:

> Sunt etenim multi tales qui verba colorant,
> Qui pascunt aures, aurea verba sonant,
> Verbis frondescunt, set non est fructus in actu,
> Simplicium mentes dulce loquendo mouent:
> Set templum domini tales excludit, abhorret
> Verborum phaleras, verba polita fugit.
> Scripta poetarum, que sermo pictus inaurat,
> Aurea dicuntur lingua, set illa caue:
> Est simplex verbum fidei bonus vnde meretur,
> Set duplex animo predicat absque deo.
> Despicit eloquia deus omnia, quando polita
> Tecta sub eloquii melle venena fouent:
> Qui bona verba serit, agit et male, turpiter errat,
> Nam post verba solet accio sancta sequi.
> Quod magis alta scola colit, hii sermone polito
> Scandala subtili picta colore serunt.

Gower is borrowing again here, this time drawing various lines from Peter Riga's *Aurora*; see Stockton, *The Major Latin Works*, p. 426.

poetic words; for indeed, it seems that any wrought speech is necessarily anathema, and contrary to God's desire.[46]

The distrust of ornate speech is a topos of long standing, and one that Gower uses as well in both his first and his last vernacular. In the *Mirour de l'Omme*, Gower uses the example of the chastisement of Jerome, in a way that suggests that Latin is particularly subject to misuse precisely because it carries the flavor of clerkly authority and the appeal to scholarly pride:

> Who has knowledge of clergy,
> There's no doubt he'll glorify
> Himself, pronouncing gorgeous speech
> Instead of suiting words to teach
> And say what suits the soul's good,
> For himself and other's food.
> And in Jerome the proof's overt,
> For Tully's thought he sought, to learn
> To speak more beautifully; but God
> Rebuked his learning's vanity.[47]

The misuse of learning is not confined to scholars such as Jerome; elsehere in the *Mirour*, Temptation's representations to Man are described in this way:

> But one who heard Temptation's words—
> How sweetly flattering she urged
> Through the honey of her speech—

[46] It is a rather pleasing irony that this condemnation of poetic speech is made up of bits and pieces of someone else's poetry.

[47] *Mirour*, lines 14665–76:

> Cil q'ad science du clergie,
> Ne falt point qu'il se glorifie
> En beal parole noncier,
> Ainçois covient qu'il sache et die
> Dont soy et autres edefie
> Au bien de l'alme; et ce trover
> De saint Jerom bon essampler
> Porrons, qant il estudier
> Voloit en la philosophie
> Du Tulle pour le beau parler;
> Mais dieus l'en fesoit chastier,
> Pour ce que vain fuist sa clergie.

He'd say that never since his birth
Had such a boaster of such worth,
Of such a school, been heard; *parole*
More sweet than harp or than *citole*.[48]

Temptation's speech is here aligned to the schools and to poetry both—an alignment that continues throughout the work, as both unscrupulous clerics and storytellers are condemned.[49] And in the *Confessio*, too, Gower's discussion of rhetoric is preoccupied with the extent to which the learned manipulation of words can hide the truth:

In Ston and gras vertu ther is,
Bot yit the bokes tellen this,
That word above alle erthli thinges
Is vertuous in his doinges,
Wher so it be to evele or goode.
For if the wordes semen goode
And ben wel spoke at mannes Ere,
Whan that ther is no trouthe there,
Thei don fulofte gret deceipte;
For whan the word to the conceipte
Descordeth in so double a wise,
Such Rethorique is to despise
In every place, and forto drede.[50]

This section of the *Confessio* both praises "pleine" speech and records how often it is trumped by rhetorical display—even as the Latin verse which begins the section repeats the Augustinian notion that the plain

[48] *Mirour*, lines 505–12:

Mais cil qui lors ust bien oï
Temptacioun come il blandi
Par la douçour de sa parole,
Il porroit dire bien de fi
Que ja n'oïst puisqu'il nasqui
Un vantparlour de tiele escole:
Car plus fuist doulce sa parole
Que n'estoit harpe ne citole.

[49] For example, Temptation tells "many delightful stories [mainte delitable geste]" (line 981) at the banquet celebrating the marriage of the World to the seven daughters of Sin, and the lengthy condemnation of the clergy and of lawyers has frequent recourse to reproving their manipulation of their privileged speech.

[50] *Confessio* VII.1545–57.

truth is self-evident and pleasing: "Fair words at first are pleasing in a speech / But in the end what pleases is the truth."[51] The topos is not unusual,[52] but Gower's almost obsessive return to it, no matter when or in what language he writes, is striking, as is his tendency to be at once confident and pessimistic about the plain truth's ability to be made manifest. The recurrence of this complex attitude across his major works indicates that Gower's shift to English did not quell his anxieties about speech in general, nor about his own speech in particular.

At the opening of the *Vox*, Gower makes a Latinate appeal to his Muse: "My Muse, add shape to Latin things recalled, / And mistress, teach me words to fit your book."[53] By the time of the *Confessio*, the poet has shifted the modesty topos so that it now aligns him with the simple folk: "Thus I, which am a burel clerk, / Purpose forto wryte a bok . . ."[54] It is tempting to conclude that the poetic voice has abandoned both the Latin language and the Latinate literate culture of the *Vox* in order to become the "burel" vernacular writer of the *Confessio*—that Gower finds both his poetic voice, and unproblematic access to the truth, in the voice and forms of the common folk. Even if Gower seems to be giving us permission to romanticize the vernacular here, however, this is a temptation that should be resisted. Gower continues to worry about the common folk whose voice he apparently assumes, in both the Latin and English portions of the *Confessio*. See, for example, the Latin verses that introduce the section in the *Prologue* on the commons:

> When regal law subdues the common folk,
> They rest, and meek as lambs they take their load.
> But if they lift their heads, and if the law
> Lets go its reins, as their own will demands,
> The common folk will like the Tigris be.

---

[51] *Confessio* VII, before line 1507 "Compositi pulcra sermonis verba placere/Principio poterunt, veraque fine placent"; Echard and Fanger, p. 79.

[52] Compare, for example, Chaucer's *House of Fame*, with its progression from the re-telling of the *Aeneid* at the outset, to the vision of the House of Rumour at the end, where the dreamer sees "fals and soth compouned" and "shipmen and pilgrimes, / With scrippes bret-ful of lesinges, / Entremedled with tydynges"; Geoffrey Chaucer, *The House of Fame*, in *The Riverside Chaucer*, ed. Larry D. Benson (Boston: Houghton Mifflin, 1987), III.2108, 2122–24; I am grateful to an anonymous reader for pointing to this comparison. The appeal in the proem to Book II to "every maner man / That Englissh unders-tonde kan" (II.509–10), along with the Latinate appeals and references throughout the poem, suggest a landscape of concerns similar to those I am exploring in Gower's Latin.

[53] *Vox*, Prol., lines 53–54: "Adde recollectis seriem, mea musa, Latinis, / Daque magistra tuo congrua verba libro."

[54] *Confessio*, Prol., lines 52–53.

> Both fire and water pity lack in rule,
> But still more violent is the people's wrath.[55]

The metaphor of a river breaking its banks is repeated in the English lines that follow:

> Now forto speke of the comune,
> It is to drede of that fortune
> Which hath befalle in sondri londes:
> Bot often for defalte of bondes
> Al sodeinliche, er it be wist,
> A Tonne, whanne his lye arist,
> Tobrekth and renneth al aboute,
> Which elles scholde noght gon oute . . .[56]

In other words, Gower has not suddenly become John Ball. But there is another reason to complicate Gower's own claims about his turn to simple English, and it can be seen in the passage on the Hypocrite discussed above. That passage shows that the poetic voice rejects *aurea verba* while still *within* the privileged sphere of Latinate culture. Thus this Latinate display undermines its own grounds long before Gower claims to be a "burel clerk." And the class identification suggested here needs to be placed against the similar condemnation of honeyed speech in the *Miroure*, for the Anglo-Norman vernacular has a different class valence than does the English of the *Confessio*: while English has come to have upper-class appeal (Gower's protestations about simplicity notwithstanding), it also always carries with it the ability to be understood by a broader social spectrum. French, on the other hand, is by Gower's day more limited, being the language (or one of the languages) of the court, the upper classes, and the legal profession.[57] In using it, Gower signals his

---

[55] *Confessio*, Prol., before line 499:

> Vulgaris populus regali lege subactus
> Dum iacet, vt mitis agna subibit onus.
> Si caput extollat et lex sua frena relaxet,
> Vt sibi velle iubet, Tigridis instar habet.
> Ignis, aqua dominans duo sunt pietate carentes,
> Ira tamen plebis est violenta magis. (Echard and Fanger, p. 11)

[56] *Confessio*, Prol., lines 499–506. Gower is repeating metaphors he used first in the *Miroir*; cf. lines 26497–503; cf. also *Vox* V, lines 991–92.

[57] For a detailed discussion of Anglo-French in fourteenth-century England, see W. Rothwell, "The Trilingual England of Geoffrey Chaucer," *SAC* 16 (1994): especially 56–66. In this study of medieval English records, Rothwell concludes that "Two languages such as Anglo-French and Middle English, being used in one stratum of society

membership in yet another group—he belongs to the schools and to the gentry—and yet the concern over speech remains the same. In French, too, then, Gower both claims the right to speak and interrogates and condemns his own tribe(s).

Of course, the poetic voice of the *Vox* asserts, again and again, its truth, its desire simply to set forth a vision, according to divine command. This is, after all, what St. John did. But it is hard to do so when the truest form of relation to God's will is, in fact, shown to be silence:

> Add faith, true faith, which without sight or sound
> Believes, and hopes: this is the way, the life,
> And salvation. Where reason cannot grasp,
> Nor mind can know, faith offers arguments.
> What true faith seeks to do, it must achieve,
> Believe it possible, it will be so.
> The tongue is stilled, mouth shut, mind fails, and ears
> Won't hear; there's nothing here but faith alone.[58]

This is another place in the *Vox* where Gower shifts away from classical reference, and it is significant that the borrowings here are biblical, considering the doubts about poetic speech which I have been discussing.

---

on a daily basis by generations of scribes, officials, and scholars, simply cannot be kept apart; the idea that such people could have in their minds neat and tidy pigeonholes for each language is a product of modern, not medieval, thinking," 66. Latin and English are similarly often combined; Linda Ehrsam Voigts concluded her presidential address on the relationship between Latin and vernacular in medieval English scientific and medical manuscripts by remarking that "We must not bring modern assumptions about the integrity of monolingual texts to these late-fourteenth- and fifteenth-century English writings. If we do, we will fail to understand the bilingual culture that produced nearly half of the scientific and medical manuscripts that survive from this period, and we will overlook the variety of ways in which this bilingual culture exploited the linguistic resources of two languages"; "What's the Word? Bilingualism in Late-Medieval England," *Speculum* 71.4 (1996): 823.

[58] *Vox* II.ix.467–74:

> Adde fidem, nam vera fides, quod non videt, audit,
> Credit, sperat, et hec est via, vita, salus.
> Argumenta fides dat rerum que neque sciri
> Nec possunt mente nec racione capi:
> Vera fides quicquid petit impetrat, omne meretur,
> Quicquid possibile creditur ipsa potest.
> Lingua silet, non os loquitur, mens deficit, auris
> Non audit, nichil est hic nisi sola fides.

For the biblical borrowings, see Stockton, *The Major Latin Works*, p. 383.

Here the Augustinian notion of the absolute power of truth renders the traditional avenues of persuasion—the eyes and ears—irrelevant.[59] A poet addresses eyes and ears, and elsewhere in the *Vox* the poetic voice appears confident of its ability to ventriloquize the *vox populi* to good effect, but can it also ventriloquize the absolute truth? Or is the question, can that truth be spoken at all? The problem, of course, is that the sense of mission—to be the prophet, the public poet, the counsellor to the king, the maker of culture, to collect just a few of the epithets modern critics have given him—is at odds with Gower's deep uncertainty about the relationship between his poetic tongue(s) and the truth. Despite his caricaturing of vernacular speech in Book I of the *Vox*, I do not think that Gower exempts Latin from the uncertainties inherent in tongues. If Latin is no more stable than the vernacular(s)—or to express it somewhat differently, if Latin is no *more* able than any other tongue to reflect the ever-changing "truth" that is England at the end of the fourteenth century—then what is left? In the uncertain political and social climate in which Gower writes, how does a poet keep pace with the truth?

Perhaps he does so by giving up: the *Confessio Amantis* closes with Venus presenting the newly identified John Gower with his "Peire of Bedes blake as Sable,"[60] and the author then takes his leave of "makyng"—of books of love, he says, but perhaps of books entirely—and turns to prayer. Is this the recommended silence? Certainly there are gestures, at the beginning and at the end of Gower's poetic career, which suggest the ephemeral nature of language. In the *memento mori* that occupies a good bit of the last book of the *Vox*, the speaker tabulates the losses to death, including the loss of speech: "Say once he knew all kinds of tongues—when death / Makes mute his tongue, why then,

---

[59] The eyes and ears are first on Genius's list, in Book I of the *Confessio*, as a potential source of sin and deception: *Confessio* I, before line 289:

> Visus et auditus fragilis sunt ostia mentis,
> Que viciosa manus claudere nulla potest.
> Est ibi larga via, graditur qua cordis ad antrum
> Hostis, et ingrediens fossa talenta rapit.

> The doors of fragile mind, the eye and ear,
> So faulty are, no hand may shut them up.
> That way is broad by which the foeman goes
>   Into the heart's cave, grabs the buried gold. (Echard and Fanger, p. 19)

[60] *Confessio* VIII.2904.

he's profitless."[61] And at the end of his life, Gower turns again to Latin to express the impotence of all tongues, this time inflected explicitly as written, in the poem "Quicquid homo scribat." This short piece renders the failure of *transcribed* tongues (here through the failure of the poet's eyes):

> Whatever man may write, it's Nature writes the end;
> Who like a shadow flees, nor fleeing, comes again.
> She's dealt my end to me; I'm blind; and nevermore
> And nowhere will I write—for though my will remains,
> My power's gone, and all I long for, she denies.[62]

In the end, *all* tongues fail—but a reader cannot help noticing that Gower's silence, his abandoning of "makyng," comes at the end of a poetic career that includes the almost 30,000 lines of the *Mirour*, the more than 10,000 lines of the *Vox*, and the over 34,000 lines of the *Confessio*. As Gower himself says at the beginning of the *Confessio*, these "bokes duelle," books that Venus at the end aligns with "vertu moral."[63] And there are a few things to say about the form as well as the languages of these books, before we take final leave of John Gower.

At the outset of this essay, I noted that Book I of the *Vox*, commonly discussed separately as the *visio*, was a later addition to what was originally conceived as an estates satire. There is little doubt that the addition of Book I is politically opportune, but this kind of modification in response to current political conditions is something we see throughout Gower's career—and all of these modifications have poetic as well as political dimensions. Even within the expanded version of the *Vox*, there are changes whose effects go beyond the merely political. A first version of the *Explicit* merely gives the work's title: "Here ends the book which

---

[61] *Vox* VII.ix.751–52: "Nil sibi quod genera linguarum nouerat olim / Confert, qui muto mortuus ore silet."

[62] In Macaulay, vol. 4, p. 365:

> Quicquid homo scribat, finem natura ministrat,
> Que velut vmbra fugit, nec fugiendo redit;
> Illa michi finem posuit, quo scribere quicquam
> Vlterius nequio, sum quia cecus ego.
> Posse meum transit, quamuis michi velle remansit;
> Amplius vt scribat hoc michi posse negat.

[63] *Confessio, Prol.* 1–3: "Of hem that writen ous tofore / The bokes duelle, and we therfore / Ben tawht of that was write tho"; VIII.2925–27: "Bot go ther vertu moral duelleth, / Wher ben thi bokes, as men telleth, / Whiche of long time thou hast write."

is called the Voice of One Crying."[64] But half the manuscripts contain a much longer version of the *Explicit*.[65] All of these latter manuscripts include Gower's other political Latin poem, the *Cronica tripertita*;[66] that is, the longer version of the *Explicit* occurs only in manuscripts that bridge to the later work, with its unequivocal condemnation of Richard and praise of Henry. And the version of the *Explicit* in these manuscripts makes direct reference to the end of the *Vox* and to the *Cronica* to follow:

For there were then three nobles who were particularly moved by all these things, and they were Thomas Duke of Gloucester, who was known as the Swan; Richard Earl of Arundel, who is called the Horse; and Thomas Earl of Warwick, whose name is the Bear. These men, along with other nobles who were adherents to their cause, revolted most manfully, with strong hand and spirit, for the glory of God and the health of the realm, in order to destroy those who promoted the King's malice. Which the writer intends to show most clearly in the chronicle, which has three parts, which follows.[67]

The *Cronica tripertita* is thus presented as an addition to the *Vox*, a second wing to what then becomes a political diptych, juxtaposing two rulers. The *Cronica* confirms this structure by ending with an explicit comparison of the two men: "How far from Henry Richard's seen to be / When character is weighed and scrutinized!"[68] The *Cronica*'s end

---

[64] *Vox*, p. 313: "Explicit libellus qui intitulatur Vox Clamantis."

[65] These are Oxford, All Souls' College, MS 98; Glasgow, University Library, Hunterian MS T.2.17; London, British Library, MSS Cotton Tiberius A IV and Harley 6291.

[66] The *Cronica* covers the events of the end of Richard's reign, concluding with the assertion that Richard starved himself to death in January 1400; for a discussion of more exact dating of the copies of the *Vox* that also contain the *Cronica*, see Fisher, *John Gower*, pp. 99–109.

[67] *Vox*, p. 313:

Tres namque tunc regni nobiles super hoc specialius moti, scilicet Thomas Dux Glouernie, qui vulgariter dictus est Cignus, Ricardus Comes Arundellie, qui dicitur Equs, Thomas Comes de Warrewyk, cuius nomen Vrsus, hii vero vnanimes cum quibusdam aliis proceribus sibi adherentibus, vt regie malicie fautores delerent, ad dei laudem regnique commodum in manu forti iusto animo viriliter insurrexerunt, prout in hac consequenti cronica, que tripertita est, scriptor manifestius declarare intendit.

[68] *Cronica tripertita*, *Works*, vol. 4, III 462–63: "O quam pensando mores variosque notando, / Si bene scrutetur, R. ab H. distare videtur!" Some 15 lines follow which compare the two head-to-head, often with both contrasted in a single line. My translation expands the initials to the rulers' names, but this is a piece of aesthetic license; I am in fact tantalized by Robert W. Epstein's argument that the use of the initials is a deliberate strategy: "The opposition of Richard and Henry IV is *literally* literal: it resides in the letter. Richard II and Henry IV become simply R. and H., individual letters,

also reimagines the nature of Gower's political verse; while the *Vox* combines the vatic and visionary modes with estates satire, the *Cronica* offers itself as explicitly a mirror for princes, one imagined to speak to the future as well as to the present:

> Wise men beware, who read this here:
> If living ill, earth's rulers will
> Endure God's hate. No king is he
> Whom sin doth win; by Richard's test,
> It's manifest: his vaunting pomp's
> Reduced to naught; such was his life.
> His pride has died; this cronique stands.[69]

In shifting to leonines in these closing lines, Gower chooses a poetic form whose tight rhymes can serve to bolster the impression of confidence.[70] It seems, then, that the *Cronica* represents a confident political statement, and one which, through its association with the *Vox*, retrospectively recasts the earlier poem's political positionings in a more triumphant light. Part of this movement can be explained by the difference between 1381 and 1400, and Macaulay for one argues that the expanded version of the *Explicit* shows that "Gower has in the end brought himself to think that the misfortunes of the earlier part of Rich-

---

arbitrary signs without positive value, interpretable only in their binary operation, the recognition of each requiring the presence of the other. . . . some fifteen years after originally opposing Henry to Richard in the *Confessio*, Gower is still defining Lancaster through opposition rather than essential unity"; "Literal Opposition: Deconstruction, History, and Lancaster," *Texas Studies in Literature and Language* 44.1 (2002): 22, 23.

[69] *Cronica tripertita*, III 484–89:

> Hoc concernentes caueant qui sunt sapientes,
> Nam male viuentes deus odit in orbe regentes:
> Est qui peccator, non esse potest dominator;
> Ricardo teste, finis probat hoc manifeste:
> Post sua demerita periit sua pompa sopita;
> Qualis erat vita, cronica stabit ita.

[70] Compare the Latin verse at the end of the *Confessio*; whether commending the book to Richard or to Henry, Gower again shifts to leonines. However, he also uses the form throughout the *Cronica tripertita*, a work in which he is not always triumphant or confident in tone. Perhaps it is the contrast, rather than the verse form itself, which is important here. A. G. Rigg points out that "the Leonine rhyme and the fondness for onomastic wordplay" are common features of fourteenth-century political poetry; A. G. Rigg, *A History of Anglo-Latin Literature 1066–1432* (Cambridge: Cambridge University Press, 1992), p. 291.

ard's reign were intended as a special warning to the youthful king . . . and that the tyranny of his later time sprang naturally out of his disregard of this preliminary chastisement."[71] Without wishing to discount the effects of a changing domestic political scene, I would point out that, in adding one poem to another and writing a new "hinge," Gower has also clearly reimagined the shape of his work. The longer version of the *Explicit* is thus necessitated as much by the new form of the *Vox-Cronica* diptych as by politics.

The various versions of the *Quia vnusquisque*, referred to above, speak, as the changes in the *Vox Explicit* do, to politics—earlier versions of that part of the colophon which describes the *Vox* excuse Richard, on account of his youth, from responsibility for England's situation, while the latest version condemns him:

First recension: The second book, composed in Latin hexameter and pentameter verses, deals with those amazing things which happened in England in the time of King Richard the second, in the fourth year of his reign, when the serfs rebelled rashly against the nobles and the freeborn men of the kingdom. The innocence of the aforesaid King Richard is declared on account of his youth, and it is clearly shown that terrible things happened to men, not because of Fortune, but because of other faults. And the title of this volume, whose order contains seven pages, is the Voice of One Crying.

Third recension: The second book was written in Latin verses, and deals with the various misfortunes which befell in England in the time of King Richard the Second. Because of these misfortunes, not only did the nobles of the kingdom and the common people experience torments, but also that most cruel king, falling from the heights through his own faults, was finally cast into the pit which he had dug for himself. And the name of this volume is the Vox clamantis.[72]

---

[71] Macaulay, vol. 4, p. lvii.

[72] First recension: Secundus enim liber, sermone latino versibus exametri et pentametri compositus, tractat super illo mirabili euentu qui in Anglia tempore domini Regis Ricardi secundi anno regni sui quarto contigit, quando seruiles rustici impetuose contra nobiles et ingenuos regni insurrexerunt. Innocenciam tamen dicti domini Regis tunc minoris etatis causa inde excusabilem pronuncians, culpas aliunde, ex quibus et non a fortuna talia inter homines contingunt enormia, euidencius declarat. Titulusque voluminis huius, cuius ordo Septem continet paginas, Vox clamantis nominatur (*English Works*, vol. 2, pp. 479–80).

Third recension: Secundus enim liber sermone latino metrice compositus tractat de variis infortuniis tempore Regis Ricardi Secundi in Anglia contingentibus. Vnde non solum regni proceres et communes tormenta passi sunt, set et ipse crudelissimus

I present the description of the *Vox* in full here in order to show how poetic self-presentation travels in tandem with political moves, as all versions of the colophon, whatever their political content, subordinate everything to the prefacing statements about the language of poetic composition. It is also noteworthy that the first recension version of the colophon—dating to a more politically uncertain time—also offers more detail about the actual form of the *Vox*. That is, the poet's works are described first in terms of their form and language, and only secondly in terms of their (political) content. One could then see the revisiting of the descriptions in the *Quia vnusquisque*, even if occasioned by politics, as providing yet another opportunity for Gower to redescribe, to reframe, his poetic *oeuvre*, just as the extended *Explicit* to the *Vox* did.

Gower reworked his poetry most famously in response to politics in the differing English openings and conclusions to the *Confessio*. Macaulay divided the manuscripts of the *Confessio Amantis* into three recensions, based primarily on these aspects of the work; broadly stated, first recension manuscripts attribute the inspiration for the poem to Richard and dedicate the work to him, while third recension manuscripts rewrite certain sections in order to shift the focus to Henry.[73] But once again, the changes are not merely political. In the rewritten version of the *Prologue*, for example, Gower not only shifts his allegiance from Richard to Henry; he also removes the credit for the work's inspiration from Richard, and does *not* set Henry up in Richard's place, at least not in relation to his poetics. In an essay on the responses of Chaucer, Gower, and Clanvowe to the political situation of the 1390s, Lynn Staley has recently suggested that these shifts, in moving from an address to King Richard to an address to the nation, reconfigure the *Confessio* as a more generally national poem, rather than as a mirror for (receptive) princes.[74] In the Latin concluding matter, too, the poet shifts from attributing the work to Richard to praying for the peace of the whole realm; again the

---

rex suis ex demeritis ab alto corruens in foueam quam fecit finaliter proiectus est. Nomenque voluminis huius Vox Clamantis intitulatur (*English Works*, vol. 2, pp. 479–80).

[73] In "Gower's Boat," Grady points out that readers have tended to accept the commission story told at the beginning of the Ricardian version of the poem as truth; he argues it is simply part of the "poetic fiction" (p. 4) of the *Confessio*.

[74] Lynn Staley, "Gower, Richard II, Henry of Derby, and the Business of Making Culture," *Speculum* 75.1 (2000): 78. That is, a shift in the political culture of the court has meant that personal appeals to the monarch are no longer welcome. She also suggests that Henry may be co-opting a poet with a reputation for integrity, 96.

political emphasis moves from the personal to the national. But it is also true that, as a result of the changes in both the English and the Latin end matter, the *Confessio* also comes to be more clearly Gower's own production, whatever his declared political allegiances and anticipated audiences might be.[75] Finally, the *Confessio* can itself, like the two parts of the *Vox* and like the *Vox-Cronica* diptych, be understood as a composite text, for though the poem announces its concern with love, its *Prologue* contains, albeit in shorter space, the same concerns about both the corruption of the realm and the danger represented by the peasants as we find in the two parts of the *Vox*. And these political concerns are partnered by poetical ones—by the familiar panoply of modesty *topoi*, deferrals to authority, and claims of ill health and old age. That is, Gower has a lifelong habit of aggregating, as well as of revising, his texts. I would extend the argument I have been making about tongues to say that we see here as well Gower's constant—almost obsessive—desire to revisit his poetic mission, this time in terms of the overall making of poetry to which he apparently bids farewell at the end of the *Confessio*.[76] In other words, politics is not trumping poetry; rather, for Gower, the realms are inextricable, his endless experiments with the latter traveling with his lifelong attempts to encompass the former. Rather than moving toward any kind of simple resolution of the dilemmas inherent in poetic speech, it seems that Gower might in fact have recognized that his own multilingual, multiversioned *oeuvre* was in the end the closest approach he could make to truth, if he were *not* simply to fall silent and pray.

At the end of the first book of the *Vox*, the speaker has a vision of the island of Britain, whose origins are explained to him by an old man:

[75] I develop these arguments more fully in "Last Words."

[76] For another discussion of Gower's political affiliations in terms of complication, irony, and anxiety, see Frank Grady's careful analysis of Gower's late English poem "To King Henry the Fourth, in Praise of Peace," in "The Lancastrian Gower and the Limits of Exemplarity," *Speculum* 70.3 (1995): 552–75. Grady offers this poem as another example of the kind of poetic/political aggregating I have been describing here. He remarks that "The dedication of the *Confessio* to Henry and the address of 'In Praise of Peace' to Henry force the two poems into a hypotactic relation; in adapting his illustrative tales for Henry's royal status, Gower implicitly challenges both Henry's memory of the *Confessio* and his understanding of history and historical writing," 558. The argument in "Gower's Boat" about the degree to which the dedications participate in the poet's overarching, fictive program underlines the importance of seeing the ancillary material in the Gower manuscripts as part of an aesthetic and poetic, as well as a political, program.

This land is born of varied stock, and blood
And war and slaughter hold it in their grip.
The fields, deformed, give bitter wormwood birth,
And by this fruit the land's harsh savour's shown.
Yet if true love was found among these men,
I think there'd be no finer race on earth.[77]

Gower's mastery of tongues suits him, then, to speak to his nation—a nation that is mixed, and still in search of the mutual love necessary to bind it. That division is as much present in the *Confessio* as it is in the *Vox*; one could indeed argue that it is more present, as the *Confessio*'s prologue addresses itself to how "divisioun" came into the world—and to how that division is first seen in the dividing of tongues at the Tower of Babel. The fact that Gower's last book is in English, then, needs to be understood in terms of the contest of tongues in Gower's whole life's work, as well as on his island. Recent interest in the status of vernacular English has tended to concentrate on the process by which English moved from being a minority language to being not only a prestige language but also a patriotic one, the true "mother tongue" of the island of Britain.[78] Gower's Anglo-Norman and Latin writings are easily framed by this interest as part of a natural evolution. Thorlac Turville-Petre has pointed to the linguistic shift that allows Chaucer, at the end of the *Troilus*, to announce the Englishness of his book in a way that would not have been possible in the first part of the century,[79] and I do

---

[77] *Vox* I.xx.1977–82:

> Hec humus est illa vario de germine nata,
> Quam cruor et cedes bellaque semper habent:
> Tristia deformes pariunt absinthia campi,
> Terraque de fructu quam sit amara docet.
> Non magis esse probos ad finem solis ab ortu
> Estimo, si populi mutuus esset amor.

Ovid is again the source; see Stockton, *The Major Latin Works*, p. 372.

[78] For a useful survey of these studies, see Nicholas Watson, "The Politics of Middle English Writing," in *The Idea of the Vernacular*, pp. 331–52.

[79] Thorlac Turville-Petre, *England the Nation: Language, Literature, and National Identity, 1290–1340* (Oxford: Oxford University Press, 1996); pp. 216–17. While Turville-Petre is dealing with a period earlier than Gower's, it is worth quoting his assessment of the linguistic situation in the South-West Midlands at the beginning of the fourteenth century: "Three languages existed in harmony, not just side by side but in symbiotic relationship, interpenetrating and drawing strength from one another; not three cultures but one culture in three voices," p. 181.

not mean to suggest here that by the 1390s, Gower retains any doubt about the triumph of English. The *Confessio*, whether "for kyng Richardes sake" or "for Engelondes sake," is indeed written "In oure englissh."[80] But the progression from the *Vox* to the *Confessio*, and through the various revisions of each of these works, is not an evolution, if that means a discarding of outdated languages or modes. It is, instead, an accumulation, in response to the recognition that England is a complex political space, requiring of its poet an equally complex poetic voice. Gower's head rests on three books, not one, and Latin remained with England's poet to his dying day, and beyond it.

---

[80] *Confessio, Prol.* 22–24: "And for that fewe men endite / In oure englissh, I thenke make / A bok for Engelondes sake (A boke for king Richardes sake)." Of course by the time Gower wrote the *Confessio*—and certainly by the time of the Henrician revisions—it simply is not true to say that "few men" make poetry in English—another reason to treat with some suspicion Gower's statements about language.

Love and Disease in Chaucer's *Troilus and Criseyde*

Sealy Gilles
Long Island University

IN BOOK 4 of Geoffrey Chaucer's *Troilus and Criseyde,* Criseyde, beset by her impending transfer to the Greek camp, draws our gaze upon herself and cries out:

> Whoso me seeth, he seeth sorwe al atonys—
> Peyne, torment, pleynte, wo, distresse!
> Out of my woful body harm ther noon is,
> As angwissh, languor, cruel bitternesse,
> Anoy, smert, drede, fury, and ek siknesse. (4.841–45)[1]

In giving this doleful catalogue to the heroine, Chaucer inverts Boccaccio's more straightforward, even comic, account of a world transfigured by lovers' grief. In *Il Filostrato,* Pandaro, having just come from the distraught Troilo, looks upon the weeping Criseida and complains: "wherever I go today, it seems to me I hear everywhere sorrow, torments, weeping, anguish, and loud woes, sighs, pain, and bitter lamentation" [che dovunque oggi vo, doglia sentire, / tormenti, pianti, angoscie ed alti guai, / sospiri, noia ed amaro languire].[2] In dramatic contrast to the hyperbolic panorama of Pandaro's complaint, Criseyde's claustrophobic lament turns inward to situate the world's torments

---

[1] Geoffrey Chaucer, *Troilus and Criseyde, The Riverside Chaucer,* 3d ed., ed. Larry D. Benson (Boston: Houghton Mifflin, 1987). All Chaucer quotations will be taken from this edition. I wish to take this opportunity to thank the NY Meds for challenging my anachronisms, Erica Gilles for introducing me to the plague tractate, and Sylvia Tomasch for being, as always, the ideal reader.
[2] Giovanni Boccaccio, *Il Filostrato,* ed. Vincenzo Pernicone, trans. Robert P. apRoberts and Anna Bruni Seldis (N.Y.: Garland, 1986), pp. 236–37.

within her own "woful body." Apart from that body, she tells us, there are no evils—no pain, no fear, no illness. The stanza surrounds the body with a catalogue of woes that, paradoxically, that same body contains, or at least that are contained nowhere else. The awkward construction, "out of . . . there noon is," and Chaucer's final addendum to Boccaccio's catalogue of woes, "ek siknesse," coalesce in linguistic and bodily unease. This discomfort, moreover, is distilled within the body of the woman, voicing itself as the object of our indiscriminate gaze: "whoso me seeth, he seeth sorwe al atonys." Within her corpus, public danger and private suffering lie entangled, only to be sorted out, eventually, by the translation of one body and the transcending of another. Troilus will shake free of "feynede loves" (5.1848), but at a price, for his transcendence rests upon the construction of the woman as pathogenic, as source of "siknesse." Shaped by the insidious configurations of *amor hereos* and by a sea change in late medieval pathology, Criseyde's body first infects her lover, then cures him, only to sicken and kill through absence and betrayal when that remedy is withdrawn.

Readers have long noted the emphasis on death and illness in Chaucer's version of Boccaccio's romance.[3] Several critics, moreover, have remarked upon the intervening cataclysm that struck Europe in the mid-fourteenth century.[4] *Troilus and Criseyde* and *Il Filostrato*, although only a half-century apart, emerge from very different worlds in terms of disease and contagion. Whereas the young Boccaccio completes *Il Filostrato* in 1335, twelve years before the plague enters Italy, Chaucer writes in an England devastated first by the pandemic of the Black Death in 1348–49 and then by a series of lesser epidemics, or "grey deaths," in 1361, 1369, 1374–79, and 1390–93. While Chaucer's hero suffers from one type of affliction, he and his beloved are forged in a world shaped by another, far more lethal disease.

At first glance, lovesickness and plague inhabit radically different realms. Even as, by the mid-fourteenth century, the diagnosis and treatment of lovesickness had become as much game as earnest, the brutal

---

[3] See, for example, Mary Wack, "Pandarus, Poetry, and Healing," *SAC* 2 (1986): 127–33, for Pandarus's use of medical language; Wack, "Lovesickness in Troilus," *Pacific Coast Philology* 19 (1984): 55–61; Richard Firth Green, "Troilus and the Game of Love," *ChauR* 13 (1979), pp. 201–20; Karen Arthur, "A TACT Analysis of the Language of Death in *Troilus and Criseyde*," in *Computer-Based Chaucer Studies*, ed. Ian Lancashire (Toronto: Centre for Computing in the Humaniities, 1993), pp. 67–85.

[4] For example, Arthur, "TACT Analysis," p. 74.

irruptions of "real" disease beginning in Europe in 1347 and in England in 1348, compelled radical epistemological shifts in the understanding of somatic boundaries. The Black Death, manifested in grotesque swellings and effusions, killed with terrifying consistency. The comprehensiveness of the epidemic combined with the painful inadequacy of medical responses to it forced a rewriting of bodies, which were found to be both more permeable and more dangerous than contemporary medical literature suggested. These reconfigurations are particularly visible in contemporary chronicling of the disaster, as eye witnesses struggled to explain what they saw. Chronicles and tractates that bear witness to the catastrophic powers of the plague also reveal paradigmatic shifts in European understandings of the body, shifts that permeate the imaginative literature of the period. The sense of bodies as capable of doing damage to others left its mark on the literature of *fin' amors* and, I will argue, on Chaucer's version of *Il Filostrato*. Chaucer invests Boccaccio's *roman de Troie*, already a story haunted by invasion, with a pathology of bodily violation and culpability.

The Critics

Even as Criseyde's body, in 4.841–45, is construed as exclusive receptacle for all the world's suffering, the poem begins and ends with masculine somatics. We encounter Troilus's body burning with passion, immobilized in bed, plunging into battle, reveling in the act of love, and, finally, repulsed by its own *psyche*. Readers of *Troilus and Criseyde* have long been troubled by its hero's psychosomatic suffering and by the question of Criseyde's culpability for that pain. Discussions of Troilus's lovesickness have ranged from the deeply sympathetic to the derisory. Richard Firth Green calls the "notion that a man might die of unrequited love . . . one of the commonest and most exaggerated of all erotic fictions in the Middle Ages." The threat is "patently hyperbolic and only the most obtuse literalism could possibly lift it out of the realm of metaphor."[5] Nevertheless, the "elaborate make-believe"[6] in which Troilus and Pandarus indulge becomes all too real when Troilus refuses to relinquish his "fantasie" (5.329 and 623) for healthier fare.

[5] Green, "Game of Love," p. 204.
[6] Green, "Game of Love," p. 205.

Anxiety about the woman's role in turning game to earnest perme-
ates decades of criticism around the poem. The poet seems at first to
grant Criseyde extraordinary subjectivity and agency and then to use
that gift to indict, try, and condemn his heroine. Thus, vindications of
Criseyde inevitably fail in the face of the narrative, even as indictments
of her violate the woman we feel we have come to know. As Jill Mann
notes: "The character of the betrayer is one with which events invest
her, not one we are persuaded is hers from the beginning."[7] For many
critics, "changeableness" alone is enough to convict the heroine. R. A.
Shoaf, in his student edition of the poem, maintains that "as much as
[Criseyde's] actual betrayal of [Troilus] for Diomede it is her *being* 'slydynge of corage' that diseases Troilus's imagination and breaks his will
to live."[8] Others lament the corrosive impact she has on her princely
admirer, who has become "a slave to his desire, a victim of Cupid," and
who has "so abandoned reason that he has practically no free will left."
In blaming Cupid here, D. W. Robertson argues that the woman is
incidental to the tragedy and has been constant in her self-centeredness:
"She meant to be true to Troilus too, but she is actually faithful only to
her own selfish desires of the moment. Her beauty is the sensuous
beauty of the world, and her fickleness is the fickleness of Fortune."[9]

Perplexity with Criseyde's treachery has led to agonized justifications,
many of which seek to defend Chaucer as much as his heroine. For
example, Alastair Minnis and Eric J. Johnson argue that Criseyde's fear
is "a natural response" to her positions, both in Troy and in the Greek
camp, and that, therefore, Chaucer's portrayal of her as fearful stands in
opposition to "blatantly misogynistic inscriptions of the tale."[10] Others
find Criseyde, as an object of adoration, to be the vehicle that eventually
facilitates access to the divine. Alfred David, for example, finds that

[7] Jill Mann, *Feminizing Chaucer* (Cambridge: D.S. Brewer, 1991/rev. 2002), p. 18.
[8] R. A. Shoaf, Introduction, Geoffrey Chaucer, *Troilus and Criseyde* (East Lansing,
Mich.: Colleagues Press, 1989), p. xxi.
[9] D. W. Robertson Jr., *A Preface to Chaucer* (Princeton, N.J.: Princeton University
Press, 1962), pp. 494, 498.
[10] Alastair Minnis and Eric J. Johnson, "Chaucer's Criseyde and Feminine Fear" in
Medieval Women: Texts and Contexts in Late Medieval Britain. Essays for Felicity Riddy, ed.
Jocelyn Wogan-Browne, Rosalynn Voaden, Arlyn Diamond, Ann Hutchison, Carol
Meale and Lesley Johnson (Belgium: Brepols, 2000), p. 200. See also David Aers, "Cri-
seyde in Medieval Society" in *Critical Essays in Chaucer's* Troilus and Criseyde *and His
Major Early Poems,* ed. C. David Benson (Toronto: University of Toronto Press, 1991),
pp. 128–148. See Alfred David, *The Strumpet Muse: Art and Morals in Chaucer's Poetry*
(Bloomington, Ind.: Indiana University Press, 1976), pp. 29 ff., for an argument that
Chaucer was unwittingly "of Criseyde's party."

Troilus's love for Criseyde is transformative and "contains an intimation of love for the human God." Its "brevity and fragility" only make it more precious.[11]

Feminist studies tend to cast Criseyde's fickleness as either a legitimate response to the threat of rape or as an inevitable collaboration with masculine systems of exchange. Arlyn Diamond sees her volatility as a function of masculine need:

In the course of the tragedy, Criseyde undergoes a complex series of identifications and transformations which rise not out of a central core of character that we as critics can identify but out of the shifting and contradictory needs of the masculine world she inhabits within and beyond the work.[12]

Carolyn Dinshaw goes further to argue that feminine instability is a structural necessity within patriarchy:

The "slydynge" of Criseyde's "corage" . . . turns out to work in conformity to masculine structures of control, to work as a function of her structural role as woman in Troy's patriarchal society.[13]

Subsequent studies read that structural role in a variety of ways. From a psychoanalytic perspective, Gayle Margherita sees Criseyde's abjection as crucial to the poem's melancholic project to reconstitute the male subject in the face of loss:

Through Pandarus, the narrator disavows the remediable difference of the historical or material world, by inscribing that difference onto the body of Criseyde; through Criseyde, material losses are made good as poetic or metaphoric gains. In situating itself over and against feminine interiority or lack, male subjectivity is shown to be coherent and whole.[14]

[11] David, p. 32–33. David cites T. P. Dunning, "God and Man in *Troilus and Criseyde*" in *Studies Presented to J. R. R. Tolkien,* ed. Norman Davis and C. L. Wrenn (London: Allen & UnWin, 1962), p. 174.

[12] Arlyn Diamond, *"Troilus and Criseyde:* The Politics of Love" in *Chaucer in the Eighties,* ed. Julian N. Wasserman and Robert J. Blanch (Syracuse, N.Y.: Syracuse University Press, 1986), pp. 99–100.

[13] Carolyn Dinshaw, *Chaucer's Sexual Poetics* (Madison: University of Wisconsin Press, 1989), p. 39.

[14] Gayle Margherita, *The Romance of Origins: Language and Sexual Difference in Middle English Literature* (Philadelphia: University of Pennsylvania Press, 1994), p. 117.

In my reading, this redemptive function, the feminine body's efficacy in the reconstitution of the masculine whole, rests upon prior construction of that body as first pathogenic, then curative. The beloved infects, then cures, only to prove by her willful absence and fickleness that that earthly salve is illusory. The masculine coheres, in the end, through the treacherous withdrawal of the feminine remedy.

Amor hereos

The volatile somatics of Chaucer's poem and, in particular, the instability of the woman's body testify to the fraught intersection of two pathologies: the *amor hereos* tradition and the diverse and often conflicting responses to the plague. The first of these, the science of lovesickness, had become, in the fourteenth century, as much psychodrama as clinical practice. Nevertheless, the hubristic Troilus who falls prey to Love's arrow at first conforms to the medical paradigm that Chaucer, servant of the servants of love, inherited from late classical and early medieval clinicians. The young victim, made vulnerable by his own humoral tides and disturbed by beauty, fastens upon a love object and falls ill. In many late classical and early medieval clinical texts, the beloved, far from being the fulcrum of the condition, is discussed primarily in the context of other causes and remedies. Constantinus Africanus's *Viaticum* (late eleventh century) and its glosses, for example, revolve around the lovesick patient, with the beloved playing a minor role as occasion for disease. Constantine argues that the cause of lovesickness may simply be the need to rid oneself of excess humors ("necessitas in multa humorum superfluitate expellenda"), a remedy accomplished easily enough through sexual intercourse. However, he concedes that on occasion beauty can contribute to *eros*:

Aliquando etiam eros causa pulchra est formositas considerata. Quam si in sibi consimili forma conspiciat, quasi insanit anima in ea ad uoluptatem explendam adipiscendam.

[Sometimes the cause of eros is also the contemplation of beauty. For if the soul observes a form similar to itself it goes mad, as it were, over it in order to achieve the fulfillment of its pleasure.][15]

[15] *Viaticum* I.20; ed. and trans. Mary F. Wack, *Lovesickness in the Middle Ages: the* Viaticum *and its Commentaries* (Philadelphia: University of Pennsylvania Press, 1990), pp. 188–89.

Glossators of Constantine's *Viaticum* differ on many issues—whether *amor hereos* is a disease of the estimative or imaginative faculty, whether it is a suffering (*passio*) of the heart, the brain, or the testicles, whether it occurs in hot or cold complexions—but, as in the *Viaticum* itself, the concentration throughout is on the internal world of the patient, who, in the medical literature of the eleventh and twelfth centuries, is usually a man.[16] Although the beloved is occasionally cited as an individual, she is seldom specific to the illness and not necessary for its cure. In fact, one of the suggested remedies is coitus with prostitutes, implying that the cure is effected by the release of pent-up bodily fluids into one female body or another.[17] In another cure, the equivalence of women with each other and with objects is assumed: "in the cure of lovesickness, plasters or women are applied to the testicles" [in cura amoris hereos applicantur emplastra vel mulieres ad testiculos].[18] This exchangeability will surface in Book 4 (lines 400–427) of Chaucer's poem as Pandarus attempts to mitigate what he sees as Troilus's excessive response to the trading of Criseyde.

In later medical literature, the balance shifts slightly. The early fourteenth-century commentator Bona Fortuna says that "the beauty of a woman and the necessity of expelling superfluities" are "coadjuvant," but he places greater emphasis on the apprehension of the woman:

Sed ego dico quod est tamen una causa principalis, scilicet extrinsicum apprehensum quod putatur conveniens et amicum, sicut forma alicuius mulieris que est ita fortiter apprehensa et ita firmiter a cogitatione amplexata quod placet ipsi patienti super omnia.

[But I say that there is, however, one principal cause, namely an extrinsic apprehension that is thought fitting and congenial, such as the form of any

---

[16] On gender and lovesickness, see Wack, *Lovesickness*, pp. 110–13. Wack points out that although in the imaginative literature lovesick women are common, the medical literature is more likely to see the lovesick man as a problem and a candidate for diagnosis and treatment. Also see Maud Burnett McInerney, "'Is this a mannes herte?': Unmanning Troilus Through Ovidian Allusion," in *Masculinities in Chaucer: Approaches to Maleness in the* Canterbury Tales *and* Troilus and Criseyde, ed. Peter G. Beidler (Cambridge: D. S. Brewer, 1998), p. 223. For medieval discussion of gendered susceptibility see Peter of Spain's list of *Questiones super Viaticum* in Wack, *Lovesickness*, pp. 223–25.

[17] Authorities differ on the effectiveness, and the morality, of this cure. For an early opposing argument see Caelius Aurelianus, *On Acute Diseases and on Chronic Diseases*, ed. and trans. J. Drabkin (Chicago: University of Chicago Press, 1950), pp. 557–59. Also see Gerard de Berry in Wack, *Lovesickness*, pp. 199–205.

[18] Peter of Spain, *Questiones super Viaticum* (Version A) lines 71–72 in Wack, *Lovesickness*, pp. 218–219.

woman that is so strongly apprehended and so firmly embraced by the thought that it pleases the patient above everything.][19]

Nevertheless, even when the external apprehension of beauty wreaks havoc in the lover, the beloved herself is not held responsible for the struggle waged within the afflicted body. In fact, according to Peter of Spain, the lover's excited vision lights upon its object almost at random:

In amore hereos estimat virtus estimativa aliquam mulierem an aliquam aliam rem esse meliorem vel pulchriorem omnibus aliis cum non sit ita, et tunc inperat virtuti cogitative ut profundet se in formam illius rei.

[[I]n lovesickness, the estimative faculty judges some woman or some other thing to be better or more beautiful than all the rest, even though it might not be so, and then it orders the cogitative faculty to plunge itself in the form of that thing.][20]

In this scenario, the lover's deranged fancy creates a false and unstable other who conforms to the demands of his illness even as she over-whelms his faculties. In a moment of self-annihilating penetration, he loses himself "in formam illius rei." The patient, in other words, pro-duces his own pathogen and that product of lovesickness becomes, *ipso facto,* cause and source of loss.

When we turn from clinical treatises to manuals on the arts of love, we find a similar dynamic. In Ovid's playful verses, the beloved, even though she is designated the occasion for disease, is not necessarily im-plicated in the disintegration of the lover; her lack of agency protects her from blame. In *Remedia Amoris,* Ovid characterizes Eros, not the beloved, as wounder and healer alike:

> Discite sanari, per quem didicistis amare:
> Una manus vobis vulnus opemque feret.
> Terra salutares herbas, eademque nocentes
> Nutrit, et urticae proxima saepe rosa est

[Learn healing from him through whom ye learnt to love:
one hand alike will wound and succour. The same earth

[19] *Tractatus super Viaticum,* lines 33–37 in Wack, *Lovesickness,* pp. 256–57.
[20] *Questiones super Viaticum,* Version A, lines 37–40 in Wack, ibid., pp. 216–17.

fosters healing herbs and noxious, and oft is the nettle
nearest to the rose][21]

However, the Roman poet also insists that love is a game—a war-game
sometimes, but nevertheless not the real McCoy. Thus, even as he tells
us in the *Remedia* that Cupid can be a killer, he also insists that death
from love is inappropriate:

> Qui, nisi desierit, misero periturus amore est,
>   Desinat; et nulli funeris auctor eris.
> Et puer es, nec te quicquam nisi ludere oportet:
>   Lude; decent annos mollia regna tuos.

[He who, unless he give o'er, will die of hapless love,—let him give o'er; and
thou shalt be the death of none. Thou art a boy, nor does aught save play
become thee: play then; a tender rule becomes thy years.][22]

The poet further argues that if Phyllis, Dido, Medea, and Paris had used
his remedies the course of history would have been transformed. In this
fantasy, infanticide, suicide, and the Trojan war can all be canceled. Lovers simply need to learn the difference between game and reality, and
history, with its cumulative losses, fades away, neutralized by elegiac
remedy. Far from being inevitable, the course of lovesickness is posted
with choices, for patient and god alike. Such an illness, the pastime of
idle hours, bears little resemblance to the life-threatening disease to
which Chaucer's hero succumbs.

In medieval love literature, Ovid's playful language of morbidity and
mortality is amplified into elaborate rhetorical games of self-conscious
hyperbole, of antithesis and paradox, of wordplay and foreplay. In
twelfth-century troubadour lyrics and in Andreas Capellanus the Ovidian game undergoes a crucial shift, a shift that is manifest in Chaucer's
poem. Andreas retains the sense of the male body as insular and afflicted
from within, but gives the beloved a larger and less benign role:

Quod autem illa passio sit innata, manifesta tibi ratione ostendo, quia passio
illa ex nulla oritur actione subtiliter veritate inspecta; sed ex sola cogitatione

---

[21] *Remedia Amoris,* 43–46. Selections from Ovid are from *The Art of Love and Other
Poems,* trans. J. H. Mozley (Cambridge: Harvard University Press, 1979, repr. 1985).
They are identified by title and line numbers.
[22] *Remedia Amoris,* 21–24.

quam concipit animus ex eo quod vidit passio illa procedit. Nam quum aliquis videt aliquam aptam amori et suo formatam arbitrio, statim eam incipit concupiscere corde; postea vero quotiens de ipsa cogitat, totiens eius magis ardescit amore, quousque ad cogitationem devenerit pleniorem.

[I can demonstrate by a clear argument that the feeling of love is inborn. A careful scrutiny of the truth shows that it arises not from any action, but solely from the thought formed by the mind as a result of the thing seen. When a man sees a girl ripe for love and fashioned to his liking, he at once begins to desire her inwardly, and whenever subsequently he thinks about her, he burns with love for her more each time, until then he reaches the stage of more detailed reflexion.][23]

Here, as in Bona Fortuna's later account, the woman is inert, a pathogenic phantasma shaped by the gaze of the diseased: seemingly a far cry from the loving heroine of *Troilus and Criseyde*. Nevertheless, Andreas's "aliquam aptam amori," the product of humoral vulnerability and diseased cogitation, might also be seen as prefiguring the Criseyde Troilus encounters in the temple.

In twelfth-century troubadour lyrics, the intensifying focus on the male body as infected and endangered is accompanied by the implication of the lady as culpable source of harm. Ovid's playful privatization of history persists, but agency changes and with it the assignation of guilt. Medieval lyrics that use the language of wounding and illness indict the woman, not the god, as murderer.[24] The dangerous role assigned to the woman does not require action on her part; instead her passivity and her malleability ensure her destructiveness. She is turned against herself, and, unlike the mischievous divinity in Ovid's court, she is threatened with the consequences of the powers she unwittingly exerts:

> e si·l maltraich no·m restaura
> ab un baisar anz d'annou
> mi auci e si enferna.

[23] *Andreas Capellanus on Love*, ed. and trans. P. G. Walsh (London: Duckworth, 1982), Book 1, cap. 1, sections 8–10, pp. 34–35.

[24] There are, of course, exceptions to this, most notably the *Roman de la Rose* in which Guillaume de Lorris keeps the Ovidian dynamic between god and human lover. The rose remains a passive third.

[If she does not cure me of this torment
with a kiss before new year's,
she murders me and sends herself to hell.][25]

This shift, which we also see in Andreas Capellanus's *De Amore*,[26] elides Ovid's mischievous Eros and exerts a polarizing and powerfully heterosexual pressure on the love relationship. Unlike Cupid, the woman is susceptible of judgment and retribution. Whereas, in the charmingly ambiguous relationship between the adult poet and the boy-god, the Ovidian persona must present himself as a penitent as well as a chastising older friend, his medieval disciples are free to take on the roles of victim, prosecutor, jury, and judge, often concurrently.

The protean pathology of *amor hereos* in twelfth- and thirteenth-century texts remains sketchy, abstract, and to some extent disembodied. Lovesick bodies in romance, for example, often seem interchangeable. Masculine and feminine bouts of *amor hereos* may carry the same symptoms and submit to the same laws, as in Chrétien's *Cligés* or Marie de France's *Guigemar*. Susan Crane points out that "waiting, longing, and victimization in love may sound oddly feminine" in an early text like *Eneas,* but she argues that, rather than emasculating the lover, the re-gendering of traits associated with the feminine is used to establish the masculine experience as representative of human experience *in toto*: "Masculinity is expanded rather than feminized."[27] In Chaucer's poem, the extrapolation of the human from the masculine will figure in the condemnation of Criseyde and in the apotheosis of her lover.

The imbrications of masculine identity and communal values that Crane notes in the romances also resonate in both Boccaccio and Chaucer. Ovid's claim, that *eros* has the power to negate history, is shown to be wishful thinking. In Boccaccio's *Il Filostrato,* love's transformative power is preempted by communal necessity. Here, the privatizing of

[25] Arnaut Daniel, "L'aur'amara," in *Lyrics of the Troubadours and Trouvères: An Anthology and a History,* ed. and trans. Frederick Goldin (Gloucester, Mass.: Peter Smith, 1983), pp. 218–19. Also Guillaume IX #7, III, ll. 15–18, #8 V, l. 26, in Goldin; Andreas Capellanus *De Amore,* Dialogue F, 1.6.283, pp. 120–21 (here the rhetoric of death is used by a noble lover to seduce a peasant woman).

[26] See Dialogue E, 1.6.206–8, pp. 98–101. For a discussion of the language of death in Andreas, see Mary F. Wack, "Imagination, Medicine, and Rhetoric in Andreas Capellanus' *De Amore,*" in *Magister Regis: Studies in Honor of Robert Earl Kaske,* ed. Arthur Groos (New York: Fordham University Press, 1986), p. 109.

[27] Susan Crane, *Gender and Romance in Chaucer's* Canterbury Tales (Princeton, N.J.: Princeton University Press, 1994), pp. 25–26.

history, which serves to guarantee love's playfulness in Ovid, is turned on its head when the intimate world of the lovers falls victim to the exigencies of war. Troilo first glories in the primacy of his love:

> Segua chi vuole i regni e le ricchezze,
> l'arme, i cavai, le selve, i can, gli uccelli,
> di Pallade gli studi, e le prodezze
> di Marte, ch'io in mirar gli occhi belli
> della mia donna e le vere bellezze
> il tempo vo' por tutto, che son quelli
> che sopra Giove mi pongon, qualora
> gli miro, tanto il cor se ne innamora

[Let him who wants to, pursue power and riches, arms, horses, wild beasts, dogs, birds, the studies of Pallas, and the valorous deeds of Mars; I wish to spend all my time in gazing at the beautiful eyes of my lady and her true beauties, which are those things which place me above Jove whenever I gaze at them, so much is my heart enamored of her.][28]

Later he must conform to the demands of public security and to his role as prince. Chaucer, following Boccaccio's lead, also subjects the private to the needs of the polis. Far from being neutralized by lovers' games, as Ovid playfully argues, history renders those games suddenly self-indulgent and destructive. Lee Patterson points out that "Books 4 and 5 show . . . that the local enclave of love can neither withstand nor transcend the pressures of history."[29] The poem, moreover, is shadowed by a never quite completed homology between hero and city. Patterson argues against the too easy equation of Troilus with Troy, yet notes the "narrative symmetry between the fate of the city and the fate of the lovers."[30] More specifically, it is Troilus's fate, not Criseyde's, that prefigures the city's fall, and it is Troilus's body that, like the body of Troy, is invaded and overcome.

[28] Boccaccio, 3.88, pp. 178–79.
[29] Lee Patterson, *Chaucer and the Subject of History* (Madison, WI: University of Wisconsin Press, 1991), p. 111.
[30] Ibid. See Patterson's note 73 for a summary of texts in which Troilus's fate is prophetic of Troy's fall. Also see Sylvia Federico, "Chaucer's Utopian Troy Book: Alternatives to Historiography in *Troilus and Criseyde*," *Exemplaria* 11.1 (1999): 88.

Body Praxis

The homology between masculine body and polis flickers through the stanzas of *Troilus and Criseyde*. Never entirely worked out, the link is, nevertheless, intimate and physical. From early in the poem, the *soma* transcends its static role as microcosm to reproduce the social and political dynamics of a town besieged, dynamics enacted both through the performance of a concealed illness always on the verge of exposure and through Troilus's triumphal incarnation as "little Troy." Just as the poem's hero stands in for his city's elegance and valor in Books 1 and 2, the battle waged within Troilus's body in Book 5 presages Troy's own fall. Eugene Vance argues that "the individual experience of Troilus . . . is therefore but a synecdoche . . . , a fragment, of that larger historical violence occurring outside the city's walls."[31] Lover and town also co-alesce in an elegiac mode as Criseyde responds to Diomede's wooing by cloaking her allegiance to one in a prayer for the other:

> As she that hadde hire herte on Troilus
> So faste, that ther may it non arace;
> And strangely she spak, and seyde thus:
> "O Diomede, I love that ilke place
> Ther I was born; and Joves, for his grace,
> Delyvere it soone of all that doth it care!
> God, for thy myght, so leve it wel to fare!" (5.953–959)

Yet, as the narrator predicts, "er fully monthes two, / . . . bothe Troilus and Troie town / Shal knotteles thorughout hire herte slide" (5.766–69).

This conflation of the heroic body and the body politic late in the poem has little impact on Chaucer's announced purpose to construct a love story, not an epic, but it does trouble the boundaries between the two genres. The busy performance of *amor hereos* at the still center of a city under siege also disturbs the equations implied in medieval and early modern analogies between *corpus* and *polis*. As Troilus's body becomes the stage for invasion, contamination, and purgation, we can see the workings of the synergy between personal and communal agons. This dynamic is both physiologically determined and culturally enacted.

[31] Eugene Vance, *Mervelous Signals: Poetics and Sign Theory in the Middle Ages* (Lincoln: University of Nebraska Press, 1986), p. 283.

D. Vance Smith points out that, in medieval and early modern clinical literature, the post-edenic world is shaped literally and figuratively by the work of the male body, that the elements comprising that world are also the complexions of the human physiognomy, and that both world and body are difficult to control, contradictory, in need of regulation.[32] In other words, the world quite literally inhabits the body through its trace elements, the earth, air, water, and fire found in the humoral equilibrium, and the body in its turn molds the world through its labor. However, the elemental interpolation of man and world is not only found in medieval medicine; a less literal but nevertheless intimate interplay of physiognomy and culture can be seen in the "body praxis" of modern medical anthropology. In their studies of conditions such as nervios, or nevra, a mysterious paralysis that afflicts laborers working under oppressive conditions, Margaret Lock and Nancy Scheper-Hughes contend that sickness is, at least in part, a cultural act, not simply "an isolated event or an unfortunate brush with nature." This is because the body is not only a somatic or even psychosomatic entity, but also a dynamic site through whose "language of the organs . . . nature, society, and culture speak simultaneously." In particular, it is an arena for struggle: "The individual body should be seen as the most immediate, the proximate terrain where social truths and social contradictions are played out, as well as a locus of personal and social resistance, creativity, and struggle."[33]

In this reading of the body, the microcosm takes on a new, extended valence. It expands to embrace the agonistic dynamics of the larger world. However, even as they argue for an expansive understanding of the body, medical anthropologists maintain the reflective distance between inner and outer, mirror and image.

[32] D. Vance Smith, "Body Doubles: Producing the Masculine *Corpus*," in *Becoming Male in the Middle Ages,* ed. Jeffrey Jerome Cohen and Bonnie Wheeler (New York: Garland, 1997), pp. 4–6, 15.

[33] Margaret Lock and Nancy Scheper-Hughes, "A Critical-Interpretive Approach in Medical Anthropology: Rituals and Routines of Discipline and Dissent," in *Medical Anthropology: A Handbook of Theory and Method,"* ed. Thomas M. Johnson and Carolyn F. Sargent (New York: Greenwood, 1990), p. 71. See also Scheper-Hughes, "Embodied Knowledge: Thinking with the Body in Critical Medical Anthropology" in *Assessing Cultural Anthropology,* ed. Robert Borofsky (New York: McGraw-Hill, 1994), pp. 229–42. For a detailed survey of the lexicon for these conditions, see Setha M. Low, "Embodied Metaphors: Nerves as Lived Experience" in *Embodiment and Experience: The existential ground of culture and self ,* ed. Thomas J. Csordas (Cambridge: Cambridge University Press, 1994), pp. 139–62.

This distance collapses in Chaucer's account of troubled bodies within a besieged town. Troilus's performance of lovesickness disrupts the discrete corporeal boundaries implied both in medieval and early modern analogies between the body politic and the human corpus and in the medical anthropologists' mapping of "proximate terrain." To understand that performance, I turn to twentieth-century phenomenological critiques of the physical self, in which characterizations of the body as vehicle (through which nature and culture speak) or as terrain (upon which social and political tensions are mapped) are augmented by the performative physical self, our necessary yet fraught intersection with the world. In the work of Elaine Scarry and Drew Leder, increased attention to illness and pain invests the once clearly circumscribed essential body with an enhanced power to disrupt and reshape its world.[34] Leder argues that normally we are unaware of our bodies—they disappear into wellness. "[T]he lived body," he says, "is necessarily self-effacing."[35] However, when the body is ill, or not functioning as we expect it to, it is uncomfortably present in dysfunction, a phenomenon that he calls *dys-appearance*.[36] As pain or illness forces an internalization of experience and compels the afflicted to reorganize crucial relationships to space and time, to others and to themselves, the world ceases to be an arena for productive, purposeful activity and the body becomes alien, "something foreign to the self," "aversive, involuntary, and disruptive."[37] Leder argues that, in the Western tradition, the physical self is thus seen as a source of error—moral and epistemological—and as a source of mortality.[38] Disease also brings "a heightened thematization of the body," scrupulous attention to its every function, and an obsessive regard for symptoms. Such hyperattention, however, rather than restoring the sufferer's sense of self, in fact further obviates it, for, once taken over by disease or pain, the body is no longer under the sufferer's control. It seems instead to have capitulated to "the hegemony of an occupying force."[39]

[34] See Elaine Scarry, *The Body in Pain: The Making and Unmaking of the World* (New York and London: Oxford University Press, 1985), pp. 53 ff.

[35] Drew Leder, *The Absent Body* (Chicago: University of Chicago Press, 1990), p. 69.

[36] Ibid., p. 83.

[37] Ibid., pp. 76, 77.

[38] Ibid., p. 127.

[39] Ibid., pp. 81–82.

In a trajectory familiar to Chaucer's readers, as the body becomes more troubled, it also gains agency.[40] In his introduction to *Embodiment and Experience,* Thomas Csordas summarizes the "kind of body to which we have been accustomed in scholarly and popular thought": "a fixed, material entity subject to the empirical rules of biological science, existing prior to the mutability and flux of cultural change and diversity and characterized by unchangeable inner necessities."[41] That body has given way to a problematic, historicized, performing body/self, a "being-in-the-world."[42] Although Csordas sees this as a recent development in conceptualizations of body/world relations, evidence from the late Middle Ages suggests a similar dynamic: under the pressures of disease and social dislocation the static, bounded body beloved of ancient and medieval physicians grew increasingly problematic.

Plague

When epidemic strikes, the effects of disease are patently no longer confined within the individual body. The diseased body becomes entangled with the communal *corpus*, no longer as its microcosmic double, but rather as the infected and infective cell, both mirroring and contaminating the larger organism. As contagion further tests somatic limits, the analogy between the individual physical body and the body politic is clouded by a sense that the body is no longer inert. Rather than being simply a carrier of pathogens, an innocent host, the body is itself seen as invasive. Once valued and compliant, now compromised by retrovirus, plague, or even lovesickness, the physical self becomes at once sign, harbinger, and cause of corruption and disease. Those already defined as "other" find themselves particularly vulnerable to reconfiguration. In *Simians, Cyborgs, and Women,* Donna Haraway tells us that

expansionist Western medical discourse in colonizing contexts has been obsessed with the notion of contagion and hostile penetration of the healthy body,

---

[40] Elizabeth Robertson argues that this is particularly true of women's bodies, indeed that women gain subjectivity and agency under the constraint of rape. "Public Bodies and Psychic Domains: Rape. Consent, and Female Subjectivity in Geoffrey Chaucer's *Troilus and Criseyde*" in *Representing Rape in Medieval and Early Modern Literature,* ed. Elizabeth Robertson and Christine M. Rose (New York: St. Martin's Press, 2001), pp. 281–310.

[41] Csordas, p. 1.

[42] Ibid., p. 10.

as well as of terrorism and mutiny from within. This approach to disease involved a stunning reversal: the colonized was perceived as the invader. [43]

Haraway argues that the colonized body—whether female, queer, or non-western—is always perceived as infective. Such a body is not only infectious or *capable* of causing an infection; it will *inevitably* sicken its host. Jonathan Gil Harris locates these "pathological paradigms" in early modern political thought, particularly in political discourse that casts "Catholics, Jews and witches as the English body politic's medicinal poisons, palliatives, or purgatives."[44] However, the "discourse of infection, containment, and foreign bodies" can also be seen two hundred years earlier in the plague tractates of the fourteenth-century, and its impact extends well beyond defensive political delineations of marginal groups.

Studies of twentieth-century epidemics in the colonized world and of the AIDS epidemic in industrial nations expose etiology's role in the construal of otherness. D. Vance Smith notes that in AIDS literature, broadly construed as text and film, *and* in plague tractates, disease originates in foreign territory, territory that is also home to deviance. Thus, in the discourse emerging from the AIDS epidemic in the West, Africa becomes "the site at which specific practices are repressed, the site where the unknowable and inexplicable behavior that originally produced AIDS is located." Here, as in many of the plague tractates, "epidemiology and moral etiology have collapsed into territoriality."[45] Case studies of epidemics in Africa and India explore a similar merger of medicine, cultural anxieties, and ideology. Myron Echenberg, in his study of bubonic plague outbreaks in twentieth-century Senegal, casts that epidemic in political terms, arguing that epidemics are never solely medical events. According to Echenberg, recurring outbreaks of plague in Senegal from 1914 to 1945 "can best be understood as part of the ideological contest between the conqueror and the conquered."[46] In the course of their decades-long struggle against the plague, the Senegalese were in-

[43] Donna J. Haraway, *Simians, Cyborgs, and Women: The Reinvention of Nature* (London, Free Association Books, 1991), p. 223.

[44] Jonathan Gil Harris, *Foreign bodies and the body politic: Discourses of social pathology in early modern England* (Cambridge: Cambridge University Press, 1998), p. 15–16.

[45] D. Vance Smith, "Plague, Panic Space, and the Tragic Medieval Household," *The South Atlantic Quarterly* v. 98 (1999), p. 382.

[46] Myron Echenberg, *Black Death, White Medicine: Bubonic Plague and the Politics of Public Health in Colonial Senegal, 1914–1945* (Portsmouth, N.H.: Heinemann, 2002), p. 3. For an analysis of colonial medicine in India see David Arnold, *Colonizing the Body: State Medicine and Epidemic Disease in Nineteenth-Century India* (Berkeley: University of California Press, 1993).

creasingly characterized as dangerous and as requiring segregation and control.[47] Here, Echenberg argues, the infective other is retroactively construed to conform to the disease s/he is presumed to have caused. In other words, the etiology of disease becomes an etiology of the other through which the threat of sickness creates, defines, and delimits otherness. Alterity, delineated by the exigencies of sickness, finds its expression in the real or imagined power to infect others.[48]

According to Smith, the identification of "sites of origin and radical alterity" becomes "an essential phase of the writing of plague history."[49] We can see this siting in Gabriele de' Mussis's narrative of the siege of Caffa, in which, like Haraway's colonized invader, the deviant and infective alien penetrates a healthy society. The account begins in Caffa, a Genoese port on the Black Sea where Christian merchants held out for almost three years against "hordes of Tartars." Finally, in 1346, the enemy is stricken by pestilence. Thousands in the Tartar camps sicken and die, "morbo inexplicabili."

Quod Tartari, ex tanta clade et morbo pestifero fatigati, sic defficientes attoniti et vndique stupefacti, sine spe salutis mori conspicientes, cadavera, machinis eorum superposita, Intra Caffensem vrbem precipitari Jubebant, ut ipsorum fectore (!) intollerabili, omnino defficerent. Sic sic proiecta videbantur Cacumina mortuorum, nec christiani latere, nec fugere, nec a tali precipicio liberari valebant.

[The dying Tartars, stunned and stupefied by the immensity of the disaster brought about by the disease, and realising that they had no hope of escape, lost interest in the siege. But they ordered corpses to be placed in catapults and lobbed into the city in the hope that the intolerable stench would kill everyone inside. What seemed like mountains of dead were thrown into the city, and the Christians could not hide or flee or escape from them.][50]

---

[47] Echenberg., pp. 27–32.

[48] Mary Douglas makes a similar argument concerning witchcraft and leprosy. She points out that in the Middle Ages "the attribution of a hidden power to hurt" becomes a powerful weapon, especially against those suspected of violating the social order. "Witchcraft and Leprosy: Two Strategies of Exclusion," MAN n.s. 26 (1991), pp. 726.

[49] Smith, "Plague," p. 383.

[50] Gabriele de' Mussis, *Historia de Morbo*, ed. A. W. Henschel, "Document zur Geschichte des schwarzen Todes," in Heinrich Haeser, ed., *Archiv für die gesammte Medicin* 2, Jena, 1841/42, p. 48. Translated by Rosemary Horrox, in *The Black Death* (Manchester and New York: Manchester University Press, 1994), p. 17. For all subsequent excerpts from plague tractates I use Horrox's translations. I have reproduced editorial marks and accidentals in Henschel's edition. For a discussion of Gabriele de' Mussis, see Vincent Derbes, "De Mussis and the great plague of 1348: A forgotten episode of bacteriological warfare," *Journal of the American Medical Association* 196 (1966): 59–62.

In a potent precursor to biological warfare, the corrupt bodies of the East penetrate the enclosed Christian town, but the invasion does not end there. The Genoese are also vulnerable to the disease, and not only from the miasma generated by decaying corpses:

Moxque toto aere inffecto. et aqua uenenata, corrupta putredine, tantusque fetor Increbuit ut vix ex Millibus vnus, relicto exercitu fugere conaretur qui eciam uenenatus alijs ubique uenena preparans, solo aspectu, loca et homines, morbo Infficeret uniuersos. Nec aliquis sciebat, uel poterat viam Inuenire salutis.

[Soon the rotting corpses tainted the air and poisoned the water supply, and the stench was so overwhelming that hardly one in several thousand was in a position to flee the remains of the Tartar army. Moreover, one infected man could carry the poison to others, and infect people and places with the disease by look alone. No one knew, or could discover, a means of defence.][51]

The violated town becomes a source of corrupted bodies, defenseless against the contagious gaze of their fellows and contagious in their turn. The *Historia de Morbo* tells us that infected survivors of the siege of Caffa boarded ships for Genoa, Venice, and other ports:

Nauigantes, cum ad terras aliquas accedebant, ac si maligni spiritus comitantes, mixtis hominibus Intererint (ierunt). Omnis ciuitas, omnis locus, omnis terra et habitatores eorum vtriusque sexus, morbi contagio pestifero uenenati, morte subita corruebant. Et cum vnus ceperat Egrotari, mox cadens et moriens vniuersam familiam uenenabat. Iniciantes, ut cadauera sepelirent, mortis eodem genere corruebant.

[When the sailors reached these places and mixed with the people there, it was as if they had brought evil spirits with them: every city, every settlement, every place was poisoned by the contagious pestilence, and their inhabitants, both men and women, died suddenly. And when one person had contracted the illness, he poisoned his whole family even as he fell and died, so that those preparing to bury his body were seized by death in the same way.][52]

In the remorseless logic of contagion the beloved body is rewritten as the agent of disease and death. Gabriele speaks in the voices of the Genoese and Venetian sailors:

[51] Gabriele de' Mussis, pp. 48–49; Horrox, p. 17.
[52] Gabriele de' Mussis, p. 50, Horrox, pp. 18–19.

Et qauia nos grauis Infirmitas detinebat. Et nobis de Mille Nauigantibus vix decem supererant, propinqui, Affines, et conuicini ad nos vndique confluebant. heu nobis, qui mortis Jacula portabamus, dum amplexibus et osculis nos tene-rent, ex ore, dum uerba uerba loquebamur, venenum fundere cogebamur.

[And because we had been delayed by tragic events, and because among us there were scarcely ten survivors from a thousand sailors, relations, kinsmen and neighbours flocked to us from all sides. But, to our anguish, we were carrying the darts of death. While they hugged and kissed us we were spread-ing poison from our lips even as we spoke.][53]

Here, the pathogenic corpus writes itself as abject and laments its own fatal power. Death's terror lies in intimacy and in the inadvertent but inevitable betrayal of those closest to us: "propinqui, affines, et conui-cini."

Gabriele's account is only the most well-known of almost three hun-dred tractates scattered throughout Europe.[54] Often subsumed within a chronicle, the plague tractate departs from the terse cataloguing of events to speculate on the causes of the disease. Smith notes that the tractates are commonly "etiological rather than . . . palliative" docu-ments that are "interested mainly in designating the inception of disas-ter . . . in the world."[55] We see this preoccupation with origins in the wide range of contemporary responses to the epidemic—in ecclesiastical orders for penitential prayers and processions, sermons, and scientific treatises, as well as in the chronicles. The sources reveal a remarkable confusion over the causes of the plague and the mechanism of its trans-mission, a confusion that persists even today.[56] In fourteenth-century accounts, the gap between scientific explanation and observed data is particularly noticeable. Even as learned medical explanations attributed the plague to vapors resulting from the malevolent conjunctions of Saturn, Jupiter, and Mars in the sign of Aquarius or to divine wrath, experience taught afflicted communities horrible object lessons in conta-

---

[53] Gabriele de' Mussis, p. 50; Horrox, p. 19.

[54] Nancy G. Siraisi estimates that at least 281 plague tractates were composed be-tween the mid-fourteenth century and 1500. *Medieval and Early Renaissance Medicine: An Introduction to Knowledge and Practice* (Chicago: University of Chicago Press, 1990), p. 128.

[55] Smith, "Plague, Panic Space, and the Tragic Medieval Household," p. 384.

[56] For a recent volley in the centuries-long dispute over causes of the plague, see Samuel K. Cohn, Jr., *The Black Death Transformed: Disease and Culture in Early Renaissance Europe* (New York: Oxford University Press, 2002).

gion.[57] Death dwelled in the touch, or the breath, or even the eyes of loved ones, visitors, and neighbors. Insular and continental sources speak of the dangers infectious bodies brought to the communities they entered. A Franciscan chronicle in Norfolk records the plague's incursion into England:

In quibus naute de Vasconia venientes quadam inaudita pestilencia epidemia nominata infecti, homines illius ville de Melcoumbe primo in Anglia inficiebant

[In [these ships] were sailors from Gascony who were infected with an unheard of epidemic illness called pestilence. They infected the men of Melcombe, who were the first to be infected in England.][58]

An Irish chronicle attributed to John Clynn, first warden of the Franciscan Friary of Carick, tells of a "pestilence so contagious that those who touched the dead or the sick were immediately infected themselves and died" [ista pestilencia sic erat contagiosa quod tangentes mortuos vel inde infirmos incontinenter et inficiebantur et moriebantur].[59] In these texts, the comfortable polarities of friend and foe disintegrate, and death locates itself within the familiar. Those closest to us, themselves taken over by disease, become the deadly other, the hostile invader.

As late medieval physicians struggle to reconcile the medicine they inherited from antiquity with the cataclysm taking place before their eyes, the body itself is reconfigured.[60] In a widely circulated treatise,

[57] For a comprehensive discussion of theoretical and practical medicine in the Middle Ages see Siraisi. Also Lucas García-Ballester, "*Artifax factivas sanitatis*: health and medical care in medieval Latin Galenism," in *Knowledge and the scholarly medical traditions,* ed. Don Bates (Cambridge: Cambridge University Press, 1995), pp. 127–50.

[58] Antonia Gransden, ed., "A Fourteenth-Century Chronicle from the Grey Friars at Lynn," *EHR* 72, (1957): 274. Horrox, p. 63.

[59] Friar John Clynn, *The Annals of Ireland by Friar John Clyn and Thady Dowling,* ed. R. Butler, *Annalium Hibernae Chronicon*, Irish Archaeological Society, 1849, pp. 36. Horrox, p. 82.

[60] Jean-Noël Biraben notes that "The plague of the fourteenth century, the Black Death, played a major part in upsetting all certainty in medical thinking. This tremendous epidemic disease, found in the writings of neither Hippocrates nor Galen, appeared exceedingly contagious in popular experience, contradicting the traditional ideas of physicians." "Diseases in Europe: Equilibrium and Breakdown of the Pathocenosis" in Mirko D. Grmek, ed., Antony Shugaar, trans., *Western Medical Thought from Antiquity to the Middle Ages* (Cambridge: Harvard University Press, 1998), p. 353. For theories of infection in classical and medieval Europe, see also Henk A. M. J. Ten Have, "Knowledge and Practice in European Medicine: The Case of Infectious Diseases" in *The Growth of Medical Knowledge*, ed. Henk A. M. J. Ten Have, Gerrit K. Kinsma, Stuart F. Spicker (Dordrecht: Kluwer Academic Publishers, 1990), p. 19.

John Jacobus (or Jean Jacmé), the papal physician and chancellor of Montpellier, notes the infectious nature of plague sores and the bodies afflicted with them. His advice survives in a fifteenth-century English translation of a Scandinavian edition:

> Pestilence sores be contagious by cause of enfecte humours bodyes and the reek or smoke of suche sores is venemous and corrupteth the ayer and therfore it is to flee fro suche persons as be infect. In pestilence time no body sholde stande in grete prece of people be cause some man of them may be infect. Therfore wise physicians in visityng seke folke stande ferre fro the patient holdying their face toward the doore or wyndowe and so sholde the servaunts of seke folke stande.[61]

Corrupt air and fluids are not the only suspects; death lives in the touch, the clothes, and even the sight of the afflicted. Infection dissolves corporeal margins and defines the corrupt body not only as lethal, but also as transgressive in invisible and irresistible ways. Some witnesses felt that the imagination itself could become contaminated. Guillaume de Nangis writes:

> Et veniebat mors prædicta et infirmitas ex imaginatione vel societate ad invicem et contagione; nam qui sanus aliquem visitabat infirmum, vix aut raro mortis periculum evadebat.

> [And death and sickness came by imagination, or by contact with others and consequent contagion; for a healthy person who visited the sick hardly ever escaped death.][62]

In 1349, another of Montpellier's doctors argues that the disease takes hold too quickly to be the result of contaminated breath. Instead, in an echo of lovesickness etiology, he indicts the *pneuma* which passes from one person to another almost instantaneously through the medium of sight:

[61] *A litil boke the which traytied and reherced many gode thinges necessaries for the* . . . *Pestilence,* reproduced in facsimile from the copy in the John Rylands Library (London: Manchester University Press, 1910), f. 3v. Horrox's translation is on p. 175. Horrox calls Jacobus's tract "one of the most popular plague tracts of the fourteenth century," p. 173.

[62] Guillaume de Nangis, *Chronique Latine de Guillaume de Nangis de 1113 à 1300 avec les continuations de cette chronique de 1300 à 1368,* ed. H. Géraud (Paris: Jules Renouard, 1843) vol. 2, p. 211. Horrox, p. 55.

Cum igitur hæc epidemia secundum aliquos habeat solo aere, solo flatu, sola conversatione contra ægros, plures occidere dicunt, quod aere inspirato infirmis et a sanis circumstantibus aspirato, ipsos lædi et necari maxime illo tunc quando sunt in agone; sed non subito, sed per intervallum, et paulatim illa necatio posset esse: sed major fortitudo hujus epidemiae, et quasi (72) subito interficiens, est quando spiritus aerius egrediens ab oculis ægroti repercusserit ad oculum sani hominis circumstantis, et ipsum ægrum respicientis, maxime quando sunt in agone: tunc enim illa natura venenosa illius membri transit de una in alia , occidendo alium.

[This epidemic, according to some people, has the power to kill large numbers by air alone, simply by the breath or the conversation of the sick. They say that the air breathed out by the sick and inhaled by the healthy people round about wounds and kills them, and that this occurs particularly when the sick are on the point of death. But that would kill gradually, after an interval rather than straight away; and the greater strength of this epidemic is such that it kills almost instantly, as soon as the airy spirit leaving the eyes of the sick man has struck the eye of a healthy bystander looking at him, for then the poisonous nature passes from one eye to the other.][63]

These burgeoning theories of contagion, more than two centuries before the microscope, are consistent with early theories of sight. Indeed, as we shall see, lovesickness initially invades Troilus's body through the eye. The eye, however, was not the only portal; the neo-Galenic body of fourteenth-century Europe, never thoroughly contained, was ripe for contagion. Awash with internal tides that prove so ungovernable that they must be "let"—released, thinned, and bled from veins and orifices —the body also ingests, taking in fluids, solids, and *pneuma* through mouth, nose, genitals, and pores. Fear of infection, moreover, is evident in the segregation of lepers. The idea that the plague, or any other disease, might travel invisibly from one body to another, rather than a watershed, was just another step in destabilizing somatic boundaries, a step compelled perhaps by the failure of the academic medical tradition to explain the evidence on the ground.

The pandemics of the fourteenth century exposed the academy's response to epidemic disease as woefully inadequate. Astrology, miasma, and even the vengeance of God: none of these satisfied as sufficient cause for the cataclysm. Thus, many fourteenth-century chroniclers of-

---

[63] "Consultation d'un Practicien de Montpellier," in L.-A.-Joseph Michon, ed., *Documents inédits sur la grande peste de 1348,* thèse pour le doctoral en médecine (Paris, J.-B. Baillière, 1860), pp. 72–73. Horrox, p. 182.

fered their own etiologies, and, in the process, reimagined the body. The plague taught its horrified witnesses that when fluids or spirits originate in a diseased body, that body, no matter how innocent or beloved, becomes a source of death. The breaching of the well body, then, implies an infectious other, and that lethal other is very likely an intimate of the one he or she sickens.[64]

Changing configurations of the body necessitated new social mechanisms. As Mary Douglas and, more recently, Donna Haraway have shown, fear of contagion compels redefinition of the bodies of others not only as dangerous but also as requiring supervision, scrutiny, and control. In many parts of fourteenth-century Europe, the plague deeply affected social relations and public policy. The understanding that friends, family, and neighbors could be immediate sources of disease and death led to the creation of a new kind of siege, in Italy and France in particular, and to policies of expulsion and compulsory isolation of the sick. Communities found themselves frantically defending their walls against peaceful strangers and even expelling their own members.[65] On January 17, 1374, Bernabò Visconti, lord of Milan, ruled that "each person who displays a swelling or tumour shall immediately leave the city, castle or town where he is and take to the open country, living either in huts or in the woods, until he either dies or recovers" [Volumus, quòd quælibet persona, cui nascentia, vel brosa veniet, statim exeat Urbem, vel Castrum, vel Burgum, in quo fuerit, & vadat ad campos in capannis, vel in nemoribus, donec aut moriatur, aut liberetur].[66] David Herlihy cites the quarantine in Ragusa in 1377 and subsequent quarantines throughout Europe as evidence that medieval towns understood

[64] Although the microscope, with its window into the world of microorganisms, is still two centuries in the future, plague tractates make it hard to argue, as does Keith Manchester, that "medieval man had no real conception of infection," "The palaeopathology of urban infections" in *Death in Towns: Urban Responses to the Dying and the Dead, 100–1600,* ed. Steven Bassett (Leicester: Leicester University Press, 1992), p. 8.

[65] An analogy can be found in the new regulatory climate developed in response to the AIDS epidemic. See Linda Singer on the logic of epidemic as justifying regulatory practices, *Erotic Welfare: Sexual Theory and Politics in the Age of Epidemic,* edited posthumously by Maureen MacGrogan and Judith Butler (New York: Routledge, 1993), pp. 30–31. For a more general study, see Peter Lewis Allen, *The Wages of Sin: Sex and Disease, Past and Present* (Chicago: University of Chicago Press, 2000). Also see Douglas, "Witchcraft and Leprosy," and Roberta Gilchrist, "Medieval Bodies in the Material World: gender, stigma and the body," in *Framing Medieval Bodies,* ed. Sarah Kay and Miri Rubin (Manchester: Manchester University Press, 1994), pp. 43–61.

[66] L. A. Muratori, ed., "Chronicon Regiense," *Rerum Italicarum Scriptores* 18 (Milan, 1731), col. 82. Horrox, p. 203.

the danger of contagion and took steps to isolate themselves.[67] Walls were erected and gates barred, not against enemies carrying weapons in their hands, a visible and external threat, but against family, friends, and neighbors bearing disease within familiar bodies. Far more pervasive, precipitous, and deadly than leprosy, King Death could not be confined to lazar houses. Although England was late to employ official quarantines, in the mid-fourteenth century Geoffrey le Baker of Swinbrook tells us that

Glovernienses illis de Bristollia ad suas partes denegarunt accessus, quolibet putante anelitus vivencium inter sic morientes fuisse infectivos . . . Vix aliquis infirmum ausus est contingere, relicta mortuorum quondam et nunc preciosa tamquam infectiva sani fugiebant.

[the people of Gloucester denied admission to people from Bristol, believing that the breath of those who had lived among the dying would be infectious . . . Hardly anyone dared to have anything to do with the sick. They fled from the things left by the dead, which had once been precious but were now poisonous to health.][68]

The sick, their possessions, and their bodies were shunned.[69] In times of epidemic disease, not only is the diseased body itself assessed as infectious; its very margins are dissolved and reconstituted to include and indict all traces and links, human and material. Compatriots, belongings, dwelling places—all these, once precious, must now be abhorred.[70]

---

[67] David Herlihy, *The Black Death and the Transformation of the West* (Cambridge: Harvard University Press, 1997), p. 71. See also Grmek, "The Concept of Disease" in *Western Medical Thought from Antiquity to the Middle Ages,* pp. 241–58. England was late in using quarantines; Paul Slack says the first quarantine was declared by Cardinal Wolsey in 1518, "The Response to Plague in Early Modern England: public policies and their consequences" in *Famine, disease and the social order in early modern society,* ed. John Walter and Roger Schofield (Cambridge: Cambridge University Press, 1989), pp. 167–87, but Chaucer may have encountered the policy in his trips to the continent, in particular Genoa and Florence, in 1373. For a summary of early quarantines, see Cohn, *Black Death,* pp. 48–49.

[68] Geoffrey Baker, *Chronicon Galfridi le Baker de Swynebroke,* ed. E. M. Thompson (Oxford, Clarendon Press, 1889), p. 99. Horrox, p. 81.

[69] Compare the ostracization of the AIDS patient in the twentieth century. See Julien S. Murphy, "The Body with AIDS: A Post-Structuralist Approach" in *The Body in Medical Thought and Practice,* ed. Drew Leder (Boston: Kluwer Academic Publishers, 1992), p. 162 ff.

[70] Plague tractates do not always yield an accurate account of conditions in particular towns. Authors may exaggerate the severity of the attack for polemical reasons or pattern their rhetoric after classical or Biblical sources. Communities across Europe differed

The plague forced reconfiguration of other boundaries as well. The need to identify cause and assess blame for the epidemic led in many cases to the conflation of physical and moral disease. The increasing suspicion that crowds offered the plague opportunities to spread prompted the regulation of social gatherings. Belief that the epidemic was an instrument of divine justice afforded preachers and moralists opportunities to condemn licentiousness. Chaucer's Pardoner gives us a vignette of a corrupt town in which "Deeth, / . . . hath a thousand slayn this pestilence."[71] Morally suspect social practices, especially those in which bodies transgress gender boundaries, are said to provide occasions for disease, often by calling down the wrath of God.[72] The fourteenth-century cleric Henry Knighton inveighs against cross dressing at tournaments and strongly implies that it inspires divine retribution:

Illis diebus ortus est rumor et ingens clamor in populo, eo quod ubi hastiludia prosequebantur quasi in quolibet loco dominarum cohors affuit, quasi comes interludii, in diverso et mirabili apparatu virili . . . et tali modo expendebant et devastabant bona sua, et corpora sua ludibriis et scurrilosis lasciviis vexitabant ut rumor populi personabat.

[In those days a murmuring and great complaint arose among the people, because whenever and wherever tournaments were held a troop of ladies would turn up dressed in a variety of extraordinary male clothing, as if taking part in

---

in their reactions to the threat of plague. See Richard W. Emery, "The black death of 1348 in Perpignan," *Speculum* v. 42 (1967), pp. 620–621 for the resilience and persever-ance of one plague-ridden community, and D. W. Admundsen, "Medical Deontology and Pestilential Disease in the Later Middle Ages," *Journal of the History of Medicine* 32 (1977), pp. 403–421, for the behavior of physicians. Shona Kelly Wray notes that notarial documents from Bologna in the 1340's offer us an alternative to the tractates in their more measured and less cataclysmic account of social and personal responses to the plague. "Re-evaluating Responses to the Plague: the Evidence from Bologna," *Responses to Epidemic Diseases,* Medieval Academy of America annual meeting, 2001. Never-theless, the tractates express cultural attitudes and enact imaginary constructs.

[71] *Canterbury Tales* VI.675, 679.

[72] In a foreshadowing of moralistic reactions to the AIDS epidemic of the twentieth and twenty-first centuries, strategies of blame and control coalesce to define deviant sexuality as responsible for the plague, and the cataclysm comes to be seen as a meta-phor for the collapse of morality and social discipline. Cf. Wallman: "the breakdown of the immune system's capacity to inhibit infection . . . is a ready metaphor for the breakdown of social and sexual inhibition, which is widely believed to have caused AIDS in the first place," "Sex and Death: The AIDS Crisis in Social and Cultural Context," in the *Journal of Acquired Immune Deficiency Syndrome* 1 (1988). Also quoted in *The Anthro-pology of Disease,* C.G.N. Mascie-Taylor, ed. (New York: Oxford University Press, 1993), p. 115.

a play . . . In this way they spent and wasted their goods, and (according to the common report) abused their bodies in wantonness and scurrilous licentiousness.][73]

In Knighton's account, this decadent behavior is followed immediately by the "universal mortality of men throughout the world" [generalis mortalitas hominum in universo mundo].[74] Similarly an anonymous monk of Malmesbury, writing of the year 1362, links effeminate fashions in men to divine punishment. He condemns fashions that inadequately cover the genitals and make men look like women and warns "it is only to be expected that the Lord's vengeance will follow" [quare timendum est ne subsequatur dira Domini flagellatio].[75] In other words, the deviant body, open to illicit penetration, profligate, and self-abusive, refuses containment and thus calls down divine retribution in the shape of a disease that will, in its turn, penetrate, corrupt, and pollute the body politic.

Epidemic, then, forces both a reconfiguring of corporeal and communal boundaries and a shift in the construction of deviant others—women, foreigners, sexual transgressors. The unregulated and permeable body, in Judith Butler's words, "constitutes a site of pollution and endangerment."[76] Linking the body, by analogy, to the social order, Mary Douglas argues that "its boundaries can represent any boundaries which are threatened or precarious."[77] In Catherine Waldby's discussion of the AIDS epidemic and the body politic she makes the analogy more concrete: "the whole social order [is imagined] as itself an infected body, or more precisely a body threatened by infection." An infected person then is "assimilated to the position of the virus in the body politic."[78] In these configurations, the conflation of the individual corpus and the body politic transcends metaphor to become a powerful hermeneutic tool for understanding disease as social and moral as well as physiologi-

---

[73] Henry Knighton, *Chronicon Henrici Knighton vel Cnitthon monachi Leycestrensis*, ed. J. R. Lumby, Rolls Series, 1889–95, vol. 2, p. 57. Horrox, p. 130.

[74] Knighton, p. 58. Horrox, p. 76.

[75] F. S. Haydon, ed., *Eulogium Historiarum sive Temporis: Chronicon ab Orbe Condito usque ad Annum Domini M.CCC.LXVI*, Rolls Series, 1858–63, vol. 3, pp. 230–31. Horrox, p. 133.

[76] Judith Butler, *Gender Trouble* (New York: Routledge, 1990), p. 132.

[77] Mary Douglas, *Purity and Danger: an Analysis of Concepts of Pollution and Taboo* (New York: Routledge, 1966/2000), p. 116, qtd. Butler, p. 132..

[78] Catherine Waldby, *AIDS and the Body Politic: Biomedicine and sexual difference* (New York: Routledge, 1996), p. 15.

cal. In the course of those hermeneutics, the carrier or source of disease is recast in the image of the disease itself.

The Poem

When we turn to the works of Geoffrey Chaucer, we find surprisingly few direct references to the plague. It provides the occasion for the *Book of the Duchess*[79] and both location and context for *The Pardoner's Tale*. We also learn that the Physician of the *Canterbury Tales* Prologue "kepte that he wan in pestilence"[80] and that the Reeve is feared like the death—perhaps a reference to the "First Death." Chaucer's contemporaries, especially on the continent, were more explicit. An outbreak of disease provides the occasion for Boccaccio's *Decameron* and gives the tale collection its powerful prologue. Guillaume de Machaut sets the playful argument of the *Jugement du Roi de Navarre* against the darkness of a time when God "made death come forth from his cage, / Full of rage and anger" [Fist la mort issir de sa cage, / Pleinne de forsen et de rage].[81] Contagious disease, moreover, has a virulent afterlife in later English treatments of Criseyde. In the early fifteenth century, in John Lydgate's *Troy Book*, Diomede's bout with love-sickness is closely followed by an account of plague sweeping the Greek camp. Criseyde succumbs to leprosy in Robert Henryson's *Testament of Cresseid*, and disease stalks both the town of Troy and the Greek camp in Shakespeare's *Troilus and Cressida*.

Although Chaucer's *Troilus and Criseyde*, the English forerunner to Lydgate, Henryson, and Shakespeare, ostensibly confines its medicine to *amor hereos*, it is suffused with the language of contagion and death. Critics have attributed the medicalization of Troilus's malady and the intensification of the language of death in Chaucer's poem to a movement away from the metaphorical and toward the literal and material.[82] Wack, for example, believes that "the medical model of love provided

---

[79] For a detailed discussion of *The Book of the Duchess* in this context, see Smith, "Plague," pp. 388–92.

[80] *Canterbury Tales* I. 442, p. 30.

[81] Guillaume de Machaut, *The Judgment of the King of Navarre*, ed. and trans. R. Barton Palmer (New York: Garland, 1988), ll. 355–56, pp. 16–17.

[82] Giles Y. Gamble argues that, in *Il Filostrato*, lovesickness is a metaphor for Boccaccio's own romantic problems, whereas in Chaucer "the malady is posited as a literal fact." "Troilus Philocaptus: A Case Study in *Amor Hereos*," *Studia Neophilologica* 60 (1988): 175–78. Also Wack, "Pandarus, Poetry and Healing."

Chaucer with a materialistic, deterministic, and ethically neutral view of love." She argues that "the patient is not held 'guilty' or 'responsible' for his illness."[83] This ethical dispensation, however, is not extended to Criseyde, who worries about the social and moral consequences of the affair and who is subsequently condemned for ending it. Clearly, the "erotic materialism"[84] which excuses Troilus and Pandarus does not exonerate the heroine. Then, as now, all bodies are not equal: Troilus may retain his heroic stature and eventually transcend his earthly condition, but his beloved is delimited by the disease she causes. Moreover, in Chaucer, that conflation of disease and carrier gains an additional and devastating dimension in that Criseyde is cast as sole earthly cure of the illness that she occasions. In the end, by withholding that cure, she renders herself doubly culpable. Even though, in this, she resembles her continental predecessors celebrated in the troubadour lyrics, as well as Boccaccio's Criseida, she complicates those models as her creator grounds both illness and cure in the material body.

By medicalizing the poem, Chaucer amplifies Boccaccio's conventional portrait of a generous but fickle paramour into an elaborate study of a pathogen. In an etiological fallacy that first conflates carrier and disease, then physician and cure, Criseyde is constructed as inadvertently pathogenic, then as curative, and finally as deadly. In the poem's concluding irony, by destroying her lover, the woman guarantees for him the primal fantasy in which the earthly birth site, ground of mutability and error, is superseded as country of origin by the "gret ayr" of the empyrean.[85]

In spite of the bathos and the humor of Troilus's performance, we are never permitted any doubt that his malady is dangerous. Like Leder's bodies in pain and like de' Mussis's bewildered Genoese sailors, he experiences the body as invaded by an external force, and this occupation vitiates the wholeness and integration proper to a prince. This violation occurs early in the poem, and for Troilus, as for some observers of the

---

[83] Wack, "Lovesickness," pp. 55 and 56.
[84] Ibid., pp. 58–59.
[85] In Chaucer's translation of Boethius's *Consolation of Philosophy*, Dame Philosophia promises to fix wings to Boethius's thought so that it "despiseth the hateful erthes, and surmounteth the rowndenesses of the get ayr." In this way the soul finds its true home (*Boece*, Book 4, metrum 1). For a gendered reading of these passages, see Robert Sturges on the Orpheus myth in Boethius and Chaucer. *Chaucer's Pardoner and Gender Theory: Bodies of Discourse* (New York: St. Martin's Press, 2000), p. 115.

plague, the point of entry is the eye.[86] Troilus's princely entrance into the temple for the festival of Pallas Athena is marked by the unselfconscious, scrutinizing gaze of the well body, whole and self-sustaining:

> This Troilus, as he was wont to gide
> His yonge knyghtes, lad hem up and down
> In thilke large temple on every side,
> Byholding ay the ladies of the town (1.183–86)

As *byholding* becomes *lokynge* "on this lady, and now on that," Troilus's eye "percede, and so depe it wente,/ Til on Criseyde it smot, and ther it stente" (1.269, 272–73). That gaze, however, soon turns upon its source:

> And of hire look in him ther gan to quyken
> So gret desir and such affeccioun,
> That in his herte botme gan to stiken
> Of hir his fixe and depe impressioun. (1.295–98)

The scenario is true to a medical tradition in which every bodily opening is potentially a portal to disaster. In a classically Galenic sickening through sight, Troilus is "thorugh-shoten and thorugh-darted" (1.325).[87] The *pneuma*, rebounding upon its source, causes his heart "to sprede and rise" (1.278). Soon thereafter, "the spirit in his herte," his vitality, is said to "dyen" (1.306–7). While Criseyde stands apart and looks aslant, Troilus has, in Sarah Stanbury's words, "[shot] himself with arrows from his own eyes";[88] in effect, he penetrates himself with the

---

[86] This account of the onset of illness reminds us that the plague tractates and the discourse on love sickness rely on a common physiological tradition, in which the eye is seen as portal to the body. William Shakespeare alludes to the infectious power of vision in relationship to both diseases in *Twelfth Night* 1.5.265–68.

[87] For medieval theories of optical contamination, see the Montpellier physicians cited in Anna Montgomery Campbell, *The Black Death and Men of Learning* (New York: Columbia University Press, 1931), pp. 61–62 and Robert S. Gottfried, *Doctors and Medicine in Medieval England: 1340–1530* (Princeton, N.J.: Princeton University Press, 1986), pp. 112–13. For a summary of the medieval science of optics relevant to Chaucer's poem see Sarah Stanbury, "The Lover's Gaze in Chaucer's *Troilus and Criseyde*," in *Chaucer's* Troilus and Criseyde: 'Subgit to Alle Poesye': Essays in Criticism, ed. R. A. Shoaf and Catherine S. Cox (Binghamton, N.Y.: Medieval and Renaissance Texts and Studies, 1992), pp. 224–238.

[88] Stanbury points out that, although love dwells within "the subtile stremes of hire yen" (1.305), "Criseyde never explicitly notices Troilus in this scene," p. 232.

image of the beloved. Soon, however, agency and culpability devolve upon the lady. As the incident is replayed for Criseyde's benefit in Pandarus's disingenuous account of Troilus's dream, her beauty and her gaze take on a new and unwonted power. Pandarus purports to be quoting Troilus as the besotted prince talks in his sleep:

> For certes, lord, so soore hath she me wounded,
> That stood in blak, with lokyng of hire eyen,
> That to myn hertes botme it is ysounded,
> Thorugh which I woot that I moot nedes deyen. (2.533–536)

Pandarus's invention begins the characterization of Criseyde as the contaminant that at once infects male hero and heroic narrative. In a poem haunted by the future penetration of a beloved city by a treacherous gift—a gift, moreover, bearing within its belly the agents of destruction—this breaching of the male body bespeaks a future of agonizing loss. It also renders the source of that suffering as first precious, then abhorred.[89]

In the subsequent narrative of disease, Troilus's lovesickness mimics the progress of a viral infection. Once breached, the body performs its newly compromised identity through fever, loss of appetite, and physical disintegration:

> And fro this forth tho refte hym love his slep,
> And made his mete his foo, and ek his sorwe
> Gan multiplie, that, whoso tok kep,
> It shewed in his hewe both eve and morwe. (1.484–87)

In this process, symptoms become more than outward representations of illness: in the terms of medical anthropology, they "recreate in the internal world of the body the perceived contradictions and disorder of the external world."[90] Conversely, the multiplication of sorrows forces

---

[89] Note Emmanuel Dreuilhe's use of the Trojan horse metaphor vis-à-vis AIDS. *Mortal Embrace: Living with AIDS*, trans. Linda Coverdale (New York: Hill and Wang, 1988), p. 115. Cited in Steven F. Kruger, *AIDS Narratives: Gender and Sexuality, Fiction and Science* (New York: Garland, 1996), p. 21.

[90] K. Finkler, "The Universality of Nerves" in *Health Care for Women International* 10: 171–79. Cited in Low, p. 142.

an outward showing of inner distress. Unable to reconcile his desiring and vulnerable self with the self-contained, impregnable hero it has supplanted, Troilus pretends to an entirely somatic ailment and withdraws.

The internal disorder of the male body compels a matching construction of the cause of that disorder. Troilus has, in Leder's terms, been occupied and alienated from his former self, and Criseyde seems culpably insensible to his distress: "Ne semed it that she of hym roughte, / Or of his peyne, or whatsoevere he thoughte" (1.496–97). Her responsibility for his illness is further established through her failure to respond to apostrophes it is impossible she should hear:

> Thise wordes, and ful many an other to,
> He spak, and called evere in his compleynte
> Hire name, for to tellen hire his wo,
> Til neigh that he in salte teres dreynte.
> Al was for nought: she herde nat his pleynte;
> And whan that he bythought on that folie,
> A thousand fold his wo gan multiplie. (1.540–46)

The figure of the indirect apostrophe here and elsewhere in the poem guarantees Criseyde's function in the beginning and the end of the romance as she who can heal but will not. The poet gives her enough subjectivity to render her culpable, but not enough to make her sensible of her lover's distress.[91]

Pandarus begins the wooing of Criseyde with a conventional accusation. He employs the medical language of wounding and healing fundamental to the Ovidian arts of seduction:

> Wo worth the faire gemme vertulees!
> Wo worth that herbe also that dooth no boote!
> Wo worth that beaute that is routheles!
> Wo worth that wight that tret ech undir foote!
> And ye, that ben of beaute crop and roote,
> If therwithal in yow ther be no routhe,
> Than is it harm ye lyven, by my trouthe! (2.344–50)

This is Ovid with a difference. The Roman poet names Eros, not the beloved, as the ground that bears the healing herb. Chaucer's Pandarus

---

[91] The trope of the accusatory apostrophe returns in the end of the poem in the material form of unanswered, or misanswered, letters.

recasts the metaphor to indict Criseyde as the medicine that refuses to cure.

Criseyde recognizes the absurdity of Pandarus's threat that she will be responsible for two deaths unless she "lat [her] daunger sucred ben a lite" (2.384): "Is al this paynted process seyd—allas!— / Right for this fyn?" [2.424–25]. Nevertheless, she accepts her own perilous role in that etiology:

> Unhappes fallen thikke
> Alday for love, and in swych manere cas
> As men ben cruel in hemself and wikke;
> And if this man sle here hymself—allas!—
> In my presence, it wol be no solas.
> What men wolde of hit deme I kan nat seye;
> It nedeth me ful sleighly for to pleie. (2.456–62)

Her musings place her firmly within the matrix of disease and gender that has been charted for her by her uncle.[92]

Although Criseyde also undergoes enamourment ("Who yaf me drynke?" [2.651]), she escapes the disintegration and disorientation lovesickness brings to her admirer. Her extended inner debate in lines 2.694–812 shows us a woman determined, like the "goodlieste mayde" of Antigone's song, to lead "hire lif in moste honour and joye" (2.880, 882). Nevertheless, regardless of her precautions, her deliberations, and her conditions, Criseyde has no choice but to conform to the prescriptions of disease and the needs of her ailing suitor. She will finally be unable to withstand the logic of infection:

> [She] ay gan love hire lasse for t'agaste
> Than it dide erst, and synken in hire herte,
> That she wex somwhat able to converte. (2.901–3)

Grounded in desire for an other who has little power except the power to elicit such longing, Troilus's lovesickness seems not only to express social relations but, more potently, to shape them. Illness not

---

[92] Criseyde is only one of number of witnesses, historical and fictional, who question love's power to kill. Green cites Valescus of Taranto, John of Gaddesden, Chartier's Belle Dame, and Christine de Pisan, pp. 204–5.

only reconfigures his world; it also reshapes those who dwell within it.[93] Insofar as the relationships so created are profoundly sexed by the desire of the diseased, the lovesick body constructs the other as both origin and end, as cause and remedy. More specifically, Troilus's performance of suffering and the "telic demand" for a cure that his suffering elicits indicts Criseyde even as it empowers her.[94] That performance, coupled with interpretive work by Pandarus, forces the beloved to internalize the logic of disease, until she conforms, with a little coaching from her uncle, to the homeopathic role of pathogen and cure. As Troilus remakes the world in the image of his pain, Criseyde remakes herself in the service of that same suffering. Her nascent subjectivity, which will, in the end, give warrant to the world's condemnation of her, deepens in proportion to her internalization of the twisted logic of lovesickness.

Thus, at Deiphebus's house, Criseyde waits, a silent witness to the discussion of how best to cure Troilus of his fever, "ther sat oon, al list hire nought to teche, / That thoughte, 'Best koud I yet ben his leche'" (2.1581–82). Criseyde's subsequent visit to Troilus's bedside is laden with the conflation of desire, laughter, and death characteristic of Chaucerian *fin' amors*. She is Troilus's bier (2.1638), Pandarus abjures her to "sle naught this man" (2.1736), and introduces her to him as "she that is youre deth to wite" (3.63). Pandarus's hyperbole—at once threatening, ridiculous, and seductive—here emerges as an integral part of Troilus's love-talking and as crucial to the construction of his beloved. Troilus greets Criseyde with a garbled threat of suicide:

> Thus muche as now, O wommanliche wif,
> I may out brynge, and if this yow displese,
> That shal I wreke upon myn owen lif
> Right soone, I trowe, and do youre herte an ese,
> If with my deth youre wreththe may apese.
> But syn that ye han herd me somwhat seye,
> Now recche I nevere how soone that I deye. (3.106–12)

Criseyde is not so much resistant to the rhetoric of death as perplexed by it: "by God and by my trouthe, / I not nat what ye wilne that I seye" (3.120–21). Her capitulation is both indulgent and detached, with but

---

[93] For the impact of pain or sickness on the body's relationship to the world and to others, see Leder, *Absent Body*, p. 74 ff. and Scarry, *Body in Pain*, p. 35 ff.

[94] Leder, *Absent Body*, p. 73.

a passing reference to Troilus's psychosomatic suffering: "Now beth al hool; no lenger ye ne pleyne. / . . . Beth glad, and draweth yow to lustinesse" (3.168, 177). In spite of this carefully maintained distance, however, her capitulation to the role of *leche,* or healer, marks her as the site of two mutually constitutive systems: disease and gender converge in her infective and salutary body.

Consistent with the approved therapies for *amor hereos*, the physical consummation of the love between Troilus and Criseyde is also the cure for Troilus's ills. First, however, the lover's hysterical reaction to Criseyde's distress when she believes herself accused of treachery reminds us of the disorientation he suffers and idiomatically invokes his own metonymic relationship to Troy:

> And every spirit his vigour in knette,
> So they astoned or oppressed were.
> The felyng of his sorwe, or of his fere,
> Or of aught elles, fled was out of towne;
> And down he fel all sodeynly a-swowne. (3.1088–92)

The comic scenario of the swooning, perhaps impotent,[95] lover tossed into bed with his bewildered beloved and rubbed and coaxed out of his stupor gives way to the sublime trope of the lover's world restored:

> Troilus, al hool of cares colde,
> Gan thanken tho the bryghte goddes sevene.
> Thus sondry peynes bryngen folk in hevene. (3.1202–04)

The momentary healing of Troilus is accompanied by the bittersweet designation of Criseyde as cure:

> O, sooth is seyd, that heled for to be
> As of a fevre or other gret siknesse,
> Men moste drynke, as men may ofte se,
> Ful bittre drynke; and for to han gladnesse,
> Men drynken ofte peyne and gret distresse—
> I mene it here, as for this aventure,
> That thorugh a peyne hath founden all his cure. (3.1212–18)

---

[95] For Troilus's impotence, see McInerney, "Unmanning."

The narrator's sly joke—Troilus's first cure is far from painful—not only foreshadows the tougher remedy to come but also invokes the sacrificial lexicon of the crucifixion, a vocabulary often echoed in medical prescriptive treatises. "Ful bittre drynke" evokes Christ's drink of gall as well as the salutary bitterness of medicine. We might at one level see Chaucer's playful invocation of the medical *cum* eschatological language as parody—in particular parody aimed at Troilus's bathetic performance. Parody, however, has a way of speaking painful truth and, as the poem turns its attention to Criseyde's traded and treacherous body, the medicinal joke proves all too prescient.

Book 4's tale of a father's plea, a council meeting that must bow to the popular will, and a hostage exchange moves the *mise en scène* from the lovers' chamber to the afflicted community with wrenching clarity. The woman's mutable and salutary body must now be put to work on behalf of an endangered town. The lovesickness cure achieved in Pandarus's closet is destined, through the workings of history and the popular will, to be withdrawn. Moreover, the trade predicated on Troy's desire for Antenor's return will prove disastrous to the town. Criseyde, the unwitting and unwilling pawn, is traded for Antenor, the traitor, and that exchange proves fatal for Troy and Troilus alike.

In Troilus's and Pandarus's reactions to the Trojans' decision to trade Criseyde for Antenor, we see two radically different understandings of lovesickness and its treatment. Insisting on the specificity of the remedy, Troilus maintains that separation from Criseyde means his death: "Who shal now yeven comfort to my peyne? / Allas, no wight" (4.318–19). Pandarus returns to the classic prescriptions for lovesickness and argues that Troilus has had his pleasure and another lady, another coitus, will do as well:

> But telle me this: whi thow art now so mad
> To sorwen thus? Whi listow in this wise,
> Syn thi desire al holly hastow had,
> So that, by right, it oughte ynough suffise?
>
> . . .
>
> This town is ful of ladys al aboute;
>
> . . .
>
> If she be lost, we shal recovere an other. (4.393–96, 401, 406)

Pandarus, in his cynicism, is kinder to Criseyde than is his friend. Troilus, by casting her in the role of sole remedy, ensures that her absence constitutes a fatal betrayal. In the erotic game in which Eros and his surrogate, Pandarus, play go-betweens, no serious damage is done because lovers suffer in order to be cured, the game can always be replayed, and female bodies are interchangeable. In contrast, in Troilus's world of disease and siege, the lover suffers until he dies, the game is an end-game, and there is only one curative body. By casting Criseyde as pathogenic and desired, Chaucer renders her both abject and precious,[96] recalling us to the bewildered reconfiguration of innocent bodies in the plague tractates. By giving Criseyde, and Criseyde alone, the power to cure, the poet moves beyond notions of infection to trap her in a double paradigm—the pathogenic body is meshed with the curative.

Troilus is not the only one to reject Pandarus's Ovidian solution. Criseyde's reaction to news of the exchange establishes her body, in her own words, as the abject object, sole source of corruption and disease. The passage bears repeating:

> Whoso me seeth, he seeth sorwe al atonys—
> Peyne, torment, pleynte, wo, distresse!
> Out of my woful body harm ther noon is,
> As angwissh, languor, cruel bitternesse,
> Anoy, smert, drede, fury, and ek siknesse. (4.841–45)

Like Chaucer's Black Knight, "For whoso seeth me first on morwe / May seyn he hath met with sorwe, / For y am sorwe, and sorwe ys y" (*Book of the Duchess*, ll. 595–97), Criseyde begins by allegorizing herself. In *Troilus and Criseyde*, however, allegory turns in on itself and, in so doing, is embodied, is made material. We see, in procession, emotional and physical ills entirely configured. She embraces her role as exclusive bodily receptacle for the world's afflictions, as the corrupt inverse of the anchoritic, enclosed vessel of divine love and virginal purity.[97] This, then, is the culmination of her carefully crafted subjectivity: to be the territory of suffering, at once cause and specter of loss.[98] Her introspec-

---

[96] On Criseyde as healer and nurturer see David Aers, *Community, Gender, and Individual Identity: English Writing 1360–1430* (New York: Routledge, 1988), pp. 132–37.

[97] See Jocelyn Wogan-Browne, "Chaste Bodies: frames and experiences" in Kay and Rubin for a discussion of the anchoress's body as receptacle, p. 29. Also Charlotte Morse, *The Pattern of Judgment in the* Queste *and* Cleanness (Columbia: University of Missouri Press, 1978), pp. 12–55, especially p. 12 on blood pollution.

[98] For an extensive psychoanalytic study of Criseyde's subjectivity see Margherita, pp. 100–28.

tive scrutiny, channeled through the gaze of others, emphatically concentrates the losses of the masculine world within her own pathogenic body. As her catalogue of evils culminates in "ek siknesse" she names herself the infective other.

Even as Criseyde designates her own body as pathogenic, she, also, anticlimactically, returns to her role as healer. Consistent with her curative obligations, she promises to restrain her sorrow and search her heart—every vein—for salve to treat her lover's wound:

> Hym for to glade I shal don al my peyne,
> And in myn herte seken every veyne.
> If to his sore ther may be fonden salve,
> It shal nat lakke, certeyn, on my halve. (4.942–45)

As source of disease she is obliged to bleed herself in search of a cure for the damage she has caused. Gail Paster calls phlebotomy "menstruation's cultural inversion": voluntary instead of involuntary, controlled instead of incontinent.[99] Criseyde's abject offer further inverts phlebotomy itself. Rather than bleed herself to purify her own body, she offers to search her veins for the salve to gladden her failing lover. In so doing, she intermingles sacrifice, nurture, fluidic corruption, and purification. Caught up in the binary of nourishment and contamination, the fluids so crucial to health in humoral medicine are also vehicles for anxiety and blame.[100] Bad blood must be purged, and yet blood nourishes, saves, and heals. The blood of women, in particular, refuses containment; the menstrual blood that contaminates a man sustains a fetus, and then, transformed into breast milk, nourishes the growing infant.[101]

[99] Paster, *Body Embarrassed: Drama and the Discipline of Shame in Early Modern England* (Ithaca, N.Y.: Cornell University Press, 1993), p. 83.

[100] Compare also the role of bodily fluids in a public pathology haunted by the threat of AIDS. Wallman points out that the AIDS epidemic has been associated with "the perversion of both the vital fluids: blood and semen are normally the source of life; infected with an AIDS virus, they become agents of death," in Mascie-Taylor, p. 115.

[101] Adelard of Bath explains that the menstrual blood of the mother, retained in the uterus during pregnancy, is first used to form the limbs of the fetus and then converted into milk. "Questiones naturales," *Adelard of Bath. Conversations with His Nephew: On the Same and the Different, Questions on Natural Science and On Birds,* ed. and trans. Charles Burnett (Cambridge: Cambridge University Press, 1998), question 39, pp. 166–67. The mutable blood and milk of the mother also figure in the healing imagery of the crucifixion. See *Ancrene Wisse,* part 7, in Bella Millett and Jocelyn Wogan-Browne, *Medieval Prose for Women: Selections from the Katherine Group and Ancrene Wisse* (Oxford: Clarendon, 1990). For the dangers inherent in menstrual blood, see Danielle Jacquart and Claude Thomasset, *Sexuality and Medicine in the Middle Ages,* trans. Matthew Adam-

Criseyde's desperate offer to bleed herself in search of the salve for Troilus's wounded heart also reminds us that Troilus is not the only one to suffer from lovesickness. Criseyde, after all, comes to the point of death herself at the prospect of separation from her beloved:

"O Jove, I deye, and mercy I beseche!
Help, Troilus!" And therwithal hire face
Upon his brest she leyde and loste speche—
Hire woful spirit from his propre place,
Right with the word, alwey o poynt to pace.
And thus she lith with hewes pale and grene,
That whilom fressh and fairest was to sene. (4.1149–55)

Once traded into the Greek camp, however, Criseyde seems to be immune to the disease that once brought her to death's edge. After a brief struggle, she proves herself to be mysteriously careless of the life of her patient and all too willing to heal another. In her acquired immunity to lovesickness and in her promiscuity, Criseyde conforms to the medical paradigm of the venereal woman as one who, while contaminating others, survives unaffected by disease.[102] Like Beroul's Yseut, who can spread her legs around the supposedly leprous Tristan and assure her lover "Do you imagine I will catch your disease?/ Have no fear, I will not" [Quides tu que ton mal me prenge?/ N'en aies doute, non fera],[103] Criseyde will survive, physically healthy and morally stigmatized. Her treachery sends Troilus once more into battle, like the fourth horseman of the apocalypse, to bring death to the Greeks, "For thousandes his hondes maden deye" (5.1802), and eventually to die himself at the hands of Achilles.

---

son (Princeton: Princeton University Press, 1988), pp. 72–74; Dyan Elliott, *Fallen Bodies: Pollution, Sexuality, and Demonology in the Middle Ages* (Philadelphia: University of Pennsylvania Press, 1999), pp. 2–3, 6, 115–16; Caroline Bynum, *Jesus as Mother: Studies in the Spirituality of the High Middle Ages* (Berkeley: University of California Press, 1982). See Paster, *Body Embarrassed,* on women's blood, menstruation, and phlebotomy in the early modern period, pp. 79–83.

[102] Jacquart and Thomasset, p. 185–89. Leprosy, probably confused with venereal disease at times, was thought to be transmitted through sexual relations, and in particular through sexual relations with a menstruating woman or with a leprous woman who may not show symptoms of the disease. Adelard of Bath teaches that woman's cold and moist nature protects her from leprosy, even if she is exposed to the semen of a leprous man. That semen, however, remains active and capable of infecting another man. *Questiones naturales, q.* 41. For a modern analogue to the infectious woman, see also Waldby on women as carriers of AIDS, *AIDS,* pp. 86–87.

[103] Beroul, *The Romance of Tristan by Beroul,* ed. and trans. Stewart Gregory (Amsterdam: Rodopi, 1992), lines 3924–25, pp. 184–85. I have used Gregory's translation.

Palinode

Troilus's death seems an afterthought, a one-line addendum, to the narrator's lament over feminine corruption in Book 5; his flight to the eighth sphere continues to provoke puzzled and hostile commentary. Walter Clyde Curry inveighs against it as "a sorry performance" that "denies and contradicts everything that has gone before."[104] Readers perplexed by the collapse of the love affair have sought solace in generic pedigrees and in the elegiac. E. T. Donaldson finds that the epilogue expresses "[a]ll the illusory loveliness of a world which is man's only reality."[105] John Steadman agrees with Donaldson and, in a magisterial survey of sources and analogues for "disembodied laughter," gives the epilogue a generic pedigree. Steadman emphasizes the epilogue's Boethian resolution of "two different but complementary points of view": "the naïve and worldly attitude toward earthly prosperity and adversity, and the heavenly teachings of philosophy."[106] More recently, Catherine S. Cox finds that "excessive Christian rhetoric ends the text without concluding it, forcing the reader to contend with a jarring juxtaposition of the patriarchal security of Christian orthodoxy and the ambiguous uncertainty of the human world."[107] In these readings, Criseyde herself is erased, in spite of the narrator's insistence that there is life after Troy for his heroine, both in the Greek camp and in the narrative tradition. I suggest that, far from becoming irrelevant, the poem's unstable heroine remains central to Troilus's vexed somatics, and not simply as a foil for divine love. Ironically, or perhaps logically, it is the deviant beloved who works the ultimate cure and enables her lover to escape the earthbound cycle of contagion. The withdrawal of her body, sole earthly remedy for his disease, enables the apotheosis of the masculine. In the redemptive logic of *felix culpa*, even as woman destroys, man is reincarnated, whole and without lack. Troilus, sick with desire, is cured through the obliteration of the feminine and through excision of the corruption it entails. Moreover, in the fantasy of healing, that expulsion, or erasure, seems,

---

[104] Walter Clyde Curry, *Chaucer and the Mediaeval Sciences* (New York: Barnes and Noble, 1926/1960), p. 294.

[105] E. T. Donaldson, *Speaking of Chaucer* (London: Athlone Press, 1970), p. 98.

[106] John Steadman, *Disembodied Laughter: Troilus and the Apotheosis Tradition* (Berkeley: University of California Press, 1972), p. 85.

[107] Catherine S. Cox, *Gender and Language in Chaucer* (Gainesville: University Press of Florida, 1997), p. 52.

for a moment, to erase gender itself, replacing the dyad of male and female with that of male savior and saved:

> For he nyl falsen no wight, dar I seye,
> That wol his herte al holly on hym leye.
> And syn he best to love is, and most meke,
> What nedeth feynede loves for to seke? (5.1845–48)

Troilus's apotheosis becomes, then, a kind of retraction in which the penitent hero sheds doubt, flaw, and excess. In the poet's penultimate, formulaic prayer, he asks God to defend us from our enemies, human, diabolical, and perhaps pathogenic as well, "the visible and invisible foon" (5.1866) that haunt both his century and our own, only to compromise that totalizing circumscription with a final invocation of the feminine:

> So make us, Jesus, for thi mercy, digne,
> For love of mayde and moder thyn benigne. (5.1868–1869)

Criseyde's Prudence

Monica E. McAlpine
University of Massachusett Boston

CONCLUDING HIS DISCUSSION of the accomplishments of Prudence in Chaucer's *Tale of Melibee,* and citing those of other women counselors in the *Canterbury Tales,* David Wallace remarks: "The price of such success for women is that their complex and dangerous work of household rhetoric, vital to the health of the body politic, will not be acknowledged *as* political work; assumed to occur in private, it can expect no public acknowledgment." Similarly, speaking about actual prudent women like Joan of Kent, Carolyn Collette has proposed that such women may remain largely invisible either because they do not "perform deeds that translate into records we are used to looking for," or because "we have not looked closely enough into the available records, have not yet asked the right questions." Wallace attempts to rescue one fictional female figure from this kind of neglect by arguing that the Wife of Bath performs valuable political work by means similar to Prudence's, although critical presuppositions have blocked from view this dimension of the Wife's character. I shall argue that Criseyde is one of Chaucer's neglected prudent women, one who enacts a highly significant and especially complex anticipation of the "wifely eloquence" Wallace identifies as "the most distinctive feature of Chaucerian polity" in the *Canterbury Tales.*[1]

Initially, it seemed to me that of the two—the Wife and Criseyde—the case for Criseyde's prudence would be the easier to make, but further

---

[1] David Wallace, *Chaucerian Polity: Absolutist Lineages and Associational Forms in England and Italy* (Stanford: Stanford University Press, 1997), pp. 246, 225, and 82, respectively; Carolyn P. Collette, "Joan of Kent and Noble Women's Roles in Chaucer's World," *ChauR* 33 (1999): 358. In *Chaucer in Context: Society, allegory and gender* (Manchester: Manchester University Press, 1996), pp. 151–63, S. H. Rigby argues that "woman as help-meet," as "respected inferior," was the dominant image of woman in Chaucer's era, not those more extreme images that placed her in the pit or on the pedestal.

reflection on Criseyde's critical history has fully persuaded me of the difficulty of my undertaking. Since prudence was understood, in the medieval period, to be a moral as well as an intellectual virtue, readers who see Criseyde as the embodiment of carnality, as well as all those for whom her ultimate infidelity to Troilus must be *the* defining fact of her career, are unlikely to be willing to associate her with the chief of the cardinal virtues. A special difficulty, however, arises from the association of prudence with considered action. As Aquinas insists, "the value of prudence consists not in merely thinking about a matter, but also in applying itself to do something."[2] In arguing for the prudence of the Wife of Bath, Wallace has at least the advantage that the Wife has long and often enthusiastically been associated with agency. Criseyde, on the other hand, is ever more insistently, and usually pejoratively, identified with passivity.

"Drift," the tendency to be guided by circumstances and by others' choices, was very early attributed to Criseyde by R. K. Root; it was elevated by Charles Muscatine into the instability and ambiguity that characterizes the entire sublunar world, of which Criseyde became virtually a symbol. More recently, Gretchen Mieszkowski has seen Criseyde as the medieval equivalent of Simone de Beauvoir's "Other" objectified by men, an "extreme instance of the passive woman." Derek Pearsall's more subtle reading of Criseyde as an individual consciousness attributes to Criseyde only the will to appear—even to herself—to have no choices, as she protects her self-image from the consequences of decisions she seems not to make. Emphasizing the external constraints Pearsall downplays, Carolyn Dinshaw's powerful reading of Criseyde as a woman traded between men grants Criseyde insight into her situation but no effective way to influence it. Earlier, David Aers's groundbreaking portrayal of the poem's patriarchal society denied Criseyde even this, seeing her as a woman whose choices were dictated by internalized male values. Thus whether critics treat Criseyde as individual or symbol, as morally flawed or as innocently victimized, many tend to associate her with a high degree of regrettable or deplorable passivity—chosen, enforced, or both.[3]

[2] Thomas Aquinas, *Summa Theologiae,* 2a2ae.47.1, Reply 3. "Laus prudentiae non consistit in sola consideratione, sed in applicatione ad opus": ed. and trans. Thomas Gilby, O.P., in the Blackfriars Edition, ed. Gilby and T. C. O'Brien (London: McGraw Hill, 1964–74), vol. 36, pp. 6–7.

[3] R. K. Root, *The Poetry of Chaucer,* rev. ed. (Boston: Houghton Mifflin, 1922), pp. 104–18; Charles Muscatine, *Chaucer and the French Tradition* (Berkeley: University of California Press, 1957), pp. 153–61, esp. p. 154; Gretchen Mieszkowksi, "Chaucer's Much Loved Criseyde," *ChauR* 26 (1991): 109–132, esp. 129; Derek Pearsall, "Criseyde's Choices," *SAC,* Proceedings No. 2 (1986): 17–29; Carolyn Dinshaw, *Chaucer's*

So powerful is this consensus that resistance to it may well seem quixotic. Those several scholars who have clarified the medieval ideal of passive heroism, however, have challenged the assumption that all types of passivity are, or were, objectionable, and have shown that the very distinction between action and inaction was often made in now unfamiliar ways. Drawn from both classical and Christian sources, the ideal of "active suffering," as Jill Mann has termed it, was closely associated with patience, the most frequently discussed aspect of the cardinal virtue of fortitude. This mode of heroism was also especially compatible with the Boethian attribution of a crucial, irreducible degree of freedom, and thus responsibility, to actors even in the most constrained and desperate of straits. The most limited opportunities for initiative—if only in the form of deciding *not* to do something—could be of the highest moral significance, and as we shall see, the exercise of prudence often involved deciding, and counseling others, not to do something.[4]

So far these concepts around "active suffering" have been applied either to male characters (Troilus, Theseus) or to Chaucer's other suffering and prudent women (Constance, Griselda, Melibee's Prudence).[5] I

Sexual Poetics (Madison: University of Wisconsin Press, 1989), pp. 28–64; David Aers, *Chaucer, Langland, and the Creative Imagination* (London: Routledge and Kegan Paul, 1980), pp. 117–42. For David Williams, see note 9 below. A welcome departure from this trend is Carolyn Collette's "Criseyde's Honor: Interiority and Public Identity in Chaucer's Courtly Romance" in *Literary Aspects of Courtly Culture*, eds. Donald Maddox and Sara Sturm Maddox (Cambridge: D. S. Brewer, 1994), pp. 47–55. Studying Criseyde's widowhood, Collette finds "a Criseyde much more complex, knowing, and aware than what I will refer to as the more romanticized versions of Criseyde as lovely, timid, and indecisive" (p. 55).

[4] See Georgia Ronan Crampton, *The Condition of Creatures: Suffering and Action in Chaucer and Spenser* (New Haven: Yale University Press, 1974), pp. 1–44, for the history of the topos *agere et pati,* and for Chaucer's poem, see her "Action and Passion in Chaucer's *Troilus,*" MAE 43 (1974): 22–36. The concept of active suffering is central to Jill Mann's *Geoffrey Chaucer* (Atlantic Highlands, N.J.: Humanities Press, 1991); see esp. pp. 182–85. On patience, see Ralph Hanna III, "Some Commonplaces of Late Medieval Patience Discussions: An Introduction" in *The Triumph of Patience: Medieval and Renaissance Studies,* ed. G. J. Schiffhorst (Orlando: University Presses of Florida, 1978), pp. 65–87. For Boethius, see Monica E. McAlphine, *The Genre of "Troilus and Criseyde"* (Ithaca, N.Y.: Cornell University Press, 1978), pp. 47–85. Katherine L. Lynch's study of voluntarism in the *Parlement of Foweles,* in *Chaucer's Philosophical Visions* (Cambridge: D.S. Brewer, 2000), pp. 83–109, shows Chaucer exploring the human ability to choose within constraints such as those imposed by Nature. The ultimate proof of such ability is the decision not to do something: see esp. pp. 97–105.

[5] For Troilus and Theseus as "feminised" heroes, see Mann, *Geoffrey Chaucer,* pp. 165–82; on Theseus and the "unheroic" image of man in Chaucer, see J. A. Burrow, *Richardian Poetry: Chaucer, Gower, Langland and the "Gawain" Poet* (New Haven: Yale University Press, 1971), pp. 93–129. On Chaucer's women characters, see Mann, esp. pp. 120–25, 128–43, and 146–64, and Wallace, *Chaucerian Polity,* pp. 182–211, 212–46, and 261–293.

propose to place Criseyde in this company as a prudent woman who, suffering with Troilus the diminished freedom of citizenship in a doomed city, rightly rejected the option of violent action on her last night in Troy, instead urging patient acceptance of her exchange. Long before taking Diomede as her new lover, Criseyde had completed her "political work," in Wallace's phrase, both for Troilus and Troy, by prudently counseling a prince to reject a treasonable elopement in time of war.[6] Indeed, important as Chaucer's scenes of female prudence in the *Canterbury Tales* are, he was, arguably, never again to examine the phenomenon as complexly as he did in the *Troilus,* where the extraordinary intricacy of his treatment opens out vistas on Chaucer's own ethical assessment of the three eyes of Prudence.

Prudence, *Trouthe,* and the Future

Criseyde's principal exercise of prudent counsel is, in one sense, clearly marked as such in a passage original with Chaucer which also constitutes one of the earlier appearances of the term "prudence" in English.[7] Criseyde, now a prisoner in the camp of the Greek enemy, recalls her anguished discussion with Troilus on their last night together in Troy. Rehearsing her failure to foresee the full difficulty of her new circumstances, she claims two forms of prudence and laments her lack of a third:

> Prudence, allas, oon of thyne eyen thre
> Me lakked alwey, er that I come here!
> On tyme ypassed wel remembred me,
> And present tyme ek koud ich wel ise,
> But future tyme, er I was in the snare,
> Koude I nat sen; that causeth now my care.[8]

[6] Although mention is made of other aspects of Book 4, Mark Lambert's discussion of the "unheroic" Criseyde does not treat this key decision: see "Troilus, Books I–III: A Criseydan Reading" in Mary Salu, ed., *Essays on "Troilus and Criseyde"* (Cambridge: D. S. Brewer, 1979), pp. 105–25. The same is true of Pearsall's "Criseyde's Choices." There has been a general neglect of this key moment in Criseyde's career.

[7] *Prudence* achieved currency in English only in the fourteenth century, according to J. A. Burrow: see "The Third Eye of Prudence" in *Medieval Futures: Attitudes to the Future in the Middle Ages,* ed. J. A. Burrow and Ian P. Wei (Woodbridge, Suffolk: Boydell Press, 2000), p. 42. Burrow cites but does not discuss the *Troilus.* Chaucer's Prudence stanza is an addition not found in his chief source, Boccaccio's *Il Filostrato.*

[8] Book 5.744–49. All references to Chaucer's work are to Larry D. Benson, gen. ed., *The Riverside Chaucer,* 3d ed. (Boston: Houghton Mifflin, 1987). The text of *Troilus and Criseyde* is edited by Stephen A. Barney; subsequent references will appear in the text.

Critical attention has naturally focused on Criseyde's admitted lack of prudence,[9] and there is not a fully explicit identification, I grant, of the occasion on which she exhibits the first two forms of prudence. Implicitly, though, Chaucer's principal reference is clearly to the very incident whose recollection provokes her reflection: her counseling of Troilus in Book 4. Like the typical actions of all the characters, Criseyde's counsel is undoubtedly driven by a mixture of motivations, including her fear of the violence and public exposure of elopement. Nevertheless, there is ample evidence, I hope to show, that Criseyde prudently remembered the past—the negative example of Paris and Helen—and prudently viewed the present—the significance of that earlier example for herself, for Troilus, and for Troy. Her self-assessment is exact, and worthy of being taken seriously as one key to the intricacies of her ethical history.[10]

No other Chaucerian heroine, however, differentiates distinct aspects of prudence or, subsequent to her enactment of the virtue, accuses herself of a deficiency in it. The interconnections of the scene of counsel in Book 4, which has been called the primary site of *trouthe* in the poem, and the scene of lament in Book 5, whose action has aptly been labelled "Future contingents," are extraordinarily complex.[11] On that last night in Troy, Criseyde commits her *trouthe* to a highly circumstantial plan to return to the city within a specific time frame. Later, in the Greek camp,

[9] The major studies of Criseyde and prudence are by David Burnley, in *Chaucer's Language and the Philosophers' Tradition* (Cambridge: D. S. Brewer, 1979), pp. 59–63, and in "Criseyde's Heart and the Weakness of Women: An Essay in Lexical Interpretation," *SN* 54 (1982): 25–38. In the first, Burnley attributes to Criseyde imprudent haste, as seen in her decision to accept Troilus as her lover. In the second study, citing Albertus Magnus, Burnley finds Criseyde capable only of false prudence or *astutia*, as a consequence of her status as woman. In both studies, Burnley ignores the choices made in Book 4; but if Criseyde had been astute, she would presumably have chosen the elopement Troilus proposed. In *"Distentio, Intentio, Attentio:* Intentionality and Chaucer's Third Eye," *Florilegium* 15 (1998): 37–60, David Williams invokes an Augustinian formulation of time which the pagan Criseyde fails to grasp. Largely ignoring Book 4, Williams insists, like other critics, on Criseyde's passivity, her ethical emptiness: she lacks "inner substance," "an inner life"; she has "no sense of self" (p. 52).

[10] Susan Schibanoff is unusual in associating the passage with Paris and Helen; she suggests that the audience views the story with Prudence's three eyes—looking back to Paris and Helen and forward to the sorrows of Troilus and Criseyde even as we experience the present of the lovers' love. See "Prudence and Artificial Memory in Chaucer's *Troilus,"* *ELH* 42 (1975): 513. Crampton, "Action and Passion in Chaucer's *Troilus,"* finds "Criseyde's own self-analysis [in this passage] . . . as competent as any of her by others" (p. 35).

[11] Barry Windeatt, *Oxford Guides to Chaucer: Troilus and Criseyde* (Oxford: Clarendon Press, 1992), p. 249, and Henry Ansgar Kelly, *Chaucerian Tragedy* (Cambridge: D. S. Brewer, 1997), pp. 107–17, respectively.

she recognizes what the third eye of Prudence, focused on the future, might have shown her—the near impossibility of carrying out the plan—and she appears to regret the counsel she gave Troilus:

> Allas, I ne hadde trowed on youre loore
> And went with yow, as ye me redde er this!
> Than hadde I now nat siked half so soore.
> Who myghte han seyd that I hadde don amys
> To stele awey with swich oon as he ys? (5.736–40)

That is, Criseyde now sees her counsel, entangled as it became in a promise and a hope to return, as in some sense *im*prudent.

Yet, as I shall show, the understanding of *trouthe* in fourteenth-century England, as recovered by Richard Firth Green, tends to confirm the prudence of Criseyde's counsel against elopement.[12] Was she, then, both prudent and imprudent? Could prudence, the virtue without which, it was famously said,[13] no other virtue was possible, be at odds with *trouthe*? Clearly, a full analysis of Criseyde's enactment of prudence requires an ethical examination both of her promise to return to Troy and of the third eye of Prudence itself, anticipation of the future. Her failure to keep her promise has for too long obscured the significance of her prudent counsel, and the attention she calls to the third eye of Prudence offers an invitation not yet fully accepted by critics to explore the several connections between knowledge of the future and ethical choice and ethical judgment in Chaucer's poem.

The very collocation of the words "prudence" and "future" is an ex-

[12] In my argument *trouthe* has the senses "loyalty" and "integrity." As Richard Firth Green has shown, in *A Crisis of Truth: Literature and Law in Ricardian England* (Philadelphia: University of Pennsylvania Press, 1999), pp. 8–31, such ethical senses of the term, now rare, were predominant in the fourteenth century. Legal senses were the oldest; theological senses recent; and intellectual senses very new, in the fourteenth century. Green does not imply, nor do I, that newer senses eliminated older ones. For another discussion of *trouthe* in Chaucer's post-feudal society, see Paul Strohm, *Social Chaucer* (Cambridge: Harvard University Press, 1989), pp. 102–9.

[13] Aristotle, *Nichomachean Ethics*, Book 6, Chap. 13. "Now true virtue cannot exist without prudence any more than prudence without virtue." The translation is J. A. K. Thomson's in *The Ethics of Aristotle* (London: Allen & Unwin, 1953), p. 168. For Aquinas, see *Summa Theologiae*, 1a2ae, Ques.58, art. 4 and 5, ed. and trans W. D. Hughes, in the Blackfriars edition (see note 2), vol. 23, pp. 72–79. In "Third Eye" Burrow observes: "The modern word 'prudence' is a chilly term for a much shrunken concept . . . for Chaucer and his age [it] represented a still rich and living complex of moral ideas" (pp. 45–46). See also Josef Pieper, *Prudence* (London: Faber and Faber, 1959), esp. pp. 10–11.

traordinary aspect of this key passage; for just as "prudence" was seemingly a relatively new word in English, "future" was apparently a neologism in English introduced by Chaucer himself.[14] His linguistic adventuresomeness was matched by a broad interest in varied aspects of time and the future. Studies of his knowledge of traditional ways of telling time, of his acquaintance with the mechanical clock—a new invention in the fourteenth century—of his *chronographiae,* or time-telling passages, and of his astrological investigations, find him to be learned and sophisticated.[15] These interests may well have been shaped in part by the many-sided contemporary philosophical controversies over future contingents, human free will, and God's power and foreknowledge. As Gordon Leff has said of the late fourteenth century, "for the first time the future came to constitute a real problem."[16] Moreover, philosophical controversies once limited to the universities were now entertained by newly literate lay audiences, and as Katherine Lynch has freshly and convincingly argued, Chaucer was not only a member of his audience but also a philosophical poet who wrote for it.[17]

[14] Windeatt, *Oxford Guides,* p. 255, remarks that "such innovative diction points to how *Troilus* is concerned to explore human ways of perceiving the past and future in relation to the present." On Chaucer's very first use of "future" in his *Boece,* see below, p. 220. Chaucer's priority in using "future" has not been challenged, although Christopher Cannon, in "The Myth of Origin and the Making of Chaucer's English," *Speculum* 71(1996): 646–75, has documented the tendencies of the *OED* and *MED* to give Chaucer undue credit for earliest use of words.

[15] Derek Brewer, "Arithmetic and the Mentality of Chaucer" in *Literature in Fourteenth-Century England,* eds. Piero Boitani and Anna Torti (Cambridge: D. S. Brewer, 1983), pp. 155–64; Linne R. Mooney, "The Cock and the Clock: Telling Time in Chaucer's Day," *SAC* 15 (1993): 91–109; Peter Travis, "Chaucer's *Chronographiae,* the Confounded Reader, and Fourteenth-Century Measurements of Time," *Disputatio* 2 (1997): 1–34. J. D. North, in *Chaucer's Universe* (Oxford: Clarendon Press, 1988), p. ix, characterizes the poet as a "meticulous calculator" who may well have had a serious interest in judicial astrology. North assigns little weight (pp. 229–30) to what has often been thought Chaucer's rejection of judicial astrology as "rytes of payens" (*Astrolabe* 2.4.57–60). For T. A. Shippey on Chaucer and number, see note 70.

[16] Gordon Leff, *Medieval Thought* (Harmondsworth: Penguin, 1958), p. 275. The problem of future contingents dominates his discussion of "The Fourteenth Century: Scepticism versus Authority," pp. 262–303. See also Calvin Normore, "Future Contingents" in *The Cambridge History of Later Medieval Philosophy: From the Rediscovery of Aristotle to the Disintegration of Scholasticism, 1100–1600,* eds. Norman Kretzmann, Anthony Kenny and Jan Pinborg (Cambridge: Cambridge University Press, 1982), pp. 358–91.

[17] See Janet Coleman, *Piers Plowman and the Moderni* (Rome: Edizioni di storia e letteratura, 1981), pp. 147–70, and *Medieval Readers and Writers, 1350–1400* (London: Hutchison, 1981), pp. 232–80; William Courtenay, *Schools and Scholars in Fourteenth-Century England* (Princeton: Princeton University Press, 1987), pp. 356–80; and Ann W. Astell, *Chaucer and the Universe of Learning* (Ithaca: Cornell University Press, 1996), esp. pp. 3–11 and 32–60. Courtenay cautions against exaggerating the influence of the more speculative philosophical questions on secular literature, finding the chief influence

In the *Troilus,* as Windeatt observes, Chaucer "makes both the craving and the feasibility of . . . prediction part of the thematic preoccupation . . . with the boundaries of human knowledge and freedom."[18] The Prudence stanza dramatizes that craving in its explicit lament over a failure of foresight, and reflects on the boundaries of freedom by suggesting intricate relations between knowledge or ignorance of the future and *trouthe.* The linkage of the Prudence stanza with its referenced passages in Book 4 produces a multifaceted analysis of prudence that opens the way to some tentative formulations about the poet's own attitudes toward knowledge of the future. In what follows, I shall argue that Criseyde's deficiency in anticipating the future, while personally disastrous for her, is not ethically significant, and that in ethical matters, at least, Chaucer, an innovative student of the future within a "fundamentally memorial" culture, ultimately privileged the first two eyes of Prudence over the third.[19]

Prudence

The importance of prudence to the crises in which Criseyde finds herself in Books 4 and 5 is signaled by the variety of ways in which Chaucer exploited the fit between the virtue's history and Criseyde and her circumstances.[20] First, Criseyde's reflection on prudence should be added

---

to be mainly ethical and concerned with "the conflicts and ambiguities that life presented to the average Christian" (p. 380). In *Chaucer's Philosophical Visions* (see note 3), Lynch insists that Chaucer's interest extended to speculative philosophy as well (pp. 1–30). She revives arguments for Chaucer's having university education, but also sees the poet as "a formidable autodidact" (p. 20) not dependent on such exposure for his philosophical knowledge.

[18] Windeatt, *Oxford Guides,* p. 259.

[19] The phrase is Mary Carruthers's in *The Book of Memory: A Study of Memory in Medieval Culture* (Cambridge: Cambridge University Press, 1990), p. 8. In her Appendix B, Carruthers translates Tractatus 4, Quaestio 2, Article 2 of Albertus Magnus's *De Bono,* which reads in part: "Among all those things which point towards *ethical* wisdom, the most necessary is trained memory, because from past events we are guided in the present and the future, and not from the converse" (p. 275; emphasis mine). At the same time, medieval people, of course, attempted to use knowledge of the future to guide effective actions of various kinds in the present. Recent studies include Burrow and Wei, *Medieval Futures* (see note 5), and Chris Humphrey and W. M. Ormrod, eds., *Time in the Medieval World* (York: York Medieval Press, 2001). I. F. Clarke traces changes in Western mentality concerning the future in *The Pattern of Expectation, 1644–2001* (New York: Basic Books, 1979).

[20] In this section, I select those aspects of prudence I think most relevant to the *Troilus* and ignore others. I do not believe this poem invites concern, for example, with the relation of the natural, cardinal virtues to the supernatural virtues, a relation at the

to the list of Chaucer's classicizing elements in the *Troilus*. The virtue's classical origin was well known and frequently invoked long after prudence and its three companion "cardinal" virtues—justice, fortitude and temperance—had been integrated with Christian virtues and knowledge of them disseminated to both preachers and lay people.[21] Designated a "natural" virtue, prudence could be practiced, though in an imperfect form, by good pagans without the aid of grace, and the example of good pagans was sometimes cited as an inspiration or a rebuke to Christians.[22] A reference to prudence, then, linked Chaucer's Christian audience to his pagan heroine ethically, as a virtue to which they commonly aspired, even as it recalled the distance between them theologically.

Also, prudence was often understood to be essentially a form of knowledge. Aristotle classified it as an intellectual virtue, and Aquinas considered it both an intellectual and a moral virtue.[23] More specifically, prudence was understood as the pre-eminent form of *practical* knowledge. Aquinas distinguishes it from wisdom, science, and art, all of

---

center of David Aers's study of another Chaucerian work: "Chaucer's *Tale of Melibee: Whose Virtues?*" in *Medieval Literature and Historical Inquiry: Essays in Honour of Derek Pearsall,* ed. David Aers (Cambridge: D. S. Brewer, 2000), pp. 69–81.

[21] Rosemond Tuve, in "Notes on the Virtues and Vices," Part 1, *Journal of the Warburg and Courtauld Institutes* 26 (1963): 267, identifies Aristotle's *Nichomachean Ethics* (Book 6), Cicero's *De Officiis* (1.13–19) and *De Inventione* (2.53), Macrobius's *Commentary on the Dream of Scipio,* and the "Pseudo-Seneca," Martin of Braga's *Formulae vitae honestae,* as the four "streams" conveying knowledge of the classical virtues to later times. For the Christianization of the cardinal virtues, see Francis A. Yates, *The Art of Memory* (Chicago: University of Chicago Press, 1966), pp. 57–81; Alexander Murray, *Reason and Society in the Middle Ages* (Oxford: Clarendon Press, 1985), pp. 132–37; and Carruthers, *Book of Memory,* pp. 64–71. For an overview of works of instruction, see Richard Neuhauser, *The Treatise on Vices and Virtues in Latin and the Vernaculars (pre-1800 Works)* (Turnholt: Brepols, 1993), esp. Chap. 2 for a discussion of the development of this genre, pp. 127–35 on the influence of the Fourth Lateran Council of 1215, and pp. 142–50 on English vernacular works.

[22] "A God, how we schulde be a-ferd, whan þei þat were heþen and wiþ-out any lawe y-write, þat wisten no þing of þe verray grace of God ne of þe Holi Gost, and ȝit clombe þei vp to þe hil of parfiȝtnesse of lif bi strengþe of here owne vertue . . . & we þat ben cristene and hadde þe grace and þe bileue veraliche and connen þe comaundementes of God and han þe grace of þe Holi Gost . . . we lyuen as swyn here byneþe in þis grottes of þis world!": *Book of Vices and Virtues,* ed. W. N. Frances, *EETS,* o.s. 217 (London: Oxford University Press, 1942), p. 124. This work is a fourteenth-century translation of the *Somme le Roi* of Lorens de'Orléans. Tuve, "Notes," pp. 265 and 280, refers to similar discussions in John of Wales' *Breviloquium de virtutibus* and in Jehan Mansel's *Fleur des histoires.* Philippe Delhaye cites Alain de Lille on the practice of the natural virtues by pagans: "La vertu et les vertus dans les oeuvres d'Alain de Lille," *Cahiers de civilisation médiéval* 6 (1963): 19–21.

[23] *Summa Theologiae,* 1a2ae, Ques. 56, art 2 and 3 and Ques. 58, art 3, ed. Hughes, in the Blackfriars edition, vol. 23, pp. 58–61 and 83–85.

which involve elements of the theoretical or speculative, insisting on prudence's confinement to the realm of practical reason; following Aristotle, he associates prudence with a variety of spheres of practical activity, including the political.[24] Chaucer may well have matched prudence to the character as well as the pagan status of his heroine, confirming the often pragmatic outlook of Criseyde that has been so widely recognized, and somewhat variously interpreted, by critics.[25]

The cardinal virtues were also closely associated with rulers from the time of Cicero's *De Officiis* and Macrobius's *Commentary*.[26] Treatises on the cardinal virtues were often bound with advice-to-rulers literature; John of Wales's *Breviloquium* combined a treatment of the cardinal virtues with examples drawn from history and with advice to princes.[27] The Middle English *Gouernaunce of Prynces or Pryvete of Pryveteis* (1422) devotes twenty-two chapters to the cardinal virtues, illustrated by "olde stories."[28] Aquinas specifies that prudence concerns "the common good of the people," not just the individual's private good; while emphasizing "kingly prudence," he insists that there is a prudence appropriate to subjects, too, and observes that "to furnish good advice is an office of prudence."[29] Prudence was inarguably an appropriate virtue to invoke

[24] *Summa Theologiae,* 2a2ae, Ques. 47, art. 2 and Ques. 50, art. 1–4, ed. Gilby, in the Blackfriars edition, vol. 36, pp. 8–11 and 82–93. Both Burnley, in *Chaucer's Language* (see note 9) and Burrow, in "Third Eye" (see note 7), emphasize the varied practical fields to which prudence was related.

[25] In one critical tradition, Criseyde's pragmatism is seen as opposed to *trouthe* and spirituality, and implicitly at least as virtually identical with *astutia,* the false form of prudence. See, for example, Donald Rowe, *O Love, O Charite! Contraries Harmonized in Chaucer's "Troilus"* (Carbondale: Southern Illinois University Press, 1976), esp. pp. 78–82; and Winthrop Wetherbee, *Chaucer and the Poets: An Essay on Troilus and Criseyde* (Ithaca, N.Y.: Cornell University Press, 1984), pp. 179–204. Some dissenters from this tradition view Criseyde's pragmatism neutrally, as an aspect of a personality type complementary to Troilus's different type, or even approvingly: see Monica McAlpine, *Genre,* pp. 193–94; Stephen Knight, *Geoffrey Chaucer* (Oxford: Blackwell, 1986), esp. pp. 47 and 57; and Alfred J. Frantzen, *Troilus and Criseyde: The Poem and the Frame* (New York: Twayne, 1993), esp. pp. 107–11.

[26] Neuhauser, *The Treatise on Vices and Virtues,* pp. 110–11, notes that Martin of Braga's *Formula,* "the first Latin representative of the genre dealing with the cardinal virtues," was written for the Suevic king Miro and his court. William O. Harris offers a convenient summary in *Skelton's Magnyfycence and the Cardinal Virtue Tradition* (Chapel Hill: University of North Carolina Press, 1965), pp. 145–56.

[27] Tuve, "Notes," p. 294; Newhauser, *Treatise,* pp. 131–33.

[28] This work is one of many versions of the *Secreta Secretorum,* an eighth-century work supposedly containing Aristotle's advice to Alexander. See *Three Prose Versions of the Secreta Secretorum,* ed. Robert Steele, *EETS,* o.s. 74 (London: Kegan Paul, 1898), 145–95.

[29] *Summa Theologiae,* 2a2ae, Ques. 47, art. 12 and Ques. 49, art. 5, reply, ed. Gilby, in the Blackfriars edition, vol. 36, pp. 38–41 and 72–73. Lorenzetti's fresco on Good

in a circumstance—Criseyde's proposed exchange—that concerned the integrity of a prince and the survival of a kingdom.

Largely because of the association with rulers and their counselors, prudence was sometimes associated primarily with men. Carolyn Collette suggests, however, that by the late fourteenth century a new "sociolect" found in French texts had refashioned prudence as "a form of female aristocratic virtue." Women were to act as "agents of restraint" (p. 428), practicing self-effacement while directing men away from violence and folly through indirection, correction, and patience. Both Collette and Paul Strohm have also analyzed such behavior in historical figures—Joan of Kent and the queens Philippa and Anne, respectively.[30] For Chaucer's works, David Wallace provides a detailed paradigm for the poet's staging of female counsel: female rhetoricians, relying in part on their bodily relationships to the threatening male and acting in private spaces, deploy speech and silence, both carefully timed, to redirect the violent desires of the suffering male while repressing their own pain.[31] As we shall see, on her last night with Troilus, Criseyde displays many of the characteristics these scholars associate with a female-gendered prudence.

Finally, the relations of prudence to time and specifically to the future have a long history. The formula in Cicero's *De Inventione* from which Chaucer's passage derives centers on time,[32] and etymologically, as

---

Government in the Palazzo Publico at Siena (1337–40) shows the Common Good surrounded by the three supernatural and the four natural or cardinal virtues. *Prudentia* points to an inscription that identifies her concern with past, present, and future. See Tuve, "Notes," pp. 290–95; and Yates, *Art of Memory,* p. 92 and plate 2 (facing p. 81).

[30] Carolyn Collette, "Heeding the Counsel of Prudence: A Context for the *Melibee,"* *ChauR* 29 (1995): 416–33; Paul Strohm, "Queens as Intercessors" in *Hochon's Arrow: The Social Imagination of Fourteenth-Century Texts* (Princeton: Princeton University Press, 1992), pp. 95–119. In "Joan of Kent" (see n. 1) Collette contends that noble women's roles were more powerful than Strohm allows. On Queen Philippa, see further Monica E. McAlpine, "The Burghers of Calais: Chapters in a History" in *Retelling Tales: Essays in Honor of Russell Peck,* eds. Thomas Hahn and Alan Lupack (Cambridge, U.K., and Rochester, N.Y.: D. S. Brewer, 1997), pp. 231–58.

[31] Wallace, *Chaucerian Polity,* pp. 223–46.

[32] Cicero, *De Inventione,* 2.53: "Partes eius: memoria, intellegentia, providentia. Memoria est per quam animus repetit illa quae fuerunt; intellegentia, per quam ea perspicit quae sunt; providentia, per quam futurum aliquid videtur ante quan factum est." [Its parts are memory, intelligence, and foresight. Memory is the faculty by which the mind recalls what has happened. Intelligence is the faculty by which it ascertains what is. Foresight is the faculty by which it is seen that something is going to occur before it occurs.] The Latin text and English translation are taken from the Loeb Classical Edition, ed. and trans. H. M. Hubbell (Cambridge: Harvard University Press, 1949), pp. 326–27.

Aquinas recognized, the word "prudence" is derived from *providentia,* with the sense "foreseeing."[33] Both Aquinas and Boccaccio privileged *providentia* over the other temporal aspects of prudence.[34] Iconographical traditions, too, expressed Prudence's temporal dimensions and specifically her link with the future. Although the triciput Prudence as in Titian's "Allegory of Prudence" is well known,[35] no less significant are works showing Prudence with a single head holding a triple mirror, or with two heads and a mirror, the latter interpreted as the third "face" of Prudence, its aspect as *providentia.*[36] The mirror images cited here

[33] *Summa Theologiae,* 2a2ae, Quaes. 49, art. 6, ed. and trans. Gilby, in the Blackfriars edition, vol. 36, pp. 76–77. "Et ideo nomen ipsius prudentiae sumitur a providentia sicut a principaliori sua parte": "And so prudence takes its very name from providence, that being its main feature." In "Third Eye," pp. 42–47, Burrow cites the overlapping significances of *prudence* and *providentia* and related terms in several fourteenth-and-fifteenth-century English and Scottish works. Before the Reformation, "providence" referred principally to human, not divine, agency: see Peggy Knapp, *Time-Bound Words: Semantic and Social Economies from Chaucer's England to Shakespeare's* (London: Macmillan Press; New York: St. Martin's Press, 2000), pp. 113–29.

[34] *Summa Theologiae,* 2a2ae, Ques. 49, art. 6, ad 1. "Hoc providentia est principalior inter omnes partes prudentiae; quia omnia alia quae requiruntur ad prudentiam, ad hoc necessaria sunt ut aliquid recte ordinetur in finem"; "Prevision is principal among the components of prudence, for the others are necessary in order that a deed be rightly directed to the end": ed. and trans. Gilby, in the Blackfriars edition, vol. 36, pp. 76–77. For Boccacio, *Il Decameron,* see the speech of Dioneo at the end of Day 10. "Il senno de mortali non consiste solamente nell 'avere a memoria le cose preterite o conoscere le presenti, ma per l'una e per l'altra di queste sapere antiveder le future e da' solenni uomini senno grandissimo reputato": *Il Decameron,* ed. Cesare Segre, fourth edition (Milan: Mursia, 1974), p. 669. "The understanding of mortals consists not only in having in memory things past and taking cognizance of things present; but in knowing, by means of the one and the other of these, to forecast things future is reputed by men of mark to consist the greatest wisdom": from the John Payne translation revised and annotated by Charles S. Singleton (Berkeley: University of California Press, 1982), pp. 791–92.

[35] Erwin Panofsky, "Titian's *Allegory of Prudence*: A Postscript," in *Meaning in the Visual Arts* (Chicago: University of Chicago Press, 1982; originally published 1955), pp. 146–68, and see Figure 28. Panofsky cites a three-headed Prudence in a relief attributed to the school of Rossellino, and another in a niello in the pavement of Siena Cathedral. A cartoon for the niello, viewed in the Museum of the Duomo, shows the triple-headed Prudence holding a triple mirror.

[36] Giotto's triple-faced Prudence in the Arena frescoes in Padua (1306) is probably the earliest of these works, which include a fresco by Perugino in the Collegio del Cambio in Perugia; images by Pisano adorning the Campanile of the Duomo in Florence and a door to the Baptistry; a painting by Raphael in the Stanza della Segnatura in the Vatican; and a ceiling tondo by Lucca della Robbia at San Miniato. Pisano's image for the Campanile is reproduced by Raimond Van Marle in *Iconographie de L'art Profane au Moyen-Age et a la Renaissance* (New York: Hacker Art Books, 1971), Figure 24, and a second relief by della Robbia is reproduced by Heinrich Swarz in "The Mirror in Art," *The Art Quarterly* 15 (1952), Figure 5. For the significance of the mirror, see Herbert Grabes, *The Mutable Glass: Mirror Images in Titles and Texts of the Middle Ages and English*

have an Italian provenance, as do the three eyes of Chaucer's image; examples have been found in other parts of Europe as well, however.[37] In England, Lydgate shows himself familiar with Prudence's mirror of providence.[38] This iconographical tradition, bolstering the evidence of etymology and authoritative texts, suggests that Prudence's strong association with the future—an obvious but critically neglected fact[39]— qualified the virtue as one of several sites for Chaucer's exploration of the vexed issue of knowledge of the future in the *Troilus.*

The multiple threads connecting prudence to Criseyde and her circumstances, and to broader themes in the *Troilus,* indicate that Chaucer's invocation of the virtue constitutes far more than a decoration for a poignant speech of regret. There can be little doubt that Chaucer thoughtfully assigned a reflection on prudence to a pagan woman with a pragmatic turn of mind who is called upon to advise a prince in urgent personal and political circumstances that required difficult projections

---

Renaissance, trans. Gordon Collier (Cambridge: Cambridge University Press, 1973; rpt. 1982), pp. 158–60.

[37] The rare image that Chaucer uses, three eyes rather than three heads, is probably borrowed directly or indirectly from Dante's *Purgatorio,* Canto 29, 130–33: see Lloyd Matthews, "Chaucer's Personification of Prudence in *Troilus* (V.743–749): Sources in the Visual Arts and Manuscript Scholia," *ELN* 13 (1976): 249–55; and *"Troilus and Criseyde,* V.743–749: Another Possible Source," *NM* 82 (1981): 211–13. A Spanish poem of 1396 describes a two-headed Prudence holding a mirror: see Archer Woodford, "Mediaeval Iconography of the Virtues: A Poetic Portraiture," *Speculum* 28 (1953): 521–24. Also outside of Italy a Prudence with two faces and a mirror appears on the tomb of Don Garcia Osorio from the chapel of Sangre de Cristo in Ocaña, a fifteenth-century work housed in the Worcester Art Museum in Massachusetts, and on the double tomb (1502–07) of Frances II, Duke of Brittany, and his second wife, Marguerite de Foix, from the Cathedral of St. Pierre, Nantes, and now at the Carnegie Museum in Pittsburgh.

[38] John Lydgate, "A Mumming in London," line 143: "hyr myrrour, called provydence"; see *The Minor Poems of John Lydgate,* eds. H. N. MacCracken and M. Sherwood, (London: Oxford University Press, 1934), vol. 2, p. 686. For the importance of prudence in Lydgate's works, see C. David Benson, "Prudence, Othea, and Lydgate's Death of Hector," *American Benedictine Review* 26 (1975): 115–23, and James Simpson, " 'Dysemal daies and Fatal houres': Lydgate's *Destruction of Thebes* and Chaucer's *Knight's Tale"* in *The Long Fifteenth Century: Essays for Douglas Gray,* eds. Helen Cooper and Sally Mapstone (Oxford: Clarendon, 1997), pp. 15–35.

[39] Burnley, in *Chaucer's Language* and "Criseyde's Heart" (see note 9), does not explore prudence's connection with the future, and there has been very little discussion of Chaucer and the future. For the *Troilus,* see Windeatt, *Oxford Guides,* pp. 255–59, and Sylvia Federico, "Chaucer's Utopian Troy Book: Alternatives to Historiography in Troilus and Criseyde," *Exemplaria* 11(1999): 79–106. Federico argues that in the *Troilus,* a utopian vision of an alternative future is ultimately overtaken by a predestined history. In " 'What Man Artow?': Authorial Self-Definition in *The Tale of Sir Thopas and The Tale of Melibee,"* *SAC* 11 (1989): 117–75, rpt. in his *Chaucer and the Subject of History* (Madison: University of Wisconsin Press, 1991), Lee Patterson suggests that the absent child, Sophia, may serve as a figure of the future in the *Tale of Melibee.*

about future outcomes. My claims for the importance of the Prudence stanza in Book 5 must rest, though, in the first instance, on a convincing analysis of Criseyde's final private meeting with Troilus in Book 4 as a scene of prudential female counsel.

Prudence and *Trouthe*

The political crisis of Book 4 and Criseyde's response to it anticipate in detail the features Wallace has identified as characteristic of Chaucer's depictions of female prudence in later works. Male violence or the threat of it is the catalyst, and a woman's body is placed in jeopardy to ward it off.[40] The Trojans have just lost a costly battle, and they hope that Criseyde's exchange for Antenor will prevent a greater disaster. And, as Troilus recognizes, elopement would be another kind of "violence" (4.561–62). Further, as in the *Tale of Melibee,* a large and diverse group of people are shown to give faulty counsel (Wallace, p. 235). A majority of the Trojan parliament, ignoring Hector's principled objection (4.179–82) and egged on by the people acting under a "cloude of errour" (4.183–201), agrees to the exchange. The involuntary instrument of Trojan war policy, Criseyde voluntarily places herself in danger to prevent Troilus's violence. Her submission to the exchange is ethically of a different nature than the parlement's acceptance of the Greek proposal.

The meeting of the lovers exhibits several additional features of Wallace's paradigm. Meeting at night in Pandarus' house, they occupy a private space and exhibit their intimate relationship (Wallace, pp. 234–35). They retire to bed to confer, and later have intercourse. The woman represses the expression of her own pain as fully as possible (Wallace, pp. 231–32). Although Criseyde initially weeps and involuntarily swoons, the shock of Troilus's proposed suicide enables her to return to her first purpose of assuaging his pain.[41] Like Melibee's spouse (Wallace, pp. 232–34), Criseyde is attuned to the present moment, and identifies the appropriate times for addressing the crisis (4.1242–46, 1254–60).

[40] Wallace, *Chaucerian Polity,* p. 230. Additional references appear in my text.
[41] Jennifer Campbell, in "Figuring Criseyde's 'Entente': Authority, Narrative, and Chaucer's use of History," *ChauR* 27 (1993): 243–58, argues that Criseyde's stance is dictated by Pandarus's advice (4.876–938) and is "not her own" (p. 353). My reading is that the involuntary swoon is a marker that indicates the authenticity of her subsequent behavior even if it superficially conforms to Pandarus's earlier advice. See Mann, *Geoffrey Chaucer,* pp. 104–7, on the limitations of Pandarus's agency and especially its relation to Troilus's swoon in Book 3.

Like Melibee (Wallace, pp. 240–41, 243–44), Troilus does not make steady moral progress, but reverts to his "violent" purpose, urging elopement a second time after seeming to accept the opposing counsel Criseyde had offered with urgent appeals to his honor and hers (4.1600–03; 1555–89). And like Prudence, Criseyde replies with vehemence (4.1604–05), in the process offering Troilus an interpretation of himself (4.1667–80) as Prudence did with Melibee. Finally, just as Prudence opposed Melibee's "lykyng" and "wylle" with wisdom (Wallace, pp. 235–36), so Criseyde rejects the "hete" and "delit" which Troilus himself has usually "bridlede" with "resoun" (4.1583, 1678).

Suggestive as these paradigmatic features are, however, the argument for Criseyde's prudence requires that her position against elopement be shown to be the ethically necessary one. Here the story of Paris and Helen looms over the crisis, the linchpin that links the love of Troilus and Criseyde to the fate of Troy. What Baswell and Taylor call "the dialectic of private desire and public imperative," and the "incalculable aftermath in history" when the former prevails are among Chaucer's themes, as they always have been in stories of Troy.[42] Chaucer's audience was well prepared, by romance, history, iconography, and mythography, to link Troilus and Criseyde with Paris and Helen.[43] The connection is made explicit by both Troilus and Pandarus. " 'Artow in Troie,' " Pandarus asks, " 'and hast non hardyment / To take a womman which that loveth the . . . . Thenk ek how Paris hath, that is thi brother, / A love; and whi shaltow nat have another?' " (4.533–34, 608–09). Troilus is equally direct in rejecting this advice: ". . . syn thow woost this town hath al this werre / For ravysshyng of wommen so by myght, / It sholde nought be suffred me to erre, / As it stant now, ne don so gret unright" (4.547–50). Criseyde is almost equally explicit in warning Troilus of the dangers to his honor: ". . . awey thus for to go / And leten alle youre frendes, God forbede / For any womman that ye sholden so, / And namely syn Troie hath now swich nede / Of help" (4.1555–59). Everyone would say "That love ne drof yow naught to don this dede, / But lust voluptuous and coward drede" (4.1572–73). In Book 4 we wait to see

[42] Christopher Baswell and Paul Beekman Taylor, "The Faire Queene Eleyne in Chaucer's *Troilus*," *Speculum* 63 (1988): 293–311.

[43] In addition to Baswell and Taylor, see Patricia Orr, "Pallas Athena and the Threefold Choice in Chaucer's *Troilus and Criseyde*," in *The Mythographic Art: Classical Fable and the Rise of the Vernacular in Early France and England,* ed. Jane Chance (Gainesville: University of Florida Press, 1990), pp. 159–76.

whether the "ravyshyng" of a woman, the original sin in Chaucer's tale, will be repeated.[44] It is not repeated; Criseyde neither contributes to making Troilus another Paris, in Pandarus's devastating phrase, nor does she choose Helen's path for herself.[45] She rejects what would have been the gravest betrayal of Troilus, and her own later infidelity is a matter of private sorrow, not public catastrophe.[46]

A unity of ethical outlook is not on overt display in the bedroom scene of Book 4, however, and could not be if Criseyde is to act the role of prudent counselor to a male tempted to violent folly. An astonishing aspect of the scene is that "true Troilus" argues against accepting the exchange and for flight. Could he ever have been an exemplum of *trouthe* if he had deserted Troy for Criseyde, even if he had loved her faithfully for the rest of his life? Despite the wishes of many modern readers, the answer has to be "no." Criseyde is right (4.1555–75): his name would have been destroyed forever. If we celebrate his ultimate fidelity to Criseyde (5.1695–1701) even in the midst of her final infidelity to him, we are able to do so partly because we can still assume his loyalty to Troy: he is no Calkas, no Antenor—and no Paris.

How has Troilus escaped criticism, then, for urging elopement? Partly, the shock and pain of the crisis earns sympathy for at least the momentary entertainment of almost any mode of response. More important, though, is Chaucer's handling of Troilus's dual role as courtly lover and Trojan prince. The lovers' meeting still occupies that private space in which the claims of love are expected to be paramount: if Troilus seems a failed lover to some because he does not carry Criseyde away, how much more would he seem to have failed as love's servant if he had urged her to accept her going to the Greek camp. On the other hand, we know that he has already soberly rejected the option of flight because of what he judges to be his obligation to the "townes gode" (4.547–53). At the same time, he is not in any simple sense hypocritical since he

---

[44] Rowe, *O Love, O Charite* (see note 26), pp. 76–77.

[45] This theme is also hinted at in both of the passages where Troilus and Criseyde refer to stealing away. It is folly, Troilus says, recommending elopement, "whan man may chese, / For accident his substaunce ay to lese" (4.1504–05). That he might lose his "substaunce," understood as his honor, by eloping is implied again when Criseyde asks, in one of Chaucer's typically multivalent rhetorical questions, "Who myghte han seyd that I hadde don amys / To stele awey with swich oon as he ys?" (5.739–40). If they had stolen away, Troilus would not have remained "as he ys."

[46] I agree with Patterson, *Subject of History,* that "the poem will not allow us to say that the failed love of Troilus and Criseyde causes the fall of Troy nor that the fall of Troy causes the failure of the love affair" (p. 152).

defers to his lady's decision, as a lover should.[47] Can we be sure he wouldn't have abandoned Troy, then, if Criseyde had asked it? No, I think not, but what we can be sure of is that "true Troilus" was very fortunate in his choice of a lady: at this moment of moral crisis for him, she plays her role perfectly. Like the prudent women described by Wallace and Collette, she correctly interprets his public obligations, and shows the love itself to have been more than a game and more than sensuality by connecting it, in a moving speech (4.1667–87), to the very *trouthe* that must characterize what the people call a "holder up of Troye" (2.644).

In the private world of courtly love, however, the lady, once having accepted the risk of love itself, usually plays her role as educator and judge without peculiar risk to her own happiness and safety. In the public crisis of the exchange, Criseyde is peculiarly at risk; as Pandarus says, there was never "ruyne / Straunger than this" (4.387–88). And still she is the good counselor, advising a prince without regard to her own interests, at least as they concern physical safety, continued enjoyment of his love—everything indeed except her own honor (4.1576–82), which here, as elsewhere, she excepts from her service to others.[48] Derek Pearsall has rightly identified the ability to accept the involuntary as voluntary as one of the tests of *trouthe,* but he finds Criseyde incapable of such acceptance.[49] I submit that there is no better or comparable instance in the poem of making the involuntary voluntary than Criseyde's submission to the exchange, her unresisting departure to the camp of the feared Greek enemy, against so many interests of her own, and in the service of Troilus's *trouthe* and her own honor.

But why should the lovers' *trouthe* be identified with the terms of the exchange or even with the fate of Troy? Chaucer clearly delineates the scandal of the exchange itself, initiated by the traitor Calkas, executed in spite of Hector's objection, and fated to expose Troy to the eventual treason of Antenor. David Aers's powerful challenge to identifying Trojan values with *trouthe* is well known. Far from viewing Criseyde as an admirable courtly lady and counselor in Book 4, he sees her as a female

[47] See McAlpine, *Genre,* pp. 160–65, for an extended analysis of the complications surrounding Troilus's choice and behavior.
[48] Lisa J. Kiser, in *Truth and Textuality in Chaucer's Poetry* (Hanover, N.H.: University Press of New England, 1991), p. 80, argues that Criseyde's concern for her honor and reputation is not a character flaw. See also Richard Firth Green, "Troilus and the Game of Love," *ChauR* 13 (1979): 201–20, and Collette, "Criseyde's Honor" (note 3 above).
[49] Pearsall, "Criseyde's Choices" (see note 3), p. 29.

victim who has internalized the values of the patriarchy, discounting her love in favor of "the cohesion of the male aristocracy," and accepting "crude militaristic notions" of honor allied to "anti-feminist norms."[50] Aers's analysis captures part of the truth. But it is also true that Troy cannot be identified solely with a bonded group of male aristocrats. It is a beloved home the loss of which Criseyde laments in her exile (5.708–11, 729–33), and the prey of Greeks like Diomede who are plotting its utter destruction, down to the last man, woman, and child (5.883–96). Such, Chaucer seems to say, are the political contradictions among which one must often choose either self-interest or the common good; such is the arena in which treason may suddenly appear as a possibility, and *trouthe* be tested—and validated, even if self-sacrifice fails to produce its intended effects or produces unintended effects.

My assignment of Criseyde's advice to Wallace's category of "political work" receives further support from the contemporary concern in English politics with issues of loyalty and disloyalty. According to Richard Firth Green, "treason," as the "principal antonym" of *trouthe*, was also a key word in fourteenth-century England, and a crisis in treason accompanied the crisis in *trouthe*.[51] Edward III's Statute of Treason of 1352, the first official definition of treason, reflected a struggle between an older definition based on personal relationship and a newer one based on institutional loyalties (pp. 207–10). Troilus's situation—as a citizen and defender of the city of Troy whose personal relationships to his brothers and his father are prominently discussed—provides grounds for a charge of treason under both definitions. Moreover, covertness was seen as an aggrevation of treason under both definitions (Green, p. 211), and both Troilus and Criseyde characterize their elopement to frustrate her exchange as "stealing away" (4.1503; 5.739–40). As regards Cri-

---

[50] Aers, *Chaucer, Langland, and the Creative Imagination* (see note 3), pp. 133–34. Aers's interpretation requires Chaucer to imagine radical changes in his society's values. I agree with Arlyn Diamond that Chaucer exposed the deformations of love in a feudal patriarchy, but, unable to imagine alternatives, generalized those deformations as human weakness and worldly imperfection. See *"Troilus and Criseyde:* The Politics of Love" in *Chaucer in the Eighties,* eds. Julian N. Wasserman and Robert J. Blanch (Syracuse, N.Y.: Syracuse University Press, 1986), pp. 93–103. For additional comment on Aers's reading, see Kelly, *Chaucerian Tragedy* (see note 11), pp. 122–24, and Mann, *Geoffrey Chaucer,* pp. 183–84. Kiser, *Truth and Textuality,* pp. 79–81, observes that Criseyde does not articulate an awareness of the social forces that constrain her nor of others' manipulation of her.

[51] Green, *Crisis of Truth,* pp. 207, 230. Subsequent page references will appear in my text.

seyde in her role as adviser, to give wicked counsel was itself regarded as a species of treason (Green, p. 214), even as, we may recall, to give good counsel was an aspect of the virtue of prudence. It seems impossible to deny that questions of treason, and therefore of *trouthe,* which Chaucer and his audience would have taken seriously are raised by the lovers' dilemma.[52]

The lovers' crucial mutual choice not to elope, a choice based on *trouthe* and honor, becomes entangled, however, with Criseyde's simultaneous commitment of her *trouthe* to a highly circumstantial plan to return to Troy within a specific time frame. Here Green's researches are again of assistance; Criseyde's commitment might well be seen as a kind of rash promise. According to Green, such a promise is typically offered gratuitously, binds only one party, and proves to involve unforeseen difficulties.[53] Criseyde's promise is gratuitous since she offers her plan initially as a way to blunt Troilus's immediate pain and to offer him hope; she is under no obligation to find or to effect single-handedly a solution to their dilemma. In the second place, all of the responsibility for execution of the plan falls to Criseyde; Troilus undertakes no reciprocal responsibility. Finally, Criseyde does carry out her promise insofar as she attempts to persuade her father to allow her to return to Troy, though this scene is not directly represented (5.694–5). Not surprisingly, the project turns out to be as unlikely of success as Troilus himself feared (4.1450–84), though it does not meet the standard of literal impossibility (Green, pp. 320–23.) Moreover, by the end of the conversation, Criseyde seems clearly to intend to be bound by the promise (Green, pp. 305–16), though the confused, emotion-laden process by which she arrives at this unanticipated conclusion from what began as a set of hypotheses offered to console (4.1289–95) is also made clear by Chaucer. Unfortunately, Criseyde did not think to add specific conditions to her promise (Green, p. 309).

As Green's research shows, medieval persons would have been much more inclined to require the fulfilment of such a promise than moderns might be; he notes that Criseyde reflects this understanding when she says of Troilus "[He] shal in his herte deme / That I am fals, and so it may wel seme" (5.697–98). The intricacy of the poet's design suggests

---

[52] In "Treason in the Household" in *Hochon's Arrow* (see note 31), Paul Strohm comments on the newly expansive concept of treason which could embrace "court and bedchamber, state policy and personal desire" (pp. 122–23).

[53] Green, *Crisis of Truth,* pp. 293–335.

that Chaucer is probing the requirements of *trouthe* more deeply than his hero, however. It is fair to wonder why Troilus, who clearly understood the difficulties of the plan from the beginning, does not later, on reflection, absolve Criseyde of her commitment to return to Troy. He requires her to fulfill a condition he knows to be impossible, or nearly so, holding her in a double bind much like a critical tradition that, lamenting Criseyde's supposed tendencies toward "calculation" in earlier scenes, deplores the ineffectualness of her clearest, most overt attempt at what might legitimately be called calculation.[54]

Finally, in the Prudence passage Chaucer complicates matters further by having Criseyde link in a *new* way her plan to return with her decision not to elope with Troilus. *If* she had known that her plan would fail, she says, she would have accepted Troilus's plea to flee Troy with him. Here we come to the crux presented by Criseyde's reflection on Prudence as itself a moment of ethical significance, distinct from the crisis of her last night with Troilus. Does not Criseyde's regret strip her of all the credit I have argued she deserves for the decision not to run away? My answer is no: no more than Troilus's arguing for elopement and thus passing responsibility for making the right choice to Criseyde, *after* having made the proper ethical analysis himself, strips him of all credit for choosing not to be another Paris. Would Criseyde indeed have decided differently on that fateful night if she had clearly foreseen that once in the Greek camp, she would have had no possibility of returning? The question is unanswerable, even as we cannot know for certain what Troilus would

---

[54] The attribute of "cool calculation," as well as "drift," appears in Root, *The Poetry of Chaucer* (see note 3), p. 108. Other early critics rejected the characterization: G. L. Kittredge, *Chaucer and His Poetry* (Cambridge: Harvard University Press, 1915), pp. 133–34; C. S. Lewis, *The Allegory of Love* (New York: Oxford University Press, 1936; rpt. 1958), pp. 182–83. A powerful alternative reading of Criseyde's quality of mind was offered by Donald R. Howard, "Experience, Language, and Consciousness: '*Troilus and Criseyde*,' II, 596–931," in *Medieval Literature and Folklore Studies,* eds. Jerome Mandel and Bruce A. Rosenberg (New Brunswick: Rutgers University Press, 1970), pp. 174–92; rpt. in *Chaucer's "Troilus": Essays in Criticism,* ed. Stephen A. Barney (Hamden, Conn.: Archon Books, 1980), pp. 159–80. The older view survives, however, as in Sheila Delaney's description of Criseyde's character as including, among other qualities, "conscious and manipulative self-presentation, coyness, calculation, [and] egocentricity": see "Techniques of Alienation in "Troilus and Criseyde" in *The Uses of Criticism,* ed. A. P. Foulkes (Bern: Peter Lang, 1976), pp. 77–95; rpt. in *Chaucer's* Troilus and Criseyde: *"Subgit to alle Poesye": Essays in Criticism,* ed. R. A. Shoaf (Binghamton: Medieval & Renaissance Texts and Studies, 1992), pp. 29–46. Williams, "Intentionality and Chaucer's Third Eye" (see note 9), recreates the double bind, describing Criseyde as a " 'chip off the block'," that is, Calkas, whose "inability to construct a realistic plan to return to Troilus" nevertheless proves "her lack of guiding values" (pp. 55, 53).

have done if Criseyde had asked him to flee Troy. What we do know is that Criseyde's lack of a clear vision of the future facing her did not impede, on that fateful last night in Troy, the making of the better, bitter choice. For that choice, the first two eyes of Prudence were sufficient.

Trouthe and the Future

Even if Criseyde's regret does not wholly cancel out ethically her earlier exercise of Prudence's first and second eyes, is not her lack of the third eye still a significant moral deficiency? Certainly, Chaucer took some care to construct a narrative sequence that draws attention to her deficiency, whether moral or intellectual. As Windeatt indicates, Chaucer made substantial changes to Boccaccio's story in Book 4, turning what were retrospective speeches in his sources into predictive speeches. Briseida's upbraiding of Calchas, in the camp, for his earlier behavior, in Benoit and Guido, becomes Criseyde's rehearsal of arguments she *will* make to her father once in the camp, and Troilus's recriminations against Criseyde later in the *Il Filostrato* become *anticipatory* misgivings before her departure from Troy in the *Troilus*.[55] Then in another innovation of his own, the Prudence stanza, Chaucer shows Criseyde living in and lamenting a future she failed to foresee accurately.

Assessing the moral significance of Criseyde's "deficiency" involves consideration of at least two questions: whether it is a deficiency peculiar to her, and whether its opposite, knowledge of the future, has a claim to moral superiority. Within Chaucer's poem, I believe the answer to both questions is "no." Criseyde's "deficiency" defines a universal human limitation even as Troilus's questioning of Jupiter's foreknowledge does, and it distinguishes her from Calkas and Cassandra, of whose uses of knowledge of the future Chaucer is critical. Indeed, Chaucer's treatment of characters who do and do not have knowledge of the future suggests that we should reframe what might seem the natural question. The pertinent question concerns how *knowledge* of the future, *not* lack of it, may deform ethical choice and judgment.

First of all, Criseyde's distinction among the three eyes reflects the common medieval teaching that, especially with respect to knowledge of the future, prudence must always be imperfect. Aquinas observes:

---

[55] Windeatt, *Oxford Guides,* p. 258.

"Now because the subject matter of prudence is composed of contingent individual incidents, which form the setting for human acts, the certitude of prudence is not such as to remove entirely all uneasiness of mind."[56] Moreover, the reoccurrence of the word "future" in the Prudence stanza, after Chaucer's initial use of the term in his translation of Boethius's *Consolation of Philosophy,* identifies the stanza as a Boethian addition to the *Troilus* and links it to Troilus's soliloquy in the temple.[57] Prose 6 of Book 5 of the *Consolation,* in the translation of which Chaucer made his first use of the term "future,"[58] presents the conclusion of Philosophy's answers to the very questions about divine foreknowledge and human freedom raised by Troilus in the temple scene (4.953–1085). As a related reflection on knowledge of the future, the Prudence passage constitutes the Criseydan parallel to Troilus's temple soliloquy. Characteristically, Troilus addresses the issue of the future theoretically and in relation to divine knowledge, while Criseyde addresses it concretely and in relation to human knowledge. Characteristically, too, Troilus finds a possible flaw in the universe, while Criseyde finds a deficiency in herself.[59] The two passages, however, are of equal validity in their application to the universal human condition.

[56] *Summa Theologiae,* 2a2ae, Ques. 47, art. 9, ad 2. "Quia vero materis prudentiae sunt singularia contingentia, circa quae sunt operationes humanae, non potest certitudo prudentiae tanta esse, quod omnino sollicitudo tollatur": ed. and trans. Gilby, in the Blackfriars edition, vol. 36, pp. 30–31. As John of Salisbury explained in his *Metalogicon,* Book 4, Chapter 14, "handicapped as it is by errors begotten by sense perceptions and opinions, human prudence can hardly proceed with [entire] confidence in its investigation of the truth, and can scarcely be [completely] sure as to when it has comprehended the latter": trans. Daniel D. McGarry (Berkeley: University of California Press, 1962), p. 224. "Et quidem propter fallacias sensuum et opinionum, uix in eius inuestigatione fideliter incredit, uis est in comprehensione secura": J. B. Hall, ed., *Corpus Christianorum,* Series Latina, vol. 98 (Turnholt: Typographi Brepols, 1991), 152. See C. David Benson, *Chaucer's Troilus and Criseyde* (London: Unwin Hyman, 1990), pp. 174–76, on the theme of "inescapable ignorance" in the *Troilus.*

[57] See Windeatt, *Oxford Guides,* p. 107. Tim William Machan, in *Techniques of Translation: Chaucer's "Boece"* (Norman, Okla.: Pilgrim Books, 1985), observes that very few of the neologisms in the *Boece,* of which he counts 247, were used in other works of Chaucer (pp. 50–57; 114–16).

[58] The word appears ten times, in several grammatical forms, in prose 6. In the first of these instances, Chaucer glosses his English plural noun *futures* as "tyme comynge," and in the second instance, he glosses *futuris* as "that ne ben nat yit," suggesting that the term was indeed a neologism unfamiliar to his audience.

[59] The dominant view, as in Pearsall's "Criseyde's Choices" (see note 3.), appears to be that Criseyde regularly shirks responsibility; but see McAlpine, *Genre* (see note 4), p. 196, where the excuses of Criseyde and Troilus are compared. To the passages cited there may be added Criseyde's spontaneous and general request for forgiveness (3.1182–83).

As these related speeches of hero and heroine dramatize, human blindness with respect to the future is indeed cause for painful and legitimate lament. But what if more perfect knowledge of the future were possible? Would its ethical consequences be benign? Chaucer raises this question and suggests some answers to it through two characters, Calkas and Cassandra, who possess the kinds of knowledge of the future that Criseyde lacks. In granting these characters some accurate knowledge of the future, Chaucer is certainly guided by the tradition of the Troy story; but logically, too, some such reliability must be granted if Chaucer is to pursue the implications and limits of knowledge of the future. Significantly, both Calkas and Cassandra foresee catastrophes or at least unhappy events. The future was typically seen as a site of disaster, and perhaps the most common medieval defense of seeking knowledge of the future was the claim that it would allow people to prepare for or protect themselves in some degree from misfortune.[60]

As Alastair Minnis has argued, Chaucer does not challenge the "science" of prediction, even if exercised by pagans, when those predictions are "general": that is, concerned with major events affecting large numbers of people, a type allowed by Christian thinkers.[61] Calkas's prediction of the fall of Troy is of this type. It is precisely here, though, that knowledge of the future may encounter the demands of *trouthe,* for the expedient response in the face of disaster will not always be the ethical one. As Chaucer's contemporary and critic of astrology Nicole Oresme put it: "the astrologers themselves say that the stars can give to man no greater misfortune than to be inclined against his faith and against his

---

[60] These observations are made by A. J. Gurevich in "What is Time?" in *Categories of Medieval Culture,* trans. G. L. Campbell (London: Routledge & Kegan Paul, 1985; original publication in Russian, 1972), p. 116. A passage in Chaucer's *Boece* brings together calamities, the future, prudence, and the imagery of eyes: "What other thyng is flyttynge Fortune but a maner schewynge of wrecchidnesse that is to comen? Ne it suffiseth nat oonly to loken on thyng that is present byforn the eien of a man; but wisdom [Latin *prudentia*] loketh and mesureth the ende of thynges" (2. pr. 1, 81–86). "Quid est aliud [fugax] quam futurae quoddam calamitatis indicium? Neque enim quod ante oculos situm est suffecerit intueri, rerum exitus prudentia metitur": *Consolatio philosophiae,* ed. Ludovicus Bieler, *Corpus Christianorum,* Series Latina, vol. 94: 2. pr. 1, lines 38–41.

[61] Alastair Minnis, *Chaucer and Pagan Antiquity* (Cambridge: D. S. Brewer, 1982), pp. 46–47 and 80–81. See also Laura Ackerman Smôller's discussion of the distinction between general and particular predictions in the thought of Pierre d'Ailly in *History, Prophecy and the Stars: The Christian Astrology of Pierre D'Ailly* (Princeton: Princeton University Press, 1994), pp. 25–42.

law."[62] Calkas is Chaucer's textbook case of this possibility as one "that falsly hadde his feith so broken" (1.89). Brewer puts it only a little too simply when he says of Calkas's knowledge of the future: "That is why he is a traitor. Calculation destroys values such as loyalty."[63] Although several critics have linked Criseyde's eventual infidelity with Calkas's treason, the more appropriate comparison, in my view, is quite different: Calkas misused knowledge of the future to betray Troy; Criseyde, lacking such knowledge, properly used knowledge of the past and present to serve Troy.

Cassandra's prophecy extends Chaucer's skeptical analysis of knowledge of the future by asking how such knowledge might affect moral judgment of others' actions. Her prophecy involves particulars, a form of prediction condemned by Christian theorists as undermining a proper understanding of free will.[64] Commentators usually emphasize the broad sweep of Cassandra's review of Theban history, but she is interpreting one person's dream and her prophecy concerns three specific persons only. As a particular prediction, Cassandra's prophecy illustrates another limitation to human knowledge of the future identified by Oresme: even if we could foresee the effects of certain choices, "we could not know the details of the particular results."[65] Indeed, Cassandra may not know which woman her prophecy concerns. She refers to Troilus's lady "wherso ["wherever" or perhaps "whatever"] she be" (5.1516). It appears that Troilus has not identified his lady as the Criseyde recently traded so publicly to the Greeks. And Cassandra's more profound ignorance or lack of interest is indicated by her famously abrupt conclusion: "This Diomede is inne, and thow art oute" (5.1519). Cassandra foresees the infidelity of Troilus's "lady"—but in terms that seriously obscure Criseyde's experience of love, *trouthe* and *untrouthe*. Moreover, the textual

[62] "Les astrologiens mesmes dient que les estoilles ne peuent donner a homme plus grant infortune que d'estre enclin contre sa secte et contre sa loy": ed. and trans. G. W. Coopeland, *Nichole Oresme and the Astrologers: A Study of His Livre de Divinacions* (Cambridge, Mass.: Harvard University Press, 1952), pp. 84–85.

[63] Brewer, "Arithmetic" (see note 15), p. 4. On Calkas, see Minnis, *Chaucer and Pagan Antiquity*, pp. 78–83; Stanley B. Greenfield, "The Role of Calkas in *Troilus and Criseyde*," *MAE* 36 (1967): 141–51; and R. M. Lumiansky, "Calchas in Early Versions of the Troilus Story," *TSE* 4 (1954): 5–20.

[64] Minnis, in *Chaucer and Pagan Antiquity*, discusses particular predictions but makes no application to Cassandra. Instead he associates her prophesy with dream lore, finding her prophesy to be true because Troilus's dream is itself a "gift of grace" granted to a "noble pagan" (p. 76).

[65] "Et pose que elle fust sceue, si ne puet on savoir les particuliers effects avenir": ed. and trans. Coopland, *Nichole Oresme,* pp. 82–83.

status of Cassandra's prophecy, its derivation from a highly compressed twelve-line summary of Statius's twelve-book work, reflects its distance from the intricacies of experience. This late, factual, but insufficient recitation of *events* is similar in quality to the late, tantalizing but insufficient *character* portraits of Diomede, Criseyde, and Troilus in Book 5 borrowed from Joseph of Exeter (5.799–840).[66] Cassandra's prophetic speech announces certain inarguable facts, but obscures deeper truths that our whole experience of the narrative present of Chaucer's story should prepare us to appreciate.[67] Thus Chaucer explains why all "particular" predictions should be viewed with the skepticism that crude, reductionist versions of human experience deserve.[68]

The implications of my analysis for Chaucer's attitudes toward knowledge of the future are several. First, Chaucer agreed with the orthodox distinction between general and particular predictions and made a more pointed use of this distinction in the *Troilus* than has so far been recognized. Next, he saw even in the permitted general predictions a temptation for some to pursue self-interest instead of *trouthe*. Third, he distrusted particular predictions not only, presumably, because of their implied threat to the doctrine of free will, but also (and this was of the greatest importance to him as a poet) because of their inability to capture the always intricate complexities of any human exercise of that will. Finally, despite exhibiting a multifaceted interest in knowledge of the future and an empathic understanding of the craving for such knowl-

[66] Windeatt, *Oxford Guides* (see note 11), p. 46, observes that both the twelve-line argument from Statius and the portraits are known to have circulated separately.

[67] John Ganim demonstrates how the reader is immersed in the present, the temporal linearity of the narrative: "Consciousness and Time in *Troilus and Criseyde*" in *Style and Consciousness in Middle English Narrative* (Princeton: Princeton University Press, 1983), pp. 79–102. For Ganim, however, the present is mainly a site of change, instability, and imperfection (p. 101). I emphasize its status as locus of complex and consequential choices.

[68] Winthrop Wetherbee, in *Chaucer and the Poets: An Essay on "Troilus and Criseyde"* (Ithaca, N.Y.: Cornell University Press, 1984), p. 130, remarks on how Cassandra's recitation reduces history to "a mere sequence of events" and individuals to "pawns." See also Patterson, *Subject of History* (see note 40), p. 131: "Cassandra invokes a historiography that merely restates the problem of the relation of individuals to events without providing an answer." For an unqualified defense of Cassandra's speech, see John Fleming, *Classical Imitation and Interpretation in Chaucer's 'Troilus'* (Lincoln: University of Nebraska Press, 1990), pp. 225–27. Valerie A. Ross, in "Believing Cassandra: Intertextual Politics and the Interpretation of Dreams in *Troilus and Criseyde*," *ChauR* 31 (1997): 339–56, sees in Cassandra's interpretation of Troilus's dream an attempt by Chaucer to attribute to a woman character agency and authority not found in his sources. "Chaucer's audience knows that Cassandra is right" (p. 334).

edge, he ultimately regarded remembrance of the past, with its instructive examples, along with responsiveness to the requirements of the present moment, as more reliable guides to ethical decision-making than any actual or potential knowledge of the future.[69]

This study of Criseyde's prudence argues that in the crisis of her proposed exchange, she exhibited the two kinds of prudence Chaucer valued most highly. Like other medieval exemplars of female prudence, she restrained a highly placed male from a violent action that threatened the common good. Yet, as she suffered the personally disastrous consequences of her virtuous choice, made in unfortunate but innocent ignorance of the future, she was vulnerable to doubt and regret. Her ethical history does not follow the comparatively simple trajectories some have traced for her as an unfaithful woman; her costly "political work" for Troy must always find a place in the history of her career.

Her creator's study of the future exhibits a parallel degree of complexity. His extraordinary interest in knowledge of the future rested not on personal intellectual curiosity only, but on the shared longing for effectual means to confront the disasters the future always seems to promise. At the same time he clearly feared the potential of such knowledge to distort ethical judgment, both in making choices for oneself, as in Calkas's case, and in understanding the choices made by others, as in Cassandra's. Chaucer seems to have been a man of two minds if not exactly of two worldviews: the one, pragmatic and somewhat new; the other, moral and essentially conservative.[70]

The Prudence stanza, with its painful retrospection from the future on an ethical choice rightly made in the past—and with its distinction between the virtue's first two eyes and its third—opens valuable perspectives on the divided frames of mind of both heroine and poet. Both coveted Prudence's third eye; but Criseyde may have been saved from the worst treason of all by her lack of it, and Chaucer seems to have distrusted it as much as he prized it.

[69] A similar threefold pattern appears in the *Nun's Priest's Tale,* with a similar privileging of knowledge of the past and present over knowledge of the future. Chantecleer might have escaped the fox if he had remembered the fate of his father and/or attended to his own instinct, even if he had had no predictive dream. See Monica E. McAlpine, "The Triumph of Fiction in the *Nun's Priest's Tale*" in *Art and Context in Late Medieval Narrative,* ed. Robert Edwards (Cambridge: D. S. Brewer, 1994), pp. 79–92.

[70] In "Chaucer's Arithmetical Mentality and the *Book of the Duchess,*" *ChauR* 31 (1966), T. A. Shippey concludes that Chaucer is "a man between two worlds"—that of the "'numerological mentality' which remained traditional, moral, and conservative" and that of the "pragmatic, novel, commercial, 'arithmetical mentality'" (pp. 197–98).

Troilus and Criseyde and the "Treasonous Aldermen" of 1382

Tales of the City in Late Fourteenth-Century London

Marion Turner
King's College London

*T*ROILUS AND CRISEYDE is emphatically a product of the 1380s.[1] It is a text informed by the discourses and politics of the time, deploying and manipulating the languages and concerns prevalent in late fourteenth-century London. Prominent among these concerns is an anxiety about betrayal and urban division, a concern that could easily be explored through the story of Troy—indeed, Christopher Baswell has recently discussed the fact that the *Aeneid* and the Peasants' Revolt were compared by one late-medieval annotator.[2] While scholars have drawn connections between *Troilus and Criseyde* and the Wonderful Parliament of 1386,[3] little has been said about the implications of documents about the Peasants' Revolt for the "textual environment" of Chaucer's poem.[4]

---

[1] Paul Strohm suggests that Chaucer may have worked on *Troilus and Criseyde* from late 1381 to late 1386, arguing that it was probably completed by late 1385. See Paul Strohm, *Social Chaucer* (Cambridge: Harvard University Press, 1989), p. 207, note 41.

[2] Christopher Baswell, "Aeneas in 1381," *New Medieval Literatures* 5, ed. Rita Copeland, David Lawton, and Wendy Scase (2002): 7–58. For the traditional connection between Troy and London see Geoffrey of Monmouth, *History of the Kings of Britain*, trans. Sebastian Evans, rev. Charles W. Dunn (London: Dent, 1963). See also John Clark, "Trinovantum—the Evolution of a Legend," *Journal of Medieval History* 7 (1981): 135–51; Francis Ingledew, "The Book of Troy and the Genealogical Construction of History: The Case of Geoffrey of Monmouth's *Historia Regum Britanniae*," *Speculum* 69 (1994): 665–704, and Heather James, *Shakespeare's Troy: Drama, Politics and the Translation of Empire* (Cambridge: Cambridge University Press, 1997).

[3] See, for example, Lee Patterson, *Chaucer and the Subject of History* (London: Routledge, 1991), p. 158.

[4] For the concept of the "textual environment," see Paul Strohm, "The Textual Environment of Chaucer's 'Lak of Stedfastnesse,'" in *Hochon's Arrow: The Social Imagination of Fourteenth-Century Texts* (Princeton: Princeton University Press, 1992), pp. 57–74, p. 57.

In order to maintain a "respect" for the text, it is necessary to historicize it by placing it within the cultural context of contemporary discourses.[5] J. G. A. Pocock writes that "languages are the matrices within which texts as events occur," adding that texts "are actions performed in language contexts that make them possible, that condition and constrain them but that they also modify."[6] This useful formulation emphasizes the fact that the text is both produced by and produces its world. The existence of urban dissent and division is by no means unique to the period in question, but the way in which such fragmentation is manifested and represented is a product of a specific historical moment. *Troilus and Criseyde* can profitably be read alongside a coeval set of texts, also produced in 1380s London, and also dealing with issues of urban tension and betrayal. These texts accuse certain London aldermen (John Horn, Walter Sibyl, and Adam Carlisle) of betraying the city during the Peasants' Revolt by opening the gates of the capital to the rebels (accusations that were almost certainly without foundation and politically motivated).[7] Both the accusations of the aldermen and *Troilus and Criseyde* serve to illustrate the changing allegiances and betrayals that dominated London politics in the 1380s.[8] Reading these texts side by side allows us to situate *Troilus and Criseyde* within contemporary discourses of treason and urban fragmentation, discourses that were under particular pressure in the closing decades of the fourteenth century.[9] In this article, I am

[5] Paul Strohm, *Theory and the Premodern Text* (Minneapolis: University of Minnesota Press, 2000), p. xiii.

[6] J. G. A. Pocock, "Texts as Events: Reflections on the History of Political Thought," in *Politics of Discourse: The Literature and History of Seventeenth-Century England*, ed. Kevin Sharpe and Steven N. Zwicker (Berkeley: University of California Press, 1987), pp. 21–34, pp. 28–29.

[7] John Fresh, a mercer, and William Tonge, a vintner, are also implicated. See Ruth Bird, *The Turbulent London of Richard II* (London: Longmans, Green, 1949), pp. 53, 57–61.

[8] Northampton, for example, was allied to grocers in 1371, a group that were later to become his great enemies; he was variously supported by Gaunt and by Richard; he was twice arrested, once only a year after being the king's declared favorite; and he was pardoned in the wake of Richard's anger against Exton (Brembre's successor and Northampton's principal opponent), who had allowed the Lords Appellant to enter London. See Pamela Nightingale, "Capitalists, Crafts and Constitutional Change in Late Fourteenth-Century London," *Past and Present* 124 (1989): 3–35, especially pp. 6–7 and pp. 26–31, and Bird, *Turbulent London*, p. xxii.

[9] See Richard Firth Green, *A Crisis of Truth: Literature and Law in Ricardian England* (Philadelphia: University of Pennsylvania Press, 1999). The idea of a "crisis of truth," which Green himself modifies in his introduction to *Crisis of Truth* (p. xiii) in order to stress the "chronic" nature of the phenomenon, is in some ways misleading. In the present investigation, it is not being claimed that *trouthe* disappeared at a certain point in history. Rather, I would suggest that fragmentation is expressed at this specific mo-

interested in examining both the similarities and the differences between *Troilus and Criseyde* and the accusations of the aldermen, and in exploring the differing ways in which these texts deal with ideas of social antagonism, betrayal, and stasis. Ultimately, I offer a reading of *Troilus and Criseyde* as a poem about the inevitability and omnipresence of social fragmentation and betrayal.[10]

The "Treasonous" Aldermen of 1382

The Rolls of Parliament record John More's accusation against Walter Sibyl, John Horn, and Adam Carlisle. More, a prominent supporter of Northampton, says:

sist il je ne die mye expressement que einsi est, mais je die, que commune fame & parlance est en nostre Citee, que Johan Horn, Fisshemonger, & Adam Karlill de Londres estoient en dit rumour les primers & principalx conseillours, confortours, abettours, & excitours que les Communes de Kent & de Essex nadgairs treiterousement levez & assemblez encontre le Roi & son Roialme approcheassent leur Citee, & entrassent en ycelle: Et que le dit Wauter suist le primer & principal destourbour a William de Walleworth lors Mair, & a diverses autrez persones foialx nostre Seignur le Roi q'ils ne poaient a cell foitz clore les Portz de la Citee, ne lever le Pount, ou defendre mesme la Citee, encontre les ditz Treitours.[11]

---

ment in the pressured arena of sworn relations: in the language of *trouthe* and *treason,* and in critiques of new forms of affinity and association.

[10] My argument is thus very different from the claim that *Troilus and Criseyde* acts as a warning or moral lesson. Eugene Vance, whose depiction of *Troilus and Criseyde* as a fragmentary text depends upon the idea that Chaucer was a stern moral idealist, claims that Chaucer believed that the city could progress. He writes: "this war will be perpetrated yet again and again through successive erotic transgressions in that 'future' which is our past and also *(unless we use signs properly)* the future of England itself." See Eugene Vance, *Mervelous Signals: Poetics and Sign Theory in the Middle Ages* (Lincoln: University of Nebraska Press, 1986), p. 283, emphasis mine. Equally, C. David Benson says that *Troilus and Criseyde* contains "pertinent lessons" for Chaucer's London (C. David Benson, *Chaucer's Troilus and Criseyde* [London: Unwin Hyman, 1990], p. 71). In Vance's interpretation, Christian teleology is celebrated in the poem, and the message of *Troilus and Criseyde* is basically religious and moralistic. This point of view is in direct contrast with that outlined here. I argue not only that divided Troy reflects contemporary London itself in many ways in this text, but also that the text demonstrates the inevitability of social fragmentation in any and every city.

[11] Rev. John Strachey, ed., *Rotuli Parliamentorum; ut et petitiones et placita in Parliamento tempore Ricardi II,* vol. 3 (London, 1767–77), p. 143. Abbreviations have been silently lengthened. Translations are my own.

[If I did not say my express reasons thus, it is merely because what I said is common rumour and talk in our city, that John Horn, fishmonger, and Adam Carlisle of London were, by the said rumor, the major and principal counselors, advisers, abettors, and instigators, when the commons of Kent and of Essex recently traitorously rose and assembled against the king and his realm; they approached their city and entered into there. And that the said Walter was the main and principal disturber against William Walworth, our mayor, and against many other people loyal to our master the king, who were not able on this occasion to close the gates of the city, nor to raise the bridge or defend the said city against the said traitors.]

An investigation was made into these aldermen by the sheriffs and jurors of London, the results of which appear in two letters dated 4 November and 20 November 1382. The letters serve as damning indictments of the aldermen, and as grave descriptions of urban betrayal, conspiracy, and deceit.[12] In the letter of 20 November, particular pains are taken to emphasize the treachery of the aldermen. John Horn "cum principalibus insurrectoribus conspiravit" [conspired with the principal rebels], and Walter Sybil was "de suis coniva, consilio et conspiracione precogitatis" [of his covin, council, and premeditated conspiracy].[13] Their specific treason to the king is shown by the fact that Horn is "capiens super se regalem potestatem" [taking upon himself the power of the king], and acting to the "adnullacionem regie dignitatis ac legis terre ac pacis regis" [annulment of the royal dignity and the law of the land and the peace of the king].[14] Horn's treachery is summed up decisively: "sic idem Johannes Horn fuit unus principalium insurrectorum contra regem et principalis eorum malorum consiliator" [in this way the same John Horn was one of the principal rebels against the king and a principal counselor of those evil men].[15] There are also many references to their

[12] For the later report and part of the report of 4 November, see André Réville, *Le soulevement des Travailleurs D'Angleterre en 1381* (Paris: Picard, 1898), pp. 190–99; also Charles Oman, *The Great Revolt of 1381* (London: Greenhill Books, 1989), pp. 206–13. The earlier report is printed in B. Wilkinson, "The Peasants' Revolt of 1381," *Speculum* 15. 1 (1940): 12–35, 32–35. Wilkinson comments that neither account can be accepted as "anything but a biased and misleading representation of events" (p. 13).

[13] Réville, *Le soulevement*, pp. 190, 192. Translations are my own. For published translations see R.B. Dobson, *The Peasants' Revolt of 1381*, 2d edition (London: Macmillan, 1983), pp. 213–26.

[14] Réville, *Le soulevement*, p. 192.

[15] Réville, *Le soulevement*, p. 193. For example, when Sir John Gerberge was accused of treason, his crime was "'against his allegiance usurping to himself royal power within the king's realm.'" Cited in Green, *Crisis of Truth*, p. 206.

conscious oath-breaking, a manifest demonstration of treachery and bad faith. Thus John Horn:

in contemptum ejusdem domini regis, felonice, false et proditorie contra ligeanceam suam, dixit eisdem: *Venite Londonias, quia unanimes facti sumus amici et parati facere vobiscum que proposuistis, et in omnibus que vobis necessaria sunt favorem et obsequium prestare,* sciens regis voluntatem et majoris sui mandatum suis dictis contraria fore.[16]

[In contempt of that same master, the king, feloniously, falsely, and treacherously against his allegiance, he spoke in these very words: 'Come to London, because, sharing a common purpose, we have become friendly and ready to do with you that which you have proposed and to show compliance and favor in all that is necessary to you,' knowing that his words were spoken in opposition to the inclination of the king and to the order of the mayor.]

Blame is further heaped onto the accused by the fact that an impressive list of crimes is attributed either to them, or to their agency. More than once it is claimed that *all* of the most heinous and notorious offences of the revolt occurred because of the aldermen's perfidy. For example:

sic *per* predictum Johannem Horn et Walterum Sybyle predicti felones et proditores domini regis introducti fuerunt in civitatem, *ob quam causam* carcera [sic] domini regis de Newgate fracta fuit arsiones tenementorum prostraciones domorum, decapitaciones archiepiscopi et aliorum facte fuerunt, et alia plura mala prius inaudita perpetrata per ipsos tunc fuerunt.[17]

[In this way, *through* the aforesaid John Horn and Walter Sybil the aforesaid felons and traitors to the king were introduced into the city, *by which cause* the king's prison at Newgate was broken open, buildings were burnt, homes razed, the archbishop decapitated and other things done, and many evil things previously unheard of were perpetrated then through them.]

These sweeping accusations, which state not that the aldermen personally committed all these crimes but that they occurred because the aldermen enabled them, rely on the premise that the aldermen betrayed London by inviting the commons of Kent and Essex into the city and by opening the gates to them. Thus, "Willelmus Tonge portam illam

[16] Réville, *Le soulevement*, p. 192; emphasis in original.
[17] Ibid., emphasis mine.

male aperuit" [William Tonge evilly opened that gate], and Walter Sybil "reliquit portas civitatis apertas" [left the city gates open].[18] The eagerness of the aldermen to encourage the rebels to enter the city and to stress the support of the city is a central theme; John Horn is said to have reassured the rebels, insisting:

quod ad civitatem cum turmis suis venirent, asserens quod tota civitas Londoniarum fuit in eodem proposito sicut et ipsi fuerunt, et quod ipsi deberent in eadem civitate ita amicabiliter esse recepti, sicut pater cum filio et amicus cum amico.[19]

[that they might come to the city with their company, claiming that the whole city of London had the same intention as themselves, and that they themselves ought to be received in the same city just as lovingly as a father with his son, or a friend with his friend.]

The untruth of such a statement—that the whole of London was in agreement—and the divisiveness of the actions of the "traitor aldermen" is asserted with descriptions of these aldermen repulsing those who were loyal to the crown and to the mayor. Walter Sybil, about to give to the rebels the freedom of "introitum et egressum" [entry and exit] to the gates, is portrayed impeding those who come to resist the Kent men.[20] The aldermen are also accused of having attempted to prevent members of the city from opposing the revolt on other occasions. Walter Sybil and John Horn are said to have ridden back to London when the king was at Smithfield, in order to try to close the gates and to delay any help reaching Richard: they "impediverunt homines ad succurrendum domino regi et majori" [impeded men from assisting the king and the mayor].[21] Even more explicitly, in a strong accusation of treachery, the letter asserts:

si cives civitatis festinancius se non expedivissent, auxilium domino regi et majori minus tarde advenisset, causa verborum et factorum predicti Walteri Sybyle et Johannis Horn.[22]

---

[18] Ibid., pp. 196, 194. William Tonge was accused of opening Aldgate, location of Chaucer's house, where he lived from 1374–c. 1386. See *Chaucer Life-Records*, ed. Martin M. Crow and Clair C. Olson (Oxford: Clarendon Press, 1966), p. 147.
[19] Ibid., p. 190.
[20] Ibid., p. 193.
[21] Ibid., p. 194.
[22] Ibid., p. 194.

[if the citizens of the city had not hurried with all speed, help would have come to the king and the mayor too late, by the cause of the words and deeds of the aforesaid Walter Sybil and John Horn.]

The jurors claim that the peasants "prius in proposito fuerunt ad hos-picia sua revertendi" [before had in mind to turn back to their lodgings], and were only persuaded to enter the city by John Horn's urgings.[23] Further:

per ipsum et per predictum Walterum Sybyle felonice et proditorie malefact-ores prenominati *excitati et procurati* fuerunt veniendi Londonias.[24]

[Through [John Horn] and through the above-mentioned Walter Sybil, the felonious and treacherous malefactors above named were *aroused and incited* to come into London.]

The inference is that the ideology and meaning of the revolt originated with the aldermen themselves, and that the specific grievances of the peasants are immaterial. The aldermen do not merely fail to protect the city or to dissuade the rebels; the letter implies that, were it not for the treachery of the aldermen, the peasants would not have been a threat at all. Indeed, the authors' determination to condemn the aldermen was so strong that the first version of the accusation was rewritten within a fortnight to damn the aldermen more conclusively.[25]

The accusations made against the aldermen have their roots in very specific historical circumstances. London of the 1380s was, as is well known, a site of high-stakes factional conflict and political intriguing, most notably between John Northampton's and Nicholas Brembre's "parties."[26] In 1381 and 1382, Northampton and his supporters (promi-nent among whom was John More), held sway, and his opponents, in particular the fishmongers (including among their number Walter Sybil and John Horn), suffered. Northampton sought to implement anti-fishmonger measures and to exclude the victuallers from office. During Northampton's trial, the suggestion was made that the accusations

---

[23] Ibid., p. 206.

[24] Ibid., p. 193, emphasis mine.

[25] See Wilkinson, "Peasants' Revolt," p. 13.

[26] See Bird, *Turbulent London*, p. 2. However, as I suggested at the start of this essay, the changing alliances and betrayals that dominated London politics make it difficult to talk of any one specific political party: such groups were formed, operated for a while, and were soon altered or discarded.

against the aldermen were trumped up by John More, and that he suppressed evidence in their favor:[27] indeed, More accused them in the context of a debate about the ordinances against the fishmongers. Pamela Nightingale has also posited a direct connection between these events. She writes:

To quash the opposition which the London fishmongers raised in parliament, John More accused the two fishmongers Horn and Sybil and the grocer Adam Carlille, all three of them aldermen, of treachery by opening the City gates to the rebels.[28]

The fact that in the Gloucester parliament of 1378, dominated by John of Gaunt, the victualler adherents of the Calais staple had been attacked, aliens supported, and special privileges given to the drapers (such as Northampton) and the mercers, might seem to give the aldermen a motive.[29] After all, the principal targets of the rebels included Gaunt and his palace, the Savoy, and immigrant traders and workers. The accusation of these merchant-capitalists nonetheless seems deeply untenable but it could be made and sustained under the protection of Northampton's mayoralty, especially when he enjoyed the strong support of the king, who personally recommended his re-election in 1382. It is highly improbable that the "conservative"[30] merchant aldermen would have supported a subversive mob, and the indemnity and continued civic importance of the accused reveals that they were not generally

[27] See Edgar Powell and G. M. Trevelyan, eds., *The Peasants' Rising and the Lollards: A Collection of Unpublished Documents Forming an Appendix to "England in the Age of Wycliffe"* (London: Longmans, Green, 1899), p. 30, for a transcription of the relevant document (Coram Rege Roll, Hill. II Ric II 507, Rex 39). Wilkinson describes the jurors who authored the report as "strongly and unscrupulously partisan" ("Peasants' Revolt," p. 19).

[28] See Pamela Nightingale, "Capitalists," pp. 26–27. However, rather surprisingly, Nightingale seems to take the accusations against the aldermen at face value in her more recent book, *A Medieval Mercantile Community: The Grocers' Company and the Politics and Trade of London 1000–1485* (New Haven: Yale University Press, 1995). She writes: "The evidence certainly suggests that the alderman-fishmonger, John Horn [. . .] actively encouraged [the rebels], and even brought back several of the leaders to lodge at his house" (pp. 266–67). Her reading of the letters here seems to be entirely uncritical.

[29] See Nightingale, "Capitalists," pp. 22–24.

[30] These aldermen were generally part of the group described by Bird as "wealthy merchant capitalists" (*Turbulent London*, p. 1). Although the groups and factions in London politics were perhaps more fluid than Bird implies, this term is still useful: the fishmongers and their associates were certainly among the richer and more prominent London citizens.

viewed as traitors.[31] The existence of these accusations suggests that a
fear of urban collapse was being manipulated by More and others, who
were exploiting contemporary anxieties in order to further a political
agenda. The letters thus serve to demonstrate two layers of urban intrigue: first, the aldermen are accused of treachery; second, these accusations appear to have been trumped up to be used in pursuit of factional
advantage. The matter of the (un)reliability of the documents is of secondary importance here, however; the crucial issue is the availability
and easy deployment of the idea and language of civic betrayal and
treachery.[32]

The accusations seem to have become common currency, as versions
of them occur elsewhere. They are transmitted, however, in distorted
form. Froissart states that:

En la ville de Londres avoecques le maieur a XII eschevins. Li IX estoient pour
ly et pour le roy, sicom il le monstrèrent et ly troy de la secte de ce mescheant
peuple

[together with the Mayor, the City of London has twelve aldermen. Nine were
with him and the King, as their actions showed, and three were on the side of
those evil men.][33]

When he accuses Londoners of inviting in the rebels, it is the commons
and not the aldermen that he specifies, but his phrasing is significant.
Going a step further than the letter of 20 November, cited above, Froissart claims that the entire impetus for the revolt originated in London,
and that the rebels only rose at all because they were told to do so by
the city dwellers. He writes:

De la parolle de la vie et des oeuvres de Jehan Balle, furent aviset et enfourmet
trop grant fuisson de menues gens en la cittè de Londres, qui avoient envie sus
les rices et sour les nobles, et commenchièrent à dire entre euls que li roiaulmes

[31] Adam Carlisle, for example, was alderman of Aldgate in 1390, 1391, and 1393,
sheriff in 1388, and M.P. for the City in 1388. For an account of the civic offices
subsequently held by the accused aldermen, see Bird, *Turbulent London*, p. 60.

[32] The unreliability of all of the documents surrounding this issue is such that, in
relation to the account in the Letter-Book, for example, Bird comments that "it is
impossible to believe that it was not censored" (Bird, *Turbulent London*, p. 53).

[33] The original is from Jean Froissart, *Chroniques*, in *Oeuvres*, ed. Baron Joseph Marie
Kervyn de Lettenhove, 25 vols. (Brussels: Victor Devaux, 1867–77), vol. 9, p. 402. The
translation is from Jean Froissart, *Chroniques*, trans. and ed. Geoffrey Brereton (Harmondsworth, Middlesex: Penguin Books, 1968), p. 219.

d'Engletière estoit trop mal gouvernès et que il estoit d'or et d'argent des-roeubès par ceulx qui se nommoient nobles. Si commenchièrent ces mescheans gens en Londres à faire les mauvais et à yaulx reveler et segnefyer à ceulx des contrèes dessus dites que il venissent hardiement trouveroient Londres ouverte et le commun de leur acord.

[The things (John Ball) was doing and saying came to the ears of the common people of London, who were envious of the nobles and the rich. These began saying that the country was badly governed and was being robbed of its wealth by those who called themselves noblemen. So these wicked men in London started to become disaffected and to rebel and they sent word to the people in the counties mentioned to come boldly to London with all their followers, when they would find the city open and the common people on their side.][34]

The emphasis on London's treason remains, but this treason is not driven by the aldermen in Froissart's account. It is the common people who open the gates, and, despite his mention of the "traitor aldermen," Froissart stresses that the division in London was largely between classes. Urban division nonetheless remains the focus of the account: Froissart's general implication is that the city betrayed itself.

The "Traitors" in *Troilus and Criseyde*

The accusations of the aldermen are particularly resonant if read along-side *Troilus and Criseyde*, another text of the 1380s concerned with a city destroyed through internal corruption and betrayal.[35] Both resort to equivalent strategies of highlighting urban division and demonstra-ting its catastrophic results. In both texts, the infiltrator, the alien at-tacker of the city (the rampaging rural peasantry, the marauding Greeks), is partially (and crucially) elided: blame is allocated to the trai-tors *within* the city, and the classic idea of a Sinon preying on a town is ejected from the text. The silence of Chaucer's text on this point speaks volumes. Sinon is glaringly absent from this Trojan tale. The emphasis on Trojan traitors in *Troilus and Criseyde* is especially significant in the

[34] Original from *Chroniques*, ed. de Lettenhove, pp. 389–90; translation from *Chroni-ques*, trans. Brereton, p. 213.

[35] The connections between Chaucer's Troy and contemporary London have often been discussed: C. David Benson comments, for example, that "the Troy of *Troilus and Criseyde* is also familiar and medieval. Its architecture and furnishings are those of fourteenth-century London." See C. David Benson, *Chaucer's Troilus and Criseyde* (Lon-don: Unwin Hyman, 1990), p. 60.

context of other Chaucerian texts that refer to Troy, in which the dominant emphasis seems to be on the figure of slippery Sinon (just as many accounts of the Peasants' Revolt focus on the rural peasants). The demonizing of Sinon serves to emphasize Troy's innocence and credulity, and to detract from the idea of Troy destroying itself, stressing Greek rather than Trojan guilt; the guilt of the outsider, not the betrayer. Of the fifteen references to Troy in Chaucer's work (excluding *Troilus and Criseyde*), six focus on (or imply a focus on) Sinon, two more also focus on Greek penetration of the city, and the remaining seven are generally incidental, or simply refer to Troy's destruction. There are three specific references to Sinon bringing Troy to destruction:

> Whan Troye brought was to destruccioun
> By Grekes sleyghte, and namely by Synoun,
> Feynynge the hors offered unto Mynerve,
> Thourgh which that many a Troyan moste sterve;
> (*Legend of Good Women*, lines 930–33)

> O newe Scariot, newe Genylon,
> False dissymulour, o Greek Synon,
> That broghtest Troye al outrely to sorwe!
> (*Nun's Priest's Tale*, lines 3227–29)

> Or elles it was the Grekes hors Synon,
> That broghte Troie to destruccion,
> As men in thise olde geestes rede
> (*Squire's Tale*, lines 209–11)[36]

In these references, the blame is unambiguously attributed to Sinon as agent of Troy's downfall; he is accused in all of them of actively bringing misery to Troy, which itself is helpless, has no agency, and is the innocent victim. His culpability is also emphasized in the *House of Fame*:

> First sawgh I the destruction
> Of Troye thurgh the Grek Synon,
> [That] with his false forswerynge,
> And his chere and his lesynge,
> Made the hors broght into Troye,

---

[36] All references to Chaucer's works are to *The Riverside Chaucer*, ed. Larry Benson, 3d edition (Oxford: Oxford University Press, 1987).

Thorgh which Troyens loste al her joye
(*House of Fame*, lines 151–56)[37]

Here the guilt of the Trojans is pointedly ignored. The idea of the real enemy being within the city, society, the protective/exclusive walls, is occluded.[38]

In *Troilus and Criseyde*, internal division and betrayal are consistently decried as the cause of the war and Sinon is written out of Trojan history entirely. Instead of stressing the guilt of the (quasi) outsider, this poem shifts the emphasis onto bona fide Trojans—Calchas, Antenor, and Criseyde, all of whom are depicted as faith-breaking traitors—while the Greeks are sidelined.[39] The subject of Calchas's treachery is broached near the very beginning. We are told how he, a man of "gret auctorite" (I. 65) (an interesting detail given the supposed treason of the authorita-

---

[37] There is another reference to the Trojan horse (*Squire's Tale*, lines 306–7) and an implied reference to Sinon in the *Canon's Yeoman's Tale*, when the teller claims that the Canon "wolde infecte al a toun," even if it were as great as "Rome, Alisaundre, Troye, and othere three" (*Canon's Yeoman's Tale*, lines 973, 975). The audience is left in an uncomfortable position, unsure whether it is the Canon or the storytelling Yeoman who is the real Sinon. (This is pointed out by David Wallace in *Chaucerian Polity: Absolutist Lineages and Associational Forms in England and Italy* [Stanford: Stanford University Press, 1997], p. 251). The other two references to the destruction of Troy by outside forces come in the "Man of Law's Tale," in a mention of Pyrrhus breaking the walls of the city (lines 288–89), and in *Boece*, when Agamemnon is blamed for the "destruccioun of Troye" (Book 4, metrum 7, l. 4). In the other passing references to Troy, there is no implication that Troy destroyed itself and was itself guilty. (These other references are in the *Book of the Duchess*, line 326 and line 1066, the *House of Fame*, line 146, the *Knight's Tale*, line 2833, the *Squire's Tale*, line 548, the *Franklin's Tale*, line 1446, and the *Legend of Good Women*, line 1026).

[38] It is important to note, however, that the language of betrayal sneaks into the characterization of Sinon. Despite the fact that Sinon is a Greek, and a loyal Greek, many Chaucerian references emphasize his *treachery*: he is "newe Scariot" and a "false dissymulour," who destroys Troy through "false forswerynge," " 'feynynge,' and 'lesynge.' " Sinon can be classified as a partial insider, and therefore as a traitor, but he also remains a foreigner, unassimilated to the system: the town evades guilt, and blame is attached to the lying Greeks, and to this one adopted Trojan. Troy itself is merely a dupe, but, even in these Trojan references which seem to be emphasizing the guilt of the outsiders, there is still a hint of betrayal, of treason as the inevitable cause of urban collapse.

[39] Of course, it could reasonably be suggested that Chaucer is following Boccaccio in this exclusion of Sinon. However, the fact that Chaucer inserts into his text many extra intimations of internal betrayal reveals *Troilus and Criseyde*'s specific concern with internal, Trojan deceit rather than Greek guilt. These added intimations include the anticipation of Antenor's treason, in Book 4, lines 197–210, the dinner party at Deiphoebus's house with its manifest implications of internal division, in Book 2, lines 1569–1757, and Criseyde's excessive oath-swearing in Book 4, lines 1534–54, which serves later to stress her oath-breaking.

tive aldermen), decided "out of the town to go" (line 75) and "ful pryvely" (line 80) stole away. He is then described as a "traitour" (line 87) and as "hym that falsly hadde his feith so broken" (line 89); his actions are a "false and wikked dede" (line 93). After this, Criseyde is oppressed by "Hire fadres shame, his falsnesse and tresoun" (line 107) until Hector tells her to "'Lat youre fadres treson gon'" (line 117). Shortly after this, Troilus and Criseyde have their first encounter at the festival of the Palladium (a resonant occasion if we bear in mind Antenor's later treachery in selling the Palladium to the Greeks).[40] The lovers' relationship is engendered at the site of political betrayal, and Criseyde is marked out as the daughter of a traitor. When Criseyde abandons Troilus, her actions are described in language very similar to that used to portray Calchas's acts. Troilus asks:

> "Where is youre feith, and where is youre biheste?
> Where is youre love? Where is youre trouthe?"
> (Book 5, lines 1675–76)

Criseyde's breaking of her oath and her faith is stressed, just as Calchas was described as one who had "his feith so broken." Pandarus goes on to describe Criseyde's behavior as "'this tresoun'" (line 1738), and, just as Criseyde earlier had to deal with her father's shame, now Pandarus is "shamed for his nece" (line 1727). Her "treason," like her father's, is a symptomatic betrayal of Troy from within.

Criseyde is also specifically linked with Antenor, the Trojan traitor for whom she is exchanged, and their betrayals are implicitly juxtaposed. In Book 2, mention is made of the fact that "Antenor and Eneas" (line 1474) have been allied with Poliphete in a campaign against Criseyde. Aeneas, legendary betrayer of women, is referred to not for his heroism or his later founding of New Troy (Rome), but in connection with Antenor, his partner in betraying Troy.[41] This selective and unique mention of Aeneas can be read as an attempt to hint that the betrayer of women was also a betrayer of the city, a political as well as a personal traitor. Antenor's treachery is emphasized much more explicitly. In a section with no source in the *Filostrato*, Antenor is demonized as one

---

[40] See *Riverside Chaucer*, p. 1045, note to lines 202–6.

[41] This episode appears in Dares, *De excidio Troiae historia*. See Barry Windeatt, *Oxford Guides To Chaucer: "Troilus and Criseyde"* (Oxford: Clarendon Press, 1992), p. 75.

that brought hem to meschaunce,
For he was after traitour to the town.
(Book 4, lines 203–4)

Chaucer's text explicitly foregrounds the treason of this figure. The names of Antenor and Criseyde—the two "traitors"—are frequently linked in this passage: for example, "axed was for Antenor Criseyde" (line 149); "For Antenor how they wolde han Criseyde" (line 177); " 'That al oure vois is to forgon Criseyde.' / And to deliveren Antenor they preyde" (lines 195–96); "For Antenor to yelden out Criseyde," (line 212). The frequent association of Criseyde with traitors and treachery gains resonance if we consider that "treason" in the fourteenth century was a concept "sufficiently expansive to embrace court and bedchamber, state policy and personal desire."[42] As Strohm points out, a woman's private challenge to a man could be seen as a challenge "to commonly held notions of civil order and the state."[43] Just as, in the *Westminster Chronicle*, a woman's murder of her husband is juxtaposed with accounts of the 1388 treason trials,[44] so Criseyde's betrayal of Troilus could arguably be described as the same basic crime as Antenor's betrayal of Troy. Many years ago, Robertson commented:

Like most medieval men, [Chaucer] regarded political and social problems as moral problems, not as difficulties to be overcome by reorganization and legislation. And moral problems in a Christian society were essentially problems of love.[45]

In other words, there is no simple division between the personal and the political in Chaucer's texts: indeed, in *Troilus and Criseyde*, Chaucer uses a romance plot to comment on sociopolitical behavior and, in particular, on treason and betrayal.[46] Contemporary legislation and chronicles tell

---

[42] Strohm, "Treason in the Household," in *Hochon's Arrow*, pp. 121–44, pp. 122–23.

[43] Strohm, "Treason in the Household," p. 123.

[44] See Strohm, "Treason in the Household."

[45] See D. W. Robertson, *A Preface to Chaucer: Studies in Medieval Perspectives* (Princeton: Princeton University Press, 1962), p. 462.

[46] In *Troilus and Criseyde*, the narrator maintains a façade of not being interested in history/politics, but the personal story is made to tell the political one nonetheless. This is done through occupatio ("how this town com to destruccion / Ne falleth naught to purpos me to telle," Book 2, lines 141–42), through direct, seemingly incidental references (" 'Se, Troilus / Hath right now put to flighte the Grekes route!,' " Book 2, lines 612–13), through the language of war constantly employed by the characters to talk about love (" 'desir so brennyngly me assailleth,' " Book 1, line 607) and through the movement of the plot. As the poem progresses, it exposes the impossibility of constructing a "private" world, as history proves inexorable and the scene of the action shifts

us that political structures were seen to depend upon—or at least to mirror—familial ones.[47] A narrative about personal betrayal could not escape political relevance in the 1380s.

In *Troilus and Criseyde*, treason extends into the heart of Trojan society, and is not contained within the obvious "traitor" figures. As Calchas attests, the gods are angry with all of the "folk of Troie" (Book 4, line 122) as they refused to pay for the building of the walls. Troilus openly asserts that the corruption within Trojan society is to blame for the conflict with the Greeks, saying that:

> "First, syn thow woost this town hath al this werre
> For ravysshyng of wommen so by myght,"
>
> (Book 4, lines 547–48)

The irony of Troilus's comment lies in the fact that his own "'ravysshyng of wommen'" has caused him to neglect the welfare of his city and, in a sense, to betray Troy and Priam, who is both his own father and the king. Eugene Vance has commented on the "politically anarchic force of Troilus's very conventional sentiments of love."[48] Troilus's love is so excessive that it leads him to neglect his city and the war, and to prioritize his personal desire over every other concern. This is evident throughout his speeches; he asserts he would rather have Criseyde's love than "a thousand Troyes" (Book 2, line 977) and he laments that

> "desir so brennyngly me assailleth,
> That to ben slayn it were a gretter joie

---

from private chambers to the battlefields outside Troy. See Vance, *Mervelous Signals*, pp. 256–310, for an excellent discussion of the role of history and language in *Troilus and Criseyde*. Gayle Margherita comments that "the poem seems committed to forgetting the past. The narrator, Troilus, and Pandarus all contribute to the poem's disavowal of the historical real and its deferral of historical knowledge," and goes on to discuss the "feminization and marginalization of the past," in the poem. See Gayle Margherita, *The Romance of Origins: Language and Sexual Difference in Middle English Literature* (Philadelphia: University of Pennsylvania Press, 1994), pp. 111, 112. This ostensible forgetting and marginalization of the past is problematized throughout the poem: the tragedies of the poem can happen precisely because the characters ignore history, and participate in an inexorable traffic in (and therefore marginalization of) women.

[47] Strohm writes, "if the master or husband or priest is understood to occupy a position 'like' that of the king, then his position must be protected lest the king suffer analogical or derivative slights" ("Treason in the Household," p. 125).

[48] Vance, *Mervelous Signals*, p. 288.

> To me than kyng of Grece ben and Troye."
>> (Book 1, lines 607–09)

In Book 4, Troilus's words to Fortune express explicit disloyalty to his father:

> "Why ne haddestow my fader, kyng of Troye,
> Byraft the lif, or don my bretheren dye."
>> (Book 4, lines 276–77)

Discussing this speech, Larry Scanlon comments that Troilus

values Criseyde beyond his patrilineage [. . .] It reveals the extent to which that desire enacts itself precisely as a conflict with the Law of the Father, as an attempt to wrest control of a woman outside the normal channels of exchange. This characterization will surface twice more in this lament, first in the invocation of Oedipus two stanzas later, and in the final, abrupt attack on Calkas.[49]

These lines involve Troilus in treason: he ignores the duty he owes to his brother and his father and, at the same time, flouts the duty that he owes to his king. The juxtaposition here of "fader" and "kyng of Troye" neatly encapsulates just how close personal and political betrayal can be: for the son of the king, they cannot be divided. Troilus's desire makes him traitorous, as he rebels against the patriarchal power that "should" control the exchange of women, and to which he should submit himself as son and as subject.

Truth and Treason

Both the accusations of the aldermen and *Troilus and Criseyde* situate their investigations of division within the troubled discourse of truth and treason. Richard Firth Green has recently and persuasively described the pressures on the semantics of *trouthe* and *tresoun* in the late fourteenth century. He considers the two terms to be closely related to each other, frequently referring to treason as the "antonym" of truth.[50] A citation

---

[49] Larry Scanlon, "Sweet Persuasion: The Subject of Fortune in *Troilus and Criseyde*," in *Chaucer's "Troilus and Criseyde:" "Subgit to alle Poesye": Essays in Criticism*, ed. R. A. Shoaf and Catherine S. Cox (Binghampton, N.Y.: Pegasus, 1992), pp. 211–23, p. 221.

[50] Green, *Crisis of Truth*, pp. xiv, 207.

from the *Parson's Tale* illustrates the interdependence of the two words: ". . . he that wikked conseil yeveth is a traytour. For he deceyveth hym that trusteth in hym" (X. 639).[51] Green emphasizes that the word "traitor" "meant primarily someone who had betrayed a trust."[52] Further, he claims that both terms were sites of contention and shifting semantic possibilities in the late fourteenth century.

Green argues that, at this time, the meaning of *trouthe* shifted from "integrity" to "conformity to fact," and that this change was connected with a growing emphasis on the written over the spoken, encouraged by the spread of vernacular literacy. Trothplight began to be replaced by written contract, trust in people by trust in documents, as these decades saw a "widespread loss of faith in the word of trusted neighbours."[53] At this time, the development of so-called "bastard feudalism" and the trend for the formation of temporary affinities and opportunistic groups (appropriating the associational modes of bastard feudalism) may have led to a devaluing of the notion of sworn allegiance.[54] Green also describes the meaning of *tresoun* as shifting from "personal betrayal" to "a crime against the state" in these decades, arguing that "the overriding political issue in the last two decades of the fourteenth century was the legal definition of treason."[55] In the texts under consideration in this

[51] Green cites this in *Crisis of Truth*, p. 214.

[52] Green, *Crisis of Truth*, p. 214.

[53] Ibid., pp. 1–4 and p. 40.

[54] For discussions of bastard feudalism and the livery and maintenance debate, see K. B. McFarlane, *England in the Fifteenth Century: Collected Essays* (London: The Hambledon Press, 1981), pp. 23–43 and *The Nobility of Later Medieval England: The Ford Lectures for 1953 and Related Studies* (Oxford: Oxford University Press, 1973), pp. 102–21, and Maurice Keen, *English Society in the Later Middle Ages 1348–1500* (London: Penguin Books, 1990), pp. 1–24. See also R. H. Britnell and A. J. Pollard, eds., *The McFarlane Legacy: Studies in Late Medieval Politics and Society* (New York: St. Martin's Press, 1995), where both G. L. Harriss and Linda Clark voice useful correctives warning against emphasizing "bastard feudalism" too much. Harriss comments that "The proclivity of bastard feudalism to escalate gentry disputes has perhaps been exaggerated"; Clark (discussing parliament) that, "we should be careful not to exaggerate the role played by magnates in determining the composition of the lower house" as the majority of members "lived lives largely untouched by 'bastard feudalism.'" See G. L. Harris, "The Dimensions of Politics," in *McFarlane Legacy*, pp. 1–20, p. 4, and Linda Clark, "Magnates and Their Affinities in the Parliaments of 1386–1421," in *McFarlane Legacy*, pp. 127–53, pp. 134, 136.

[55] Green, *Crisis of Truth*, p. xiv, p. 213. With his revision of the Statute of Treason, Richard tried to silence all attempts at criticizing him, terming anyone who purported to advise or to counsel him a traitor. In response to a petition concerning the expense of the royal household, Parliament declared that "if anyone at all, whatever his status or condition, should encourage or incite the commons of Parliament or any one else, to remedy or reform anything which concerns our person, our rule, or our regality, he should, and shall, be held a traitor." Cited in Green, *Crisis of Truth*, p. 222.

essay, "truth" and "treason" function as key concepts and terms, as a struggle emerges for control over the meaning of these words.

In *Troilus and Criseyde* the language of truth is crucial. Troilus is concerned with the idea of truth as reputation and integrity, in other words with the "older" notion of "trothplight." He urges Criseyde to "thynketh on youre trouthe" (Book 5, line 1386), claims that her "name of trouthe / Is now fordon" (lines 1686–87), because she "nolde in trouthe to me stonde" (line 1679), and accuses her of having "bytrayed" (line 1247) him by failing to keep her "trust" or "feyth" (line 1259). Yet, if we think of truth as "conformity to fact," Troilus himself has hardly behaved "truthfully" throughout the courtship which has, as Robertson points out, been "grounded on a tissue of lies, rather than on 'trouthe.' "[56]

Criseyde too is deeply concerned with the issue of her *trouthe,* as is demonstrated in her lament in Book 5 (lines 1051–85). It opens:

> But trewely, the storie telleth us,
> Ther made nevere womman moore wo
> Than she, whan that she falsed Troilus.
> She seyde, "Allas, for now is clene ago
> My name of trouthe in love, for everemo!
> For I have falsed oon the gentileste
> That evere was, and oon the worthieste!"

After another stanza in which she mourns her approaching notoriety, Criseyde worries about future generations of female readers who will berate her lack of truth:

[56] Robertson, *Preface*, p. 496. Robertson contextualizes this point by claiming that the ultimate " 'sentence' of *Troilus and Criseyde* is 'What nedeth feyned loves for to seke?' ", (p. 501), that the meaning of the poem is grounded in Christian morality and closure. My view is that, rather than celebrating Christian teleology, the text fails to end: Rosemarie P. McGerr has argued that the ending demonstrates a "resistance to closure"; that it is "conventional but inconclusive," and that its incongruity reveals the difficulties encoded within the idea of an ending. She adds that the poem "ultimately makes clear the difficulty of determining meaning and the need for resisting the illusion of closure in our pursuit of understanding." See "Meaning and Ending in a 'Paynted Proces': Resistance to Closure in *Troilus and Criseyde,*" in *Chaucer's "Troilus and Criseyde": "Subgit to alle Poesye,"* ed. Shoaf and Cox, pp. 179–98, pp. 181, 180, 198. E. Talbot Donaldson famously described the ending of *Troilus and Criseyde* as "a kind of nervous breakdown in poetry." See "The Ending of Chaucer's *Troilus,*" in *Early English and Norse Studies,* ed. Arthur Brown and Peter Foote (London: Methuen, 1963), pp. 26–45, p. 34. Patterson also makes an illuminating comment that the scornful laughter from the spheres, at the end of the poem, mirrors the scornful laughter in the temple at the beginning. See Patterson, *Chaucer and the Subject,* p. 151.

"Thei wol seyn, in as muche as in me is,
I have hem don deshonour, weylaway!
Al be I nat the first that dide amys,
What helpeth that to don my blame awey?
But syn I se ther is no bettre way,
And that to late is now for me to rewe,
To Diomede algate I wol be trewe.

"But, Troilus, syn I no bettre may,
And syn that thus departen ye and I,
Yet prey I God, so yeve yow right good day,
As for the gentileste, trewely,
That evere I say, to serven feythfully,
And best kan ay his lady honour kepe."
And with that word she brast anon to wepe.

"And certes yow ne haten shal I nevere;
And frendes love, that shal ye han of me,
And my good word, al sholde I lyven evere.
And trewely I wolde sory be
For to seen yow in adversitee;
And gilteles, I woot wel, I yow leve.
But al shal passe; and thus take I my leve."

The passage is informed by an awareness of untruth and falsity. In the first stanza, the word *falsed* is twice repeated within four lines. Criseyde goes on to lament her "deshonour" and the loss of her "name of trouthe," promising to be "trewe" from now on—within these few stanzas the word *trewely* is repeated three times. Having acknowledged her own falsity and the loss of her reputation for truth, Criseyde goes on to assert that she will be "trewe" to Diomede, and to qualify her assertions with the word *trewely*. She simultaneously admits her *untrouthe* while depending on a belief in her *trouthe* to make her words meaningful. Criseyde is saying that, although she has lost her "name" for truth—that is, society's idea of truth—she can personally still be true to Diomede. She acknowledges the validity of two different semantics of truth; in one sense it refers to public honor and permanent integrity, or appearance of integrity, in the other meaning, it refers to a changing, but honestly meant intent.[57] However, Criseyde's intent is not even clear in

[57] See also Elizabeth Archibald, "Declarations of 'Entente' in *Troilus and Criseyde*," *Chau R* 25 (1991): 190–213.

her words; we cannot know if she "truly" intends to keep her faith with Diomede, or if she means what she says. She also uses the word with the meaning "conformity to fact," when she declares that Troilus is "trewely" the "gentileste" man, and when she says that she would "trewely" be sorry to see him in "adversitee." This meaning of "truth" coexists with the idea of truth as "trothplight," and both meanings are available in these lines. Moreover, the disingenuous narrator himself uses the term *trewely*, and repeats it immediately after the conclusion of Criseyde's "untruthful" lament. He comments:

> But trewely, how longe it was bytwene
> That she forsok hym for this Diomede,
> Ther is non auctour telleth it, I wene
> (Book 5, lines 1086–88)

He is using the word *trewely* with the meaning "conforming to fact," but we know that the narrator is profoundly unreliable in this poem. The dissimulation and "untruth" of the narrator on the matter of his sources, for example, has already been made clear; he too is a prevaricator when it comes to the idea of *trouthe*.[58]

In *Troilus and Criseyde*, the word *trewe* proves to be ambiguous, and the importance of gaining control over its meaning is expressed in Criseyde's attempts to harness it to her own behavior and in Troilus's forgetfulness of his own untruth. With its emphasis on the way that personal division and sexual deviancy lead to political dissent, and on the connections between petty and high treason, as evinced in the insistent connections between political traitors (Antenor, Calchas) and a personal traitor (Criseyde), *Troilus and Criseyde* also draws heavily on the differing conceptions of treason available at this time. *Troilus and Criseyde* suggests that fragmented personal relationships imply a fragmented society and city, and that macrocosmic as well as microcosmic groups are corrupted and treasonous. In this text, the meaning of treason is often unclear: Criseyde, for example, betrays both Troilus, and Troy, as she goes over to the Greeks, and indirectly causes Troilus's

---

[58] My argument—that in *Troilus and Criseyde* (and in the culture in which it was produced) the meaning of *trouthe* is contingent and fluctuating—is very different from Vance's belief that *trouthe* functions as a metaphysical absolute in the poem. See Vance, *Mervelous Signals*, p. 309. Green too suggests that Chaucer feels "nostalgia for the vanished stability of the old trouthe" (*Crisis of Truth*, p. 164). I would argue that *Troilus and Criseyde* can be read as a meditation on the absurdity of nostalgia itself.

death. This seals the fate of Troy, which cannot survive without Troilus.[59] The "older" conception of treason as personal betrayal remains crucial in this text, and is emphatically connected with high treason itself.

Equally, within the textual accusations of the aldermen, a struggle can be seen for control over the terms of truth and treason. In the reports of the actions of the aldermen, the same, clearly emotive words of accusation frequently recur: they act "felonice, false et proditorie contra ligeanceam suam" (feloniously, falsely, and traitorously against their allegiance), "false, felonice et proditorie, contra fidem et ligeanciam suam" (falsely, feloniously, and traitorously against their faith and allegiance), "contra ligeanciam et fidem suas domino regi debitas" (against the allegiance and faith owed to their king).[60] Throughout the text, the "traitors" are insistently described as "false," as acting against their "fidem" or "ligeanceam," as men who break their word and oath, and fail to do what they "deberent." The key words and concepts are insistently repeated, hammering home the idea of the *untrouth* and deceitfulness of the accused. Throughout the letter of 20 November, the aldermen are accused of high treason, of betraying their allegiance to their king.

Yet, at one point in the text, we can glimpse both a different conception of treason, and a different construction of where the treason in society is to be found. Thomas Farringdon is depicted saying: "*Vindica me de illo falso proditore priore, quia tenementa mea false et ffraudilenter de me arripuit.*"[61] ["Avenge me on this false, treacherous prior, because he has falsely and fraudulently seized from me my houses."] In this short phrase, the language of accusation is bounced back from the rebel-figures to the objects of their attack, who become the traitors. Farringdon is here portrayed as twice using the word "false," and he also uses the key term of "treason." The prior and his ilk are false, and therefore the rebels, by implication, are true. Moreover, the words attributed to Farringdon introduce a competing construction of treason, as he accuses the prior of being a traitor because he has seized his house. Farringdon

---

[59] See Sylvia Federico, "A Fourteenth-Century Erotics of Politics: London as a Feminine New Troy," *Studies in the Age of Chaucer* 19 (1997): 121–55, p. 123, note 8. She notes, "Criseyde's betrayal of her lover, Troilus, was [. . .] seen as a direct cause of the fall of Troy, since Troilus's survival was thought necessary for the survival of the city."

[60] Réville, *Le soulevement*, pp. 192, 195, 194.

[61] Ibid., p. 195; emphasis in original.

is clearly here trying to settle a personal score, and is making use of the older conception of treason as personal betrayal. In this attribution of a voice to the rebels, the report taps into some of the linguistic and political issues that most troubled the rebels and, ironically, it provides matter for their defense. The peasants, after all, insisted on their self-identification as the "trew communes,"[62] and on defining their enemies as traitors. Indeed, the revolt participated in a number of ways in the fourteenth-century debate concerning "new and illicit forms of association."[63]

Strohm describes the way that accounts of the revolt often include suggestions that the insurgents are using "new forms of association for purposes of rebellion"; they use livery, they force people to swear to support them, they swear fealty to each other.[64] He suggests that the chronicle accounts involuntarily demonstrate the rebels' ability "to manipulate existing forms creatively in order to constitute themselves as a new kind of community."[65] Green's work has a slightly different emphasis: he claims that the peasants were actually trying to hold on to *traditional* notions of oaths, trothplight, and truth that were being eroded by the encroaching emphasis on written documents and bureaucracy. He writes:

the outlaw tradition can only be understood in the light of a genuine and documented late-medieval resistance to central authority which many historians would discuss as mere endemic lawlessness, but which I prefer to characterize as a last-ditch appeal to older legal strategies. In our period, the most extreme, though far from the only, example of such resistance is the Peasants' Revolt.[66]

He argues that the peasants' grievance was that "truth," embodied in folklaw and tradition, was being supplanted by judicial writing, which sought to remove ancient rights and liberties, among other things. Ste-

---

[62] See, for example, V. H. Galbraith, ed., *The Anonimalle Chronicle, 1333–1381* (Manchester: The University Press; Longmans, Green, 1927), p. 139.

[63] Strohm, "'A Revelle!': Chronicle Evidence and the Rebel Voice," in *Hochon's Arrow*, pp. 33–56, p. 39.

[64] Ibid., "'A Revelle!'," p. 39.

[65] Ibid., "'A Revelle!'," p. 40.

[66] Green, *Crisis of Truth*, p. 164. See also Jesse M. Gellrich, *Discourse and Dominion in the Fourteenth Century: Oral Contexts of Writing in Philosophy, Politics and Poetry* (Princeton: Princeton University Press, 1995), especially chap. 5, "The Politics of Literacy in the Reign of Richard II," pp. 151–91.

ven Justice too argues for *trewþe* as that which the insurgents "intend to repossess."[67] In this context, it is the peasants who are the traditionalists, the authorities the radicals who are seeking to redefine the concepts of truth, and indeed treason. The penchant of the nobles and the king for encouraging temporary forms of association by employing novel forms of livery and maintenance, and the growing legal importance of written contract over trothplight, would support this interpretation.[68] The insistence in the report on the aldermen on the treason and truth-breaking of the accused could itself be seen as a backlash against the accusations heaped on the crown and government.[69] Moreover, other groups, also demonized as rebels against authority, took as their agenda the reclaiming of *trouthe*. For example, the possibility of a "Lollard sect vocabulary," dominated by an emphasis on "trewe prechoures," "trewe men," and "trewe cristen men" has been mooted.[70] Claiming rights over the language of truth was of crucial importance at this time. Both the reports on the aldermen and *Troilus and Criseyde* place the terms of division within the context of the debate over the idea of truth, and both betray an awareness that the language of accusation is unstable in the extreme.[71]

The ambiguities of the concepts of "truth" and "treason" in these texts complicate the attribution of blame to specific individuals. While the idea of betrayal and high treason implies that there is a coherent

[67] See Green, *Crisis of Truth*, p. 201, and Steven Justice, *Writing and Rebellion: England in 1381* (Berkeley: University of California Press, 1994), p. 94 and also p. 188. Justice discusses the importance of the idea of *trewþe* in John Ball's letters and in *Piers Plowman* at length in this work.

[68] In *Writing and Rebellion*, Justice further discusses the importance of "personal pledging" (p. 183) in village life.

[69] Green describes the way that "centralized law sought to redefine social loyalties by turning old, local folklaw virtues into new crimes against authority" (*Crisis of Truth*, p. 163) and emphasizes the peasants' anger against and resistance to new legal strategies (pp. 163–64).

[70] Anne Hudson, "A Lollard Sect Vocabulary?," in *Lollards and Their Books* (London: The Hambledon Press, 1985), pp. 165–80, pp. 166–67.

[71] In his analysis of the annotations on MS London, B.L. Additional 27304, Baswell suggests that Horn's work can be seen, from within a "broad-based urban perspective," as "peacemaking and containment," adding that the nature of Horn's actions—"loyalty or treachery"—is "a question of highly interested perspective, of hermeneutics in effect, not fact." See "Aeneas in 1381," pp. 29, 27. Similarly, Carolyn Dinshaw comments, "When [Criseyde] chooses to shift her allegiance from Troilus to Diomede, she in fact acts in the best interests of Troy in the repair of its losses in battle and in the reestablishment of truce." Carolyn Dinshaw, *Chaucer's Sexual Poetics* (Madison: University of Wisconsin Press, 1989), p. 57. Furthermore, at the end of Book 4, Criseyde advocates and predicts peace (lines 1345–58).

and unified society to be betrayed, the faction-fighting and multiple divisions evident in the body of these texts, as well as in the circumstances of their production, suggests that division is deeply rooted in society. In the accusations of the aldermen, a more general sense of social division is evident in *what has been suppressed*: the factional circumstances of the texts' production, the suggestion of a more widespread urban guilt during the revolt. Indeed, Wilkinson has suggested that it was in the jurors' interests to indict a few specific traitors, rather than implicating a more "considerable section of the citizens," who may have been to blame.[72] Further, inside the texts themselves, the imagined Farringdon, who implies that there is a more general treachery within society, and the imagined Horn, who claims that many Londoners support the peasants, voice what the text is trying to silence. Their words infiltrate the structure of the text and chip away at its edifice, by introducing the possibility of a broader urban division. The mere suggestion of such division, and its strident denial, might encourage readers to imagine a guilt that extends much further than the authors wished to allow. However, overt references to the general urban fragmentation that may have contributed to the revolt and that certainly motivated the production of the letters are excluded from the text (presumably because of the agenda of the jurors). The emphasis remains strongly on the individual traitor aldermen. In *Troilus and Criseyde*, as has been shown, specific figures of social importance—Calchas, of "gret auctorite" (Book 1, line 65), Criseyde, and Antenor—are singled out for blame. But, as my brief discussion of Troilus's "treachery" implied, Chaucer's text is more expansive than the accusations of the aldermen can be. In *Troilus and Criseyde*, internal division resonates throughout urban society and is not confined to specific traitors: rather, the emphasis is on the culpability of all the Trojans, and on division within the protective/exclusive walls. The traitor figures are not essentially different from the other characters; rather, they are representative of the chaos within Trojan society. The final part of this article will focus on the fragmentary nature of the urban society depicted in *Troilus and Criseyde*.

The Divided City: Social Impossibility in *Troilus and Criseyde*

Urban division is exemplified in the episode in Book 2 at Deiphoebus's house, in which the idea of betrayal within the walls of the house—a

---

[72] See Wilkinson, "Peasants' Revolt," p. 19.

microcosm of the city—is crucial. This is particularly demonstrated when Troilus and Pandarus use a ruse to get Helen and Deiphoebus out of the way, and make "'the townes prow'" (line 1664) (the town's profit), the excuse. The ideal of common profit is opportunistically invoked to allow Troilus and Pandarus the chance to pursue their private intrigues. Throughout this section, all of the characters seem to be duplicitous and divisive in some way. Pandarus is the most obvious example as he has lied his way into Deiphoebus's house, and is masking his *entente*, as he "Deiphebus gan to blende" (line 1496), saying "For I right now have founden o manere / Of sleyghte" (lines 1511–12). The hosts are explicitly described as "they, that nothyng knewe of his entente" (line 1665). Pandarus is manifestly using and manipulating his host and abusing his trust. He has also deceived Criseyde, who is "Al innocent of Pandarus entente" (line 1723)—although we can never be sure of how much or little she understands—persuading her that "some men wolden don oppressioun, / And wrongfully han hire possessioun" (lines 1418–19). Troilus too is complicit in the general deception: he acts "His brother and his suster for to blende" (Book 3, line 207). This is especially significant in the context of the fact that Deiphoebus is Troilus's most beloved brother (Book 2, line 1398) and Pandarus's second most beloved friend (lines 1403–4). Pandarus's and Troilus's conduct demonstrates their lack of concern for the bonds of fraternity in the face of their selfish needs. This unconcern for the ties of brotherhood can also be seen in a seeming declaration of the importance of common profit: "Anhonged be swich oon, were he my brother!" (line 1620), a sentiment declared by all present.

An added sense of intrigue, incest, and internal secrets and division is suggested by the choice of Deiphoebus and Helen as hosts and counselors of the session.[73] Far from being the innocent parties, they may be

---

[73] From the Fourth Lateran Council of 1215, incest was defined as sexual intercourse between those related to the fourth degree: thus one was proscribed from having sex with one's parent, sibling, aunt, uncle, first, second or third cousin. These rules also applied to relationships of affinity (e.g., one could not marry someone who had previously slept with one's sibling) and of spirituality (e.g., one's godparents). It was a commonplace to associate incest with social division and destruction. Georgiana Donavin, for example, discusses the fact that Thomas Aquinas defended exogamy on the grounds that it cements social relationships by encouraging ties outside the family and by discouraging exploitation within it, and comments that in the *Confessio amantis*, there are many "tales of incest resulting in social chaos" and that "the actually incestuous family is a microcosm of and a catalyst for the social decay. Actualized incestuous desire both represents and contributes to the discord." Georgiana Donavin, *Incest Narratives and the Structure of Gower's Confessio Amantis* (Victoria, B.C.: English Literary Studies University of Victoria, 1993), pp. 10, 11, 51. The best article on incest in *Troilus and*

easy to deceive because they themselves are intent upon their own deception. According to tradition, Deiphoebus was Helen's second Trojan husband, killed by Menelaus in their bedchamber after the Greek entry into Troy.[74] In the *House of Fame*, reference is made to Aeneas meeting Deiphoebus in the underworld: in the *Aeneid*, this meeting involves Deiphoebus telling Aeneas about Helen's treachery to Troy and to him, her husband.[75] Perhaps the depiction of the close relationship between Deiphoebus and Helen and their obvious intimacy in *Troilus and Criseyde* implies something more, and that they too are eager to seize on the "townes prow" as an excuse for disappearing together. Their putative affair could be seen as a mirror to that of Troilus and Criseyde, especially as both relationships involve women who are unfaithful to their lovers and also to Troy itself, women whose autonomy and motivation remain always opaque.[76]

One more incident clearly demonstrates the falsity of the appearance of fraternity and honesty at the meeting in Deiphoebus's house. In reaction to Criseyde's worries about her enemies,

> Pleynliche, alle at ones, they hire highten
> To ben hire help in al that evere they myghten.
>
> (lines 1623–24)

Yet this declaration proves utterly hollow when Criseyde faces a real threat—her expulsion from Troy—and neither Deiphoebus nor Paris, whom Helen "may leden" (line 1449), nor even Troilus speaks out for her or supports Hector in the parliament. Indeed, in the parliament scene, the self-destruction of the Trojans and the unreliability of group opinion is clear. The deceptive nature of unity is demonstrated in the use of the chorus-like group, characterized as the "peple," who represent

---

Criseyde is Richard W. Fehrenbacher, "'Al that which chargeth nought to seye': The Theme of Incest in *Troilus and Criseyde*," *Exemplaria* 9 (1997): 341–69. Much can be gained from adding a consideration of Helen and Deiphoebus to his argument.

[74] See McKay Sundwall, "Deiphobus and Helen: A Tantalizing Hint," *Modern Philology* 73 (1975–76): 151–56.

[75] See the *House of Fame*, line 444, and *Aeneid*, Book 6, lines 509–29, in P. Vergili Maroni, *Opera*, ed. R. A. B. Mynors (Oxford: Clarendon Press, 1969). Deiphoebus here recounts how Helen, his wife, removes all the weapons from his house and his sword from next to his head, and invites Menelaus into his bridal chamber to murder him.

[76] See Louise Fradenburg, *Sacrifice Your Love: Psychoanalysis, Historicism, Chaucer* (Minneapolis: University of Minnesota Press, 2002), p. 230.

ignorant public opinion and provide a commentary on the action.[77] They are described thus:

> The noyse of peple up stirte thanne at ones,
> As breme as blase of strawe iset on-fire;[78]
> For infortune it wolde, for the nones,
> They sholden hire confusioun desire.
> "Ector," quod they, 'what goost may yow enspyre
> This womman thus to shilde and don us leese
> Daun Antenor—a wrong wey now ye chese—
>
> "That is so wys and ek so bold baroun?
> And we han nede to folk, as men may se.
> He is ek oon the grettest of this town.
> O Ector, lat tho fantasies be!
> O kyng Priam," quod they, "thus sygge we,
> That al oure vois is to forgon Criseyde."
> And to deliveren Antenor they preyde.
>
> (Book 4, lines 183–96)

Here the people are depicted as blind and thoughtless, obeying a mindless mob mentality, which will lead them to destroy themselves.[79] They

---

[77] The exact social level of the people is ambiguous: those who argue that they are a figure for the parliamentary commons would raise them to a level above the general mob. Patterson, for example, says that the Trojan parliament provides a "mordant commentary" on the Wonderful Parliament of 1386: if the "peple" represent the people of the English Commons they are by no means of low class. I would not agree that they are such a straightforward reflection of the English parliament. The "peple" do not seem to me to be a figure for the peasantry either; rather they represent group opinion or thinking. See Patterson, *Chaucer and the Subject*, p. 158.

[78] The possible reference to Jack Straw and the Peasants' Revolt is significant here: the present investigation has discussed the transference of blame for the revolt to those within the city in the accusations of the aldermen and in some chronicle accounts. In the above-cited stanzas too, if a reference to the revolt is implied, it is again the urban dwellers who are blamed, rather than the rural peasants. John Ganim discusses the allusion to "straw" and also suggests that the "peple" could here reflect both the rebels *and* the Parliament of 1386. See John M. Ganim, "Chaucer and the Noise of the People," *Exemplaria* 2 (1990): 71–88, p. 74.

[79] Depictions of mob madness are, of course, common in the wake of the Peasants' Revolt, in particular in chronicle accounts, and, famously, in Gower's depiction of the peasants in the first book of the *Vox clamantis*. In an article about Chaucer's reference to the Peasants' Revolt in the *Nun's Priest's Tale*, Peter Travis says of the chroniclers of the revolt that they were apparently "as disturbed by the revolting noise of the peasants as by the fact that the peasants were revolting." See Peter W. Travis, "Chaucer's trivial fox chase and the Peasants' Revolt of 1381," *Journal of Medieval and Renaissance Studies* 18 (1988): 195–220, p. 217. See also Justice, *Writing and Rebellion*, especially Chap. 5,

disregard Hector—"holder up of Troye!" (Book 2, line 644)—and invite the return of Antenor, who will betray the city through his removal of the Palladium. The idea of the folly of the people is emphasized by this stress on Antenor's behavior, as the "cloude of errour" (Book 4, line 200) of the masses is described. The unreliability of popular opinion is also referred to at other points in the poem. For example, Pandarus declares in Book 2, at Deiphoebus's house, that:

> "In titeryng, and pursuyte, and delayes,
> The folk devyne at waggyng of a stree;"
> (Book 2, lines 1744–45)

Yet the views of these people are frequently held up as important throughout the poem and Criseyde, in particular, often relies on their opinion.[80]

As well as the "peple," a group that illustrates the dangerous aspects of social "unity," many other social groupings—or factions—within the poem are portrayed as divided. Trojan society, like contemporary London, is splintered into a wide variety of "meynees," affinities, and fraternities.[81] Both Troilus and Criseyde have their own social groups, or "meynees" that they systematically deceive, hiding the truth of their relationship and feelings under a mantle of overt friendship and honesty. Troilus acts "his meyne for to blende" (Book 5, line 526) and Criseyde feels "wo and wery of that compaignie" as "hire herte on othir thyng is" (Book 4, lines 707, 696). The scene at Deiphoebus's house analyzed above acts as a paradigm for the way that Troilus and Criseyde consistently treat their closest companions throughout the text. Social groups are never transparent or unproblematic in this text.

Indeed, in my view, society in Chaucer's texts is underpinned not by "natural amiability," but by an idea of "natural antagonism."[82] In Slavoj Žižek's words, this "dimension of radical negativity [. . .] defines *la condition humaine* as such."[83] Augustine's characterization of earthly

---

"Insurgency Remembered," pp. 193–254, for a discussion of the ways in which the peasants' actions were memorialized as inarticulate and insane.

[80] See, for example, Book 2, lines 730, 748.

[81] See McFarlane, *Nobility of Later Medieval England,* p. 105, for a discussion of the meaning of "meinie."

[82] Wallace discusses "natural amiability" in Chaucer's texts in *Chaucerian Polity,* p. 67.

[83] Slavoj Žižek, *The Sublime Object of Ideology* (London: Verso, 1989), pp. 4–5.

societies illuminates this concept of inevitable antagonism: "human society is generally divided against itself, and one part of it oppresses another."[84] Throughout the *City of God*, Augustine often repeats and elaborates on this idea, at one point commenting that "the earthly city is generally divided against itself by litigation, by wars, by battles, by the pursuit of victories that bring death with them or at best are doomed to death."[85] Augustine uses the city as an image of community: "the society whose common aim is worldly advantage or the satisfaction of desire, the community which we call by the general name of 'the city of this world.'"[86] He emphasizes the fact that the city is particularly associated with antisocial activity, commenting that: "The first founder of the earthly city was [. . .] a fratricide."[87] The examples of Cain and Romulus illustrate the fragmentary nature of human fellowship— Augustine writes that the story of Romulus and Remus demonstrates "the division of the earthly city against itself."[88] It is often suggested that ideas of social fragmentation are crystallized in an urban environment: the *polis* frequently acts as an image for society or civilization.[89] Elaine Scarry connects the "unequivocally negative connotations to city-dwelling" in the Old Testament with the Old Testament's prohibition of "human acts of building, making, creating, working."[90] In other words, living in a city is associated with being a social/political animal; the city foregrounds ideas of society/community, with their concomitant problems.[91] In *Troilus and Criseyde*, the fragmentation of the city, and of human society, is laid bare.

[84] Augustine of Hippo, *City of God*, trans. Henry Bettenson (London: Penguin Books, 1984), Book 18, Chap. 2, p. 762.
[85] Ibid., Book 15, chap. 4, p. 599.
[86] Ibid., Book 18, chap. 2, p. 762.
[87] Ibid., Book 15, chap. 6, p. 600.
[88] Ibid., Book 15, chap. 6, p. 601.
[89] Giorgio Agamben is a recent participant in a long line of writers who discuss the (Aristotelian) idea that the city is associated with civilization, the human, while the forest is linked with savagery and the animal. See *Homo Sacer: Sovereign Power and Bare Life*, trans. Daniel Heller-Roazen (Stanford: Stanford University Press, 1998), p. 105. See also Jacques Le Goff, 'Lévi-Strauss in Broceliande: A Brief Analysis of a Courtly Romance,' in *The Medieval Imagination* (London: University of Chicago Press, 1988), pp. 107–31, especially pp. 110, 115.
[90] Elaine Scarry, *The Body in Pain: The Making and Unmaking of the World* (New York; Oxford: Oxford University Press, 1985), pp. 221.
[91] The city is associated with human endeavor and social groupings, and these groupings are always already destructive and negative. Fradenburg comments: "The idea of the city seems so often to raise the specter of ontological crisis," and adds that, "the city—not exclusively, but with a particular kind of power—poses the problem of how human beings construct and produce their world." Louise Fradenburg, *City, Marriage,*

The inevitable fragmentation of social groups is a central theme of the poem. Within *Troilus and Criseyde*, an integrated community can only exist if it is based on exclusion and repression. This is evident at the start of the poem, when Hector advises Criseyde to "'Lat youre fadres treson gon / Forth with meschaunce, and ye youreself in joie / Dwelleth with us'" (Book 1, lines 117–19). Criseyde must forget and ignore what has happened, in order to continue living happily. At the end of Book 3, the peak of Fortune's wheel, the moment of the greatest plenitude and completion in the poem, the falsity of imagining a perfected community is made manifest. Troilus's ecstasy is described in this way:

> In suffisaunce, in blisse, and in singynges,
> This Troilus gan al his lif to lede.
> He spendeth, jousteth, maketh festeynges;
> He yeveth frely ofte, and chaungeth wede,
> And held aboute hym alwey, out of drede,
> A world of folk, as com hym wel of kynde,
> The fresshest and the beste he koude fynde;
>
> That swich a vois was of hym and a stevene,
> Thoroughout the world, of honour and largesse,
> That it rong unto the yate of hevene;
> And, as in love, he was in swich gladnesse
> That in his herte he demed, as I gesse,
> That ther nys lovere in this world at ese
> So wel as he; and thus gan love hym plese.
>
> (Book 3, lines 1716–29)

Picking up Troilus's own characteristic hyperbole, the narrator idealizes the group that he collects, describing them in superlatives as the "fresshest and the beste" and terming Troilus the happiest lover "in this world." The language of these stanzas emphasizes the fact that Troilus has cocooned himself in a little group which he believes constructs the whole world: he has "A world of folk" and the talk of him that penetrates "Thoroughout the world" clearly only has resonance within this very specific social milieu. He keeps these people with him "alwey" and lives "al his lif" in this joy—there is a pretence that such happiness

---

Tournament: Arts of Rule in Late Medieval Scotland (Madison: University of Wisconsin Press, 1991), pp. 3, 9.

can be sustained. The most notable aspect about these stanzas is their incongruity: this seemingly ideally happy little community exists in a war zone, in a besieged city overshadowed by the threat of death every day. The reality of the horror and trauma going on throughout Trojan society is repressed by the desperately partying, leisured few, who try to excise all awareness of the pervasive fragmentation and destruction in Troy.

The poem suggests that a happy community is deceiving itself—the very structure of the text emphasizes the idea that Fortune's wheel is ever turning, destruction always overshadowing social groups, and that they can only construct a veneer of coherence through repression. The bleak idea that society is *inevitably* divided is further born out by *Troilus and Criseyde's* examination of the nature of fellowship. The idea that social idealism per se is undermined in this text is demonstrated in the fact that Pandarus, master of linguistic duplicity and fragmented relationships, is the defender of social ideals. He is loud in his approval of ideologies of fellowship, but exposes the ultimate destructiveness inherent within such idealism through the extremity of his beliefs. In Book 1, Pandarus is a passionate defender of fellowship, arguing strongly for the importance and validity of fraternal bonds. He yokes the language of proverbs to his service, giving his words the character of time-honored maxims, as well as his personal approval. He says:

> "Men seyn, 'to wrecche is consolacioun
> To have another felawe in hys peyne.'"
> (lines 708–9)

The fact that such words are spoken by Pandarus encourages us to question the validity of these ideas themselves—especially as he later contradicts himself, revealing the easy manipulation of proverbial wisdom, declaring that the "'firste vertu is to kepe tonge'"[92] (Book 3, line 294) and adding that he can prove this through "'Proverbes'" (line 299). In his defense of fellowship, he asserts:

> "The wise seith, 'Wo hym that is allone,
> For, and he falle, he hath non helpe to ryse';

[92] Such proverbial wisdom is also manipulated in the *Manciple's Tale,* when the verbose mother repeatedly insists that her son must "keep wel thy tonge" (line 319, line 333, line 362).

And sith thow hast a felawe, tel thi mone;"
(Book 1, lines 694–96)

This passage finds no source in the *Filostrato*.[93] By putting such words in Pandarus's mouth and making him the defendant of the concept of fellowship, Chaucer's text fundamentally problematizes such beliefs.

Moreover, such moral musings on the value of friendship and brotherhood are greatly undermined when Pandarus takes his friendship to its logical extreme, and unwittingly exposes its perversion. His sense of the importance of fellowship is so strong that he will condone incest and Troilus's betrayal of his own brother if necessary (Book 1, lines 676–79). Similarly, when Pandarus acknowledges that he has become " 'swich a meene / As maken wommen unto men to comen' " (Book 3, lines 254–55), Troilus reassures him, partly by offering to be the same kind of man himself and giving Pandarus the choice of his sisters, but also by a manipulation of the language of fellowship: he insists that "bauderye" (line 397) is *"compaignie"* (line 396, emphasis mine) and encourages Pandarus to "calle it gentilesse, / Compassioun, and *felawship*, and trist" (lines 402–03, emphasis mine). Pandarus's own idea of fellowship seems to be both violent and selfish, a bond that overrides all other considerations and is demonstrable through bloody conflict. The most damning exposé of his concept of fellowship comes in Book 4, when he swears that

"Theigh ich and al my kyn upon a stownde
Shulle in a strete as dogges liggen dede,
Thorough-girt with many a wid and blody wownde;
In every cas I wol a frend be founde."
(Book 4, lines 625–28)

The viciousness implicit in Pandarus's concept of fellowship is shown here in his use of violent images of death and destruction, and is further demonstrated by his total lack of understanding of Troilus's plight. The implication of his early use of words of friendship is that these words and ideas are deployed to mask internal selfishness and corruption—as demonstrated in the episode in Deiphoebus's house. In this episode, in

[93] The proverbial tone of the passage comes from its source in Ecclesiastes 4:10. See Geoffrey Chaucer, *Troilus and Criseyde: A New Edition of 'The Book of Troilus,'* ed. Barry Windeatt (London: Longman, 1984), p. 129.

the Parliament scene, in the depictions of social cliques, of close friend-ships, and of sexual relationships, division and antagonism are perva-sively evident.

Troilus and Criseyde reveals what the accusations of the aldermen imply: that the discourse of treachery and the scapegoating of individual traitors is a smokescreen to cover up a more general and pervasive social antagonism. Žižek suggests that society maintains itself and its illusion of harmony through displacement:

> the basic trick of anti-semitism is to displace social antagonism into antagonism between the sound social texture, social body, and the Jew as the force corro-ding it, the force of corruption. Thus it is not society itself which is "impossi-ble," based on antagonism—the source of corruption is located in a particular entity, the Jew.[94]

This classic strategy of displacement is operative in the accusations of the aldermen, in which an awareness that "society 'doesn't work'" is partially elided by strident scapegoating.[95] Chaucer's poem questions and problematizes the idea of containing blame for civic division within a few individuals—a pertinent issue indeed in the 1380s—and suggests that urban fragmentation cannot be contained or limited. In *Troilus and Criseyde*, the consistent depiction of fragmentary social groups implies that there is no possibility of escape from a social antagonism that proves to be relentless: the text offers no hope of an alternative society, it contains no social group or relationship that is undivided or nonde-structive. Instead, the poem shows "the impossibility of 'society,'" the fact that "society never manages fully to be society."[96]

---

[94] Žižek, *Sublime Object*, p. 125.
[95] *Ibid.*, p. 127.
[96] Ernesto Laclau and Chantal Mouffe, *Hegemony and Socialist Strategy: Towards a Radi-cal Democratic Politics*, trans. Winston Moore and Paul Cammack, 2d edition (London: Verso, 2001), pp. 122, 127.

All Dressed Up with Someplace to Go

Regional Identity in *Sir Gawain and the Green Knight*

Rhonda Knight
Coker College

A theory of the border offers a method of historical analysis that confronts the paradoxes that inhere in limits and boundaries. The figure of paradox inhabits all boundary concepts because of the line of the limit seeks to institute an absolute difference at the place of most intimate contact between two spaces (or concepts, or peoples, or times, or . . .)

Michelle R. Warren, *History on the Edge*

ICHELLE R. WARREN'S WORK on border historiography acknowledges that place—region, city, nation—is a principal factor in the constitution of cultural identity, but also points out the paradox: what is imagined outside the borders of any location is equally fundamental to the formation and maintenance of that same identity.[1] Her analysis of border writing as a method to stake "territorial claims—over space, ethnicity, language and time"[2] enables us to think about borders in creative and productive ways: boundaries and borders need not impose binary thinking about the entities located on one side or the other. "The other" here is a loaded term because border writing challenges the dichotomy of self/other. The border as meeting place is a crucible where we can see the cultural work of identity being performed and negoti-

I am grateful to Marilynn Desmond, who read several incarnations of this article, for her comments and support. In addition, my thanks go to *SAC*'s editor and two anonymous readers for their insights.

[1] Michelle R. Warren, *History on the Edge: Excalibur and the Borders of Britain, 1100–1300*, (Minneapolis: University of Minnesota Press, 2000), p. 2.
[2] Warren, *History*.

ated.[3] Like Warren, Doreen Massey, in *Space, Place and Gender*, argues that what lies outside a border is paramount in understanding what lies inside. She explains:

The identities of place are always unfixed, contested and multiple. And the particularity of any place is, in these terms, constructed not by placing boundaries around it and defining its identity through counterposition to the other which lies beyond, but precisely (in part) through the specificity of the mix of links and interconnections *to* that "beyond."[4]

In this study, I am interested in how the ideas of region and border inform *Sir Gawain and the Green Knight* (*SGGK* hereafter) and how the poem might demonstrate the fluidity and interdependence that Warren and Massey indicate.

Many factors contributed to the development of regional identities throughout late fourteenth-century England. Historical invasions and settlement patterns influenced language, linguistic development, social customs, and legal codes. In the north and the west, contact with England's colonies, Scotland and Wales, along with the responsibility of guarding these colonial borders, significantly affected the disposition of those regions. Furthermore, geographical features rendered some areas centers of trade or transportation, giving these regions a very concrete sense of identity and purpose, while simultaneously ushering in outside

---

[3] Warren's book participates in an emerging conversation in medieval studies concerning colonialism, ethnicity, and nation. Yet these very words are loaded with modern and postmodern connotations that are in many ways incompatible with the medieval world we want to discuss. The following discussions explore the problems of thinking in terms of nationalism and colonialism: Patricia Clare Ingham, *Sovereign Fantasies: Arthurian Romance and the Making of Britain* (Philadelphia: University of Pennsylvania Press, 2001), pp. 7–10. In Ingham's negotiation of the term "nation," she rejects the idea of a "progressive chronology, imagining the history of 'a people,' as a teleological trajectory from early origins to a fully realized national present" (p. 9); Jeffrey Jerome Cohen, "Introduction: Midcolonial," in *The Postcolonial Middle Ages*, ed. Cohen (New York: St. Martin's, 2000), pp. 1–17; in which the author suggests that we need to think "midcolonially" rather than "postcolonially" about the Middle Ages. He offers an important list of ways to "open up what the medieval signifies" (pp. 6–7); see also the other engaging and important essays contained within this volume. The essays contained in Kathleen Biddick's *The Shock of Medievalism* (Durham: Duke University Press, 1998) contain foundational understandings of what is at stake when we read the Middle Ages and works about the Middle Ages through ahistorical (or apolitical) lenses. The 1995 volume *Concepts of National Identity in the Middle Ages* edited by Simon Forde, Lesley Johnson, and Alan V. Murray (Leeds: Leeds Studies in English) provides a seminal look at these issues, as does Thorlac Turville-Petre's *England the Nation: Language, Literature and National Identity* (Oxford: Clarendon, 1996).

[4] Doreen Massey, *Space, Place, and Gender* (Minneapolis: University of Minnesota Press, 1994), p. 5.

elements that offered multiple opportunities for intercultural contact and thus cultural change.

A visual representation of "regional" England would not, however, be a Rand McNally map with the typically carefully delineated chunks of yellows, pinks, greens, and blues. Instead, a collage would be a more correct representation. This mode of representation would allow us to perceive the overlapping and texturing of cultural influences. Feminist art critic Lucy Lippard notes that the significance of the collage lies in its ambiguity. In her words, the collage "put[s] things together without divesting them of their own identities," but it also "willfully takes apart what is or is supposed to be and rearranges it in ways that suggest what it could be."[5] Because the collage communicates wholeness and individuality, actuality and potentiality, construction and deconstruction, it serves as a suitable metaphor for regional identity in fourteenth-century England.

Sir Gawain and the Green Knight gives us another perspective on regional identity as it employs the collage motif in its own way. The text narrates contact between two courts that represent two distinctly different conceptions of region.[6] Two characters in the poem, Gawain and Bertilak, coupled with Bertilak's alternate persona the Green Knight, embody the characteristics of their respective regions through their appearance and actions. The poem's attention to the bodies of these characters and the processes of their embodiment exteriorize the multiple influences in regional identities. In other words, regional identity is an accretion of ethnic, political, sexual and gender identities that simultaneously compete, overlap, blend and remain independent.

Of late, analyses of gender and sexual identities have dominated *SGGK* scholarship. Geraldine Heng and Sheila Fisher have examined the place of feminine authority and power within the text.[7] Heng claims that the poem enables feminine authority, while Fisher disagrees, ar-

---

[5] Lucy R. Lippard, *The Pink Glass Swan: Selected Feminist Essays on Art* (New York: The New Press, 1995), p. 209 and p. 25.

[6] On the differences between the two courts, see Lauren Lepow, "The Contrasted Courts in *Sir Gawain and the Green Knight*," in *The Medieval Court in Europe*, ed. Edward R. Haymes, Houston German Studies 6 (Munich: Wilhelm Fink, 1986), pp. 200–209; and Heinz Bergner, "The Two Courts: Two Modes of Existence in *Sir Gawain and the Green Knight*, in *Actes du 14e Congrès International Arthurien* 2 (Rennes: Presses Universitaures de Rennes, 1984), pp. 707–21.

[7] Geraldine Heng, "Feminine Knots and the Other *Sir Gawain and the Green Knight*" *PMLA* 106, 3 (1991): 500–514; Geraldine Heng, "A Woman Wants: The Lady, Gawain, and the Forms of Seduction" *Yale Journal of Criticism* 3 (1992): 101–34; Sheila Fisher, "Taken Men and Token Women in *Sir Gawain and the Green Knight* in *Seeking*

guing that the poem only gives the illusion of feminine power, which is quickly dispersed by the homosociality of the court. Carolyn Dinshaw's work, which I will discuss at length below, interrogates the homoerotics of the text. Her "Getting Medieval: *Pulp Fiction*, Gawain, Foucault," begins to consider the identities of place and gender as relational. Using Michael J. Bennett's study of Cheshire and Lancastershire[8] and positing these counties as the primary audience of the poem, Dinshaw notes that "the relative abundance of young, single, mobile men [in this area] . . . was likely to have touched off particular anxieties about homosocial relations" because of their threat to an already threatened system of primogeniture.[9]

Patricia Clare Ingham smoothly integrates postcolonial issues with gender issues in her recent reading of *SGGK*.[10] Her study converges with mine at many points. Besides our desires to examine the identities of place and gender as interdependent, Ingham and I are both concerned with the dichotomies of center/periphery, colonizer/colonized, court/frontier that the poem seems to articulate. She argues that *SGGK* addresses "the problems and pleasures of an intimate frontier, a borderland between linked, yet also distinct, insular cultures."[11] In addition, *SGGK* attempts to "forget" the "cultural heterogeneity" that such relationships produce. The poem itself, she claims, enacts strategies that "disappear" the differences of the border.[12] I argue the inverse: that the poem challenges the very idea of homogeneity and that the figure of the Green Knight/Bertilak aggressively disrupts Camelot's attempts to create such an illusion.

This illusion is first contested by the surprising entrance of the Green Knight into Arthur's court at the beginning of the text. His entrance immediately defines through juxtaposition the two regions under consideration, namely the Anglo-Welsh border and the metropolitan court. The cultural separation between the two regions becomes immediately

---

the *Woman in Late Medieval and Renaissance Writing*, ed. Sheila Fisher and Janet Halley (Knoxville: University of Tennessee Press, 1989), pp. 71–105.

[8] Michael J. Bennett, *Community, Class and Careerism in Cheshire and Lancashire Society in the Age of* Sir Gawain and the Green Knight, Cambridge Studies in Medieval Life and Thought, 3d ser., vol. 18 (Cambridge: Cambridge University Press, 1983).

[9] Carolyn Dinshaw, "Getting Medieval: *Pulp Fiction*, Gawain, Foucault," in *The Book and the Body*, ed. Dolores Warwick Frese and Katherine O'Brien O'Keeffe (Notre Dame: University of Notre Dame Press, 1997), pp. 116–163, at p. 135.

[10] See Ingham's chap. 4, "'In Contrayez Straunge': Sovereign Rivals, Fantasies of Gender, and *Sir Gawain and the Green Knight*."

[11] Ibid., p. 108.

[12] Ibid., p. 109, p. 134.

apparent. The poet tells us of Arthur's quaint feast day custom that invites "otherness" into the feasting hall:

> And also an oþer maner meued him eke
> Þat he þurȝ nobelay had nomen, he wolde neuer ete
> Vpon such a dere day, er hym deuised were
> Of sum auenturus þyng an vncouþe tale,
> Of sum mayn meruayle, þat he myȝt trawe,
> Of alderes, of armes, of oþer auenturus,
> Oþer sum segg hym bisoȝt of sum siker knyȝt
> To joyne wyth hym in iustyng, in jopardé to lay,
> Lede for lyf, leue vchon oþer,
> As fortune wolde fulsun hom, þe fayver to haue[13]

[And also another custom influences him (Arthur), that he had taken it upon a point of honor that he would never eat upon such a feast day before he had first heard an strange tale of some adventurous thing, of some great marvel of kings, knightly contests or other adventures in which he might believe; or some man might beseech him that some brave knight might join with him in jousting, to lay in jeopardy, life for life: each to allow the other, as fortune would help him, to have the advantage.]

When a green figure comes galloping in on his green horse, the spectacle is stranger, more of a "mayn meruayle" than the courtiers anticipate. They deem him a "fantoum and fayryȝe" [phantom and a faery] (line 240). The poem points out that the courtiers are "experienced" in their observation of marvels, but they had never seen anything like the Green Knight before. The Green Knight's antagonism and his invitation to play the beheading game further confuses the courtiers: should they be afraid of or entertained by the spectacle they are witnessing?

After the Green Knight's departure, Arthur decides that they should interpret the Green Knight in terms of a performance, but his reading of the event signals the cultural distance between the two regions. Arthur remarks that the Green Knight must have been some kind of court interlude planned for the holidays:

> Wel bycommes such craft vpon Cristmasse,
> Laykyng of enterludeȝ, to laȝe and to syng

[13] *Sir Gawain and the Green Knight*, ed. J. R. R. Tolkien and E. V. Gordon, 2d ed., rev. Norman Davis (Oxford: Oxford University Press, 1967), lines 90–99. Further citations will be made by line number in the text. All translations my own.

> Among þise kynde caroles of knyȝte and ladyeȝ.
> Neuer þe lece to my mete I may me wel dres,
> For I haf sen a selly, I may not forsake. (lines 471–75)

[Such doings are fitting at Christmas time, the playing of interludes, laughing and singing among these courtly carols of knights and ladies. Nevertheless, I can now direct my attention to my meal, because I have seen a marvel that I may not forsake.]

The interlude was a short dramatic vignette between the courses of a feast that often depicted marvelous events or beings. Susan Crane characterizes them as events that are celebratory in conception. They are generally performed during special feasts ("consolidating a host's dominant position, making a nationalist statement to foreign visitors, celebrating a religious holiday or a wedding").[14] She concludes that they are "condensed, intensified enactments of elite superiority."[15] However, this interlude does not glorify Arthur or his court. Rather, the opposite occurs, leaving Arthur confused but ready to eat his meal. Arthur is correct in interpreting the Green Knight's actions as a performance, but his performance has nothing to do with holiday festivities.

The Green Knight, despite his size and color, is not a phantom, a faery, nor a court interlude: he is a visitor from the provinces, specifically, the Anglo-Welsh border, who proclaims this identity through his physical appearance. His dress, while matching his color, seems a contrast to his marvelous physical attributes:[16]

> Ande al grayþed in grene þis gome and his wedes:
> A strayt cote ful streȝt þat stek on his sides,
> A meré mantile abof, mensked withinne
> With pelure pured apert, þe pane ful clene
> With blyþe blaunner ful bryȝt, and his hode boþe,
> Þat watz laȝt fro his lokkeȝ and layde on his schulderes. (lines 151–156)

[And this man and his clothing are all arrayed in green: A very straight coat that clung to his sides, a fair mantle above it, adorned within with plain,

---

[14] Susan Crane, *The Performance of Self: Ritual, Clothing, and Identity During the Hundred Years War* (Philadelphia: University of Pennsylvania Press, 2002), p. 159.

[15] Crane, *Performance of Self*.

[16] The "unsettling mixture of the monstrous and the decorous" in the Green Knight has a long critical tradition, see Greg Walker, "The Green Knight's Challenge: Heroism and Courtliness in Fitt I of *Sir Gawain and the Green Knight, ChauR* 32 (1997): 111–128, from which the above is taken (p. 112) and the critics cited therein.

trimmed fur, the facing elegantly trimmed with bright lovely ermine, and his hood, too, that was drawn back from his hair and laid on his shoulders.]

This description of the Green Knight resists a single reading. Bella Millett calls the Green Knight a "cluster of signs . . . that actively resist rational interpretation. Some of them are bizarre, some of them apparently contradictory."[17] However, as Greg Walker notes, the Green Knight is not "a confrontation of irreconcilable opposites but a far more complex encounter."[18] He appears as a "cluster of signs" or collage of different cultural stereotypes. His size and greenness recall the Otherworld often associated with Wales, while the fashionable clothing and fine materials relate to the conspicuous finery of metropolitan court culture. The juxtaposition of elements demonstrates the hybridity of his border culture. His spectacular collage is both a dramatic representation of misreadings and misunderstandings between the centralized, metropolitan court and the provincial, Anglo-Welsh border court and a testament to the middle position his own court occupies, geographically, socially, and ideologically.

This scene, to which we will return later in this essay, is the first in a series of encounters that the poem stages between the two regions. Yet, before we can understand the impact of these encounters, we must understand something about these regions. The first, King Arthur's court, belongs to Britain's historical imaginary and does not correlate to any physical region in fourteenth-century England. While its borders are theoretical, Arthur's court suggests the constructedness of the English metropolitan court. *SGGK* was composed during the reign of Richard II, who cultivated a powerful court. Historian Nigel Saul describes the late medieval court of Richard II as "the social and ceremonial setting

---

[17] Bella Millett, "How Green Is the Green Knight?" *Nottingham Medieval Studies* 38 (1994): 138, [138–151]. On the unintelligibility of the Green Knight, Wendy Clein writes: "The introduction of the challenger underscores the necessity for readers to remain uncommitted to any single point of view, for the Green Knight does not conform to romance, heraldic, or moralist patters for an opponent of chivalry. The challenger troubles twentieth-century critics as much as he does the court at Camelot" in *Concepts of Chivalry in* Sir Gawain and the Green Knight (Norman, Okla.: Pilgrim Books, 1987), p. 79. For some early critics troubled by the hybrid nature of the Green Knight, see Larry Benson, *Art and Tradition in* Sir Gawain and the Green Knight (New Brunswick, N.J.: Rutgers University Press, 1965), pp. 62–95 ; J. A. Burrow, *A Reading of* Sir Gawain and the Green Knight (New York: Barnes and Noble, 1966), pp. 12–23; John Speirs, *Medieval English Poetry: The Non-Chaucerian Tradition* (London: Faber and Faber, 1957), pp. 225–30.
[18] Walker, "The Green Knight's Challenge," 112.

of monarchy."[19] As simultaneously "the means and the expression of royal power,"[20] the court possessed an ephemeral, transcendent quality. Saul explains, "Contemporaries could recognize the court, and very often they could describe it. But in the last resort it was a mental or perceptual construct—the rationalization of those who beheld it."[21] The court of Richard II imagined itself to be *supra-regional*, England's ideological center, and the locus from whence came diplomacy, fashion, and literature.[22] Its spectacle and vast cultural influence were powerful discourses that equated English and courtly identities.

The inestimable role of the court meant that the king and his courtiers remained culturally central no matter where they resided. While *SGGK*'s Arthur stays at Camelot, other English Arthurian romances portray Arthur's court as mobile, often moving from between Carlisle, Winchester, Caerleon, and Camelot. The movements of Richard II confirm that a metropolitan court needed no fixed abode.[23] He often spent time in the North and in the Northwest Midlands; in fact between 1397 and 1399, Richard spent most of his time (when he was not campaigning in Ireland) in the Northwest Midlands. The king and his entire household set up residence in local abbeys, monasteries, manors and castles[24] and evidence shows that Richard's traveling court did not lack the lavishness nor the spectacle of a centralized court. Saul describes the ethos of Richard's court: "Courtly life can be seen as a series of unfolding set-pieces or occasions: occasions at which visitors were received, business transacted, gifts bestowed and the splendor of the king's majesty revealed to his subjects."[25] He concludes "the 'capital' of England in

[19] Nigel Saul, *Richard II*, Yale English Monarchs Series (New Haven: Yale University Press, 1997), p. 327.

[20] Ibid.

[21] Ibid., p. 328.

[22] See Gervase Mathew, *The Court of Richard II* (New York: W. W. Norton, 1968).

[23] Nigel Saul has reconstructed a typical year's travel for Richard: "The Christmas festivities of the court were generally held at Westminister, Windsor, or Eltham, where the grandest surroundings were to be had. Usually in the spring the king moved out into the provinces. . . . In April it was invariably his habit to return to Windsor for the annual Garter ceremonies. Then in May or June he would set out on his travels again. By tradition he held his midsummer court at a major town. . . . Generally he devoted part of each summer to the pleasures of the chase. . . . At the beginning of autumn he would return to the south-east. . . . In October or November he would fit in visits to Kennington or Sheen; and in December he would move on to Westminister for Christmas" (*Richard II*, p. 337). See also the itinerary in Saul, *Richard II*, pp. 468–74.

[24] Chris Given-Wilson, *The Royal Household and the King's Affinity: Service, Politics, and Finance in England, 1360–1413* (New Haven: Yale University Press, 1986), p. 37.

[25] Saul, *Richard II*, p. 337.

Richard's reign was not Westminster . . . ; it was wherever the king happened to be."[26]

In contrast to the ideological supra-region of the metropolitan court, the location of Bertilak's court for the most part relates to a specific place, the Anglo-Welsh border. Even though the poet is careful to locate his poem in this region through textual cues, this region is often under-theorized in the study of *SGGK*. The poet meticulously traces Gawain's journey to find the Green Knight and supplies ample geographical markers:

> Now rideȝ þis renk þurȝ þe ryalme of Logres,
> Sir Gauan, on Godeȝ halue, þaȝ hym no gomen þoȝt.
> Oft leudleȝ alone he lengeȝ on nyȝtez
> Þer he fonde noȝt hym byfore þe fare þat he lyked.
> Hade he no fere bot his fole bi frytheȝ and douneȝ,
> Ne no gome bot God bi gate wyth to karp,
> Til þat he neȝed ful neghe into þe Norþe Waleȝ.
> Alle þe iles of Anglesay on lyft half he haldeȝ,
> And fareȝ ouer þe fordeȝ by þe forlondeȝ
> Ouer at þe Holy Hede, til he hade eft bonk
> In þe wyldrenesse of Wyrale; wonde þer bot lyte
> Þat auþer God oþer gome wyth goud hert louied. (lines 691–712)

[Now this knight rides through the realm of England; Sir Gawain, for God's sake—although no one thought about him—often lodged companionless at night, when he did not find before him any food that he liked. Alongside the woods and hills, he had no companion but his horse nor anyone along the way but God to talk to, until he entered well-nigh into North Wales. He kept all the isles of Anglesey on his left side and went over the fords by the headlands at Holy Head, until he had once made land in the wilderness of Wirral. Little lived there that either God or man loved with good heart.]

This geographic specificity implies the poet's familiarity with north Wales, the Northwest Midlands, and the lands of the northern Anglo-Welsh border. These references have energized scholars to look for phys-ical sites corresponding to Hautdesert and the Green Chapel.[27] Simi-

---

[26] Nigel Saul, "Richard II, York, and the Evidence of the King's Itinerary," in *The Age of Richard II*, ed. James L. Gillespie, (New York: St. Martin's P, 1997), p. 87.

[27] For a careful and comprehensive examination of *SGGK*'s locations, see R. W. V. Elliott, *The Gawain Country*, Leeds Texts and Monographs, New Series 8 (Leeds: The University of Leeds, 1984). See also Thorlac Turville-Petre, "The 'Pearl'-Poet in his

larly, the poem's dialect has motivated scholars to locate the poet within a particular region. While attempts to identify a correspondence between the poem and local topography are fraught with the methodological dangers of conflating fiction and history, such investigations respond to the poem's own emphasis on region and location.[28] Through his examinations of the poem's dialect, Angus McIntosh demonstrates the linguistic correspondence between the poem and the Northwest Midlands region of the late fourteenth century. McIntosh specifically places the poem's dialect in Cheshire or Staffordshire.[29] In addition, Ralph V. W. Elliott's historical and topographical research presents a compelling argument that correlates physical features in medieval and modern Cheshire and Staffordshire to Hautdesert and the Green Chapel.[30] Similarly, Michael J. Bennett has vigorously argued that *SGGK* represents Richard II's close connection to the Northwest Midlands and to the principality of Cheshire in particular.[31] However, as the stanza above shows, the poem's setting is not simply the Northwest Midlands but the border area within that larger region.

A long history of colonial relations with Wales shaped the daily lives of inhabitants living within this border area. These inhabitants of Chesh-

---

'Farye Regioun,'" in *Essays on Richardian Literature in Honour of J. A. Burrow*. ed. A. J. Minnis, Charlotte C. Morse, and Thorlac Turville-Petre. (Oxford: Clarendon P, 1997), pp. 276–94; John McNeal Dodgson, "Sir Gawain's Arrival in Wirral," in *Early English and Norse Studies Presented to Hugh Smight in Honour of His Sixtieth Birthday*. ed. Arthur Brown and Peter Foote (London: Meuthen,1963), pp. 19–25; Andrew Breeze, "Sir Gawain's Journey and Holywell, Wales," *Selim* 5 (1996): 116–18; P. L. Heyworth, "Sir Gawain's Crossing of Dee," *Medium Ævum* 41 (1972): 125–27; Isaac Jackson, "*Sir Gawain and the Green Knight*. Considered as a 'Garter' Poem," *Anglia, Zeitschrift für Englische Philologie*" 37 (1913): 393–423; M. W. Thompson, "The Green Knight's Castle," in *Studies in Medieval History Presented to R. Allen Brown*, (Wolfeboro, N.H.: Boydell, 1989), pp. 317–326.

[28] Ingham, *Sovereign Fantasies*, writes: "no one has yet considered the relation of the text's interest in regions—exterior as well as interior; wild as well as domesticated—to its other scrutinized obsessions" (i.e., honor, identity, gender and sexual politics) (114).

[29] Angus McIntosh, "A New Approach to Middle English Dialectology," *English Studies* 64 (1963): 4. McIntosh's location is generally uncontested among contemporary scholars. Locations for the poem's provenance cited earlier are South Lancashire, Yorkshire and Derbyshire, for which see J. P. Oakden, *Alliterative Poetry*, vol. 1. (Manchester: Manchester University Press, 1930), pp. 82–87; Robert J. Menner, "*Sir Gawain and the Green Knight* and the West Midlands," *PMLA* 37 (1922): 503–26; Mary S. Serjeantson, "Dialects of the West Midlands in Middle English," *RES* 3 (1927): 327–28; and Henry Littleton Savage, *The Gawain-Poet: Studies in His Personality and Background* (Chapel Hill: University of North Carolina P), pp. 128–33.

[30] Elliott, *The Gawain Country, passim*.

[31] Michael J. Bennett, "*Sir Gawain and the Green Knight*" and the Literary Achievement of the North-West Midlands: The Historical Background," *Journal of Medieval History* 5 (1979): 63–88.

ire and Staffordshire, as well as people living in Shropshire, Worcestershire, Gloucestershire, and Herefordshire, had developed a complicated interdependency with Wales during a period characterized by both aggression and coexistence. Edward I's Welsh campaign (1276–83), which was a concentrated effort to bring all of Wales into his imperial control, relied on military service from the area. However, after Edward I completed his conquest of Wales in 1283, the border inhabitants' involvement with Wales and its people changed significantly. They no longer needed to be aggressors; instead their new roles demanded that they become part of the bureaucracy in colonial Wales as administrators and peacekeepers.

These inhabitants of the border shires contributed to a complicated system of governance designed by Edward, which included annexation of land, the creation of new administrative offices and the building of new castles and garrisons.[32] R. R. Davies describes the governmental apparatus introduced at this time:

A new governmental dispensation, with its centres at Caernarfon, Carmarthen, and Chester, was installed; new offices and units, notably the shire and its sheriff created; new surveys of financial dues compiled, and at the higher echelons of government a new exclusively non-Welsh administrative cadre took over the running of the conquered lands.[33]

Persons from the border counties not only formed a large part of the "administrative cadre" of Wales, but they also worked as laborers who built new castles and repaired existing ones. In the period 1282–83, royal officials in Wales conscripted masons, diggers, carpenters and woodcutters from all over England for a substantial castle-building project. Almost four thousand workers gathered in Chester, whence they proceeded to the sites of specific castles in North Wales.[34] Many of the skilled laborers, such as masons and carpenters, came from the border shires.

The occupation of Wales also provided employment for residents of the border counties as the constables of the castles that their predeces-

[32] Davies, "Edward," p. 2. See also J. G. Edwards, "Edward I's Castle-Building in Wales," *Proceedings of the British Academy* 32 (1950): 15–81.

[33] R. R. Davies, "Edward I and Wales," in *Edward I and Wales*, ed. Trevor Herbert and Gareth Elwyn Jones (Cardiff: University of Wales Press, 1988), pp. 1–10, at pp. 1–2.

[34] Ifor Rowlands, "The Edwardian Conquest and its Military Consolidation," in *Edward I and Wales*, ed. Herbert and Jones, pp. 41–72 at p. 52 and p. 62.

sors built. These posts were often testing grounds for more prestigious and lucrative positions: "castellanies [i.e., constableships] offered soldiers the chance to gain experience in and to display their talents for varied fields of government."[35] As a result, constables of Welsh castles might later win themselves positions as sheriffs, bailiffs, or stewards in Wales, or their ambition might carry them to the upper levels of governance, such as the position of the justicar.[36] Michael Bennett also notes that many Cheshire soldiers "acquired land and lordships in border areas" or "put down roots in the boroughs of North Wales."[37]

Bertilak represents another category of frontiersmen who found employment through England's colonization of Wales. Bertilak's castle, which Gawain encounters in his search for the Green Chapel, indicates his role as a border lord, who holds the border with Wales. The passages describing his castle has been much scrutinized. Some critics argue that the architectural image the poet creates is illogical and more a product of fantasy than reality. Others look for corresponding sites and ruins that could have served as the poet's model.[38] Whether the castle is real or imaginary, its importance is evident in the thirty-five lines (767–802) the poem devotes to describing the architecture of the castle and palisade. These descriptions combine the technically precise language found in alliterative verse with a focus on the castle's defenses. This emphasis on defense reminds Gawain and the poem's audience that the castle stands in a frontier zone. A "depe double dich" encloses the castle, while a wall equipped with watchtowers encircles the hall (line 786). Many of the seemingly decorative aspects of the castle offer strategic advantages. As Robert Cockcroft points out, some aspects that seem to be merely decorative reveal a "subtle and extensive technology of defence."[39] For example, M. W. Thompson reads the poet's detail "enbaned vnder þe abataylment" (790) as "enbaued," meaning that the castle has "machicolations," defensive attributes that allowed the castle's inhabitants to "overlook the foot of the wall and drop projectiles on an enemy."[40] Thompson notes that the castles built in Wales during the late thirteenth century were considerably different from those built later on the

[35] Bennett, *Community*, p. 179.
[36] See R. R. Davies, *The Revolt of Owain Glyn Dwr* (Oxford: Oxford University Press, 1995), pp. 43, 53; and Bennett, *Community*, pp. 179–80, and p. 201.
[37] Bennett, *Community*, p. 180.
[38] See Robert Cockcroft, "Castle Hautdesert: Portrait of Patchwork?" *Neophilogus* 62 (1978): 459–77, and Thompson, "The Green Knight's Castle."
[39] Cockcroft, p. 473.
[40] Thompson, "Green Knight's Castle," pp. 319–21.

English side of the Welsh border. For example, machicolation rarely occurred "before the mid-fourteenth century," and machicolations were very scarce in Edward I's castle-building projects in Wales.[41] This emphasis on defensive characteristics—the ditches, the towers, the barbican—serves as a reminder that this fortification is close to the Welsh colony, an occupied land, dotted with castles that are similar in purpose, if not in architectural style. Likewise, the description of the castle emphasizes the role of its master, Bertilak, as a keeper of that border.

In the late fourteenth century, border lords like Bertilak continued to hold borders that were becoming increasingly unstable, as the cultures on either side became increasingly hybrid. Trade and commerce as well as social interaction contributed to the development of hybrid cultures. Merchants in border towns from Chester in the north to Bristol in the south carried on lucrative trade with Wales. Many English merchants maintained regular routes into Wales; others moved into one of the castellated towns, "oases of Englishness."[42] The reason for the English merchants' interest in Wales emerges from the fact that they had a monopoly on almost all imports and exports, only having to compete with foreign merchants for the right to export Welsh wool and hides.[43] The English merchants who lived in Welsh boroughs valued their commercial privileges, authorized by English laws. The governmental and economic structures that the English imposed in colonial Wales provided economic opportunities for skilled and unskilled laborers, bureaucrats, merchants and tradespeople who lived in the border shires. The evidence suggests that these frontier people also had significant emotional and physical investments in colonial Wales, fostered by their continued associations with the land and its people.

By the time *SGGK* was composed, such deep connections between the border shires and colonial Wales had existed for about a century. The level of engagement between the Welsh and the English had moved from the early intensity of conquest and occupation to a more settled coexistence in the course of the late fourteenth century. Marriage between the settler and native populations aided the processes of coexistence. By the second quarter of the fourteenth century, Welsh burgesses lived in English plantation boroughs established by Edward I, which were formerly limited to English burgesses. The Welsh also lived in areas designated for English settlers called Englishries, while the English

[41] Ibid., p. 321.
[42] Davies, *Revolt*, pp. 27–28.
[43] Ibid., p. 5, p. 28.

settled in the corresponding Welshries.[44] However, as R. R. Davies makes clear, "Wales in the fourteenth century may have been a country at peace; but it was also a country where the distinction between conqueror and conquered, settler and native, English and Welsh, was more clearly defined in formal and institutional terms than ever before."[45] The Welsh rural and urban landscapes testified to assimilation and coexistence, while expressions of bureaucratic power, such as laws and charters, continued to assert ethnic distinctions. Davies cites these kinds of bureaucratic documents in his argument that it is precisely when ethnic differences become "archaic and unreal," that "artificial attempts are made to sustain and enforce" ethnic difference.[46] In other words, the energy that lawmakers and officials put toward enforcing segregation only attests to the fact that their efforts were not working. On both sides of the border, hybrid identities and communities existed.

The physical description of the Green Knight cited above also reflects the hybridity of the border. Within his person, the Green Knight combines the liminality of the border with the otherworldliness often associated with Wales.[47] The poem focuses on the liminality of the border space in its attention to landscape Gawain traverses. His journey begins in England, continues into Wales and then he crosses the border back into England, after failing to locate the Green Knight in Wales. In this return border crossing, he enters a liminal landscape full of wonders and dangers, exactly the sort of place where a creature like Green Knight should reside:

> So mony meruayl bi mount þer þe mon fyndeʒ,
> Hit were tore for to telle of þe tenþe dole.
> Sumwhyle wyth wormeʒ he werreʒ, and with wolues als,
> Sumwhyle wyth wodwos, þat woned in þe knarreʒ,
> Boþe wyth bulleʒ and bereʒ, and boreʒ oþerquyle,
> And etayneʒ, þat hym anelede of þe heʒe felle. (lines 718–23)

[So many a marvel the man finds among the hills, it is too difficult to tell the tenth part of them. Sometimes he wars with dragons and with wolves also,

---

[44] R. R. Davies, *Conquest, Co-existence and Change: Wales, 1063–1415* (Oxford: Clarendon Press, 1987), pp. 421–22.

[45] Ibid., p. 419.

[46] Davies, *Revolt*, p. 69.

[47] See Patrick Sims-Williams, "The Visionary Celt: The Construction of an Ethnic Preconception," *Cambridge Medieval Celtic Studies* 11 (1986): 71–96 and Ingham, *Sovereign Fantasies,* pp. 116–19.

sometimes with woodwoses, who dwelled in the crags, with both bulls and bears and other times with boars, and with giants, who pursued him off the high fell.]

The poem's placement of these creatures in this border space encourages its readers to question the integrity of the border and the constitution of borderlands. The otherworldliness of Wales spills over into the borderland and illustrates that the border, in the words of Owen Lattimore, renowned historian of the frontier, "is not a line but a zone."[48] In its attention to geographical and imaginary location, *SGGK* overlays various discourses of the Anglo-Welsh border in order to create a hybrid space that accommodates the coexisting otherworldly and colonial elements.

Through a collage of these disparate attributes, the Green Knight performs the hybridity of the border zone as he stands before Arthur's court in the scene discussed earlier. Yet a closer look at his dress shows that his appearance has a more subversive purpose.[49] The large green man wears expensive clothing appropriate to the court. His horse is similarly attired. However, as the poem's litany of his clothing and accessories becomes longer and more detailed, this description seems to mock courtly excess. Further descriptions of the Green Knight show how his otherworldly characteristics overpower his courtly apparel, causing a disjunction in his appearance:

> Fayre fannand fax vmbefoldes his schulderes;
> A much berd as a busk ouer his brest henges,
> Þat wyth his hiȝlich here þat of his hed reches
> Watȝ euesed al vmbetorne abof his elbowes,
> Þat half his armes þer-vnder were halched in þe wyse
> Of a kyngeȝ capados þat closes his swyre. (lines 181–86)

[His fair, waving hair enfolds his shoulders; a great beard, like a bush, hangs over his chest. That (beard), along with his splendid hair which reaches from his head, was trimmed all around above his elbows, so that half of his arms were enclosed under (them) in the manner of a king's capados (a garment) that closes at his neck.]

[48] Owen Lattimore, *Studies in Frontier History, Collected Papers, 1928–58* (London: Oxford University Press, 1962), p. 127.

[49] Ingham, *Sovereign Fantasies*, puts forth a brilliant reading of the Green Knight in terms of Homi Bhabha's concept of "mimicry" (pp. 124–25).

Susan Crane poses the question "Can wildness be courtly?" in reference to the Green Knight.[50] Ultimately, her answer is yes. She speaks of the Green Knight's "stabilized wildness inside courtliness" and "his powerful stasis of wildness in courtliness."[51] As her word choice shows, Crane indicates that courtliness is dominant in the Green Knight and that as a persona—as an interlude—he represents a ritualized mode of courtly self-definition and identification.

My reading of the Green Knight is in many ways counter to Crane's. While I do see the Green Knight as a performance, I assert that wildness is his primary aspect and that his juxtaposition of wildness and courtliness is subversive to the dominant metropolitan culture. This juxtaposition, or disjunction, points out that the Green Knight is only passing as courtly, that he is wearing courtly drag. "Drag," a term that is customarily applied to transvestism and cross-dressing, is generally associated with the adoption of gender roles. Adopting gender roles often functions as a way challenge the equation of sex and gender.[52] The goal of drag in general (and the Green Knight's in particular) is not to achieve a perfect imitation but rather to provide a simulation that points out that it is a simulation.[53] Marjorie B. Garber writes that the transvestite—as "the figure that disrupts"[54]—provides "something readable, a foot that is too big, a subtle gesture, or the peculiar grain of the voice" that subverts "'passing' and points to 'performance.'"[55] Anne McClintock, in her study of the Victorian couple Arthur Munby and Hannah Cull-

---

[50] Crane, *Performance*, p. 163.

[51] Ibid., p. 168.

[52] Jeffrey Escoffier, "Sexual Revolution and the Politics of Gay Identity" *Socialist Review* 15 (1985): 119–53, at 141. Drag, in this sense, is closely related to camp. As Susan Sontag and Jack Babuscio have shown, camp is much easier to point out than to define; see Susan Sontag, "Notes on 'Camp,'" in *Against Interpretation and Other Essays* (New York: Noonday Press, 1961), pp. 275–92; Jack Babuscio, "Camp and the Gay Sensibility," in *Gays and Film*, ed. Richard Dyer (London: BFI, 1980), pp. 40–57; and also Andrew Britton, "For Interpretation: Notes Against Camp," *Gay Left Collective* 7 (1978–79): 11–14. What drag and camp share, however, is the ability to expose that gender behavior is a role, "something that can be adopted, changed, or dropped" (Escoffier, p. 140). The slipperiness of "camp" as term that can be "applied" to a text, an action, a character or an object—in addition to camp's presumptuous self-awareness and aggressive excess—make it unsuitable for my discussion of the Green Knight's appearance at Arthur's court. The subtlety of drag is more appropriate here.

[53] Anne McClintock, *Imperial Leather: Race, Gender, and Sexuality in the Colonial Contest*, (New York: Routledge, 1995), p. 175.

[54] Marjorie B. Garber, *Vested Interests: Cross Dressing and Cultural Anxiety* (New York: Routledge, 1992), p. 70.

[55] Ibid., p. 149.

wick, has shown the ways in which cross-dressing traverses race and class lines as well as gender boundaries.[56]

I want to open up the term "drag" in the same way, considering it as a strategy of dress and performance that disrupts notions of *any* identity and provides a site that enables the inquiry into the presumed "naturalness" of one identity and the privileging of one identity over another. While drag, in Judith Butler's terms, points to the "way in which genders are appropriated, theatricalized, worn, and done,"[57] we can see that other identities besides genders can be "appropriated, theatricalized, worn and done." As Carole-Anne Tyler points out in her analysis of the camp aspects of drag, "one 'does' ideology in order to undo it, producing knowledge about it."[58]

The Green Knight's drag performance "does" metropolitan court culture, but by overdoing it, he calls into question the accepted conventions of all identities (and their presumed naturalness). The Green Knight's drag makes identity—in all its forms—available for discussion.[59] His actions and appearance highlight the dichotomy in the chivalric, courtly identity of Camelot. The luxurious courtly life of the knights that the opening of the poem describes seems incompatible with the heroic knights whose *rous* (fame, reputation) spread throughout the land. Their actions in court support the incompatibility. The knights' slowness in responding to his challenge signals their fear and prompts him to remark:

> What, is þis Arþureʒ hous, . . .
> Þat al þe rous rennes of þurʒ ryalmes so mony?
> Where is now your sourquydrye and your conquestes,
> Your gryndellayk and your greme, and your grete wordes?
> Now is þe reuel and þe renoun of þe Rounde Table
> Ouerwalt wyth a worde of on wyʒes speche,
> For al dares for drede withoute dynt schewed. (lines 309–15)

[56] *Imperial Leather*, pp. 133–80.

[57] Judith Butler, "Imitation and Gender Insubordination," in *Inside/Out: Lesbian Theories, Gay Theories*, ed. Diana Fuss (London: Routledge, 1991), pp. 13–31, at p. 21.

[58] Carole-Anne Tyler, "Boys Will Be Girls: The Politics of Gay Drag," in *Inside/Out: Lesbian Theories, Gay Theories*, ed. Diana Fuss (London: Routledge, 1991), pp. 32–70, at p. 53.

[59] See Jill Dolan, *The Feminist Spectator as Critic* (Ann Arbor: UMI Research Press, 1988), p. 116.

[What, is this Arthur's house . . . about which all the fame spreads through so many realms? Where now are your pride and your conquests, your ferocity and your wrath and your great words? The reveling and renown of the Round Table is now overthrown with a word from one man's speech, for all (of you) cower for fear without a blow offered.]

The Green Knight's challenge to the chivalric identity of the court shows that this identity, while seeming natural, authentic, and unified, is too a collage as fractured and complex as his border identity. His courtly drag begins the work of dismantling the idea of a cohesive, natural identity, which he finishes by pointing out the vast difference between the court's *rous* and its reality. One of the public relations concerns of any hegemony, in this case Camelot, is to make cultural identity appear authentic and seamless. The Green Knight's drag and his challenge highlight the cracks in the façade of the metropolitan court that become more apparent in Gawain's dressing scene.

This scene prepares Gawain for his next encounter with the Green Knight, demonstrating the metropolitan court's desire to project a whole, unified identity. Before Gawain leaves to search out the Green Knight, the poem gives a long description of his arming:

> Þennne set þey þe sabatounȝ vpon þe segge foteȝ
> His legeȝ lapped in stel with luflych greueȝ,
> With polayneȝ piched þerto, policed ful clene,
> Aboute his kneȝ knaged wyth knoteȝ of golde;
> Queme quyssewes þen, þat conyntlych closed.
> His thik þrawen þyȝez, with þwonges to tachched;
> And syþen þe brawden bryné of bryȝt stel ryngeȝ
> Vmbeweued þat wyȝ vpon wlonk stuffe
> And wel bornyst brace vpon his boþe arms,
> With gode cowters and gay, and gloueȝ of plate,
> And alle þe godlych gere þat hym gayn schulde
> þat tyde. (lines 574–85)

[Then they put the steel shoes on the man's feet, wrapped his legs in steel with exquisite greaves with brightly polished knees pieces attached to them, fastened with knots of gold. Then elegantly wrought, fine thigh-pieces enclosed his thick muscular thighs attached with laces. And next the linked mail-shirt of bright steel rings enveloped that man in lovely stuff, and well burnished arm-pieces upon both arms, with good and bright elbow-pieces and gloves of steel, and all of the fine gear that should be useful to him then.]

This passage highlights the effort that goes into armoring a knight, but it also demonstrates the disappearance of Gawain and his replacement by an icon of Arthur's court. As Claire R. Kinney points out, the process of arming disembodies Gawain: his corporeality disappears with the ad-dition of each piece of armor.[60] Each piece of armor adds to an image of wholeness and impenetrability that represents not just the knight but the desires of the culture he represents. The construction of Gawain as cultural icon must be a communal process. The knight is unable to dress himself: it takes the whole community to invest him with the armor, the ideologies, and the values that the court wants to transmit.[61] The fact that Gawain proceeds in armor is in itself significant, for this contra-dicts the Green Knight's appearance at Arthur's court. When the Green Knight arrives at Camelot, he remarks that he has left his martial accou-trements behind and his "wedez ar softer" (268–71). Because Gawain goes questing into the unknown, he wears armor, which protects him as it advertises the public persona that Arthur's court wants to project.

Gawain's arrival at Hautdesert advances the query of metropolitan identity that the Green Knight's visit to Camelot begins. When Gawain finally reaches Bertilak's court, he wears the same armor, albeit it is more travelworn. The reactions of the courtiers mark him as a cultural outsider. Their inquiries into the mysterious knight's origins indicates their caution:

Þenne watȝ spyed and spured vpon spare wyse
Bi preué poynteȝ of þat prynce, put to hymseluen,
Þat he beknew cortaysly of þe court þat he were
Þat aþel Arthure þe hende haldeȝ hym one,
Þat is þe ryche ryal kyng of þe Rounde Table,
And hit watȝ Wawen hymself þat in þat won sytteȝ. (lines 901–6)

[60] Clare R. Kinney, "The (Dis)Embodied Hero and the Signs of Manhood in *Sir Ga-wain and the Green Knight,*" in *Medieval Masculinities: Regarding Men in the Middle Ages,* ed. Clare A. Lees (Minneapolis: University of Minnesota Press, 1994), pp. 47–57, at pp. 47–51.

[61] See Kinney where she provocatively argues that in key passages it is Camelot itself that is "speaking Gawain" and "conferring upon him (and, by extension, upon the community he represents) an exemplary character and and exemplary history" (p. 50).

[Then that prince was tactfully asked about himself through discreet questions to which he courteously confessed that he was of the court that noble Arthur the gracious held alone, who is the rich royal king of the Round Table and that it was Gawain himself who sat in that dwelling.]

Their precise, cautious questions also demonstrate regional concerns. As Patricia Clare Ingham argues, the military aspects of the frontier culture mean that the inhabitants must always negotiate the "categories of identity, loyalty, and honor" through the "complications of space and territory."[62] At the same time that the members of Bertilak's court welcome Gawain, they display the cautious behavior of a people who must always be on their guard. Their caution suggests that identity itself is a potentially volatile issue in the frontier.

Yet when Bertilak's court learns of Gawain's identity, they look to him, a representative of the metropolitan court, as a standard of courtly behavior. David Aers notes that Hautdesert "receives [Gawain] as an ideal model stepping out of a courtesy book.'"[63] Aer's image of Gawain as iconic reinforces the idea that he is a fabrication, a collection of histories, codes, behaviors and ideas, that Camelot has assembled and sent out into the world to represent metropolitan culture. The statements of Bertilak's courtiers reinforce Gawain's iconic status:

> Vche segge ful softly sayde to his fere:
> "Now schal we semlych se sleȝteȝ of þeweȝ
> And þe teccheles termes of talkyng noble,
> Wich spede is in speche vnspurd may we lerne,
> Syn we haf fonged þat fyne fader of nurture." (lines 915–19)

[Each man said very softly to his companion: "Now we shall see the arts of knightly conduct and the faultless expressions of noble conversation, now we may learn, without asking, what profit there is in speech, since we have entertained that fine father of good breeding" (i.e., manners).]

Gawain's *rous* precedes him, albeit this is a different *rous* than the Green Knight has previously assigned to Arthur's court. Hautdesert focuses on

---

[62] This citation comes from Patricia Clare Ingham's dissertation, which shares a name with her book, "Sovereign Fantasies: Arthurian Romance and the Making of Britain" (University of Santa Barbara, 1995), p. 92.

[63] David Aers, *Community, Gender, and Individual Identity: English Writing, 1360–1430*, (London: Routledge, 1988), p. 162.

his knightly conduct rather than his martial skills. Nevertheless, as the Green Knight has previously pointed out in his visit to Camelot, the difference between reputation and reality can be vast. Like the disjunction between the elements of the Green Knight's drag, the disjunction between Gawain's *rous* and his actions at Hautdesert exposes Gawain as a collage of competing and overlapping identities, struggling to project a cohesive wholeness. This wholeness is troubled by the melange of Christian morality, chivalric codes, and sexual indeterminacy that Gawain tries to reconcile. With the assistance of Bertilak and his wife—and without the benefit of his armor-container—Gawain's identity begins to disintegrate.

The bedroom scenes emphasize the ruptures in Gawain's identity. The naked Gawain, trapped in his bed by Bertilak's wife, is unable to perform to the standards that his *rous* has set. In this instance, the poet is playing with Gawain's reputation as a lover, which appears in French Arthurian romances. Ad Putter describes a scene in the *First Continuation* of Chrétien's *Perceval* in which a maiden must first test Gawain's appearance against an embroidered image that she has of him before she takes him as a lover. [64] In other texts, women measure him against a statue or an engraving in a ring.[65] Like a modern celebrity, Gawain's reputation leads to his iconization and to idol-worship. Apparently, Bertilak's wife knows these romances and uses his reputation against him. In the first bedroom scene, she tells him: "Your honour, your hendelayk is hendely praysed / With lordez, wyth ladyes, with alle Þat lyf bere." [Your honor, your courtliness is courteously praised by lords, by ladies, by all that bear life.] (lines 1228–29). When Gawain does not perform up to her expectations, Bertilak's wife does not question the validity of Gawain's reputation as courtly, but instead questions his identity:

> Bot þat ȝe be Gawan, hit gotȝ in mynde.
>
> .   .   .   .
>
> So god as Gawayn gaynly is halden,
> And cortaysye is closed so clene in hymseluen,
> Couth not lyȝtly haf lenged so long wyth a lady,
> Bot he had craued a cosse, bi his courtaysye." (lines 1293, 1297–1300)

---

[64] Ad Putter, Sir Gawain and the Green Knight *and the French Arthurian Romance* (Oxford: Clarendon, 1995), pp. 109–10.
[65] Ibid., 111.

[But it is in doubt that you are Gawain. As good as Gawain is held to be and so completely embodied with courtesy, he could not easily have stayed so long with a lady and not asked for a kiss, by his courtesy.]

Her assumption provides a stark example of the Green Knight's earlier point—one should not equate reputation and reality. His interaction with Lady Bertilak enables Gawain to see the fractures in his own identity, fractures caused by the vast differences between who he thinks he is and who others think he is.

Carolyn Dinshaw has read these bedroom scenes and their concomitant hunting scenes in terms of "corporeal disaggregation." She argues that the scenes of animal evisceration and butchering are "visual representation[s] of Gawain's knightly identity's failing."[66] She concludes:

When such identity fails, the body perceptually disaggregates, because it's that identity matrix, that interlocking knot of Christian chivalric characteristics and behaviors here, that ideally and ever tenuously accords unity to this knightly body in the first place. The chivalric behavior that Gawain performs is so fundamental that without its guarantee of unity he is subject to—or, better, subject *of*—corporeal disaggregation.[67]

This "corporeal disaggregation" that Dinshaw discusses is another way of conceptualizing the fragments of Gawain's cultural collage. The trap set by Bertilak and his wife highlights the ambiguity within Gawain's cultural collage.

The triangulation of Bertilak's hunting scenes, Gawain's bedroom adventures and Bertilak's and Gawain's kissing game serves to expose cross-gendered facets of knightly identity. Susan Crane discusses cross-gendering in romance. She explains that the adventure elements of romance often place the knight in a stereotypically feminine position, yet she points out that "adventure is often a clearly masculine pursuit in which to be helpless is not to be feminine."[68] Gawain is helpless through much of the romance. He never appears more so than when he lounges in bed, fending off the advances of a beautiful woman, while Bertilak hunts beasts in the forest. Elizabeth Kirk notes that "Gawain's perfec-

[66] Dinshaw, "Getting Medieval," p. 134.
[67] Ibid.
[68] Susan Crane, *Gender and Romance in Chaucer's* Canterbury Tales, (Princeton: Princeton University Press, 1984), pp. 185, 186.

tion remains a hot-house plant by comparison with the interpolated feats of Sir Bertilak; the man trapped in bed because he cannot even get up without indecency looks comic if not effeminate by contrast with a hunter slaying holocausts of deer and facing wild boars."[69] According to Crane, Gawain is not effeminate, but experiencing a "metonymic experience with the feminine."[70] In any case, the poet deliberately sets up an opposition between passivity and activity in his transitions between Gawain's and Bertilak's simultaneous, but extremely opposite, activities: "Þus laykes þis lorde by lynde-wodeȝ eueȝ, / And Gawayn þe god mon in gay bed lygeȝ" [Thus plays this lord in the eaves of the linden-wood and the good man Gawain lies in a gay bed] (lines 1178–79).[71] Bertilak's hunting exploits, especially his trials with the boar, hyperbolize his masculinity; Gawain's encounters with Lady Bertilak closely examine his ability to perform within the expectations of courtly love. Both of these are "masculine" pursuits, yet Gawain avoids both.

Even though Gawain refuses to "prove" himself to her, his encounters with Bertilak also serve to keep his homosocial identity intact. Dinshaw asserts that the kisses that Gawain and Bertilak exchange propose the possibility of homoerotic desire in order to represent its "unintelligibility":

the poem both produces the possibility of homosexual relations *and* renders them unintelligible. The narrative, that is, produces the possibility of homosexual relations only to—in order to—preclude it, in order to establish heterosexuality as not just the only sexual legitimacy but a principle of intelligibility itself.[72]

While we have to wonder about Bertilak's agency and his intentions in the exchange-of-winnings game, we must notice that the poem con-

[69] Elizabeth D. Kirk, " 'Wel Bycommes Such Craft Upon Cristmasse': The Festive and the Hermeneutic in *Sir Gawain and the Green Knight*," *Arthuriana* 4.2 (1994): 122 [94–137].

[70] Crane, *Gender*, p. 187.

[71] See also the lines 1468–71; 1560–62; 1729–31; 1893–94.

[72] Carolyn Dinshaw, "A Kiss Is Just a Kiss: Heterosexuality and Its Consolations in *Sir Gawain and the Green Knight*," *diacritics* 24.2–3 (1994): 206, [205–226]. See also David Boyd, "Sodomy, Misogyny, and Displacement: Occluding Queer Desire in *Sir Gawain and the Green Knight*," *Arthuriana* 8.2 (1998): 77–113. Boyd argues "by setting up a potentially queer situation and then rejecting it, *Sir Gawain* ultimately frees both heterosexual activity and homosocial relations from perversity by relegating sodomy and homosexual desire to the realm of a transgressive Other" (88).

structs Gawain as the real question mark: Will he or won't he return the advances of Bertilak's wife? Will he or won't he kiss Bertilak when the time comes? How will he reciprocate Bertilak if he succumbs to the advances of Bertilak's wife? The games that Bertilak and his wife play with Gawain offer up sexual possibilities that the metropolitan knight is able to accept or reject. Courtly love and homosocial bonding, as they are constructed in this text, do not provide Gawain solace in making his decisions but rather indicate the delicate balance required in maintaining both gender roles and sexual desires.

Gawain's return to Camelot completes *SGGK*'s inquiry into metropolitan identity. His experiences at Bertilak's court give Gawain the insight to examine the foundations of this identity. He comes to see and understand the disjunctions and incompatibilities between all of the identity fragments in his own cultural collage, which he signals in his adoption of the green girdle. Gawain brings home a piece of the Anglo-Welsh border culture and makes it a part of himself:

> And þe blykkande belt he bere þeraboute
> Abelef as a bauderyk bounden bi his syde,
> Loken vnder his lyfte arme, þe lace, with a knot,
> In tokenyng he watȝ tane in tech of a faute. (lines 2485–88)

[And the shining belt he bore thereabout (around his neck), obliquely as a baldric bound at his side; the lace, fastened under his left arm with a knot, to indicate that he had been detected with the stain of a fault.]

By wearing the girdle, he expresses his desire to incorporate his experience of the border culture into his identity collage. Gawain's actions and new appearance reinforce the Green Knight's earlier demonstration of the fragmented nature of identity.

The poem lodges one last critique of metropolitan culture, which appears through Camelot's treatment of the returning Gawain. When he confesses his failure to the court and recounts his actions to them, the nobles laugh. Gawain's hardships and lessons become nothing more than entertainment to them, in the same way that the Green Knight had provided entertainment for them a year earlier. The court good-naturedly adopts Gawain's badge in order to raise his spirits and accept his reentry into their community. Elizabeth D. Kirk argues that in *SGGK* a community is "the sum of the experiences and meanings brought into it by the experience of individuals."[73] This community constructs itself through the appropriation of these "experiences and meanings." However, appropriation is not a politically neutral act. The community "may appropriate a new experience it can see value in, but assimilating it necessarily means redefining it."[74] Consequently, the meaning that the court invests in the girdle must be something other than what Gawain has told them.[75] Their act of assimilation takes a symbol of shame and failure and transforms it into an icon of fellowship.

In *Cannibal Culture*, Deborah Root explores how national identities form through the same kinds of assimilative acts. She argues that once colonizing cultures feared difference because of its capacity to contaminate them. Later, the colonizers found native objects interesting and prized them because of their aesthetic value. This value led to the desire to consume. Eventually, commodities appropriated from elsewhere and instilled with new patriotic meanings became the symbols of the colonizing culture.[76] This process requires a deliberate negotiation of "difference." Root explains:

To consume the commodities that have come to stand for other cultures is to neutralize the ambivalence cultural difference is able to generate and to extract excitement precisely from this ambivalence. . . . In order to work, the objects, events, and experiences that are commodified and marketed as cultural difference are dependent on concepts of cultural and aesthetic authenticity. In other words, difference has to be seen as real.[77]

In the case of *SGGK,* the court does see the commodity that they consume, the green girdle, as a real artifact of the Anglo-Welsh border, but they do not understand that the girdle represents heterogeneity rather than homogeneity. Their actions denote their ultimate inability to understand the world outside the one that they have constructed. Camelot is quick to deem objects and persons as "other" and then to try to absorb them and invest them with new meaning, rendering them safe and consumable. Despite their desire to consume, the court does not incorporate the knowledge that comes with these objects, persons,

[73] Kirk, " 'Wel Bycommes,' " p. 119.
[74] Ibid., p. 119–20.
[75] Ibid., p. 120.
[76] Deborah Root, *Cannibal Culture: Art, Appropriation and the Commodification of Difference,* (Bolder: Westview Press, 1996), pp. 68–69.
[77] Ibid., pp. 69–70.

and encounters. They remain as blissfully solipsistic as they were in the opening of the poem. The poem's audience and Gawain, however, are able to see that the poem explodes the idea of cultural homogeneity that it seems to uphold by pointing out binary oppositions between province and court. Yet, this idea cracks under the slightest pressure. *Sir Gawain and the Green Knight* advertises its own identity as a border text in order to show that all identities are constituted through what remains outside the borders that peoples draw or imagine around themselves.

COLLOQUIUM: *THE MANCIPLE'S TALE*

Chaucer's Poetics and the *Manciple's Tale*

Marianne Børch
University of Southern Denmark

O VID'S NARRATIVE of the god of poetry as adapted by Chaucer can be, and has increasingly been, read metapoetically. I wish to address the tale from a similar angle and to discuss the implications of the tale for an appreciation of the *Canterbury Tales* as a whole. Briefly, I shall argue that *The Manciple's Tale* points backwards and forwards, Janus-like. On the one hand, it may be viewed as a nightmare version of Chaucer's own poetic as this may be gleaned from *Canterbury Tale*'s pageant of beautiful lies, for instance, *The Knight's Tale*. On the other hand, the treatment of the literal in *The Manciple's Tale* differs greatly from that in *The Knight's Tale*; the systematic erasure of clues that might lead to varying, perhaps even mutually discordant, interpretations of signs in *The Manciple's Tale* might suggest a reading of the tale as a travesty of the didactic, single-authority narrative. Such a view of *The Manciple's Tale* might, in turn, problematize the authority of *The Parson's Tale*. However, *The Parson's Tale* seems to offer a third approach to language as an epistemological tool, a way that, while it departs from the poetic of *The Knight's Tale,* is nevertheless compatible with it. *The Knight's Tale* (as representative of the general Chaucerian poetic) and *The Parson's Tale* share the desire to "see and ask" of life, old books, and "sentences" as a way towards self-knowledge.

As a Chaucerian crux, *The Manciple's Tale* is perhaps only emulated by the ending of *Troilus and Criseyde*. William Wordsworth found the tale excellently suited to its teller, and until recently the tale-teller link was how the tale was salvaged for the claim of unerring Chaucerian excellence.[1] Few have found anything to recommend in the tale as such,

---

[1] Wordsworth is quoted by an approving Earle Birney in "Chaucer's 'Gentil' Manciple and his 'Gentil' Tale," *Essays on Chaucerian Irony*, ed. Beryl Rowland (Toronto: University of Toronto Press, 1985), p. 126. Other critics who find tale suited to teller in the tradition of "roadside drama" are, among others, Richard Hazelton in "The *Manciple's Tale*: Parody and Critique," *JEGP* 62, (1963) 1–31; Britton Harwood "Language and the Real: Chaucer's Manciple," *ChauR* 6 (1972): 268–79; and John P. McCall,

despite Burke Severs's valiant attempt in "Is the *Manciple's Tale* a Success?"[2] Most scholars, understandably in an age suspicious of rhetoric, accepted Manly's equation of "rhetorical" with "bad," and, perhaps less understandably, of "bad" with "early";[3] the hugely influential Chaucer edition edited by F. N. Robinson transmitted Manly's evaluation and dating up to 1987, when the revised Riverside made a U-turn to cite and adopt Neville Coghill's view that the tale "issue[s] from Chaucer's most sardonic maturity";[4] in the meantime, Donald Howard had come forward to claim, again influentially, that *The Manciple's Tale* "is a perfect choice for the last tale: its effect is astonishing, and it prepares perfectly for the Parson's Prologue and the Tale which follow."[5]

Increasingly, *The Manciple's Tale* has been held to be about language, critics detecting in this thematic concern Chaucer's need to explore the mechanics and hegemonic potential of the romance genre, a courtly poet's role, a "new man's" problematic class consciousness, or the dangers of Chaucer's own poetic practice (a stance that finds in the tale a veritable "anti-poetic").[6] The view of language, or specifically

---

Chaucer Among the Gods (University Park: Pennsylvania State University Press, 1979), p. 130.

[2] J. Burke Severs, *JEGP* 51 (1952): 1–16. Critical dislike may generally be inferred *ex silentio*, although the scattered critical remarks suggest widely different assessments from Ian Robinson's verdict of "pure entertainment" (*Chaucer and the English Tradition* [Cambridge: Cambridge University Press, 1972], p. 47) to emphases upon the tale's tragic or anarchistic ethos, e.g. Coghill cited by Scattergood in the *Riverside Chaucer*, ed. Larry Benson (London: Oxford University Press, 1988), p. 952, see quotation cited in note 4 below.

[3] Manly criticized the tale for being developed "rhetorically, not imaginatively." He calculated rhetorical elements in percentages of the total number of lines and concluded that "highest . . . stands the *Monk's Tale*, with nearly 100 per cent. Next comes the *Manciple's Tale* with 61 per cent. . . ." Quoted p. 283 in reprint of *Chaucer and the Rhetoricians*, Warton Lecture on English Poetry 12 (London, 1926), 95–113 in *Chaucer Criticism*, ed. Richard J. Schoeck and Jeromes Taylor, eds., vol. 1 (Notre Dame: Notre Dame University Press, 1960), pp. 268–90.

[4] *Riverside*, p. 952.

[5] Donald Howard, *The Idea of the Canterbury Tales* (Berkeley: University of California Press, 1978), p. 300. Helen Cooper, in *The Canterbury Tales*, Oxford Guides to Chaucer, concludes that "it is extremely hard to imagine any context for it outside the *Canterbury Tales*" (Oxford: Oxford University Press, 1989), p. 384.

[6] In 1963, Richard Hazelton broke new ground with "The *Manciple's Tale:* Parody and Critique" (see n. 1), as he addressed the tale's literary rather than dramatic aspect. I disagree, however, with a reading that holds *The Manciple's Tale* a genre take-off analogous with *Sir Thopas*. No scholarship was ever needed to identify the comedy of *Thopas*; and the rhetorical/tonal instabilities of *The Manciple's Tale*, as well as its inconsistencies of content, suggest that Chaucer had other axes to grind than that of generic play. Britton Harwood went beyond generic analysis in "Language and the Real: Chaucer's Manciple" (see note 1), pp. 268–79. Very influential in the same field has been Donald Howard with *The Idea of the Canterbury Tales*, see note 5, pp. 302 ff. See further Gruber &

poetry, as the tale's central theme adds special urgency to the question
of its place in the *Canterbury Tales*, since the implications of *The Manciple's Tale's* particular brand of "divine poetry" must carry special weight
if placed immediately before the Parson's abrupt dismissal of poetry in
preference for penitential discourse.[7] The present reading assumes that
The Manciple's Tale stands where every manuscript has in fact placed it,
although the *Prologue* suggests that more tales might still be pending.
However, its central argument is not dependent upon that assumption
for its basic validity, only for its relative weight.

The views of language presented in *The Manciple's Tale* are basically in-
congruous: Rhetoric as such is denied authority as vehicle of truth at the
level of story as well as narration; at the same time, however, both
narrator and protagonist engage in extensive glossing and symbolic constructions to consolidate their authority. Phoebus uses rhetorical lies to
protect the myth of his wife's innocence, later even elaborating the lie
into an elegiac eulogy "of operatic proportions," as Howard has it.[8]
However, to restore and embellish his wife's reputation—as is necessary
if his own is to shine—Phoebus has to not only "rewrite" but to erase
altogether the original text, that is, he must silence his wife absolutely,
demolishing her potentially alternative meaning(s) along with her life.
Instead of an intransigently live and speaking woman, Phoebus' ideal
text is thus a dead body ventriloquized into perfection by himself. Phoebus, moreover, makes sure that he alone is the interpreter, for not only
does he kill his wife, he also reduces the crow's singing and whiteness
to croaking and blackness, mute signs whose vaguely sinister associations may be freely elaborated and articulated by Phoebus himself. If
silence is pronounced golden, then, speech saves Phoebus's face, effacing

---

Johnson, eds., *New Views on Chaucer: Essays in Generative Criticism* (Denver: Society for
New Language Study, 1973), 43–49. Mel Storm sees the tale as an apology for quietist
or relativist writing at a time badly in need of a serious "mirror of princes" in "Speech,
Circumspection, and Orthodontics in the Manciple's Prologue and Tale and the Wife of
Bath's Portrait," *Studies in Philology* 96 (1999): 109–26. Louise Fradenburg, esp. inspired by Zumthor and Poirion, anatomises *The Manciple's Tale* in Lacanian terms to
view it as depicting "Chaucer's awareness" of the "limitations" of the courtly poetic of
"pluralized carnival" before he passes on to "penitential prose," p. 111 in "The Manciple's Servant Tongue: Politics and Poetry in the Canterbury Tales," *ELH* 52 (1985):
85–118. See further note 21.
  [7] Helen Cooper argues that there is "near certainty that IX and X (Manciple and
Parson) were . . . linked by Chaucer himself," *The Structure of the Canterbury Tales* (London: Duckworth, 1983), pp. 61–2.
  [8] Howard, *Idea*, p. 300.

what defaces him by filling up the silence of the wife with the "reputaci-oun" her preference for Phoebus should guarantee. Turning to the level of narration, the Manciple engages in similar *glossing* as *glossing over* when he eulogizes Phoebus, although he pronounces beautiful rhetoric void (see below for further elaboration); similarly, the crow's excellence is warranted by its elaborately described whiteness and nightingale's voice, as well as by the known worth of its singing teacher, all boosting the crow's merit in a way that aggravates the shock when finally we hear the bird itself speaking its "Cokkow" (IX, 243) to debunk beauty, moral integrity, and divine control.[9] Going beyond the Tale to the *Prologue*, we see the Manciple suppressing the behavioral analogue of unglossed hostility by means of kiss and drink. There is, in other words, a consis-tent undermining of the very rhetoric employed by the the Manciple and by its own god, Phoebus. The undermining extends to rhetoric or poetry as such, not only its abuse: if words must correspond to the deed (208), here beautiful words have no "deeds" to refer to except the vanity of the self-deceiver, but are the hot-air tools of the demagogue, and, however empty, difficult even for him to keep in the air. Devoid of intrinsic worth, fair appearances must be kept up by a sustained and most likely futile effort: Phoebus may do "al that he kan" (line 256), but "blered is [his] ye,"(line 252), and his subsequent acts show him as slave to pragmatic necessity rather than free agent. Successively en-raged, murderous, penitent, and vindictive, Phoebus's statements are always tactical, playing to delude a credulous world by suppressing the ill effects of "rakel" (line 289) action, in a way reminiscent of the Manci-ple's swift retraction in the *Prologue*.[10] Even as Phoebus can save face by revising two bad things (adultery and betrayal of noble estate) into a true and doting (if dead) spouse, even so in the *Prologue*, the Manciple is able to patch up enmity and the danger of exposure with acts of token friendship, turning "rancour and disese" into "acord and love" (lines 97–98).

The tale features no single noble act. The opening eulogy of Phoebus sets the standard: Among many a "noble worthy dede" (line 111), the

---

[9] All quotations are from *The Riverside Chaucer*, gen. ed. Larry D. Benson (Boston: Houghton Mifflin, 1987).

[10] The Manciple's nihilism goes beyond that of the Pardoner: The Pardoner protests that pardon, responsibly administrered, works. The Manciple boasts that success in establishing a beautiful and reputable facade is grounded in demolishing the very notion that beauty and honesty might exist.

slaying of Python comes off as less than glorious, as the monster is killed in his sleep (lines 109–10), the rhetorical figure thus undermining the proposition it pretends to support.[11] The reference to Amphion may be similarly suspect. Besides, priorities seem oddly twisted, as when the after-thoughtish "in signe eek" in the following refers to the all-important symbolic bow, the very bow, moreover, which is later to be broken after serving Phoebus in another noble, worthy deed, to wit an erratic, ignoble murder.

> This Phebus, that was flour of bachilrie,
> As wel in fredom as in chivalrie,
> For his desport, *in signe eek* of victorie
> Of Phitoun, so as telleth us the storie,
> Was wont to beren in his hond a bowe. (IX, 125–9)

Looking about for an anchor of value, a point of identification, the reader discovers none. Phoebus is a violent and hysterical manipulator. The truth-telling witness's merit is tarnished by its malicious timing (lines 240–43). Phoebus's wife is a whore, Chaucer having removed every individuating detail and basis for sympathy from the portraits found in his sources.[12] Any action that is orderly and controlled is exposed as pragmatic, with its gains balanced by its losses, since successful manipulation entails enslavement of the manipulator to his own schemes. All nobility or culture is thus exposed as a prison of natural impulses—like that which keeps a bird in its cage, a cat on its beautiful cushion, or a wife virtuous (lines 160–95).[13] Staying in culture's cage remains a chore, never a natural choice, since natural man is an animal, given to desires that have no respect for reputation, honor, or decency (lines 212–22).

The disillusioned view of beautiful rhetoric as a façade covering up a sordid truth in the name of opportunism and hegemonic power arguably casts a long shadow back over every Canterbury Tale up to this, the last of the tales "proper," which at the same time leads up to the very different *Parson's Tale*. The tale's position, as well as echoes tying Chaucer to

[11] See Michael Kenzak, "Apollo exterminans: The God of Poetry in Chaucer's *Manciple's Tale*," *Studies in Philology* 98 (2001): 143–57. Kenzak casts light on traditions that depicted Apollo as respectively violent and inept.
[12] Chaucer elides from Ovid the wife's name, her pregnancy and lament, and the pathos of Phoebus's attempts to save her.
[13] In none of Chaucer's sources is the bird kept in a cage.

the Manciple (see below), arguably make one's reading of the tale critical to an assessment of the entire *Canterbury Tales*. And *The Manciple's Tale*, indeed, stands as a touchstone of two, or possibly three, different poetics at work in the *Tales*.

First, with its exposure of rhetoric, *The Manciple's Tale* might cast a galled eye back upon *The Knight's Tale*, which, although the first and grandest tale of all and different from *The Manciple's Tale* in ethos and scale, nevertheless has many features in common with it: *The Knight's Tale* is a classicized philosophical romance in which heroic ideals are explored through tragic action viewed in a context of divine agency; it employs a classical pagan framework to explore values in a secular perspective, unaided by Christian authority; it clearly demonstrates the connection between discourse and outlook, notably in Theseus's final speech; and its principal settings and imagery, of prison and imprisonment, suggest a human predicament of helpless restraint.[14] As is often noted, and as in *The Manciple's Tale*, the form of *The Knight's Tale* seems to groan under the pressure of its content.[15] Its prison images and structures encage the erratic contingencies of plot and passionate motivation up to the moment when, Phoebus-like, Theseus speaks a world of tragic experience into sense and teleological direction. Moreover, the "sorwes two" which produce "O parfit joye, lastynge everemo" (I, lines 3071–72) might well spring to mind when Harry Bailey rejoices at the transformation of "rancour and disese" to "acord and love" in *The Manciple's Prologue* (IX. 97–98). With such resonances, *The Manciple's Tale* might be read as an acrid critique of the implied poetic of *The Knight's Tale*, suggesting that rather than bringing out an inherent order in things, eloquence and philosophy are reductive fabrications (a suggestion the more disturbing as it is already latent in the *The Knight's Tale* itself). Indeed, the Manciple seems to beat Theseus in the art of myth-making: Theseus can only ever be a substitute god, as sadly and sighing (I. 2185) he makes the best of a bad situation. But the Manciple stands apart from his environment, and so is able to manipulate it, along with "an heep of lerned men" (*General Prologue*, line 575). This stance makes him god of his own life, like his protagonist who, in a grotesque take-off of the creative act, speaks reality into being. Furthermore, salvaging his

---

[14] As subtly analysed in Kolve's *Chaucer and the Imagery of Narrative* (London: Arnold, 1984); anticipated by K. Nakatani, "A Perpetual Prison: The Design of Chaucer's the *Knight's Tale*," *Hiroshima Studies in English Literature* 9 (1963): 75–89.

[15] The seminal text here remains Charles Muscatine, *Chaucer and the French Tradition* (Indiana, Berkeley: University of California Press, 1966), pp. 175–90.

wife's good name (and his own) by killing her, Phoebus dramatizes the way Theseus's speech transforms Arcite's ugly death into the happy means by which his reputation is preserved: Arcite is dead, long live his reputation (I. 3047–56).[16]

However, the Manciple's and the Knight's tales are worlds apart, the difference resting in their respective treatments of the literal level, or more precisely in the way the author mediates between his matter and his audience. *The Knight's Tale* presents a rich view of features that problematize its philosophical standpoint as articulated by Theseus and implied by its form: both human suffering and human generosity (including some on Theseus's own part) are depicted in a manner which makes it difficult to accept Theseus's mechanical equation of human life with oak, stone, or river (I. 3017 ff.); the unruly gods, in turn, are portrayed in ways which clash with the conception of an Aristotelian First Mover (lines 2987 ff.); we are allowed to wonder, finally, at the convenient way in which Theseus's cosmology underpins his political authority, as he tones down old conflicts and places himself "as he were a god in trone"(line 2529). So perhaps Arcite's question "What asketh men to have?" (line 2777) is not satisfactorily answered by Theseus's "Why Grucchen we?" (line 3058). It may be the only possible answer, but the reader is allowed to ask along with Arcite.

In contrast to *The Knight's Tale*, the Manciple and his protagonist both establish a unified message through suppression of the literal (otherwise eloquent in itself and potentially problematizing). And this in a context that declares such suppression at the same time godlike and violent. The "gloss" here is not an interpretation, but a supersession that precludes active interpretation by listener or reader. The line of communication may be thus represented:

narrative → exegete-narrator with message → reader

In *The Knight's Tale*, however, the inclusion of discordant features establishes a triangular relation that allows for multiple, variable, and continuing interpretation. The poetic of *The Knight's Tale* cannot deceive in the way that Phoebus's glossing can, because its form accommodates difference without concealing it. There may be an overt message, but

---

[16] I paraphrase and quote my own analysis in *Chaucer's Poetics: Seeing and Asking* (Copenhagen: Own, 1993), p. 442.

the crow or wife (understood as metonymic of "difference from" or "resistance to" the stated meaning) is not killed—silenced—by it, a communicative pattern that may be represented thus:

narrative—exegete-narrator's message/moral

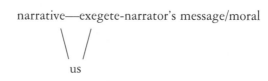

us

A modern critic celebrates this type of readerly access and freedom. However, violence done to the literal in the glossed, single-meaning text is quite normal, even mandatory, in many a medieval text. Exegetical practices are notoriously neglectful of the literal level.[17] And if such grotesque flaunting of the literal may ultimately be grounded in the piously Augustinian desire to salvage Egyptian gold, or preserve the vase without the vipers, Chaucer likes to demonstrate the many bad-faith possibilities of "glosynge," as with the Friar in *The Summoner's Tale* (III. 1788–96), Chauntecleer in *The Nun's Priest's Tale* (VII. 3163–6); or even Nicolas in *The Miller's Tale*, less often cited in this context, but who supersedes the Flood narrative of Genesis and Miracle Play with his own (I. 3534 ff.). *The Manciple's Tale* may serve the same end as a critique of the didactic poet, the glossator who, like the Manciple's Phoebus, controls the meaning of his text by monopolizing its meaning—a text, then, whose propagation, even perhaps of orthodox truth, depends upon a violation of the literal (as when the wife's adultery is beautified by its erasure), treats form as essentially redundant ("lady or lemman," no matter), and encourages in, indeed forces upon, the audience a passively receptive attitude, rather than a critical one (since it cannot monitor or critique Phoebus' story).[18]

The Knight's Tale, allowing different, even contradictory, discourses to act upon the reader, is clearly an approach less easily controlled by its author than the Manciple's approach, but it is Chaucer's usual choice.

---

[17] For a hilarious and lucid example of a story from *Gesta Romanorum* allegorized, *De Jactantia*, consult Helen Cooper's *The Structure of the Canterbury Tales* (see note 7), pp. 10–11.

[18] Britton Harwood notes that Phoebus uses description "to control attitude," "Language and the Real," p. 271. Alastair Minnis argues that Chaucer questions "the traditional relationship between literally-fictious *narratio* and allegorically-true *moralizatio*" and "shows how the technique of moralization can be misused or abused by a moralizer of dubious moral standards," *Chaucer and Pagan Antiquity* (Cambridge: D. S. Brewer, 1982), pp. 19–20.

Chaucer generally allocates to his reader an extremely active role, as his tales often encourage, and occasionally dramatize, several possible responses to the same story, even simultaneously contradictory ones, for instance, in the *Canterbury Tales* links' display of different pilgrims' responses, or in the way Chaucer in *The Clerk's Tale* dramatises two responses to incite us to active engagement rather than either unthinking acceptance or unquestioning outrage, even as in *Troilus and Criseyde* the narrator's voice defines possible variables of response. Increasing readerly autonomy is further encouraged once Chaucer begins to experiment with an idiosyncratic narrator whose "auctoritee" must itself be open to interpretation (as in the Wife of Bath's case). This approach makes for intelligent, consciousness-raising reading, even as it insures that the meaning of a tale will always transcend its teller's intention, pious or perverted. But it also provides a dangerous poetic in that it may seduce not only the sinful, but also the merely unintelligent (unintelligent responses are dramatized in *Canterbury Tales* in, for instance, the Reeve's response to the Miller). The approach might also be cowardly in a time that needs clear speaking out on princely obligations.[19] Or bespeak the ambivalent responses of a courtly poet as a servant whose identity is subsumed in that of his superior.[20] If Truth may deliver (and ambiguity "sownen into synne" or sublimate quietist grovelling), why insist upon such a wide scope for the reader?

Whether *The Manciple's Tale* be understood as a critique of exegetical practice or as a self-castigating Chaucerian moment of truth—the moment when he confronts and exposes the deceptions and violences done to truth by beautiful, godlike control—may well depend upon what follows after, and *PsProl* and *Tale* might well suggest the moment of truth: the Parson spurns fables and, like the Manciple, refuses to gloss or be textual, a literalism already demonstrated in an earlier appearance (II. 1170 ff.). His tale is not a multiple-ambiguity fable, but straight prose exposition, offering an uncompromising view of right and wrong, sin and virtue. Then follows the *Retraction* with Chaucer worrying about texts which "sownen into synne" (X. 1086). So, possibly, *The Canterbury Tales* issues in Chaucer's rejection of his own poetic, prefaced with the Manciple's exposure of rhetorical abuse. After all, the Manciple shows us one of Chaucer's faces, even if that face is a mask, and the poet has

[19] As suggested by Mel Storm in "Speech, Circumspection, and Orthodontics in the *Manciple's Prologue and Tale* and the *Wife of Bath's Portrait*".
[20] As argued by Louise Fradenburg in her, who brilliantly stitches together the narrative and the strange "my sone" sequence in "The Manciple's Servant Tongue: p. 111.

even taken pains to highlight his affinity with the Manciple and other churls of the Canterbury pilgrimage. He defends the need to match word with deed in exactly the same suspect context as does the pilgrim narrator—where is the necessity in giving words to deeds of drunkenness or promiscuous sexuality (I. 3173–5; IX. 207 ff.)?—and rejoices that wine can turn earnest into game, a defense that somehow did not seem convincing in the Miller's ale-befuddled case (I. 3136–40; IX. 99–100). The pilgrim at this point has already placed himself with the churls in *GP*, lines 542–44, possibly an indicator of a poet's uncertain status, or of Chaucer's in general as one of those "new men."[21]

The Manciple, then, is arguably aligned with Chaucer in his least attractive role as poet, a Chaucer in need of priest and Grace. On the other hand, as we have seen above, the *The Manciple's Tale* may equally be read as an attack on texts that stuff truth down people's throats, a reading that threatens the authority of the Parson, who would appear to prefer precisely such stuffing. However, *The Parson's Tale* allows for, indeed on a closer look encourages, a third reading of his procedure: as neither a negation of the Chaucerian poetic of which *The Manciple's Tale* is a nightmare reflection, nor as doctrine stifling readerly freedom. The Parson's poetic is far from continuous with *The Manciple's Tale*'s repressive rhetoric, but rather bears affinities with Chaucer's more common practice.

The Parson and Phoebus/Manciple equally reject glossing, but Phoebus/Manciple's refusal to gloss legitimizes removing the discrepant "literal" detail of the speaking wife; and even filling the silence left by that wife. Glossing is reductive, then; or it is creative, since Phoebus's glossing extends to filling that silence. In contrast, the Parson, rather than removing the literal "text" or "deed" of a sin, rejects a glossed-over or

---

[21] *Riverside* suggests that Chaucer may have depicted the Manciple from his own experience, since "the Manciple does not appear in traditional estates satire" (p. 821). Possibly the Manciple's liminal position between superior and inferior, buyer and seller (in a community where the development of the third estate threatened to blow up the tripartite division of society altogether), may have invited some degree of identification with Chaucer as a court poet, similarly placed in an intermediary position. The reflection of a court poet's situation in the tale has been discussed at length in Fradenburg and earlier by V. J. Scattergood in "The Manciple's Manner of Speaking," *Essays in Criticism* 24 (1971): 124–46. Sheila Delany argues in her psychoanalytical reading that the tale "does . . . emanate from Chaucer, representing his atttitudes and fantasies," "Slaying Python: Marriage and Mysogyny in a Chaucerian Text," *Writing Woman: Women Writing and Women in Literature, Medieval to Modern* (New York: Schocken Books, 1983), pp. 47–75.

silenced truth in favor of its exposition—his is glossing as unveiling, revealing; his practical guide to confession advocates speech that lays open and explores as he invites, in effect, self-narrative. The procedure abides by old traditions, but does not stifle individual self-discovery in the now.[22] The Parson's strategy encourages each pilgrim, figuratively "stond[ing] upon the weyes": "seeth and axeth of olde pathes" (X. 77). Jerome's metaphor of asking old paths and ways links such devotional practice with the *Canterbury Tales*'s structural metaphor of the pilgrimage; and even more specifically with the way individual tales allow people to ask, with Arcite, "what asketh men to have?" in a life where often "we witen nat what thing we preyen heere" and therefore "goon wrong ful often" (I. 2777, 1260, 1267). The work thus suggests three ways of clarifying individual human "entente": storytelling, the study of stories and "sentence," and the self-exploration of confession. The role of language in clarifying motivation through meticulous exploration, then, links the Parson's poetic with that of Chaucer. And it separates both poetics from the Manciple's repressive one.

[22] Thomas H. Bestul has studied evidence that Chaucer was inspired by treatises on meditation, and characterizes the Parson's conservative tract as "al of the newe jet" in at least its attention to "affective Passion themes" which looks forward to *"devotio moderna,"* pp. 618–9 in "Chaucer's Parson's Tale and the Late-Medieval Tradition of Religious Meditation," *Speculum* 64 (1989): 600–19. The role played by the individual as listener to *The Parson's Tale* is also suggested as Parson in his Prologue, where he adopts the other tellers' appeal to his listeners (if they "list") to accept his "tale," and his willingness, unlike Phoebus, to "stonde to correccioun" (X, 45–60).

"For sorwe of which he brak his minstralcye": The Demise of the "Sweete Noyse" of Verse in the *Canterbury Tales*

John Hines
Cardiff University

THE PLACE of *The Manciple's Prologue and Tale* as the penultimate fragment of and contribution to the *Canterbury Tales*, followed by the *Parson's Tale* and then Chaucer's own leave-taking and retractions, is not without textual and dramatic problems.[1] Nevertheless its position here in every early collection of the *Tales* worthy of critical consideration means that we have to treat it as a fact. There are then two possible interpretations of the location of *The Manciple's Tale* that are truly irreconcilable opposites. One is that its place here should not be attributed any intrinsic meaning at all. The messiness of its links both to what precedes it and to what follows—that the Host seems not to know that the Cook abortively began to tell the last tale of Fragment I (IX. 4–19); a time-shift from morning to afternoon between this and the *Parson's Prologue* (IX. 16; cf. X. 1–9); and references to the Yeoman, Merchant and Franklin as the tellers of the previous tale in some versions of the first line of the *Parson's Prologue*—imply that its presence here is that of a leftover from an incomplete re-organization of the whole work. This comes, moreover, immediately after *The Canon's Yeoman's Tale* has forcefully ruptured the explicit dramatic framework of the *Tales*. It is thus easy to imagine that *The Manciple's Tale* has simply been parked—if not dumped—at the back of the *Tales*.[2]

[1] Larry D. Benson et al. (eds.), *The Riverside Chaucer*, 3d ed. (Oxford: Oxford University Press, 1988), pp. 951–55. All quotations from Chaucer in this paper are taken from this edition. Norman F. Blake, *The Textual Tradition of the Canterbury Tales* (London: Edwin Arnold, 1985), pp. 58–62.

[2] Thus J. M. Manly, "Chaucer and the rhetoricians," *Proceedings of the British Academy* 12 (1926): 95–113, at pp. 108–9. He describes *The Manciple's Tale* as "one of the least known and least interesting of the tales . . . the tale is not particularly appropriate to the Manciple or indeed to any other of the pilgrims, and . . . no effort is made to adapt it to him."

The alternative view is that the crucial position of *The Manciple's Pro-logue and Tale* allows them to bring the presentation of major themes in the *Canterbury Tales* to a climax: a climax that, together with the re-sponse of Fragment X, concludes the discussion of such themes in the whole work. It is hardly surprising that scholarly critics have largely preferred a positive and constructive view of this kind. Such, for in-stance, was my view when writing an extended study of the fabliau in English, in which Chaucer's *Canterbury Tales* inevitably played a leading part, and with that reconsidering *The Manciple's Tale* as a story concerned with sexual liaisons and cuckolding.[3] Prior to this point, Chaucer's fabli-aux in the *Tales* have developed and emphasized the unfamiliar image of the contented cuckold prefigured by, and possibly adopted from, Boc-caccio—the husband who is happy as long as he is ignorant of his wife's sexual misdemeanors:[4] a slightly different figure from the complaisant *wittol*, who is undisturbed by his wife's blatant adultery. The Miller forcefully advocates the complicit happiness of this position, in answer-ing the Reeve (I. 3151–66), and ending with the memorable couplet:

> . . . So he may finde Goddes foyson there,
> Of the remenaunt nedeth nat enquere.

It is ironic that the famous concept of "God's plenty" was thus intro-duced with specific reference to the inexhaustible sexual capacity of women, but this does not render Dryden's adoption of that phrase as an encapsulation of Chaucer's positive moral vision wholly inappropriate.[5] This contended cuckold subsequently reappears as *The Shipman's Tale*'s merchant, and *The Merchant's Tale*'s January.

In *The Manciple's Tale*, such happy illusions are utterly shattered. Phoebus learns of his wife's adultery and is intensely hurt by it. He kills his wife and turns the crow black, also taking away its "sweete noyse." Likewise he destroys his musical instruments, followed by the Cupidean symbols of his bow and arrows (IX. 262–308). This may in a way prove the point that the cuckold is happy as long as ignorant, but, in contrast to the Miller's willing ignorance, *only* as long as he remains ignorant: most significantly, this tale destroys the illusion that ignorance of adul-tery can be a stable and tenable situation. *The Manciple's Tale* would thus

[3] John Hines, *The Fabliau in English* (London: Longmans, 1993), pp. 200–202.
[4] The relevant tale of *Il Decamerone* is Day 6, tale 7. See Hines, *Fabliau*, pp. 237–38.
[5] John Dryden, Preface to *Fables Ancient and Modern,* in *The Poems of John Dryden,* ed. James Kingsley, 4 vols. (Oxford: Clarendon, 1958), pp. 1455–1463.

appear to be well-placed at the transition from the sweet and seductive noise of poetry to the solemn prose and penitential theme of the Parson, and subsequently to Chaucer's retractions, particularly in respect of the tales "that sownen into synne."

This, of course, is by no means the only possible interpretation of *The Manciple's Tale*'s thematically important position. A reading of the tale that represents it as concluding the discussion of an issue that has been developed through the *Tales* certainly attributes a degree of literary re-flexivity to the *Tale*, but other approaches have predictably applied this recently dominant line of Chaucer criticism in a more general way. Christopher Cannon has newly revised and revived the argument that *The Manciple's Tale* is "about language," suggesting that it provides one of Chaucer's most serious dramatized analyses of the power of language, and thus, implicitly, the power of rhetoric and poetry.[6] As the speech of the crow converts knowledge into action, such discourse is revealed as a potentially destructive force, having been misused here to produce the very opposite of its ideal function of allowing individuals to construct a moral community by communicating with one another. Cannon also proposes *The Nun's Priest's Tale* as the positive counterpart to *The Manciple's Tale*: even if in a comical manner, speech there defers the execution of decisive and destructive acts of power.

The story of Phoebus and the crow was a conventional exemplum on ill-advised speech that redounds to the detriment of the speaker: this is confirmed by other medieval English versions of the tale, such as Gower's version in Book III of *Confessio Amantis*.[7] This book is concerned with the sin of Wrath, but the point at issue here is not the ruinous wrath of Phoebus; it is rather the disastrous consequences that quarrelsome and angry words (*cheste*) can have. This interpretation of the tale is a markedly Christian one, quite different from its presentation by Ovid in Book II of his *Metamorphoses*, the source of the medieval ver-

---

[6] Britton J. Harwood, "Language and the Real: Chaucer's Manciple," *ChauR* 6 (1971): 268–79; Michael Kersak, "The Silences of Pilgrimage: *Manciple's Tale, Paradiso, Anticlaudianus*," *ChauR* 34 (1999): 190–206; Christopher Cannon, paper read at the inaugural London Chaucer conference, School of Advanced Studies, University of London, April 2002.

[7] John Gower, *Confessio Amantis*, III. 782–817, in *The Complete Works of John Gower*, ed. G. C. Macaulay, 4 vols. (Oxford: Clarendon, 1899–1902), ii.247–8. See also the Middle English *Seven Sages of Rome*, ed. Karl Brunner, EETS, o.s. 191 (London: Oxford University Press, 1933), where a version of the exemplum is used in lines 2193–292 as warning against rash actions by those in power, and the bird is eventually vindicated.

sions.[8] The Christian reading does adopt Ovid's moral censure of the petty malice of the bird rather than the infidelity of Coronis (the woman), but does so at the expense of Ovid's crucially important critique of Phoebus's enraged and destructive reaction. Completely excised from Chaucer's and Gower's versions is the fact that Coronis is pregnant and that in slaying her Phoebus also loses his own unborn son. With his characteristically impressive, almost Olympian moral audacity, Ovid's mythic, pagan, and humanist tale asks us to face the essential rule that active and available female sexuality—and with that, potential female promiscuity—is essential to the maintenance of the reproductive cycle and thus of human life itself. Phoebus's pain is a price he has to be prepared to pay for the ability to enjoy his own sex life and to beget a son.

Comparison of *The Manciple's Tale* with Gower's version emphasizes the degree to which Chaucer elaborated and developed the exemplum.[9] Gower's version is brief, following Ovid a little more closely, for instance in naming the woman (Cornide), but is otherwise a rather mechanical summary of the story. The one flash of striking literary art in Gower's narrative is the line (III. 791) in which he expresses Cornide's infidelity, emphatically deemphasizing it and presenting it as a mundane if tragic inevitability:

> So it befell upon a chance
> A yong kniht tok hire acquentance
> And hadde of hire al that he wolde. (*Confessio Amantis*, III. 789–91)

This enables Gower practically to dismiss adultery as the moral topic of this exemplum. It most certainly does not efface the act of adultery as a fault, but is enough for him successfully to declare that it is not the issue of importance: it is a fact that can be accepted without emphasis or even reflection.

If Chaucer's *Manciple's Tale* is a reflection upon speech, however, it is not just concerned with language in general, but also with speech-acts and the contexts of those acts—contexts that crucially include the mat-

---

[8] Ovid, *Metamorphoses*, II. 531–632. Cf. *Ovide Moralisé*, lines 2130–548. Both sources are quoted in W. F. Bryan and Germaine Dempster (eds.), *Sources and Analogues of the Chaucer's Canterbury Tales* (Chicago: University of Chicago Press, 1941), pp. 701–9.

[9] Cf. William Cadbury, "Manipulation of sources and the meaning of the *Manciple's Tale*," *Philological Quarterly* 43 (1964): 538–48.

ter the utterance is referring to. If speech has consequences, it also has causes of its own, and relates no less to the circumstances out of which it arises. The exemplum proper in *The Manciple's Tale* does not begin with a speech–act: it begins by introducing characters and setting, and narrating an event that takes place:

> And so bifel, whan Phebus was absent,
> His wyf anon hath for hir lemman sent. (IX. 203–4)

As if to emphasize this, the narrator also monopolizes the field of speech-act, moving into an ostentatious, self-referential analysis of his own performance:

> Hir lemman? Certes, this is a knavyssh speche! (line 205)

In Aristotelian terms, the crow's words and tone are the formal and efficient causes between the preverbal material cause (the act of infidelity/adultery) and the final cause of Phoebus's destructive fury: they are intermediary between the original sexual misdeed and the effects of pain and violence. In representing the facts, moreover, not just any words will do:

> The word moot need accorde with the dede (line 208)

If we are, then, to regard *The Manciple's Tale* as a reflection upon the capacity of language and discourse to define and evaluate human transgressions, we should not consider that as being done in the abstract and at some sort of universal level of generality, but rather in connection with a specific case. This nicely reconciles the divergent moral potential and use of the exemplum: on the one hand as a warning about ill-advised speech, which we may regard as ethically superficial and only justified by highly local dramatic relevance (to a Manciple who has been caught out being too freely critical of the Cook); on the other its significance that is particularly recognizable as a result of its place in the *Canterbury Tales*, as a reflection upon the destructive consequences of adultery—or perhaps even sexual passion more generally. Despite where the attention of Chaucer scholars and critics has principally lain for the past three decades, I would not try to distinguish between sexual mores and the sanctity of marriage, on the one hand, and the critical capacity and moral power of literature, on the other, as the more serious and dominant theme of the *Canterbury Tales*. Neither is merely a local or an occasional issue.

The Problem of the Manciple

The restoration of a practical connection between the powerful act of speech and the situation and events that precede that act and to which it refers reactivates the problem of how we should regard the tale as some sort of reflection upon its teller. The 104-line *Prologue* to the *Tale* provides a small vignette putting the character and motivation of the teller squarely at the center of the picture. The Manciple is scornfully and openly abusive of the drunken Cook, drawing a rebuke and warning from the Host that the tables can be turned and the Manciple's own fraudulent manipulation of his employers' accounts be revealed. The Manciple accepts this reproof in a glib and ostentatious manner, and then apparently tells an exemplary tale reinforcing the cynical lesson of which he has just been reminded: hold your tongue even in the face of manifest vice, lest you draw attention to yourself and your own misdeeds come under scrutiny. This is not the virtuous principle of "Let him amongst you without sin cast the first stone" but a pragmatic conspiracy of infectious corruption.

Looked at in realistic terms, it is simply unconvincing for a Manciple who supposedly wishes to divert attention from himself to tell a tale that is a sort of confession—not least when it is a pragmatically black one in which he actually admits to not having been immoral or amoral enough to repress his disgust at the Cook. One possible reading, inevitably, is that it is a Vice, virtually personified, and not a character that is offered for examination here. But that is a difficult position to defend in relation to Chaucer's *Canterbury Tales*, and to the pilgrims in particular, when such approaches—and the normative moral assumptions they represent—have long been out of favor. Critics have generally been more willing to take the view that the Manciple is one of a number of the pilgrims whose vicious characters are gradually revealed in the progress from their *General Prologue* introductions through their interactions in the dramatic framework to the tales they tell themselves.[10] There is,

---

[10] Earle Birney, "Chaucer's 'gentil' Manciple and his 'gentil' tale," *Neuphilologische Mitteilungen* 21 (1960): 257–67; Richard M. Trask, "The Manciple's Problem," *Studies in Short Fiction* 14 (1977): 109–16; Arnold B. Davidson, "The logic of confusion in the 'Manciple's Tale,'" *Annuale medievale* 19 (1979): 5–13.

however, no other convincing example of a pilgrim-character that Chaucer has created solely to condemn so utterly, in such an insidious way, out of his or her own mouth. Even the outrageously corrupt characters—the Friar, Summoner, and Pardoner—have strangely redeeming features in their ability to tell extraordinarily powerful moral tales against specific sins, and against other sinners than themselves. In respect of the fabliaux, it proved important to discuss, but also possible to argue substantially against, such a widely held "black" view of the Shipman, Reeve, and Merchant.[11]

It could be held that those last three characters had simply been critically "misunderstood," but it is less easy to construct a case that can rescue the Manciple's good character. Yet the *General Prologue* portrait of the man actually seems rather positive. He is sly, certainly, but in a way that seems clever rather than evil. There is no basis for or hint of any sympathy for his "victims," who seem first just to be merchants that he is able to outsmart in the buying-and-selling business:

> A gentil MAUNCIPLE was ther of a temple,
> Of which achatours myghte take exemple
> For to be wise in byynge of vitaille;
> For wheither that he payde or took by taille,
> Algate he wayted so in his achaat
> That he was ay biforn and in good staat. (I. 567–72)

It is then revealed that he acts in the same way in his dealings with his lawyer masters, whom he "setteth hir aller cappe" (I. 586). Above all, the Manciple is a figure of wit:

> Now is nat that of God a ful fair grace
> That swich a lewed mannes wit shal pace
> The wisdom of an heep of lerned men? (I. 573–75)

All in all, this would appear to set him up as another example of the socially humble character to whom real strength of insight and abilities are attributed. In character he could thus contribute significantly, if unremarkably, to the criticism of contemporary society and social ideology propounded through the *Tales*.

This is at least sufficient for it to be valid, even important, to consider

---

[11] Hines, *Fabliau*, esp. 73–80, 125–39 and 182–96.

why it should be the figure of a manciple selected to be presented thus, and to tell this tale—to suggest that, despite the hesitancy or uncertainty implied by the textual problems already referred to, Chaucer's final choice is unlikely to have been entirely arbitrary. Historically, the Manciple, especially as he is presented in the *General Prologue*, is markedly associated with distinct and modern, urban and urbane phenomena of the late fourteenth century. While the Inns of Court were highly specialized and a distinctly London feature, they functioned as a rather lofty variant of the craft guild—especially with their collegiate lifestyle, focussed on the hall: the very situation that provides the Manciple with his opportunities to profit.[12] The five guildsmen of what must be construed as a religious confraternity are scornfully lampooned in the *General Prologue* (I. 361–78) in a way that must at least predispose the reader toward a tolerant sympathy for the Manciple's discreet and painless skills rather than judgmental disapproval.

The origins of guilds, both religious and professional, can be traced back as far as the tenth century, and guilds were unquestionably a powerful and influential presence on the urban scene by the later thirteenth century. It was in the second half of the thirteenth century that provisions made by Henry III and Edward I to remove the administration of the common law from the clergy laid the foundations on which the Inns of Court, including the Inner and Middle Temple, evolved, significantly in the area between the Cities of London and Westminster. However, the thirteenth century by no means exhausted the guilds' capacity for development and even further enhancement, especially in the extensively changing economic and social circumstances across western Europe of the second half of the fourteenth century. It is important to appreciate in which areas especially they were a major—and still growing—social force in Chaucer's time; as institutions that were superseding conventional orders of society and ideas of propriety. The fraternity of the guild, in a far more real and practical manner than the notional brotherhood of chivalry, was exercised in strategies of mutual help, for the material and spiritual welfare of the group's admitted members.

---

[12] See G. Rosser, "Going to the Fraternity Feast: Commensuality and Social Relations in Late Medieval England," *Journal of British Studies* 33 (1994): 430–46; Rosser, "Crafts, guilds and the negotiation of work in the medieval town," *Past and Present* 154 (1997): 3–31; Sir Robert Megarry, *Inns Ancient and Modern: A Topographical and Historical Introduction to the Inns of Court, Inns of Chancery and Serjeants' Inns* , Selden Soc. Lecture, 14 July pp. 1971 (London, 1972), esp. 6–14; John H. Baker, *The Third University of England: The Inns of Court and the Common-Law Tradition*, Selden Soc. Lecture, 4 July 1990 (London, 1990).

While not an alternative to the church, the guild was able, financially, to appropriate a considerable amount of power from the church, for instance by effectively buying up space and manpower, employing chantry priests in chantry chapels. Socially, it provided a complete contrast to the idealized and strictly hierarchical, rural-feudal model of reciprocal services of dependency and obligation between knights and ploughmen. The Inns and guildhalls were also becoming significant cultural centers: social foci for the performance of literature, music, and, in due course, drama.[13] In this way they were direct counterparts to the royal and aristocratic courts—but were disconcertingly alternative to those cultural centres, not just flatteringly minor and junior imitations of them.

One possible explanation of the whole representation of the Manciple could, then, be as a vehicle for a Chaucer with courtly and conservative allegiances to undermine the embryonic utopianism and republicanism of the bourgeois guild movement. This attack would reside not only in the ridicule of the "heep of lerned men," but even more in the fact that the institution is shown to be subverted from within; not by some heroic, lovable, or admirable figure who offers an alternative model for emulation, but rather by a cynical parasite spawned by that system itself. Just as damning, although less reassuring from Chaucer's standpoint, would be to read the character in his portrait, *Prologue*, and *Tale* as a recognition that here in the already thriving urban professional classes were the best-adapted survivors and profiteers within the emerging order of the early modern world.

An aspect of conceptual development from the later medieval to the early modern periods that is of special relevance to the characterization of the Manciple is the redefinition and revaluation of the quality of *wit*. In English usage from the fourteenth century to the beginning of the seventeenth one can trace a steady shift of range and salience in the meaning of the word, from denoting knowledge and practical ability to denoting dexterity of mind and general adaptability. There are examples—particularly clear ones in the French *Les Cent Nouvelles Nouvelles* of the 1460's—of how wit as a quality served to ameliorate the breakdown of an old social hierarchy: a knight and a miller might still be far apart

---

[13] Especially relevant to a consideration of Chaucer and Gower and their time is the institution of the London *puy*. See John H. Fisher, *John Gower: Moral Philosopher and Friend of Chaucer* (New York: New York University Press, 1964), pp. 78–83; Derek Pearsall, *The Life of Geoffrey Chaucer: A Critical Biography* (Oxford: Blackwell, 1992), p. 22 and note 7.

in terms of inherited social rank, but could concede equality in terms of innate wit.[14] The first instance of an individual having the identity of "a wit" occurs in English around the same date.[15] Chaucer strikingly anticipates this development in the approbation granted to the "subtiltee and heigh wit" of the churl at the end of *The Summoner's Tale* (III. 2290–91). The Manciple also has wit. Oddly, though, his is still a purely practical wit, and subtle, discursive wit is conspicuously lacking in all we see of him.

What is tantalizing about *The Manciple's Tale* is that, like the powerfully admonitory *Pardoner's* and *Friar's Tales*, there is a remarkable divergence between intention and moral: between the dramatic motivation of the telling of the tale and the significance of its contents. In this case, the discrepancy is between the Manciple's reflexive but public memorandum to himself—"Kepe wel thy tonge . . . ," attributed to his mother's lore[16]—and the paradoxical fact with which I began: namely, that within the overall structure of the *Canterbury Tales* the Manciple effectively reinstates precisely the sort of moral orthodoxy we should normally (rightly) associate with Gower, by reasserting the Commandment: "Thou shalt not commit adultery." This, I would propose, is another instance of the crucial power of a text to break free in moral terms from the immediate circumstances of its performance that is a key revelation of the carefully and elaborately crafted dramatic framework of the *Canterbury Tales*. We could even then claim that the tale's intrinsic moral value is reinforced rather than subverted by the dramatic inconsistencies and social confusion from and through which it emerges. There is a message there that survives, irrespective of the virtues, or lack of them, of whoever happens to read the tale, or of however inappropriate the circumstances may be in which it is read. For Chaucer the ultimate recourse against the failure of any faith in the perfectibility of human society he may ever have had, was to the permanent Christian values represented by the end of the *Canterbury Tales*, not to siding with one social party against another.

[14] *Les Cent Nouvelles Nouvelles*, Book III, ed. F. P. Sweetser (Geneva, 1966).

[15] See *OED*, 2d ed., s.v. WIT, 9.

[16] It can, of course, and has been argued that the explicit introduction of a female speaker here is significant in relation to the much-discussed issues of sex and gender related to speech and discourse in Chaucer's writings. I am not personally persuaded that any particular force and importance need be attributed to the brief attribution of this collection of proverbial lore to "my dame" at the end of line 317 beyond the equally conventional claim that such practical advice is learned at one's mother's knee. Certainly, the persistent use of a vocative "my sone" in this 45-line exordium to the tale may be held to reinforce the characterization of the speaker, although it would be equally at home in the speech of a prolix and sententious priest.

Murdering Fiction: The Case of *The Manciple's Tale*

Eve Salisbury
Western Michigan University

F ROM THE PHYSICAL DISPUTE between Alisoun and Jankyn, the litany of spousal homicides in Jankyn's *Book of Wicked Wives*, the abuse of children and spouse in the *Clerk's Tale*, Constance's domestic tribulations in the *Man of Law's Tale*, the killing of children in the *Prioress's Tale*, the *Physician's Tale*, the *Tale of Melibee*, to the Hugolino story in the *Monk's Tale*, and even the fabliaux (of the Miller, the Reeve, and the Merchant) where household violence is defused by laughter, the *Canterbury Tales* is a work strewn with dead and/or mutilated bodies.

Included in this catalogue of violent tales, but often neglected in discussions of the meanings of domestic violence in Chaucer's work, is the *Manciple's Tale*, the narrative in which an angry and jealous husband murders his adulterous wife and then silences the talking crow who discloses the infidelity. Though the husband of the tale, Phoebus Apollo, expresses remorse for having murdered his wife, the body of the deceased woman is not mentioned; the narrative focus shifts to Apollo's curse on the talking bird whose white feathers are forever changed to black and whose power of speech is lost. At this point in the telling the Manciple's attention turns to the negative effects of thoughtless language use as he recounts what his mother taught him about the kind of indiscreet speech she calls "janglyng"; harmful speech acts, and not spousal homicide, is the subject of the tale.

The implications of the *Manciple's Tale*—that the murder of a wife is something to be glossed over or mitigated—are rendered more unsettling by the next speaker, the Parson, who considers the *Manciple's Tale* to be "fabel" and therefore not worthy of further discussion. Fables are not "truthful" narratives, in the Parson's view, neither to be told nor believed. The Parson "quits" the Manciple's tale and, seeming to take his cue from the Manciple's mother, begins his homily with a warning to his audience about harmful speech acts, particularly those that command or counsel homicide.[1] Certainly a medieval audience would understand the importance of these particular kinds of speech acts given the value that medieval society placed on verbal contracts.[2]

Soon afterward the Parson begins to describe four kinds of "manslaughtre," ending with homicidal acts that revoke the procreative goal of medieval marriage—contraception, onanism, and abortion. Both men and women are warned about the gravity of murdering children in this section of the homily (which the Parson calls a "myrie tale"). Yet neither men nor women are warned about the gravity of murdering a spouse. Is Chaucer allowing the *Manciple's Tale* and the Parson's response to raise questions about spousal homicide? Is there an implicit approbation of the murder of an *adulterous* wife? Or is Chaucer allowing an audience to render judgment on its own, deliberately murdering the fiction, to expose the legal issues of the time?

However we read the events of the *Manciple's Tale*, the deflection of attention from spousal homicide to other matters of concern, particularly when read in conjunction with the absence of an indignant response from the Parson, render the murderous act significant. When I say "murdering fiction" I mean to call attention to the point at which narrative fiction collapses to reveal the legal realities of everyday life. Every violent moment in the *Canterbury Tales*, every injury or homicide of an intimate familiar or household member, murders the fiction constructed around that event and exposes the deficiencies of a legal system divided by jurisdiction—secular and ecclesiastical—intended to assure stability, protection, and justice.

Chaucer's knowledge of the laws of his time—his acquaintance with the Inns of Court as well as his personal experiences with litigation—are generally accepted as factual. But also important in any discussion of what Chaucer knew is his experience as justice of the peace, a position he held while he was working on the *Canterbury Tales* in the late 1380s.[3] The office, which developed significantly in the fourteenth century, was

---

[1] The argument presented here assumes Fragment 10 to be Chaucer's intended ending to the *Canterbury Tales*.

[2] Richard Firth Green, *The Crisis of Truth: Literature and Law in Ricardian England* (Philadelphia: University of Pennsylvania, 1999), passim.

[3] See Derek Pearsall, *The Life of Geoffrey Chaucer: A Critical Biography* (Blackwell: Oxford, 1992), p. 205.

intended to provide law enforcement assistance to local sheriffs; by Chaucer's time its officers came to be known as "the keepers of the peace" (*custodes pacis*).[4] As one of the ten justices of the peace for the county of Kent Chaucer was "charged with enforcing the statutes for keeping the peace, taking surety for good behavior from those who threatened bodily harm or arson, and hearing by sworn inquest all manner of felonies, trespasses, ambushes, and the like."[5] My point here is to suggest that Chaucer's knowledge of the laws of his time includes an intimate familiarity with procedures required to bring a case of homicide first to public attention then to the attention of the courts.

As Chaucer likely knew, the discovery of a dead body could be a noisy business since it was the duty of the first finder to raise the hue and cry to call attention to it. He or she was then to notify neighbors, who in turn informed the bailiff, who in turn informed the coroner; if foul play were suspected the coroner was expected to bring his findings to the proper authorities, including the sheriff and the justice of the peace. Of course, the first finder risked being suspected of having committed the crime, and a body could be passed by many times before anyone would be willing to accept responsibility for setting a public inquest into motion.[6] In the *Manciple's Tale* there is neither a first finder nor a public hue and cry following the death of the wife. Rather, the scenario of events begins when the talking bird discloses the adulterous affair when he utters a well-known euphemism for cuckoldry—Cokkow! Cokkow! Cokkow!—and provides an eyewitness report:

> "Phebus," quod he, "for al thy worthynesse,
> For al thy beautee and thy gentilesse,
> For al thy song and al thy mynstralcye,
> For al thy waityng, blered is thyn ye
> With oon of litel reputacioun,
> Noght worth to thee, as in comparisoun,
> The montance of a gnat, so moote I thryve!
> For on thy bed thy wyf I saugh hym swyve." (IX. 249–56)

[4] James Root Hulbert, *Chaucer's Official Life* (New York: Phaeton Press, 1970), p. 53.
[5] Donald R. Howard, *Chaucer: His Life, His Works, His World* (New York: Fawcett Columbine, 1987), p. 384.
[6] R. F. Hunnisett, *The Medieval Coroner* (Cambridge: Cambridge University Press, 1961). Hunnisett explains, "the 'first finder' in law, the man who ultimately raised the hue and cry, might often have been more correctly termed the 'last finder,' many having previously noticed the body in silence and hurried by" (11).

A few lines later an irate Phoebus shoots an arrow into his adulterous wife: "And in his ire his wyf thanne hath he slayn. / This is th'effect; ther is namoore to sayne" (lines 265–66). The intense remorse that Phoebus demonstrates immediately thereafter moves him to break all the implements of his art—harp, lute, cithern, and psaltry—as well as the murder weapons—his bow and arrows. Then, turning to the only eyewitness to the murder, the crow, whom he blames for having brought him to "confusioun," he utters a curse that silences the calumniating fowl forevermore:

> Now shaltow, false theef, thy song forgon,
> And eek thy white fetheres everichon,
> Ne nevere in al thy lif ne shaltou speke.
> Thus shal men on a traytour been awreke;
> Thou and thyn ofspryng evere shut be blake (IX. 295–99)

When Apollo's histrionics subside, the Manciple launches into a moral diatribe that emphasizes the necessity for silence and discretion. The implication, by virtue of the Manciple's spin on things, is that had the crow restrained his speech, Phoebus's jealous anger would not have been provoked and the crime would not have been committed. The shift in subject is noteworthy, but what happens immediately after the murder is also noteworthy, particularly in view of what I have said about the role of the coroner and the justice of the peace. Rather than raise a hue and cry—the duty of *any* witness to a homicide—the eyewitness is silenced by Apollo's curse and narrative attention is diverted away from the wife's corpse to Apollo's self-recriminations. Though we could say that Apollo does indeed raise a hue and cry it is certainly not the kind intended to render the felonious deed public. Rather, the attention of the audience is directed away from the truth as an elaborate coverup begins. Without a body or a murder weapon as evidence, a case for homicide cannot be made.

As many scholars have pointed out, the significant variations between the *Manciple's Tale* and Chaucer's source for it in Ovid's *Metamorphoses* help to fill in some of the gaps in the narrative action. Chaucer, like other Ricardian poets, uses a rhetorical technique to point to underlying texts by a method of comparison called *collatio*. As described in Geoffrey of Vinsauf's *Poetria Nova*, a text that Chaucer knew well, comparison could be made overtly (*aperta*) by explicit resemblance or in a hidden way (*occulta*) by a comparison made "with dissembled mien, as if there were no comparison there at all, but the taking on, one might say, of a new form marvelously engrafted, where the new element fits as securely into the context as if it were born of the theme."[7] By pointing to Ovid's narrative in this "occult" manner, Chaucer allows Ovid to tell parts of the story that he does not.

In Ovid's account Phoebus's beloved is a beautiful maiden named Coronis who is not Phoebus's wife but rather his mistress, a significant difference, according to Sheila Delany, since by making Coronis a wife Chaucer eradicates her free agency and the "gratuitous murder becomes a punishment, harsh but not necessarily unjust."[8] But if marital status is a glaring alteration to the source text, far more conspicuous is Chaucer's lack of description of the dying woman and the state of her body at death. In Ovid the description of the dying maiden is graphic: her groans, the flow of blood from her wounded body, the agonizing extraction of the arrow, the fall of body temperature as she "lay cold in death," and her heretofore unrevealed pregnancy all lend pathos to the scene.[9] Other noteworthy omissions in Chaucer's version include the wounded woman's assent to the murderous act, her confession and admission of guilt, and Apollo's attempt to revive his dead mistress and rescue his unborn child "from his mother's womb."[10] Neither does Chaucer mention the god's transfer of the apparently viable fetus to the centaur Chiron, Achilles' famed mentor.

Chaucer's omission of the pregnancy and the events surrounding the domestic homicide is telling. If, as many scholars have suggested, such

---

[7] Geoffrey of Vinsauf, *Poetria Nova*, trans. Margaret F. Nims (Toronto: Pontifical Institute of Medieval Studies, 1967), 25.

[8] Sheila Delany, "Slaying Python: Marriage and Misogyny in a Chaucerian Text," in *Chaucer: Contemporary Critical Essays*, ed. Valerie Allen and Ares Axiotis (New York: St. Martin's Press, 1996), pp. 77–107.

[9] "Icta dedit gemitum tractoque a corpore ferro candida puniceo perfudit membra cruore et dixit: 'potui poenas tibi, Phoebe,' dedisse, sed peperisse prius; duo nunc moriemur in una. hactenus, et pariter vitam cum sanguine fudit; corpus inane animae frigus letale secutum est." [The smitten maid groaned in agony, and, as the arrow was drawn out, her white limbs were drenched with her red blood. "Twas right, O Phoebus," she said, "that I should suffer thus from you, but first I should have borne my child. But now two of us shall die in one." And while she spoke her life ebbed out with her streaming blood, and soon her body, its life all spent, lay cold in death]. See Ovid, *Metamorphoses*, ed. and trans. Frank Justus Miller (Cambridge: Harvard University Press, 1944), p. 102.

[10] Other changes between the two narratives have been documented as well. Those above look only to the events surrounding the murder.

omissions create sympathy toward Apollo's all-too-impulsive killing of his "adulterous" wife—an act predicated upon the testimony of a talking bird—then these omissions are significant. Had Chaucer included the pregnancy, any sympathy that might have been elicited from a medieval audience would certainly *not* arise when that same audience realized that Apollo also murdered his unborn child. Neither could there be a narrative strategy to rescue the fetus in the way invented by Ovid, since Chaucer has already committed the tale to a social world in which such medical miracles (at least those done by a pre-Christian deity such as Apollo) would be precluded.

If the rhetoric of the *Manciple's Tale* is significant in its elusive maneuvers, then so too is the Parson's response to it. When the *Manciple's Tale* ends in a warning against telling tales—"Be noon auctour newe of tidynges, weither they been false or trewe" (IX. 59–60)—the Parson's perfunctory dismissal calls attention to itself. Instead of rejecting spousal homicide in the most ardent language possible he launches into a homily on the seven deadly sins.[11]

In the most relevant section in his tale—that on anger—the Parson describes four kinds of bodily homicide: 1) by law, 2) by necessity, 3) by accident, and 4) through contraception, onanism, and abortion. He does not explicitly address killing one's adulterous wife, perhaps because it would be understood to be an act not needing explanation. After all, anger is a sin, not a crime. This is a point further clarified as the Parson distinguishes the "good" kind of anger from the "bad." The former constitutes a zeal for goodness, an anger against the sin of anger, while the "bad" form of anger is of two kinds: "withouten avisement and consentynge of resoun," and the "wikked wil to do vengeance." The former is a less serious form of compulsive behavior while the latter constitutes premeditated murder.

What is striking about the Parson's discussion of homicide, notwithstanding its grounding in penitential discourse, is the remarkable resemblance it bears to Henry Bracton's definitions of homicide in the

---

[11] Most scholars consider the *Parson's Tale* to be more closely aligned with penitential manuals than with legal codes. The most recent compilation of sources and analogues, for instance, lists the following: Raimundus de Pennaforte, *Summa de Paenitentia*, *Compileison de Seinte Penance*, Guilelmus Peraldus, *Summa de Vitiis*, *Summa de Vitiis "Quoniam,"* *Summa vitiorum "Primo,"* *Summa virtutum de remediis anime*, and Anselm of Canterbury's *Meditation on the Last Judgment*. See *Sources and Analogues of the Canterbury Tales*, vol. 1, ed. Robert Correale and Mary Hamel (Rochester: D. S. Brewer, 2002), p. 529. There are no legal codes listed here.

thirteenth-century legal code *De Legibus et Consuetudinibus Angliae*.[12] Just as Chaucer's Parson defines four kinds of bodily homicide, so too does Bracton. Three of the four categories of homicide—by law, by necessity, and by chance or accident—correspond almost word for word to the Parson's outline. It is only in the fourth category (conception and abortion) that the two narratives differ somewhat: whereas the Parson explicates various actions taken to preclude pregnancy, Bracton discusses various forms of homicide before getting to this question. The language each uses is strikingly similar. Witness the Parson: "Eek whan man destourbeth concepcioun of a child, and maketh a womman outher bareyne by drynkynge venenouse herbes thurgh which she may nat conceyve, or sleeth a child by drynkes wilfully, or elles putteth certeine material thynges in hire secree places to slee the child . . . yet is it homycide."(IX.575–76). Now compare it to Bracton's definition: "If one strikes a pregnant woman or gives her poison in order to procure an abortion, if the foetus is already formed or quickened, especially if it is quickened, he commits homicide."[13] That Chaucer's Parson and Bracton recognize the harm done to a pregnant woman and her unborn child tells us something about why those details may have been omitted in the *Manciple's Tale*. That is, the murder of an adulterous wife might be permitted under certain circumstances while presumably the murder of a pregnant woman would not be.

Also important in a comparison of the Parson and Bracton is the similarity in their definitions of homicide. Bracton's corporal homicide, defined as committed "by word," "by counsel," or "by command" is echoed by the Parson: "Bodily manslaughtre is, whan thow sleest him with thy tonge in oother manere, as whan thou comandest to sleen a man or elles yevest hym conseil to sleen a man" (line 569). Both Bracton and the Parson agree that spiritual homicide, the category under which harmful speech acts reside, is "discharged by penance" (p. 341). And while Bracton suggests that homicide by deed (under the various categories mentioned above) would accrue a variety of punishments, he does not specifically address wife murder. Neither, of course, does the Parson.

What is revealed in this all-too-brief comparison of the Parson's

[12] *Bracton, De Legibus et Consuetudinibus Angliae*, vol. 2, ed. George E. Woodbine, trans. Samuel E. Thorne (Cambridge: Belknap Press, 1968).

[13] Ibid., 341. The Latin reads: "Si sit aliquis mulierem praegnantem percusserit vel ei venenum dederit, per quod fecerit abortivum, si puerperium iam formatum vel animatum fuerit, et maxime si animatum, facit homicidium."

"myrie tale" and Henry Bracton's *De Legibus* is a convergence of penitential and civil law codes both in definitions of homicide and in their punishments. The two categories of law governing human behavior in the Middle Ages—secular and ecclesiastical—categories that modern law separates, are conjoined and interwoven into Chaucer's fiction. Given that fact I would like to reiterate why it is important to read the tales at the point of rupture. If Chaucer is indeed directing his audience(s) to the legal issues of the time in every act of violence in the *Canterbury Tales* then the tale of spousal homicide told by the Manciple prompts us and those before us to ask questions about the relation of the violent act to the fiction. Are the Manciple and the Parson subtly assenting to and/or willing to consider mitigating circumstances—a husband's jealous rage—as grounds for acquittal of wife murder? As the *Manciple's Tale* reveals and the penitential and legal codes on homicide seem to corroborate, the answer is "yes." What Chaucer tells us by blending secular and ecclesiastical law in the *Parson's Tale* is that sin and crime could often be conflated and penalties for serious infractions such as spousal homicide could be reduced to penance and/or dismissed entirely.[14] The poet tells us that fictions surrounding private acts of violence could cleverly elude indictment and allow irate husbands to get away with murder. That cold hard fact is attested to in the *Manciple's Tale* by the silent witness of a woman's corpse.

---

[14] Witness Robert of Flamborough's *Liber Poenitentialis*: "You have murdered your wife without [incurring] the death penalty. Enter a monastery; observe with a simple spirit all those things that will be ordered unto you" [Occidisti uxorem tuam sine causa mortis. Ingredere monasterium; observa cuncta simplici animo quae tibi fuerint imperata]. *Robert of Flamborough, Liber Poenitentialis: A Critical Edition with Introduction and Notes*, J. J. Francis, ed. (Toronto: Pontifical Institute of Mediaeval Studies, 1971), p. 225.

See also James A. Brundage's discussion of the ambivalence of canonists to prosecute this crime: "There was general agreement that adultery was a serious crime and that it often led to further crimes. The canonists stressed that although folklaw might permit a husband to slay his wife if he discovered her in bed with another man, canon law absolutely denied him this right. . . . But despite the protest of canonists, customary practice usually held husbands blameless in these situations" (p. 388). In *Law, Sex, and Christian Society in Medieval Europe* (Chicago: University of Chicago Press, 1987).

The Manciple's Phallic Matrix

Peter W. Travis
Dartmouth College

I N THE FOLLOWING REMARKS, I would like to attempt an answer to one seldom asked question: Why does Chaucer's last poem, *The Manciple's Tale*, conclude with the voice of "my dame" (IX.317), the narrator's logorrheic mother?[1] Or, put a slightly different way, why should an etiological fable about the destructive un/truth of poetic fiction achieve resolution via a mother's mind-numbing declamations to her son that he should learn to keep his mouth shut? Certain psychoanalytic theories that view the artistic field of masculine creativity as a complex deferral of the maternal will be helpful in answering this question because they provide a critical lens that links art, masculinity, and the maternal—all of which are on display in this unsettling and enigmatic tale. Fred Botting, for example, in *Sex, Machines, and Navels: Fiction, Fantasy and History in the Future Present*, defines the masculine field of artistic creation as the "matrix, locus of the extremes of a distinctly masculine desire," a symbolic space which "is also a mode of suppression, a means of overcoming the creative matter associated with mater, the mother."[2] I contend that *The Manciple's Tale* is an especially tortured version of this archetypal "matrix," an example of a narrator's strenuously repressing the maternal yet subliminally negotiating its inevitable return. More specifically, the *Tale* is a site of fierce requitals, a self-infantilizing fable of desires and denials in contention over the matter of origins and endings. There are several closely related phenomena in the *Prologue* and the *Tale*, all of them projecting from the infant's primal relation to the mother, that support this thesis: namely, sensorimotor disorder, oral

---

[1] Quotations from the *Manciple's Tale* are drawn from Larry Benson, gen. ed., *The Riverside Chaucer*, 3d ed. (Boston: Houghton Mifflin, 1987), with fragment and line numbers in parentheses.

[2] Fred Botting, *Sex, Machines, and Navels: Fiction, Fantasy and History in the Future Present* (Manchester: Manchester University Press, 1999), pp. 169–70.

consumption, human aggression, language, and the demonized feminine.

One of the most remarkable features of the *Tale* is its author's obsession with orality and sensorimotor disorders. From the tale's *Prologue* to
its concluding *moralitas*, there is something about the Manciple that
causes him to fixate on the oral cavity—the mouth sucking, spewing,
engorging, swallowing and consuming. In the *Prologue*, for example, the
Manciple forces all in his company to behold the drunken Cook's
speechless and stinking maw, yawning agape "As thogh he wolde
swolwe us anonright" (IX.36). "Hoold cloos thy mouth, man," the
Manciple commands the Cook, "The devel of helle sette his foot therin!"
(IX.38–9). There is likewise something in the Manciple that despises
yet nevertheless identifies with the physical disorder and nonverbal impotence of the infant, mimed in the *Prologue* by the same drunken
Cook—yawning, tottering, swinging his arms, "fnes[ing]" through "his
nose" (IX.61–2), falling into the dungy mire—and attributed repeti-
tively to the Manciple himself by his infantilizing mother at fable's end:
"My sone," she shushes, "spek nat, but with thyn heed thou bekke"
(IX.346).

To be sure, much of the *Tale*'s dramatic frame involves the competitive production and ownership of food: the Cook prepares food for a
living; the Manciple, the Cook's social/sibling rival, practices "byynge
of vitaille" (I.569). But there is, I believe, a more primal and self-contra-
dicting level to the Manciple's ambivalences about oral consumption
and production, contradictions that are grotesquely captured in the
image of the Cook, forced by the Manciple to drink wine to sober up,
"poup[ing] in this horn" (IX.90). "To poup" in Middle English means
"to puff, to blow," as in the peasants' "howp[ing] and powp[ing]"
(VII.3399–4000) their wind instruments in the raucous fox chase of *The
Nun's Priest's Tale*. Here, however, blowing out appears indistinguishable
from taking in, imbibing is equivalent to vomiting. The Cook, the Manciple's first object of oral fascination and aggression, thus begins to fix
our attention on the mouth as a site of introjection and rejection, of
desire and disgust, even, perhaps, of life and death.

The Manciple's Tale is a tale about what comes out of the mouth, as
well as what goes in. Having completed his fable's tortuous narrative,
the Manciple feels compelled suddenly to cite his mother as the fount
of nurturing wisdom. But from her mouth spew forth forty-four itera-
tive lines (IX.318–62) that naggingly command her own son: Shut your

mouth; contain your treasonous tongue; lock it inside your teeth and lips; say little, or, better yet, say nothing at all. The mouth's most dangerous emanations are thus seen by the Manciple to be words. The aggressive words of the truthful crow, for example, are shown to cause death to his mistress, as well as pain and humiliation to his master and himself. Similarly, the Manciple deploys his own words as weapons as if they were Apollo's phallic arrows: in his sadistic defamations of the speechless Cook, his language is typically brutal, violent, and hypermasculine. Yet, perhaps paradoxically, the Manciple attempts to demonstrate in his *Tale* that words *qua* words are feminine, slippery, dishonest, and cheating. Female nature, no matter how men may nurture it, is at bottom bestial, he argues: any bird, any cat, any she-wolf will follow her fleshly appetites (IX.162–186). And so it is with words, which are no different from women. Although verbal signifiers of the same referent may differ—as with *wyf* (IX.213), *lemman* (IX.220)), *lady* (IX.218), and *wenche* (IX.220)—at bottom they are all tawdry wenches, the lowest and most plebian denominator. And yet what is most puzzling in this regard is that the Manciple does not remain consistent, either in his assessment of the nature of the feminine, or in his valuation of his own words. Is Apollo's wife, in truth, a lemman" (IX.204–5)? This narrator's implicit and unstable answer is: No/Yes/No (IX.39, 256, 275). In a similarly conflicted fashion, after citing several illustrations of women's falsity, he suddenly reverses his condemnation of women by faulting men and letting women off the hook: "Alle thise ensample speke I by thise men/ That been untrewe, and nothyng by wommen" (IX.187–88). Either the Manciple is incapable of understanding the basic principles of the meaningfulness of language, or he is unable to confront the deep import of his conflicted attitude toward the import of his own words.

Thus *The Manciple's Tale* is an utterance that cannot be trusted by any wary reader: whatever its narrator says is said only that it may be gainsaid. This, in part, is what makes the *Tale* so gnarled and primitive. The *Tale*'s multitude of narratorial contradictions provides none of the cerebral pleasures of a Cretan Liar paradox, for example. Nor does the *Tale* explore the *mise-en-abyme* mysteries of riven intentionality, as in the Pardoner's celebrated "I wol yow nat deceyve" (VI.918). The *Tale*'s "meandering, shambling gait,"[3] its diastole-systole narrative rhythms,

---

[3] J. Campbell, "Polonius Among the Pilgrims," *Chaucer Review* 7 (1972): 143.

are likewise anti-aesthetic, reader-unfriendly, and disequilibrating. And as a poem that is always in some ways about poetry, the *Tale* is also a deliberately crude denigration of art. Yet, if we accept the *Riverside* sequence,[4] this undigestible lump of a tale is Chaucer's last poem, written at the end of his career, at the height of his poetic powers. Its leading man is none other than Apollo, the God of Poetry (albeit satirically euhemerized), and its avian protagonist—the white, melodious, and truthful crow—serves as a sardonically idealized image of the poet himself. But by the *Tale*'s end the crow is humiliated, disempowered, and, as it were, castrated. In fact, Apollo destroys all the instruments of his art (a form of artistic self-castration), and he "rashly" murders his own wife, his "gemme of lustiheed" (IX.274). How then might we understand the Manciple's peculiar matrix of oral aggression, verbal slipperiness, sensorimotor disorder, and distrust of the feminine? What, if anything, is to be learned from this orally conflicted and self-consuming artifact?

Carol Dever's *Death and the Mother from Dickens to Freud*, a study of the role of the absent and repressed mother in the Victorian novel, sheds light on the significance of the return of the aggressive mother in narrative fiction generally—a topic of central importance to understanding the sudden appearance of "my dame" at the end of *The Manciple's Tale*. According to Dever, "The function of maternal absence, and even more problematically, the function of maternal return, indicate a crisis of origin that is configured as a crisis of causality. . . . [T]he more aggressively the mother returns, the more aggressively she challenges exclusionary structures of signification and narrative."[5] This crisis of maternal absence and return is, in a nutshell, what I see as the central motif of *The Manciple's Tale*. In a psychoanalytic model such as Dever's, the crisis of origins of the self and the function of the maternal imago begins with the infant's originary experience of ambivalence toward the maternal breast. According to Freud, the infant's primary identification involves a wish to merge with the mother through oral ingestion. Yet this desire is balanced by a need to fend off total infusion, to reject immersion, to keep the other from rapaciously consuming his identity. This infantile ambivalence is provided symbolic representation later in childhood, as analyzed in Freud's celebrated account of his grandson's *fort/da* game,

[4] See *The Riverside Chaucer*, Explanatory Notes, pp. 951–52.
[5] Carol Dever, *Death and the Mother from Dickens to Freud* (Cambridge: Cambridge University Press, 1998), p. xiii.

whereby the child, thrusting and retrieving a spool over the side of his crib while repeating the sounds *fort/da*, has learned to employ material and vocal symbols as signs representing and substituting for his mother: once present, now absent, and yet magically-soon-to-return. As a sememe, as the pared-down essence of figuration, language, and song, the child's *fort/da* locution asserts itself as both replacement and aggressive displacement of the mother. A dialectic of emotional ambivalence is thus embodied in these material and linguistic signs—pleasure in the control afforded by the symbolic presentation of the desired other, displeasure in face of the mother's absence, her treasonous desertion. According to Freud, this drama of emotional ambivalence concerning the fullness or emptiness of signifiers, verbal and otherwise, follows us through life.

Jacques Lacan similarly understands the preverbal stage of kinesthetic sensations and minimal motor control as characterized by swings between "desiring to devour/to be devoured, between keeping something inside one's self/ being kept inside someone" else.[6] But in his version of the mother-child dynamic during the Oedipal crisis, Lacan famously foregrounds language as the sign of the phallus, to which the child must subject himself in order to enter into the symbolic domain of social laws, moral restrictions, and the creative arts. Lacan's own shifting silences and uncertainties about the role of the mother in relation to the symbolic order of phallic signifiers form a telling narrative in their own right, but generally it can be said that Lacan tends to characterize the archaic imago of the mother as demonic and castrating, threatening to engulf the subject's acquired phallic powers of symbolic self-representation.[7] In *Seminar XVII*, for example, Lacan forcefully writes: "The mother is a big crocodile, and you find yourself in her mouth. You never know what may set her off suddenly, making those jaws clamp down. That is the mother's desire." And he continues: "There is a roller, made of stone, of course, which is potentially there at the level of the trap and which holds and jams it open. That is what we call the phallus. It is a roller which protects you, should the jaws suddenly close."[8]

Following Freud's and Lacan's analytical templates and Dever's appli-

---

[6] As explained by Shuli Barzilai, in *Lacan and the Matter of Origins* (Stanford: Stanford University Press, 1999), p. 121.

[7] On the role of the mother in Lacan's schematics, see especially Barzilai, *Lacan*.

[8] Translated in Bruce Fink, *The Lacanian Subject: Between Language and Jouissance* (Princeton: Princeton University Press, 1995), pp. 56–57.

cation of these templates to the narrative designs of literature, we can now see that much of the Manciple's *agon* —consumption, self-castration, infantilization, fear of/desire for the feminine other—is an aspect of his fundamental life-and-death struggle with language itself as a surrogate replacement and displacement of what has been lost and is longed-for, desired and reviled. While Robert Trask and others have noted that the Manciple has a "mother problem,"[9] and while Britton Harwood and others have argued that the *Tale* is "about" language,[10] I am suggesting something more: to be very precise, The *Manciple's Tale* is an etiological fable about the crisis of the origins of the self played out in the field of linguistic signs. Or, to use Dever's terms, the "maternal return" in *The Tale* "indicate[s] a crisis of origin that is configured as a crisis of causality." The *Tale*'s oft-noted *non sequiturs* in narrative design, its characterological inconsistencies, its distrust of lexical nuance and sliding signification, are all therefore "crises of causality" caused by an originary trauma. The particular trauma whose mature effects are enacted throughout the tale we may imagine as an extreme version of the primary shock all infants theoretically suffer at the moment of separation from the maternal Other. But rather than being unique, it is a pathological variant of a trauma that in other contexts has produced matrices of the imagination that prove to be artistic masterpieces. In her study, Dever explores the "positive" creative energies male novelists can generate and sustain in part because they are able to repress and displace the maternal imago with elegant "structures of signification and narrative." I would argue here, in contrast, that Chaucer's Manciple reveals himself to be a negative, infantilized, and self-castrating narrator, whose destructive "structures of signification and narrative" are jammed desperately into the crocodile's mouth like Lacan's phallic roller.

If the Manciple's is this self-infantilizing and aggressive, then how destructive is the maternal figure of his tortured imagination? About as destructive and threatening, it would appear, as the frightful mother of Lacan's similarly inventive worlds of fantasies. In "The Phallus and the Insatiable Mother," Lacan describes the unsatisfied mother as appearing to the child like an open mouth or muzzle, resembling the petrifying

[9] Robert Trask, "The Manciple's Problem," *Studies in Short Fiction* 14 (1977): 109–16.

[10] Britton Harwood, "Language and the Real: Chaucer's Manciple," *ChauR* 6 (1972): 268–79.

THE MANCIPLE'S PHALLIC MATRIX

Gorgon. Correlating this maternal mouth with the phantom counterpart of the life-giving womb, Lacan equates the gaping aperture with *Das Ding*, with "whatever is open, lacking, or gaping at the center of our desire."[11] *The Manciple's Tale*, we might argue, is also "about" *Das Ding*, for it is possible to sense the awful power of this hole at the center of human desires in the strange movements of the *Tale* itself. In its sudden shifts from *abbreviationes* to *amplificationes*, from high romance diction to low fabliau, from plotty *longeurs* to narrative freeze-frames, the *Tale* seems to be sucking in air and blowing it out, "fnes[ing]" in spasmodic and bitter paroxysms. Impotent and self-hating, "poup[ing]" into the poisonous horn of plenty, the Manciple-as-poet, more than anything else, is caught in the grip of the death drive.

The Manciple's originary trauma leaves tracings, like psychical scars, throughout his *Tale*. For example, the Manciple's pathologically conflicted relation to the maternal makes it a certainty that Apollo's wife never had a chance. Even before her adulterous affair, she had been fully coded as the reviled object of erotic desire, a surrogate for the castrating mother, the lost original. Thus Apollo's weirdly inconsistent assessment of his wife's value, from lady to whore to lady, his killing what he loves and then loving what he kills, is but a horrific variant of the Manciple's entangling and strangling desire for, and hatred of, "my dame." Along the same continuum, Apollo's assessment of his wife's lover as a "man of litel reputacioun" (IX.199) can be seen as an alter-egotistical projection of his own self-loathing. Similarly, whereas in Ovid's version Apollo's sudden remorse is caused by his discovery that his wife is pregnant, in the Manciple's sterile fable Apollo's child is significantly erased. Indeed, even if he were known to be alive *in utero*, his son would likely have been viewed by Apollo as sibling rival rather than as innocent offspring. In the same vein, Chaucer changes his Ovidian source once again by choosing to include Apollo's slaying of the Python—not in an epic battle, however, but "as he lay/ Slepynge agayn the sonne" (IX.109–110). Apollo's slaughter of the limp snake clinches the Manciple's murderous relation to the mother: as Elizabeth Bronfen has observed in another context, the Python was the son of Gaia as well as the guardian of the *omphalos*, which suggests that Apollo's killing of the

[11] Jacques Lacan, *The Ethics of Psychoanalysis*, trans. Dennis Porter (New York: Norton, 1992), p. 118.

Python is a masculinist victory over the original matrilineal order of the "phallic" Mother.[12]

If it is inevitable that in medieval narratives the displaced maternal will eventually return in some form or other, ranging from the erotic to the sublime, from the nurturing to the consuming, from the red rose to the white, then it is also perhaps inevitable that masculinist makers of fiction will project a distorting and self-serving image of the returning mother in order to offset, validate, and bring to closure the matrix of their own literary art. This having been said, it remains to be asked whether the battle between the Manciple's aggressive verbal matrix and the consuming mother of his literary imagination embodies Chaucer's definitive view of poetry's relationship to the maternal. To arrive at an adequate answer, we would first need to decrypt all present and absent images of the maternal throughout *The Canterbury Tales*, from the *General Prologue* to the Retraction. While an undertaking of such magnitude is beyond the scope of this essay, I would nevertheless caution against domesticating, sublimating, or sentimentalizing the extraordinary power of the Manciple's mother as a controlling figure in the *Tales*. It is essential that we acknowledge the Manciple is an integral part of Chaucer, as a sibling rival within his imagination, even, perhaps, as his darkest alter-ego. But that does not make the Manciple-in-Chaucer the sole author and origin of *The Canterbury Tales*. Rather, he is a misogynistic gainsayer intent on destroying the truth-bearing achievements of the verbal arts. And *his* mother has very big teeth.

---

[12] Elizabeth Bronfen, "Death: the Navel of the Image," in *The Point of Theory*, ed. M. Bal and I. Boer (Amsterdam: Amsterdam University Press, 1994), pp. 79–90.

Friendship, Association and Service in *The Manciple's Tale*

Stephanie Trigg
University of Melbourne

L IKE MANY OF THE TALES told on the way to Canterbury, *The Manciple's Tale* offers a closely observed meditation on power relationships. More precisely, I suggest that this tale is specifically concerned with the difficulties involved in performing a series of subordinate and overlapping roles in hierarchically organized structures: that is, the roles of courtier, servant, and poet. Like many other commentators, I read the tale as self-reflexive, though rather than finding an expression of purely poetic anxiety, I identify an anxiety that is primarily social, about how to speak—or write—in the context of courtly service or literary patronage. In my reading, the tale dramatizes, though it does not resolve, the question of when and how to speak to one's superiors. But I also want to foreground the *Tale's* thematic and moralizing concern with the question of friendship, to suggest that the idea of a relationship among equals provides a powerful counterpoint to the Manciple's interest in the relationships between servant and master, and between courtier and lord. This counterpoint is almost always problematic, however: at what point, if ever, can the discourses of friendship overlap with those of service? And what are the social and political implications of such crossover? To summarize: I want to argue that the tale sets up two principal axes of relationship among men: a horizontal axis of friendship, or at least of homosocial identity; and a vertical axis of service. At the same time, the tale's narrative works to confound that distinction. The resultant uncertainty dramatizes Chaucer's own position as poet and servant. Like the Manciple perhaps, he too is writing, or telling stories, for both his superiors and his friends.

Many recent critics foreground the self-reflexive aspects of this tale, in its context as the penultimate contribution to the storytelling context and as the ultimate narrative in the collection. It can easily be read as foregrounding the problem, even the mortal danger, of speech and truth-telling. On that reading, and in the context of a concern with master/servant relations, and with respect to the genre of etiological narrative, the fate of the crow constitutes a cautionary tale with the most profound consequences for courtiers. Thinking to please his master Phoebus, the crow says the wrong thing, and is both punished and dismissed from his lord's service. And once we foreground the crow's role as storyteller or as singer, his case is even more extreme: thinking to please his patron, the crow sings the wrong song, and is not only punished and dismissed, but loses his poetic gift. The fact that this gift was bestowed on him by his master, the god of music, has the dramatic effect of debasing him further. As the master raised him up and bound him to service in the cage, so he can dismiss him and release him, make him not only unemployed but unemployable.

In considering this relationship, we must revisit one of the most suggestive essays on the *Manciple's Tale*, written by Louise Fradenburg in 1985. In this essay Fradenburg uses Lacanian theories of subjectivity-in-process to develop an argument about late medieval courts as "historical spaces produced by, and producing, certain kinds of relationship between certain types of subjects and others."[1] In this context, there is no "given" kind of discourse or subjectivity at court. Rather, the mode of master, like the mode of servant, is continually being negotiated, either informally, in the day-to-day encounters of the household, or more formally, in the rhetorical or narrative productions of the court poet. Fradenburg is principally concerned with psychoanalytic relations and linguistic structures, but if we insist on thickening our sense of the sociohistorical frame of the tale, we can see how much more acute the situation becomes in a context where the vernacular is in process of becoming an acceptable medium for court poetry and court discourse, in a period of radical social change and class mobility. If it is tricky to address one's lord in French, how much more difficult to write for him in English?

Fradenburg argues that understanding subjectivity in this mutually constitutive way helps us read what she calls "poetic concessions to the desire of a patron" as "the marks of a meditation on the other which penetrates every aspect of courtly poetics." But sometimes the negotia-

[1] Louise Fradenburg, "The Manciple's Servant Tongue: Politics and Poetry in *The Canterbury Tales*," *ELH*. 52 (1985): 85–118, at p. 87.

tions are more violent and aggressive than the vocabulary of "meditation" would imply; since it's not simply a case of negotiating and renegotiating rival subjectivities. As she says, the courtly subject in a way "has had to renounce being. . . ." This is the extreme case of courtly subjection, and here Fradenburg draws an analogy between the woman and the crow in the tale: both are to serve being, not to possess it, that is, to be "hadde," in his house, by Phoebus, and not to have. ("Now hadde this Phebus in his hous a crowe," line 131; "Now hadde this Phebus in his hous a wyf," line 139.)[2] In Gower's version of the tale, the bird Corvus belongs to Phoebus's lover, Cornide: Chaucer's version underlines the similar situation of Phoebus's pet and Phoebus's wife. It is also true that Phoebus is the only player whose point of view is focused through the tale. The tale is concerned with his jealousy, his pride, his disbelief, his murder, his remorse, his lament, his punishment of his wife, and his revenge on his crow. His crow, his wife, his wife's lover, in decreasing order of realized subjectivity, fade away into beinglessness.

Chaucer's poem thus affirms the hierarchy that grants higher or deeper subjectivity to those who enjoy material and political power. To that extent, it parallels the situation in *The Book of the Duchess* where, although the narrative focus shifts from dreamer to duke, it is patently apparent that the duke's tragedy outweighs in moral and rhetorical importance the dreamer's own problems of love and insomnia. Similarly, there is no question about Phoebus's wife's lover being "a man of litel reputacioun, / Nat worth to Phebus in comparisoun" (lines 199–200). In fact, the crow repeats the Manciple's phrase, almost word for word, in his report to the god (lines 253–54). The superiority of Phoebus doesn't even depend on his divinity but simply on his "reputacioun": this assumption naturalizes his enjoyment of lordly power. Phoebus is an absolutely powerful lord, not through his birth or his divinity or any royal favor, though these elements are all important contexts. He is simply "the better man."

The question of being "the better man" is, of course, quite important to the Manciple, whose professional role is that of a servant to lords. Indeed, more than half his *General Prologue* portrait is dedicated to a discussion of his relations with his masters, the more than thirty learned men whom he is nevertheless able to outwit, for all their legal training

---

[2] All quotations from Chaucer are taken from *The Riverside Chaucer*, gen. ed. Larry D. Benson (Oxford: Oxford University Press, 1987).

and their supposed superiority. But Chaucer also reminds us that a lord can also be a servant, as a dozen of the Manciple's lords are "Worthy to been stywardes of rente and lond / Of any lord that is in Engelond" (lines 579–80). In another context, these lawyers would also do what the Manciple does: that is, provide, in one way or another, for their superiors. The hierarchical and essentially feudal nature of service allows us to extend Fradenburg's point: while it is true that service relationships are constantly being negotiated, this is in large part because a lord in one context may well be a servant in another.

In addition to the many hierarchical relationships in this *Tale* and its surrounding texts (and I set aside, for the moment, the relationship between the Manciple and his mother that concludes the *Tale*), there are also a number of horizontally organized ones. As a key example of late medieval "association," David Wallace draws attention to the relationship between Cook and Manciple that is explored in the *Manciple's Prologue*.[3] Wallace is particularly concerned with how these two Londoners are presented in relation to each other, and the barely emergent sense of a shared London discourse, in this case one that resolves itself through amity—and wine. It is the simplest resolution of the estates context or professional rivalry drama in the *Tales,* and even though the medium is wine, it is still a drama of reciprocity. As the Host reminds the Manciple:

> . . . Another day he wole, peraventure,
> Reclayme thee and brynge thee to lure;
> I meene, he speke wole of smale thynges,
> As for to pynchen at thy rekeynynges,
> That were nat honest, if it cam to preef. (lines 71–75)

Here the rivalry can be turned around: commercial and professional rivalry is a question of taking turns to have the mastery, to invoke knowledge of the other's misdealing. This very reciprocity, this participation in the same enterprise, means there is no question of one partner either having or losing "being," in Fradenburg's usage, even though they may take turns in having the upper hand. The reminder of this reciprocity is enough to reconcile the two. The Manciple is clearly motivated by self-interest, and the Host is perhaps over-generous in his ac-

---

[3] David Wallace, "Chaucer and the Absent City," in *Chaucer's England: Literature in Historical Context*, ed. Barbara Hanawalt (Minneapolis: Minnesota University Press, 1992), pp. 59–90.

count of "rancour and disese" being turned benignly into "acord and love." Nevertheless, this social rupture is very quickly healed.

There is an even stronger indication of the importance of relationships among equals in the long *moralitas* at the end of the tale, spoken by the Manciple's mother. On a minor note, it is symptomatic of much Chaucer criticism that this authoritative set of pronouncements spoken by a woman is generally agreed to be ridiculously prolix and repetitive, as if ironically enacting the sin against which it preaches. But I'm less concerned here with its gender politics than its message. Twice the Manciple's mother draws attention to the need to speak discreetly to protect friendship: "My sone, keep wel thy tonge, and keep thy freend" (line 319), and again, "A tonge kutteth freendshipe al a-two" (line 342).

Read back against the tale, this encourages us to see the relation between the crow and Phebus as a relationship of amity and friendship rather than that of servant and master. According to the moral, the crow has erred not by telling the truth to his courtly superior, but rather in telling a friend of his wife's infidelity. The crow has presumed a relationship of homosocial identity with Phoebus, at the expense of the wife, whose sexuality has become the currency of exchange between them. When the crow speaks to Phoebus, there's one of those lovely moments in Chaucer when bird subjectivity intersects with human subjectivity, as in the *Parlement of Foules* and *The Nun's Priest's Tale*. The first example we hear of the bird's wonderful speaking and talking is the repeated call, "Cokkow! Cokkow! Cokkow!" (line 243). When challenged, the bird speaks to Phoebus directly, as an equal, even addressing him as "thou," the same form the god uses to him. In the pronominal forms of address, then, theirs is a friendship, a reciprocal relationship. But Phoebus reveals himself firmly the master, with power over the crow's voice and his very being, with devastating effect. He calls him "false theef," and "traytour," turns his white feathers black, takes back the voice he had given him, kicks him out of doors, and sends him to the devil.

And indeed, this is the other side of the mother's advice. In addition to the theme that candid speech ruins friendship, she remarks, in the lines that conclude the tale:

> He is his thral to whom that he hath sayd
> A tale of which he is now yvele apayd.
> My sone, be war, and be noon auctour newe
> Of tidynges, wheither they been false or trewe.

Whereso thou come, amonges hye or lowe.
Kepe wel thy tonge and thenk upon the crowe. (lines 357–62)

The ease with which what seems like a friendship can suddenly turn
into a hierarchically organized relationship of "thraldome" is profoundly
disturbing. The mother's advice to her son as he leaves home to enter a
life of service, perhaps, warns against the dangers of such relationships
and the ease with which they can be refigured. The terminology of
"tale" and "tidynges" can refer to stories as well as news. It's not a big
step from the idea that offending someone enslaves you to them, to the
idea that telling a displeasing story has the same effect. It is a lesson
that is, potentially, quite damning of the whole Canterbury enterprise,
based as it has been on reciprocity, community, association, amity, and
the competitive exchange of narrative. A relationship that is deeply hierarchical and classbound comes back to haunt the idea of telling stories
and narratives as a friendly rivalry over the price of a dinner. It is the
complete obverse of the relatively amicable reconciliation of Manciple
and Cook in the *Prologue*: no wonder it's the last story! Technically, the
Manciple's mother has the last word, counseling against tale-telling, but
if we know anything of Chaucer, we know that he has a problem with
closure, that endings are rarely endings—perhaps because closure is
often concerned very much with hierarchy. Still, in its extremity, it's a
disturbing note to strike.

Reading the *Prologue and Tale* together, then, we see Chaucer setting
two forms of relationship against each other, in order to explore some
of the difficulties and uncertainties experienced by the courtier. His lord
seems to be a good friend to him, and this is what the courtier wants;
but the lord can always invoke his superior powers, can always dismiss
the servant and set him free. And where the courtier-servant is a courtier-poet, he is doubly vulnerable. In his dramatization of these dynamics
among friends, associates, and servants, Chaucer seems especially conscious of the analogous power relations that pertain in the act of storytelling. Given what we know of Chaucer's difficulties with endings, we
should not be surprised that the tale closes with the familiar dynamic of
ventriloquism and self-parody, of fractured voices and uncertain tone,
since speech, and its reception, has been rendered so problematic, and
indeed so dangerous.

The Manciple's Tale: Response

Warren Ginsberg
University of Oregon

A
S AN ENSEMBLE, these five papers on *The Manciple's Tale* provide a snapshot of some of the ways we Chaucerians read today. Essays that investigate ways in which language is deployed in the tale also ponder the protocols of interchange between masters and servants in late fourteenth century England; essays that historicize the fable by invoking London's guilds or the legal construction of homicide as contexts seem equally interested in assessing the effect of the Manciple's performance on *The Canterbury Tales* as a whole. Even Peter Travis's essay, which remains steadily focused on structures of language and the formation of subjectivity, implicitly sets its insights in dialogue with Louise Fradenburg's use of Lacan to discuss the negotiation of social identity in Richard II's court.[1]

The intersection within a single paper of psychoanalytic, new historical, or rhetorical concerns is, I think, neither a sign of critical confusion nor an indication that methodological eclecticism is an emerging mode of Chaucerian interpretation. The proliferation of approaches seems to me a rejoinder to the annulments the Manciple attempts to enact both in his *Prologue* and in his *Tale*. Phoebus's murdered wife and the excision of her corpse command Eve Salisbury's attention, as befits a reading that advances its arguments by comparing the events in the narrative to the events the law required to establish a case of homicide. Stephanie Trigg sees in the crow's impolitic revelation and subsequent punishment evidence that Chaucer challenged his audience to consider not only the diffident servility a subordinate needs to adopt when speaking to his superiors but also the associative parity that lets friends converse on equal terms. The lies Phoebus tells in the aftermath of his slaying under-

[1] See Louise Fradenburg, "The Manciple's Servant Tongue: Politics and Poetry in the *Canterbury Tales*," *ELH* 52 (1985): 85–118.

331

writes Marianne Børch's view that the tale's negation of rhetoric positions it between the Knight's and the Parson's tales in Chaucer's
Canterbury poetics. For John Hines, the Manciple's malfeasance, which
we hear about in his portrait and which he half confirms in his exchange
with Harry Bailly, licenses Chaucer's incipient critique of the guilds. For
Peter Travis, the Manciple's mother's (re)turn at the end of the tale
lays bare the psychic mechanisms that transform his simple story into a
terrifying etiology "about the origin of the self played out in the field of
linguistic signs." Face to face with a text whose *moralitas* insists we
should "say nothing, nothing at all," these authors, however else they
differ, all say much that is "fructuous" in little space. Their unequivocal
commitment to breadth seems something more than the reflex of scholars who know they have limited time to deliver their remarks. By expanding their scope in defiance of the Manciple's exhortations to be
silent, these critics assert their profession's right to be by speaking as
commentators. In so doing, they repeat Chaucer's own response to his
villicus iniquitatis.

As readers of this journal know, I have argued that in the *Manciple's
Prologue*, and, by extension, in his tale as well, Chaucer reenacts the
ineluctable, never-resolved battle that antiphrastic irony and allegorical
polysemy wage to author figurative language.[2] Even though the Manciple would leave the unhorsed Cook stuck and muddied in the mire,
Hogge of Ware's fall and rise outside Bobbe-up-and-doun restage Paul's
conversion on the road to Damascus. Even though the Manciple would
filch from the Cook a chance to do penance by telling a tale, his words
evoke countervailing words from others, from Harry Bailly to the Parson to Chaucer himself. Even though the Manciple will conclude by
contending that muteness, not truth-telling, is the better course, the
beast fable he relates to make this point recalls the Nun's Priest's, whose
final lesson is "Al that writen is, / To oure doctrine it is ywrite, ywis."
That Chaucer would array a host of associated voices against his conniving steward's compulsion to nullify utterance entirely suggests he had
the figural propensities of his own "ernest and game" very much in
mind. As his pilgrims approached Canterbury, he decided, it would
seem, that the best way—maybe the only way—he could vindicate his
poetry as doctrine was to present a character who denied, again and
again, that it could have any.

[2] "Chaucer's Canterbury Poetics: Irony, Allegory, and the *Prologue to the Manciple's
Tale, SAC* 18 (1996): 55–89.

No pilgrim spends more time interrupting his tale to comment on it than the Manciple; because his asides invert in order to efface, because the goal they aim to reach is the empty silence of an evacuation, every pilgrim and reader is implicated in his denials, since they ultimately deny the possibility of answering.[3] Each time the Manciple intrudes, he follows the same pattern: first he collapses opposites by making both consequences of the same cause, then he renders the cause null and void by denying that it is real or that it matters. Early in the tale the Manciple breaks and enters to remark on Phoebus's jealousy, which makes him fear his wife will "byjape" him unless he keeps her closely under guard. Lost labor, the Manciple says, for a faithful wife should not be treated as if under house arrest, and a shrew will do as she pleases no matter how closely a husband keeps an eye on her. Although the good woman is defended, and the bad one censured, the differences between them disappear when they solicit the same response. According to the Manciple, each should be dealt with by doing nothing: "This holde I for a verray nycetee, / To spille labour for to kepe wyves" (lines 152–53).

By itself, such a conclusion is sufficiently caustic to make morality seem a form of cynicism; in context, its corrosiveness is doubled. The Manciple had begun his fable by briskly describing qualities of word and deed that certify Phoebus as a model of knighthood. His prowess in arms has its fit symbol in his bow, with which he slew the Python; his mastery of "minstralcie" corroborates his courtly refinement. In short order, of course, Phoebus will renounce both these attainments; however, before the Manciple turns courage and art into deluding vices, he noticeably repeats himself. In rapid succession he tells us once again that Phoebus always carried a bow in token of his victory over the Python (lines 125–29); that Phoebus had a crow ("Whit . . . as is a snow-whit swan," line 134) which could speak and sing a hundred thousand times better than any nightingale; and that he also had a wife. By reverting to Phoebus's chivalric achievements, we expect the Manciple to complete the pattern by referring to another instance of his gentle breeding. This the Manciple does and does not do when he tells us that the crow sings as well as its owner. As in beast fables, the bird has taken on human attributes; by the next line, however, the Manciple already seems to have sneered at the equation, as if to imply that aristocratic

---

[3] With some changes, I have drawn the following paragraphs from my recent book, *Chaucer's Italian Tradition* (Ann Arbor: University of Michigan Press, 2002): 85–88.

manners and animal instinct really amount to the same thing. For he immediately levels crow and wife by reiterating a syntactic pattern: "Now hadde this Phebus in his hous a crowe" (130); "Now hadde this Phebus in his hous a wyf" (139).

These repetitions make repetition as such an agent of antiphrastic irony. With more than a hint of resentment, the Manciple confirms Phoebus's lordly standing by showing that he thinks of his crow and his wife as possessions to be kept caged up in his house—much the way we may suspect the Manciple feels the lawyers of his Inn treat him. At the same time, the Manciple abolishes every right of rank by identifying Phoebus with his crow and his wife. If each can stand in for the other, what is nobility but a phantasm, a fiction of preeminence where no distinction actually exists? Instead of sponsoring the construction of correspondence between dissimilar things, the Manciple's repetitions blot out both. Instead of sustaining the creative potency of metaphor, the Manciple's repetitions homogenize its multiple senses in order to render each a figure of the vanity of meaning.

Precisely because the annulments of the Manciple's irony haunt all extra-literal language from within, his reiterations are likewise philoprogenitive. After they beget the counsel that Phoebus should confront his jealousy by doing nothing about it, they immediately breed the three successive exempla that outspokenly justify the repudiation of humankind that to this point the Manciple had been content merely to suggest. People *are* beasts, he now says, for, as he said before, it is wasted effort to restrain the natural impulses that nature (note the doubling) sets in creatures:

> But God it woot, ther may no man embrace
> As to destreyne a thyng which that nature
> Hath natureelly set in a creature (lines 160–62).

A caged bird, the Manciple continues, no matter how dainty its food and tender its care, would still rather be free to eat worms "and swich wrecchednesse" in the forest (lines 163–74); give a cat all the milk and meat you will, let it see a mouse and its "lust" and "appetite" will put "discrecioun" to flight (lines 175–82); the she-wolf in heat will couple with the "lewedste wolf . . . leest of reputacioun" she can find (lines 183–86).[4] In each case, human traits consort and become interchange-

---

[4] In the first two examples, of course, the Manciple ironically implicates himself in his condemnation by emphasizing the importance of supplying provender.

able with animal characteristics so that the Manciple can dispatch animal and human both.

Out of repetitions that reveal the emptiness of everything on earth this wise child of his generation thus generates a discourse that obliterates the world. Nothing escapes the Manciple's purview, not even his own words. Each of the "ensamples" he has just recited repeats *in parvo* the form of the story he is telling; since all beast-fables carry an interpretive moral, the Manciple offers his:

> Alle thise ensamples speke I by thise men
> That been untrewe, and nothyng by wommen,
> For men han evere a likerous appetite
> On lower thyng to parfourne hire delit
> Than on hire wyves . . . (lines 187–91)

The application seems almost defiantly preposterous in the way it contradicts the plain sense of the matter that it glosses; not a second before the Manciple had castigated the she-wolf for its lechery, and Phoebus's wife is poised to commit adultery with a "man of litel reputacioun" (line 199). The Manciple misidentifies the object of his reprobation, of course, so that he can defend women by extending his contempt for them to men. At the same time, by demonstrating that black and white can be made to repeat each other, he exposes the arbitrariness of all commentary. With one ethical parenthesis he effectively wipes blank all the records of moral philosophy. Men are the same as women who differ not a bit from wolves in their lewdness: each frictionlessly substitutes for the other in the Manciple's parables of abrogation.

Little wonder then that Chaucer countered the Manciple's ironies with a chorus of contrapuntal voices and his consumptive moralizing with an allegory of conversion. Little wonder also that these essays, by putting pressure on different aspects of the tale, together supplement in fruitful ways the vision each advances alone. After reading Eve Salisbury's paper in conjunction with Peter Travis's, for instance, I felt convinced that Phoebus's slaying of his wife in the tale is closely connected to the surprising appearance of the Manciple's mother at its end. By introducing the latter woman, who is the antithesis of both the Wife of Bath's dame and her mistress, that old master of the arts of licentiousness, the *lena*, he expunges the former a second time, as Salisbury and others have said. The Manciple is not the sort of person, one sees, who would rob himself of the pleasure of repeating Apollo's vendetta; instead of the untruths the god told to take the place of the adulteress he had murdered, however, this spiteful steward fills the space he has cleared by rehearsing the homebred wisdom he learned as a child. The Manciple wraps himself in his mother's skirts, one imagines, to suggest that, unlike Apollo, he's neither rash nor a liar; in the process, he also manages to make a mockery of Melibee by recruiting feminine counsel to help execute summary justice on treacherous women.

At the same time, the hammer-beat bombardment of precept after precept conjures a scene from the Manciple's youth in which he invites us to see him as the victim of an educational drubbing; not altogether unlike the Prioress's little "clergeoun," he seems to be repeatedly pummeled by the blunt instrument of maternal lore. And yet, despite argument after argument less *ex* than *a silentio*, the Manciple clearly ignored his mother's admonitions when he disparaged the Cook. Whether or not he intended it, his disobedience, in light of Peter Travis's analysis, is unnerving. The Manciple undoubtedly wants his audience to associate him with the crow; does he also wish that we surreptitiously associate his expostulating instructress with Apollo and the wife he kills? In the *Prologue*, the Manciple struck at Roger by speaking for him; in his peroration he speaks for his mother. Just as Phoebus's eulogy pays self-canceling homage to his dead wife, the Manciple's extended quotation of his mother eliminates her presence with the very words that resubmit him to her authority. Sadomasochism does not seems an inappropriate diagnosis for this mixture of a child's servility and Melibean desire to strike back; Chaucer, however, would more likely say the Manciple is a narcissist turned inside-out. Like yet unlike many pilgrims in the *Tales*, he thinks all characters are repetitions of what he is not.[5]

The conjoining of perspectives that *The Manciple's Tale* stimulates in responses to it also invites us to scrutinize points where the five critics diverge. John Hines, for instance, detects Chaucer distancing himself from the guilds; Stephanie Trigg sees him championing the comradeship we have come to associate with them. Eve Salisbury feels *The Parson's Tale* contributes to the occlusion of homicide; Marianne Børch believes its conversion of language into an epistemological tool makes it a third path in Chaucer's fiction. Like many others I welcome studies that place

---

[5] In this regard, I think the Manciple's egregious interpretation of the she-wolf is meant to remind readers of Amans's equally egregious interpretation at the "mirëors perilleus" (*Roman de la Rose*, lines 1507–10).

the *Tales* amid the social discourses of the time. Perhaps because it is a beast fable, however, the Manciple's tale has the peculiar effect of catching those who relate it to historical institutions in the ironic act of fabricating allegories of their own. Even if, like Gower, one feels the crow reports what he has seen with malice in his heart, he does not lie; to enjoin speaking entirely can, I suppose, remedy envy or rancor, but in this case the advice is an affront to truth. Nevertheless, however misguided such a moral may be, the gap between it and the tale is no greater than the gap between the tale and an interpretation that sees it as a reminder of the curbs a courtier must put on his tongue when he addresses his lord. The tale may indeed be Chaucer's cautionary comment about his experience at court; if it is, though, the Manciple is certainly a strange figure for him to have chosen to voice the lessons he learned there. My point, though, is that while the Manciple's ineradicable presence in the tale virtually forces us to read his words other than he has, every attempt to make them honest has to remove the mean-spirited steward from what he says in exactly the way he would remove from others the chance to say something else.

For similar reasons, the Manciple's "manner of speaking" troubles the notion that Chaucer rejected the bridled talk of subordinates in favor of unconstrained dialogues between friends or guild members. Who doubts that Chaucer preferred unfettered exchange? But Harry Bailly's praise of the wine that has restored amity between the Manciple and the Cook is the single example of such amicable speech; I hope no one thinks me mean-spirited if I surmise that the companionability the Host celebrates has the shelf-life of a hangover.

Were I to weave my own allegory of reading social history in the *Manciple's Tale*, the figure I would discover in the carpet would be the classroom as a theater of violence.[6] The threads that would form my allegory's warp would be spun out of the fact that beast fables were staple school texts;[7] its woof's filaments would connect *The Manciple's Tale*, via the *The Nun's Priest's Tale*, to *The Prioress's Tale*, in which maternal teaching is also juxtaposed with homicidal fury. But whenever it is that I sit down to elaborate my design, I would return to these essays for guidance and inspiration.

---

[6] Especially relevant here is the work of Bruce Holsinger on the connection between violence and what he calls the "pedagogical body." See *Music, Body, and Desire in Medieval Culture* (Stanford: Stanford University Press, 2001), pp. 259–92 and the relevant bibliography Holsinger cites.

[7] See, for instance, Peter Travis, "*The Nun's Priest's Tale* as Grammar-School Primer," *SAC* 1 (1984): 81–91.

REVIEWS

DAVID AERS, ed. *Medieval Literature and Historical Inquiry: Essays in Honor of Derek Pearsall.* Cambridge: Boydell and Brewer, 2000. Pp. xvi, 212. $75.00.

A. J. MINNIS, ed. *Middle English Poetry: Texts and Traditions, Essays in Honour of Derek Pearsall.* Woodbridge, Suffolk; Rochester, N.Y.: York Medieval Press, 2001. Pp. xv, 304. $85.00.

Over the past two decades, Derek Pearsall has emerged as the Godfather of Middle English literary studies. It would not be an exaggeration to say that the themes and topics of current English medieval literary scholarship—a shift in emphasis to the fifteenth century, innovation in editorial scholarship, a concern with the material conditions of literary production, exhaustive historical contextualization of texts and authors—have been influenced and shaped directly or indirectly by his encouragement or his example. Moreover, his influence has been transatlantic, and even transpacific, in scope. He has also been an exemplary scholarly citizen, involving himself in the largest issues and smallest details of the profession. If he has championed an unsentimental good sense over theoretical speculation, he has done so in such a way as to encourage rather than stifle dialogue. It is not a surprise, then, though it is something of a puzzle, that he should be honored with not one but two *festschriften.*

A brief survey of the contents gives some idea both of the depth and breadth of these volumes. The Minnis volume begins with Christopher Cannon's "The Unchangeable Word," which chooses the citation "misleading" to investigate how and why the MED and OED are misleading as accounts of the history of words. He determines that the recursiveness of the MED's definitions, which sometimes shuttle between record and probable composition dates, results in a thick description of words and meanings, not always fixable in time or sequence. Estelle Stubbs reviews the evidence for the possible involvement of Augustinian friars and canons in the copying of CT manuscripts, possibly explaining their many shifts of allegiance. Elizabeth Solopova argues that the punctuation in Hengwrt and Ellesmere may be traceable to Chaucer's original and may not be entirely scribal. Charlotte Morse suggests that part of the potential of the electronic Canterbury Tales Project would be to make available all of Manly-Rickert's data in such a way as to promise a true critical edition of the *Canterbury Tales.* Morse reports that her experience editing the *Clerk's Tale* for the *Variorum* validates Manly-Rickert's skepticism about early circulating copies. (One respects her convincing conclusions, but not her ad hominem aspersions against all living defenders of Ellesmere.) Moving on to Gower, Siân Echard clearly and elegantly demonstrates that the visual design of some *Confessio* manuscripts, especially the location of the Latin elements, to a greater or lesser degree aid the reader in remembering, understanding, and interpreting its structure and meaning. Kate Harris describes the little-known Longleat House MS 174, which extracts Gower in such a way as to present the *Confessio* as a repository of scientific and medical knowledge rather than as a story collection. John Scattergood reviews the inconclusive evidence for and controversies surrounding the connection of Cotton Nero AX with the Massy family of Chester and its possible authorship by one of several John Massys. Scattergood is able to connect a John Massy with another manuscript, Trinity College Library MS 155, a collection of Rolle and other largely devotional texts. Carol Meale adds to her many original studies of Middle English romance by reading *The Tournament at Tottenham* as a carnivalized text with unstable social energies. Tottenham's position as a recently gentrified town previously inhabited by relatively prosperous peasants and artisans meant that the satire on bumpkins and the burlesque of chivalry could have been received in different ways by different sectors of is "audience." (Alas, one of the volume's few typographical errors at p. 110, note 27, cites me under the apparent pseudonym of "Gavin," but I shall look the other way). S. S. Hussey, whose own collection of essays on Langland was a formative influence on the current explosion of Langland studies, considers the "outsider" status of Langland, whom he identifies autobiographically with the dreamer, geographically, intellectually and physically, suggesting that the relative calm of the C-text is a result of his return to more familiar Malvern surroundings. Kathryn Kerby-Fulton offers an extensive comparison of two Langland manuscripts, Huntington Library HM114 and the Ilchester MS (Senate House Library MS V.88), the latter copied by the notorious Scribe D, to support the notion that passages in both represent early examples of Langland in his revision process and that the scribal habits are therefore of considerable importance for the establishment of the C-Text. John Burrows, whose own earlier editorial work on Hoccleve has cleared the way for some interesting recent books on the poet, compares autograph versions of Hoccleve's *Series* with other manuscripts to deduce that unmetrical lines almost always represent scribal "mismetrings," as Chaucer puts it, a conclusion with implications for the editing of both Chaucer and Gower. John J. Thomson explains the peculiar coincidence of both Tottel's and Wayland's printings of Lydgate's *Fall of Princes* by their religious and personal differences and the uncertain implications for printers, both Catholic and reformed, during Mary Tudor's reign. And in an essay that is as much art history as literary history, Martha Driver analyzes the illustrations as well as the text of Pierpont Morgan M 876, which includes Lydgate's *Troy Book,* demonstrating that they represent Lydgate's classical past in the same way as the Beauchamp Pageants and other examples represent the English present, in terms of heroic memorialization and grand narrative. Linne R. Mooney argues that the content and the hands of several booklets of Trinity College MS R.319 and R.3.21 point to a late assembly of the manuscript, perhaps by John Stow himself, one of the scribes and an owner of the MSS. A. S. G. Edwards informs us that British Library Additional 11814 contains the unique Middle English translation of Claudian's *De Consulatu Stilichonis,* with the Latin on the page facing the Middle English, a rare arrangement. The work may have been meant to associate Stilichonis and Richard VI, but perhaps also links Richard with Duke Humfrey and his program of classical learning. Finally, Julia Boffey notes that the influence of Chaucer's *Legend of Good Women* has been recognized in similar collections in the fifteenth and sixteenth centuries, but that the symbolic number of women is significant. Cambridge Trinity College MS R.3.19 contains "Nine Ladies Worthy," which slipped into the Chaucerian apocrypha. Other evidence, often visual, suggests a tendency to celebrate heroic women in groups.

Given the time lag between conference, book preparation, and publication, some of the arguments in both volumes are now familiar to readers of this journal in somewhat different forms, as single-authored books and so forth. If there is a general theme to the Aers volume, it is perhaps best summed up in Elizabeth Fowler's citation of a comment by Elizabeth Kirk to the effect that criticism should turn its attention to how "theological inquiry can be carried out in a medium other than discursive argument" (57). Kirk herself wrote one of the seminal studies of the current *Piers Plowman* revival and the quotation suggests how Langland, rather than Chaucer, has become the normative poet of current literary study. That is, we have learned to read Chaucer, as Anne Middleton once suggested we should, as part of the "Age of Langland." It would require a review of Pearsall's own career to explain how he is part of this shift, but one could argue that he accorded a clearer and more forceful intentional program to Langland than to Chaucer, at least by questioning so many of the assumptions of traditional Chaucer scholarship. The state-of-the-art critical historicism of the Aers volume reflects this reversal of fortune and inversion of what we value in late medieval poetry.

The Aers volume begins with some lovely tributes by Aers himself and by Derek Brewer, once Pearsall's teacher. In the articles that follow, we can observe Langlandian urgency displacing Chaucerian irony. Nicolette Zeeman contributes a lengthy exploration of Langland's *kynde* as a state of "lack," a somatically experienced negative state that must be endured to achieve spiritual rewards. C. David Benson presents *Piers Plowman* as a sort of public pillory, and explores the similarity to and transcendence of the pillory and the system of justice it represents in the crucifixion sequences. Elizabeth Fowler adds to her important articles on the political philosophy implicit in late medieval narratives by defending the *Man of Law's Tale* as a "thought experiment," exploring the complexities of dominion and consent, especially in regard to the conflict of laws. David Aers makes an important contribution to the growing body of commentary on Chaucer's *Melibee*. He notes that the near-total absence of the Church and its sacraments renders *Melibee's* discussion of Prudence analogous to controversial stoic, secular humanist, and even Wycliffite positions; Prudence herself ignores the orthodox Thomistic stress on the intent and effect of prudence. Hence, *Melibee* needs to be delinked from the *Parson's Tale* as an example of Chaucer's orthodoxy. In the next essay, Lynn Staley explores the startling possibility that the subject of *Pearl* is Isabel, daughter of Thomas of Woodstock, given as an oblate to the Minoresses in London. Staley's supporting evidence concerning patronage and the status of aristocratic women in Ricardian England is as arresting as her argument. Paul Strohm discusses the possibly apocryphal "Complaint for My Lady of Gloucester" as a "Lydgatean" poem. Against the recent tendency to accord Lydgate a certain degree of critical agency and moral independence, Strohm suggests that compared to historical documents detailing the situation of Jacque of Holland, Lydgate is again defending royal interests and policies, and any apparent subversion is a function of poetic language itself, not of

Lydgatte's intention. Lee Patterson's contribution, "The Heroic Laconic Style," is one of his most remarkable essays, an exploration of the reticent male hero from Beowulf through its reemergence in the late nineteenth century, exemplified in the Edwardian popular novel *The Four Feathers*. Patterson's essay is a defense, rather than the usual critique, of the often maligned silent male hero, whom he argues suffers from an excess of inner consciousness rather than its lack. He begins and ends his essay with Captain Lawrence Oates's famous last words as he sacrifices himself for Scott and his other comrades in the Antarctic. (At the time of his writing, of course, Patterson could not have known that Oates had plenty to be silent about, given the recent revelation that the adult Oates had fathered a child with a twelve-year-old girl.) Christopher Cannon, the only contributor to both volumes, writes on "Malory's Crime," describing Malory's representation of the conflict between a fixed ethics of rivalry and the positional morality of fifteenth-century politics, resulting in a series of portrayals of knights who are always already criminals. Sarah Beckwith concludes with another one of her searching analyses of the mystery plays and their theology of community, demonstrating how the theater itself was appropriate to the theological complexities of representing the presence and absence of Christ's body. The resurrection is embodied in the community of believers, just as the audience participates in dramatic performance.

The *festschrift* is too often dismissed as an avenue of scholarly publication. It is remarkable how enduring and important in Middle English studies alone have been the articles that have appeared in volumes dedicated, for example, to Bloomfield, Donaldson, Kane, Tolkein, Wenzel, and to contributors to these volumes such as Hussey and Burrow. I would expect the volumes under review to join this company, given the remarkable quality of the essays and the distinction of the contributors. Nevertheless, we should pause to consider how many recent collections of essays have played a crucial role in shaping Middle English studies as we know it today, potentially at the expense of the traditional journal. The older defense of such collections, that they may be acquired by individuals and libraries who would or could never subscribe to journals, is being turned upside down by electronic publishing and library internet access. We will need to consider how work of this quality is distributed, not just to specialists, but to a wide sector of readers and users. Derek Brewer's wise and unnecessarily modest preface to the Aers volume should remind us of how central his own innovative publishing ventures have been to our enterprises over the past quarter century, and how we will need to respond as creatively to new economic and technological circumstances.

JOHN M. GANIM
University of California, Riverside

ELIZABETH ARCHIBALD, *Incest and the Medieval Imagination.* Oxford: Oxford University Press, 2001. Pp. xv, 295. $70.00.

Elizabeth Archibald's literary history of the incest motif in medieval romance and *exempla* is a welcome survey of a subject paradoxically most discussed and most taboo in both the medieval and modern eras. In clear and often witty prose, Archibald's book provides excellent coverage of medieval incest tales, as well as their classical forebears and early-modern cousins. As a result, this book will be especially useful to those in need of a literary context for single incest narratives or a collection.

In her introduction, Archibald states the purpose of her study: "I think of my project as a literary archaeology, and I hope that other literary critics will build on the foundations I have excavated, using whatever approach they find most useful, just as historians build on the fieldwork of archaeologists" (p. 2). While Archibald hints that others may bring theoretically informed readings to the tales she unearths, she herself eschews the use of psychoanalytic or anthropological methods as anachronistic. For the most part, Archibald succeeds in sustaining her desired distance from theoretical entrenchment, and even though a strong focus of the book is "the representation of women in medieval incest stories" (3), neither does she place herself in a single camp of feminism. Some will think this repudiation of postmodern theory a strength in that it allows for an objective, thorough presentation, and others a weakness in that it does not foster in-depth analysis of the literature. Archibald's own readings rely on formalist cues that identify patterns in incest narratives throughout the medieval era and beyond.

Before a discussion of the popular incest narratives, Chapter 1 reviews "Medieval Incest Law: Theory and Practice" (p. 9). Archibald presents a lucid, extensive history of the changes in incest law from the classical period through the middle ages. Employing law codes—civil and ecclesiastical—as well as penitentials, she traces the early evidence that in-junctions against incest are constructs of culture rather than reflections of natural revulsion. For example, she explains the laws against inter-course with affines, such as godparents, as a reflection of the Roman Catholic Church's conception that all people are brothers and sisters in Christ. In this chapter, Archibald chronicles well the extension of incest laws under eleventh-century clerics who were zealous about church power and issues of chastity, and the relaxing of these laws under the burdens of enforcing them. While James A. Brundage's *Law, Sex and Christian Society in Medieval Europe* stands as the classic work in English on this subject, Archibald's survey is still incredibly useful for its sharp focus and distillation of a variety of legal and moral texts into a reason-ably short chapter. Students of the middle ages to whom this topic is new will enjoy an immediate familiarity with the most important ques-tions and determinations on incest during this period.

Most of the fine points of medieval incest law dwell on defining this sin and determining to which degree of consanguinity sexual relations are incestuous. As the eleventh-century churchmen mandated, is inter-course with almost any family member immoral and illegal? Or as the Fourth Lateran Council proposed, is a prohibition to the fourth degree sufficient to promote chastity and exogamy? Archibald herself notes that in contrast to ecclesiastical discussions, popular literature is hardly at all interested in cousin marriage or the spiritual pollution of sleeping with a member of one's godparent's family. Instead, popular medieval *exempla* and romance portray more often than not parent-child or sibling incest. Archibald posits "Perhaps one reason why popular medieval in-cest stories almost always deal with nuclear family incest is that in these cases there can be no argument about the severity of the sin, or the need to regularize the situation" (p. 50). While this may be true, it does not explain why the history of incest law in Chapter 1 is essential to an understanding of the incest literature to follow. Throughout the book, Archibald makes an occasional reference to the legal history of her first chapter. For instance, in her study of *La Manekine* she remarks that when the pope grants permission for the King of Hungary to marry his daughter Joie, "this must be a reflection, if not a criticism, of the Church's notorious leniency in sanctioning aristocratic marriages with the prohibited degrees of kinship" (p. 165). Nevertheless, the connec-tion between the discussion of incest prohibitions and the history of medieval incest literature seems tenuous.

The book is strongest in chapters 2 through 5, where Archibald charts the sources and types of incest narratives. These chapters represent Archibald's careful and wide-ranging literary research; together, they add up to an impressive presentation of the great variety of medieval incest tales and their readers. Chapter 2 relates "The Classical Legacy" for medieval incest tales (p. 53). One of the surprises for contemporary students familiar with post-Freudian theory is the way in which medieval authors downplay the Oedipus story, although both the *Roman de Thèbes* and Statius's *Thebaid* made it available. Archibald explains that medieval writers were interested in the political consequences of incest and often connect this sexual crime to murder, tyranny, and chaos; therefore, the war between Oedipus's two sons Polynices and Eteocles takes precedence in medieval accounts, for instance Boccaccio's *De casibus virorum illustrium* of Lydgate's *The Fall of Princes*. More often than Oedipus's story, medieval authors circulated romanticized tales of incest from their classical heritage, such as the *Historia Apollonii* (splendidly edited by Archibald for Cambridge in 1991) and Ovid's poems of forlorn women. Such tales were easily adapted to medieval romances and lais.

Since medieval readers were often introduced to classical incest tales along with the Christian marginalia that interpreted them, Archibald argues that "it was almost impossible . . . to separate the plot itself from the moralizing tradition in which it had become cocooned" (p. 54). For medieval adapters of classical incest tales such as John Gower, who in the *Confessio Amantis* retold the tale of Canace from Ovid's *Heroides,* the *Historia Apollonii* and others, the "moralizing tradition" encouraged a casting of judgment upon the incestuous, either for their runaway passion or lack of public responsibility. For medieval authors of newly invented incest tales, the tendency to preach against incestuous sin in the commentaries led to a focus on the need for penance. Chapter 3, on "Mothers and Sons," illustrates this focus, especially through its evaluation of the "medieval Oedipuses" Judas and Gregorius (pp. 104, 107). The *Legenda aurea* tells the events of Judas's life as it relates the story of St. Matthias, who eventually took the betrayer's place as an apostle. Like Oedipus, Judas is separated as an infant from his parents after a premonition about the disaster he will wreak upon the household. When he returns to Jerusalem as a man, he does not recognize his parents and unwittingly murders his father in a dispute over stolen fruit and marries his mother. The fact that Judas does not repent after recognizing his crimes demonstrates the extent of his evil and foreshadows his betrayal of Jesus. In contrast, the penitence of the hero in Hartmann von Aue's *Gregorius* illustrates the power of Christ's forgiveness in raising in incestuous sinner to the office of pope. Gregorius is the abandoned child of sibling incest, who returns to his homeland and unknowingly marries his mother. When this misfortune is discovered, Gregorius implores a fisherman to chain him to a rock in an isolated lake, and there the miserable penitent remains for seventeen years. When the pope dies, two churchmen dream that Gregorius is to be successor, and thus repentance not only erases incestuous sin, but lifts the sinner up to glory.

Archibald notes in Chapter 4, "Fathers and Daughters," however, that repentance and sainthood are not options for daughters trapped in incestuous relationships with fathers in medieval tales (p. 145). Perhaps this is because daughters are generally raped or seduced in these portrayals and cannot repent a choice they could not exercise in the first place. The characters who should express contrition, the fathers, are generally tyrants past reform, as in the opening scene of the *Historia Apollonii* that Chaucer's Man of Law much laments. There Antiochus rapes his daughter after the death of his wife; his brutality is a metonym for his political savagery. Other well-known medieval stories, whose origins are probably folkloric, begin with such a scene of a bereft widower who would destroy his daughter in his grief. In cases where the daughter escapes, or the Flight from the Incestuous Father tales, the threat of incest propels the heroine out into the world of adventures and functions as a sign of the great sinfulness both at home and abroad. Such a tale is *Emare,* an analogue to the Constance tales, in which the fleeing daughter survives misfortune as well as she can, not actively as a male hero, but passively trusting to God's protection. Archibald employs *La Manekine* as the best example of these tales, including all of the thematic and structural features of the Flight from the Incestuous Father tales.

Chapter 5, "Siblings and Other Relatives" (p. 192), emphasizes the Arthurian saga and presents a revision of Archibald's "Arthur and Mordred: Variations on an Incest Theme" (*Arthurian Literature* 8, ed. Richard Barber [1989]: 1–27). The Arthur and Mordred story is an example of the double incest plot that pervades medieval literature: Mordred is the child of Arthur's sibling incest with Morgause and later pursues Guinevere, his stepmother. As Archibald points out, though, the Arthurian story reverses the usual pattern of double incest in medieval tales in that parent-child incest is usually followed by that between siblings.

Much is unusual in the presentation of the incest theme in the Arthurian saga, the most surprising point being that while a brother-sister affair is generally treated less seriously than a parent-child liaison in medieval literature, for Arthur, as well as for Charlemagne, sibling incest signals the downfall of a kingdom.

In a provocative Conclusion, Archibald sums up the features of medieval incest tales by comparison to Renaissance plays. Drawing an even more significant contrast, she cites a great exception among the characters in medieval incest narratives: the Virgin Mary. Depicted as *mater et filia,* and reigning queen of heaven at Jesus's side, Mary's "incest" with the Father and the Son is paradoxically a sign of great purity and of the human potential to conform to God's will. Much work might be done on this aspect of medieval representations of the Virgin. Elizabeth Archibald, however, has left little to do in canvassing the great variety of medieval tales that represent incest. Now, as she suggests, it is for literary critics to build an interpretive house upon the foundation she has laid.

GEORGIANA DONAVIN
Westminster College

SARAH BECKWITH. *Signifying God: Social Relation and Symbolic Act in the York Corpus Christi Plays.* Chicago: University of Chicago Press, 2002. Pp. xviii, 294. $35.00.

This is a deeply religious book, in both its thematic focus and its mode of thinking. It argues that English pre-Reformation civic theater can best be understood as sacramental. For Beckwith this theater is not an experience or expression of religion: it is the very condition of possibility of late medieval Catholic sacramentality. To see the dead come to life in the bodies of the living is to participate in both theater and resurrection. Such a meaning has been lost to us not only because iconoclasm has made this drama inaccessible, but also because the dominant narrative of new historicist theater studies sees religion in terms of power and ignores the embodied practices of theater. What is at stake is precisely embodiment. In this drama "forgiveness has been embodied . . . not bought or acquired" (p. 121), but so thoroughly did the Reformation redefine our ways of seeing that this theater's powerful, and powerfully communal, modes of signification have been occluded. In Beckwith's words, "what accompanied the suppression of Corpus Christi theater was also the very means of its understanding" (p. 122). At the heart of this book's redemptive project is also an attempt to heal the rift of the Reformation.

That project marks a significant (even startling) shift in Beckwith's writing. Her earlier work is characterized by its scrupulous attention to the minutiae of socioeconomic and sociohistorical analysis and its rigorous pursuit of a clear Marxist agenda. In fact, half of the current book (chapters 1, 2, 3, and 5) is previously published material from this earlier era. The voice in these chapters speaks of the political mechanisms of labor regulation in York, of the importance of non-idealist modes of thinking, of understanding ritual in nonfunctionalist terms. The later voice speaks of very different things: of a desire for a time before the Reformation, of religiosity, of a quasi-unified community. Both voices are present in the book, but the later voice all but drowns out the earlier one. It is not so much that the earlier pieces have been radically overhauled in line with this new theological focus (they have not been), but that their effect is changed, their voice muted by the changed context. It's as if Beckwith hasn't been able entirely to abandon her old self, but still believes in some way that it is compatible with her rebirth as theologian. This is especially true of Part 2 (chapters 2 and 3) which, significantly, receives only perfunctory attention in the Introduction. These chapters simply do not fit with the rest of the book's emphasis on sacramental theater.

There is another awkward lack of fit in the book's framing chapters, which address the question of whether the passion and resurrection story is still meaningful and in what senses it can be performed for modern audiences. The opening chapter, on the post-1951 revivals of the cycle in York, is a trenchant critique of the plays as commodifications of "heritage." The closing chapter deals with two twentieth-century works (Denys Arcand's film *Jesus of Montreal* and Barry Unsworth's novel *Morality Play*). But the point that actors, not priests, keep alive spirituality in both Unsworth's novel and Arcand's film is somewhat dissipated through too much plot telling. And it is hard to reconnect this point to the wider historicist argument about the effects of the Reformation on York's drama. Twentieth-century Quebec is not medieval York; a novel isn't a play. Turning to the work of two modern directors, Bill Bryden and Katie Mitchell, Beckwith asks how Christ is represented in the professional theater: in Bryden's "workerist" (p. 163) production of The Mysteries and Mitchell's 1996–97 Royal Shakespeare Company production of the medieval drama. Beckwith is properly skeptical of the idea that The Mysteries are "a demotic challenge to elitism" (p. 181). Mitchell, in attempting to put religion back in, ends up with a very Protestant production, one that suffers from a "crippling version of medievalism . . . [and] of Christianity" (p. 188). The book ends by acknowledging that we cannot recreate the religious dimensions of Corpus Christi theater, but then sounds a rather priestly and elegiac note: we might learn to love these plays precisely for their chronic anachronism.

Yet we cannot ignore the other kinds of cultural work that this theater performs. An exclusively theological focus cannot address that work. So there is no discussion of gender or cross-dressing, no psychoanalysis, and no attention to the Play's others: to what has had to be violently repressed within medieval Christian sacramental theology in order for it to emerge at all (despite the brief mention of one of the most shameful episodes in York's anti-Semitic past, the Clifford's Tower massacre of 1190). Instead, the book's title, *Signifying God,* points to its core concern with the undoubtedly "theological" and ongoing activity of fixing meaning in relation to a stable and authoritative signified. Its presiding geniuses (in the volume's three epigraphs) are the Jesuit poet Gerard Manley Hopkins, the American philosopher Stanley Cavell, and the social anthropologist Mary Douglas, to whom it owes its subtitle. Cavell's repeated mantra "Nothing can be present to us to which we are not present" is understood as the essence of both sacramentality and theater: just as theater can only happen in the present, so the absent Christ can only be present to a community of believers. This is theater as transubstantiation (an experience of simultaneous presence and absence) and criticism as at-onement: an attempt to seal up the gap between modern secular sensibility and medieval religiosity. But Beckwith's point that theological meaning lies in the "enactment," not beyond, behind or through it, is important. This is (perhaps) where Marxism meets medieval sacramental theology: in their shared insistence on the inescapably embodied nature of social practices.

But the "return to religion" here is emphatically not the same as that taking place in other parts of the academy, medieval or otherwise. I'm thinking of Derrida's notion of untranslatability as the "becoming-sacred" of literature, or of Simon Gaunt's recent work on the troubadour poet Bernart de Ventadorn, work that seeks to understand the religious and ethical dimensions of sacrificial desire (see "A Martyr to Love: Sacrificial Desire in the Poetry of Bernart de Ventadorn," *JMEMS* 31). Although this book asks about the power of the sacred today and about what kinds of experiences still count as sacred, it does not explore the literary dimensions of the drama (and is not really interested at all in their textuality) nor the complex psychoanalytic dynamics of its sacrificial aspects. Literature and religion come together here, insofar as they both engage with the abyss of and in the Other's desire that is represented by the Real (that which lies beyond symbolization). In Gaunt's words, "Art organizes itself around the abyss, religion tries to avoid it" (p. 499). This does not mean that art and religion are opposed; it means rather that they both have a relation to desire.

This is not an easy book to read or to get along with. Nearly every sentence feels wrung from its author. Paradoxically, it seems unable to elucidate the texture of medieval popular devotion or identify the sources of its pleasure, then or now. For Beckwith, "the separation of theology and theater, of religious and theatrical history" (p. 123) has been "disastrous." But disastrous for whom? What this difficult and intellectually challenging book still leaves unanswered is how the plays continue to be meaningful today without casting our responses as either false consciousness or wilful misunderstanding of their theology.

RUTH EVANS
University of Stirling

JOHN M. BOWERS, *The Politics of* Pearl: *Court Poetry in the Age of Richard II*. Cambridge: D. S. Brewer, 2001. Pp. xx, 236. $75.00.

In *The Politics of* Pearl, John Bowers makes a strong argument for an affinity between the *Pearl*-poet's interests and those of Richard II's court in the late 1380s and 1390s. As he asserts in an opening Excursus, Bowers seeks to recover *Pearl*'s "public life" (p. 16), lost in more traditional formalist readings of the poems of BL MS Cotton Nero A.x. The book is organized into three main sections, "*Pearl* and the Politics of Class," "Court Poetry in the Age of Richard II," and "Love and Loss at the Ricardian Court." The image of the *Pearl*-poet that emerges from his chapters on the chief issues of the period, including anticlericalism, Wycliffite heresy, and the labor crisis, is that of a staunch royalist from the same Cheshire milieu as many of Richard's most loyal retainers. Bowers gathers an immense amount of contextual material in order to bolster his claims about the king's direct patronage of this author, situating the poem's concerns within the myriad intentional courtly discourses of the late fourteenth century. Bowers describes his methodology as an "heuristic argument" to recover "a previously overlooked specimen of court poetry operating according to a cultural logic that renders each of the poet's literary decisions suggestive of whole registers of social meaning" (p. 37).

Pearl itself and the other poems attributed to its author remain, however, curiously elusive in Bowers's account of Ricardian culture. Perhaps this is because these aesthetically intricate works do not lend themselves easily to a coherent ideological program. Indeed, as Bowers puts it, the poet is neither a royal apologist like Lydgate nor a critic like the author of "Richard the Redeless" (p. 21). The so-called "Poems of the *Pearl* Manuscript" and the similarly alliterative "St. Erkenwald," whether they were composed by one hand or more, are suffused with loss, moral failure, and notoriously unfixed meanings. In *Pearl,* the dreamer's own desire undoes him when his frenzied plunge into the stream that separates him from the *Pearl*-maiden wakes him up and prevents him from learning more of the "new city of Jerusalem." Gawain, in *Sir Gawain and the Green Knight,* reacts to the revelation of the beheading-game as a second fall from Eden and wears the green girdle as a "token of untrawthe" until Arthur and his merry knights reinterpret it as a badge of honor. In *St. Erkenwald* the "roynyshe" letters that adorn the pagan judge's tomb remain untranslated, a narrative forever lost. Moreover, Bowers often replicates the poet's own ambiguities by gesturing toward competing interpretations of several of the poems; for example, he reads *Cleanness* as an affirmation of Richard's own obsession with purity, yet later suggests that its virulent attack on homosexuality accords with the terms of Richard's harshest critics, who accused him of "unmentionable acts" (p. 173).

The Politics of Pearl is most successful when Bowers evokes the stunningly rich culture of the Ricardian court through its artefacts. The *Pearl*-poet, as he argues, was clearly familiar with this glittering world. He persuasively shows how the sensuous language of *Pearl*'s "kingdom of heaven" recalls the Wilton Diptych, Richard Maidstone's *Concordia inter Regem Riccardum II et Civitatem Londonie* and Chaucer's *Legend of Good Women*. Indeed, Bowers's juxtapositions of Ricardian court productions as disparate as Roger Dymmok's *Liber contra XII Errores et Hereses Lollardorum* and Philippe de Mézières's *Epsitre au Roi Richart* make fascinating reading aside from the question of *Pearl*. Bowers's penultimate chapter, on "Courtly Love," reads the poem within the specifically Ricardian culture of mourning inaugurated by the king following the death of Queen Anne of Bohemia. He brilliantly recreates this historical moment, a high point in Richard's "theatrical" behavior, during which he beat up the Earl of Arundel for arriving late to the funeral and ordered the destruction of the palace of Sheen, where Anne had died. Bowers's abundant intertextual evidence for *Pearl*'s participating in Richard's specific style of courtly lament is thoroughly convincing. His argument falters, however, when he tries firmly to identify the *"Pearl* Queen" with Anne herself and dismisses the poem's rather clear description of the Pearl as a two-year old child and a virgin, who had never even learned how to pray "nawther Pater ne Crede." His suggestion that Queen Anne may well have remained a virgin, given Richard's devotion to the idea of chaste marriage, is certainly intriguing, but it doesn't convincingly decode the dreamer's anonymous longing for the otherworldly Pearl.

Bowers's final chapter argues that the deposition of Richard II in 1399 not only spelled the end of the *Pearl*-poet's literary career but consigned his works to near oblivion. The *Politics of* Pearl itself does much to recover these poems and their social and political world. The book will be of great value to anyone interested in Richard's eventful reign and courtly politics in general. In Bowers's marvelous recreation of the Ricardian era, the *Pearl*-poet once again speaks in a public voice.

RUTH NISSÉ
University of Nebraska—Lincoln

MARY FLOWERS BRASWELL. *Chaucer's "Legal Fiction": Reading the Records.* Cranbury, N.J.: Fairleigh Dickinson University Press; London: Associated University Press, 2001. Pp. 170. $34.50.

Mary Flowers Braswell's study dips into that venerable current of literary criticism that tracks down representations of legal practices in literary texts. Specifically, she traces how Chaucer threads plots and characters from the medieval court records into his texts and how legal protocols shape his texts and his ways of thinking about style, audience and narration. Referencing a wide range of medieval law books—from those teaching legal precepts and recording actual legal cases to those disseminating law—Braswell's readings provocatively suggest that Chaucer's juridical interests animate his verse.

The extent of Chaucer's direct involvement with legal practice has been an open question since the fifteenth century. Although knowledge of both the law and legal procedure was expected of every citizen, details from Chaucer's life records and his ease with legal terminology and protocol would seem to associate him more closely with the courts, even if in ways that are broader and less reliant on institutional credentialing than we are accustomed to. Whatever Chaucer's role in England's legal system, Braswell contends that the poet's intimate knowledge of courtroom protocol makes legal practice a natural subtext for his poems. Chaucer is transforming legal practice into a new poetics when he opens his poems with a Prologue introducing characters and the core event, relies on dialogue, uses set speeches, demonstrates unusual concern with word precision, and understands that each text can have multiple meanings capable of manipulation.

Turning to the way legal culture shaped *House of Fame,* she first examines the legal implications of fame in medieval England. Invoking various contexts that include twelfth-century ecclesiastical inquisitions and thirteenth-century baronial courts, she explains that one's *publica fama,* or reputation within the community, determined the form of trial received. Those of bad fame had their cases tried by a judge, who ideally was a wise and prudent arbiter of justice. In this context, Chaucer's Fame represents a defendant's worst fears, an imprudent and arbitrary judge. According to Braswell, Chaucer prepares the reader for this legal context earlier in the *House of Fame* by introducing laws on reputation, setting up examples of how to read like a lawyer, and depicting a catalogue of "tydynges" presented by "Loves folk" as legal documents. If Braswell is correct in her suppositions, then this infusion of legal motifs and concerns supports the tradition that the *House of Fame* was originally performed for lawyers. Perhaps a more careful explication of the legal practices contextualizing the *House of Fame,* showing clearly how it perverts the legal process and explores the implications of reading and writing like a lawyer, would make a more important contribution toward understanding this enigmatic text.

Just as Braswell infers that the inquisitional courtroom provides the backdrop for the *House of Fame,* she speculates that the Manor Courts would have provided Chaucer, as a justice of the peace, ringside seats to the mélange of individuals who presented tales to promote their own interests at the courts' assembly each spring. Beginning with the legal terminology that pervades Harry Bailly's proposal to the pilgrims gathered at the Tabard Inn, she explains how the *Canterbury Tales* follow the legal exemplar established by the Manor Courts. There defendants tell their own tales without the aid of a legal surrogate by presenting the facts of the case to their own advantage; in turn, each "tale-teller" is opposed by another who retells the same core narrative, but with a slant questioning the defendant's version of the tale. As a poet, Chaucer interweaves these two different tales, creating an ambiguous text and transforming the reader into the judge who must determine which tale best accounts for the evidence. Coupled with these legal methodologies are the ordinances that form the subtexts for the pilgrims' tales. For instance, the *Reeve's Tale* develops around characters who take the law into their own hands and misapply legal maxim and property law. And the *Shipman's Tale* in some ways resembles borough laws covering a husband's liability for his wife's debts.

Braswell also demonstrates how the *Tales* express social concerns reflected in contemporaneous ordinances and court cases that attempt to deal with individuals who seek their own gratification rather than the commonweal. Thus the Pardoner's and the Canon's Yeoman's subtexts deal with confidence men brought to court for scamming both the innocent and the greedy. Likewise, the *Friar's Tale* and the *Miller's Tale* examine the schemes of individuals who do not observe the traditional social bonds.

Finally, Braswell explores the ways the *Tales,* with their multiple and fragmentary explorations of common themes and less-than-oblique references to other pilgrims, create a reading experience much like the twenty-first-century reader experiences when perusing medieval legal texts. Because the extant legal records are often memoranda and abbreviated versions of complex and convoluted cases, the legal narratives often are full of tantalizing lacunae, as in the *Tales'* fragmentary and disjointed presentation of the Cook. Not only does the *Cook's Tale* break off, but its teller reappears in the *Tales* and in the documentary records (as Roger Warre). Despite these glimpses, our understanding of the Cook is not made more complete by the additional information; instead, the additional details entice us to ask more questions. Although Braswell introduces this fragmentation as an aspect of storytelling that Chaucer must have learned from reading legal texts and documents, the cases she cites could have easily been circulating as common gossip or tavern news. Moreover, if Chaucer did glean his information from codices of legal documents, I wonder if he encountered texts so frustratingly incomplete. It seems imprudent to impose our own frustrations with lost documents onto fourteenth-century readers.

In short, Braswell shows that sometimes the law provides a source for Chaucer's poetics, a way of writing and reading that has been previously delineated but whose debt to legal techniques and sources has been underacknowledged. Braswell's plausible readings of Chaucer's texts would be strengthened, however, by more systematic and heavily theorized discussions of medieval law and legal protocol.

CANDACE BARRINGTON
Central Connecticut State University

MARÍA BULLÓN-FERNÁNDEZ. *Fathers and Daughters in Gower's* Confessio Amantis: *Authority, Family, State, and Wriging.* Publications of the John Gower Society. Cambridge: D. S. Brewer, 2000. Pp. viii, 241. $90.00.

In *Fathers and Daughters in Gower's Confessio Amantis: Authority, Family, State and Writing,* María Bullón-Fernández draws our attention both to the remarkably large number of father-daughter relationships highlighted in the *Confessio Amantis,* and to the variety of ways in which these relationships are presented. Bullón-Fernández suggests that this focus allows Gower to consider the role and limits of patriarchal authority in fourteenth-century England, and that his examination of authority is not confined to familial relationships. One of Bullón-Fernández's major points is that Gower's critique extends to explore how legitimate and illegitimate authority is configured in other discursive arenas. As she argues, Gower's tales of father-daughter relationships also "become vehicles for the examination of other relationships of authority such as that between king and subjects, as most of his fathers are kings or some type of governor, and that between an artist and his work, and, more specifically, between a literary author and his text" (p. 2). As Bullón-Fernández goes on to assert, in the *Confessio Amantis* Gower views patriarchal authority as abusing its power in father-daughter relationships when incest occurs, just as the king is "infringing on his subject's private rights" (p. 2), and the author who attempts "to impose a one-sided interpretation on his work, trying to prevent it from producing meanings beyond its control" (p. 2), abuses his power. However, Gower's attempts to distinguish between legitimate and illegitimate uses of authority are troubled by the theme of incest that runs throughout his text. Ultimately, Bullón-Fernández asserts, Gower's considerations of both the taboo's foundational role in establishing patriarchal authority, as well as the incessant violations (threatened and real) of that taboo in his own text, leads him to recognize "the inherent transgressive nature of such authority" (p. 215).

The book's first chapter, "Fathers and Daughters: Defining Authority," lays out this ambitious project, and includes a fine overview of the "post-structuralist" (p. 5) methodology Bullón-Fernández employs throughout the book. Thus her examination of the incest taboo's foundational nature and transgressive pull in father-daughter relationships is informed not only by medieval thinkers such as Aquinas and Augustine, but also by more contemporary critics like Judith Butler, Jacques Derrida, and Claude Levi-Strauss. The chapter also discusses fourteenth-century and contemporary notions of authority as manifested in the political relationship between king and subject, and the literary relationship between author and text. These discussions engage profitably with contemporary criticism, but at times Bullón-Fernández's sudden shifts in discursive field and critical idiom—for example, from familial to political relationships, from feminist psychoanalytic to new historicist approaches—underline the differences, rather than the congruities, between how authority is configured in the familial, political, and literary realms. More typically, however, Bullón-Fernández's overview does an excellent job of demonstrating the common concerns of both these schools of criticism and spheres of authority.

The book's following chapters are arranged thematically, each examining two or three father-daughter narratives. Chapter 2, "Redeeming Daughters: Thaise, Peronelle, and Constance," focuses on "good" daughters who "play crucial roles in complying with the system of ex-

change and in helping their fathers when they are in potentially dangerous or socially problematic situations" (p. 42). The fathers in these tales
are never tyrannical, and no incest occurs between the father and the
daughter. Although these tales would seem to display exemplary instances of proper patriarchal authority, Bullón-Fernández astutely demonstrates how in each tale there lurks beneath this surface compliance a
displaced incestuous and transgressive desire that ultimately works to
undermine these ostensible examples of proper authority.

Chapter 3, "Fathers as Husbands, Husbands as Fathers: Supplanta-
tion and Exchange in the 'Tale of the False Bachelor' and the 'Tale of
Albinus and Rosemund',", examines how these two tales' emphasis on
the interchangeability of the father and husband blurs the distinctions
the incest taboo attempts to draw between father-daughter and hus-
band-wife relationships. Bullón-Fernández argues that the tales thus reveal that legitimate authority in such relationships is determined less by
"natural" categories of consanguinity and more by the performative and
gendered category of "man." The chapter closes with a discussion of the
performative nature of chivalry, and what Bullón-Fernández takes to be
Gower's assertion that such a self-absorbed, "incestuous" institution was
incommensurate with legitimate political authority.

The next chapter, "Limiting Authority: Leucothoe, Virginia, and Canace," discusses how the character of Genius attempts in these tales to
limit patriarchal authority by defining a public sphere in which such
authority is legitimate and a private sphere in which it is not. Unfortunately for each of the women in these tales, such a definition is shown
to be unsustainable, as each of their fathers violate their private spheres
by ordering their deaths. Ultimately, Genius's desperate attempts to
establish this distinction in the text lead him to abuse the authority of
the author as he insists upon privileging his own univocal interpretations
of the tales.

The book's final chapter, "Textual Fathers and Textual Daughters:
The 'Tale of Rosiphelee,' The 'Tale of Jephthah's Daughter,' and 'Pygmaleon and the Statue," makes the claim that in these tales Gower sees
the relationship of the author and the text as participating in the same
dynamic of authority as the father-daughter narratives. In these tales,
Genius attempts to exercise interpretive authority over his texts; the
incestuous overtones of the Pygmaleon story, however, call such authorial control into question.

The book is well-written and nicely edited, and the bibliographic information is well-organized and thorough. Although I find myself in agreement with much of what Bullón-Fernández suggests, the book can at times be a frustrating read, mostly due to its ambitious scope. Bullón-Fernández's attempts to draw analogies between the familial, political, and authorial spheres can seem at times strained, and it must be said that while the similarities between familial and political authority are highlighted throughout the bulk of the text, her discussion of the author-text relationship appears only late in the book, and is somewhat underdeveloped and unconvincing. Overall, however, Bullón-Fernández has done Gower scholarship a great service in this book, which unflinchingly brings contemporary critical approaches to bear on what has traditionally been a very ticklish subject.

RICHARD W. FEHRENBACHER
University of Idaho

GLENN BURGER AND STEVEN KRUGER, eds. *Queering the Middle Ages.* Medieval Cultures 27. Minneapolis: University of Minnesota Press, 2001. Pp. xxiii, 318. $49.95 cloth, $19.95 paper.

Queen theory is old enough by now to ask how it might remain queer unto itself. Like resistance theory in composition studies or any marginalized discourse, it runs the danger of finding itself if not at the center at least at the center of the margin. In *Queering the Middle Ages,* editors Burger and Kruger seek less to uncover a medieval queer here or there than to goose an historical body primly buttoned up in the periods that shape our identities—medieval, renaissance, modern, postmodern. In this they distinguish their work from that of some contemporary queer theorists and some "gay/lesbian and feminist" medievalists for whom this linear temporality remains unproblematic. Once you queer medievalism, ask the editors, what happens to contemporary categories of (post)modernity, which implicitly define themselves as everything the middle ages is not? The historiographical repercussions of posing such a question are explicitly addressed by Kathleen Biddick, who explores the fetishistic logic of periodizing the middle ages as pre-modern, whether decked out as a utopian site of unrepressed pleasures or a dark age of bigotry.

The volume's ten essays fall into three sections, each of which concludes with a response by a guest contributor. The rationale behind the tripartite division is not wholly clear, although the final section, where medieval and (post)modern texts rub up suggestively against each other, seems the most coherently connected of the three; certainly Larry Scanlon provides the most substantial and critical of the three responses (by Karmie Lochrie and Francesca Canadé Sautman and himself). Diversity in this collection is all; the book explores an early fourteenth-century marginal of Brunetto Latini in hell; the inquisition proceedings of Arnaud de Verniolle, arrested for heresy and sodomy; Froissart's account of the face-off between Isabella and Hugh Despenser, boyfriend to her husband Edward II; cigars à la Clinton and Lewinsky; gay porn; HIV/AIDS; and a sketch of the visit of Oscar Wilde to Harvard in 1882, published in the college rag by a young George Lyman Kittredge, all of which keep the reader engaged throughout.

Two essays were particularly entertaining; pleasure after all lies at the heart of getting queer/medieval, and earnest preaching against heteronormativity (of which there are occasional touches) can be a passion killer. Michel Camille looks at the "first 'flaming queen' in medieval art" (p. 58), Brunetto Latini, who, in this particular illumination from the Chantilly manuscript, stands with one arm on hip, the other extended in mannered pose. Camille considers the flamboyant "self-statuary" (p. 70) of the stance, oratorical yet perversely sensuous. The illumination straddles the inner spine of the book, leaving Latini and Dante to face each other across the divide of the page. Camille characteristically foregrounds the corporeality of the reading process, reimagining the inner spine of the book as an ass-crack with teacher and pupil spread out on the nates of the pages, touching only when the book is closed. This is Camille at his most impish, striking his own campy pose within the piece "as a twenty-first-century sodomite and scholar of the Middle Ages" (p. 58); the essay has latterly acquired the cachet of being one of the last publications of a scholar already much missed.

Garrett P. J. Epp's witty "Ecce Homo" considers the display of Christ's flesh in medieval theater, arguing strongly for its erotic appeal. At first blush, the claim of eroticism seems located in the author's personal proclivity: "the onstage display of a seminaked male body does indeed have an inherent erotic potential for me" (p. 238). Epp's point, however, is that Christ's radiant flesh, perpetually offered to the worshipper's gaze and tongue, is as physically beautiful as it is spiritually wholesome, that the passion of a medieval Passion play is meant in its fullest possible sense. From the work of scholars such as Aers and Staley, we understand more about the contiguity of the sacred and the political; here, we are arrested by the sensuality of worship, a queer thought indeed to a culture thoroughly used to thinking of religion as bad sex.

Both these essays display queer signatures: one a sodomist, the other an aroused spectator of Christ. Camille and Epp are not the only ones in the collection to name themselves thus. Compare Lochrie's self-insertion "as a queer female medievalist" (p. 95), and Burger, who when speaking of the damage Chaucer studies has done to queer subjectivities, asks whether "*we* would be better off without Chaucer altogether" (p. 213). What do these confessional tropes signify? Camille's signature extends our awareness of the corporeality of reading; the writer's own bodily desire weighs upon us as we read about the bodies of medieval readers and of the medieval book, itself made out of an animal's body. Epp's insinuating admission of failure to achieve what Dante describes as the "sinfully distended muscles" is as in-your-face as the thought of Christ with a hard-on. The effect of Camille's and Epp's declarations is ultimately rhetorical. Their confessional pose may happen to be autobiographical, but it is also knowingly theatrical, their selfhood worn like a gay costume, their authorial identities as much textual constructs as those of Latini or Christ. The revelatory topoi of Burger and Lochrie seemed less gay in plumage by comparison, more like the *nakyd* intent of Wycliffite discourse. To ventriloquize briefly through Epp, "I do not feel included here" (p. 249). If the task of queer medievalism is to come out and to out, it will also inevitably and as a consequence leave out. This collection, very oddly indeed, leaves out lesbian desire, Lochrie's lone phrase excepted.

However, the collection largely and inclusively celebrates the "rich stew" that medieval sodomy is. Witness Sautman's exploration of Arnaud's love between the thighs where interfemoral sex eschews the "perfected" act of penetrating that devil's hole, the anus. The vice of sodomy subsumes every (in)conceivable position, partner, and orifice, except for penile penetration of the vagina where the man is atop the woman. But if the sixteenth-century theorist of criminal law, Jodocus Damhouder, can opine in his *Practica Rerum Criminalium* that coition between a Christian and a Jewess (or vice versa) constitutes sodomy (propriety of position and orifice being assumed), then all sex, missionary position included, is sodomy when either is unbaptized. At this rate, I don't know anyone who isn't a sodomite.

While Burger's and Kruger's collection may not turn on some of the more hard-core historians, the sodomite is, after this book, less easy to dispatch as mere emblem of spiritual sterility: take Claire Sponsler on Froissart's construction of Despenser as political and familial threat. Arguably, historical periodization itself has made us medievalists a bit queer. Here is a challenge really to bugger up the eras.

VALERIE ALLEN
John Jay College of Criminal Justice, City University of New York

LESLEY A. COOTE, *Prophecy and Public Affairs in Later Medieval England.* York: York Medieval Press; Woodbridge: Boydell and Brewer, 2000. Pp. ix, 301. $90.00.

In *The Political Prophecy in England* (New York: Columbia University Press, 1911) Rupert Taylor cautions that approaching the study of medieval prophetic writings from a chronological perspective is a difficult undertaking because the number of texts "soon become too numerous and too short, and deal with too many different things to be treated and discussed in a general study" (p. 48). Undaunted by Taylor's warning, Lesley Coote has undertaken just such a project: *Prophecy and Public Affairs in Later Medieval England* examines political prophecies in England from 1135 to 1485, paying close attention to the historical context of the manuscripts as well as to matters of ownership, audience, and circulation. Coote's attentive and detailed analysis makes *Prophecy and Public Affairs* a useful text for the literary scholar as well as the historian, and her "Handlist of Manuscripts" is a valuable tool for anyone interested in political prophecy in medieval England.

The book is comprised of an introduction and five chapters; the introduction and the first chapter set up the terms of Coote's analysis. Whereas Taylor classifies political prophecy as a genre, Coote characterizes it as a "discourse" (p. 13). Traditional views that derive from Taylor see prophecy as "a kind of code, or puzzle-language, put together by the initiated, in order that other initiated persons might then decipher it," (p. 1), but Coote sees prophecy as accessible to—and popular with—a much larger potential audience: "If we are to conclude that political prophecy was an intellectual game, or a series of coded messages for the initiated, then either the game was extremely popular among a large group of intellectuals, or the number of initiates was very large indeed" (p. 6). Coote sees prophecy as "living language" in which "people communicated their feelings about people, king and nation to one another" (p. 14). Thus, in the study of political prophecy, "the emphasis should be placed less upon the writer and his text, than upon the audience and their interpretation of texts" (p. 15).

From the introduction and Chapter 1, Coote moves on to the main material of her study. Chapter 2, "The Second Arthur: The King as Hero c. 1135–1307," examines some of the most popular prophetic texts in this period—including the "Prophecia Merlini," the "Sibille generaliter" and the "Pseudo-Methodius"—and details the attributes of what Coote calls the "prophetic hero" who comes to be associated with the king, a figure who has the important quality of "Englishness" (p. 65). Henry III and Edward I deliberately exploited the popularity of these prophetic texts, seeking to align themselves with the hero-ruler, often described as *Arthur redivivus*. Chapter 3, "Expectation and Disappointment: 1307–1340," discusses Edward II and Edward III making particular use of the text known as "Adam Davy's dreams." Here Coote argues that Edward I's son and grandson made little deliberate use of prophecy as propaganda because "political prophecy had become so well established among the governing and administrative classes as discourse of 'Englishness' that it no longer needed official stimulation" (p. 92). Chapter 4, "Debate and Crusade: 1340–1399," engages with the prophetic texts "Erceldoune," the "Alliterative Becket," and a text that Coote calls "Bridlington." Coote argues that despite numerous troubles—the plague, the Uprising of 1381, and the death of the Black Prince, to name a few—the "audience of prophecy was too optimistic to be dismayed for long" (p. 145), and prophecy proved itself to be "flexible" enough to be transferred with ease from the Black Prince to his son, Richard II. In Chapter 5, "The Imperial Hero: 1399–1440," Coote focuses extensively on "coded messages" and "opaque" prophecies that could be "interpreted in many ways" and thus "were potentially subversive" (p. 165). She expands her argument about the "flexibility" of prophecy, detailing how prophetic texts could be reread and reinterpreted to demonstrate that Richard II's deposition had been foretold, as had Henry IV's coming to the throne as a "prophetic saviour" (p. 168).

Likewise, the seeming disaster of the infant Henry VI's accession to the throne was viewed as a "great advantage" by the writers and audience of prophetic texts who characterized the infant king as "the sinless successor" (p. 178). In her final chapter, "Cadwallader and the Angelic Voice: The Rationalization of Chaos 1450–1485," Coote describes the use of prophecy as a "partisan tool." She traces an increased interest in prophetic texts among both commons and nobility, noting "a broadening of the basis of ownership of prophecy in the fifteenth century" (p. 213).

Coote turns again and again to issues of ownership and audience, emphasizing that earlier studies have neglected to note that "the part played by the audience of a text was as important as that of the writer and copyist" (p. 42). Indeed, she concludes her study by stating that political prophecy "expresses the political consciousness of an important section of the English national community" (p. 238). However, Coote herself indicates on numerous occasions that determining exactly what or who constitutes that "important section" is nearly impossible. Her claims about general shifts in patterns of ownership, production, and circulation of prophetic texts from 1135–1485—that we see more texts belonging to lay people, and more texts written in English rather than Latin—could easily be applied to other types of literature composed and circulated during the same period. When Coote states "the demand for political prophecy was not created by the production of literary texts; rather, it was the demand which stimulated the production of text" (p. 43), one is compelled to ask, on what evidence? On more than one occasion, Coote seems to have caught herself in a "chicken and egg" problem, in which she argues that the popularity of prophecy helps explain the large number of prophetic texts in circulation, which in turn suggests that prophecy was popular.

The "audience problem" would not loom so large if Coote did not keep insisting on its significance. The work she has done in reading, analyzing, and describing the various manuscripts that contain political prophecy is truly impressive and a significant contribution to the field. Although at times her attention to the details of the individual manuscripts slows the pace of her argument, this would seem to be unavoidable in such a complex and comprehensive study. Coote's careful analysis of the manuscript evidence and equally careful historical contextualization is one of the book's great strengths. She provides a fresh perspective on this most interesting topic, even though *Prophecy and Public Affairs* is by no means the final word on the matter of political prophecy. As Coote herself notes, her study is "a contribution, not a final solution" (p. 7).

DORSEY ARMSTRONG
Purdue University

RITA COPELAND, *Pedagogy, Intellectuals, and Dissent in the Later Middle Ages: Lollardy and Ideas of Learning.* Cambridge Studies in Medieval Literature 44. Cambridge: Cambridge University Press, 2001. Pp. xii, 243. $65.00.

Rita Copeland has given much too modest a title to a book that ranges, with great learning and authority, across fifteen hundred years and from north Africa to northern England. In *Pedagogy, Intellectuals, and Dissent in the Later Middle Ages,* Copeland draws complex lines of intellectual and social filiation that link the early Roman Empire to the England of the Lancastrian kings. The book tracks the mutually defining yet often mutually hostile preserves of elementary pedagogy and advanced hermeneutics, particularly as they used the surprisingly complex notion of "literal sense."

For most of this time, the agents of advanced hermeneutics made themselves a small and carefully guarded elite, largely in service to more militant forms of power. Elementary education was the space of literal and then (more oppressively, because more permanently) metaphorical childhood, even infantilization, an arena of hierarchy and strict control. Copeland uncovers, though, the brief flowering of a medieval English counter-tradition of subversive pedagogy, at once generating and serving a marginal, dissenting community of belief. Heretical learning itself was nothing new. The truly radical move, the genuine paradigm shift that Copeland identifies among the Lollards, is their ambition to integrate sophisticated exegetics with the moment and space of elementary pedagogy. This is long history of a daring sort, that consciously resists "a certain pressure to forget or simply to ignore the force of long-established orders of discourse" (pp. 5–6) in recent study of the Lollards. Modestly declining to draw much attention to this aspect of its project, then, the book offers a powerful alternative to the tendency of some

New Historicism toward historical narrowness, even exquisite miniaturism.

A general introduction entitled "Pedagogy and Intellectuals" opens the book. Its first part, "Pedagogy," argues that ancient pedagogy and its heirs produced an orthodoxy quite separate from theology. Its most influential legacy was the separation of biological childhood from social and political childishness, a status perpetuated in Christian clerical discourse about the laity as children. The adult students of Lollard conventicles, however, were taught through active discussion, a less hierarchical procedure with intriguing analogies to recent "liberationist" critiques of pedagogy as an oppressive regime; Lollard teaching thus decoupled elementary knowledge from the status of childhood. The second part of the introduction, "Intellectuals," asks whether there was a category of Lollard intellectual, and how that might relate to broader late medieval notions of the intellectual and of intellectual labor. Using both Jacques Le Goff's and Alain de Libera's explorations of a professional "craft" of medieval learning, Copeland argues that Lollard pedagogy "aims to deprofessionalize intellectual identity" (p. 42).

Lollard pedagogy undermined the hierarchies of traditional pedagogy and the preserves of its elite by eliding what had been, for more than a millennium, two important but incompatible notions of the literal sense. It is this dual tradition and its subversive Lollard elision that are articulated in a quite dazzling display of erudition in Part One, "From pedagogies to hermeneutics: childhood, the literal sense, and the heretical classroom." From Mediterranean antiquity onward, the acquisition of literacy was joined inevitably to the literal sense, but even advanced study of grammar and style was restricted to the textual surface. Access to textual depth was the preserve of the philosopher. This divide, initially porous, took on increasing solidity in the declining empire, and increasingly mirrored lines of class. At the same time, however, ancient grammarians had developed their pedantic erudition of the textual surface far beyond the elementary level, while in the Middle Ages, the literal level took on increasing importance and complexity in biblical exegesis. Hence two entrenched but incompatible, even hostile, discourses of the literal sense developed, pedagogical and hermeneutic, with the vulgar and childish crowd studying the one debarred from access to the other, with its attendant social powers.

Chapter 2, "Lollardy and the politics of the literal sense," explores how Lollard teachers (broadly conceived) worked to collapse these two discourses of the literal sense by bringing its most ambitious hermeneutic use into the setting of an elementary pedagogy liberated from disenfranchised childishness. In smaller and affordable form, and in English, the apparatus of university hermeneutics is exported to the Lollard classroom. In reaction, Henry Knighton writes about the Wycliffite Bible as casting pearls before swine. (Copeland shows how Lollards are dismissed and oppressed as "children;" Knighton's phrase suggests they were deemed something lower yet: beasts.) Lollard pedagogy, then, moves "horizontally towards an open community of lay, adult readers" (p. 114) which is inevitably politicized as it is driven underground by regulations such as the fifth Arundel Constitution.

A literal sense that fused its roles in elementary teaching and sophisticated biblical hermeneutics was perceived as dangerous both theologically and politically; its Lollard proponents often faced the alternatives of recantation or prison . . . or burning. Part Two, "Violent representations: intellectuals and prison writing," turns to two Lollard prison texts. Richard Wyche's clandestine letter about his examinations by Walter Skirlaw, bishop of Durham, during an incarceration in 1402–3, transforms the prison—the ultimate space of enforced hierarchy and oppression—into a pedagogic space. Wyche's letter schools his clandestine readers in the rhetorical techniques of examination and evasion, which derive from the university world of exercises in scholastic disputation, and in the legal notion of "mental reservations" in the taking of oaths. It is an irony Copeland might have developed further, though, that when he was burned as a relapsed heretic in 1440, Wyche was treated as a martyr, incipiently a saint. Church authorities repressed the cult, but the cult of saints and pilgrimages were repugnant to Wyclif's followers. If Lollard pedagogy could export university discourse to a dissident community, Lollard martyrs could be imported into a discourse of sainthood. Orthodoxy and heresy are always mutually constitutive, and their boundary, however policed, is mutually permeable.

William Thorpe's narrative of his examination of Archbishop Arundel presents himself retrospectively as a last survivor of Wyclif's Oxford circle, which he tries to rescue from erasure in the atmosphere of the Arundel Constitutions. Indeed, it is only Thorpe's status as a renegade from the elite, Latinate university world that earns him Arundel's lengthy and exasperated attention. Yet Thorpe might have been an archaic survival from the perspective of the Lollard cells as much as his own. The huge project of vernacular translation and annotation—the Bible, Glossed Gospels, and sermon cycles—had created a body of English books that could be studied locally and without the need necessarily of further university guidance. Hence the survival of local Lollard groups for more than a century.

This bald summary does no justice to the density and wide, often recondite learning of Copeland's book, which includes fluent translations from some difficult Latin; it especially fails to account for the several theoretical discourses that inform her arguments, Gramsci most importantly, but also Althusser, Benjamin, and theoreticians of liberationist pedagogy. Indeed, *Pedagogy, Intellectuals, and Dissent in the Later Middle Ages* is a fiercely intellectual book, and makes considerable, demands upon its reader—although the reader's effort is richly rewarded. At the same time, Copeland makes admirable strategic use of provocative questions within her exposition which invite her reader to be a responsive participant in the complex discussion that may follow. It is a Lollard procedure.

The author's questions also stimulate the reader's, of course, and every medievalist reader will no doubt wish his or her own were more fully explored. I found myself curious about the wider context of vernacular religious text production, which was seriously restricted but not wholly arrested by the Arundel Constitutions. Arundel famously patronized Nicholas Love. Other vernacular texts, despite their technical orthodoxy, undertake their pedagogy in explicitly threatened circumstances, contaminated and endangered (whatever their content) by Lollard vernacularity. If a move underground was the Lollard reaction to attacks from the church hierarchy, other vernacular writers sheltered under the influence of noble secular protectors, as the author of *Dives and Pauper* suggests he did, in the sermons of MS Longleat 4. Together these texts suggest an array of vernacular pedagogies among which the Lollards represent an innovative (and undoubtedly the most important) extreme.

What is most important about Copeland's book, though, is its superb tracking of the meeting place of, and struggle between, traditional pedagogy and dissent—that is, between two great forces that respectively perpetuate and alter social order in any era. This makes it a very current book, which acknowledges its own situatedness within the university milieu toward which Lollard pedagogues were so ambivalent. Copeland's exploration of the prison as a site of writing and dissident pedagogy is troublingly current in a nation whose prison population is burgeoning, and whose prison institutions are becoming, in some states, centers of profit. Copeland mentions (among others) the prison writing and pedagogy of Nelson Mandela. I kept thinking of the more recalcitrant instance of Eldridge Cleaver's *Soul on Ice,* and his long afterlife of apostasy and reconciliation with the state, intriguingly like that of Richard Wyche. It remains to be seen if the universities of the twenty-first century will export the sort of egalitarian interventions that, as Copeland shows, they briefly but spectacularly did in the fifteenth.

CHRISTOPHER BASWELL
University of California, Los Angeles

KATHLEEN FORNI. *The Chaucerian Apocrypha: A Counterfeit Canon.* Gainesville: University Press of Florida, 2001. Pp. xviii, 261. $55.00.

In his 1977 essay "Outstanding Problems of Middle English Scholarship," George Kane made the salutary but unnerving point that "no one has worked out a rationale of ascription" and that we accept works as Chaucer's, for example, largely out of collective habit. Assessing this process of authorial canon-formation historically, Kathleen Forni's book does admirable service by examining the accretion of spurious works in the folio editions of the sixteenth century and then the banishment of these works, often on very questionable grounds, during the nineteenth century when our collective habits were established.

In her Introduction, Forni distinguishes four separate phases in the development of Chaucer's oeuvre, beginning with the "manuscripts canon" of fifteenth-century collections, then the "print canon" of Caxton, Pynson, and early black-letter editions, and eventually the "institutional canon" devised by Skeat for the university curriculum and fixed in its present form by 1900. Her book concentrates on the third phase of the "folio canon" in which spurious or counterfeit pieces appeared in early editions of the *Works* by Thynne, Stow, Speght, and Urry. She is particularly interested in the ways that these works, attributed to Chaucer throughout the nineteenth century, came to generate the literary image of the author that, to some extent, endured even after Skeat's *Chaucerian and Other Pieces* (1897) banished these fakes from the official corpus.

Chapter 1 examines the creation of the folio canon out of the manuscript sources used by these early Tudor editors, with an eventual total of fifty-one apocryphal works. Authorial ascription for the shorter works was not strongly supported by manuscripts collections such as Bodley 638 and Tanner 346, which typically have no names attached to individual pieces. Since Thynne consulted manuscripts that are no longer extant, it is entirely possible that the process of assigning later texts to the poet was begun prior to these omnibus editions. But since Stow was perfectly capable of ascribing to Chaucer works that he knew from TCC R.3.20 were Lydgate's, other principles of inclusion must have operated, such as the desire to preserve whatever contributed to the conceptual milieu of courtly and urbane poetry.

Chapter 2 situates these folio publications within the political and commercial contexts of the Tudor age. Chaucer's name had come to possess so much cultural value that the particular contents of the volumes, including the accretions, operated in the marketplace as a sort of "celebrity endorsement." Each folio collection represented a particular inflection of courtly taste. Thynne introduced Chaucer as an advisor to princes and an admirer of ladies, Stow converted the poet into an antifeminist spokesman and satirist of courtly conventions, and Speght used the volume's contents as well as his biography of the poet to emphasize Chaucer's aristocratic affiliations, treating the author as a "classic" with full editorial apparatus and linking his literary career to royal biography.

Chapter 3 looks at some specifics. Speght's first biography in 1598 was based on the allegorical life in *The Testament of Love* that actually belonged to Thomas Usk. On evidence of *The Court of Loue* and *The Plowman's Tale,* the Elizabethan editor was also confident that Chaucer had studied at Oxford where he became a follower of John Wyclif. Rather than damaging the poet's reputation, these works lodged themselves securely into the sixteenth-century canon precisely because they confirmed Chaucer's identity as a precursor of the Reformation and victim of Richard II's tyranny ended by the coming of the Lancastrians. By the same token, editorial omission of the Retraction for almost two hundred years eliminated the implications of this Catholic-styled confession.

Chapter 4 examines how the *Testament of Cresseid* appeared following Chaucer's *Troilus* as the "sixth book" in all of these folio editions, altering the toning and conclusion of the overall story. Specifically, Henryson's ugly characterization of the Trojan lady descended to Shakespeare for his own deeply troubling portrayal of the love story in *Troilus and Cressida*.

Chapter 5 traces the reception history of the *Flower and the Leaf*. This charming dream-vision was printed by Speght, modernized by Milton, lauded as a masterpiece by Pope, and celebrated in a sonnet by Keats—and thereafter praised throughout most of the nineteenth century as the clearest expression of Chaucer's childlike simplicity and touching descriptions of nature. Forni demonstrates how the poem was widely considered "good" when readers believed its author was Chaucer, but almost universally disdained as "worthless" after Skeat decided the author was not Chaucer. This test case shows how the perception of literary value is historically contingent, here partly tied Modernism's reaction against the aesthetic judgments of the Romantics. Bothered by the fact that their predecessors had got the attribution wrong, twentieth-century readers also rejected a childlike Chaucer rhapsodizing about the beauties of the countryside. So the *Flower and the Leaf* was definitely out.

Chapter 6 examines the processes by which Skeat disattributed spurious works in order to create the authenticity of the Chaucer canon according to principles that are no longer considered valid—theories of grammar and versification based on the *Ormulum* (c. 1200)—while the results themselves remain almost universally unchallenged. Like Tyrwitt, Skeat's aesthetic judgments, which were based on personal taste, operated as the silent determiner for rejecting some pieces such as *Praise of Women* while including others such as *Proverbs*. Showing that the textual evidence for establishing the prevailing canon of Chaucer's works is not nearly so obvious and inevitable as asserted by modern editions, including *Riverside 3,* Forni offers the sobering conclusion that our current institutional canon might reflect the real historical Chaucer no more accurately than did the manuscript and folio canons.

This book's research is remarkable for its coverage of primary and secondary materials. Forni allows the works of theorists such as Barthes, Foucault, Jauss, and Bourdieu usefully to inform her discussions without succumbing to the pretentiousness of needless jargon. Appendix 1 catalogues the spurious works found in folio editions; Appendix 2 lists the manuscripts that contain texts later incorporated into the folio apocrypha.

JOHN M. BOWERS
University of Nevada, Las Vegas

ALAN T. GAYLORD, ed. *Essays on the Art of Chaucer's Verse*. Basic Readings
in Chaucer and His Time. New York: Routledge, 2001. Pp. viii,
449. $95.00.

The contributors to this splendid volume are united in their agreement
that "Chaucer criticism has tended, and still tends, to treat Chaucer as
if he were a writer in prose" (p. 1). The essays collected here by Alan
Gaylord set out to restore this curious imbalance by showing "just how
intricate and how essential the analysis of Chaucer's *verse* can be" (p. 3,
my italics).

After an unusually detailed and helpful introduction, showing precisely where each contributor is coming from, the book is divided into
three sections: Part One, Historical and Theoretical Essays (Thomas
Tyrwhitt, "Essay on the Language and Versification of Chaucer: Part
the Third"; George Saintsbury, "Chaucer's Prosody"; Gaylord's own
groundbreaking study from 1976, "Scanning the Prosodists"; Derek
Pearsall, "Chaucer's Meter: The Evidence of the Manuscripts"; Steven
R. Guthrie, "Prosody and the Study of Chaucer: A Generative Reply to
Halle & Keyser"; and Stephen A. Barney, "Chaucer's *Troilus:* Meter and
Grammar"); Part Two, Essays Combining History, Theory, and Close
Reading (a new essay from Richard H. Osberg on "Chaucer's Artful
Alliteration"; a chapter from James I. Wimsatt's *Chaucer and His French
Contemporaries* on "Natural Music in Middle French Verse and Chaucer";
and an exuberant talk by Emerson Brown, not previously published, on
"The Joy of Chaucer's Lydgate Lines"); Part Three, Essays on Prosodic
Practices (a new essay by Winthrop Wetherbee on "Theme, Prosody
and Mimesis in the *Book of the Duchess*"; a chapter from David Wallace's
Chaucer and the Early Writings of Boccaccio on "The Making of *Troilus and
Criseyde*"; a contribution specially commissioned from Charles A. Owen
on "Witty Prosody in the General Prologue"; Howell Chickering's
"Comic Meter in the *Miller's Tale*"; and Stephen Knight's chapter on
the *Nun's Priest's Tale* from his *Rymyng Craftily*).

Agreement on many more points emerges as the book progresses.
Studies of versification cannot be based on published editions (which
already embody the editors' theories of versification), but must return
to the manuscripts (Pearsall, Barney, Brown, Chickering). Chaucer's
verse must be performed (or at least mentally *heard*) by anyone who is
going to comment on it (and no one has done more than Gaylord himself in the way of performance for the Chaucer Studio). As most com-

mentators have argued, Chaucer's rhythm is basically iambic (Barney shows this beyond dispute, though for Chaucer's commonest line he prefers the term "five stress alternating rhythm" to "iambic pentameter", p. 168); but it embraces much greater "freedom, variety, and flexibility" (Pearsall, p. 144) than the iambic pentameter that we are used to from Shakespeare, Milton, and company (so all those scribes and editors who emend *causa metri* to produce smooth pentameters are not entirely wrong, they just overdo it, and in forcing Chaucer into the straitjacket of regularity lose much of his audacity and inventiveness). His rhythm owes more to French *décasyllabe* than to Italian *endecasyllabo* (Guthrie, Wimsatt); nevertheless (as Wallace shows), Chaucer was a fluent Italianist, in complete control of what he was doing with Boccaccio and Dante. Even his alliteration (which appears much more frequently than in the well-known passages describing the tournament in the *Knight's Tale* and the Battle of Actium in the *Legend of Good Women*) owes more to Romance than to native English models (Osberg).

The rhythmic variations include lines with fewer stresses and more anapests than we are used to, including lines with weak-position stress at position 7, such that "when proud Bayard has his moment—'Than thynketh he//though I *praunce* al byforn' [*TC* 1.221]—we should allow him his gait as well" (Guthrie, p. 159). Such variations (as this example shows) are always purposeful. They include those notorious broken-backed Lydgatian lines, with a weakly stressed syllable missing in the middle of the line, throwing two heavy stresses together: "Hath in the Ram his *half cours* yronne," "And whan the *fox saugh* that he was goon" ("the mother of all Lydgate effects," as Brown calls it, p. 275). The "Lydgate effect" can occur at other points in the line, too, and if "Her grettest ooth was but by *Seint Loy*" as opposed to the metrically less interesting "by Seinte Loy" the effect may perhaps "distance the poet from his pilgrim narrator's obvious admiration for the Prioress" (Brown, p. 275). One interesting phenomenon is how long it can take for us to break completely free of the iambic shackles we are accustomed to, even if we are liberally minded to begin with: both Pearsall and Barney remark in their essays that they would now accept more Lydgate lines than they did in their editions of (respectively) *NPT* and *TC* (pp. 139–40, 187).

A point on which all the contributors are implicitly agreed (though I do not recall its being explicitly stated) is that one of the reasons for Chaucer's having been treated as if he were a writer in prose is that his verse is so skilful as not to draw attention to itself. It seems "natural." It is the art that conceals art. The treasures are there if we look for them, but we have to do the looking. When we do look, we are likely to be astonished by the jewels that have been there all along. This is everywhere apparent in the essays in Part Three of the volume, perhaps nowhere more so than in Chickering's piece, which shows how very much funnier the *Miller's Tale* is in Chaucer's riming couplets than it might have been if written in prose; or in Wetherbee's demonstration of how the prosody of the *Book of the Duchess* portrays "the delicate psychological process the poem describes" (284); or in Owen's tour de force of close readings both of the portraits and of the linking passages in the *General Prologue.* (Surely there couldn't have been any more to be said about the poetry of the *GP?* Read this essay and think again.)

"Talking about meter is a hazardous business," as Pearsall remarks with his usual crispness (p. 131); but this volume shows that it *should* be done, and that it can be done with style. The remarkable fact that ten of the fourteen essays brought together here (all but the first three and the last) have appeared in the last twenty-five years—and most of them in response (directly or indirectly) to Gaylord's "Scanning the Prosodists"—shows how much the study of Chaucer's verse owes to his prodding. He may justly take pleasure in the thought that this volume can "fill our hearts with joy" as (in Brown's words) "we tap our feet and hear—far off but distinct—Geoffrey Chaucer swing" (p. 278).

T. L. BURTON
University of Adelaide

ANA SÁEZ HIDALGO, trans. *Geoffrey Chaucer: Troilo y Criseida.* Clásicos Medievales. Madrid: Gredos, 2001. Pp. 262. $21.40.

Sometime between 1433 and 1454 the Spanish author Juan de Cuenca translated John Gower's *Confessio Amantis.* Although Cuenca based his work on a Portuguese translation of the poem, as far as we know Cuenca's constitutes the first translation into Spanish of a major English literary work. Such an early translation may seem to have heralded a Spanish interest in translating Middle English works, but the subsequent history of Spanish translations has not lived up to its auspicious beginning. It was not until the twentieth century that Spanish translators and publishers started to show a significant interest in Middle English literature. Most of the attention has concentrated on Arthurian works, such as *Sir Gawain and the Green Knight* or Malory's *Morte d'Arthur,* as well as Chaucer's *Canterbury Tales,* the only non-Arthurian Middle English work that has been translated numerous times over the course of the twentieth century. All other works by Chaucer have been translated at least once, with the exception of *The Legend of Good Women,* which has never been rendered in Spanish. Antonio León Sendra produced the first translation of *Troilus and Criseyde* in 1985, a book that is now difficult to find. Translations of Chaucer's other works have not been widely published either. Ana Sáez Hidalgo's is the second translation of *Troilus and Criseyde* ever to appear in Spain. It is published by a major Spanish publisher, Gredos, which should ensure that this new translation will be more easily available.

Troilo y Criseida is handsomely produced. It includes a useful introduction in which Sáez Hidalgo discusses Chaucer's biography and analyzes the date of *Troilus and Criseyde,* the origin of the story (including a comparison to Boccaccio's *Il Filostrato*), the formal elements, and the genre of Chaucer's poem. The introduction ends with a discussion of the poem's manuscript tradition and an explanation of the translator's methodology. The introduction takes into account some recent work on *Troilus and Criseyde,* and does a thorough job of explaining structural, genre, and source issues, but it does not identify any of the issues raised by feminist, new historicist, or post-structuralist criticism. It includes an important mistake that is probably no more than a typo: Boethius is said to have lived in the first century A.D. rather than in the fifth and sixth centuries A. D. (p. 21). This is a rare mistake in an introduction that has no other errors and has been carefully researched.

Translators always face several significant and difficult choices, which are especially hard to make when the work translated is in verse and is written in a language that is not contemporary with the writer's. Faced with these choices, Sáez Hidalgo has made some wise decisions. Like all Spanish translators of Chaucer, she renders his verse in prose. Sáez Hidalgo justifies this choice by citing "el carácter narrativo del texto original" [the narrative character of the original text] (p. 34). Her decision may also be related to her wish to produce a version that is faithful to the sense of the original, something difficult to do when the translator is concerned with maintaining the Spanish meter. This prose translation of *Troilus and Criseyde* is thus fairly accurate and emphasizes its narrative character. Nevertheless, like all prose translations of verse, it does so to the detriment of its lyrical qualities. In this sense, one wishes that Sáez Hidalgo had tried to render at least the lyrical passages, such as the *Cantici Troili,* in verse.

In translating Chaucer's language, Sáez Hidalgo generally and wisely avoids using archaisms. One of the few moments she does use them is in the case of the second person singular pronoun. Her decision to render "ye" and "you" as Spanish "vos" instead of "usted" seems appropriate. It is a subtle reminder that the work is medieval and it also helps convey some of the nuances of the relationships between the characters. For instance, the fact that "thou" (or "tú") is the predominant mode of address between Pandarus and Troilus, while "you" (or "vos") is the predominant one between Criseyde and Pandarus suggests that their relationships are qualitatively different. More significantly, whenever the characters change their usual mode of address, as they do a few times, we know that Chaucer is signalling something significant about their relationship.

Throughout, common phrases and sayings are generally skillfully translated. For instance, "to don thyn eris glowe" (II.1022) is rendered as "que te zumben los oídos" (p. 101), rather than as "que te brillen las orejas," which would be a literal but nonsensical translation in Spanish. At times, though, sayings are not as skillfully handled. For instance, in the lines "Dredeles, it cler was in the wynd / Of every pie and every lette-game" (III.526–27), the expression "it cler was in the wynd" is glossed in Benson's edition as "downwind, safe from discovery." Sáez Hidalgo translates these lines by rendering the expression literally ("estaban libres los vientos de cualquier cotorra o aguafiestas," p. 131). This sounds awkward in Spanish. There are a few other awkward moments in the translation, which are the result of arguable choices made by the translator. Sáez Hidalgo notes in her introduction that she respects "las repeticiones léxicas del texto inglés" [the lexical repetitions of the English text] (p. 35). Thus she translates every single word, even in cases when it seems clear that Chaucer is using certain words for the sake of the meter. The resulting repetitiveness makes the reading slightly cumbersome at times.

Based on both Stephen A. Barney's edition in Benson's *Riverside Chaucer* and Barry Windeatt's in his *Troilus and Criseyde: A New Edition of "The Book of Troilus,"* Sáez Hidalgo's translation is reliable, accurate, and generally well written. The problems pointed out do not detract fundamentally from the translation. The text is glossed by numerous, but never excessive, footnotes that clarify specific issues in the text, explain literary, historical, or mythological references, point to sources, and generally illuminate the poem. This volume is a welcome contribution to the cultural exchange between the Spanish- and English-speaking worlds. Spanish-speaking readers now have an opportunity to enjoy the richness of Chaucer's work beyond *The Canterbury Tales.* For those who teach Chaucer in the English-speaking world and who may have students whose primary language is Spanish, this translation could be an aid to their teaching.

María Bullón-Fernández
Seattle University

Robert Hollander, *Dante: A Life in Works.* New Haven: Yale University Press, 2001. Pp. xvi, 222. $25.00.

This "intellectual biography" introduces Dante through a chronological survey of his writings, aimed at showing the value of the earlier works for understanding the *Commedia.* It is more prescriptive than biographical, and prescriptive in a way that clearly reflects Robert Hollander's large and distinctive contribution to Dante studies over several decades. (In the index, "Hollander, R." easily outscores the Bible, Vergil, Jesus, and Bruno Nardi.) The "biography" that emerges is quasi-allegorical, less a matter of describing Dante's intellectual and artistic development than of pondering the possible significances of the various *Donne* who appear at crucial stages in his writings. In addressing the *Commedia* itself Hollander departs from biography altogether, offering instead what amounts to a set of rules for reading the great poem.

   This is not to say that one cannot learn a great deal here. An impressive body of learning is very skillfully digested in the earlier sections, and the book as a whole might best be seen as a "guide" or handbook to Dante. But its comprehensiveness comes at a stiff price. At no point are we brought into close engagement with Dante's poetry as such, or with his reflections on the issues that most concerned him as he developed his art. Appropriate space is assigned to the *Rime,* early and late, but too much of this space is occupied with inventorying and classifying the lyrics in terms of theme, occasion, or dedicatee. At no point are we given a specimen passage to illustrate the developing character of Dante's verse. (Remarkably, nowhere in the entire book is there a passage of poetry long enough to merit indented quotation.) The account of the *Vita nuova* offers information on numerology and the sources of Dante's Latin quotations, but almost nothing on the work's complex literary strategy—the dialectic of remembered lyric and retrospective prose; the elaborate self-authorizing gesture implicit in the form and method of Dante's packaging of his verse; or his pregnant comments on "love," the making of poems, and poetic tradition.

This unconcern with poetry as such is still more marked in the surprisingly long discussion of the *De vulgari eloquentia,* long largely because so much of it is summary, and a reenumeration of particulars already enumerated at length by Dante. Again, some close examinations of examples illustrating Dante's stylistic criteria would have made this a useful discussion. As it is, one would do better to read the text itself.

The treatment of the *Convivio* is similarly limiting. Apart from a helpful discussion of Dante's ideas about allegory (a subject with which Hollander deals very well throughout the book), the main emphasis is on the biographical implications of the *canzoni,* and on the reasons why we should be hesitant to take the larger project of the *Convivio* too seriously, given the number of points at which the *Commedia* "corrects" the earlier work. We are given no real sense of what Dante is up to in the *Convivio,* of the complex universe of learning it sets in orbit around his poems, or what reason a student of the *Commedia* might find for reading it. The final paragraph of Hollander's discussion leaves me uncertain as to what he thinks he has accomplished in providing us with "evidence" about the treatise:

The point of this assemblage of evidence is not to see how often in the *Comedy* Dante is in polemic with his own previous work, only that he sometimes is. It is not convincing to say that when we read the poem, we are not licensed to consider the text of *Convivio* as relevant to its meaning—either because in 1300, within the fiction, Dante had not yet written it and could not make its contents part of his consciousness as character in the poem, or because the work had little or no diffusion. It is more helpful to observe that the later poem at times tackles the task of clearing the record of errors in *Convivio.* And it is clear that some of these are not trivial. (p. 90)

What I get from this passage is a clear sense of how concerned Hollander is with "license," with the ways in which we are and are not "authorized" to read Dante's poems, singly or in relation to one another. These terms recur in the course of the book, and they are implicitly present at many points. What licenses us to read this way but not that way, apparently, is Hollander's view of Dante's view of what his own poetry "really means." The quoted words are Hollander's (p. 40), and they carry with them the message that there are all too many wrong ways and perhaps only one right way to read the poems, though Dante's genius is fortunately such that many kinds of reader can gain pleasure from them, even such readers as Dante "would surely have disdained." Sometimes, of course, even Dante did not know what something really meant—*Amore* in the *Vita nuova,* for example. Sometimes, as in his comments on Latin and vernacular in the *Convivio* and *De vulgari eloquentia,* he contradicts himself. Elsewhere the lines are clearly drawn.

To read the *Commedia* properly is to recognize its central concern with justice: "Everything in God is just; only in the mortal world of sin and death do we find injustice. . . . It is small wonder that Dante believes that only few of those alive in his time will find salvation" (p. 106). We may be led to sympathize with what seem the attractive features of this or that sinner in the *Inferno,* but to do so is to remain in a moral vacuum. "It is probably better," Hollander suggests in the most remarkable sentence in the book, "to believe that we are never authorized by the poem to embrace such a view" (p. 107). Better to withhold sympathy, like Cato, or the Angel of *Inferno* 9, and accept that everybody has gotten what he or she deserved.

It may well be that something like this is the poem's stern final message for us, but as formulated by Hollander it has no proper bearing on any reader of Dante's poetry but Hollander. Great poetry does not impose itself on its readers as Hollander would impose the *Commedia* on us. It is capacious, generous, true enough to human experience to help us realize for ourselves us that our sympathies are sometimes misdirected, and our judgments at least equally so. No doubt a Dante, a Vergil, a Milton, with every line he had ever written alive in his mind as he composed each new line, can be seen to have censored his work retroactively as he evolved. But it is at least as important that all of their poems are continuously in play, echoing and illuminating one another, and a recognition of this is an important part of the sort of reading a "life in works" ought to promote. Poetry, like being itself, is a great sea, and getting through it requires certain skills, as Hollander rightly teaches us. But rather than going straight to life-saving, we should first learn to take pleasure in swimming.

WINTHROP WETHERBEE
Cornell University

BRUCE W. HOLSINGER. *Music, Body, and Desire in Medieval Culture: Hildegard of Bingen to Chaucer.* Figurae: Reading Medieval Culture. Stanford: Stanford University Press, 2001. Pp. xxiv, 472. 21 illustrations, 3 figures. $65.00 cloth, $24.95 paper.

This is a joyful, often dazzling study of the musical body in medieval culture. Holsinger's subject covers the sensuous embodiment of medieval musical performance but also medieval visions of singing bodies and a range of metaphors based on the musical body, above all that of Christ's crucified body as the taut strings of a harp or lyre. The book takes us from Clement of Alexandria's vision of the New Song resonating through the bodies of the faithful, Peter Damian's claim that chanting ten psalms is the equivalent of receiving a thousand blows with the whip, and Augustine's gradual softening of his early Manichaean hostility to music's carnality, through the erotic pleasures of Hildegard of Bingen's chant and Notre Dame polyphony, to literary images of music, including the polyphonic singing of Chaucer's Pardoner and Summoner, the debased chorus of the snoring and farting Symkyn and his family in the *Reeve's Tale,* and the rational discipline of teaching plainsong that the Prioress's "litel clergeon" avoids. *Music, Body, and Desire* filled me with gratitude—for its rich and surprising bibliography, its unusual insights, its attention to Latin wordplay, the lucidity with which it explains medieval notation and other musicological technicalities, and its sheer gall—as when Holsinger characterizes Augustine's claim in the *Confessions* that God had freed him from his sensuous enjoyment of music as "the self-assured defensiveness of an addict" (p. 74).

   In his introduction, Holsinger tackles the philosophical question of whether music exists prior to performance. Rejecting the Platonic and Pythagorean understanding of music as transcendental harmony that can only be stained or tainted by its embodiment, Holsinger argues for the materialist claim that music only exists when embodied. Embodied music, however, is inherently sensual and disruptive. *Music, Body, and Desire* is thus an explicit challenge to the vision of ordered hierarchy D. W. Robertson propounded in his famous *Preface to Chaucer,* although in its subtle allegories it is also an indirect tribute. (The suggestion that the turn to theory of the last twenty years constitutes "a final break from Robertsonianism" (p. 28) is one of the few moments of naïvete in this very sophisticated book.) So, in his exegesis of the *Prioress's Tale,* Holsinger interprets the grain the abbot removes from the boy's tongue not as a soul winowed from the body but as the "soul miraculously enduring *within* the body" (p. 289, emphasis in original). This reading might also be called incarnational. One of Holsinger's central claims is that medieval theologians and musicians did not monolithically reject embodiment but sometimes explored and even embraced it. He makes a strong case.

A good many will respond with skepticism to Holsinger's initial claim that in the middle ages "the intermingling of same-sex voices in plainchant and polyphony allows composers and performers to explore through sonority unsanctioned forms of desire" (p. 1). As Allen Frantzen has argued in *Before The Closet: Same-Sex Love From Beowulf to Angels in America,* (1998), in a passage cited by Holsinger, the drive in some recent criticism "to show that everything is about sex, same-sex in particular, especially when it claims to be about something else" has sometimes led to readings that demonstrate "the ingenuity of the critics and the malleability of medieval texts," but little more. Holsinger himself has on occasion allowed his desire for medieval texts to express coded sexual transgression to run away with him and he uses *Music, Body, and Desire* as an occasion to modify some of his earlier claims about Hildegard. This time round Holsinger is not just preaching to the choir. Anyone who doubts that certain formal features of Hildegard's music, such as its broad melodic range, might express unsanctioned desire, need simply turn for confirmation to Cistercian condemnations against such "lawless license" or to the Cistercian statute of 1134 declaring "It befits men to sing with a manly voice and not in a womanish manner" (p. 113).

Reviewers often reveal more about themselves than about their subject. The chapter I found most powerful is also the most methodologically conservative, drawing on an unedited manuscript to reconstruct a lost textual community. Picking up on Craig Wright's identification of Leoninus as a canon at Notre Dame de Paris in the 1180s (although not without acknowledging that this identification is still tentative), Holsinger explores Leoninus's unedited verse epistles in Paris, Bibliothèque Nationale, MS Latin 14759. He compares the veiled eroticism of "De anulo," written to an anonymous friend at the papal Curia, which alludes to Ovid's *Amores* 2:15, to the far more explicit verse epistle that follows, urging an unnamed friend to join Leoninus in Paris for the Feast of Fools, where they can then embrace "dear breast against dear breast" [*pectore tunc caro pectora cara,* p. 150]. Holsinger then considers the less tolerant atmosphere at the end of the twelfth century, including the attacks against sodomy in some of the pieces in the *Magnus liber organi,* the great compilation of liturgical music that contains, among much else, the polyphonic compositions of Leoninus. Drawing on other poets, such as Walter of Chatillon, and moral critics, especially Alan of Lille, Holsinger establishes convincingly that in the late twelfth and thirteenth centuries, polyphonic singing was widely regarded as "homoerotic musical spectacle" and that even the layout of the notation on the page was sometimes condemned as "improper coupling" (p. 170).

The sharpest contrast to this closely focused study comes in Chapter 7, "Orpheus in Parts." In deliberate emulation of the anxious mythographers who fragmented Ovid's account of Orpheus, thus avoiding his later days when he turned from women to boys, Holsinger ranges from the poems of the eleventh-century Baudri of Bourgeuil, through the *Ovide Moralisé,* Dante's *Purgatorio,* and Guillaume de Machaut's "Dit de la harpe," to Thomas Heywood's seventeenth-century tragedy *A Woman Killed With Kindness* and Lydgate's *Fall of Princes.* Despite the brilliance of many of the readings, the virtuoso leaps left me frustrated. Others will appreciate the methodological innovation.

One aspect of the book troubled me. Although he makes a few allusions to the excesses of New Age sentimentality, Holsinger never refers to a single specific modern performance of a medieval work. This is a puzzling lapse. Holsinger's account of medieval performance often turns on individual notes and is quite technical. He argues, for example, that the erotic spaciousness in Hildegard's hymn "Ave generosa" is reinforced because it is accomplished "not through conjunct motion (i.e., step-by-step progression), but rather through disjunction, where a rising fifth is followed immediately by a rising fourth and intervallic leaps are emphasized throughout" (p. 115). Much as I appreciated the clarity of the exposition and the careful integration of the figures and musical examples into the argument, I was disappointed to receive no guidance as to where I might hear more. This silence works against Holsinger's declared principles of empathy and performativity, the need to be "honest and straightforward concerning our love and even desire for the music we study" (p. 348), pulling us back from the body to the world of intellectual discourse. It is an easy slip. In his preface Holsinger describes the recent work of Hiroshi Chu Okubo, a "Virtual MIDI body percussionist," who straps electronic sensors to his own body, plugs them into a computer, and plays on his own appendages. A living instrument, Hiroshi offers an avant-garde demonstration of Holsinger's subject. Hiroshi's website, for which Holsinger provides the URL, is richly illustrated but, as of November 2002, was still silent.

ANDREW TAYLOR
University of Ottawa

TONY HUNT, *Three Receptaria from Medieval England: The Languages of Medicine in the Fourteenth Century*. Medium Aevum Monographs, n.s. 21. Oxford: Society for the Study of Medieval Languages and Literatures, 2001. Pp. viii, 263. With the collaboration of Michael Benskin. $25.00.

This work is an edition of medical *receptaria* found in three texts from the first half of the fourteenth century: one in Bodleian MS Rawlinson C. 814, designated R, and two in Corpus Christi College Cambridge MS 388, designated C and CC. Most of the recipes in R are in Anglo-Norman (64 percent), the remainder in Latin. Middle English makes its appearance in C, where the language division is roughly that of equal thirds. All the recipes in CC, save one in AN, are in ME. This volume also includes Michael Benskin's discussion of the language of the Corpus manuscript (C and CC), glossaries of AN and ME words, and an index of ailments treated by the 1,500 medical recipes. Hunt describes this monograph as initiating his efforts to establish a taxonomy for recipe collections from medieval England.

Hunt's undisputed expertise and extensive publications in the study of AN *Fachliteratur* make this work a welcome one, but the fact that he comes late to the study of ME medical writings means that any reader primarily interested in ME will be required to supplement this edition with information from other resources. Hunt compares recipes to published editions of ME prose, but those texts are all fifteenth century and represent only a fraction of surviving writings. He does not cite published editions of ME verse, nor references that provide extensive information on ME texts in manuscript, for example, *The Index of Middle English Verse* and *Supplement;* George Keiser's *A Manual of the Writings in Middle English 1050–1500,* vol. 10 (New Haven, 1998); or Patricia Kurtz's and my database, *Scientific and Medical Writings in Old and Middle English: An Electronic Reference,* CD-ROM (Ann Arbor, 2000), here cited as eVK. It is possible that Hunt's volume was in press when this last reference appeared.

In the case of C, for example, the reader will have to look elsewhere to learn of ME versions of two striking AN texts. Hunt edits (on pp. 88–89) the AN metrical prologue that begins this compendium with the lines "Ypocras se livere fyt, / A le emperour Cesar myt." He refers (at p. 85) to edited ME compendia with similar rubrics but does not mention the many ME versions of this verse. ME metrical versions are IMEV/S 1603 (eVK 3098, 3099 [Sloane 3466, not cited in IMEV/S 1603], 3100) and IMEV/S 1605 (eVK 3108). Another text, IMEV 1604, is relevant although deleted in IMEVS as prose. IMEV/S 3422 and 4182 (additional manuscripts supplied in eVK) are related as well. The tradition also includes eVK 7426 (Wellcome 405), not in IMEV/S.

Other Latin and AN texts on uroscopy and fevers precede the recipes in C and are edited by Hunt. One of them, an AN uroscopy text (pp. 92–93) begins "Si le urine seyt blanche de tut le matyn e ruge aprés manger signefiet sainté." The ME scholar should be aware that Hunt does not cite any ME versions (e.g., eVK 6592, 7809–10, 7835, 7838–40 & c.), but what is particularly unfortunate is that Hunt does not mention that there is a ME version of this AN text in the very same manuscript. He says only in his introduction to the manuscript (p. 86) "finally (ff. 53vb-54rb) comes a treatise in English on urines beginning 'He[r] mayst you knowen urines be coloures.'" That text is in fact a ME version of Hunt's AN text beginning "Si le urine seyt blanche . . ." The ME text on f. 53v of Corpus 388 begins "Urine white at morn and brown after mete that is sign of good hele . . ." (spelling modernized). This text in Corpus 388 is eVK 7835).

There are also ME texts related to the Latin uroscopy treatise Hunt edits (pp. 89–90) from C (eVK 1647–48), and the ME remedies for head wounds, C53 and C54, are similar to ME recipes in many manuscripts (eVK 1214, 1723, 2025, 3436, 3446, 4999, 5185, 5816), including those of the *Liber Medicinalium* of John Arderne. They also share similarities with eVK 5193 (three manuscripts including Sloane 2584, edited by Hunt in 1990 in *Popular Medicine in Thirteenth-Century England*).

In the case of the third compendium, CC, instructions for preparation of the first recipe (p. 163) begin "Make lye of vervain or of betony or of filles or of wormwood and therewith wash thine head thrice in the week" (spelling modernized). Of this incipit Hunt says, "the reference to 'filles' is unique to the present text and to C, which actually has 'or filles of wormod' i.e. leaves of wormwood" (p. 185). That statement cannot be supported, as "filles" is used similarly in other, unrelated ME texts (e.g., eVK 440 and 4289). More important is the fact that this recipe is much more common as the first text in ME compendia than Hunt suggests. This incipit, using the word "filles," begins the compendia eVK 3451, 3455, 3458–59, 3462–65 (3464 is CCCC 388), 3468, 3471–75 (3473 conflates incipits from 2 MSS), 4969, 5139–41, 5608, 6463–66; in short these words initiate *receptaria* in at least twenty-three surviving instances.

Hunt's edition includes from R (p. 64) the Latin poem "Signa Mortalia" and from CC (p. 184) three short ME texts on the signs of death. There are many more versions of these Latin and ME texts than are cited here; similar surviving ME texts on the signs of death include eVK 2417–18, 2590, 2670–71, 7611, 7939, 7953–55, 8226 and 5651.

Two additional suggestions may be helpful to the reader of this book. The first is that, although the volume lacks an Introduction, much valuable introductory information is provided in the Acknowledgements, which should not be overlooked. The second is that there are other works the reader may wish to consult in using this book, in addition to the ME research tools mentioned above. It is standard practice to identify Latin texts with the relevant column number in Lynn Thorndike and Pearl Kibre, *A Catalogue of Incipits of Mediaeval Scientific Writings in Latin,* rev. ed. (Cambridge, Mass., 1963). Hunt cites this reference on p. 3 (with ThK instead of the usual sigil TK), for a text he does not edit, but does not use it to identify other Latin texts in the two manuscripts containing R, C, and CC. For example, he edits from R (p. 64) the Latin verse "Signa Mortalia," but does not identify it as TK 628M and 629D (10 manuscripts). The reader should also have to hand Juhani Norri's *Names of Sicknesses in English, 1400–1550* (Helsinki, 1992). Norri's valuable dictionary is listed in the bibliography, but Hunt's "Index of Medical Conditions Treated" does not always draw on it.

Although other resources should be called on in using this volume, especially for those who work with ME texts, Hunt has made a valuable contribution with this careful edition of three fourteenth-century recipe compendia. A taxonomy of medieval *receptaria* from England is surely a desideratum, and Hunt's plans to work to that end should only be encouraged.

LINDA EHRSAM VOIGTS
University of Missouri, Kansas City

KATHRYN JACOBS. *Marriage Contracts from Chaucer to the Renaissance Stage.* Gainesville: University of Florida Press, 2001. Pp. viii, 181. $59.95.

Jacobs argues that between the early thirteenth century and the Hardwicke Act of 1753, marriage laws and their variations are reflected in a special way in the "popular literature" of the times, ranging from the *Canterbury Tales* to the mystery plays to secular Renaissance drama. Only in works such as these, she asserts, is it possible "to trace without disguise the literary effect of marriage as an institution" (p. viii).

Paralleling her literary thesis is a legal one: Gratian's law of 1140 ("consent" plus "consummation" equals "marriage") gave way in the thirteenth century to precise laws governing spoken vows, where specific phrasing and verb tense became crucial and consummation and cohabitation ceased to be important. The relationships between Chaucer's characters reflect these concerns. Characters in the plays of Shakespeare and other Renaissance dramatists, however, took a still different turn: individuals are obsessed with every aspect of the marriage law, not just the spoken vows. Still later, by the seventeenth century, the old laws—medieval and Renaissance—had become "unjust or inadequate." *Marriage Contracts* proposes to explain this shift in perception, "comparing and contrasting the very different literary reactions to a common stimulus" (p. vii). This method is uncommon, Jacobs argues, since critics rarely relate marriage law and literary presentation, and those who do are "usually content to compare marriage formation as it was dramatized onstage with the law on the books, note the correction, and then move on" (p. 156).

In her section on the *Canterbury Tales,* Jacobs makes some challenging assertions. She suggests that Chaucer might have considered adultery as an alternative when a marriage contract was violated; that the delayed consummation between his illicit lovers is directly patterned on the formal marriage contract; and that he popularized the "nonmarital 'accord'" in literature. Jacobs claims that Chaucer initiated a new type of widow into the canon—disadvantaged, realistic—arguing against the lusty, conniving stereotype. In the section on Renaissance drama, Jacobs discusses the "trailing spouse" motif and the reintroduction of the "lusty widow myth" (p. 135) as a character born of wish fulfillment. Throughout the book she suggests insights into marriage not available through the history texts.

Although at times provocative, *Marriage Contracts* presents some real difficulties for this reviewer. In the Preface Jacobs notes that, although most of the work centers on Chaucer and his marriage contracts, the project actually began as an investigation of marriage on the *Renaissance* stage. In other words, she worked backwards. Perhaps these facts account for the lack of unity in the book. In addition, Jacobs states that *after* noting the various treatments of marriage laws, she turned to "historians" for an explanation, and she lists a number of important scholars. But with the exception of Pollock and Maitland (her bibliography lists *The History of English Law Before the Time of Edward I*—i.e., *before* 1239) these are not precisely *legal* historians, and that poses a problem.

In adhering so closely to the "literary" text and only then seeking an historical explanation, Jacobs has ignored the very legal records that would illuminate that text (or provide a proper background for it). Documents from the *Letter Books,* the *Memorials of London and London Life,* the *Munimenta Gildhallae Londoniensis,* and the various volumes of the Selden Society, which contain a wealth of material on medieval married life and law, are nowhere to be found in her study. There are, in fact, no primary legal materials listed in the bibliography. Quoting legal passages from the *Canterbury Tales* and the Renaissance plays, Jacobs speculates on what the audience might have known. The answers, however, lie in the legal texts where the "law" is revealed as multifaceted and where any such exploration must begin. The "audience," who understood that law on various levels, would not have thought with a single mind.

Missing, too, from the bibliography are authoritative secondary sources on Chaucer and Shakespeare that should have been consulted, some of which belie Jacobs's assertion that critics have neglected to discuss marriage law in its relationship to literature. (Hornsby's *Chaucer and the Law,* for example, is conspicuously missing.) A more thorough exploration of Chaucer's own oeuvre would have been helpful here. In Chapter One, for example, Jacobs suggests that if one's spouse did not live up to his or her part of the marriage contract, "adultery [would] be a moral alternative available to good people" (p. 27), and she cites the *Shipman's Tale,* and the *Franklin's Tale* as "case studies" in this approach to the law. Unless Jacobs is suggesting that the Shipman and the Franklin *themselves* advocate this "moral alternative" (an assertion impossible to prove), then it is *Chaucer* who is doing the advocating. How, then, is one to interpret the Parson's remarks that "Avowtrie" is a "cursede synne . . . the gretteste thefte that may be, for it is thefte of the body and soule"?

Jacobs's book is not easy reading. Her argument skips about and her paragraphs often veer away from their topic sentences. Sometimes a concept is not explained as soon as it should have been (the "widow problem," for example). Arguments are often structured as post hoc and straw men are set up. There are frequent slang or clichéd expressions that should have been edited out: "Chaucer *chickens out*" (p. 24), "the *guy* deserves it" (p. 25), "let them *off the hook*" (p. 27), "No priest of church has *had a finger in* [Walter's] union with Griselde" (p. 30). Jacobs does not indicate the audience level to which she has directed her book. Although she diligently translates all references to Chaucer's text, even passages that are self-evident, such as "Certainly he did not 'folwe hir wyl in al' (749) [follow her will in all]," she occasionally neglects to translate difficult phrases from the drama, such as "My fadir thynkis to flitte full ferre."

Despite my criticism of this book, its premise is an attractive one. Literature *does* reflect the law and close attention to diction and word nuances often reveals much about historical and ideological mutability. Marriage contracts are not to be taken lightly and their form does not remain static. There is considerable potential for research in this area. Jacobs's wish that "some of my readers, at least, will be moved to further the studies thus begun, and to take them in new directions undreamt of, perhaps, in this volume" (p. 158), may ultimately be granted.

MARY FLOWERS BRASWELL
University of Alabama, Birmingham

ANDREW JAMES JOHNSTON, *Clerks and Courtiers: Chaucer, Late Middle English Literature and the State Formation Process*. Angelstiche Forshungen 302. Heidelberg: Universitätsverlag C. Winter, 1998. Pp. 410. $58.00.

Clerks and Courtiers is an extremely ambitious book. Not only does it put forward a broad historical thesis about the parallel emergence of English literature and the English state, but it also sets out to critique the bulk of recent scholarly work on late medieval English vernacular writing. Although the book's subtitle singles out Chaucer, this is by no means a purely Chaucerian analysis; Johnston includes chapters on Gower, Hoccleve, Boethius, and Pecock, and intersperses his discussions of Chaucer with commentary on contemporary theoretical trends and perspectives. As with many books that cast their nets widely, there is a tension in *Clerks and Courtiers* between the overall argument advanced in the Introduction and the individual readings adduced in support of the thesis, especially in the discussions of Chaucer—a poet always difficult to submit to a confining historical narrative. Nonetheless, *Clerks and Courtiers* is a book worth reading; though many will find themselves in disagreement with its claims, and occasionally frustrated by a lack of nuance in its readings, it is a thorough response to the groundbreaking work of scholars like Lee Patterson, Paul Strohm, and Richard Firth Green, and as such, deserves serious attention.

The thesis of *Clerks and Courtiers* and the author's debts to various theorists are described in a long introductory chapter that focuses on the "problem of the middle strata" and the "state formation process." Put simply, Johnston argues that the notion of state formation derived from Norbert Elias provides a historical perspective that evades the problems inherent in Whiggish narratives of the rise of the middle class. It does so by constructing an account of the development of court society, the transformation of warriors into courtiers, and the emergence of a clerkly class of bureaucrats, especially lawyers, and by insisting on the court as the point of origin for the modern state. Johnston argues that Chaucer must be situated with reference to a foundational tension between the clerkly class and the courtiers, one produced in part by rivalry for power within the court, and particularly in relation to the king. Johnston's Chaucer is neither clerk nor courtier; he stands between the two dominant groups, resisting the two literary models they represent: moral didacticism and *fin amor*. In their place, Chaucer and his friends— chamber knights like Clanvowe and Philippe de la Vache—substituted a notion of poetry for poetry's sake, an "aesthetic of social spacelessness" (p. 378) that is ironic, ambiguous, purposeless, and formally experimental. It is, finally, an aesthetic of originality, one produced by specific social dynamics but defined in opposition to the social function of literature in its historical moment.

This brief summary of the book inevitably leaves out a number of steps in the argument, including Johnston's careful analysis of bastard feudalism, his discussion of the emergence of the clerkly class, and his examination of the notion of the "middle strata," all of which are characteristically thorough. But even this necessarily brief recounting of the thesis of *Clerks and Courtiers* illustrates the paradox that undergirds the book: on the one hand, Johnston is prone to making sweeping generalizations about historical development that are presented as wholesale revisions of commonly accepted versions of state formation and of Chaucer's place within literary history. On the other, the conclusions he reaches—with which many readers will have some sympathy—are nevertheless tried-and-true formalist claims about the Chaucerian aesthetic. In a sense, Johnston marries New Historicism and New Criticism, deriving from their union a notion of the social situatedness and historical specificity of art for art's sake, which he suggests was a revolutionary idea emerging from the particular nexus of interests at the court of Richard II. He further argues that after Chaucer—in figures such as Hoccleve, Lydgate, and Pecock—the clerkly class came to dominate literary production, coopting Chaucer as one of their own and eliminating the space he carved out for experimentation and innovation. Again, this is a familiar narrative of the fifteenth century's inability to comprehend and appreciate Chaucer's achievement, one that fits poorly with Johnston's insistence upon the careful analysis of literature *as literature*—an insistence that seems to apply largely to Chaucer alone.

Johnston develops his thesis with an extended series of readings of Chaucer—of the *Squire's Tale,* the *Franklin's Tale,* the *Tale of Sir Thopas,* the *Tale of Melibee,* the *Man of Law's Prologue and Tale,* the *Clerk's Tale* and the *Legend of Good Women*—and through analysis of Usk, Scogan, Gower, Hoccleve, Lollardy, Pecock, and visual representations of Chaucer. In the short space available here, it is impossible to do justice to the variety, depth, and complexity of these readings, each of which forms part of the overall thesis of the book and also puts forth a distinct argument. Readers will find much to engage them in each of these chapters; they are painstakingly researched and precisely argued. But as an exercise in literary criticism, *Clerks and Courtiers* is perhaps hampered by its own exhaustiveness; so broad is its scope and so thorough its attention to the critical tradition that the very qualities it identifies as distinctively Chaucerian—ambiguity, nuance, density, and complexity—are often given short shrift.

In sum, *Clerks and Courtiers* advances a thesis about Chaucer's relationship to the dominant forms of poetic identity in the fourteenth century that is well worth considering; though it is less groundbreaking than its author claims, the argument of this book will give critics much to think about as work on the emergence of English vernacular literature continues. Fifteenth-century scholars will no doubt find themselves the least satisfied with the argument rendered here, which tends to undervalue the capacity of Chaucer's immediate successors for understanding and perpetuating his poetic project, but they too will find insight in Johnston's readings of Hoccleve and Pecock. Ultimately, it is the salutary ambition of *Clerks and Courtiers* to articulate a broad vision of Chaucerian poetics and its influence; though it will not radically revise our understanding of Chaucer, the book thoroughly fulfills that ambition.

MAURA B. NOLAN
University of Notre Dame

HENRY ANSGAR KELLY. *Inquisitions and Other Trial Procedures in the Medieval West.* Variorum Collected Studies Series. Aldershot, Hants., and Burlington, VT: Ashgate Publishing, 2001. Pp. xxvi, 354. $105.00.

In the introduction to this collection of some of his important articles on medieval law, the author writes of having taken part in a television program called *The Inquisition.* When the program was aired, he found to his horror that his full and measured statements had been reduced to "a few snippets," apparently in order to make it look as though he had characterized the medieval church's inquisitorial methods as having been brought into being designedly to convict and burn alleged heretics. He seemed also to be arguing that the inquisitors were not bound by any notion of due process. He had in fact said just the reverse. Many academics will recognize the experience and remember their own chagrin in similar circumstances. In this volume, Professor Kelly has the chance to redress the balance and to present his own conclusions more fully and accurately, and he does so.

The first eight of the ten essays deal with various aspects and incidents in the history of inquisitorial process. It was introduced, or at least formally authorized for the church, by Pope Innocent III and the Fourth Lateran Council (1215). Thereafter it was taken up and used in most parts of the Western church to deal with routine disciplinary matters, including, but by no means limited to, heresy cases. Its essence was to shift the burden of prosecution from private parties (*accusatio*) to the court itself. The judge and his staff took over the function of preparing the case and carrying it forward. They could lawfully do so, however, only if there was sufficient *fama publica* to make it reasonable to suspect the person of a crime—roughly equivalent to modern "probable cause." This was important. Under the medieval *ius commune* there was to be no trial for secret faults, and due process was to be afforded to those who were brought before the courts of the church. It is quite true that these protections were not always afforded in fact. These essays show the gaps between theory and practice. But they were abuses of what was otherwise a quite legitimate method of proceeding.

In a few of the areas treated here, one might differ slightly on some questions of emphasis. An example is the right to counsel. Kelly argues forcefully that, contrary to what other historians have said, defendants before an inquisitorial tribunal were entitled to counsel. This is true in one sense. They were entitled to consult with an advocate, even to be furnished with one if poverty prevented them from obtaining counsel. But when most people today think of the "right to consel," they have in mind the ability to be represented by a lawyer and to have that lawyer conduct the defense for the benefit of the accused. The system keeps the defendant, who is by definition unsophisticated in the intricacies of legal practice, from making mistakes that may lead to his conviction. This, however, is not what the medieval *ius commune* provided. The accused had to appear in person and answer the questions put to him by the judge or the judge's agent. His lawyer could not do it for him. It was not an abuse of inquisitorial procedure to exclude participation by lawyers in this central part of the trial. It was of its essence. No proctor was permitted to take the place of the accused.

However, even where there may be differences of opinion, readers will learn much from these essays. They show clearly that there was no such thing as "The Inquisition" in the sense of there being a single and fearsome tribunal. There were many courts using the methods of the inquisition. The essays also illuminate varied aspects of European history during the middle ages, including the lives of Joan of Arc, John Wyclif, and William Lyndwood. They shed light on the literature of the time, and they convey information about several aspects of the prosecutions for witchcraft and sorcery that occurred toward the end of the middle ages. The essays also contribute materially to a subject of current scholarly interest: the history of the natural rights in the medieval *ius commune*.

In the last two essays (occupying about a third of the total number of pages), Kelly takes a leisurely look at the possible meanings of the term *raptus* in English law. Although some scholars have thought otherwise, he shows that "abduction" was more commonly meant than "rape" in the modern sense. No sexual violation was necessarily involved, and sometimes the woman herself used the court procedures to escape from an unwanted or invalid marriage. As in the first eight essays, Kelly is alert to mistaken readings and shortcomings when he detects them in the writing of other scholars. It is good to have the results collected in the Variorum Studies.

R. H. HELMHOLZ
University of Chicago

KATHRYN KERBY-FULTON and MAIDIE HILMO, eds. *The Medieval Reader: Reception and Cultural History in the Late Medieval Manuscript.* Studies in Medieval and Renaissance History, 3rd ser. vol 1. New York: AMS Press, 2001. Pp. xviii, 256. $82.50.

Like the contributions that make up a *festschrift*, the essays in *The Medieval Reader* belong together more because of the personal relationships of their authors—all were trained at the University of Victoria—than because of common subjects, methodologies, or intellectual concerns. Still, this collection seems unusually diffuse, for its offerings range from analytical studies to transcripts and editions, and concern subjects as diverse as Augustine's *Confessions* and the guide to parliamentary procedure known as *Modus tenendi parliamentum.* The essays are grouped loosely as case-studies in "professional reading" on the one hand, and "vernacular reading" on the other, but this general categorization raises more questions than it resolves. Following Malcolm Parkes, the editors and contributors understand "professional reading" to be done by those in the book-making business, those who prepare—and adapt—texts for the reading public (xi). "Vernacular reading," then, is presumably the reading done by that public for more private purposes, most often in vernacular languages rather than Latin. As the editors acknowledge, the two categories are not wholly distinct, nor do they seem wholly to account for the varieties of reading studied in this volume.

Derek Pearsall introduces the three essays on professional reading by invoking the familiar analogy between codicology and archaeology. Maidie Hilmo, the author of the first study, has indeed approached British Library MS Cotton Nero A.x archaeologically, using modern devices such as a Video Spectral Comparator and an IC8 Integrator Comparator to uncover some of the secrets of the book, its celebrated poems, and its much-maligned pictures. Hilmo suggests that the famously poor quality of the images can be meaningfully appreciated in the particular terms of contemporary iconoclastic controversies. She further proposes that the images accompanying *Pearl,* when properly understood, lead readers on an internal journey towards a "vision of peace" that is the New Jerusalem. One might not find all the details of her argument equally convincing—I was more persuaded by the comparison between the vessels at Belshazzar's feast and the furnishings of the mass, for example, than by the comparison between the *Pearl*-dreamer and the Ninevite to whom Jonah preaches. But it is clear that the pictures are relevant to the poems, and that more thinking about them is needed.

The next two essays offer interesting accounts of the evidence to be gleaned from medieval readers' (rather than medieval artists') interactions with texts. Linda Olson's study of an abridgment of Augustine's *Confessions* from Norwich shows that the local contexts in which that important text was read and the pedagogical uses to which it was put could be more important than the values of textual integrity that modern readers might presuppose. Tanya Schaap's study of two layers of marginalia in a *Piers Plowman* C-Text (MS Digby 102) neatly bridges the divide between professional reading and private (or vernacular) reading. The first annotator seems to have designed his commentary as the copy of the poem was created, whereas the second seems to have marked what interested him, only perhaps secondarily signaling to others what he considered highlights of the poem. I see no reason to assume, as does Schaap, that an interest in sexual morality meant that he was annotating for his family (90), and I wonder why "liberal" thinking on the question of Trajan's salvation is necessarily evidence of "early Protestant tendencies (91)". But the two layers of annotation, however interpreted, do provide compelling and important perspective on early readings of Langland.

This last essay might be considered to address the question of vernacular reading, since it concerns a copy of a vernacular poem annotated at least in part in English, and at least in part by a reader, rather than a producer, of the manuscript. But the "vernacular reading" section of *The Medieval Reader* begins officially with a short essay by Nicholas Watson, which introduces the three studies to follow. The first of these, Patricia A. Baer's study of Cato in *Piers Plowman,* demonstrates a deep integration of Latin with vernacular reading, arguing for the importance of Cato's *Disticha* in *Piers Plowman,* and for the increasing reverence shown Cato as the poem was revised from A- to B- to C-texts. Langland's engagement with the *Disticha* would seem to exemplify neither "professional" nor "vernacular", but a species of "authorial" reading—clearly it cannot be dismissed.

What is even more valuable than the analytical arguments advanced by the authors of this collection is their careful excavation (continuing the archaeological metaphor) of the contents of the manuscripts with which they have worked. Schaap provides helpful information in the form of appendices detailing the annotations in MS Digby 102, and the last two essays in the volume take this sort of contribution as their main goal. Arne Jönsson and Rosalyn Voaden have produced a facing-page comparison of the Middle English and Latin texts of the *Epistola solitarii ad reges* of Alfonso of Jaén, and Kathryn Kerby-Fulton and Ruth Hodie have transcribed the French *Modus tenendi parliamentum* in the Courtenay Cartulary. These are two texts from quite distinct realms of experience—mystical and parliamentary—but they both demonstrate the late-medieval importance of the vernacular, in the largest sense of the term.

The presentation of this edited material varies in its usefulness: Schaap's list provides a practical bridge between the annotations in one manuscript and a critical edition of *Piers Plowman*. Jönsson and Voaden present their two texts in a convenient juxtaposition, even though the Middle English is not a translation of the Latin; one of the benefits of such an alignment, in fact, is to highlight gaps and omissions. But the editors' choice to include the Middle English manuscript line numbers in the body of the text is less helpful, since the parenthetical numbers interfere significantly with the experience of reading. Kerby-Fulton and Hodie record the same important information about manuscript layout in a more friendly form.

I found the archaeological work of transcription and editing the most constructive aspect of *The Medieval Reader,* in part because I found the organization of essays into cases of "professional reading" and "vernacular reading" unsatisfying. Nevertheless, the strengths of this collection lie in its particularities, and the varieties of inquiry included here do provide a number of useful perspectives on late-medieval manuscript studies.

JESSICA BRANTLEY
Yale University

ETHAN KNAPP. *The Bureaucratic Muse: Thomas Hoccleve and the Literature of Late Medieval England.* University Park: Pennsylvania State University Press, 2001. Pp. x, 210. $40.00.

The central contention of Ethan Knapp's monograph is that, in addition to perceiving "Lollardy and the Lancastrians" as the shaping forces of early fifteenth-century writing, we should add a third term, "bureaucracy." Whereas we have come to think of literary and bureaucratic discourse as wholly distinct if not inimical to each other, in fact the relation of these two kinds of writing bears closer inspection. The fifteenth century witnessed three key developments: the continued separation of the principal bureaucratic offices from the king's household; the adoption of English as an official language of state; and the growing laicization of the staff of the central writing offices. Knapp situates Hoccleve within these developments, and argues for his importance "not as an eccentric but as a representative of a significant alternative to the aureate predecessors confirmed as a lineage" by later critics (p. 12).

This is a promising opening gambit; the Hoccleve of this book is indeed enmeshed in fundamentally bureaucratic culture. While Hoccleve does not emerge as exactly "eccentric," Knapp's book consistently does present him as a difficult and peculiar poet, balanced on representational knife-edges. He is more the companion of, say, Langland or Margery Kempe than he is of urbane Chaucer. Recent studies have focussed on Hoccleve as public poet (for instance, Paul Strohm's *England's Empty Throne: Usurpation and the Language of Legitimation 1399–1422* [1998], or Nicholas Perkins' *Hoccleve's "Regiment of Princes": Counsel and Constraint* [2001]). Despite the inevitably public orientation of bureaucracy, the Hoccleve of this book is, by contrast, an agonized and private figure, seeking, yet never achieving, a relation of protective and abiding presence with the powerful. The focus remains consistently on Hoccleve's works.

The title is a little misleading, since "the literature of late medieval England" doesn't get a look in. On the contrary, Knapp takes any post-Hocclevian poets out of the picture by arguing that Hoccleve has "no progeny" (p. 11). This is a missed opportunity to consider that other intensely bureaucratic fifteenth-century poet, George Ashby, whose *Prisoner's Reflections* open with a very clear reference to the opening of Hoccleve's *Series*.

Chapter 1 establishes the frame of the argument with the examples of Hoccleve's own book of bureaucratic models, the *Formulary,* and "La Male Regle." Hoccleve's bureaucratic position was liminal, poised as it was between the status of scribe and that of gentleman, between a gift and a wage economy, between membership in the king's household and a state bureaucracy. Scrutiny of both the *Formulary* and the petitionary text reveals a Hoccleve whose autobiographical particularity emerges from that liminality; it emerges only out of its obverse, bureaucratic anonymity: "The language of bureaucracy and that of autobiography are, in effect, mutually constitutive" (p. 36). After this conceptual frame the rest of the book is, reasonably enough, a largely chronological march through Hoccleve's oeuvre, beginning with *The Letter of Cupid* (Chapter 2), *The Regement of Princes* (Chapters 3 and 4), Hoccleve's polemical, anti-heretical, and devotional works (Chapter 5) and, finally, a chapter on the *Series,* which is in fact focused on the "Complaint" and "Dialogue."

(There is no sustained discussion of "Lerne to Die," a text that could have illumined the general argument).

In my view Knapp hits one real bull's eye, in his penetrating discussion of Hoccleve's Marian lyrics. The premise of the discussion is that bureaucratic patrons and divine intercessors perform very similar functions, and that Hoccleve's divine intercessors turn out to be just as unsettlingly evanescent as the earthly patrons. Knapp reveals the representational peculiarity and sophistication of Hoccleve's Marian invocations with great acumen; he argues that these texts, like the secular invocations for protection, expose their own constructedness: Mary "presents an impossible causality," in which she "remembers the faithful because of their memory of her but in which the memory of the faithful is said to be founded on Mary's precedent" (p. 153). The properly complex argument points persuasively to "a peculiarly self-reflexive spirituality" (p. 153), and to a situation in which Hoccleve is inventing his own patronal relations.

This is an account of isolation, whereby a bureaucratic intervention of sorts is designed to produce a protective presence; it threatens to fail, however, as it exposes its own making, the patron's absence, and the text's own recursiveness. Very much the same argument shapes the other chapters. Chapter 2 doesn't sort out the issue of where Hoccleve comes down in his translation of the *Epistle of Cupid* (ironic or non-ironic?), precisely because this Hoccleve isn't so decisive; instead the voice is "fragmented at its core" (p. 75). In the *Regement,* Hoccleve produces "a complaint that endlessly defers consolation, that circles back recursively . . . and never allows that consolatory dialogue to resolve itself into the monologic text of counsel" (pp. 104–5). In the same chapter, with regard to the image of Chaucer in the *Regement,* we read that "the relation of image to text does not establish Chaucer as an authority underlying Hoccleve's text but rather creates a circuit of authority, one in which Chaucer's authority supports that of the text, but is also itself created by the text" (p. 123). In the next chapter, Knapp argues that Hoccleve evokes Oldcastle's presence yet underlines his absence in the "Remonstrance." The final chapter has it that the "Dialogue" can only replicate the existential instabilities of the "Complaint": "The most significant fact about the dialogue between Hoccleve and the Friend, however, is the extent to which the formal transformation of textual complaint into verbal dialogue fails to make the problems of the earlier 'Complaint' any less insoluble" (p. 176). The presence of the friend can only point, that is, back to the solitary Hoccleve of the "Complaint," whose authentic self is an uncertain category.

At his best Knapp reads with a Derridean finesse, revealing just how strange and unsettling Hoccleve's position is. Not all the writing is at that level: some is so sophisticated as to be unconvincing (Chapter 2), and occasionally wrinkles in the book's thematic statements seem not to have been ironed out. The final sentence offers an example: we hear Hoccleve's voice not as that of "personal alienation but as a voice shaped by a shared culture" (p. 186). The actual argument is that bureaucratic writing is the product of a shared culture that repeatedly produces personal alienation.

In sum, this (beautifully produced) book advances one avenue of Hoccleve studies; it thickens the scholarly texture in laudable ways; it by no means exhausts present possibilities.

JAMES SIMPSON
University of Cambridge

KATHRYN L. LYNCH. *Chaucer's Philosophical Visions.* Chaucer Studies, vol. 27. Cambridge: D. S. Brewer, 2000. Pp. viii, 178. $75.00.

In *Chaucer's Philosophical Visions,* Kathryn Lynch proposes to take seriously the longstanding view that Chaucer is a philosophical poet, a view held during and immediately after Chaucer's own lifetime by Deschamps, Hoccleve, and Usk among others, yet one which has never been adequately conceptualized in modern criticism. As Lynch's title suggests, her focus is Chaucer's dream visions; after an initial chapter that lays out her project, she proceeds chapter by chapter through the *Book of the Duchess,* the *House of Fame,* the *Parliament of Fowls,* and the *Legend of Good Women,* with a final chapter sketching possible extensions into Chaucer's later poetry. Like most recent critics who have tried to develop the idea of a philosophical Chaucer beyond Christian moralizing and the citation of a few passages from Boethius, Lynch links Chaucer's writings to technical debates in medieval logic, epistemology, and the theory of action. Her central claim is that Chaucer knew these technical debates and engaged them directly, without thereby becoming a dogmatic poet: that he was less interested in taking up a philosophical position than in the underlying philosophical problems that provoked the debates. I find Lynch's focus on problems rather than positions to be utterly right, and some of the connections she draws to technical arguments are quite suggestive. But the book too frequently flattens out the philosophical issues it takes up, collapsing arguments and problems that are in fact distinct, and linking technical arguments to the poetry in hurried, unconvincing ways. I will concentrate on Lynch's chapter on *Parliament of Fowls;* I think it is the book's best, and taking time to lay out the issues it raises will clarify the book's strengths and limitations better than would a chapter-by-chapter survey.

Lynch begins her discussion of the *Parliament* by claiming that the erotic blockage it represents dramatizes a problem of the will rather than one of understanding. The formel eagle's stasis and inability to choose a mate is not, Lynch argues, the sign of an intellectual failure; she knows everything she needs to know to make her choice. Chaucer instead uses her stasis, like that of the narrator earlier in the poem, to explore the difficulty of accounting for agents' dispositions to act. Contrary to the Platonic argument in one standard reading of it, agents do not always pursue that which they know or believe to be good. On the other hand, part of the poem's joke in having a bird be deaf to Nature's call is that neither is there anything in nature—such as a naturally determined desire—that explains why agents act as they do. Lynch is right, I think, in arguing that Chaucer has a genuinely philosophical interest in the theory of action, that he understands what is at stake in both rationalistic and naturalistic attempts to explain action, and that the *Parliament of Fowls* investigates the appeal and the limitations of both forms of reductionism. But as she pursues her argument she gets that set of issues muddled up with others that are substantially different, with the result that none are articulated as clearly as they need to be.

The main confusion occurs in repeated shifts back and forth between questions of how to explain action and the old philosophical problem of determinism and freedom of the will. Depending on some broad assertions concerning the history of medieval ideas of the will, Lynch argues that the *Parliament* stages an unresolved debate between a determinism exemplified by the narrator and a defense of the will's freedom exemplified by the formel eagle: the narrator's paralysis is associated with a theory according to which choice is determined by one's intellectual capacities, while the formel's resistance to Nature's demands amounts to a challenge to the view that natural desire determines action. This

400

argument, however, rests on a confusion between two distinct kinds of determination. The metaphysical problem of determinism and freedom of the will concerns the question of whether agentive explanations of human behavior are compromised by the ability to explain that behavior as determined by outside forces; "determined" here usually means caused. But theories according to which action is determined by the intellect or by desire do not *compete* with agentive explanation, they *depend* on it. In both cases, the idea is not that the language of action involves a reference to an illusion, however comforting or necessary, but rather that the right way to understand action is to see how it is motivated by reason or desire. That being said, it is easy to confuse agentive and causal explanation, and naturalism in many of its forms does just that. But an analysis of naturalism should not duplicate its confusions; and furthermore, Lynch's argument concentrates on the intellectualist position, and it is very clear in all but the craziest examples of such theory that the idea that action can be explained by the intellect's grasp of one's ends is not the idea that the intellect *causes* us to act, but rather that the *reason why* we act as we do is that our intellect has grasped an end. In this sense the intellect determines the will; but there is no question here of a causal explanation, or of any other kind of explanation that could threaten to make agentive explanation seem bankrupt and so raise questions of determinism and freedom.

The book as a whole is marked by a similar failure to capture the nuances of the philosophical issues it raises. So, for example, a promising discussion of the *Book of the Duchess* as an experimental recasting of philosophical dialogue proceeds to collapse technical logical discussions of universals and singulars with epistemological skepticism, and skepticism with solipsism, and solipsism with relativism; and a discussion of the *House of Fame* that rightly locates that poem's interest in linguistic truth gives such brief attention to philosophical logic that its claim that the poem calls logic itself into question remains hyperbolic and unsubstantiated. In these and other cases, the basic difficulty is the book's reliance on a broad-strokes history of ideas that takes the place of any sustained philosophical discussion, and that practically requires for the telling of its story the lumping together of disparate arguments and problems. This has the unfortunate effect of making the book's contribution seem less significant than it is. For Lynch at times makes a compelling case that Chaucer would have had access to technical medieval philosophy and that he showed an ongoing interest in it; her discussion of John

Duns Scotus stands out for me in this regard. And even when she misarticulates the issues, she often does so in a way that reveals something important about the poetry, as she does in her discussion of the *Parliament of Fowls,* where the tendency to conflate agentive and causal explanation is part of what Chaucer is interested in and seeks to understand. From time to time Lynch worries that she must defend her picture of Chaucer against the charge that it is overly philosophical, that it loses sight of what has been called Chaucer's genial humanism by making him out to be an intellectual poet. But the genial Chaucer is pretty much dead in the water by now, and Lynch is absolutely right in stressing the intellectual seriousness of Chaucer's work. She has taken an important step in connecting that seriousness to the philosophical discussions of the thirteenth and fourteenth centuries, and towards making the idea of a philosophical Chaucer once again compelling.

MARK MILLER
University of Chicago

DAVID MATTHEWS, *The Invention of Middle English: An Anthology of Primary Sources.* Making the Middle Ages, vol. 2. Turnhout, Belgium: Brepols Publishers, 2000. Pp. x, 244. $50.00, cloth, $19.95 paper.

David Matthews has put together an anthology of selections about Middle English language and literature from George Hickes (1680) to James Murray (1915), some familiar, but many quite fresh. His title is somewhat misleading because the critical commentary far outweighs the linguistic, 181 pages to 40, simply because there was more discussion of literature than of language. He does allow that the delimiting events for Middle English were the Norman conquest and the Tudor accession, although he makes no reference to the influence of Chancery and Henry V. Matthews observes that the concept of "Middle English" is recent. Indeed, when I was at the University of Pennsylvania in the 1940s, the philological course was called "Middle English Dialects," not "Middle English." Until the middle of the nineteenth century, early Middle English pieces like Layamon's *Brut* and the *Ancrene Riwle* were designated "Semi-Saxon" and attached to Anglo-Saxon studies.

In the first selection, in Latin—conveniently translated by the editor—George Hickes (1703, p. 13) distinguishes between Anglo-Saxon, Semi-Saxon into which Anglo-Saxon developed after the Conquest, and English *(Anglicanus)* which Hickes does not date. In the third piece, Jacob Grimm in *Deutsche Grammatik* (1819, p. 22) introduces the term "Middle English" *(Mittelenglische),* adapted from his concept of "Old," "Middle," and "New" or "Modern" German. George Craik is the next to use the term "Middle English" (1851, p. 28). Eduard Mätzner, *Englische Grammatik* (1865, trans. 1874, p. 30) begins describing the Middle English inflections, but the brief selection here does not do credit to his detailed analysis of the language in the full grammar that really began to distinguish Middle English as an autonomous stage in the development of the language. George Marsh (1862, p. 33) and Carl Friedrich Koch (1868, p. 39) still designate the language as "Semi-Saxon." George Marsh is the only American to be admitted to the anthology. John Earle (1871, p. 42) uses the term "Middle English" and describes the language used by Chaucer and Gower as "the language that had formed itself in the court about the person of the monarch" (p. 48), which is a step toward recognizing Chancery and Henry V. Henry Sweet, *A History of English Sounds* (1873, p. 53), argues against any use of the term "Saxon" and for Grimm's designations that have now become standard: "Old English," "Middle English," and "Modern English." The other selections in Part One are from Thomas Warton (the selections in Part Two are more satisfactory), Gordon Latham, T. L. Oliphant, Richard Morris, and James Murray. It is unfortunate that there is nothing from Oliver Ferrar Emerson's *Middle English Reader* (1905). Indeed, it is unfortunate that Matthews' anthology is so confined to British and Continental authors. By 1890 American scholars were making substantial contributions to the invention of Middle English.

Part Two of the anthology is devoted to selections from editions and literary histories. Matthews begins with selections from the preface to Thomas Hearne's 1724 edition of the *Chronicle* of Robert of Gloucester (1300), evidently the first instance of Middle English's recognition as a distinct entity. There had been continuing allusions to and editions of Chaucer, Gower, Wycliffe, the Mystery Plays, and so on, but these had been merged into a general sense of medieval or gothic. Hearne recognizes the *Chronicle* as a significant historico-cultural document. He discusses the manuscripts and the language and his principles of editing, describing a scholarly procedure (familiar from the Classics) for the sort of editions that become standard with EETS, the Hunterian Society, the

Roxburghe Club, and other publishing societies that created the Middle English oeuvre. Matthews follows with nine pages (pp. 67–78) from various commentaries in Thomas Percy's *Reliques* (1767) which again present Middle English poetry as an autonomous body. Percy was especially interested in the bardic performance of the romances, and this topic runs through several of the following selections. Next (p. 79) come selections from various parts of Thomas Warton's *History of English Poetry* (1778), which begin to assemble the Middle English oeuvre systematically: Robert of Gloucester, Robert Manning of Brunne, Langland, Chaucer, the romances, and so on. Next come twenty-five pages of selections from five different books by Joseph Ritson (1783ff, p. 92), criticizing the content and presentation of Percy's *Reliques* and adding Layamon, Laurence Minot, Gower, Langland, Lydgate, and Malory to the Middle English list. There follow twenty-two pages of selections from prefaces to early English pieces from editions by George Ellis. In *Specimens of the Early English Poets* (1801, p. 117) Ellis published sections from and commentary on Layamon's *Brut,* the *Ormulum,* the *Land of Cokaine,* Richard Rolle, Laurence Minot, *Piers Plowman,* Chaucer, Gower, Lydgate, and several others. In *Specimens of Early English Metrical Romances* (1805, p. 133) he published and commented on various romances and poems—assembling in the six volumes most of what we now regard as the Middle English oeuvre. The twenty pages from Sir Walter Scott's edition of *Sir Tristrem* (1804, p. 138) are devoted largely to Scott's argument that the romance is by Thomas of Erceldoune, which few today accept. There are nine pages from the introduction of Thomas Whitaker's edition of *Piers Plowman* (1813, p. 170).

I shall not follow the other ten selections through in detail. Robert Southey (1817, p. 187) has some prefatory remarks about Arthurian romance in his introduction to Malory. James Heywood Markland (1818, p. 188) discusses the plays in the preface to his edition of the *Chester Mysteries.* Henry Hallam has a very sensible paragraph (1837, p. 205) on the transition from Anglo-Saxon to "English," as he calls it, without distinguishing the type of English. The selections from Thomas Wright (1846, p. 219) discuss the Robin Hood ballads. The final selection is the transcription of notes by W. W. Skeat for a lecture on "The Language of Chaucer" from the backs of exam books (ca. 1900, p. 227)—this really belongs in Part One of the anthology—followed by questions for an examination in English literature (1866, p. 239) which suggest how much students were expected to know about both the language and the content—it was a great deal. There are also selections from Henry Weber, Edward Utterson, David Laing, Frederic Madden, James Halliwell, John Robson, and Francisque Michell.

The material in the volume is interesting. Some of it is unfamiliar; it has been scrupulously annotated. But the choice and arrangement of the selections is arbitrary, and the commentary makes no effort to weave them together. There is no "argument" to the book. The selections on Language in Part One average three pages in length, which does little more than to acknowledge the existence of Semi-Saxon or Middle English. The longest, nine pages by John Earle, provides an epitome of the development of the language from Old to Modern English, but much of the space is devoted to citing Middle English texts, which might be better in Part Two. The selections in Part Two on literature average ten to twenty pages, although there are still several bits of one and two pages. And the absence of any American representative after George Marsh severely limits the comprehensiveness of the collection.

JOHN H. FISHER
University of Tennessee, Knoxville

ALASTAIR MINNIS. *Magister amoris: The* Roman de la Rose *and Vernacular Hermeneutics.* Oxford: Oxford University Press, 2001. Pp. xvi, 352. $74.00.

The great virtue of *Magister amoris,* but also the source of some difficulty in following its argument, is its simultaneous engagement with three closely related topics: medieval responses to Ovid and his poetry; the intellectual inheritance and cultural legacy of Jean de Meun's *Roman de la Rose;* and the medieval European tradition of scholastic Latin textual commentary/exegesis and its *translatio* into "vernacular hermeneutics." (This last subject has undergirded Minnis's scholarship and criticism since his *Medieval Theory of Authorship* [1984].) Minnis sees the *Rose* as the linchpin of his argument, an important point of intersection between medieval Ovidianism and the interpretive techniques of an intellectual/scholastic/clerical elite, and an analogously influential point of departure from which both traditions entered, separately and in a variety of interactions, into vernacular culture. As he puts it, "medieval literary theory, as channeled by commentary-tradition and its beneficiaries, helped to shape the reception of the *Rose,* just as it had contributed to the formation of the poem itself" (26).

The book's structure has two contextualizing chapters framing four on various aspects of Jean de Meun's *Roman de la Rose.* Chapter One, "Academic Prologues to Ovid and the Vernacular Art of Love," examines several French translations/adaptations of Ovid's *Ars amatoria* which "mark the move from classroom concerns to secular interests and fashions" (12), including the courtly rhetoric of *fin'amors,* and, in the case of *L'Art d'amours* (an anonymous adaptation by two different thirteenth-century authors), "medical discourse, which counterbalances (or perhaps challenges) the moralizing discourse . . . inherited from Latin literary theory" (13). And to complement this analysis the chapter considers "sermon prologues" to two texts much influenced by Ovidian love lore, Juan Ruiz's *Libro de buen amor* and Richard de Fournival's *Bestiaires d'amours.*

In Chapter 2, "Lifting the Veil: Sexual/Textual Nakedness in the *Roman de la Rose,*" Minnis rejects two contradictory responses to Jean's poem: the reductionism of those (such as D. W. Robertson and John Fleming) who insist on reading its myths and metaphors as consistent allegories, or *integumenta,* concealing a moral and Christian message; and the unmitigated censure by others of the *Rose*'s apparent endorsement of misogynist rhetoric, Ovidian techniques of seduction, and (in its conclusion) brutal rape. He appeals instead to the tradition of satirical writing inherited from the ancients that Jean knew and (in his "apologia" within the *Rose* [line 15221 f.]) appears to embrace: a penchant for plain speaking, as opposed to the "integumental" style (in imitation of Macrobian *narratio fabulosa*) of the twelfth-century learned Latin poets to whom Jean owed the figures of Nature and Genius. The satiric "naked text" could also be invoked to appropriate for satire Ovid's misogyny, sexual frankness, and supposed instruction in how to seduce *puellae.*

Chapter 3, *"Parler proprement:* Words, Deeds, and Proper Speech in the *Rose,*" examines Jean's "pronouncements on speech which is plain, 'proper,' and directly significative of its referents" (120). Several meanings of "proper" were at play in Jean's French, based on Latin linguistic and rhetorical theory, including literal (as opposed to metaphorical) signification, and unembellished (as opposed to ornamented) diction. These different though overlapping areas of opposition and polemic provided grist for what Minnis sees as Jean's "donnish humor" (158) when the poet has Raison defend the use of vulgar words—*coilles, coillon, vit*—to signify the genital organs, on the grounds of speaking "properly," and again when Jean describes the dreamer's ravishing and impregnating of the Rose in an extended pilgrimage metaphor which does nothing to hide the meaning (or diffuse the violence) of the sexual encounter. Chapter 4, "*Signe d'estre malles:* Genre, Gender, and the End of the *Rose*," explores the poem's problematic ending as a final instance of its "uncontrolled, subversive" wit, exemplifying "a medieval clerical sense of humor, the product of an exclusively male academic environment" (178). This environment had earlier generated the twelfth-century Latin *comediae*, which play (often crudely and in a misogynist register, but also anxiously) with the idea that "learning hinders a man's sexual performance" (181) or, in today's parlance, somehow renders him effeminate, but also suggest, especially in the widely diffused *Pamphilus*, that women, whatever their feigned resistance to male sexual desire, are in fact there for the taking (as argued in Book 1 of *Ars amatoria*).

By concluding the *Rose* with a representation of sexual intercourse calculatedly transgressive in both its use of religious imagery (pilgrims, relics) and its insistence on the act as one of male dominance, if not actually rape (which Minnis denies it is [197]), Minnis argues that Jean undercuts the religious and philosophical elements in the long speeches of Nature and (especially) Genius—not to say the courtly patina of Guillaume de Lorris's depiction of Amans's quest for the Rose. He also with this taps into "a complicated matrix of ideas which highlight male anxieties relating to emasculation and frustrated or fractured virility" (169).

Chapter 5, "Theorizing the *Rose:* Crises of Textual Authority in the *Querelle de la Rose*," examines the *prises de position* in that famous row in order to demonstrate how, in it, "a common body of ideas from commentary tradition were [sic] manipulated to serve two utterly opposed and irreconcilable points of view" (254). The participants in the *querelle* draw their arguments from principles enunciated in the *accessus Ovidiani*—for instance, that poetry of erotic love and seduction is the product of undisciplined youth; that it is instead composed as a negative example for the instruction of others; that one must distinguish between the virtue of a poet and the vices of some of his characters. They were thus able with equal authority to exalt or stigmatize Jean de Meun, re-enacting in a more serious vein the *licentia disputandi* of the schools, according to which "the same texts (*auctoritates*) could be alleged in support of diametrically opposed positions" (211). And Chapter 6, "Pruning the *Rose:* Evrart de Conty and European Vernacular Commentary," closes the frame opened in the first chapter by "seek[ing] to relocate the [anonymous, late fourteenth-century] *Eschez amoureux* and its commentary within the reception history of the *Rose*" (265). Minnis demonstrates how the labors of Evrart de Conty, author of the commentary, constitute "an attempted erasure of a substantial part of jean de Meun's legacy as *magister amoris*," substituting "a more comprehensive vision of married love" for "Jean's narrow concern with male performance of desire" (265).

Minnis endeavors to contextualize both the formation and the reception of Jean de Meun's *magnum opus* by casting a wide net across late medieval western Europe's intellectual and literary scene. But having so many texts and topics in play can have a disorienting effect on the reader. In addition, *Magister amoris* brings together material previously published in several places [see p. viii], and the repetition, sometimes literal, of observations and quotations in different chapters suggests incomplete editorial integration of this material. Furthermore, *Magister amoris* shows some signs of insufficient proofreading. (Page 172 provides a good [or bad] example: it has Jean de Meun translating the *Letters* of Abelard and Heloise in 1380, and a few lines later refers to "feeings of sexual desire.") But whatever its imperfections, Minnis's latest excursion into European cultural history not only offers a compelling new reading of Jean de Meun's *Roman de la Rose;* it also consolidates its author's reputation as a premier commentator on the shaping of later medieval vernacular literature by traditions of learned commentary on the classical *auctores.*

R. W. HANNING
Columbia University

JAMES H. MOREY. *Book and Verse: A Guide to Middle English Biblical Literature.* Urbana and Chicago: University of Illinois Press, 2000. Pp. xix, 428. $34.95.

This is a most useful finders' list of versions of the biblical narrative in Middle English. When, for example, Nicholas Love claims that he need not deal with the Lord's Prayer *in extenso* because it is already treated in many places, in both Latin and English, it is useful to be able to check just how many Middle English translations of the Lord's Prayer there were, in how many manuscripts, and where to find them in print. The guide is divided into "Comprehensive Old and New Testament Works" (for instance, *Cursor Mundi,* but also "Versions of Robert Grosseteste's *Chateau d'Amour"* and *The Charter of the Abbey of the Holy Ghost*), "Primarily Old Testament Works," "The Psalter," "Canticles and Hymns," "Miscellaneous Old Testament Pieces," "Primarily New Testament Works," "*Temporale* Narratives," "Passion Narratives," "Miscellaneous New Testament Pieces," "Lectionaries," "Prose Commentaries and Lives of Christ," "Epistles" and "Versions of Revelation," with a comprehensive bibliography and indices of references to individual chapters of the Bible; of people, places, and events; and of manuscripts. The introduction to the volume discusses, in separate chapters, "The Medieval Idea of the Bible," "The Official Reception of Biblical Literature," "The Place of English in Post-Conquest England," and "Genre, Audience, and Self-Representation." The tenor of this introduction, as of the volume as a whole, may be summed up in a statement from its conclusion: "Once aware of the number, variety, and extent of vernacular materials which transmitted a sense of biblical literature to lay audiences from the twelfth into the fifteenth century in England, one is tempted to ask facetiously, 'who needed Wyclif?'" (85).

In this attitude, Morey joins Wyclif's fourteenth- and fifteenth-century critics and, like them, he misses the point. For what Wyclif's supporters and followers wanted was not "material" that "transmitted a sense" of biblical "literature." As Kantik Ghosh in particular has recently demonstrated, the traditional "literature" of the Bible consisted primarily of narratives with built-in interpretations, narratives that increasingly, in the face of Wycliffite pressure, became conscious of their own dubious textual authority. What the Wycliffite movement accomplished was a transformation of the discursive field in which what counted as knowledge of the Bible was completely changed, and literature that transmitted only a sense of what the Bible said was no longer sufficient.

This anti-Reformation bias, posed in pre-postmodern critical terms (one thinks of Eamon Duffy's *Stripping of the Altars* here) does not decrease the utility of Morey's guide in the least. The only problems that I found with it were its tendency to depend entirely on already printed sources (the section on the Lord's Prayer, for example, "covers only those versions . . . that appear in print," and refers the reader Aarts' *Paster Noster of Richard Ermyte*), and an inclination to uncritical fullness similar to that which Morey describes in Peter Comestor: "Differences between authorities were not ignored, and though [the author] presented various readings . . . he was more interested in weighing than in resolving them" (6).

For example, the McGill University Library manuscript often described as a fragment of the *Cursor Mundi* (although, at 8 × 13 cm and 22 lines per page, the complete manuscript would—at 500 + folios—have been far thicker than it was wide or long) is listed among *Cursor* manuscripts here, with a note that M. G. Sargent demonstrated years ago that it was actually a fragment of the Southern English poem on the Assumption, a poem that the *Cursor* author himself admits to inserting into his own narrative. The "Southern Assumption," on the other hand, since its narrative is extra-biblical, is not listed in Morey's guide, and its other manuscripts are not referred to. The mistaken attribution of the poetic "Meditations on the Supper of Our Lord" to Robert Manning of Brunne is duly recorded as "has been doubtfully attributed," when it would have been far more helpful to note that George Howard Naish (and note Idelle Sullens's edition of Brunne's *Handlyng Synne*) really did settle the question years ago. This is an important error, since it still misleads discussions of the dating, and thus the attribution, of the *Meditationes Vitae Christi*. Or again: the Wycliffite sermon cycle edited by Anne Hudson and Pamela Gradon, despite Hudson's able demonstration that there are no surviving English works by John Wyclif, is described as "Wycliffe's own sermon cycle."

There are also, as always in such surveys, gaps that one would have liked to see filled. The two most obvious sources of lay knowledge of scripture in the Middle English period, for example, the drama and sermons, are given short shrift. The drama is excluded categorically (as all too often in such surveys), and only printed collections of sermons are included.

A few times, there is a failure to follow up on bibliographic ramifications: William Dunbar's and Walter Kennedy's poems on the passion of Christ are both referred to their partial source, the *Vita Christi* of Ludolph of Saxony; but unless the reader already knows that it was Elizabeth Salter who demonstrated this textual dependence in her article on the Middle English versions of Ludolph, he or she will not know where to find the argument. But complete cross-referencing would, of course, have resulted in an unmanageable book. These problems aside, Morey's is still an extremely useful source book, and a welcome addition to any Middle English scholar's set of reference tools.

MICHAEL G. SARGENT
Queens College and the Graduate Center, City University of New York

RUSSELL A. PECK, ed., with Latin translations by Andrew Galloway. *John Gower: Confessio Amantis, Volume 1*. Kalamazoo: Medieval Institute Publications, Western Michigan University, 2000. Pp. x, 363. $20.00, paper.

This is the first part of a projected three-volume TEAMS edition of the whole of Gower's *Confessio Amantis*. It contains the Prologue (in both original and revised forms), and Books I and VIII. Subsequent volumes will include Books II–IV and V–VII respectively. At first blush, the decision to abandon a strictly chronological sequence in this first volume is curious, but the pedagogical case for doing so is strong: to have the key opening and concluding parts of the narrative in one volume is of clear value for teaching so long a work.

The text itself is primarily based on Bodleian, Fairfax 3, with some parallel passages from Bodley 902 and Bodley 294 (where the former is defective) for the variant portions of the Prologue. It has been regularized according to the established principles of this series. There are on-page modern glosses for the Middle English. The text itself is preceded by a lengthy Introduction and Bibliography (pp. 1–59) and followed by Explanatory Notes (283–355), Textual Notes (356–58) and Glossary (359–63).

In his Preface Peck pays proper tribute to Macaulay's great edition and his text generally seems to follow his predecessor's. Occasional forms seem either mistranscribed or to require emendation, as at 1.2092, which reads here "His brother ne was redi there." The sense seems to require "His brother he was . . ."; at 8.2175 where the form "briest" is rhymed with "prest"; presumably it should be "brest"; at 8.2226 "ayer" should perhaps be "a yer."

The greater potential value of Peck's work must lie less in textual innovation than in its capacity to make the work accessible to a student audience through its glossing and annotation. Glossing is always where an editor will give most hostages to fortune, especially with Gower, where the extent of the difficulty in producing succinct and accurate modern renderings of his Middle English is considerable. At the beginning of Book I, for example, I found myself needing help with such formulations as "loves lawe is out of reule" (I.18) and "Of love tempre the mesure" (I.23), but not finding any. Elsewhere, glossing seems inexact, at times; thus in "the rihte salve of such a sor" (1.33), "sor" is glossed as "ailment"; but in the context of "salve" it clearly means "sore." Again, at 1.565: "I am topulled in my thought," "topulled" is glossed as "pulled to pieces"; it surely means "pulled this way and that." Throughout I found a steady trickle of words or phrases likely to pose difficulty not just to the undergraduate. Conversely, it hardly seems necessary to gloss "daies olde" (1.2272) as "olden days."

The annotation is largely quite hopeless. The bulk of the notes are not actually annotation but the text and translation of the Latin glosses to the *Confessio* (not always happily presented; see, for example, 8.1141 ff. where one finds such forms as "Qualtier" and "relinguqens"). But this seems the only consistent element in the notes. Although occasionally proverbial phrases are noted from Whiting, a number are not; for example, 1.35 = Whiting L 518; 8.2102-3 = Whiting F 466. At times, passages are asserted to be proverbial but no Whiting number is given (see 8.2412; the omission is understandable since the phrase is not).

Nor are other suggestive forms of words noted, including ones with insistent Chaucerian resonances. Thus, 1.47: "For love is blind and may noght se" seems to invite some reference to CT IV. 1598, or indeed to 8.2104 ("Thus love is blind and can noght knowe"). Similarly, 1.100–101: "And that was in the monthe of Maii, / Whan every brid hath chose his make" seems to recall *PF,* 309–10; "For this was on Seynt Valentynes day, / Whan every foul cometh there to chese his make." Again, the reference to "Some of the lef, some of the flour" (8.2468), clearly invites some reference to the Prologue to *Legend of Good Women* or to the numerous other references to this courtly game.

Other explanatory notes have in common a lack of clarity or tendentiousness. At 1.45 the phrase "herte rote" prompts a note running to nearly a page on medieval amatory and medieval views of the heart, when all that is required is a gloss. At 1.1339–40, the play on "forme

. . . enforme" prompts a lengthy and scarcely intelligible summary of seemingly unrelated arguments by James Simpson. At 1.1769 ("go we to bedde"), the reader is referred to an article "on Gower's use of subjunctive mood rather than imperative mood, which he uses very little" (317). It would seem more useful simply to gloss the imperative. There are quite a lot of these "woods-for-trees" problems here, at times seemingly the product of considerable confusion. For example, this note on 8.1696:

Avoi. An exclamation of surprise, fear, or/and remonstrance. Perhaps the best gloss would be something like "Ouch," combined with "What do you take me for?" "Stop it!" "Hold on!" or "Don't do that!" (341)

The prolix futility of all this is underscored when one turns to the text and finds the perfectly adequate gloss "Desist!" (238).

The commentary would have benefited from far more succinctness as well as more consistency. Above all, it would have benefited from regular consultation of, and reference to, Peter Nicholson's *Annotated Index to the Commentary on Gower's* Confessio Amantis (1989), the existence of which makes any commentator's life a lot simpler.

It is easy to snipe at any edition in a short review, especially an edition aimed at a student audience, where the expository rather than the scholarly is the proper mode. I feel the examples I have noted are representative of the problems in this edition, not just isolated aberrations. It does seem that an opportunity to present Gower constructively to students has been missed. Yet I must end by commending Russell Peck for producing an edition that is certainly going to be used for teaching purposes and also for his much wider services both to Gower and the TEAMS series, of which he has been general editor since its inception. In these respects he deserves our gratitude as scholars and teachers.

A. S. G. EDWARDS
University of Victoria

JIM RHODES. *Poetry Does Theology: Chaucer, Grosseteste, and the Pearl Poet.* Notre Dame: University of Notre Dame Press, 2001. Pp. xi, 324, $54.95 cloth, $24.95 paper.

As Jim Rhodes demonstrates in this readable and extremely intelligent book, the diverse ways in which Chaucer, Grosseteste, and the *Pearl-*

poet treat theological themes are intricate and subtle. Unlike many other scholars who have recently brought theology to bear on medieval poetry, Rhodes seeks "to offset the growing tendency to reduce poetry to the status of a document and to show that poetry is a significant discourse unto itself and that it has its own interests" (2). True to plan, Rhodes repeatedly invokes general literary and philosophical authorities alongside his principal medieval primary and secondary sources—for instance, Adorno, Bakhtin, Bataille, Benjamin, Iser, Ricoeur, Rorty, and Rushdie rub shoulders with Anselm, Aquinas, Boccaccio, Bultmann, Courtenay, Dante, Kötting, Pelikan, Pieper, and Southern—and illuminating conjunctions abound.

Chapter 1, "Poetry and Theology," includes a useful survey of the variety and vitality of late medieval English theology. The chapter ends with an excellent essay on Chaucer's *Nun's Priest's Tale* and the contrasting *Monk's Tale* (a prolepsis of the book's final chapter, which treats four other tales by Chaucer, also paired off for comparative analysis). What we begin to appreciate, and what the rest of the book illustrates in detail, is the way Chaucer and other late medieval vernacular poets could "do theology" creatively, and often with passion, at a time when many writers were afflicted by a sense of "the absence of God's truth" (25).

Chapter 2 starts from Grosseteste's *Le chateau d'amour,* a mediocre Anglo-Norman poem by an important English theologian, and ends with a postscript on the topos of the Four Daughters of God in *Piers Plowman*. Rhodes focuses his analysis on the Anglo-Norman text but also draws on a fuller Middle English version in order to point out additions, omissions, and alterations in a work that "gave medieval audiences a greater purchase on the christological and incarnational elements apparent in the poetry of Chaucer, Langland, and the *Pearl*-poet" (51). Rhodes claims, convincingly, that the poem's main argument on behalf of "the goodness of the Creation and the centrality of human beings in it epitomizes what is most English about English theology" (55). (A recent book by Hugh White, *Nature, Sex, and Goodness in a Medieval Literary Tradition* [Oxford, 2001], makes a similar case—and tends to confirm Rhodes's main insight, because it does so with reference mainly to vernacular texts other than those featured in Rhodes's book.)

In Chapter 3, on the *Pearl*-poet, Rhodes makes the painful decision to omit *Sir Gawain and the Green Knight,* presumably because the theological themes in *Sir Gawain* have already called forth several books and

414

at least a few dozen major articles. In his interpretations of the other three poems by the *Pearl*-poet *(Cleanness, Patience,* and *Pearl),* and in a closing section on the anonymous but stylistically and thematically related *Saint Erkenwald*, Rhodes proves the relevance of theological trends explored in previous chapters (in addition, medieval Aristotelian and other political theories are helpfully brought to bear on *Saint Erkenwald*).

In a twenty-page essay that from now on should be on any short list of the best criticism of *Pearl*, Rhodes adopts a Bakhtinian dialogical approach. In analyzing the use of the Vineyard parable, Rhodes finds that the *Pearl*-poet "prefers to sustain the paradox built into the parable and its several levels of meaning so that the impasse between the parties serves as a provocation that frustrates closure and allows questions about social justice and divine justice to arise naturally from the situation that exists" (141). (The shrewd discussion of the Vineyard parable, like that of the Wedding Feast parable discussed in relation to *Cleanness,* would have been enriched had Rhodes consulted Stephen Wailes's *Medieval Allegories of Jesus' Parables* [Berkeley, 1987].)

Rhodes's reading of *Patience*—my favorite in the *Pearl*-poet chapter— entails a spirited defense of Jonah, in all his flawed humanity. Rhodes's convincing treatment of the *Pearl*-poet's paraphrase of the Book of Jonah includes, among other rewarding surprises, a strikingly apt comparison between Jonah in the Middle English poem and the figure of Samson in Milton's *Samson Agonistes*. Finally, the argument for a recuperated Jonah is brilliantly summed up in a concluding paragraph:

Jonah is, then, a far better example of the beatitude than anyone could have anticipated at the outset. This prophet, this all-too-human everyman, this visionary and this willful example of short-sightedness, this emissary from eternity and this man mired in human time, is the "point," the dividing line between time and eternity, sacred time and human time, who binds us to God's will at the same time that he liberates us from it. This is the *Patience*-poet's vision. . . . the last line of *Patience* does not lead us out of this world or out of the poem; it leads us inexorably back to the beginning—back to the world, back to ourselves, back to Jonah—but, as a new beginning. (125)

Chapter 4 treats four of the *Canterbury Tales,* discussed in pairs: Prioress–Second Nun, and Reeve-Pardoner. "Dramatic" readings of individual Canterbury tales in relation to the personalities of their pilgrim-tellers are currently out of fashion, but they get a new lease here, as

Rhodes proves that Chaucer used "theological discourse" as material to be "dramatized or worked out" in the tales of all the pilgrims in the *Canterbury Tales* (6). Though the limitations of space forbid me, it would be easy to show how Rhodes's analyses of Chaucer's tales move beyond familiar interpretive conclusions by expanding upon or cogently revising those conclusions in light of the theological themes each tale explicitly or implicitly contains.

In closing, some technicalities: the book is handsomely designed and solidly constructed, and the proofreading seems close to flawless. To sum up: Rhodes's book definitely breaks new ground by advancing our understanding of the theological facets of Ricardian literature. Questions, of course, remain: for example, in addition to the absence of *Sir Gawain,* one might also ask, where is Gower? And surely other Canterbury Tales could be illuminatingly discussed from a similar interpretive perspective? One assumes that Rhodes will want to address these and other questions in future essays and books; the excellent quality of the present book suggests that his answers should be eagerly awaited.

LAWRENCE BESSERMAN
The Hebrew University of Jerusalem

ELIZABETH ROBERTSON and CHRISTINE M. ROSE, eds. *Representing Rape in Medieval and Early Modern Literature.* New York: Palgrave, 2001. Pp. ix, 453. $45.00.

This stunning collection of well-written, rigorous essays responds to the social and moral imperatives in our reading and teaching of medieval and Renaissance literature, perceiving a political "urgency," particularly for "feminist readers." Robertson and Rose, dedicating the work to their fathers but also to "mothers, daughters and sisters everywhere" (p. i), want us to learn to see in the history of representations of rape the history of violation, violence, legal control, and oppression that exists beyond the fiction, beyond the trope, beyond the often male-authored literary use of rape. As Rose, reversing Chaucer's Miller, puts it, "(wo)men *shal* maken ernest out of game" (22). Some of the individual readings seem, at first, outlandish: the *Reeve's Tale* is a scene of "double rape"; Sir Gawain is metaphorically raped; Spenser metaphorically rapes

Queen Elizabeth in Book 3 of the *Fairie Queene*. But however extreme these formulations may initially seem, they purposefully draw our attention to the complicated implications of texts in which rape or the threat of rape signals a social, legal, physical reality not readily apparent on the surface and not necessarily part of the text's intended meaning.

Robertson and Rose want to lift the veil and expose a dark underside so as to provide for students and readers of these texts the empowerment of agency and resistance. "Espousing a paradigm of reading that is relevant for feminist scholars and teachers," they want to expose the control of the processes of knowing in the history of representations of rape and to draw attention to "overlook[ed] sexual violence" so as to articulate the "complex aesthetic response required of readers attuned to reading rape" (8). The editors' goal throughout is to prove that "stories of sexual violence against women serve as foundational myth of western culture," that "the contours of sexual violence have altered surprisingly little over the past thousand years" (15), and that rape "makes manifest the specifics of a given culture's understanding of the female subject in society" (2). The essays "explore the artistic thread that links early depictions of rape to contemporary rape, a thread that although twisted in different ways, at different times will remain unbroken as long as sexual access to women is controlled by patriarchal structures" (7). The editors and the author of the afterward, Christopher Cannon, know that they are being provocative and daring, and they invite readers to challenge the ways in which the essays read rape (and read "not-rape" as "rape"). Thus, even though Cannon's afterward (portrayed here as an "aftermath") (411 ff.) explicitly "hope[s]" that the book's readings of these "happenings" will be "accepted and confirmed, extended and repeated," he nonetheless avers that this might be as great a failure as if they were to be "implicitly or explicitly reversed." The editors are less interested, then, in providing unalterable objective answers than in undoing the traditional processes of certainty authored throughout history by men and woven into the tropes and images of literary rape.

The essays vary in the intensity with which they adopt the book's provocative thesis and are thus by no means univocal, but they all provide important and detailed analysis of the literary and cultural history of rape as they confront English, French and Latin texts from the twelfth to the sixteenth century. The first three essays comprise "Reading and Teaching Rape." First, Rose reads the *Reeve's Tale* as the scene of "double rape" in an attempt to undo simple fabliau laughter. Her chapter con-

417

tinues the theoretical and pedagogical imperatives outlined in the introduction, arguing that reading rape in Chaucer "can be a way to sensitize our students and to help effect social change. . . ." potentially "spawn[ing] a society that encourages fewer rapists" (3). Mark Amsler makes telling and important distinctions between the reception of Ovidian tales of rape in academic commentaries and in the hands of Christine de Pizan and Chaucer, who often transcend potentially sterile mythographic allegories and "regender narratives of rape" (93), though the approaches of these two vernacular authors differ greatly. Monica Brzezinski Potkay makes the bold assertion that Gawain is metaphorically raped in *Sir Gawain and the Green Knight* but makes a convincing argument for violence in the poem by arguing that "courtesy, the language of seduction, can all too easily slide into a language of compulsion that at least threatens the use of physical force against women" and finally that Gawain is "subjected to an experience that, like rape, destroys his physical and psychic integrity" (99).

The next section, on "The Philomel Legacy," begins with a reprint of E. Jane Burn's classic essay on the Old French *Philomena* in which she argues that the actions of the sisters, these "violent, creative women," "kill off the conventions that oppress them," and form an "alternative bonding between women" (156, 155). Working on the same text, Nancy Jones plays upon puns based on Philomena (fil = thread, fille = daughter) and compellingly explores female expression and the fragility of twelfth-century familial relations and marital practices. In an essay with deeply tragic overtones, Robin Bott explores Chaucer's *Physician's Tale* and Shakespeare's *Titus*, where the raped woman becomes analogous to a disease that harms family and society, "making the destruction of the raped woman not only permissible, but also highly desirable" (190). In another deeply disturbing but hopeful piece, Karen Robertson studies how *Titus* reinforces "Tudor homiletic prohibitions of anger for women" by excising Procne and thus "transform[ing] the gender of the avenger" (214–15). Robertson was inspired by a class where one-fifth of the women admitted that they had been raped and insisted that the text be understood "from the position of their twentieth-century experience of sexual violence" (229).

Part Three concerns "law, consent and subjectivity," beginning with Anne Howland Schotter's "Rape in the Medieval Latin Comedies," "texts written by clerics in northern France during the twelfth-century revival of classical learning as rhetorical exercises for adolescent males learning the trivium" (214); these texts can condone rape but can also advocate seduction over ravishment, reflecting attitudes in canon law that privilege the couple's will and freedom over parental consent. Chapter 9 reprints of one of Chris Cannon's essential articles on Chaucer and the Chaumpaigne release, here exploring how in our uncertainty in defining the meaning of the release, we have not listened adequately to how Chaucer's own writing "shows him to have defined such grayness with precisely the situational and philosophical specificity we have lacked" (257). Co-editor Robertson then discusses rape, consent, and female subjectivity in the *Troilus,* reading Criseyde's plight through legal and ecclesiastical documents on rape and ravishment, documents that alternately abrogate female consent and confirm the autonomy of the female will and soul. Criseyde thus represents an "emergent female subject" whose "subjectivity" even "Chaucer cannot know or control," however "little efficacy" this offers her, as a woman "with no social identity or role outside of a sexual one" (304). Amy Greenstadt explores in Sidney the tension between "rapture" as an "aesthetic experience and as an immoral sex act" in the *Old Arcadia* and in the *Apology for Poetry.*

Part Four concerns the "canonical artist, the feminist reader, and male poetics," beginning with Susan Frye's argument that Spenser in the rape of Amoret in *Fairie Queene,* Book 3, conducts metaphorical rape of Queen Elizabeth in an attempt to "enforce the meaning of chastity as male-determined and male-possessed" (355). In the volume's final essay, Katherine Eggert explores how the *Fairie Queene* "schizophrenically careens" between "a poetics of rapture and a poetics of rape" (401).

The editors begin the collection with a strong appeal: "we urge readers to face squarely the literal violence against women so often represented and too often easily passed over as merely metaphoric in Western art, while stressing our need to scrutinize the ways in which these representations reveal the deep structures of cultures that tolerate rape" (7–8). Readers will have to decide if such an interpretation of art, culture, and social history will be part of their scholarship and pedagogy, as Rose and Robertson so dramatically urge. But however one evaluates the viability of the book's sociological aims, the level of scholarship and close textual analysis in the entire volume is so high that it will be difficult to read the texts studied here without confronting the real histories of power and violence that lie behind the tropes and fictions we have been accustomed to accept. The editors rightly call this confrontation feminist resistance, but I see it also as a testimony to the works themselves, which indeed invite us (most clearly in Chaucer) to read beyond the initial representations, as the scholars here have compellingly done. They have lifted the veil from the poetic illusion. What we do with the often harsh reality beneath will have to be answered in the unfolding future of our criticism and pedagogy.

MICHAEL CALABRESE
California State University, Los Angeles

SARAH SALIH, *Versions of Virginity in Late Medieval England.* Cambridge: D. S. Brewer, 2001. Pp. ix, 278. $75.00.

Versions of Virginity provides a welcome reassessment of established assumptions about the place of virginity in medieval culture. Sarah Salih's explicit aim is to redefine the way virginity has been interpreted, especially by feminist scholars, and the resulting study amply bears out her Lévi-Straussian claim that "virgins are good to think with" (9–10). She sees chastity as a "strategy"—a "deployment, not a denial, of the body" (8). She therefore takes exception to the exclusive model based on work of Caroline Bynum that conceives of female piety only in terms of "fleshliness and abjection." She also claims that "there is no single authoritative 'Church's view of virginity,' just as there is no single church, but a 'site of many competing discourses of piety and politics'" (21).

After her introductory challenge to current scholarship on medieval women and a fundamental chapter, "Towards a Theory of Virginity," Salih develops her ideas about virginity as "multiple and unstable identity" and "ongoing process/performance" in discussions of hagiographic texts of virginity (focusing on the Katherine group), historical practices of virginity in the convent, and the *Book of Margery Kempe.* Unlike some studies whose theoretical introduction is more or less forgotten once the main texts are engaged, Salih's exploration of virginity maintains its theoretical vigor and rigor throughout the five chapters of the book. Despite the fact that her book makes for continuously interesting reading, the value of this study is less in new readings of specific texts and practices than in the redefined theory of virginity for which they are test cases.

"Performing Virginity," the wide-ranging third chapter, examines the thirteenth-century texts known as the Katherine group—consisting of legends of virgin martyrs Katherine of Alexandria, Margaret of Antioch, and Julian of Niocomedia, with didactic works on virginity and the anchoritic life. Virginity of the martyr type is then compared to that of repentant prostitutes and virgin transvestites in other hagiographic genres. Salih reads saints as cultural constructs that may be variably appropriated rather than proposing one inevitable and ahistorical interpretation of such figures. She asserts that "Different readings and rewritings of hagiography are likely to occur because saints' lives tend to point to areas of contested value" (44).

She builds on the work of Karen Winstead, Jocelyn Wogan-Browne, and Sheila Delany to argue against the conventional feminist reading which assumes a universal and unchanging meaning to the violence enacted upon the female body in medieval legend and literature. Judith Butler's concept of an "embodied performance" of gender identity provides the theoretical basis for moving away from influential theories of spectatorship, especially Laura Mulvey's, in which the "active male gaze on the passive, eroticised female spectacle" is the "paradigm for reading the torture scenes" in martyr legends (80). For Salih, the virgin martyr is in control of her own performance because "she understands the politics of spectacle" (78). Salih rejects readings of martyrdom as pornographic or as symbolic rape, positing instead that the torture victim may be in a position of power and resistance to social norms, while the spectator may be not just misguided but vulnerable. The martyr legends seek to distinguish voluntary virgins from other women, while legends of transvestite virgins or penitent prostitutes reveal the fluidity of gender negotiations, also destabilizing the gender binary.

Chapter 4, "Containing Virginity," takes up the historical space reserved for virginity, the nunnery. Although nuns did read legends of the virgin martyrs, which often functioned to oppose worldly gender norms, monastic practice envisaged a different configuration of virginity as "feminized, communal, and recoupable" (109). Salih examines various Rules and other monastic texts, including Christina of Markyate's *Life* and visitation records, to show how monastic discourse produced virginity as *habitus* in Bourdieu's sense of embodied practice. Heloise, who asserted that her perfect external discipline to the Rule masked a rebellious will, thus challenges the assumption that exterior discipline produces the proper spiritual interior.

Salih takes up the vexed question of whether nuns should be regarded as a subcategory of women or of monks, concluding that "the fragility and fleshliness of secular, sexually active women are thus held to be relevant to nuns, despite their consecration" (118), and the result was a demand for stricter enclosure of female monastics in order to preserve their virginity. The story of Christina of Markyate shows how tenuous that virgin identity was, for Christina had escaped her parents' marital plans for her dressed as a man, then adopted monastic dress while remaining in hiding for several liminal and culturally unintelligible years, until she could take a public vow of virginity with its legible signs of veiling and affiliation with a community.

The chapter also traces the tension between calls for strict enclosure of nuns (the 1298 decretal *Periculoso*) and the more relaxed Rules that allowed monastic walls to be "permeable membranes rather than watertight seals," in the words of Penelope Johnson (140). Monastic virginity was a process in which the boundary between the ideal and the historically contingent was in constant negotiation. Salih argues that "the texts which are most informative about the logic of monastic virginity are those which deal with its failures" (165), that is, Christina of Markyate, Heloise, and the nun of Watton.

Chapter 5, "Like a Virgin?" focuses on the *Book of Margery Kempe,* an account of a performance of virginity that takes place in public, outside monastic enclosure. Margery attempts to create "her own codes of virginity, to perform an identity" other than bourgeoise, wife, and mother, and, in the process, "rediscovers the radical potential of hagiographic virginity" to offer "oppositional power" (166). Like the virgin martyrs, Margery makes a spectacle of herself, flaunting her difference because spectacle is a position that can be manipulated to generate her "disruptive sanctity" (216). Given the overwhelming amount of recent scholarship on the *Book* and Margery Kempe, Salih does a creditable job of acknowledging the work of others while—like Margery—negotiating her own distinctive path among competing discourses of sanctity, conversion, martyrdom, and virginity. Salih argues that Margery develops her personal version of remade virginity as the basis for her socio-religious career as apostoless and mystic (180), and she further argues that "Margery's virginity is so provisional and unstable because she pushed the cultural resources available to her to the limit" (185). Ultimately, Salih suggests that Margery, in her semiotic multiplicity performing the "messiness" of historical process, may herself be the "paradigm of virginity on earth" (241).

Versions of Virginity is a rewarding study of a complex topic. Although the book focuses on later medieval English texts and practices, Salih draws on materials from a thousand-year span, and her insights are pertinent across many disciplines. What I most appreciated about the book, however, was the strong and flexible argumentative voice and the courage with which it intervenes in the politically-laden discussion of medieval women's piety.

KATHLEEN ASHLEY
University of Southern Maine

VICTOR I. SCHERB. *Staging Faith: East Anglian Drama in the Later Middle Ages.* Madison, N.J.: Fairleigh Dickinson University Press; London: Associated University Presses, 2001. Pp. 273. $45.00.

East Anglia, as Victor Scherb astutely observes, was the "West End or Broadway" of late medieval England. On the basis of linguistic and codicological evidence, nearly one-third of the pre-Reformation corpus of religious drama in English can be ascribed to the East Anglian counties (Norfolk, Suffolk, and portions of Essex and Cambridgeshire). Yet for most of the twentieth century, critical emphasis on the northern biblical cycle plays obscured this important statistic, and only recently has the concept of a regionally specific East Anglian dramatic tradition begun to figure in scholarly accounts of late medieval English literature and culture. *Staging Faith* is the first study to focus exclusively and comprehensively on that dramatic tradition.

The title of this book succinctly condenses its argument: late medieval East Anglian drama was a theater whose expressions of spiritual and religious interest were inseparable from the public performances through which these were conveyed. Like Gail McMurray Gibson's influential formulation of an East Anglian "theater of devotion," Scherb's "stages" of faith recognize the nondramatic components of this expression, the material monuments as well as the "more scripted cultural forms" (12) that collectively have come to be seen as signatures of East Anglian piety in the late Middle Ages. But this book departs from Gibson's through its central focus on the modes of theatrical practice and organization that characterize performances of East Anglian devotional theater and its systematic consideration of all of the region's major dramatic texts. Although it incorporates material from a number of Scherb's previously published articles on East Anglian drama, this book presents that material in the context of an overarching argument about regional theatrical traditions that is wholly new.

Early sections of the book "set the stage" for the detailed analyses of these texts that occupy its later chapters. Chapter 1 briefly surveys the extant corpus of East Anglian dramatic texts and fragments, ranging from the thirteenth-century *Cambridge Prologue* to the late fifteenth- and early sixteenth-century plays of the Digby manuscript, and provides an overview of salient features of late medieval East Anglian society, spirituality, and textual production. Looming large in the region's rich field of cultural activity is dramatic performance, whose sophisticated theatricality and variety of venues, methods, and auspices are attested to in extant dramatic records and, more intriguingly, in notices of performance practice that appear regularly in East Anglian dramatic texts. Chapter 2 examines religious dimensions of theatrical practice, emphasizing East Anglian drama's penchant for devotional and mnemonic spectacle and its frequent representation of sacred rite and discourse. These preoccupations are reinforced by conventions of staging that enable and encourage the manipulation of dramatic images for ideological and symbolic effects.

Subsequent chapters demonstrate the convergence of devotional aim and dramatic technique, cutting across more familiar ways of structuring analyses of the plays, such as by genre or manuscript, and grouping them instead in terms of possibilities afforded by specific types of staging. Chapter 3 analyzes what Scherb calls "simple place-and-scaffold" staging in the Croxton *Play of the Sacrament* and in two plays from the Digby manuscript, *The Killing of the Children* and *The Conversion of Saint Paul*. This flexible mode of performance employs techniques such as dramatic tableaux and processions to "dramatize conversion, transformation, and transcendence" (66–67). The shifting theatrical spaces of this type of staging produce fluid relationships between audience and performance; whereas the *Play of the Sacrament,* for example, formally includes its audience in the procession that embraces a newly integrated Christian community near its conclusion, *The Conversion of Saint Paul* liminally positions its audience between sacred and profane spaces.

Mankind and *Wisdom,* the subject of Chapter 4, exhibit even more indeterminate conventions of staging. Contributing to wide-ranging speculations about possible auspices for these plays, the absence of formal settings in each case also underscores the "intimate relationship between actor and audience" (107). Performance under these conditions involves the audience directly in the very dilemmas faced by the plays' protagonists, who must choose between the formal rhetoric and stately expression of icons of virtue such as Wisdom and Mercy, and the carnal and kinetic pleasures offered by the vice figures who command such a large part of these plays' indeterminate stage. Scherb's analysis of the intricate relationship between dramatic action, image, and spiritual intent in these Macro moralities has the additional benefit of emphasizing their structural and ideological similarities more than any previous study has done.

In Chapter 5 Scherb turns to the East Anglian plays of broad theatrical and spiritual ambition, the large-scale, multiple scaffold and platea stages of *The Castle of Perseverance,* the N-Town Passion Plays, and the Digby *Mary Magdalene.* Depicting the sweep of universal, biblical, and human time, these plays nonetheless employ the same repertoire of techniques as other forms of staging identified by Scherb; they "serve as virtual *summas* of East Anglian dramatic practice" (146). The same might be said of the N-Town Plays as a whole, which Scherb addresses in his conclusion. The account of each of these texts underscores its singularity in Middle English as well as East Anglian dramatic traditions. Yet what emerges most prominently from the analysis of these more "epic" dramas and the multiplay N-Town compilation is the commonality of their overall intent: "staging faith" in an eclectic, expansive theater of spiritual aspiration that was at once meticulously attentive to the claims of the world and committed to modeling an idealized spiritual community.

Approaching the analysis of medieval dramatic texts and performance through their impact on audiences can be a tricky business. Largely undocumented, responses to dramatic performances, as Claire Sponsler and Kathleen Ashley have argued, must have been as conflicted and varied as the personal and social circumstances of the individuals who patronized them. Scherb's study wisely navigates this difficult terrain, remaining attentive to the "diverse, conflicted, and complex culture" (202) of late medieval East Anglia while making a compelling argument for the coherent contours of its dramatic traditions. With its measured and learned approach to its subject, this book makes a welcome and original contribution to East Anglian studies and to the history of early English drama.

THERESA COLETTI
University of Maryland

BRENDA DEEN SCHILDGEN. *Pagans, Tartars, Moslems, and Jews in Chaucer's* Canterbury Tales. Gainsville: University Press of Florida, 2001. Pp. 183. $59.95.

Brenda Deen Schildgen begins her most recent book with a striking observation on Chaucer's worldview from Jorge Luis Borges: that the western passage from realism to nominalism took place one day in 1382 when Chaucer translated Boccaccio's allegorical phrase "E con gli occulti ferri i Tradimenti" ("And Treachery, with hidden weapons") as the surprisingly particularized "The smyler with the knyf under the cloke" (4). In her Introduction, Schildgen establishes as a working premise that Chaucer, who may not indeed have regarded himself as a nominalist, nevertheless lived and wrote in "an Ockhamist atmosphere" (6) and that the *Canterbury Tales* reflects the collapse of the "implacable singular view of reality" expressed, for example, in Dante's *Commedia* (7). The tales of the Knight, Squire, Franklin, and Wife of Bath she finds to be "infused with pagan philosophy," to introduce "heterodox concerns," and to "resist closure," in contrast to those of the Man of Law, Second Nun, and Prioress, which, in a Dante-like manner already old-fashioned by Chaucer's day, "divide the world between redeemed and unredeemed" (11).

From this good start, some readers will and some will not follow Schildgen's leap to her thesis: "Taken together, the tales probe various ethical systems and *raise doubts about the ideology of a monolithic Christian West"* (12, reviewer's emphasis). This is no doubt the way *The Canterbury Tales* has usually been taught in American classrooms over the past fifty years, but whether raising doubts about Christianity was Chaucer's *intention* is quite another question. Readers who balk at seeing Chaucer as an avuncular proponent of religious and ethnic diversity, poking gentle fun at those of his Pilgrims who evince more conservative (for instance, anti-Semitic) views, would be advised to ignore Schildgen's "intentional fallacy" passages and focus on what she has to say about these tales, their sources, and contemporary *comparata*.

One of the virtues of *Pagans, Tartars, Moslems, and Jews* is its surprising and suggestive pairings of tales. The *Knight's Tale* is discussed over two chapters with the *Squire's Tale,* while the *Wife of Bath's Tale* shares a chapter with that of the Franklin, and the Prioress's with the Monk's. What commonalities are highlighted by this arrangement? In the case of the Knight's and Squire's tales Schildgen shows that both adopt pagan philosophical perspectives, the Knight's the Stoic and the Squire's the Epicurean, neither of which, according to Schildgen, can "be assumed into a Christian worldview" (14). Yet, as she herself shows, these philosophies were widespread throughout Christian medieval Europe, not least in the romance, which would appear to undercut her main point on these two tales, that they "embrace a 'posttraditional morality' that refuses to impose Christian norms" (47). Much of her discussion of these two tales is given over to astrological matters, but there is also an interesting section on reflections in the *Squire's Tale* of both Mandeville's and Marco Polo's stories of the Tartars.

With the *Man of Law's Tale,* Schildgen focuses on "binary spatial oppositions" (49)—actually, more of a triptych, with Rome flanked by Islam and English heathenism. She shows how a thoroughgoing medieval distinction between "intellectual and political Islam" (53) could have allowed Chaucer both to cite Moslem scientists as authorities and to echo vicious Crusader propaganda, but ultimately, I believe, she overreads the (fairy)Tale with Edward-Said-supported talk of "an unregenerate history of interconnected sexual-political conspiracy and betrayal" (62) and so on. We learn little about medieval views of Moslems in this discussion that is not already clear in the Tale.

The chapter on the *Wife of Bath's Tale* and the *Franklin's Tale* presents some interesting analogues for what Schildgen calls "the green world" of the *Wife's Tale* and the garden of the Franklin's (although not many readers are likely to be able to take in references to gardens in Virgil, Statius, and Ovid, given so speedily that they are all in one sentence [78]). Pagan philosophies reappear here, as the *Franklin's Tale* "puts both Epicureanism and Stoicism on trial" (80). An important section is devoted to various medieval views of oath-taking, as these apply to the folktale promises made by the Franklin's Dorigen and the Wife's unnamed knight.

The Tales of the Prioress and the Monk are presented as a "deliberat[ion] on the Christian teleological or pagan nonteleological view of history" (93), with the Monk, of course, arguing "against any providential order in pagan, Christian, or contemporary history" and the Prioress for teleology. Anti-Semitism is discussed as it appears in the several contemporary literary genres and in official actions, but too much, in my view, is made of the Prioress's anti-Semitism being "out-of-date" (104) in her reference to the thirteenth-century Hugh of Lyncoln (105). Also puzzling in this chapter is Schildgen's mention of the Monk's praise for Caesar's manhood in light of the latter's reputation for homosexuality (107)—but no evidence that Chaucer knew of this reputation is brought to bear.

Rounding out the book is Schildgen's discussion of the *Second Nun's Tale,* in which contemporary sex-based notions of holiness are usefully examined. I was not convinced by her conclusion, however, that this Tale demonstrates Christianity's vulnerability (120). Still, Schildgen's Conclusion, with its emphasis on Chaucer's lifetime as the "end of a united Latin Europe" (121), goes a long way toward explaining why the Tales informed by the binary "redeemed/unredeemed" opposition must be set "in another time, when such simple polarities perhaps prevailed" (122)—or were nostalgically supposed by Chaucer to have prevailed.

The scholarship informing *Pagans, Tartars, Moslems, and Jews* is impressive, and the book will serve many readers as a mine for references to a wide array of both primary and secondary literature. Unfortunately, however, the book is not easy of access. References to *comparata,* as mentioned above, are normally so severely compressed as to discourage the non-researching reader from following up in the endnotes. Many citations are gratuitous, as for example a reference to Isidore's *Etymologies* VIII.vi.9 to support Dorigen's view that virtue is a precondition for happiness (80), or a Latin quotation from St. Augustine to describe the Plowman (111). At least one of Schildgen's sources, Fanon, does not appear in the Works Cited, while another, Said, is misquoted (62). That the book has not been edited adequately is also evident in scattered misreadings of Chaucer: in the *Franklin's Tale,* the phrase "of aventure or grace" does not, pace Schildgen, posit *grace* as a synonym of *aventure* (83), and in the *Manciple's Tale,* the admonition "My sone, thy tonge sholdestow restreyne" is addressed to the Manciple by his mother, not by the Manciple to the reader (117). Perhaps oddest of all are the several instances of redundancy and repetition, which one would not expect in a text this short, a mere 125 pages before the 50-odd pages of apparati, as for example the seven citations over four pages (70–73) of the Wife's funny but insignificant aside concerning friars and limitors lurking about the countryside. Added to this, an excessive amount of unnecessary use of Middle English words in quotation marks, a tendency to use back-to-back quotation marks and parentheses, and a generous sprinkling of virgules in poetic quotations within the text results in pages that sometimes resemble OED entries.

LOIS BRAGG
Gallaudet University

R. ALLEN SHOAF. *Chaucer's Body: The Anxiety of Circulation in the Canterbury Tales.* Gainesville: University Press of Florida, 2001. Pp. xvi, 162. $55.00.

R. Allen Shoaf's new book takes the body in Chaucer's *Canterbury Tales* as its subject and circulation as its governing metaphor, exploring circulation from a variety of perspectives, including somatic and social circulation and most importantly the circulation of ideas embodied in and represented by language, which is presented as both communication and communicable: "Infection," he says in the introduction to the book, "the consequence of contagion, itself the result of circulation, threatens the human body. And the most infectious agent there is . . . is language itself" (2). Shoaf postulates the inherent, existential isolation of individual bodies, a condition that necessitates efforts of communication and at the same time generates fears about communication as a potential source of infection, pathogenesis, and degeneration (7).

Throughout this book Shoaf proclaims his interest in bodies, and indeed considers the physical bodies Chaucer creates for his characters—the Prioress's body and its relationship to food, the Nun's Priest's body and its protean, substantial relationship to the power conferred by language skillfully marshaled are but two examples—but his real focus is that circulation of language that reception theory and semiotic theory seek to explain: the often labyrinthine and highly individual patterns of response that signs and groups of signs evoke. Over the course of the book Shoaf investigates, queries, and performs the circulation, contagion, and anxiety that is its topic, reading Chaucer's words broadly and imaginatively against the context of his own reading and literary experience. In their promotional materials the publishers have included Julian Wasserman's opinion that the book "breaks new critical ground" as Shoaf "casts his reading of Chaucer somewhat in the tradition of Wordsworth's *Prelude*." While it is doubtful that this book constitutes the education of either a poet or a critic, it does foreground the crucial role of the reader in responding to a literature designed to foreclose simple, unidimensional interpretations.

Shoaf develops his twofold argument through five closely argued, dense chapters that defy summary. The opening chapter, "The Care of the Self," devoted to Fragments VII and II of the *Tales,* examines a series of selves, linking the physical body and its prepossessing qualities to the effectiveness of tale-telling: "Only after the Priest has told his delightful tale . . . does Harry, perceiving the substance in it and in him, recognize the body of the Priest—the substance is *between them*" (18). The second chapter, "The Pestilence of the Sentence," reads Fragment VI, the tales of the Physician and the Pardoner, as tales that "repeat in a different and darker perspective the same binarism or duality of the . . . *Monk's Tale* and the *Nun's Priest's Tale*" (47). The third chapter, "Etym-Alchemy," discusses the secrets, transformations, and vital flow of language and life at work in Fragments VIII and III. The fourth chapter, "Magic versus Rhetoric," explores language's seemingly magical ability to transform and transmute by exploring the rhetorical magic of metonymy in Fragments V and I. The final chapter "Grant Translateur," dealing with Fragments IX, X, and IV, suggests that the "psychology of someone who defends against the anxiety of circulation with metonymy and reduction [i.e. Chaucer] is also the psychology of a translator: not an originator, the translator creates fragmentarily out of the archive of others' originals that, like the story of Tereus, threaten to 'infect' and 'envenom' him unless he inoculates himself with his own versions of them" (102).

Throughout these explorations Shoaf interweaves a variety of theoretical perspectives, classical rhetoric, and tropes of his own naming. Early in the book he announces that the rhetorical category "most important" to his argument is "epideixis *(genus demonstrativum)*": "I assume that the *Canterbury Tales* depend in part on epideictic oratory, or praise and blame *(laudando et vituperando)*" (8). The rhetorical term most central to his argument is metonymy, literally metonymy as "change of name" (8–9), the process by which metaphor and metonymy occlude, or erase, parts of what they represent. He also develops his own theory of *juxtology* to explain the apparent illogicality and arbitrariness by which metonymy selects elements of a whole by which to signify that whole: "Juxtology suggests that what appears initially illogical in metonymy may have, to the contrary, deep structure of relationships beyond coincidence, beyond logic" (89–90).

Along the way Shoaf presents cogent insights into the nature of language and of Chaucer's art (the discussion of metonymy in Chapter 4 is particularly rich), as well as some disappointingly familiar readings of the *Tales*. Is it news to conclude that the Nun's Priest differs from the Pardoner not through sexuality but through intention, the former interested in the moralities of stories, their *fruyt,* the latter single-mindedly intent on gain (55)? Or to read the Franklin as an insecure *parvenu* (77)? But interpretations of Chaucer's work ultimately emerge as secondary in Shoaf's project. Throughout the book Shoaf foregrounds himself by taking constant care to let the reader know how his mind has found, used, judged the information it has sought, as in this passage: "I am personally most attracted to the applications made by Lacan, which I intend to discuss at length elsewhere, but I am also instructed by the work in the late 1970s of David Lodge, on which I will draw now" (89). Footnotes cite texts that Shoaf notes in passing, that he has read, that he says influenced his thinking, that he promises to return to in future pages. This book is a tour de force of Chaucer criticism, in that it focuses on the processes of the mind of the critic—an astute, informed critic, without doubt, but one whose wealth of referents, interpretants, and semiotic experiences is, if not unique, highly idiosyncratic, as this passage from a discussion of the tales of Fragment VII shows: "Waste, we see, is a concern. The fragment, in fact, is full of shit, most ominously in the *Prioress's Tale*. But other forms of waste also fill the fragment, from wasted time to wasted money to wasted life. This is the p-a-t-h-o-s adumbrated by T-h-o-p-a-s. And if Chaucer goes on, at Harry's urging, to tell 'a litel thyng in prose,' the antiphrasis 'litel' (the *Tale of Melibee* is 16,925 words long!) only underscores the difficulty of dieting in a world where Sophie's body is so vulnerable and frangible" (22). Finally, the experience of reading this book is not so much one of gaining insight into Chaucer's art as into the processes of Allen Shoaf's mind.

CAROLYN P. COLLETTE
Mount Holyoke College

D. VANCE SMITH. *The Book of the Incipit: Beginnings in the Fourteenth Century.* Medieval Cultures 28. Minneapolis and London: University of Minnesota Press, 2001. Pp. 296. $34.95.

Smith's intricately philosophical reading of *Piers Plowman* contemplates the poem as endlessly beginning again yet struggling to found any originary position, and posits for this a widespread context of medieval concerns—especially in scholastic and "terminist" thought—with the nature of beginning. The study is deliberately nonlinear, generally satisfyingly so, but its utility for further work would be improved if it had a cumulative statement about the late medieval "problem of beginning" that constitutes its novel context for *Piers Plowman.* I venture the following: in late fourteenth-century England, the general medieval "problem of beginning" finds its purest possible expression—that is, the sense that current existence does not match or faithfully conform to its beginnings is uniquely acute on multiple levels of culture, from the 1381 Rebellion to terminist scholastic treatises. This sense partly derives from doubt about just what beginning is meant for significant action; the possibilities range "from the beginning of the world itself to the beginning of a text" (12), a range of beginnings that, Smith argues, "cannot really be separated" (12) but also cannot shake the sense of their arbitrariness or presentist manipulations (15, 113). The period's uncertainty about where and how any institution or moral action begins, intensified by a pervasive sense that actions and identities should have authoritative foundations, is complicated by emphases on penance, which supplants extrinsic beginnings of moral action by establishing beginnings for action based on the will alone (34–36, 154–55). This in turn is complicated by doubt about how much human will can establish any kind of beginning, given the originary power of God's grace and creation (174–83). The "merit vs. works" debates of the period thus show the ultimate difficulty of locating any kind of beginning needed for moral action, even while the terms of moral action demand some sort of beginning to be defined. Medieval theories of narrative, especially in academic prologues, emphasize that narrative form is predicated on preexisting authorial intention, and also understood to be useful for the subsequent ethical responses of its readers; thus medieval theories of narrative open onto the period's widespread debates about just what and where beginnings are (for instance, 75–77).

All these "problems" of beginning define, for Smith, the explanation for and functions of *Piers'* unusual literary form, along with a number of its notoriously difficult theological and intellectual issues. The repeated narrative beginnings in *Piers,* the continual recommencing of dream-visions (best known from Anne Middleton's argument that Langland's poem vastly extrapolates the form, literary authority, and authorial self-portrayal of the opening of the *chanson d'avanture* ["The Audience and Public of *Piers Plowman,*" in *Middle English Alliterative Poetry and its Literary Background,* ed. David Lawton (Cambridge: D. S. Brewer, 1983), 102–23]), show the poem's continual "nostalgic" sense of "pure beginnings" but also its sense of lacking any foundational power, any moral or theological ability to make a fresh start for "moral" action (not otherwise defined, except as progressing to salvation). The study's best local results are in the readings of the C.5 "autobiographical" passage, where the narrator's assertion of making a new beginning is shown to be paradoxical in ethical terms but efficacious in defining the poet's "absolute, inextricable relationship with his writing," a vocation "that can only be justified by its execution—the continuation of the poem" (59). Another splendid section is the sustained reading of the "grammatical analogy," where Smith claims the poem's focus is on relations between origins and present choices, not on the origins themselves. "'Relacoun rect' is not an absolute affirmation of the value of political and social structure," Smith states—commenting on perhaps the most elusive term in the "grammatical analogy"—"but a reminder that social relations, like grammatical relations, are uncertain and have no intrinsic being" (164). As with the reading of the "autobiographical passage," the poem's sense of the arbitrary in claims to origins is here deftly displayed. Less effective is the final reading of Patience's riddle, where the exposition vanishes in abstraction, suggesting an unwillingness to think through that or any textual moment in terms of the genres invoked.

Such are the treasures and penalties of an approach "mainly interested not in the shape that texts have, but in the things that they do, in the things they make us do or not do, in the reasons they give us for doing or not doing things" (p. ix). This rejection of formalism as an end in itself succeeds in showing how many academic authors as well as a very select number of vernacular literary authors see "finished" authorial intentions as predefining narrative form, and also in showing how *Piers* both unravels and extends the philosophical, theological, and formal dimensions of what might be called "incipit theory." These yields are accompanied by the useful conviction that philosophical and theological problems are fundamentally important for how we interrogate social history and literary form. But materiality in the simple sense of engaging texts and plotting historical causality is not given enough direct attention, and in consequence it reappears in some implausible forms. To pursue "the things that [texts] do" and "make us do" promises some history of reception, but while there is consideration of how scribes used rubrics to simplify the poem, most of the exposition focuses on how scholastic thought defines the issues in *Piers,* rather than how the poem exerts power on anything else (the claims for how *Piers* shaped John Ball's notions and those of the other rebels in 1381 [92–93, 114–16] offer no convincing new evidence of such influence, and are better seen as contrasting thought forms). The emphasis on using scholastic writing to explain *Piers* runs risks familiar from other excessive claims of medieval literature's dependence on intellectual traditions, dangers all too clear when Smith declares the whole poem "a kind of dilated scholastic prologue" (125).

That position merely licenses us to do what much scholarship on *Piers* has done on other grounds: ignore it as a poem in relation to other poems. And to the extent that the emphasis on scholastic concerns can be defended as registering or articulating broader cultural concerns with beginning, that indirectly raises the question of whether any other poems of the period were much involved with so broad an issue. There are remarkably few readings here even of *Piers,* in the sense that "readings" used to have: elucidations that allow the reader some abandonment to aesthetic and formal appreciation, from which the critic returns having somehow learned new points relevant to the argument. Given this paucity of poetic engagement, minor mistakes or exaggerations loom larger than they might: B.15.456–60 is not "the poem's only explicit etymology" (26: C.9.213–18 has another); "shepe" at B.Prol.2 does not clearly mean "shepherd," *pace* Skeat (91), since no genuine medieval example parallels that sense (the rebel name or pseudonym "John Schep," which Smith claims responds to *Piers*'s opening "shepe," is not necessarily another instance [92], since that name may be from the "Chapman" tradition); C.5.2 does not present the only time we glimpse the narrator's domestic setting (118: the end of B.18/C.20 presents another example). Occasionally the weight on details in nonliterary materials strains plausibility. The rhetorical trope of *captatio benevolentiae* seems light-years away from scholastic concerns with the problems of *voluntas* into which it is here collapsed (76–78). The forays into scholastic traditions are based on sparse and relatively outdated scholarship, and present at least one mistake: while it is true that the verb *incipere* is described as a syncategorematic term in treatises on syncategoremata, it is not the chief one—the other examples, mostly adverbs, are more often the concern of late-medieval academics (20–21)—and the reason that *incipit* (along with *desinit*, "it ends") is one of the very few verbs treated along with adverbs as syncategorematic is not because "it belongs to a class of words that carry with them their own implicit negation" (19), as Smith misleadingly defines syncategoremata, but instead because syncategoremata's signification gains definiteness only from words adjoined to them: precisely the opposite of their carrying definite implicit meanings.

Given Smith's abilities to show such metaphysical problems in literary terms, I still wish for a book that would consider the issue as a distinctly literary problem throughout the middle ages or even simply throughout the late fourteenth century, a book that might dip into literary texts more often than once every few pages and keep their details tangibly before the reader rather than swallowed up by philosophical discourse, medieval and modern. (For example, is not the problem or complex condition of making a beginning a central matter for the dual-authored, thirteenth-century *Roman de la Rose* and the vast literary tradition it spawned or influenced—to a significant degree including, I think, *Piers Plowman*?) Yet Smith's study is itself often densely lyrical, and its evasions of sustained literary appreciation or connections to literary history seem deliberately to follow the spare style of a prolegomenon. In 211 pages of text Smith covers an extraordinary quantity of difficult intellectual material, medieval and modern, with impressive deftness and accuracy, offers insights into a remarkable array of difficult points in *Piers Plowman*, and links medieval thought to modern theory with powerful suggestiveness. He closes by defining his work as merely a way for other readers to "begin to read the poem." This is no false modesty, but an accurate characterization for this study's seminal value and sustained level of suggestive abstraction. The handful of puns, ironies, and paradoxes in *Piers* it presents are thin but representative, touching the center of the challenge that any reader taking up the poem will encounter; and the continual transformation of local focuses to significant generalization reveals that Smith's heart really is in reading this poem lovingly and repeatedly. The best passage in the book, at the end of the chapter "Thema," is a marvel of eloquent philosophical formalism concerning the broad effects in *Piers* of the problem of making a beginning in all the ways Smith shows obtained in the period. That the study leaves me wanting more and denser literary engagement, and more connected or discriminated historical contexts for the topic it takes up, is a sign that it succeeds in putting before us a major and novel task.

ANDREW GALLOWAY
Cornell University

ESTELLE STUBBS, ed. *The Hengwrt Chaucer Digital Facsimile.* Leicester, UK: Scholarly Digital Editions, 2000. 1 CD-ROM. $110.00 for individual purchase, $240 for institution or library purchase.

The Hengwrt Chaucer Digital Facsimile is the third electronic publication undertaken by the Canterbury Tales Project. The previous publications—*The Wife of Bath's Prologue on CD-ROM* (1996) and *The General Prologue on CD-ROM* (2000)—provide the reader with hypertexts of their respective narratives, and thus include all the manuscripts of those narratives. In contrast, this digital facsimile offers us the *Canterbury Tales* almost in its entirety, as it appears in one single but very important manuscript: Aberystwyth, National Library of Wales, MS. Peniarth 392D. It is generally agreed that the Hengwrt Chaucer dates to soon after Chaucer's death in 1400, and that it therefore constitutes the earliest extant copy of the *Tales,* a poem never completed or fully revised by its author. The manuscript, however, was somewhat crudely made and is now in a bad condition: rats have chewed the parchment, and the removal of its boards in the 1930s and rebinding in the 1950s caused further damage. The CD provides color images of each folio of this battered codex, enabling readers to examine layout and quiring, positioning of headers and glosses, and changes in ink color and scribal hands. Links are provided alongside the images of the folios, which take the reader to notes on any distinctive codicological features. The high-resolution images are, arguably, easier to read than the manuscript itself (which is cumbersome as well as fragile), and some exciting new discoveries have been made in the process of the digital capture.

The reader of *The Hengwrt Chaucer Digital Facsimile* is effectively being presented with a highly sophisticated "best text" of the *Canterbury Tales,*

436

in that many of the assumptions underlying this type of editing manifest themselves in the surrounding apparatus. Of course, the choice of the Hengwrt Chaucer as best text (not to mention the decision to reproduce a best text in the first place) is controversial. The majority of editors and scholars continue to assert the superiority of the slightly later Ellesmere Chaucer (San Marino, California, Huntington Library, MS. EL 26 C9). And although Norman Blake, one of the co-general editors of the Canterbury Tales Project, produced an edition of the *Canterbury Tales* based exclusively on Hengwrt in 1980, he has until recently been pretty much a lone voice extolling Hengwrt's virtues. The debate about the respective merits of Hengwrt and Ellesmere hardly needs rehearsing here, and, in her editor's introduction, Estelle Stubbs provides a concise and up-to-date overview of various critical opinions on the date, condition, and strengths of both manuscripts, although her prejudices against Ellesmere—the Prince to Hengwrt's Pauper (to adapt Stubbs's own description)—are fairly evident. For example, Stubbs draws our attention to Kathleen Scott's work, which suggests the possibility of an earlier date for the Ellesmere Chaucer, and, by implication, also for Hengwrt, placing the latter within Chaucer's own lifetime, and thus giving it even more authority. This conclusion is reinforced in the article on the language of the Hengwrt Chaucer by Simon Horobin, (published in the CD), which argues that the spelling in the Hengwrt manuscript comes closest to and retains elements of Chaucer's own. I am perfectly happy to be persuaded by the findings of Scott and Horobin, although Stubbs could, I feel, have accorded more weight to the counter-arguments in favor of Ellesmere.

The Hengwrt Chaucer Digital Facsimile is an excellent research tool and a fine teaching resource and should prove invaluable, especially for postgraduate instruction in paleography and textual criticism. Indeed the editor's introduction, the detailed manuscript description by Daniel W. Mosser, the articles on the language of the Hengwrt Chaucer and on its digital capture, the observations on the folios, and the bibliography make the CD particularly suited to such a purpose. In the past decade, innovations such as this have revolutionized—and, one hopes, extended—the teaching of codicology and bibliography. Now academics and students from all over the world can closely examine manuscripts previously only accessible to those who are privileged enough to be based near libraries with major holdings of medieval texts, or fortunate enough to be in receipt of substantial research funding. However, for this reader at least, the real achievement of *The Hengwrt Chaucer Digital Facsimile* is the extent to which it provides us with what Stubbs calls the "holistic view of the manuscript as artefact" (Editor's Introduction). This is facilitated by the inclusion of images of the so-called the Merthyr Fragment (three folios surviving from a very early manuscript, comprising part of the *Nun's Priest's Prologue* and *Tale*). The fragment is described by Mosser, and contextualized by Ceridwen Lloyd Morgan. It is Lloyd Morgan's historical introduction, combined with her edition and translation of the Welsh marginalia, which reinforces our awareness of the fragment's current geographical location, and by extension that of the Hengwrt Chaucer, in the heartland of Welsh-speaking Wales. Any text—whether it is a manuscript, an early printed text, a scholarly edition, a hypertext, or a facsimile—is always also a product of the cultures that produced and preserved it. The Hengwrt Chaucer is no exception. The full circumstances of its composition will never be fully known, and although we can ascertain that it arrived in Cheshire and then Wales at a fairly early date, those that account for its survival have only partially been explained. Yet it is, perhaps, a fitting irony that a poem written in English at a time when the English vernacular was challenging the dominance of Latin should find itself in a place where Welsh continues its struggle for survival against what is now often thought of as a colonialist tongue. *The Hengwrt Chaucer Digital Facsimile* returns the Hengwrt Chaucer to the center of the English-speaking virtual world, while, thankfully, the manuscript remains at the contested margin of its real equivalent.

DIANE WATT
University of Wales, Aberystwyth

STEPHANIE TRIGG. *Congenial Souls: Reading Chaucer from Medieval to Postmodern.* Medieval Cultures 30. Minneapolis: University of Minnesota Press, 2002. Pp. xxiv, 280. $57.95 cloth, $22.95 paper.

Stephanie Trigg's title comes from Dryden's account of reading Chaucer in his *Fables Ancient and Modern,* published in 1700: "(If I may be permitted to say it of myself) I found I had a Soul congenial to his." Her book is a study of the various forms of commentary on Chaucer over the centuries, from Lydgate to herself, and in particular of the progression from the reading of his works to criticism on them. Analogous studies could be written about any canonical author, but there is one respect in which Chaucer is unique, and that is the degree to which readers of all centuries cast him as a personal friend. No one to my knowledge has claimed such kinship with (for instance) Milton, and identification with Shakespeare is typically extended to his characters rather than himself—as in Coleridge's notorious "I have a smack of Hamlet about me, if I may say so." That same air of apology hangs around the many remarks about personal acquaintance with Chaucer too, as if everyone who claims it recognizes its impossibility, its arrogance, and, in the present state of criticism, its theoretical incorrectness; but even that last handicap has tended to result not in the motif's deletion but in its application to other people—the great and good retiring Chaucerians who are acclaimed for such affinity with the Master.

The recurrence of that sense of personal intimacy forms a continuing theme throughout Stephanie Trigg's book, across all the different categories of reception she charts—Lydgate and the fifteenth century; the early printed editions; Dryden and the Enlightenment efforts to keep Chaucer in the forefront of public consciousness; the promotion of popular appeal in the work of Furnivall, Chesterton, and Woolf; and the latest developments in Chaucerian criticism for both student and professional readerships. Her starting point is the cover of the paperback edition of *The Riverside Chaucer*: a detail of the famous illustration to Lydgate's *Siege of Thebes,* which shows Lydgate himself and some of the other pilgrims setting out from Canterbury (the city is visible in the background) on their return journey. She stresses the *supplementary* quality of both the picture and the tale: "a moment that is dependent on but conspicuously absent from *The Canterbury Tales*" (xv), the presentation of which combines an illusory realism with a fulfillment of our desire to extend our interaction with Chaucer's characters, or with Chaucer through them. Both the unfinished nature of the pilgrimage and the manifestly incomplete state of the manuscript record invite such supplementary intervention, and Lydgate is only the first of many to provide it.

Two further qualities encourage the illusion of intimacy with Chaucer. One is the model of the work as a company, argumentative but convivial, with its implied promise that anyone can join; and the second, the openness of the *Tales,* not just in the textual sense but in terms of interpretation. That openness has been abundantly demonstrated by the reception history of the work over the centuries, and in extreme form over the last four decades. The early supplements, in particular the *Siege of Thebes* itself, the *Beryn* prologue, and the two *Ploughman's Tales* (one pious Catholic and one fiercely Lollard), can be taken as exemplary for much of what has followed: Chaucer as the father of English poetry in both language and content, imbued with all the "high seriousness" that Matthew Arnold so notoriously accused him of lacking; the naturalistic and humorous Chaucer ("genial Chaucer") who held the stage from Dryden through the 1950s and who continues to hold the literal stage or screen; the Robertsonian Chaucer, a single-minded spokesman for universal certainties; and the dissident Chaucer, an alternative voice subversive of the dominant hierarchies of both Church and State. However much individual critics may insist that their own reading is the correct one, the nature of Chaucer's work, with its multiplicity of contrasting voices, effectively prevents any such closure. Attempts to divide the tales into the serious and the ironic themselves rely on the critic's unstated claim to a particular intimacy with Chaucer's mind, in implicit competition with every other critic.

Such attempts at laying bare Chaucer's intentions are curiously at odds with his own opacity, as shown in his reluctance to "sign" his work—the subject of Trigg's second chapter. His authorship is something that later readers, editors, and printers have had in various ways to construct: a process going back so far that it requires an effort to recognize the constructedness at all. Yet it is "this modern emphasis on authorship that allows us to develop our elaborate theories of narrative voice and impersonation" (56), and even the postmodern deconstruction of authorship has left many such approaches largely intact. One reason for this is that they represent an accessible, common-sense approach to Chaucer such as is invaluable for teaching: if students are to continue to read Chaucer—if they are to join the company of Chaucerians, whether as generalists or as professionals—this is where they will start. And for all her recognition of the inadequacies, even the fallacies, of such an approach, Trigg is also acutely aware of the need to keep Chaucer alive, and that the discourses addressed by professionals to fellow professionals are not going to do that. Those Chaucerians of the dissident persuasion, whose political instincts would urge a deconstruction of the canon, are conscious that they are sawing off the branch they are sitting on, which may be one reason why Chaucer is proving such fertile ground for feminist, queer, multicultural, and postcolonial approaches. That these approaches have produced such interesting results may be secondary to the urgent need to re-inscribe a very dead white male within the whole postmodern agenda, just as Reformation England had to define him as proto-Protestant. The one thing that in contrast to earlier readers we cannot say, which "we have taught ourselves to repress" in writing for publication, is "the love of Chaucer and his poetry that barely dares to speak its name in contemporary criticism, but that remains one of the reasons why we keep writing and thinking about his work" (144). The careful formulation of that statement, as an assertion of repression rather than an assertion of the repressed, is itself a measure of how dogmatic the orthodoxies of academic discourse now are.

Any process of self-examination, such as Trigg offers for the whole Chaucer industry, invites readers to turn its tools on their wielder. She is, however, engagingly open about her own inscription in the discourses she analyzes; and although she does not altogether excise her own opinions, she is interested in explanation, not judgment. She is studying a historical process, every step of which (including the work of the last decade) has its own historical contexts and therefore its own justifications. She is an attentive and accurate reader, not least of people such as Furnivall and Chesterton whom it has become fashionable to decry or ignore; she notes that Chesterton "seems to prefigure the more self-conscious political criticism of Marxist and materialist readers" (193), and that Virginia Woolf's much-overlooked commentary on Chaucer is embedded, when not read in anthologies of criticism, in an account of historical reception that anticipates academic interests of decades later. She is perhaps a little hard on Furnivall's homosociality, despite her acknowledgment of his support for women's education and scholarship; the poor man can hardly be expected to revolutionize society before he starts editing Chaucer, though his belief that the two went together says more for his conviction of Chaucer's importance than our own repression would ever allow. The intelligence, wide knowledge, and fair-mindedness with which she approaches the whole topic make it that very rare thing, a critical book that one might wish had been longer.

HELEN COOPER
University College, Oxford

RAINER WARNING. *The Ambivalences of Medieval Religious Drama.* Trans. Steven Rendall. Stanford: Stanford University Press, 2001. Pp. xx, 308. $60.00.

This translation of *Funktion und Struktur: Die Ambivalenzen des geistlichen Spiels,* originally published in 1974, makes available to Anglo-American audiences an important study of medieval religious theater by a prominent continental literary and cultural theorist. Up to now, these readers most likely would have encountered Warning's analyses of medieval religious theater in an essay, "On the Alterity of Medieval Religious Drama," which presented excerpts from this book's arguments for a ground-breaking special issue of *New Literary History* dedicated to "Medieval Literature and Contemporary Theory" (no. 10 [1979]).

Hans Ulrich Gumbrecht's foreward to this new translation usefully situates Warning's study in relation to the intellectual moment of its genesis and the theoretical engagements that marked German humanist scholarship in the late 1960s and early 1970s. Critical debates then current in medieval theater studies also provide a significant informing context for Warning's endeavor. Focusing on hypotheses about the origins and development of religious drama, scholars had embraced evolutionary and genealogical models that posited organic relationships between Latin liturgical and vernacular traditions. Even with the abandonment of the idea that liturgical ceremony had moved gradually from sacred to secular space as it was translated from Latin into the European vernaculars, the medieval drama scholarship that motivated Warning's intervention was captive to a positivist historiography preoccupied with texts and sources. Its objects of study were sometimes evaluated by aesthetic criteria "normatively defined by reference to Shakespeare" (2), or, in the case of Germanic texts, for evidence of folkloric continuities that reinforced their nationalistic character. The humor and naturalism of medieval religious theater were understood as the entertaining yeast that ecclesiastical sponsorship had added to leaven the drama's fundamentally moral and didactic aims.

Warning challenged such traditional methodologies and findings by mobilizing paradigms from social anthropology, structuralism, systems theory, and theories of play and laughter to counter the "general hermeneutic helplessness" (2) that he identified in the field of religious drama studies. His major contribution to that field involves his book's argument about vernacular religious drama's discontinuity with both liturgical ceremony and medieval Christian theology. Rather than further the aims of the Christian cult, vernacular religious drama opposes them, drawing its power from enactment of a different kind of ritual, the very archaic, mythological beliefs that Christian theology labored to exclude. Presented as an effort to theorize and explain the cultural functions of religious drama, this book also seeks to recuperate—it was the first study to do so—graphic, profane, and obscene elements of vernacular theater such as the sensationalized tortures of French Passion dramas or the obscene banter of German *hortulanus* scenes, which had resisted analysis by any conventional critical paradigm.

The book considers both insular and continental dramatic texts, but it focuses on liturgical ceremony and French and German plays. It is divided into three major sections. Part One focuses on the *visitatio sepulchri* and later vernacular Easter dramas, principally German, that secularize and profane the same scriptural events enacted in the liturgical ceremony. Part Two examines the twelfth-century *Ordo representacionis Ade,* or the *Play of Adam,* as a theoretical test case for the coincident emergence of vernacular religious drama and the promulgation of theories of redemption articulated in Anselm's *Cur Deus Homo.* Part Three discusses how late medieval French Passion plays bear witness to popular reception of the fundamental tension between a theology focused on the bloodless sacrifice of the Mass and the fact of Christ's bloody sacrificial death. In each case Warning posits that the interests of vernacular drama diverge from those of the theology that ostensibly motivated it. Drama discloses latent functions that are tied far more to pre-Christian ritual elements than to dogma, thereby exposing the ambivalence at its core. Marks of these ritual elements and the ambivalence produced by their incorporation into sacred drama are evident, for example, in *hortulanus* scenes that present a resurrected Christian deity who is also the pagan year-god; in the importance accorded to Jesus's apocryphal struggle with Satan in *descensus ad inferos* episodes and the *Adam* play; and in the scapegoat rituals that elucidate Passion dramas whose violent elaborations are otherwise unexplained by Christian theology or Passion mysticism.

The appearance of this translation over a quarter of a century after this book's initial publication raises questions about its ongoing relevance to medieval drama studies. In the intervening years medieval drama scholarship has continued to explore drama's relation to ritual, its appropriations of theology and spirituality, and its problematic embodiment of sacred mysteries. Recent studies by Lawrence Clopper (*Drama, Play, and Game: English Festive Culture in the Medieval and Early Modern Period* [Chicago, 2001]); Michal Kobialka (*This is My Body: Representational Practices in the Early Middle Ages* [Ann Arbor, 1999]); and Sarah Beckwith (*Signifying God: Social Relation and Symbolic Act in the York Corpus Christi Plays* [Chicago, 2001]) in particular have provided important reckonings with topics that preoccupied Warning, and are in many ways more engaging and accessible. Seen through the lens of these comparably ambitious studies on medieval religious drama, the bold thesis of his book has to appear a little less provocative than it did nearly thirty years ago. But this recent work also reinforces the importance of the issues that Warning's book engaged and points to a vital twenty-first-century context for its reception.

The lack of a translation of Warning's book up to now has obviously limited its influence on Anglo-American study of medieval religious drama, compared, for example, to that of another German scholar who was also invested in developing new theoretical paradigms for the study of early theater. Robert Weimann's *Shakespeare and the Popular Tradition in the Theater,* available in English since 1978, has long been an important resource for early English drama studies. Granted that the attention Weimann's book received is partially a function of its popular subject matter, the example furnished by this work nonetheless raises questions about the prospect that this new translation of Warning's study will lay a foundation for his belated influence on the field. Those prospects will not be enhanced by the strenuous difficulty of this book's prose. My random comparison of several passages with versions of the same text that also appeared in Warning's 1979 article, the work of a different translator, suggests that responsibility for these difficulties must be shared by Warning and his translator, whose sentences tend to reproduce grammatical constructions of the original German rather than render them in more idiomatic English. More frustrating is the abstraction and obliquity of this book's arguments, which are frequently presented as intricate dialogues with other drama scholars and theorists whose positions are explained in only the briefest ways. The book often reads as a transcript of one voice in a conversation in progress among scholars intimately familiar with each others' ideas, rather than as a text that has the rhetorical aim of communicating with a broader audience. Gumbrecht's foreward prepares the reader for these features, tactfully emphasizing the book's "(academico-) cultural otherness" (x) and announcing in its first sentence that this study "is very demanding reading by any standards" (ix).

Hindsight provided by several decades of medieval drama scholarship and a theoretically informed medieval studies invites scrutiny of this book's monolithic conceptions of liturgy, ecclesiastical institutions, and academic theology, as well as of its investments in a religious drama originating in a festive, communal piety "that was largely theologically unenlightened." Warning asserts, but provides little evidence for, the authorship of this drama by members of a "lower clergy" whose interests were stirred more by the "mythical religiosity of their bourgeois clients" than by the "dogmatic claims of university theology" (236). His ambitious thesis about the manifest divergence from dominant ecclesiastical structures of the cultural impulses that give rise to religious theater eschews analyses of virtually all specific contexts—social, regional, economic—for the authorship, production, and reception of religious drama. While this approach to medieval religious theater might be challenged at every turn for its utter lack of interest in such details, this book's insistence that medieval vernacular religious theater drew powerfully from mythic, ritual resources that resisted recuperation by Christian officialdom underscores the ideological, symbolic, and social complexity of medieval dramatic performance in ways that few studies have done. It is precisely this book's commitment to theorizing, however problematically, these shadowy, undocumentable influences on the medieval religious stage that still merits attention.

Theresa Coletti
University of Maryland

Judith Weiss, Jennifer Fellows and Morgan Dickson, eds., *Medieval Insular Romance: Translation and Innovation.* Cambridge: D. S. Brewer, 2000. Pp. xi, 196. $75.00.

Medieval romance is such a comfortably familiar category, so often invoked in literary criticism only in opposition to the supposedly greater individualities of texts in other times and of other types, that some might doubt whether there is really anything radical to be said about its practice either of "translation" or of "innovation." Yet, as is repeatedly demonstrated in this collection of papers from the conference on Romance in Medieval England held in April 1998 at Robinson College, Cambridge, current studies in Middle English and Anglo-Norman romance have a tendency to unsettle even the most established of literary-historical and interpretative paradigms. Rosalind Field, for example, clearly demonstrates that our understanding of the distinctively Anglo-Norman culture that invented such heroes as Guy of Warwick and Bevis of Hampton has been dangerously simplified by the critical neglect of the *Roman de Waldef,* the longest and certainly the least read of these so-called "ancestral" romances. In the light of what she sees as this ultimately "deeply pessimistic" text (38), the development of an idea of "England" in this period, not just as matter for romance, but also as an ideological construct, starts to look more nervous and uncertain than is usually assumed. She concludes that *"Waldef* is something of a black hole in Insular narrative—so long ignored as to be virtually invisible, its existence explains the movements around it" (39). This formulation might be applied to several of the romance texts that are newly observed and analyzed in the course of this volume. In Helen Cooper's account of "the Elizabethan Havelok," the medieval hero is discovered in the relative obscurity of William Warner's *Albions England* (unprinted since 1612), where he exists in a context disconcertingly remote from his ancestral Grimsby. Here he is incongruously pastoralized and pressed into the service of a very different kind of politics of inheritance, that which finds "its justification and its point of rest in [Queen] Elizabeth" (183): in this way he serves to illustrate both the depth of Tudor indebtedness to medieval romance and also the ways in which this indebtedness could be strangely distorted.

W. A. Davenport's essay, like Field's, aims at the critical rehabilitation of a text that is relatively invisible to modern scholarship, in this case *Sir Degrevant.* The neglect of this text, he argues, has largely been justified in terms of a breach of generic decorum: *Sir Degrevant* blends and balances plot-motifs that traditional taxonomies of romance tend to place in separate families. Yet, as he points out, this only raises the question of why "compositeness" of this kind is seen to be a bad thing in the case of romances like *Sir Degrevant,* when it is precisely this combination of literary awareness with deliberate innovation that literary critics usually praise as a mark of individuality. Roger Dalrymple, by contrast, aims at something less than the rehabilitation of Henry Lovelich, the London skinner who produced long and pedestrian translations of the *The History of the Holy Grail* and *Merlin* at some time between 1425 and 1440. Indeed, Dalrymple only goes so far as to suggest that this "lost Arthurian" deserves further study, rightly arguing that whatever Lovelich's limitations as a writer, his very distinctness as a figure in a particular social and local milieu can only be valuable to our understanding of the reception of Arthurian material in this period.

The tension between "translation" and "innovation" is addressed most directly in this volume by Ivana Djordjević, who examines some of the ways in which medieval romances problematize, and are problematized by, contemporary translation theory. She argues that, "generally speaking, the problem of establishing what we consider to be a text is always present in medieval studies, but it seems to be much more acute in the study of Middle English romance than it is in many other genres" (19). This perspective makes the genre of romance seem less safely predictable than it is often taken to be. At the same time, Elizabeth Archibald shows that "genre" itself is a difficult concept to apply in this context, for a term such as "the Breton lay," which has long been used by scholars as a fundamental point of reference, itself depends on complex and shifting movements within the aesthetics of medieval insular romance. These approaches highlight the variety of the different linguistic and generic codes available to romancers in what Djordjević calls "the intricate socio-linguistic and socio-cultural situation in post-Conquest England" (15), but several other essays in this collection are more concerned with the range and power of the *non*-linguistic codes operating in this same situation. Morgan Dickson and Rachel Snell, for example, look at different aspects of disguise as a means of marking, and moderating between, the boundaries of social status, while Amanda Hopkins discusses the symbolic and social significance of cloth and needlecraft in *Emaré*. A group of texts on which such a range of such specific codes can operate—codes of language, of genre, of rank, of clothes, and even (as Rachell Snell points out) of food—presents particular difficulties of interpretation that make reading medieval romances too much of a continuing challenge for any sense of comfortable familiarity to be justified.

NEIL CARTLIDGE

University College Dublin / Universität Freiburg

BONNIE WHEELER and FIONA TOLHURST, eds. *On Arthurian Women: Essays in Memory of Maureen Fries.* Dallas: Scriptorium Press, 2001. Pp. xiii, 408. $39.95.

This collection of thirty-two essays in memory of Maureen Fries, many published in this *festschrift* for the first time, presents a widely ranging set of topics and perspectives on the general subject of women in the Arthurian tradition, the field to which Professor Fries devoted most of her scholarly work and her academic career. Bonnie Wheeler and Fiona Tolhurst, the volume's editors, have organized it into two major sections. "Part One: On Arthurian Women" focuses on women characters and issues related to them in the Arthuriad across a broad range of genres, media, countries, and time periods; "Part Two: On Women Arthurians" examines, in ten biographical and autobiographical essays, the contributions of women scholars to the field of Arthurian studies over the past two centuries. Taken together, these essays provide an unusually rich, varied, and detailed mapping of the complex issues involved both in studying women and in being women studying within the vast compass of the Arthurian tradition.

"Part One: On Arthurian Women" groups its twenty-two essays into seven subsections:—"Guenevere"; "Elaines"; "Sorceresses"; "Arthur's Sisters"; "The Arthurian Lady"; "Arthurian Bad Girls?"; and "The Modern Gaze." These titles suggest the range of characters, concerns, and periods covered by the collection. The preponderance of essays in this section are literary studies, whose methodologies, in many instances, represent a wide variety of feminist literary theories, from the new historicist to the psychoanalytic. While some, such as the essays on Guenevere by Rebecca Beals, Beverly Kennedy, and Edward Donald Kennedy, focus on major Arthurian women as they offer revisionist readings of them, others such as the contributions by Elizabeth S. Sklar and Michael W. Twomey, recuperate characters such as "Malory's Other(ed) Elaine" (Sklar) and "Morgan le Fay at Hautdesert" (Twomey) from their marginalization both within their texts and within the critical tradition. Throughout this section, many of the contributors acknowledge their indebtedness to Maureen Fries's numerous writings on women in the Arthuriad, and especially to her important essay, "Female Heroes, Heroines, and Counter-Heroes: Images of Women in Medieval Arthurian Tradition" (in *Popular Traditions,* ed. Sally Slocum [Bowling

Green: Popular Press, 1992], pp. 5–17; rptd. In *Arthurian Women,* ed. Thelma Fenster [New York: Garland, 1996, pp. 59–73]).

Other essays in Part One range outside literary criticism and are based in material history, in feminist spirituality, and in art historical, archaeological, and anthropological inquiry. Sue Ellen Holbrook, for example, places her examination of Nymue and her sisters within the context of elemental goddess rituals in order to study the patterns of transformation associated with them. In her essay on Morgan in *Sir Gawain and the Green Knight,* Lorraine Kochanske Stock finds a powerful "visual analogue" (121) for the *Gawain*-poet's representation of the aged Morgan in the ancient stone carvings of the Celtic Sheela-na-gigs. And Alan Lupack argues that early twentieth-century women illustrators of the Arthuriad provide their own visual revisions of telling scenes in the legends through the ways they construct and frame their illustrations of them. Taken together, the essays in Part One form a detailed and textured picture of women's place and function both in the Arthurian world and in Arthurian studies.

This range of emphases and subjects is also evident in the ten biographical and autobiographical essays in "Part Two: On Women Arthurians," which begins with Rachel Bromwich's discussion of the crucial work that Lady Charlotte Guest (1812–95) contributed to the textual accessibility of the "Mabinogion." In their accounts of women Arthurians, from the oft-discredited Jessie Laidlay Weston to Gertrude Schoepperle Loomis, Laura Hibbard Loomis, and Dorothy Bethurum Loomis, and the indomitable and indeed hula-dancing Valerie Lagorio, these essays forefront the challenges posed for these women by their work itself and by the conditions of the world in which they pursued it. Of particular note in this section is Fanni Bogdanow's powerful autobiographical essay, "From Holocaust Survivor to Arthurian Scholar," which tells the story of her journey from Nazi Germany to Great Britain in the *Kindertransport* and to the University of Manchester, where she pursued her graduate work in Arthurian studies with Eugene Vinaver. It is as moving a testimony to the power of the human spirit and the power of medieval literature as one is likely to find.

If one strand links the many and diverse essays within this volume, aside from the focus of its title, *On Arthurian Women,* it is the display of deep respect and affection for the woman Arthurian, Maureen Fries, whom these essays and their contributors honor. From Bonnie Wheeler's and Fiona Tolhurst's personal reminiscences about Professor Fries,

"'Arthurienne Extraordinaire,'" in their introduction to Donald L. Hoffman's concluding tribute to her as "Teacher, Scholar, Friend," it is clear that, in the boldness and passion she brought to her work and her life, Professor Fries was a force with which to be reckoned. Repeatedly, contributors cite the particular generosity she showed young colleagues in her mentoring relationships to them, a generosity that is amply documented in the substance and tone of these essays, as well as in their footnotes to Professor Fries's many articles and essays.

Bonnie Wheeler, Fiona Tolhurst, and Donald Hoffman all end their tributes to Professor Fries by noting that E. Y. Harburg's "Lydia, the Tatooed lady" was her favorite song. Its first line, of course, creates a neat internal rhyme between "Lydia" and "'En-cy-clo-ped-ia.'" This volume, then, is a fitting *festschrift* for the woman Arthurian who loved this song. In its pluralistic approaches, diverse methodologies, and copious range of topics, *On Arthurian Women* not only makes an important contribution to Arthurian studies, it becomes something of an "'En-cy-clo-ped-ia'" itself.

SHEILA FISHER
Trinity College

HUGH WHITE, *Nature, Sex, and Goodness in a Medieval Literary Tradition.* Oxford: Oxford University Press, 2000. Pp. ix, Pp. 278. $65.00.

Hugh White's new book on Nature (he published one on Nature and *Piers Plowman* in 1988), has a long first chapter on "Academic Natures," followed by shorter chapters on Middle English vernacular writings; Boethius and twelfth-century Latin poets like Alan de Lille; Jean de Meun; and "Further French Natures"; and concludes with longish chapters on John Gower and Chaucer. I will concentrate on the last chapters because, though the early chapters are interesting in themselves, there is little carry-over, with a few expected exceptions (e.g., the influence of the *Roman de la Rose*). A word on his method: he produces great swatches of text (slavishly following previous editors' punctuation) followed by a few observations, rather than walking us through passages. He translates all non-English passages but does not gloss even the most difficult Middle English texts.

In an introduction, White begins by listing several accounts of nature, personified or not, in medieval literature, by J. A. W. Bennett, C. S. Lewis, and others, which he considers erroneous, because they associate the natural exclusively with what is reasonable, beautiful, and moral, whereas in fact nature is sometimes taken to be just the opposite. He emphasizes the polysemous character of the word. In practice, however, he often treats nature as a single concept with contradictory attributes.

He assumes that the tradition he deals with considers both good and bad aspects of nature to exist in a postlapsarian world, whereas, it seems to me, nature and the laws of nature are often taken to exist as if no fall had ever taken place, and as if morality were simply a matter of human effort. Often such presentations are influenced by pre-Christian philosophical conceptions. (White does not mention the pagan alternative to the Fall, the gradual decline of the world from a primordial Golden Age.)

Chapter 3, "Natura vicaria Dei," begins with Boethius's accounts of beneficent natural instinct in the *Consolation of Philosophy,* especially of personified Nature (in book 3 metrum 2) as the regulating force of the universe. When we come to the twelfth-century poets such as Bernard Silvester and Alan de Lille, White makes no attempt to integrate their accounts of nature with theological concepts. He acknowledges in a note that Alan was an original theologian, but he does not treat his theological views either here or in Chapter 2, and we are left to conjecture how he would reconcile his sublime view of *Natura* with the fallen nature of Christian doctrine. He can only point to a vague unease with nature: "As well as registering what Nature cannot do, we experience discomfort about the arrangements Nature actually does make" (108–9).

In Chapter 4, on the *Roman de la Rose,* White finds a more ambiguous nature. He argues that Le Vielle parodies the Boethian nature, in that caged animals seek their freedom not for noble reasons, as in Boethius, but for base purposes, an interpretation followed by Chaucer (71–72, 117–20, 224–28). When Nature comes on the stage in her own person, White finds her insistence on active procreation disturbing: "Where, one wonders, would this leave the virgin saints, the Lamb himself and his Mother?" (128). He could have asked this sort of question of Alan de Lille.

The chapter on Gower is very methodical, concentrating mainly on the *Confessio Amantis,* with many notes further qualifying the qualifications of his main text as he attempts to deal with the contradictions, or seeming contradictions, of the work. He takes issue with the view of James Simpson that the poem ends with "a proper sense of the capacity and responsibility of human reason for controlling the natural drives" (pp. 175–76). He believes that Genius declares that love leads to misrule of the self and moral blindness, which he demonstrates by citing 8.2075–88, ending with the couplet:

> For as of this which thou art inne,
> Be that thou seist it is a Sinne.

He does not explain the last line, but seems to take it to mean, "Let it be that you see that it is a sin." But in Macaulay's edition, the sentence does not end there, so that the line seems to mean, "Since you say that it is a sin":

> Be that thou seist it is a sinne,
> And sinne mai no pris deserve,
> Withoute pris and who schal serve,
> I not what profit myhte availe.

He does not treat the headnote to 8.2377 ff. that indicates that Nature has one set of laws for the young and another for the old: "Sicut habet Maius non dat Natura Decembri." But I agree that at the end of his work (especially in his revised version), Gower seems to preclude the possibility of honest love for lovers, something that he admits throughout the work up to the end.

In the final chapter on Chaucer, White claims that one can find more of a range of meanings for nature than in Gower. When Chaucer talks about personified Nature, White believes, he is more skeptical than Gower about her benignity. However, he comes to this conclusion by making unwarranted inferences where Chaucer says nothing. Thus, in the *Physician's Tale* ("as in other works we have examined"), "Chaucer presents an apparently benign Nature, powerful and creative, only to compromise that presentation by implicating Nature in debility, disorder, depravity, and destruction" (246). But, in fact, Chaucer says nothing further about Nature, once he speaks about her endowment of Virginia with admirable attributes. The same is true in *Troilus:* by the time that things go wrong in the story, the language of nature and kind has long been dropped, and we are not invited to go back and revise what has been said earlier. It is a temporary motif.

The two-page "Conclusion" does not do justice to the good things in this book, but it points up more than ever the difficulties of speaking about nature in the Middle Ages without paying proper attention to the implications of fallen nature—the result of original sin—and classical traditions of "falling nature," or moral and physical entropy.

HENRY ANSGAR KELLY
University of California, Los Angeles

JOCELYN WOGAN-BROWNE, ROSALYNN VOADEN, ARLYN DIAMOND, ANN HUTCHISON, CAROL MEALE, and LESLEY JOHNSON, eds. *Medieval Women: Texts and Contexts in Late Medieval Britain: Essays for Felicity Riddy*. Medieval Women: Texts and Contexts, vol. 3. Turnhout, Belgium: Brepols, 2000. Pp. xv, 436. 10 figures and illustrations. $50.00.

Twenty-eight scholars, many of them Felicity Riddy's colleagues and former students at the University of York, contributed to this enormous collection of uniformly high-quality essays. As an homage to Riddy, the volume is a tremendous success. Even more impressive than the customary overview of the honoree's career to date and bibliography of her writings are the many testimonials within the essays themselves: several claim to have been inspired by conversations, collaborations, or other interactions with her; many include short paeans; most attest to her influence through citations of her scholarship.

The most striking feature of this collection is its eclecticism. To be sure, all of the essays pertain in some way to medieval women. Moreover, all but one are historicist in their orientation. Yet beyond these common threads, there is great diversity among the essays, whose subjects range from incest to Lollardy, from Marian lyrics to legal depositions, from the books women read to the houses they lived in. The editors gamely attempt to impose some coherence by dividing the essays into three categories—"Reading Matters," "Matters of Conduct," and "Household Matters"—but the essays themselves (particularly those in the "Reading" and "Household" sections) resist compartmentalization.

The issue that receives the most attention is conduct. Carolyn P. Collette discusses the influence on Chaucer's Prudence, Cecilia, and Griselda of the tradition of French conduct books for wives, with its awareness of the sociopolitical implications of female conduct and the interconnection of private and public harmony. Kim M. Phillips examines the "gestural interaction of men and women" (186) in five late-fifteenth-century books that were written for or read by women. Patricia Cullum and Jeremy Goldberg discuss the Bolton Hours as an "educational tool" (236) that Margaret Blackburn may have used to instruct her daughters, and Douglas Gray discusses Stephen Scrope's translation for an East Anglian audience of Christine de Pisan's *L'Epistre d'Othéa,* a book of advice directed at knights. In what was for me the most intriguing essay of this cluster on conduct, Nicholas Watson examines the *Book to a Mother,* whose reformist themes are anomalous in a conduct book and whose focus on a female reader is unique among major Lollard writings. The *Book,* Watson maintains, serves "as a bridge between what we think of as the separate worlds of devotion and religious dissent" and "may be an unexpectedly important piece of the jigsaw puzzle of medieval English literary history" (184).

The only author treated in more than two essays is Chaucer. Helen Phillips discusses the ambiguous, contradictory, and often riddle-like honorifics for the Virgin Mary in medieval lyrics, with special attention to Chaucer's *ABC.* Sally Mapstone looks at literary prototypes for Chaucer's Criseyde, including Homeric precedents, of which she argues medieval authors were more aware than is usually supposed. Alastair Minnis and Eric J. Johnson argue that, considered in light of medieval understandings of fear, Chaucer's allusions to Criseyde's fearfulness should not be seen as derogatory but rather as part of an overall "idealizing, antimisogynistic strategy" (213). In an equally provocative reading of incest in the *Clerk's Tale,* Anne Savage argues that Walter's proposal to marry his daughter was no sham: "It seems less likely that Walter carries out a plan to convince Griselda he will marry again than that he actually *changes his mind*" (351).

For the rest of the essays, it is easier to discern meaningful pairings than meaningful clusters. The essays by W. M. Ormrod and Noël James Menuge complement each other especially well, for both apply methods of literary analysis to materials that were once treated as sources of historical fact. Ormrod uses the disparate narratives of Joan of Kent's encounter with the rebels in the Revolt of 1381 to elucidate chroniclers' political agendas. Menuge uses the testimony in Constance de Skel-manthorpe's marriage litigation to propose that legal cases "were not won and lost upon legal circumstance, convention and technicalities alone, but also upon the skill with which events were narrated, key details brought to prominence, and background detail convincingly sketched" (129).

Other pairings reveal sharp differences in their approach to a common subject. Priscilla Bawcutt maps the largely uncharted terrain of women patrons and bookowners in Scotland, while Julia Boffey dilates upon the rather surprising circulation among women of the prose *Three Kings of Cologne*. Katherine J. Lewis and Jocelyn Wogan-Browne treat medieval interpretations of very different virgin saints: Lewis considers the mean-ing of the legendary Saint Margaret's suffering for women readers, while Wogan-Browne reads the *Life of Edith of Wilton* in terms of Lancastrian politics and propaganda, arguing, "The *Edith* life writes Wilton into a Henrician monasticism, in which the authority of this ancient Wessex nunnery and its virgin patron saint are inflected with Lancastrian con-cerns" (396). Arlyn Diamond and Jane Gilbert approach medieval ro-mance from different theoretical perspectives, Diamond using close reading to determine the contribution of the seemingly peripheral fe-male characters to the social vision of the Alliterative *Morte Arthure* and Gilbert employing Lacanian psychoanalysis to understand maternity, paternity, and monstrosity in the *King of Tars* and *Sir Gowther*.

The two contributions on Margery Kempe represent opposite ends of the spectrum of current Kempe criticism. In an essay whose findings are likely to be widely accepted, Carol M. Meale points to the importance of drama in shaping Kempe's religious consciousness and her *Book*. In what is likely to be the most controversial essay in the volume, Sarah Rees Jones argues that the *Book of Margery Kempe* is, above all, about episcopal authority and may indeed have been "written by clergy, for the instruction of clergy" (382).

The other essays in the volume certainly merit notice: Peter Biller's discussion of Northern European Cathars, whose ranks included two Englishwomen; Jane Grenville's archaeological study of two medieval townhouses in York; Ceridwen Lloyd-Morgan's introduction to those of us who know no Welsh of fascinating contributions to the "querelle des femmes" tradition by Welsh women poets; and Colin Richmond's biography of the Paston family friend Elizabeth Clere.

These brief summaries do not begin to do justice to the arguments advanced in *Medieval Women.* I do hope, however, that I have given readers some sense of the volume's scope and richness. Its editors are to be congratulated for honoring Felicity Riddy's contribution to so many facets of the study of medieval women in a volume that is bound to be read and cited extensively in the years to come.

KAREN A. WINSTEAD
Ohio State University

Books Received

Ashley, Kathleen, and Robert L. A. Clark, eds. *Medieval Conduct*. Medieval Cultures, vol. 29. Minneapolis: University of Minnesota Press, 2001. Pp. xx, 241. $49.95 cloth, $19.95 paper.

Batt, Catherine. *Malory's* Morte Darthur*: Remaking Arthurian Tradition*. New York: Palgrave, 2002. Pp. xxiii, 264. $49.95.

Blamires, Alcuin, and Gail C. Holian. *The Romance of the Rose Illuminated*. Medieval and Renaissance Texts and Studies, vol. 223. Tempe: Arizona Center for Medieval and Renaissance Studies, 2002. Pp. xxxviii, 137, 49 color plates, 16 black and white plates. $48.00.

Blumenfeld-Kosinski, Renate, Duncan Robertson, and Nancy Warren, eds. *The Vernacular Spirit: Essays on Medieval Religious Literature*. New York: Palgrave, 2002. Pp. 324. $59.95.

Boitani, Piero. *The Genius to Improve an Invention: Literary Transitions*. Notre Dame: Unversity of Notre Dame Press, 2002. Pp. xvi, 151. $35.00 cloth, $18.00 paper.

Burrow, J. A. *Gestures and Looks in Medieval Narrative*. Cambridge: Cambridge University Press, 2002. Pp. 200. $55.00.

Cenci, Elena, trans. *Robert Henryson: Il Testamento di Creseida* (Milano: Luni Editrice, 1998). With notes by Anna Torti. Pp. 97.

Chism, Christine. *Alliterative Revivals*. Philadelphia: University of Pennsylvania Press, 2002. Pp. 327. $57.50.

Crane, Susan. *The Performance of Self: Ritual, Clothing, and Identity During the Hundred Years War*. Philadelphia: University of Pennsylvania Press, 2002. Pp. 268, 4 color plates. $49.95 cloth, $19.95 paper.

Cunningham, Karen. *Imaginary Betrayals: Subjectivity and the Discourses of Treason in Early Modern England*. Philadelphia: University of Pennsylvania Press, 2002. Pp. 213. $42.50.

Edwards, Robert R. *Chaucer and Boccaccio: Antiquity and Modernity*. New York: Palgrave, 2002. Pp. xv, 205. $62.00.

Erler, Mary C. *Women, Reading, and Piety in Late Medieval England*. Cambridge: Cambridge University Press, 2002. Pp. 226. $60.00.

Evans, G. R. *Fifty Key Medieval Thinkers*. London and New York: Routledge, 2002. Pp. xxxiv, 183. $55.00 cloth, $18.95 paper.

Jeneid, Michael. *Chaucer's Checklist*. Santa Cruz: Pandion Press, 1993. Pp. 130. $24.00.

Jimura, Akiyuki, and Yoshiyuki Nakao, *Originality and Adventure: Essays on English Language and Literature in Honour of Masahiko Kanno*. Tokyo: Eihosha, 2001. Pp. v, 333.

MacDonald, Joyce Green. *Women and Race in Early Modern Texts*. Cambridge: Cambridge University Press, 2002. Pp. 188. $55.00.

Rogers, William Elford. *Interpretation in* Piers Plowman. Washington, D. C.: Catholic University of America Press, 2002. Pp. 300. $64.95.

Salisbury, Eve, Georgina Donavin, and Merrall Llewelyn Price, eds. *Domestic Violence in Medieval Texts*. Gainesville: University Press of Florida, 2002. Pp. 354. $55.00 cloth.

Scala, Elizabeth. *Absent Narratives, Manuscript Textuality, and Literary Structure in Late Medieval England*. New York: Palgrave, 2002. Pp. xix, 284. $59.95.

Seymour, M. C., ed. *The Defective Version of* Mandeville's Travels. Oxford: Oxford University Press, 2002. Pp. xxx, 234. $74.00

Steiner, Emily, and Candace Barrington, eds. *The Letter of the Law: Legal Practice and Literary Production in Medieval England*. Ithaca: Cornell University Press, 2002. Pp. 257. $45.00 cloth, $19.95 paper.

Strohm, Paul. *Theory and the Premodern Text*. Medieval Cultures, vol. 26. Minneapolis: University of Minnesota Press, 2000. Pp. xvi, 269. $42.95 cloth, $16.95 paper.

An Annotated Chaucer Bibliography
2001

Compiled and edited by Mark Allen and Bege K. Bowers

Regular contributors:

Bruce W. Hozeski, *Ball State University* (Indiana)
George Nicholas, *Benedictine College* (Kansas)
Martha S. Waller, *Butler University* (Indiana)
Marilyn Sutton, *California State University at Dominguez Hills*
Larry L. Bronson, *Mt. Pleasant, Michigan*
Glending Olson, *Cleveland State University* (Ohio)
Jesús Luis Serrano Reyes (*Córdoba*)
Winthrop Wetherbee, *Cornell University* (New York)
Elizabeth Dobbs, *Grinnell College* (Iowa)
Hisato Ebi, *Kobe Women's University*
Matsuji Tajima, *Kyushu University*
Brian A. Shaw, *London, Ontario*
Stefania D'Agata D'Ottavi, *University of Macerata* (Italy)
William Schipper, *Memorial University* (Newfoundland, Canada)
Martha Rust, *New York University*
Daniel J. Pinti, *Niagara University* (New York)
Amy Goodwin, *Randolph-Macon College* (Virginia)
Erik Kooper, *Rijksuniversiteit te Utrecht*
Cindy L. Vitto, *Rowan College of New Jersey*
Richard H. Osberg, *Santa Clara University* (California)
Margaret Connolly, *University College, Cork* (Ireland)
Juliette Dor, *Université de Liège* (Belgium)
Mary Flowers Braswell and Elaine Whitaker, *University of Alabama at Birmingham*
Denise Stodola, *University of Missouri—Columbia*
Cynthia Gravlee, *University of Montevallo* (Alabama)
Gregory M. Sadlek, *University of Nebraska at Omaha*

Cynthia Ho, *University of North Carolina, Asheville*
Richard J. Utz, *University of Northern Iowa*
Thomas Hahn, *University of Rochester* (New York)
Rebecca Beal, *University of Scranton* (Pennsylvania)
Mark Allen, *University of Texas at San Antonio*
Joerg O. Fichte, *Universität Tübingen* (Tübingen, Germany)
Andrew Lynch and Olivia Mair, *University of Western Australia*
John M. Crafton, *West Georgia College*
Robert Correale, *Wright State University* (Ohio)
Bege K. Bowers, *Youngstown State University* (Ohio)

Ad hoc contributions were made by the following: Rebecca McCracken (*University of Alabama at Birmingham*), Rebecca Sansky (*University of Scranton*), and Toni K. Thayer (*Cleveland State University*).

The bibliographers acknowledge with gratitude the MLA typesimulation provided by the Center for Bibliographical Services of the Modern Language Association; postage from the University of Texas at San Antonio Department of English, Classics, and Philosophy; and assistance from the library staff, especially Susan McCray, at the University of Texas at San Antonio.

This bibliography continues the bibliographies published since 1975 in previous volumes of *Studies in the Age of Chaucer*. Bibliographic information up to 1975 can be found in Eleanor P. Hammond, *Chaucer: A Bibliographic Manual* (1908; reprint, New York: Peter Smith, 1933); D. D. Griffith, *Bibliography of Chaucer, 1908–53* (Seattle: University of Washington Press, 1955); William R. Crawford, *Bibliography of Chaucer, 1954–63* (Seattle: University of Washington Press, 1967); and Lorrayne Y. Baird, *Bibliography of Chaucer, 1964–73* (Boston: G. K. Hall, 1977). See also Lorrayne Y. Baird-Lange and Hildegard Schnuttgen, *Bibliography of Chaucer, 1974–1985* (Hamden, Conn.: Shoe String Press, 1988); and Bege K. Bowers and Mark Allen, eds., *Annotated Chaucer Bibliography, 1986–1996* (Notre Dame, Ind.: University of Notre Dame, 2002).

Additions and corrections to this bibliography should be sent to Mark Allen, Bibliographic Division, New Chaucer Society, Department of English, Classics, and Philosophy, University of Texas at San Antonio 78249–0643 (Fax: 210–458–5366; E-mail: MALLEN@UTSA.EDU). An electronic version of this bibliography (1975–2000) is available via the New Chaucer Society Web page <*http://artsci.wustl.edu/~chaucer/*> or at <*http://uchaucer.utsa.edu*>. Authors are urged to send annotations for articles, reviews, and books that have been or might be overlooked.

Classifications

Abbreviations of Chaucer's Works

ABC	*An ABC*
Adam	*Adam Scriveyn*
Anel	*Anelida and Arcite*
Astr	*A Treatise on the Astrolabe*
Bal Compl	*A Balade of Complaint*
BD	*The Book of the Duchess*
Bo	*Boece*
Buk	*The Envoy to Bukton*
CkT, CkP, Rv—CkL	*The Cook's Tale, The Cook's Prologue, Reeve—Cook Link*
ClT, ClP, Cl—MerL	*The Clerk's Tale, The Clerk's Prologue, Clerk—Merchant Link*
Compl d'Am	*Complaynt d'Amours*
CT	*The Canterbury Tales*
CYT, CYP	*The Canon's Yeoman's Tale, The Canon's Yeoman's Prologue*
Equat	*The Equatorie of the Planetis*
For	*Fortune*
Form Age	*The Former Age*
FranT, FranP	*The Franklin's Tale, The Franklin's Prologue*
FrT, FrP, Fr—SumL	*The Friar's Tale, The Friar's Prologue, Friar—Summoner Link*
Gent	*Gentilesse*
GP	*The General Prologue*
HF	*The House of Fame*
KnT, Kn—MilL	*The Knight's Tale, Knight—Miller Link*
Lady	*A Complaint to His Lady*
LGW, LGWP	*The Legend of Good Women, The Legend of Good Women Prologue*
ManT, ManP	*The Manciple's Tale, The Manciple's Prologue*
Mars	*The Complaint of Mars*
Mel, Mel—MkL	*The Tale of Melibee, Melibee—Monk Link*
MercB	*Merciles Beaute*
MerT, MerE—SqH	*The Merchant's Tale, Merchant Endlink—Squire Headlink*

MilT, MilP, Mil—RvL	The Miller's Tale, The Miller's Prologue, Miller—Reeve Link
MkT, MkP, Mk—NPL	The Monk's Tale, The Monk's Prologue, Monk—Nun's Priest Link
MLT, MLH, MLP, MLE	The Man of Law's Tale, Man of Law Headlink, The Man of Law's Prologue, Man of Law Endlink
NPT, NPP, NPE	The Nun's Priest's Tale, The Nun's Priest's Prologue, Nun's Priest's Endlink
PardT, PardP	The Pardoner's Tale, The Pardoner's Prologue
ParsT, ParsP	The Parson's Tale, The Parson's Prologue
PF	The Parliament of Fowls
PhyT, Phy—PardL	The Physician's Tale, Physician—Pardoner Link
Pity	The Complaint unto Pity
Prov	Proverbs
PrT, PrP, Pr—ThL	The Prioress's Tale, The Prioress's Prologue, Prioress—Thopas Link
Purse	The Complaint of Chaucer to His Purse
Ret	Chaucer's Retraction {Retractation}
Rom	The Romaunt of the Rose
Ros	To Rosemounde
RvT, RvP	The Reeve's Tale, The Reeve's Prologue
Scog	The Envoy to Scogan
ShT, Sh—PrL	The Shipman's Tale, Shipman—Prioress Link
SNT, SNP, SN—CYL	The Second Nun's Tale, The Second Nun's Prologue, Second Nun—Canon's Yeoman Link
SqT, SqH, Sq—FranL	The Squire's Tale, Squire Headlink, Squire—Franklin Link
Sted	Lak of Stedfastnesse
SumT, SumP	The Summoner's Tale, The Summoner's Prologue
TC	Troilus and Criseyde
Th, Th—MelL	The Tale of Sir Thopas, Sir Thopas—Melibee Link

Truth	*Truth*
Ven	*The Complaint of Venus*
WBT, WBP, WB—FrL	*The Wife of Bath's Tale, The Wife of Bath's Prologue, Wife of Bath—Friar Link*
Wom Nob	*Womanly Noblesse*
Wom Unc	*Against Women Unconstant*

Periodical Abbreviations

AdI	*Annali d'Italianistica*
Anglia	*Anglia: Zeitschrift für Englische Philologie*
Anglistik	*Anglistik: Mitteilungen des Verbandes deutscher Anglisten*
ANQ	*ANQ: A Quarterly Journal of Short Articles, Notes, and Reviews*
ArAA	*Arbeiten aus Anglistik und Amerikanistik*
Archiv	*Archiv für das Studium der Neueren Sprachen und Literaturen*
Arthuriana	*Arthuriana*
BAM	*Bulletin des Anglicistes Médiévistes*
BJRL	*Bulletin of the John Rylands University Library of Manchester*
C&L	*Christianity and Literature*
CarmP	*Carmina Philosophiae: Journal of the International Boethius Society*
Chaucer Yearbook	*Chaucer Yearbook: A Journal of Late Medieval Studies*
ChauR	*Chaucer Review*
CL	*Comparative Literature* (Eugene, Ore.)
CLS	*Comparative Literature Studies*
CML	*Classical and Modern Literature: A Quarterly* (Columbia, Mo.)
CollL	*College Literature*
Comparatist	*The Comparatist: Journal of the Southern Comparative Literature Association*
Crossings	*Crossings: A Counter-Disciplinary Journal* (Binghamton, N.Y.)
DAI	*Dissertation Abstracts International*
Disputatio	*Disputatio: An International Transdisciplinary Journal of the Late Middle Ages*
DR	*Dalhousie Review*
ÉA	*Études Anglaises: Grand-Bretagne, États-Unis*
ÉC	*Études Celtiques*
EHR	*English Historical Review*
EIC	*Essays in Criticism: A Quarterly Journal of Literary Criticism*

ELH	*ELH*
ELN	*English Language Notes*
EMS	*English Manuscript Studies, 1100–1700*
English	*English: The Journal of the English Association*
Envoi	*Envoi: A Review Journal of Medieval Literature*
ES	*English Studies*
ESC	*English Studies in Canada*
Exemplaria	*Exemplaria: A Journal of Theory in Medieval and Renaissance Studies*
Expl	*Explicator*
FCS	*Fifteenth-Century Studies*
Florilegium	*Florilegium: Carleton University Papers on Late Antiquity and the Middle Ages*
FMLS	*Forum for Modern Language Studies*
Genre	*Genre: Forms of Discourse and Culture*
GRM	*Germanisch-Romanische Monatsschrift*
HLQ	*Huntington Library Quarterly: Studies in English and American History and Literature* (San Marino, Calif.)
InG	*In Geardagum: Essays on Old and Middle English Language and Literature*
JAIS	*Journal of Anglo-Italian Studies*
JEBS	*Journal of the Early Book Society*
JEGP	*Journal of English and Germanic Philology*
JEngL	*Journal of English Linguistics*
JEP	*Journal of Evolutionary Psychology*
JMEMSt	*Journal of Medieval and Early Modern Studies*
JournalX	*Journal x: A Journal in Culture and Criticism*
JRMMRA	*Quidditas: Journal of the Rocky Mountain Medieval and Renaissance Association*
L&LC	*Literary and Linguistic Computing: Journal of the Association for Literary and Linguistic Computing*
Lang&S	*Language and Style: An International Journal*
LeedsSE	*Leeds Studies in English*
Library	*The Library: The Transactions of the Bibliographical Society*
MA	*Le Moyen Age: Revue d'Histoire et de Philologie* (Brussels, Belgium)
MÆ	*Medium Ævum*
M&H	*Medievalia et Humanistica: Studies in Medieval and Renaissance Culture*

468

Manuscripta	*Manuscripta* (St. Louis, Mo.)
Mediaevalia	*Mediaevalia: An Interdisciplinary Journal of Medieval Studies Worldwide*
Mediaevistik	*Mediaevistik: Internationale Zeitschrift für Interdisziplinäire Mittelalterforschung*
MedPers	*Medieval Perspectives*
MES	*Medieval English Studies*
MFN	*Medieval Feminist Newsletter*
MichA	*Michigan Academician* (Ann Arbor, Mich.)
MLQ	*Modern Language Quarterly: A Journal of Literary History*
MLR	*The Modern Language Review*
ModA	*Modern Age: A Quarterly Review*
MP	*Modern Philology: A Journal Devoted to Research in Medieval and Modern Literature*
N&Q	*Notes and Queries*
Neophil	*Neophilologus* (Dordrecht, Netherlands)
NFS	*Nottingham French Studies*
NLH	*New Literary History: A Journal of Theory and Interpretation*
NM	*Neuphilologische Mitteilungen: Bulletin of the Modern Language Society*
NMS	*Nottingham Medieval Studies*
NOWELE	*NOWELE: North-Western European Language Evolution*
Parergon	*Parergon: Bulletin of the Australian and New Zealand Association for Medieval and Early Modern Studies*
PBA	*Proceedings of the British Academy*
PBSA	*Papers of the Bibliographical Society of America*
PLL	*Papers on Language and Literature: A Journal for Scholars and Critics of Language and Literature*
PMLA	*Publications of the Modern Language Association of America*
PQ	*Philological Quarterly*
Prolepsis	*Prolepsis: The Tübingen Review of English Studies*
ProverbiumY	*Proverbium: Yearbook of International Proverb Scholarship*
RES	*Review of English Studies*
Romania	*Romania: Revue Consacrée à l'Étude des Langues et des Littératures Romanes*

RSQ	*Rhetoric Society Quarterly* (University Park, Penn.)
SAC	*Studies in the Age of Chaucer*
SAF	*Studies in American Fiction* (Boston, Mass.)
SAP	*Studia Anglica Posnaniensia: An International Review of English*
SAQ	*South Atlantic Quarterly*
SB	*Studies in Bibliography: Papers of the Bibliographical Society of the University of Virginia*
SCJ	*The Sixteenth-Century Journal: Journal of Early Modern Studies* (Kirksville, Mo.)
SEL	*SEL: Studies in English Literature, 1500–1900*
SELIM	*SELIM: Journal of the Spanish Society for Medieval English Language and Literature*
SIcon	*Studies in Iconography*
SiM	*Studies in Medievalism*
SMART	*Studies in Medieval and Renaissance Teaching*
SMELL	*Studies in Medieval English Language and Literature*
SN	*Studia Neophilologica: A Journal of Germanic and Romance Languages and Literatures*
SP	*Studies in Philology*
Speculum	*Speculum: A Journal of Medieval Studies*
SSF	*Studies in Short Fiction*
TCBS	*Transactions of the Cambridge Bibliographical Society*
Text	*Text: Transactions of the Society for Textual Scholarship*
TLS	*Times Literary Supplement* (London, England)
TMR	*The Medieval Review* <*http://www.hti.umich.edu/b/ bmr/tmr.html*>
UTQ	*University of Toronto Quarterly: A Canadian Journal of the Humanities* (Toronto, Canada)
Viator	*Viator: Medieval and Renaissance Studies*
YER	*Yeats Eliot Review: A Journal of Criticism and Scholarship*
YES	*Yearbook of English Studies*
YULG	*Yale University Library Gazette*
YWES	*Year's Work in English Studies*
YLS	*The Yearbook of Langland Studies*
ZAA	*Zeitschrift für Anglistik und Amerikanistik: A Quarterly of Language, Literature and Culture*

470

Bibliographical Citations and Annotations

Bibliographies, Reports, and Reference

1. Allen, Mark, and Bege K. Bowers. "An Annotated Chaucer Bibliography, 1999." *SAC* 23 (2001): 615–99. Continuation of *SAC* annual annotated bibliography (since 1975); based on contributions from an international bibliographic team, independent research, and *MLA Bibliography* listings. 268 items, plus listing of reviews for 70 books. Includes an author index.

2. Allen, Valerie, and Margaret Connolly. "Middle English: Chaucer." *YWES* 79 (2001, for 1998): 196–226. A discursive bibliography of Chaucer studies for 1998, divided into four subcategories: general, *CT*, *TC*, and other works.

3. Allen, Valerie, and Margaret Connolly. "Middle English: Chaucer." *YWES* 80 (2001, for 1999): 183–210. A discursive bibliography of Chaucer studies for 1999, divided into four subcategories: general, *CT*, *TC*, and other works.

4. Greentree, Rosemary. *The Middle English Lyric and Short Poem.* Annotated Bibliographies of Old and Middle English Literature, no. 7. Rochester, N.Y.; and Cambridge: D. S. Brewer, 2001. x, 570 pp. Descriptive, annotated bibliography of editions and criticism of Middle English lyrics and short poems, focusing on 1900–1995 but including several editions and studies outside this range. Excludes works dedicated exclusively to Chaucer and other named authors but includes studies in which such authors and their works are discussed along with anonymous works. Includes 1,022 + cross-listed entries, an index of scholars and critics, a subject index (97 references to Chaucer), an index of first lines, and a "Temporary Index of First Lines" that covers works not included in other first-line listings.

5. Tsuchiya, Tadayuki. "A Concordance and Glossary to the *General Prologue of the Canterbury Tales* (Revised from *Win* to *Zephyrus*)." *Studies in Liberal Arts and Sciences* (Tokyo University of Science) 34 (2001): 43–62. Revised version of the portion from *Win* to *Zephyrus* in the author's privately printed *Concordance and Glossary to the* General Prologue *of the* Canterbury Tales (1975).

See also nos. 118, 133, 160.

Recordings and Films

6. Blandeau, Agnès. "Prologues et épilogues dans *I racconti di Canterbury* de Pasolini: Ellipse et dilatation du récit." In Leo Carruthers and Adrian Papahagi, eds. *Prologues et épilogues dans la littérature anglaise du Moyen Âge* (*SAC* 25 [2003], no. 98), pp. 171–82. Pasolini's *Racconti di Canterbury* uses ellipsis and expansion to produce cinematographic transformations of *CT*. Adjustments of narrative structure and original visual effects produce "tales told only for the pleasure of telling them."

7. *The Canterbury Tales*. DHP 7355. Ontario: Durkin Hayes, 1995. 2 audio cassettes; 134 min. Modern English reading (Nevill Coghill translation) of *RvT*, *ShT*, *WBP*, *FranT*, and *SumT*, each accompanied by readings of the *GP* description of the teller. Read by Fenella Fielding and Martin Starkie.

Chaucer's Life

8. Bennett, Michael. "Isabelle of France, Anglo-French Diplomacy and Cultural Exchange in the Late 1350s." In J. S. Bothwell, ed. *The Age of Edward III*. Rochester, N.Y.; and Woodbridge: York Medieval Press and Boydell Press, 2001, pp. 215–25. Seeks to "reveal a little more fully the world" in which Chaucer was trained as a page, examining the household accounts of Isabelle (BL MS Cotton Galba E.14) in the context of better-known household accounts. Bennett comments on pageantry, diplomacy, and domestic life.

9. Serrano Reyes, Jesús L. "The Chaucers in Spain: From the Wedding to the Funeral." *SELIM* 8 (2001): 193–203. Comments on Chaucer's connections with Spain, focusing on 1366, when he was married and he visited Spain, and on 1387, when many died of pestilence after accompanying John of Gaunt on his invasion of Spain in 1386.

See also nos. 114, 118, 133, 160, 184, 206, 210, 271.

Facsimiles, Editions, and Translations

10. Bly, Siobhain. "From Text to Man: Re-Creating Chaucer in Sixteenth-Century Editions." *Comitatus* 30 (1999): 131–65. Sixteenth-century editions of Chaucer's works "reflect a gradual transition from text-based definitions of what constitutes Chaucer to author-focused ones."

Bly considers Thynne's edition of 1532, Stowe's of 1561, and Speght's of 1602, discussing "visual components" of the editions, prefatory matter, and the corpus they include, observing a growing emphasis on Chaucer as a "flesh-and-blood historical personage."

11. Dalby, Richard. "Chaucer's 'Canterbury Tales.'" *Book and Magazine Collector* 199 (2000): 46–59. Surveys the sales performance of various editions of Chaucerian texts, concentrating on recent sales and auctions and on market values. Includes a brief survey of Chaucer's works and editions and responds to the auction of Caxton's first edition for £4.6 million.

12. Jimura, Akiyuki, Yoshiyuki Nakao, and Masatsugu Matsuo. *A Comprehensive Textual Comparison of "The Parliament of Fowls": Benson's, Brewer's, and Havely's Editions.* Hiroshima University Faculty of Letters Studies, no. 61.3. Hiroshima: Hiroshima University, 2001. iv, 100 pp. Comparison of three editions of *PF*.

13. Kelen, Sarah A. "Cultural Capital: Selling Chaucer's Works, Building Christ Church, Oxford." *ChauR* 36 (2001): 149–57. John Urry's 1721 edition of *The Works of Geoffrey Chaucer* was marketed to support a capital campaign to augment Christ Church, Oxford. Throughout the 1720s and 1730s, several members of the college were occupied with book sales. Despite poor evaluations of the edition, its presentation of Chaucer's works and its glossary were influential throughout the eighteenth century.

14. ———. "*Peirs Plouhman* [sic] and the 'Formidable Array of Blackletter' in the Early Nineteenth Century." In Paul C. Gutjahr and Megan L. Benton, eds. *Illuminating Letters: Typography and Literary Interpretation.* Studies in Print Culture and the History of the Book. Amherst: University of Massachusetts Press, 2001, pp. 47–67. Assesses factors in Thomas Dunham Whitaker's decision to print *Piers Plowman* in 1813 in blackletter type, even though Chaucer had been printed in roman type nearly one hundred years earlier (by Urry) and anthologists of medieval poetry such as Joseph Ritson used roman type.

15. Kim, Jae-Hwan, trans. *Turoilusuwa K'riseidu {Troilus and Criseyde}.* Seoul, Korea: Kkach'i, 2001. Korean translation of *TC*, with an introduction.

16. Lee, Dongill, and Dong-Ch'un Lee, trans. *K'ent'oberi Iyagi I {The Canterbury Tales I}.* Seoul, Korea: Hanwool, 2001. Korean translation of *GP, KnT, MilT, WBPT, ClT, FranT,* and *PardPT*. Includes an introduction.

17. Saez Hidalgo, Ana, trans. *Geoffrey Chaucer: Troilo y Criseida*. Clasicos Medievales, no. 24. Madrid: Gredos, 2001. 263 pp. Spanish prose translation of *TC*, with a biographical and critical introduction that emphasizes Chaucer's adaptation of source material.

18. Siemens, R. G. "Un-editing and Non-editions: The Death of Distance, the Notion of Navigation, and New Acts of Editing in the Electronic Medium." *Anglia* 119 (2001): 423–55. Mentions the electronic edition of Chaucer's *Wife of Bath's Prologue*, edited by Peter Robinson and others.

19. Stubbs, Estelle, ed. *The Hengwrt Chaucer Digital Facsimile*. The *Canterbury Tales* Project. Leicester: Scholarly Digital Editions, 2000. CD-ROM. Full-color complete facsimile of the Hengwrt manuscript (Hg) and the Merthyr fragment (Me) of *CT*. Includes transcriptions of Hg and the Ellesmere manuscript by Michael Pidd and Estelle Stubbs, arranged for comparison; transcription of Me by Paul Thomas and Peter Robinson; codicological descriptions of Hg and Me by Daniel W. Mosser; transcription of Hg glosses by Stephen Partridge; and an edition of the Welsh marginalia in Me, with an introduction by Ceridwen Lloyd-Morgan. Also includes a general introduction by Stubbs, a description of the "digital capture" by Gareth Lloyd Hughes and Simon Evans, and two critical articles: see nos. 35 and 74. The information is fully searchable in normal language and SGML. See also no. 369.

20. Utz, Richard. "Editing Chaucer: John Koch and the Forgotten Tradition." In Władysław Witalisz, ed. *"And Gladly Wolde He Lerne and Gladly Teche": Studies on Language and Literature in Honour of Professor Dr. Karl Heinz Göller* (*SAC* 25 [2003], no. 146), pp. 17–26. Argues that John Koch ought to be considered one of the great editors of Chaucer's works, even though he is largely forgotten by Anglophone Chaucerians who downplay German contributions to the field.

See also nos. 22, 36, 73, 75, 171, 197, 217, 248, 255, 287, 292.

Manuscripts and Textual Studies

21. Cartlidge, Neil. *"The Canterbury Tales* and Cladistics." *NM* 102 (2001): 135–50. Cladistics—the use of large-scale computer analysis of data, including variant readings—promises the possibility of identifying patterns of textual transmission. However, the inevitability of interpretive disagreement in selecting evidence or in assessing conclusions means

that present cladistic techniques cannot guarantee objective or incontestable results.

22. Gillespie, Alexandra. "Caxton's Chaucer and Lydgate Quartos: Miscellanies from Manuscript to Print." *TCBS* 12.1 (2000): 1–26. Considers 11 Caxton quarto editions of English verse (STC 17019, 17009, 17030, 1450, 17008, 17018, 17032, 4851, 5091, 5090, and 3303) that include works by Lydgate and Caxton, assessing the economy of their production and their provenances and comparing them with related manuscripts, *Sammelbände*, and booklets. Caxton sought to provide inexpensive poetry, and he printed the "component parts" of the first English poetic miscellanies. English manuscript trade and continental models influenced his decisions to produce these quartos.

23. Görlach, Manfred. "Linguistic Problems of Editing." In Christa Jansohn, ed. *Problems of Editing*. Beihefte zu Editio, no. 14. Tübingen: Niemeyer, 1999, pp. 79–88. Görlach surveys a selection of textual cruxes (Old English to Modern) that reflect the importance of linguistic evidence in editorial decisions, including two from Chaucer ("armee," *GP* 1.60; "Aueryll," *GP* 1.1) and one "quasi-Chaucerian" example (from *Mak & Morris*). Also refers to *RvT* in surmising whether *Kingis Quair* was dialectically "improved" by a Scots scribe.

24. Hanna, Ralph. "The Application of Thought to Textual Criticism in All Modes—With Apologies to A. E. Housman." *SB* 53 (2000): 163–72. Examines variants in *WBP* 3.115–17 (especially "wight" versus "wright") to identify flaws in applying cladistic theory to manuscript stemmatics. Cladistic analysis underlies the *Canterbury Tales* Project.

25. ———. "Humphrey Newton and Bodleian Library, MS Lat. Misc. C.66." *MÆ* 69 (2000): 279–91. Discusses the "household book" of Humphrey Newton and its relation to "central literary culture." MS Lat. Misc. C.66 includes a section of *ParsT* (10.601–29), a section of *KnT* (1.3047–56), and a letter imitating Troilus upon seeing Criseyde.

26. Hilmo, Maidie. "Framing the Canterbury Pilgrims for the Aristocratic Readers of the Ellesmere Manuscript." In Kathryn Kerby-Fulton and Maidie Hilmo, eds. *The Medieval Professional Reader at Work: Evidence from Manuscripts of Chaucer, Langland, Kempe, and Gower* (*SAC* 25 [2003], no. 28), pp. 14–71; 16 b&w figs. The Ellesmere miniatures are evidence of the process of text production—the shaping and preparation of the manuscript for aristocratic viewing—and a visual guide to the reading process. The illustrations foster the aristocracy's sense of superi-

ority and provide evidence for surmising the possible patron of the manuscript.

27. Jones, Alex. "The Properties of a Stemma: Relating the Manuscripts in Two Texts from *The Canterbury Tales.*" *Parergon* 18.2 (2001): 35–53. Scholars continue to reflect on whether particular readings of *CT* are authorial revisions or scribal editing and on what Chaucer's plans for the work might have been. Understanding manuscript relationships for any particular tale can help set the limits for such an enquiry. Jones constructs the stemmata that best describe manuscript relationships for *GP* and *WBP*.

28. Kerby-Fulton, Kathryn, and Maidie Hilmo, eds. *The Medieval Professional Reader at Work: Evidence from Manuscripts of Chaucer, Langland, Kempe, and Gower.* English Literary Studies Monograph Series, no. 85. Victoria, British Columbia: U of Victoria, 2001. 239 pp. An introduction and four essays suggest some methods and approaches for the recovery of medieval reader response from manuscript evidence. Two essays pertain to Chaucer studies; see nos. 26 and 29.

29. Kerby-Fulton, Kathryn, and Steven Justice. "Scribe D and the Marketing of Ricardian Literature." In Kathryn Kerby-Fulton and Maidie Hilmo, eds. *The Medieval Professional Reader at Work: Evidence from Manuscripts of Chaucer, Langland, Kempe, and Gower (SAC* 25 [2003], no. 28), pp. 217–37; 5 b&w figs. Codicological analysis of the "Taylor Gower," produced by scribe D, who also produced two manuscripts of *CT.* This scribe and his "shadow" scribe (Scribe Delta) indicate possible entrepreneurial activity among English vernacular copyists.

30. Mann, Jill. "Chaucer's Meter and the Myth of the Ellesmere Editor of *The Canterbury Tales.*" *SAC* 23 (2001): 71–107. Recent editors have privileged the Hengwrt (Hg) manuscript by attributing metrical and morphosyntactic features of Ellesmere (El) to editorial intervention rather than to scribal error. Mann traces the development of the "myth of the El editor," especially in Manly-Rickert and Norman Blake, and shows where editorial policy has depended on this myth. She argues for attention to stress (rather than syllable counting) in assessing Chaucer's meter and tabulates instances in which El/Hg variants reflect common patterns of scribal variation. She also comments on tale order in Hg and El.

31. Mayer, Lauryn Stacey. "Worlds Made Flesh: Chronicle Histories and Medieval Manuscript Culture." *DAI* 62 (2001): 565A. Studies the manuscript transmission ("more akin to gene splicing than copying") of

Old English poetry and prose, chronicle histories, and Chaucer. To establish Chaucer as a forerunner of later poetry, printers deliberately modify his works.

32. Mooney, Linne R. "Scribes and Booklets of Trinity College, Cambridge, Manuscripts R.3.19 and R.3.21." In A. J. Minnis, ed. *Middle English Poetry: Texts and Traditions. Essays in Honour of Derek Pearsall* (*SAC* 25 [2003], no. 121), pp. 241–66. Codicological analysis of the two manuscripts, which include works by Chaucer and Lydgate, Chaucerian apocrypha, and related works. Assessment of the booklets in the manuscripts and the habits of the two scribes ("scribe A" and the "Hammond scribe") indicates that the works were produced in something like a "publishing business" and perhaps compiled in their present form by John Stow.

33. Morse, Charlotte C. "What the *Clerk's Tale* Suggests about Manly and Rickert's Edition—and the *Canterbury Tales* Project." In A. J. Minnis, ed. *Middle English Poetry: Texts and Traditions. Essays in Honour of Derek Pearsall* (*SAC* 25 [2003], no. 121), pp. 41–56. Morse comments on how the *Canterbury Tales* Project may reinvigorate textual questions thought to have been answered by the Manly-Rickert edition and latent in the Variorum project. Explores such issues as tale order, tale revision, and manuscript authority, especially as they relate to *ClT*.

34. Stubbs, Estelle. "Clare Priory, the London Austin Friars and Manuscripts of Chaucer's *Canterbury Tales*." In A. J. Minnis, ed. *Middle English Poetry: Texts and Traditions. Essays in Honour of Derek Pearsall* (*SAC* 25 [2003], no. 121), pp. 17–26. Names written in manuscripts of *CT* indicate associations between these manuscripts and a number of Austin friars who were scribes; they also indicate that exemplars of some manuscripts were at Clare Priory. Friars may have copied the manuscripts piecemeal when traveling, or the manuscripts may have circulated among fraternal locations.

35. ———. "Observations on the Hengwrt Chaucer." In Estelle Stubbs, ed. *The Hengwrt Chaucer Digital Facsimile* (*SAC* 25 [2003], no. 19), n.p. Analyzes the "structural sections" of the Hengwrt manuscript (Hg) to describe the complex process of its copying and construction, concentrating on such matters as hands, inks, running titles, quiring, and the abrupt ending of *CkT*, and suggesting that the composition of Hg and that of the Ellesmere manuscripts may well have overlapped.

36. Tokunaga, Satoko. "The Sources of Wynkyn de Worde's Version of 'The Monk's Tale.'" *Library* (ser. 7) 3 (2001): 223–35. Argues that

de Worde's text of *MkT* results from collation of Caxton's second edition with a manuscript probably of the Hengwrt group. There is no sign of editing beyond the evident desire to produce a complete text of *MkT*.

See also nos. 19, 66, 74, 126, 176, 197, 199, 224, 268.

Sources, Analogues, and Literary Relations

37. Boffey, Julia. "'Forto Compleyne She Had Gret Desire': The Grievances Expressed in Two Fifteenth-Century Dream-Visions." In Helen Cooney, ed. *Nation, Court and Culture: New Essays on Fifteenth-Century English Poetry* (*SAC* 25 [2003], no. 101), pp. 116–28. Contrasts the parliaments or courts of love in *PF* and *LGWP* with those in Lydgate's *Temple of Glas* and the anonymous *Assembly of Ladies*. The later poems present "idealizing fantasies of social assimilation or integration."

38. Heyworth, Gregory George. "The Amorous Scripture: Ovidian Romance and the Rhetoric of Culture." *DAI* 61 (2001): 4375A. Transmission of ancient Greek and Roman culture through Ovid to later tradition affected romance and shaped attitudes in popular literature. Heyworth discusses works by Marie de France, Chrétien de Troyes, Chaucer (with emphasis on politics in the court of Richard II), Shakespeare, and Milton.

See also nos. 17, 67, 90, 95, 102, 108, 148, 149, 156, 161, 162, 174, 175, 181, 182, 187, 189, 190, 192, 193, 196, 199, 204, 208, 212, 213, 215, 234, 243, 249, 250, 263, 265, 266, 278.

Chaucer's Influence and Later Allusion

39. Bianco, Sue. "New Perspectives on Lydgate's Courtly Verse." In Helen Cooney, ed. *Nation, Court and Culture: New Essays on Fifteenth-Century English Poetry* (*SAC* 25 [2003], no. 101), pp. 95–115. Critical reception of Lydgate has been prejudiced by negative comparisons with Chaucer. Fuller appreciation of Lydgate's poetry depends on recognizing that, while moral and political issues in Chaucer are largely exemplary, Lydgate writes to effect moral and political change—reflecting a "new and distinct fifteenth-century poetics."

40. Boffey, Julia, and A. S. G. Edwards. "An Unpublished Middle English Lyric and a Chaucer Allusion." *Archiv* 238 (2001): 327–30. A

three-stanza poem in praise of the Virgin Mary—from a single leaf inserted after Lydgate's *Life of Our Lady* in Bodleian Library MS Bodley 120—alludes to or echoes *SqT* (5.347) and *TC* (5.1670).

41. Bowden, Betsy. "Transportation to Canterbury: The Rival Envisionings by Stothard and Blake." *SiM* 11 (2001): 73–111. The treatment of horses and horsemanship helps to contrast the "secular lightheartedness" of Thomas Stothard's 1809 painting of the Canterbury pilgrims and the "heartfelt religious fervor" William Blake sought to convey in his 1807 engraving.

42. Cohen, Jeffrey Jerome. "On Saracen Enjoyment: Some Fantasies of Race in Late Medieval France and England." *JMEMSt* 31 (2001): 113–46. Echoing Chaucer's poetry while portraying non-Christian, racialized others, the Middle English romance *The Sultan of Babylon* invokes a "Saracen Chaucer" whose status as national poet depends on such markers of difference.

43. Couch, Julie Nelson. "From Hero to Trope: Chaucer's Dissolution of the Medieval Child Subject." *DAI* 61 (2001): 3554A. Chaucer's representations of the child as pathetic and passive (in *Th* and *PrT*) contrast with images of children in romance (*Havelock the Dane*) and miracle tales (*Child Slain by Jews* and *The Jewish Boy*). Chaucer "canonizes" this negative view of children.

44. Dean, Paul. "Pericles' Pilgrimage." *EIC* 50.2 (2000): 125–44. Assesses the genre, fictional self-consciousness, and religious elements of *Pericles*, suggesting that Chaucer influenced Shakespeare's decision to include the character Gower onstage throughout the play, an aspect of its literary self-consciousness.

45. Hadfield, Andrew. "Spenser and Chaucer: *The Knight's Tale* and Artegall's Response to the Giant with the Scales (*Faerie Queene*, V, ii, 41–42)." *Spenser Studies* 15 (2001): 245–49. The passage in Spenser echoes *KnT* 1.2987–3074, Theseus's "Firste Moevere" speech.

46. Hays, Peter. "Chaucer's and Faulkner's Pear Trees: An Arboreal Discussion." *ELN* 38 (2001): 57–64. Chaucer's *MilT* may have influenced William Faulkner's *The Sound and the Fury*. Each work presents the pear tree as a central symbol in a plot focused on greed and deception, one comic and the other tragic. Chaucer's and Faulkner's narratives also share common themes: "inappropriate love relationships," physical and spiritual blindness, and tainted sexuality.

47. Hilles, Carroll. "Gender and Politics in Osbern Bokenham's *Legendary*." *New Medieval Literatures* 4 (2001): 189–212. Bokenham "strate-

gically utilizes feminine piety" and his own "dullness" to express political dissent in a style that differs from the high rhetorical style of Gower, Chaucer, and Lydgate. He rejects their "classicizing, aureate" tradition, initiating a tradition that affiliates York with the power of women through discourse that the "Yorkists would develop throughout the ensuing decades."

48. Johnson, James D. "Leigh Hunt's 'Canterbury Tale.'" *ELN* 38 (2001): 41–49. Leigh Hunt's "The Tapiser's Tale" amplifies our understanding of Hunt as a nineteenth-century Chaucerian. The poem both imitates Chaucer's language and verse and utilizes the setting, plot, and key motifs from Charles MacFarlane's account of Mandeville's *Travels*. Hunt heightens the pathos of his poem and frames it within *CT* by focusing on the perspective of a Chaucerian pilgrim, the Tapiser.

49. ———. "Walter W. Skeat's *Canterbury Tale*." *ChauR* 36 (2001): 16–27. Skeat wrote a "Canterbury tale" in Middle English that admonishes the sin of covetousness, is thoroughly grounded in the Middle Ages, and fits into the scheme of *CT*. It reveals one of the more "relaxed moments" of this great Chaucer scholar, about whom so few personal records survive.

50. King, Andrew. "'Grounded, Finely Framed, and Strongly Trussed Up Together': The 'Medieval' Structure of *The Faerie Queene*." *RES* 52 (2001): 22–58. Spenser calls attention to his sources and models in *The Faerie Queene*. *SqT*, *Orlando Furioso*, and English medieval romances are specific sources, while narrative collections such as *CT*, anthologies of romances, or perhaps Malory's *Morte D'arthur* inspired the structure of Spenser's work.

51. Martin, Ellen E. "Bookburning in Chaucer and Austen." *Persuasions* 21 (1999): 83–89. Identifies *WBP* as the inspiration for Harriet Byron's burning of a prayer book in the second act of Jane Austen's play, *Sir Charles Grandison*, noting in both works the importance of hyperbole, the manipulation of language, and ironic commentary on masculine and literary authority.

52. Patterson, Lee. "'What is me?': Self and Society in the Poetry of Thomas Hoccleve." *SAC* 23 (2001): 437–70. Examines the "uncomfortable sense of selfhood" recorded in Hoccleve's works, a sense of an individual lost within the press of responsibilities. Patterson remarks on Chaucer's influence and suggests that the older poet was beyond conventional praise for Hoccleve, who regarded Chaucer as "an instance of a particular person" with an "inimitable appearance and manner."

53. Pearsall, Derek. "The Idea of Englishness in the Fifteenth Century." In Helen Cooney, ed. *Nation, Court and Culture: New Essays on Fifteenth-Century English Poetry* (*SAC* 25 [2003], no. 101), pp. 15–27. There was no growing sense of an English nation until the time of Henry VIII, although there were momentary surges in 1290–1340 and 1410–1420, the latter focused on Chaucer. Language is crucial to nation building, and the process of "accrediting English as a language of choice" in medieval England proceeded "slowly and fitfully."

54. Price, Paul. "Trumping Chaucer: Osbern Bokenham's Katherine." *ChauR* 36 (2001): 158–83. In his account of Katherine in the *Legendys of Hooly Wummen*, fifteenth-century poet Osbern Bokenham "rebels" against his poetic fathers, namely Chaucer, Gower, and Lydgate. Bokenham allows Katherine to persuade her audience with the Nicene Creed (as opposed to rhetorical devices) and thereby opposes the strategies used by his literary predecessors.

55. Richmond, Velma Bourgeois. *Shakespeare, Catholicism, and Romance.* London and New York: Continuum, 2000. 242 pp. Explores affinities between Roman Catholic doctrine and outlook and Shakespeare's works, especially his romances and other plays that use the "romance mode." Recurrent references to Chaucer reflect his influence on Shakespeare in plot, mode, and outlook.

56. Simpson, James. "Bulldozing the Middle Ages: The Case of 'John Lydgate.'" *New Medieval Literatures* 4 (2001): 213–42. Surveys the reception of Lydgate, especially his *Dance Machabré*, and argues that the poet has been victimized by "'ageist' conceptions of cultural change" that seek to reify "the medieval." Lydgate's stature as the most public of English poets has served him poorly in reception history, but this realization enables us to reclaim him. Recurrent contrast with reception of Chaucer and his works.

57. Straker, Scott-Morgan. "Deference and Difference: Lydgate, Chaucer, and the *Siege of Thebes*." *RES* 52 (2001): 1–21. Lydgate appropriates Chaucer not so much to pay tribute as to distance himself from anticlericalism, to redeem the narrative and monastic voice, and to assert its freedom from authority, as represented by Harry Bailly. Lydgate's apparent compliance allows the monastic identity to address unwelcome truth to secular authority. While the prologue to the *Siege* is self-confidently naive, the body of the poem articulates the inability of rhetoric to affect history.

58. ———. "Dictating Authority in Lydgate's *Troy Book*." In Mar-

tin Gosman, Arjo Vanderjagt, and Jan Veenstra, eds. *The Growth of Authority in the Medieval West: Selected Proceedings of the International Conference, Groningen, 6—9 November 1997*. Groningen: Egbert Forsten, 1999, pp. 285—306. Assesses Lydgate's responses to authority in *Troy Book*: his rhetorical additions to Guido delle Colonne's *Historia destructionis Troiae* (his source), his freeing himself from the influence of *TC* (his model) by transforming Chaucer into an "institution," and his paradoxical praising and critiquing of Henry V (his patron). In *Troy Book*, Lydgate is a reformer of authorities.

59. Thompson, John J. "Thomas Hoccleve and Manuscript Culture." In Helen Cooney, ed. *Nation, Court and Culture: New Essays on Fifteenth-Century English Poetry* (*SAC* 25 [2003], no. 101), pp. 81–94. Examines Hoccleve's relations with the London book trade and the Lancastrian court to explain how his verse "managed to leak so successfully" into the Chaucer tradition. Hoccleve's manuscripts reflect his autobiographical self-fashioning and his associations with Chaucer.

60. Wolfe, Jessica Lynn. "Subtle Devices: Machinery and the Limits of Humanism, 1580–1625." *DAI* 61 (2001): 3586A. The Renaissance elicited mixed responses to machinery. Wolfe discusses reactions to Italian thought by Gabriel Harvey (including the effect on his reading of Chaucer), George Chapman, and Edmund Spenser.

See also nos. 25, 101, 102, 111, 126, 211, 280, 288.

Style and Versification

61. Barney, Stephen A. "Langland's Mighty Line." In Kathleen M. Hewett-Smith, ed. *William Langland's* Piers Plowman: *A Book of Essays* (*SAC* 25 [2003], no. 108), pp. 103–17. Compares paired samples of Langland's and Chaucer's verse to argue that Langland's are superior in both sound and sense.

62. Burrow, J. A. "Scribal Mismetring." In A. J. Minnis, ed. *Middle English Poetry: Texts and Traditions. Essays in Honour of Derek Pearsall* (*SAC* 25 [2003], no. 121), pp. 169–79. Compares authorial and scribal versions of passages from Hoccleve's verse, focusing on scribal omission of monosyllabic words, spelling variants, and terminal *-e*. Assesses what Hoccleve's practice might tell us about Gower's practice, and how the two may differ from Chaucer's less-strict habits of meter.

63. Cole, Andrew. "Rewriting Langland and Chaucer: Heresy and Literary Authority in Late-Medieval England." *DAI* 61 (2001): 2704A. Although many assume that Chaucer and Langland felt compelled to revise their works to avoid anti-Wycliffite censorship, such censorship was restricted to clerical writing. Chaucer drew on Wycliffite translation techniques to improve his skill, as seen in the contrast between *Bo* and *Astr*.

64. Gaylord, Alan T., ed. *Essays on the Art of Chaucer's Verse*. Basic Readings in Chaucer and His Time, no. 3. New York and London: Routledge, 2001. viii, 449 pp. Reprints fourteen essays, ranging historically from Thomas Tyrwhitt and George Saintsbury to recent commentary. Includes an introduction that summarizes the contributions of the essays, the notes from the original publications, and an inclusive bibliography but no index. Topics include historical and theoretical essays, essays on Chaucer's prosodic practices, and readings that combine close analysis with history and theory.

65. Karlin, Daniel. "The Figure of the Singer." F. W. Bateson Memorial Lecture. *ÉC* 50 (2000): 99–124. Surveys the relationship between song and poetry in English tradition, identifying the tenacity of the association until the end of the nineteenth century as evident in poetry and in the statuary of London's Albert Memorial. Cites evidence from *TC* and Chaucer's lyric poems to argue that in the 1300s and 1400s verse was "still steeped in music, but no longer dissolved in it."

66. Solopova, Elizabeth. "The Survival of Chaucer's Punctuation in the Early Manuscripts of the *Canterbury Tales*." In A. J. Minnis, ed. *Middle English Poetry: Texts and Traditions. Essays in Honour of Derek Pearsall* (*SAC* 25 [2003], no. 121), pp. 27–40. Compares punctuation in the Hengwrt and Ellesmere manuscripts with that of other manuscripts to argue that Chaucer's punctuation survives in the virgules of Hengwrt and Ellesmere, related to his development of the iambic pentameter line.

67. Stockwell, Robert P., and Donka Minkova. "The Partial-Contact Origins of English Pentameter Verse: The Anglicization of an Italian Model." In Dieter Kastovsky and Arthur Mettinger, eds. *Language Contact in the History of English* (*SAC* 25 [2003], no. 112), pp. 337–62. Stockwell and Minkova argue that Chaucer's prosodic innovation is rooted in his familiarity with the "Romance decasyllabic model." The article focuses on duple and triple rhythmic units, suggesting that Chau-

cer imposed native iambic rhythm on romance models found in Petrarch and Boccaccio.

See also nos. 192, 271.

Language and Word Studies

68. Blake, N. F. "Fabliaux and Other Literary Genres as Witnesses of Early Spoken English." In Hans-Jürgen Diller and Manfred Görlach, eds. *Towards a History of English as a History of Genres*. Anglistiche Forschungen, no. 298. Heidelberg: Winter, 2001, pp. 145–57. The realism of fabliaux (and some drama) makes them valuable in studying the history of colloquial language, especially sexual colloquialisms. Blake draws examples from *Dame Sirith*, *MilT*, *RvT*, *WBP*, and *MerT*, remarking on Chaucer's self-consciousness and restraint in use of sexual language.

69. Brinton, Laurel J. "The Importance of Discourse Types in Grammaticalization: The Case of *Anon*." Susan C. Herring, Pieter Van Reenan, and Lene Schøsler, eds. *Textual Parameters in Older Languages*. Amsterdam Studies in the Theory and History of Linguistic Science, ser. 4, no. 195. Amsterdam and Philadelphia: Benjamins, 2000, pp. 139–62. Traces the development of *anon* from Middle English to Early Modern English, using evidence drawn from *TC* and elsewhere. A revised version of chaper two of Brinton's *Pragmatic Markers in English* (Berlin and New York: Gruyter, 1996).

70. Burnley, John David. "French and Frenches in Fourteenth-Century London." In Dieter Kastovsky and Arthur Mettinger, eds. *Language Contact in the History of English* (*SAC* 25 [2003], no. 112), pp. 17–34. Challenges "over-simple dichotomies" between English and French in late-medieval England and illustrates the "pragmatic complexity" of the use of Anglo-French texts. Assesses grammar, style, "speaker attitudes" (with reference to *CT* and *TC*), and ambiguities of the word "French."

71. Gelderen, Elly van. "Towards Personal Subjects in English: Variation in Feature Interpretability." In Jan Terje Faarlund, ed. *Grammatical Relations in Change*. Studies in Language Companion Series, no. 56. Amsterdam and Philadelphia: Benjamins, 2001, pp. 137–57. Cites examples from Chaucer and others to show the demise of the "(slight) person split" evident in earlier English impersonal constructions.

72. Giancarlo, Matthew. "The Rise and Fall of the Great Vowel Shift? The Changing Ideological Intersections of Philology, Historical

Linguistics, and Literary History." *Representations* 76 (2001): 27–60. Reviewing the traditional narrative of the Great Vowel Shift, with its recognition by Chaucer's early editors that major changes in prosody were underway, Giancarlo suggests revision of the monolithic GVS model in the direction of a more localized and more scientifically defensible model of Modern English vowel shifts.

73. Horobin, S. C. P. "J. R. R. Tolkien as a Philologist: A Reconsideration of the Northernisms in Chaucer's *Reeve's Tale*." *ES* 82 (2001): 97–105. Challenges Tolkien's view that Chaucer aimed at a consistent representation of Northern dialect in *RvT*. Probably closest to Chaucer's autograph, the Hengwrt manuscript is neither complete nor consistent, while later scribes added Northern features and/or replaced these with Southern ones.

74. Horobin, Simon. "The Language of the Hengwrt Manuscript." In Estelle Stubbs, ed. *The Hengwrt Chaucer Digital Facsimile* (*SAC* 25 [2003], no. 19), n.p. Focuses on spelling in the Hengwrt manuscript (Hg) in light of the development of London English (from Type II to III), especially in comparison with spelling in the Ellesmere manuscript (El). Though the two manuscripts are closely related, Hg shows greater variation than El and is closer to Chaucer's own habits. El reduced early forms of "though" and increased the northernisms of *RvT*.

75. Horobin, Simon C. P. "The Language of the Fifteenth-Century Printed Editions of the *Canterbury Tales*." *Anglia* 119 (2001): 249–58. Analyzes spelling in the four printed editions of *CT* issued before 1500. Caxton (1476 and 1482) and Wynken de Worde (1498) responded individually to the perceived authority of the work, while Richard Pynson (1492) attempted to replace the nonstandard features of Caxton's editions with Chancery Standard forms.

76. Kanno, Masahiko. "A Note on Some Pregnant Words in Chaucer." *Bulletin of Aichi University of Education* 46 (1997): 1–8. Words and phrases discussed include *lust, blynde, a fewe wordes white, glosynge, ambages, amphibologie, double, sophyme, swete wordes, plesante wordes*, and *peinten*.

77. Kumamoto, Sadahiro. "Some Notes on the 'Accusative with Infinitive' Construction." *Kumamoto Journal of Culture and Humanities* (Kumamoto University) 71 (2001): 109–29 (in Japanese). Focuses on the following: (1) the kind of governing verbs; (2) the ratio of bare infinitives and (*for*) *to*-infinitives; and (3) the structure of the infinitive clause, supplementing Kenyon (1909) in many respects.

78. Markus, Manfred. "Duplication of Vowels in Middle English

Spelling." In Dieter Kastovsky and Arthur Mettinger, eds. *Language Contact in the History of English* (*SAC* 25 [2003], no. 112), pp. 217–31. Markus examines several features of Chaucer's spelling—digraphs, vowel doubling, *ee* versus *e*—drawing data from *ParsT* and arguing that inconsistencies in vowel-doubling are related to vowel length's "having lost its former phonemic identity." Uses data from the Innsbruck Computer Archive of Machine-readable English Texts.

79. Mazzon, Gabriella. "Social Relations and Form of Address in the *Canterbury Tales*." In Dieter Kastovsky and Arthur Mettinger, eds. *The History of English in a Social Context: A Contribution to Historical Sociolinguistics*. Trends in Linguistics; Studies and Monographs, no. 129. Berlin and New York: Gruyter, 2000, pp. 135–68. Mazzon demonstrates a "clear correlation between discourse strategies and pronoun use and switching" in *CT*. *You* and *thou* forms indicate "politeness" as well as social status, gender, and characterization.

80. Rinelli, Gabriele. "Scandanavian and Native Social Terms in Middle English: The Case of *Cherl/Carl*." In Dieter Kastovsky and Arthur Mettinger, eds. *Language Contact in the History of English* (*SAC* 25 [2003], no. 112), pp. 267–77. Rinelli considers Chaucer's uses of *cherl* and *carl* among evidence that distinguishes among regional uses of the terms.

81. Rothwell, W. "English and French in England After 1362." *ES* 82 (2001): 539–59. Anglo-Norman should be considered "a coherent, if constantly changing, entity from 1066 to the middle of the fifteenth century" (559), with widely different forms that influenced English in the fifteenth-century, when scribes were working in both English and French. In the *GP* portrait of Chaucer's Sergeant of the Lawe, many French legal terms have meanings particular to their use in England.

82. Vandelinde, Henry. "Wlatsom and Abhomynable: Murder and Homicide in the *Canterbury Tales*." *Clues* (Bowling Green, Oh.) 22.2 (2001): 167–76. In Chaucer's England, the legal term "homicide" ("deliberate infliction of death," justified or not) was distinct from "murder," which carried negative moral connotations but had no legal definition. In *CT*, Chaucer uses the terms precisely and suggestively.

83. Yager, Susan. "Chaucer's Peple and Folk." *JEGP* 100 (2001): 211–33. *Peple* and *folk* are marked terms in Chaucer's usage. In particular, *peple* is nearly always negative; *folk* is either neutral or positive. In Chaucer's translations (e.g., *Bo*), *folk* normally translates as *gens* or its cognates, while *peple* translates as *vulgus*, *populus*, or their cognates. In

TC and *CT*, *folk* refers to lovers; the Miller, Reeve, and Wife of Bath do not use *peple* at all. In *ClT*, *peple* refers to the citizens of Saluzzo, but Griselde is among the *folk*.

84. Yonekura, Hiroshi. "The Adverbial Suffix *-e* in Chaucer." *Cornucopia* (Kyoto Prefectural University) 11 (1991): 23–58 (in Japanese). Describes and compares Chaucer's use of adverbs ending in *-e*, formed from adjectives, and those ending in *-ly/-lice*.

85. Yoon, Minwoo. "The Use of Northern Dialect and Middle Scots in the Scottish Literature." *MES* 5 (1997): 215–41. Surveys representative examples of northern English dialect *(Alliterative Morte Arthure, RvT)*, Scottish Chaucerians (Henryson, Dunbar), and non-Chaucerian Scottish works (Barbour's *Bruce*, *The Wallace*) to identify common and distinctive linguistic features. Middle Scots is an identifiable dialect.

See also nos. 53, 99, 156, 162, 180, 185, 200, 214, 235, 239, 252, 254, 275.

Background and General Criticism

86. Aers, David. *Faith, Ethics and Church: Writing in England, 1360–1409*. Cambridge: D. S. Brewer, 2000. xii, 153 pp. Explores faith, social and political action, and theology in late-medieval England, focusing on Chaucer, Gower, Langland, the *Gawain* poet, and Wyclif. Assesses how their ideas reflect Thomas Aquinas, Ockham, and John Ball and how they responded to such phenomena as the plague and the uprising of 1381. Chaucer is not the "skeptical fideist" nor a stoic Christian, but a political poet. In *ClT*, he imagines religious "absences" that lead to social tyranny, while *SNT* asserts religious opposition to social tyranny. In *SNT* and *ParsT*, the Eucharist is "absent," reflecting the "diminished role of the sacraments," in line with Wycliffite thought. The stoicism of lyrics such as *Truth* is inconsistent with the "profoundly pessimistic representations of the contemporary Church" in *CT*. See also no. 296.

87. ———, ed. *Medieval Literature and Historical Inquiry: Essays in Honor of Derek Pearsall*. Cambridge: D. S. Brewer, 2000. xvi, 212 pp. Nine essays on medieval English literature, a preface by Derek Brewer, an introduction by Aers, and a bibliography of Pearsall's publications through 1998. Two essays pertain to Chaucer; see nos. 186 and 237.

88. Archibald, Elizabeth. *Incest and the Medieval Imagination*. Oxford: Clarendon Press, 2001. xv, 295 pp. Explores incest motifs in a wide

range of medieval texts, exploring origins and analogues. Discusses *MLT* as an example of the motif of the flight of the incestuous father and comments on incest in *LGW* (Philomena and Semiramis). See also no. 299.

89. Barr, Helen. *Socioliterary Practice in Late Medieval England*. Oxford: Oxford University Press, 2001. viii, 229 pp. Seven interrelated studies and an afterword that explore "socioliterary practice," considering literature as a material form of social behavior in "internal and dialectical relationship" with the institutions and conventions that shape it and that it helps to shape. Topics include *Pearl*, *Wynnere and Wastoure*, Hoccleve's *To Sir John Oldcastle*, Gower's *Tripartite Chronicle*, Wycliffite writings, *The Boke of Cupide*, *Mum and the Sothsegger*, Lydgate's *The Churl and the Bird*, and several works by Chaucer. An exploration of "social semantics," *ManT* "shows explicitly that literary language is a material form of social practice." With diction similar to that of more controversial texts, *LGWP* is about the policing of "orders of discourse." Engaging the uprisings of 1381, *NPT* is a radical, vernacular reflection of the struggle for social representation and empowerment.

90. Battles, Dominique. "Revising History: Narratives of Thebes in the Middle Ages." *DAI* 62 (2001): 162A. Traces the Theban legend from Statius through a twelfth-century Old French version, school texts, florilegia, commentary, Boccaccio, Chaucer (*Anel*, *KnT*), and Lydgate. Also assesses relationships with ancient and medieval history. Lydgate's version removes the Theban curse.

91. Bourgne, Florence. "Prologues et épilogues en Angleterre à la fin du Moyen Âge: Les enveloppes du texte." In Leo Carruthers and Adrian Papahagi, eds. *Prologues et épilogues dans la littérature anglaise du Moyen Âge* (*SAC* 25 [2003], no. 98), pp. 73–91. Distinguishes three major types of prologues in late-medieval English literature: organic; a dilation; and a displaced prologue, i.e., a prologue that does not correspond to the document. Examines *CT*, *LGW*, *TC*, and *Astr*.

92. Bowers, John M. *The Politics of* Pearl: *Court Poetry in the Age of Richard II*. Cambridge: D. S. Brewer, 2001. xviii, 236 pp.; 7 b&w illus. *Pearl* reflects the political and social turmoil of Richard's reign and is a product of the rich visual and verbal culture of his Cheshire coterie. Political and social allusions in the poem engage Lollardy, labor laws, court magnificence, Parliamentary upheavals, the death of Queen Anne, and other turbulences during Richard's reign. Like Langland, Chaucer, and Gower, the *Pearl* poet is a political voice. Bowers includes frequent

comparisons and contrasts to Chaucer and his works, especially *CT* and *LGW*.

93. Braswell, Mary Flowers. *Chaucer's "Legal Fiction": Reading the Records*. Teaneck, N.J.: Fairleigh Dickinson University Press; London: Associated University Presses, 2001. 170 pp. In addition to overt allusions to law and its practitioners and his depictions of legal proceedings, Chaucer weaves legal terminology into his texts and uses "embedded" references to real court cases in developing his plots and characters. Advocates and accusers in medieval courts often used creative narration to argue their cases, just as Chaucer does. As well, Chaucer uses "interrogative" rather than "declarative" style so that his audience, like courtroom participants, is expected to analyze the evidence and reach conclusions that are purposely withheld. Braswell discusses numerous courtroom cases, *HF*, *FranT*, *RvT*, *ShT*, *PardP*, *CkPT*, *CYT*, *MilT*, and *FrT*.

94. Bremmer, Rolf H., Jr. "Franciscus Junius Reads Chaucer: But Why? and How?" *SiM* 11 (2001): 37–72. Bremmer reviews the study of Chaucer undertaken late in life by the pioneering Dutch Anglo-Saxonist Franciscus Junius, as reflected mainly in copious marginalia in Junius's copy of Speght's 1598 edition of Chaucer's *Works*.

95. Bullón-Fernández, María. *Fathers and Daughters in Gower's* Confessio Amantis: *Authority, Family, State, and Writing*. Publications of the John Gower Society, no. 4 [error for 5]. Cambridge: D. S. Brewer, 2000. viii, 241 pp. Studies the incest motif in *Confessio Amantis* as a "fundamental element" in Gower's explorations of father-daughter relationships and the relationships of authority. In this context, Bullón-Fernández considers Chaucer's *MLT* and *PhyT* as analogues to Gower's versions of the tales of Constance and Virginia. See also no. 313.

96. Burger, Glenn. "Shameful Pleasures: Up Close and Dirty with Chaucer, Flesh, and the Word." In Glenn Burger and Steven Kruger, eds. *Queering the Middle Ages* (*SAC* 25 [2003], no. 97), pp. 213–35. Argues that Chaucer set the standard for discourse on heterosexuality and modernity, even though modern study has written over his "queer touch." Exemplifies the gendered instability of Chaucer's text by contrasting the normativizing power of marriage and queer performativity. See also no. 138.

97. ———, and Steven Kruger, eds. *Queering the Middle Ages*. Medieval Cultures, no. 27. Minneapolis: University of Minnesota Press, 2001. xxiii, 318 pp. Ten essays on queer issues, with responses by Kruger. Includes readings on a selection of medieval texts, including Chris-

tine de Pizan and Dante. For an essay that pertains to Chaucer, see no. 96 (and the response, no. 138).

98. Carruthers, Leo, and Adrian Papahagi, eds. *Prologues et épilogues dans la littérature anglaise du Moyen Âge*. AMAES, no. 24. Paris: Association des Médiévistes Anglicistes de l'Enseignement Supérieur, 2001. 192 pp. Eleven articles by various authors on the functions of prologues and epilogues. Five articles directly pertain to Chaucer studies; see nos. 6, 91, 151, 170, and 244.

99. Carruthers, Mary. "Meditations on the 'Historical Present' and 'Collective Memory' in Chaucer and *Sir Gawain and the Green Knight.*" In Chris Humphrey and W. M. Ormrod, eds. *Time in the Medieval World* (*SAC* 25 [2003], no. 110), pp. 137–55. Like tense-switching and first-person point of view, the use of the "historical present" by Chaucer and the *Gawain* poet illustrates how medieval authors could convincingly remember and authenticate the stories they told. The past is the time of narrative; the present is the tense of narrative. Only modern literary convention prefers past events narrated in the past tense.

100. Collette, Carolyn P., and Vincent J. DiMarco. "The Matter of Armenia in the Age of Chaucer." *SAC* 23 (2001): 317–58. Summarizes the political history of the fall of Armenia in 1375, surveying its impact on the court of Richard II and its status as a "haunting symbol" of catastrophe in Middle English literature. Discusses *SqT*, *Anel*, the description of the Knight in *GP*, *MkT*, *MLT*, *Bevis of Hamptoune*, *The King of Tars*, and other works. Levon VI, the toppled king of Armenia, sought a truce between England and France (perhaps prompting the 1387 negotiations in which Chaucer participated), promoted by Philippe de Mézières as a means to regain the Holy Land from Islam.

101. Cooney, Helen, ed. *Nation, Court and Culture: New Essays on Fifteenth-Century English Poetry*. Dublin and Portland, Ore.: Four Courts Press, 2001. 191 pp. Ten essays by various authors on the role of language and literature in fifteenth-century England, Chaucer's influence at the time, and the relations of fifteenth-century literature to earlier and later tradition. Mention of Chaucer recurs throughout, usually deemphasizing his influence. For five essays that relate to him directly, see nos. 37, 39, 53, 59, and 288.

102. Cooper, Helen. "Welcome to the House of the Dead. 600 Years Dead: Chaucer's Deserved Reputation as 'The Father of English Poetry.'" *TLS*, Oct. 27, 2000, pp. 3–4. Cooper surveys Chaucer's linguistic and poetic innovations, emphasizing that his rewritings of classi-

cal, French, and Italian models were "far from being acts of homage." Chaucer may have thought of himself as a literary heir, but he was an instinctive groundbreaker.

103. Davlin, Mary Clemente, O.P. "Chaucer and Langland as Religious Writers." In Kathleen M. Hewett-Smith, ed. *William Langland's* Piers Plowman*: A Book of Essays* (*SAC* 25 [2003], no. 108), pp. 119–41. Chaucer and Langland are both "great religious writers," although Langland is more deeply engaged in "who and what God is." Both writers are poets of religious experience: Chaucer explores pathos, and Langland confronts the "central beliefs of Christianity."

104. Dinshaw, Carolyn. "Pale Faces: Race, Religion, and Affect in Chaucer's Texts and Their Readers." *SAC* 23 (2001): 19–41. Biennial Chaucer Lecture, the New Chaucer Society, Twelfth International Congress, 14–17 July 2000, University of London. Dinshaw considers her autobiographical "queer diasporic experience" as a "pale Indian" in light of the representations of conversion, otherness, and paleness in *MLT* and the generally unnoticed presence of Indian influences on early English studies. She offers her meditative analysis to encourage other medievalists to challenge the assumptions that underlie "rationalistic, post-Enlightenment" notions of temporality.

105. Fewer, Colin D. "The Mirror in the Marketplace: Subjectivity in Late-Medieval English Culture." *DAI* 62 (2001): 1827A. The late-medieval sense of individualism (identified by New Historicists) produced anxiety among writers, including Chaucer, Lydgate, and Hoccleve. Through various genres, these writers show a need to redefine sovereignty.

106. Fisher, John H. "The Portraits in the Bedford Psalter Hours (B.M. MS Add. 42131) and the Lancastrian Literary Affinity." In Nancy M. Reale and Ruth E. Sternglantz, eds. *Satura: Studies in Medieval Literature in Honour of Robert R. Raymo* (*SAC* 25 [2003], no. 128), pp. 239–47; 36 b&w illus. Fisher comments on the series of faces or portraits depicted in the historiated initials of the Bedford Psalter, arguing that they depict members of the affinities of Richard II and Henry IV: the kings themselves and the future Henry V, Gower, Chaucer, Hoccleve, Lydgate, Henry Beaufort, and Thomas Chaucer. Suggests that the portraits follow the "doodles" of a court clerk.

107. Gertz, SunHee Kim. *Chaucer to Shakespeare, 1337–1580.* New York: Palgrave, 2001. xi, 248 pp. Gertz assesses 1337–1580 as the period of transition between the Middle Ages and the Early Modern era.

Dynastic ambition, science, exploration, and disasters provide contexts and stimuli for the literature. In their rhetorical dexterity and highly crafted images, Chaucer and Shakespeare are exceptional writers, yet Chaucer was a diplomat and bureaucrat and Shakespeare was probably an actor as well as an entrepreneur. Much of the literature of the period reflects textured engagement of contemporary concerns, evident through close reading of rhetorical and semiotic systems. Chapter Two, "Training, Religion and Treatises," discusses *WBPT*, and Chapter Five, "Narrative and Lyric Poetry," discusses *TC*.

108. Hewett-Smith, Kathleen M., ed. *William Langland's* Piers Plowman: *A Book of Essays*. Medieval Casebooks. New York and London: Routledge, 2001. x, 261 pp. Ten essays on *Piers Plowman*, including three that pertain to Chaucer. See nos. 61, 103, and 213.

109. Honegger, Thomas. "Cultural Symbols in Transition: Animal Lore in Late English and Early Scottish Poetry." *Micrologus* 8 (2000): 489–509. Whereas Robert Henryson rarely uses animals for imagery or metaphoric comparisons (outside the allegory of *Morall Fabillis*), Chaucer "exploits the rich and variegated symbolic dimension" of references to animals, even while he avoids "explicit allegorical meaning." Honegger draws Chaucerian examples from *CT* and *PF*, focusing on examples in which animals are "not in the foreground" of the plots.

110. Humphrey, Chris, and W. M. Ormrod, eds. *Time in the Medieval World*. Suffolk: York Medieval Press, 2001. viii, 176 pp. An introduction and eight essays explore various senses of time in the medieval world, assessing their influence upon life and culture. Topics include anachronism as a feature in earlier senses of time, perceptions of death and the Last Judgment, time in literary narratives, constructions of time in the professions, and clocks and calendars. For an essay that pertains to Chaucer, see no. 99.

111. Johnston, Andrew James. *Clerks and Courtiers: Chaucer, Late Middle English Literature, and the State Formation Process*. Anglistische Forschungen, no. 302. Heidelberg: Winter, 2001. 410 pp. Tripartite study that first sketches the process of state formation in late-medieval England as a struggle between clerkly and chivalric cultures. Part II locates Chaucer's poetry within this process, assessing his reaction to chivalric culture in the portraits of the Squire and the Franklin in *GP* and in *SqT* and *FranT*; also assesses Chaucer's evaluation of clerkly culture in the portrait of the Clerk in *GP*, the opening of *ClT*, and *MLP*. To determine Chaucer's own position, Johnston analyses *Th* and *Mel*. Part III traces

the reception of Chaucer's poetry by Gower, Usk, Scogan, and Hoccleve, who try to assimilate Chaucer and his poetry to their respective cultures. Includes two concluding chapters on Hoccleve and Lollardy and Reginald Pecock.

112. Kastovsky, Dieter, and Arthur Mettinger, eds. *Language Contact in the History of English*. Studies in English Medieval Language and Literature, no. 1. Frankfurt am Main: Lang, 2001. 410 pp. Seventeen essays on various issues in Old and Middle English linguistic study: language contact, borrowing, code-switching, spelling, versification, etc. Four essays pertain to Chaucer; see nos. 67, 70, 78, and 80.

113. Kerr, John M. "Proserpinan Memory in Dante and Chaucer." *DAI* 62 (2001): 163A. Dante and Chaucer elaborate on the three aspects of the classical goddess who appears as "Proserpina in hell, Diana on earth, and Luna" in heaven. Medieval commentary associates her with memory. Chaucer treats her recurrently, sometimes parodically, in *HF*, *PF*, *LGW*, *KnT*, *WBT*, *MerT*, *FranT*, and *ManT*.

114. Knight, Stephen. "Places in the Text: Topographicist Approach to Chaucer." In R. F. Yeager and Charlotte C. Morse, eds. *Speaking Images: Essays in Honor of V. A. Kolve* (*SAC* 25 [2003], no. 147), pp. 445–61. Knight calls for a critical confrontation with the semiotics of place in Chaucer, commenting on a number of topographical references in Chaucer's works, suggesting closer examination of implications of places to which Chaucer traveled (especially Genoa) and noting underexplored claims of association with Chaucer in modern tourist sites.

115. Kuhn, Wiebke. "Are Mothers Saints? Changes in the Perception of Motherhood in the Later Middle Ages." *DAI* 61 (2001): 2705A. Medieval idealizations of motherhood developed alongside the rising emphasis on the suffering of Christ and the saints. Kuhn discusses works by Jacobus de Voragine, Chaucer (*LGW*, *MLT*, *ClT*, and *PrT*), Osbern Bokenham, and Margery Kempe. The tradition survived into later centuries.

116. Kuipers, Christopher Marvin. "The Pastoral Initiation: An Ecology of Authorly Emergence from Plato to Milton." *DAI* 62 (2001): 158A. Authorial development from pastoral toward epic provides a universal creative basis, analogous to the human life span and close to nature. Assesses works by Plato, Vergil, Chaucer (*BD*), Milton, and Vladimir Nabokov (as lepidopterist).

117. Lassahn, Nicole Elise. "*Songes . . . qui ne sont mie mencongier*': Historical Context and Fictional Truth in Dream Poetry from the Time

of the Hundred Years War." *DAI* 62 (2001): 565A. Dream poems by Machaut, Froissart, and Chaucer share not only the dream frame device but also historical-political content communicated in the language of love poetry. Love, war, and politics combined show change and a model of order.

118. Lenhart, Gary. "Geoffrey Chaucer (ca. 1342–1400)." In Ron Padgett, ed. *World Poets*. Vol. 1. New York: Charles Scribner's Sons, 2000, pp. 227–36. Addressed to high school students. Surveys Chaucer's life and works, with emphasis on *CT*, emphasizing Chaucer's counterpoint between romance and realism.

119. Lochrie, Karma. "Presumptive Sodomy and Its Exclusions." *Textual Practice* 13 (1999): 295–313. Argues that sodomy in medieval literature must be understood as an "unspecified plurality of acts and intentions," which includes women as well as men. Female sodomy occupies the "silent place in the discourse" that must be acknowledged in modern discussion to understand more fully the range and nuances of medieval gender anxieties and to avoid complicity with medieval misogyny. Lochrie considers sodomy in *ParsT*, Pauline tradition, theological commentary, and Alan of Lille.

120. Mehl, Dieter. *English Literature in the Age of Chaucer*. Longman Literature in English Series. Harlow, England; and New York: Longman, 2001. xii, 252 pp. Surveys fourteenth- and fifteenth-century English and Middle Scots literature (excluding drama), with individual chapters dedicated to Chaucer, Gower, Langland, the *Gawain* poet, Lydgate and Hoccleve, the lyric, Middle Scots (James I, Robert Holland, Henryson, Dunbar, and Douglas), and Middle English prose (*Mandeville's Travels*, mystics, Margery Kempe, and Malory). Includes a timeline, bibliographies for each section, and a subject index. The treatment of Chaucer (pp. 8–59) emphasizes his adaptability and the open-ended vitality of his poetry.

121. Minnis, A. J., ed. *Middle English Poetry: Texts and Traditions. Essays in Honour of Derek Pearsall*. Woodbridge, Suffolk; and Rochester, N.Y.: York Medieval Press, 2001. xvi, 304 pp.; 40 b&w illus. Sixteen essays from the Eighth York Manuscript Conference (July 5–7, 1996) on issues in Middle English textual studies: dating, punctuation, meter, scribal practice, and book production, among others. Includes a preface (xi–xii) that celebrates Pearsall, an index of manuscripts, and an index of names and titles. Six essays pertain to Chaucer; see nos. 32–34, 62, 66, and 267.

122. Myles, Robert. "Chaucer and Character: The Heresies of Doug-las Wurtele." In Robert Myles and David Williams, eds. *Chaucer and Language: Essays in Honour of Douglas Wurtele* (*SAC* 25 [2003], no. 123), pp. 3–10. Surveys Wurtele's studies of Chaucer, clarifying the critic's consistent concern with characterization and how it relates to critical trends.

123. ———, and David Williams, eds. *Chaucer and Language: Essays in Honour of Douglas Wurtele*. Montreal and Kingston: McGill-Queen's University Press, 2001. xxii, 250 pp. Ten essays that pertain to Chaucer, plus a commemorative preface (by M. I. Cameron), an introduction (by David Williams) that summarizes the essays, a bibliography of Wurtele's publications, and a subject index. See nos. 122, 197, 200, 205, 209, 214, 221, 230, 238, and 239.

124. Orme, Nicholas. *Medieval Children*. New Haven and London: Yale University Press, 2001. xii, 387 pp.; 125 b&w and color illus. Orme surveys medieval childhood, from the seventh to the mid-six-teenth century, with emphasis on England. Topics include birth and family life, danger and death, children's literature, learning to read and reading for pleasure, play, children and the church, and growing up into law, labor, and sexuality. Passim references to children in medieval English literature, including Chaucer's works, especially *CT*.

125. Pearsall, Derek. "Eleanor Prescott Hammond." *Medieval Feminist Forum* 31 (2001): 29–36. Assessment of Hammond's contributions to Middle English and Tudor studies, including Chaucer. Includes a bib-liography of Hammond's publications.

126. ———. "The Roving Eye: Point of View in Medieval Percep-tion of Landscape." In R. F. Yeager and Charlotte C. Morse, eds. *Speak-ing Images: Essays in Honor of V. A. Kolve* (*SAC* 25 [2003], no. 147), pp. 463–77. Pearsall considers a range of medieval visual and verbal landscapes, exploring how they signify "something other" and enable the observer of the landscape to rove freely and "compose its meaning as if afresh." The essay refers to *BD, PF, LGW*, the Troilus frontispiece, and several works influenced by Chaucer.

127. Pope, Rob. *How to Study Chaucer*. 2d ed. Study Guides. New York: St. Martin's Press, 2001. x, 223 pp. Originally published in 1988. Designed for examination preparation, this guide poses a series of issues for *GP* and the individual tales in *CT; TC;* and the dream poems, espe-cially *PF*: kind of work, what it is about, characterization, the argument, narrator and narrative, and text in context. The guide also includes rec-

ommendations for writing an essay about Chaucer, a survey of current topics and debates, and suggestions for further reading.

128. Reale, Nancy M., and Ruth E. Sternglantz, eds. *Satura: Studies in Medieval Literature in Honour of Robert R. Raymo*. Donington: Shaun Tyas, 2001. viii, 279 pp.; 41 b&w illus. Fourteen literary studies that range across Old English, Old French, Anglo-Latin, Middle English, and medieval Irish, Spanish, and Italian. Three essays pertain to Chaucer; see nos. 106, 148, and 231.

129. Rhodes, Jim. *Poetry Does Theology: Chaucer, Grosseteste, and the Pearl-Poet*. Notre Dame, Ind.: University of Notre Dame Press, 2001. xii, 324 pp. Surveys the relationships between theology and poetry in late-medieval writing, assessing how Robert Grosseteste, the *Pearl* poet, and Chaucer communicate a proto-humanistic perspective, "characterized by a semi-Pelagian, anthropocentric theology" that is "roughly Ockhamist" and "incarnational." This theology "affirms human dignity and the sanctity of the human body." The most secular of the writers considered, Chaucer shows "how theological discourse has been absorbed or internalized" in his narrators. *NPT* shows that "meaning is in the story and not in the moral tacked onto the text." *PrT* and *SNT* reflect differing views on *caritas*, chastity, and their interrelations. *RvT* seeks to redefine *caritas*, while *PardT* challenges the power of theological discourse.

130. Robertson, Elizabeth, and Christine M. Rose, eds. *Representing Rape in Medieval and Early Modern Literature*. The New Middle Ages. New York and Basingstoke: Palgrave, 2001. x, 453 pp. Eleven essays about literary depictions of rape in Chaucer, Sidney, Spenser, Shakespeare, Latin comedies, Ovidian narratives, and the Philomel story. Includes an introduction by the editors, an afterword by Christopher Cannon, and a revised reprint of Cannon's "Chaucer and Rape: Uncertainty's Certainties" (*SAC* 22 [2000], 67–92; *SAC* 24 [2002], no. 10). For four new essays that pertain to Chaucer, see nos. 132, 222, 266, and 284.

131. Rogers, Laura Mestayer. "Embarking with Constance: Margaret Schlauch." *Medieval Feminist Forum* 31 (2001): 36–43. Assessment of Schlauch's career and criticism, focusing on her *Chaucer's Constance and Accused Queens* (1927; rpt. 1969). Includes a bibliography of Schlauch's publications.

132. Rose, Christine M. "Reading Chaucer Reading Rape." In Elizabeth Robertson and Christine M. Rose, eds. *Representing Rape in Medieval*

and Early Modern Literature (*SAC* 25 [2003], no. 130), pp. 21–60. Rose surveys instances of rape or threatened rape in Chaucer's works, arguing that, though Chaucer presents rape as a trope that enfigures reader response or male competition, we must recognize and confront its literal value, accepting it both in game and in earnest. Rape in Chaucer is "astonishingly prevalent and varied."

133. Rudd, Gillian. *The Complete Critical Guide to Geoffrey Chaucer.* The Complete Critical Guides to English Literature. London and New York: Routledge, 2001. xiv, 200 pp. A discursive handbook to Chaucer's life and its context, his works, and criticism of his works. The biographical portion provides basic information and notes the variety of Chaucers constructed over the years. Rudd discusses the works chronologically (including short works as well as major ones). The critical portion considers linguistic as well as literary traditions, including sources, narrative technique, historicisms, politics, feminism, and influence. All discussions are linked by a set of internal cross-listings by page number, and each section includes suggestions for further reading.

134. Salih, Sarah. *Versions of Virginity in Late Medieval England.* Cambridge: D. S. Brewer, 2001. ix, 278 pp. Explores the role of virginity in notions of late-medieval bodies, genders, identities, and social practices. The study, focusing on female religious versions of virginity, is structured around decreasing degrees of enclosure, examining hagiographic modes of virginity in Katherine Group virgin-martyr legends of the early thirteenth century, the monastic virginity of nuns, and the reclaimed virginity of Margery Kempe.

135. Salter, David. *Holy and Noble Beasts: Encounters with Animals in Medieval Literature.* Cambridge: D. S. Brewer, 2001. viii, 168 pp. A study of the representation of animals in late-medieval literature, focusing on how human identity is defined in relation to animals. Using examples from late-medieval hagiography and romance, Salter argues that medieval writers reflect on their own humanity and explore the meaning of abstract values and ideas through depictions of animals. Refers to *WBPT*, *KnT*, *FranT*, *MkT* and *MLT*.

136. Saunders, Corinne, ed. *Chaucer.* Blackwell Guides to Criticism. Oxford: Blackwell, 2001. xii, 356 pp.; 8 b&w illus. An anthology of reprinted critical discussions divided into four sections: Chaucer's reading and readership (3 essays or excerpts), dream poetry (7 essays or excerpts), *TC* (5 essays or excerpts), and *CT* (10 essays or excerpts). Saunders prefaces each selection with a summary placing the discussion

in its critical context and begins each section with an overview surveying critical trends. The book includes a selective, though extensive, bibliography and a brief subject index. All selections are from the twentieth century, most from 1965–1995.

137. Saunders, Corinne. *Rape and Ravishment in the Literature of Medieval England.* Cambridge: D. S. Brewer, 2001. ix, 343 pp. Surveys modern and postmodern theorizing of rape and addresses rape in medieval England. Topics include secular, legal notions of rape; rape in canon law, theology, and confessional manuals (especially vernacular ones); rape motifs in hagiography (especially St. Lucy); classical paradigms of rape (Lucretia and Helen of Troy) in medieval English narratives; rape in romance, especially Malory's *Morte Darthur*; and rape in Chaucer's works (pp. 265–310). Chaucer's various depictions of rape reflect a very "modern" awareness of "issues profoundly relevant to female experience." He employs classical paradigms and romance motifs, but his work never "loses a sense of the real gravity of rape."

138. Scanlon, Larry. "Return of the Repressed: The Sequel." In Glenn Burger and Steven Kruger, eds. *Queering the Middle Ages* (*SAC* 25 [2003], no. 97), pp. 284–301. A response to an essay by Glenn Burger; see no. 96.

139. Sola Buil, Ricardo. "Landscape and Description of the Natural World in Chaucer." *SELIM* 8 (2001): 77–89. Argues that landscape is a device of characterization and narrative control in fourteenth-century literature, drawing examples from Chaucer's works.

140. St. John, Michael. *Chaucer's Dream Visions: Courtliness and Individual Identity.* Aldershot: Ashgate, 2000. 226 pp. Examines the philosophical content of Chaucer's dream visions—the interplay between the soul and its courtly context—arguing that in Chaucer's world, the ideal of courtesy rather than any explicitly spiritual principle holds together a fictive community. *BD* highlights the moral dilemmas of *fin amor* viewed from a spiritual perspective. The avian parliament in *PF* offers a political ideal as an enfranchised and socially beneficial courtly desire. In *HF*, "commune profit" replaces "singuler profit" through the protocols of courtliness. *LGW* presents two aspects of courtliness: a collective body of traditions and the promotion of counsel and reason, stimulating thought about *fin amor*.

141. Strohm, Paul. "Rememorative Reconstruction." Presidential Address. The New Chaucer Society, Twelfth International Congress, 14–17 July 2000, University of London. *SAC* 23 (2001): 3–16. Strohm

calls for renewed sensitivity to historical particularity in the study of literature, especially Chaucer. Such study must acknowledge the limits of modernist empiricist assumptions and maintain deep respect for the past and its mutually constitutive relations with the present. Includes comments on the development of the New Chaucer Society.

142. Takano, Hidekuni. "The Use of Chaucer's Narrators: Up to *Troilus and Criseyde.*" *Bulletin of the Faculty of Humanities* (Seikei University) 34 (1999): 1–37 (in Japanese). Discusses the role of the narrator in *BD*, *HF*, *PF*, and *TC*.

143. Utz, Richard. "*'Chaucerphilologie'* in the Nineteenth and Early Twentieth Century." *Philologie im Netz* 21 (2002): 54–62. This account of German-speaking Chaucer philology in the nineteenth and early twentieth centuries challenges recent accusations that philology is responsible for the backward state of medieval studies. Different phases of Chaucer study are consistent with their contemporary political, historical, social, and academic contexts.

144. White, Hugh. *Nature, Sex, and Goodness in a Medieval Literary Tradition.* New York and Oxford: Oxford University Press, 2000. x, 278 pp. Questions the notion that Nature was universally considered a positive force in the Middle Ages. Although depicted as God's vicar, Nature was also aligned with sexual impulses, complicating the image. White traces depictions of and attitudes toward nature and the natural in Latin tradition, English popular tradition, and French literature as they underlie the representations of nature in Gower's *Confessio Amantis* and Chaucer's works. Gower struggles to represent Nature as good but discovers that "such belief" is impossible to sustain. In *ParsT* and *Mel*, Chaucer expresses overt scepticism about the goodness of nature; in *ManT* and *SqT*, he uses Boethian material to suggest such scepticism. He provokes scepticism in his audience with *BD* and *PF* and employs similar strategies in *PhyT* and *TC*. Chaucer's view of the human condition is "stalked by despair."

145. Williams, Deanne Marie. "Coming to Terms: The Trouble with French in Early Modern England." *DAI* 61 (2001): 3585A. Postcolonial analysis of post-Conquest attitudes toward France and French in England, considering the formulation of English identity. Williams discusses Chaucer, Corpus Christi plays, Stephen Hawes, John Skelton, Shakespeare, and continuing effects on English studies.

146. Witalisz, Władysław, ed. *"And Gladly Wolde He Lerne and Gladly Teche": Studies on Language and Literature in Honour of Professor Dr.*

Karl Heinz Göller. Kraków: Wydawnictno Uniwersytetu Jagiellonskiego, 2001. 216 pp. Nineteen essays on a variety of subjects, medieval to postmodern, literary and linguistic. Two essays pertain to Chaucer; see nos. 20 and 280.

147. Yeager, R. F., and Charlotte C. Morse, eds. *Speaking Images: Essays in Honor of V. A. Kolve*. Asheville, N.C.: Pegasus Press, 2001. xviii, 650 pp. Twenty-six essays on topics from Marie de France's *Guigemar* to Edward Burne-Jones's "Miracle of the Merciful Knight," with recurrent emphasis on the intersection between visual and verbal traditions. Includes a bibliography of Kolve's publications and lectures, a commemorative preface by Larry Luchtel, a *tabula gratulatoria*, and an index. Fifteen essays pertain to Chaucer; see nos. 114, 126, 176, 181, 182, 192, 194, 203, 204, 208, 210, 226, 227, 271, and 278.

See also no. 228.

The Canterbury Tales—General

148. Bishop, Kathleen. "*El Libro de Buen Amor* and *The Canterbury Tales*." In Nancy M. Reale and Ruth E. Sternglantz, eds. *Satura: Studies in Medieval Literature in Honour of Robert R. Raymo* (*SAC* 25 [2003], no. 128), pp. 227–37. Identifies a number of points of comparison between Juan Ruiz's *El Libro* and *CT*: wide range of genres, ecclesiastical satire, comparable characters (e.g., the Prioress and Doña Garoça; the Wife of Bath and Trotaconventos), narrators' self-deprecation, comedy and bawdy, and "outlook on the world."

149. Bishop, Kathleen A. "The Influence of Plautus and Latin Elegiac Comedy on Chaucer's Fabliaux." *ChauR* 35 (2001): 294–317. Classical and medieval Latin influences on the fabliaux are as important to analyze as are the analogues Chaucer draws upon for his tales. Specifically, a close consideration of Plautus and Latin elegiac comedy can lead to a fuller understanding of the shaping of Chaucer's fabliaux.

150. Borlenghi, Patricia, and Giles Greenfield. *Chaucer the Cat and the Animal Pilgrims*. London: Bloomsbury Children's Books, 1999. 77 pp.; color illus. A collection of animal stories set in a frame-tale of animals on pilgrimage to Assisi. Twelve children's stories from international folk traditions. Text by Borlenghi; illustrations by Greenfield. Commemorates 600th anniversary of Chaucer's death.

151. Brewer, Derek. "From the Many to the One: Chaucer's *Canter-*

bury Tales." In Leo Carruthers and Adrian Papahagi, eds. *Prologues et épilogues dans la littérature anglaise du Moyen Âge* (*SAC* 25 [2003], no. 98), pp. 55–72. In *CT*, Chaucer uses prologues to achieve great diversity, displacing himself with other narrators. He develops a counter movement in his epilogues, in which the conventions of religious epilogues communicate, however tenuously, a unified religious worldview.

152. Chan, Amado. "Causing Disorder: Chaucer's Prioress, Wife, and Amazon." *JEP* 21 (2000): 166–70. Details of the Prioress's *GP* description, *WBPT*, and Emelye's desires in *KnT* indicate that "women by nature oppose man's endeavor to rule and establish order in the world."

153. Clouet, Richard. "Les *Contes de Canterbury* et l'Espagne." *BAM* 59 (2001): 15–25. Surveys overt and covert links and references to Spain in *CT*.

154. Collette, Carolyn P. *Species, Phantasms, and Images: Vision and Medieval Psychology in* The Canterbury Tales. Ann Arbor: University of Michigan Press, 2001. xiv, 208 pp. Medieval ideas of psychology and cognition underlie the concern with sight, imagination, and *fantasye* in select tales of Canterbury, wherein Chaucer demonstrates that the only certainty in human relations is uncertainty. The male characters of *KnT* are constrained by the limits of their imaginations. In *WBPT* and *ClT*, uncontrolled male will is linked directly to problems of perception; in *MerT* and *FranT*, male and female obsessions derive from mental images distorted by desire. Beautiful images influence human "desire, judgment, and greed" in *PhyT* and *PardT*, understandable in light of Lollard anxiety about images. *SNT* and *CYT* depict successful and unsuccessful attempts to comprehend the relationship between the physical and metaphysical. *ParsT* seeks to communicate without images, and *Ret* affirms the uncontrollable nature of human imagination.

155. Dyas, Dee. *Pilgrimage in Medieval English Literature: 700–1500.* Cambridge: D. S. Brewer, 2001. vii, 288 pp. A literal journey and lifelong spiritual experience, pilgrimage involves new surroundings and new levels of understanding. Dyas discusses pilgrimage in early Christian tradition and in Old and Middle English literature, including Chaucer's choice of the pilgrimage frame in *CT* and the role of *ParsT*.

156. Fields, Peter John. *Craft and Anti-Craft in Chaucer's* Canterbury Tales. Lewistown, N.Y.: Edwin Mellen Press, 2001. v, 490 pp. Chaucer's interest in *craft* goes far beyond mere technical process. In *CT*, the word and its derivations emblematize human efforts to control the

world through personal expertise and learned tradition. Fields challenges notions of Chaucer's pluralism, assessing the self-elevation of the Wife of Bath, the resentment of the Squire, and the mystification of *CYT* and its counteractive concern with humility. He also examines privy knowledge as divine privilege and contrasts the *nova artis* and *dolus* of Venus in Virgil's *Aeneid* with the simple rhetoric of Cecilia in *SNT* and the speaker of *PrT*. Later chapters discuss craft and the development of early Christian epistemology in King Alfred's Boethius, and the craft of humanist narrative. See also no. 331.

157. Jacobs, Kathryn. *Marriage Contracts from Chaucer to the Renaissance Stage.* Gainesville: University Press of Florida, 2001. viii, 181 pp. Four chapters explore the influence of contemporary marriage law on Chaucer's imagination, and three investigate similar influences on religious and Renaissance drama. Chaucer did not merely reflect his society's concerns with marriage and its formulas; he capitalized on his reader's awareness of the formulas' consequences. In *CT*, delineation of marriage can (1) expose characters' social status and establish reader expectations; (2) reconceptualize nonmarital sexual relations by using the language of the familiar marital contract; and (3) encourage a more sympathetic view of widows by examining the straits to which marital contracts reduced them.

158. Kummerer, K. R. "A Consistent Time Frame for Chaucer's Canterbury Pilgrimage." *Journal of the British Astronomical Society* 11.4 (2001): 203–13. Discusses seven "celestial assertions" in *CT* and the reference to April 18 to show that Chaucer "accurately describes the celestial conditions he observed" in southeast England. Astronomical evidence indicates that the *CT* pilgrimage ends on April 18, 1391, "as the sun was setting and Libra and the full moon were rising." Includes several charts and appendices, including a "description and application of the astrolabe."

159. Ladd, Roger Alfred. "Merchants, Mercantile Satire, and Problems of Estate in Late Medieval English Literature." *DAI* 61 (2001): 3163A. Clerical anti-mercantile views gradually shifted as a "guardedly pro-trade ideology" emerged. Such attitudes also appear in estates satire found in *CT*, Gower's *Miroir de l'Omme*, *Piers Plowman*, Margery Kempe, the York cycle plays, and various pro-trade fifteenth-century didactic works.

160. Lawler, Jennifer. "Chaucer, Geoffrey (c.1340–1400)." In John Block Friedman and Kristen Mossler Figg, eds., with Scott D. Westram

and Gregory G. Guzman. *Trade, Travel, and Exploration in the Middle Ages: An Encyclopedia*. Garland Reference Library of the Humanities, no. 1899. New York and London: Garland, 2000, pp. 105–6. Brief description of Chaucer's travels and of pilgrimage as a frame in *CT*. Like the pilgrimage report of Felix Fabri (1441/2–1502), *CT* is important as a historical record.

161. Lewis, Celia Milton. "Framing Fiction with Death: 'The Seven Sages of Rome,' Boccaccio's 'Decameron,' and Chaucer's 'Canterbury Tales.'" *DAI* 62 (2001): 2109A. *The Seven Sages*, the *Decameron*, and *CT* share, in addition to frame structure and historical milieux, a concern with death and avoidance of it (plague), a changing sense of time, and a new concept of authorial identity (especially Chaucer). The forms encourage order and verisimilitude.

162. Minnis, A. J. "*Parler proprement*: Words, Deeds, and Proper Speech in the *Rose*." In A. J. Minnis. *Magister Amoris: The* Roman de la Rose *and Vernacular Hermeneutics*. Oxford: Oxford University Press, 2001, pp. 119–63. Explores Jean de Meun's treatment of vulgar talk in *Roman de la Rose* (15,129–272) within the context of late-medieval theories of signification. In various passages of *CT*, Chaucer also confronts direct language and low subject in literature. With Jean de Meun as his predecessor, Chaucer placed vulgarity at the center rather than in the margins, thereby calling into question value judgments.

163. O'Brien, Timothy D. "Seductive Violence and Three Chaucerian Women." *CollL* 28.2 (2001): 178–96. The Wife of Bath, the Prioress, and the wife in *ShT* represent themselves as victims of violence to make themselves attractive to men. In doing so, they draw on texts, such as medieval saints' lives and romances, that depict violence as central to the formation and maintenance of gender. The arrangement of this material suggests that Chaucer was simultaneously aware of, complicit in, and subject to this process of gender formation.

164. Pitcher, John Austin. "Equivocations: The Agency of Desire in 'The Canterbury Tales.'" *DAI* 61 (2001): 3582A. Examines the "interrelation of equivocation and desire" in *PhyT*, *ClT*, *FranT*, and *WBPT*, not in what the narrators and characters say, but through a "movement or oscillation between opposed interests." In *CT*, sexual politics can be found in the ambivalences, anomalies, and complexities of language.

165. Schildgen, Brenda Deen. *Pagans, Tartars, Moslems, and Jews in Chaucer's* Canterbury Tales. Gainesville: University Press of Florida, 2001. [xiv], 184 pp. Applying Habermas's notion of discourse ethics,

Schildgen focuses on stories in *CT* that are "set outside a Christian-dominated world." Individual chapters include discussions of *KnT* and *SqT*, *MLT*, *WBT* and *FranT*, *PrT* and *MkT*, and *SNT*. Chaucer's inclusion of these stories demonstrates his "expansive narrative interest in the intellectual and cultural worlds outside Christianity" (2). They are crucial to presenting not a single, totalizing worldview but rather an "environment" for the exchange and ultimately unresolved debate of alternative views and value systems (125).

166. Shoaf, R. Allen. *Chaucer's Body: The Anxiety of Circulation in the* Canterbury Tales. Gainesville: University Press of Florida, 2001. xvi, 162 pp. Chaucer's use of metonymy in *CT* expresses his "anxiety of circulation," which is traced through his references to the fragmented body and bodily functions, infection, magic, rhetoric, and translation. Shoaf examines relationships among tales, tellers, and Harry Bailly in the various fragments of *CT*.

167. Snell, William. "'Feloun' and 'Felonye': Violence and Violent Crime in Chaucer's *Canterbury Tales*." *Geibun-Kenkyu* (Keio University) 80 (2001): 124–41. Examines felons and felony in Chaucer's works, focusing on *CT* and how such crimes reflect on the knightly class.

168. Webb, Diana. *Pilgrimage in Medieval England*. London and New York: Hambledon and London, 2000. xviii, 317 pp. Describes the activities, theology, sociology, and psychology of medieval English pilgrimage from its roots in Anglo-Saxon tradition to criticism of the institution in the late Middle Ages. Considers English and British sites primarily, discussing topics such as early saints, penitential traditions, imagery, indulgences, royal pilgrimages, local pilgrimages, pilgrim routes and stops, and pilgrim dress. Passim references to literary pilgrimages, including *CT*.

169. Whalen, David M. "'A Little More than Kin and Less than Kind': The Affinity of Literature and Politics." *Intercollegiate Review* 37.1 (2001): 22–30. Discussion of how the political functions of literature are framed by broader ethical and moral concerns, drawing examples from Virgil, Cervantes, Robert Frost, and *CT*, where the pilgrimage frame indicates that social order—the common good—is dependent on "having an objective that is beyond" the common good.

See also nos. 2, 3, 6, 16, 19, 26, 27, 29, 30, 34, 35, 50, 66, 70, 74, 75, 79, 82, 83, 86, 91–93, 109, 124, 136, 198, 253, 275.

CT—The General Prologue

170. Kendrick, Laura. "Chaucer's *General Prologue* to the *Canterbury Tales* and the 'Lives' of the Troubadours." In Leo Carruthers and Adrian Papahagi, eds. *Prologues et épilogues dans la littérature anglaise du Moyen Âge* (*SAC* 25 [2003], no. 98), pp. 129–44. Suggests that collected *vidas*, or "lives," of the troubadours may have served as Chaucer's model for the "portraits" of the pilgrims in *GP*. Individual *vidas* open anthologies of troubadour verse in some fourteenth-century manuscripts, and Chaucer may be comically adapting this convention.

171. Kirkham, David, and Valerie Allen, eds. *The General Prologue to the* Canterbury Tales. Cambridge School Chaucer. Cambridge: Cambridge University Press, 1999. 96 pp.; b&w illus. School-text edition of *GP*, accompanied, on facing pages, by extensive glossing and pedagogical commentary and discussion questions. Also includes synoptic descriptions of Chaucer's pilgrims and brief essays on pertinent topics, including pilgrimage and social structure.

172. Schragg, E. D. "Description of the Warrener in the General Prologue and the Warrener's Prologue and Tale." *Medieval Forum* 1 (2001): n.p. Creates in reconstructed Middle English a description, prologue, and tale for an additional pilgrim, the warrener. The description and prologue are in couplets (including speeches by the Host and Prioress), and the prose tale is an adaptation of the Grail quest, modeled on Monty Python.

See also nos. 16, 23, 26, 27, 81, 111, 152, 173, 176, 177, 197, 221, 226, 252, 295.

CT—The Knight and His Tale

173. Barr, Helen. "Chaucer's Knight: A Christian Killer?" *English Review* 12.2 (2001): 2–3. The *GP* description of the Knight engages late-medieval questions of war and pacifism, confronting the audience with an "ethical and political dilemma."

174. Camarda, Peter F. "Imperfect Heroes and the Consolations of Boethius: The Double Meaning of Suffering in Chaucer's *Knight's Tale*." *Medieval Forum* 1 (2001): n.p. Chaucer leaves both suffering and heroism "open to ambiguous interpretation" in *KnT*, prompting readers to go

beyond disorder and hopelessness and discover Boethian consolation, which is anchored in recognition of the true good.

175. Johnston, Andrew James. "Wrestling with Ganymede: Chaucer's *Knight's Tale* and the Homoerotics of Epic History." *GRM* 50 (2000): 21–43. Using the wrestling scene in *KnT* 2.2959–64 as a point of departure, the author argues that the violent homoeroticism of the passage, elevated by Chaucer to a matter of state, "exposes Boccaccio's classicism as a veneer under which the traditional medieval strategies of court culture operate." The alterity of pagan antiquity, reintroduced by Chaucer, defies humanists' appropriation of the classical epic and its cultural norms.

176. Jones, Terry. "The Image of Chaucer's Knight." In R. F. Yeager and Charlotte C. Morse, eds. *Speaking Images: Essays in Honor of V. A. Kolve* (*SAC* 25 [2003], no. 147), pp. 205–36; 15 color figs. The *GP* description of the Knight suggests that he wore clothing and equipment typical of "military opportunism." More specifically, the Knight's dress and career call to mind Sir John Hawkwood, and changes to the Ellesmere portrait of the Knight may have been made to disguise the likeness to Hawkwood.

177. Sánchez Marti, Jordi. "Chaucer's Knight and the Hundred Years War." *SELIM* 7 (1997): 153–60. Characterizes the *GP* Knight based on his participation in Christian crusades and his worthy "noninvolvement" in the Hundred Years War.

178. ———. "The Representation of Chivalry in *The Knight's Tale*." *Revista Alicantina de Estudios Ingleses* 13 (2000): 161–73. In *KnT*, Theseus is "devoted to chivalry" and yet ineffectual in his attempts to achieve order. Through him, the Knight indicates the need for chivalry to undergo reform.

See also nos. 16, 25, 45, 90, 100, 113, 135, 152, 154, 165.

CT—The Miller and His Tale

179. Boenig, Robert. "Musical Instruments as Iconographical Artifacts in Medieval Poetry." In Curtis Perry, ed. *Material Culture and Cultural Materialisms in the Middle Ages and Renaissance*. Arizona Studies in the Middle Ages and the Renaissance, no. 5. Turnhout: Brepols, 2001, pp. 1–15. For medieval poets, the "hyperreality of musical instruments" was "more significant" than was their reality. In *Beowulf*, the harp signi-

fies Hrothgar's agenda of political conquest and order; in Machaut's *Remedy of Fortune*, the "instruments signify the Lady's bounty, the celestial associations of her court, and the displaced sexuality of the collector." In *MilT*, Nicholas's psaltery is a "surrogate for the female body."

180. Horobin, S. C. P. *"Phislophye* in *The Reeve's Tale* (Hg 4050) in Answer to *Astromye* in *The Miller's Tale* (3451)." *N&Q* 246 (2001): 109–10. Argues that "astromye" in *MilT* (1.3451 and 3457) is an authorial malapropism.

181. Mann, Jill. "Speaking Images in Chaucer's 'Miller's Tale.'" In R. F. Yeager and Charlotte C. Morse, eds. *Speaking Images: Essays in Honor of V. A. Kolve* (*SAC* 25 [2003], no. 147), pp. 237–54; 3 b&w figs. Mann explores Nicholas's verbal manipulation of John in *MilT*, the portrait of Alison, and the body language of the kiss scene (and some analogous fabliaux), arguing that language, imagination, and physical reality are in many ways inseparable or interdependent.

182. Nolan, Barbara. "Playing Parts: Fragments, Figures and the Mystery of Love in 'The Miller's Tale.'" In R. F. Yeager and Charlotte C. Morse, eds. *Speaking Images: Essays in Honor of V. A. Kolve* (*SAC* 25 [2003], no. 147), pp. 255–99; 8 color figs. "In-etched" reminiscences of the Annunciation strain against the dominant sexuality of *MilT*, simultaneously suggesting and denying the metonymic and synecdochaic relations between divine and earthly love. Nolan cites analogous examples of spiritual/sexual continuity from visual tradition, Boccaccio's *Decameron* 4.2, *Gilote et Johane*, mystery plays of the Annunciation, and a bawdy thirteenth-century French *Ars amatoria* by Guiart.

183. Walls, Kathryn. "Absolon as Barber-Surgeon." *ChauR* 35 (2001): 391–98. Absolon's profession is reflected in his elaborate hairstyle (rather than tonsure); in his red, white, and blue clothing; and in his choice of the cultour as a tool for revenge. With cutting blade in hand, Absolon takes his "patient" by surprise, striking with "unerring accuracy" the part of the anatomy most familiar to medieval surgeons.

See also nos. 16, 46, 68, 83, 93, 281.

CT—The Reeve and His Tale

184. Harwood, Britton J. "Psychoanalytic Politics: Chaucer and Two Peasants." *ELH* 68 (2001): 1–27. Examines the "unconscious content" of *RvT* through a number of Chaucer's own "identifications": with Sir

Edmund de la Pole, owner of the mill at Trumpington and brother of Sir Roger de la Pole; with Symkyn and the exorbitance of his social pretensions; and with John and Aleyn, who retreat to their place of privilege (Soler Hall) after beating Symkyn at his game. Harwood concludes that "ignoring textual features leading to what an author has repressed will miss an essential way the text functions within material history."

185. Pearcy, Roy J. "A Ghost Proverbial Expression from Chaucer's *Reeve's Tale*: 'Digne as Water in Dich.'" *ProverbiumY* 18 (2001): 257–60. Dialectical and textual evidence suggests that the simile in *RvT* 1.3964 means "'she is as worthy as ditch-water is stinking' that is to say 'very worthy,' with no pejorative implication."

See also nos. 7, 23, 68, 74, 83, 85, 93, 129, 180, 281.

CT—The Cook and His Tale

See nos. 35, 93.

CT—The Man of Law and His Tale

186. Fowler, Elizabeth. "The Empire and the Waif: Consent and Conflict of Laws in the *Man of Law's Tale*." In David Aers, ed. *Medieval Literature and Historical Inquiry: Essays in Honor of Derek Pearsall* (*SAC* 25 [2003], no. 87), pp. 55–67. Reads *MLT* as a "thought experiment" in which the topos of the ship (familiar in both romance and political/legal philosophy) is used to confront the "conflict of laws" among the various cultures represented: Christian, Islam, and pagan. With *ClT*, *MLT* considers consent under various kinds of coercion; *MLT* offers the principle of custom as a standard.

187. Frankis, John. "King Ælle and the Conversion of the English: The Development of a Legend from Bede to Chaucer." In Donald Scragg and Carole Weinberg, eds. *Literary Appropriations of the Anglo-Saxons from the Thirteenth to the Twentieth Century*. Cambridge Studies in Anglo-Saxon England, no. 29. Cambridge: Cambridge University Press, 2000, pp. 74–92. Frankis compares how Chaucer's *MLT* and Gower's "Tale of Constance" diminish Trevet's historiographical concern with Anglo-Saxon England. From the time of Bede, Ælle was associated with

the Christianization of the Anglo-Saxons, a motif retained by Chaucer and Gower.

188. Kikuchi, Akio. "The Legend of the 'Martyr King': Political Representation in *The Man of Law's Tale*." *Shiron* 39 (2000): 1–19. Explores the narrator's "royalist" politics in *MLT*, arguing that they are "more incomplete" than the narrator thinks. Alla is presented as a good king, and the Sultan follows the trajectory of a typical "martyr king," although the teller misunderstands the "value" of his martyrdom in the context of the court of Richard II, where the image of the martyr king was used to political advantage. Chaucer lampoons the Man of Law's political naiveté.

189. Robertson, Elizabeth. "The 'Elvyssh' Power of Constance: Christian Feminism in Geoffrey Chaucer's *The Man of Law's Tale*." *SAC* 23 (2001): 143–80. Through various alignments of Muslim and Christian characters and transgressions of social and gender boundaries, Chaucer "defamiliarizes" essentialist categories of race, class, gender, and especially religion in *MLT*. In particular, Chaucer depicts in Constance an ineffable ideal of Christianity—an unusual feminine alternative to dominant hierarchical orthodoxy, perhaps inspired by Lollardy but not congenial to many Lollard tenets. Chaucer's depictions of race and religion are similar to Wolfram von Eschenbach's in *Parzival*.

190. Rose, Christine M. "Chaucer's *Man of Law's Tale*: Teaching Through the Sources." *CollL* 28.2 (2001): 155–77. Use of sources and analogues in the classroom can provide baffled students a point of entry into the complexities of *MLT* and allow them to appreciate the importance of redaction in medieval literature. In particular, examining Chaucer's feminization of material concerning Constance and her mothers-in-law from Trevet's *Cronicles* helps students see the themes of ideal Christian passivity and the maintenance of patriarchal hegemony.

191. Spearing, A. C. "Narrative Voice: The Case of Chaucer's *Man of Law's Tale*." *NLH* 32 (2001): 715–46. A survey of selected criticism since Kittredge demonstrates that the idea of a fallible narrative voice has dominated criticism of *CT*. Spearing examines *MLT* 2.141–96 to show the difficulty of separating narrational from nonnarrational elements and of demonstrating an unreliable narrator. Focus on a fictional, narrative voice obscures the meaning of *MLT*.

192. Yeager, R. F. "John Gower's Images: 'The Tale of Constance' and 'The Man of Law's Tale.'" In R. F. Yeager and Charlotte C. Morse, eds. *Speaking Images: Essays in Honor of V. A. Kolve* (*SAC* 25 [2003], no.

147), pp. 525–57. Yeager contrasts Gower's uses of imagery in the 'Tale of Constance" with Chaucer's techniques in *MLT*, arguing that Gower is more minimalist, but that, like Chaucer, Gower challenges readers to discover the moral implications of the world he describes.

See also nos. 81, 88, 95, 100, 104, 111, 115, 135, 165, 198, 278.

CT—The Wife of Bath and Her Tale

193. Carter, Susan Ann. "Willing Shape-Shifters: The Loathly Lady from Irish Sovranty to Spenser's Duessa." *DAI* 62 (2001): 1403A. Examines loathly ladies in Irish myth, Chaucer (*WBT*), Gower ("Florent"), *Dame Ragnell*, Thomas of Erceldoune, and ballads, focusing on two loci—court and forest—and kinds of power. Also examines the political significance of the refiguration of sovereignty as evil in Spenser's Duessa.

194. Doob, Penelope Reed. "Theseus T(h)reads the Maze: Labyrinthine Empowerment/Impairment and Ariadne's Absence." In R. F. Yeager and Charlotte C. Morse, eds. *Speaking Images: Essays in Honor of V. A. Kolve* (*SAC* 25 [2003], no. 147), pp. 167–86; 4 b&w figs. Surveys relations between female literary characters and labyrinths from mythic accounts to Lady Mary Worth's *Pamphilia to Amphilanthus*, commenting on Virgil's *Aeneid*, Boethius's *Consolation of Philosophy*, Dante's *Commedia*, *WBPT*, and the anonymous *Assembly of Ladies*. The Wife of Bath constructs a rhetorical labyrinth, and the loathly lady offers the knight an "Ariadnean textual thread."

195. Dwyer, June. "Protocols of Violence: Hunters, the Wife of Bath, and Pam Houston's *Cowboys Are My Weakness*." *SSF* 35 (1998): 307–18. Two possible versions of women's attitudes toward violence appear in *WBPT*: *WBT* idealizes women as a civilizing force working to curb male violence; *WBP* portrays a woman who uses violence when other means of control fail. Both constructs of female violence can be found in Pam Houston's collection of short stories.

196. Fee, Christopher R., with David E. Leeming. *Gods, Heroes, and Kings: The Battle for Mythic Britain*. Oxford: Oxford University Press, 2001. xiv, 242 pp. Surveys the multicultural nature of medieval British literature, which combines Celtic, Roman, Anglo-Saxon, Norse, and Christian influences. Introduces the myths and heroic figures of pre-Christian cultures through synopses of various narratives and accompanying commentaries. A commentary on a synopsis of *WBT* suggests that the latter weaves folkloric motifs into a penitential pattern.

197. Kennedy, Beverly. "'Withouten Oother Compaignye in Youthe': Verbal and Moral Ambiguity in the *General Prologue* Portrait of the Wife of Bath." In Robert Myles and David Williams, eds. *Chaucer and Language: Essays in Honour of Douglas Wurtele* (*SAC* 25 [2003], no. 123), pp. 1–32, 178–91. Descriptions of the Wife of Bath in *GP* and in *WBP* are consciously ambiguous, a means of reminding us to suspend moral judgment because language is inherently ambiguous. Through glosses and textual choices, modern editions oversimplify the Wife by disambiguating her.

198. Patterson, Lee. *Putting the Wife in Her Place*. The William Matthews Lectures 1995, Birkbeck College, London, 22 and 23 May 1995. [London]: [Birkbeck College], 1995. 49 pp. Two essays: "The Place of Philology" argues that the *MLE* is Chaucer's late and revised addition to *CT* and that it is properly followed by *WBP*; Patterson confronts the manuscript evidence and suggests several structural and thematic continuities between *MLE* and *WBPT*. "The Place of History" assesses the Wife of Bath's individuality in light of medieval marital and property law, arguing that gaps, or inconsistencies, between historical facts and trends and what the Wife says about her situation indicate her desire for autonomy and a "companionate" marriage.

199. Terry, Michael. "Gofraidh Fionn Ó Dálaigh's Analogue to Geoffrey Chaucer's *Wife of Bath's Tale*." *N&Q* 246 (2001): 110–12. Proposes that "A Ghearóid déana mo dhail" (ca. 1338–56) be added to the list of analogues to *WBT*. It involves an interaction between a human and "fairy" being in which the human is rewarded for appropriate behavior; the outcome of the interaction pertains to sexual relations.

200. Wood, Chauncey. "The Wife of Bath and 'Speche Daungerous.'" In Robert Myles and David Williams, eds. *Chaucer and Language: Essays in Honour of Douglas Wurtele* (*SAC* 25 [2003], no. 123), pp. 33–43, 191–92. In light of Reason's discussion of direct language in *Roman de la Rose*, the Wife of Bath's euphemism and circumlocution characterize her as unreasonable and a misuser of language.

201. Yaw, Yvonne. "Students' Study Guides and the Wife of Bath." *ChauR* 35 (2001): 318–32. Errors in Cliffs Notes and MAX Notes guides on the Wife of Bath lead to an unsympathetic interpretation of the character and inaccurate reading of *WBT*.

See also nos. 7, 16, 18, 24, 27, 51, 68, 83, 107, 113, 135, 152, 154, 156, 163–65, 240, 281.

CT—The Friar and His Tale

202. Somerset, Fiona. "'Mark Him Wel for He Is On of þo': Training the 'Lewed' Gaze to Discern Hypocrisy." *ELH* 68 (2001): 315–34. Various late-medieval English texts (including the Wycliffite *Twelve Conclusions* and Roger Dymmok's *Reply* and other Wycliffite discourse) reflect "anxiety" about laypeople's inabilities to discern clerical hypocrisy. In *FrT*, Chaucer distinguishes between the summoner's lack of discernment and the astute discernment of the devil and the old lady. Also considers the hypocrisy of the Friar, the Summoner, and the Pardoner.

See also nos. 93, 203.

CT—The Summoner and His Tale

203. Bowers, John M. "Queering the Summoner: Same-Sex Union in Chaucer's *Canterbury Tales*." In R. F. Yeager and Charlotte C. Morse, eds. *Speaking Images: Essays in Honor of V. A. Kolve* (*SAC* 25 [2003], no. 147), pp. 301–24. Examines the "same-sex union of adoptive brotherhood" between the Summoner and the Pardoner and assesses the economic underpinnings of sworn brotherhood in *FrT* and *SumT*. Chaucer's alignment of homosexual and heterosexual issues in the Marriage Group and his presentation of the Summoner as bisexual are "coded means for inscribing" a forbidden topic in the Ricardian court, where imputations of Richard's relations with Robert de Vere were both known and kept secret.

204. Fleming, John V. "The Pentecosts of Four Poets." In R. F. Yeager and Charlotte C. Morse, eds. *Speaking Images: Essays in Honor of V. A. Kolve* (*SAC* 25 [2003], no. 147), pp. 111–41. Explores the "iconographic vocabulary" of Pentecost and its affiliations in Wolfram von Eschenbach's *Parzival*, Dante's *Inferno*, Luís de Camões's *Lusiads*, and Chaucer's *SumT*. Chaucer's version combines details from verbal and pictorial traditions and fuses respect for tradition with a "playful and expansive inventiveness."

See also nos. 6, 202.

CT—The Clerk and His Tale

205. Haines, Victor Yelverton. "Chaucer's Clerk, on the Level?" In Robert Myles and David Williams, eds. *Chaucer and Language: Essays in*

Honour of Douglas Wurtele (*SAC* 25 [2003], no. 123), pp. 83–106, 203–5. Examines several medieval notions of testing and promise-making, arguing that in *ClT* the Clerk makes fun of naïve "essentialist" allegory. Haines reads wit and sarcasm in Griselda's tone at the "portentous" line 666 and suggests that this tone helps lead readers to reject her immoral submission to Walter.

206. Hanrahan, Michael. "'A Straunge Succesour Sholde Take Youre Heritage': The *Clerk's Tale* and the Crisis of Ricardian Rule." *ChauR* 35 (2001): 335–50. *ClT* reflects aspects of Richard II's life and philosophy of kingship—and perhaps Chaucer's fanciful solutions to Richard II's political dilemma of an heirless realm: divorce or a consort advisor. The insistence on "obedience to authority" in *ClT* mirrors Richard's growing concern with disobedience as "the greatest affront to a ruler" and acquires "very real political associations for its Ricardian readers."

207. Lavezzo, Kathy. "Chaucer and Everyday Death: *The Clerk's Tale*, Burial, and the Subject of Poverty." *SAC* 23 (2001): 255–87. Griselda reflects the "ordinary peasant woman" of Chaucer's age. Her anxieties about the burials of her children are similar to concerns found in guild records; both *ClT* and the guild records indicate late-medieval interconnections among poverty, child abandonment, and infanticide.

208. Morse, Charlotte C. "Griselda Reads Philippa de Coucy." In R. F. Yeager and Charlotte C. Morse, eds. *Speaking Images: Essays in Honor of V. A. Kolve* (*SAC* 25 [2003], no. 147), pp. 347–92. Identifies "uncanny" resemblances between Griselda of *ClT* and Philippa de Coucy, wife of Robert de Vere. Similarities between the women and their treatment at the hands of their husbands (divorces) would have prompted Chaucer's immediate audience to "reflect on the political situation" in England. Events in Philippa's life may have influenced Chaucer's translation of his sources.

209. Myles, Robert. "Confusing Signs: The Semiotic Point of View in the *Clerk's Tale*." In Robert Myles and David Williams, eds. *Chaucer and Language: Essays in Honour of Douglas Wurtele* (*SAC* 25 [2003], no. 123), pp. 107–25, 205–9. Myles surveys medieval notions of natural and given signs, arguing that Griselda (and the reader with her) learns from her submission to Walter, insofar as it parallels a realist submission to quasi-nominalist understanding. Unlike Walter, Griselda eventually reflects a nascent "thesis of intentionality."

210. Olson, Glending. "The Marquis of Saluzzo and the Marquis of Dublin." In R. F. Yeager and Charlotte C. Morse, eds. *Speaking Images:*

Essays in Honor of V. A. Kolve (*SAC* 25 [2003], no. 147), pp. 325–45. Identifies possibilities for recognizing "political resonances" in *ClT*, discussing Walter's title (marquis) as it was granted in 1385 to Robert de Vere, Richard's favorite. The title was "unusual" and "short-lived" in Chaucer's experience. Olson summarizes de Vere's career and notes points of comparison with Walter.

211. Perez, Frank. "Chaucer's Clerk of Oxford: Prototype for Prufrock?" *YER* 17.2 (2001): 2–5. The Clerk and T. S. Eliot's title character in "The Love Song of J. Alfred Prufrock" share intellectual interests. In addition, both are "caught" between the external and the internal, both are reluctant to speak, and both speak allusively.

212. Valdés Miyares, Rubén. "Griselda's Sisters: Wifely Patience and Sisterly Rivalry in English Tales and Ballads." *SELIM* 8 (2001): 101–15. Explores two folkloric motifs in *ClT* and *Lay La Freine*: the patient wife and twin sisters who are rivals in love. Rooted in the same myth, the stories imagine alternatives to patriarchal culture as well as dramatizing wifely obedience and female rivalry. Long surviving as popular ballads, they show how little sensibility changed with the rise of the Renaissance.

See also nos. 16, 33, 83, 86, 111, 115, 154, 164, 186.

CT—The Merchant and His Tale

213. Baker, Joan, and Susan Signe Morrison. "The Luxury of Gender: *Piers Plowman* B.9 and *The Merchant's Tale*." In Kathleen M. Hewett-Smith, ed. *William Langland's* Piers Plowman: *A Book of Essays* (*SAC* 25 [2003], no. 108), pp. 41–67. Baker and Morrison read *MerT* as a "sustained response" to *Piers Plowman* B.9. Both works are concerned with marriage, gender, and the pursuits of appetite. Whereas *MerT* poses a woman who must live expediently, *Piers Plowman* absorbs gender into "greater, more cosmic concerns."

214. Gallacher, Patrick J. "Sense, Reference, and Wisdom in the *Merchant's Tale*." In Robert Myles and David Williams, eds. *Chaucer and Language: Essays in Honour of Douglas Wurtele* (*SAC* 25 [2003], no. 123), pp. 126–42, 209–18. Reads *MerT* for the ways it confronts and rejects skeptical nominalism. The Merchant considers the possibility that language "has sense but no reference"—that it is only games—but the absurdity of January's decision to marry undercuts this notion, and Pros-

erpina's assertion of God as the source of understanding affirms the reality of abstractions.

See also nos. 68, 113, 154.

CT—The Squire and His Tale

215. Berry, Craig A. "Flying Sources: Classical Authority in Chaucer's *Squire's Tale*." *ELH* 68 (2001): 287–313. Chaucer enhances the rhetorical authority of *SqT* by following classical authorities, using figures such as Pegasus, the Trojan horse, and Sinon's persuasive deception as models and figures for the poem's rhetorical operation. Chaucer understood and applied the methods of his *auctores* for asserting literary authority.

216. Lightsey, Robert Scott. "Monstrous Anxieties: Reading *Mirabilia* in Chaucer and His Contemporaries." *DAI* 62 (2001): 1845A. Physical and mechanical marvels suggest a mechanistic rather than a supernatural universe in *SqT*, Gower's version of the Alexander legend, and Sir John Mandeville's eastern marvels.

See also nos. 40, 50, 100, 111, 144, 156, 165, 218.

CT—The Franklin and His Tale

217. Allen, Valerie, and David Kirkham, eds. *The Franklin's Prologue and Tale*. Cambridge School Chaucer. Cambridge: Cambridge University Press, 2000. 96 pp.; b&w illus. School-text edition of the *GP* description of the Franklin and *FranPT*, accompanied, on facing pages, by extensive glossing and pedagogical commentary and discussion questions. Includes brief essays on pertinent topics, including *gentilesse*, astronomy and astrology, rhetoric, and social backgrounds.

218. Lightsey, Scott. "Chaucer's Secular Marvels and the Medieval Economy of Wonder." *SAC* 23 (2001): 289–316. Commerce in automatons, mechanical contrivances, and other marvels or *mirabilia* in late-medieval Europe diminished the wonder of such objects and encouraged scepticism. Chaucer's *FranT* and *SqT* rationalize the marvels they present in ways that indicate the poet's ambivalence, a combination of his technological awareness and the legacy of romance wonders.

219. Morgan, Gerald. "Experience and the Judgement of Poetry: A

Reconsideration of 'The Franklin's Tale.'" *MÆ* 70 (2001): 204–25. Positioned midway between aristocracy and the lower orders of society, the Franklin appropriately tells a story that emphasizes the necessity and correctness of the social order as he (and Chaucer) would have understood it. Thus, the Arveragus-Dorigen-Aurelius triangle must be resolved by mutual compromise, and in the case of Arveragus, by severe self-sacrifice that "puts the good of the beloved before one's own good" (220).

220. Oldmixon, Katherine Durham. "Otherworlds/Otherness: The Cultural Politics of Exoticism in the Middle English 'Breton' Lays." *DAI* 62 (2001):1009A. Fourteenth-century English Breton lays, such as *Sir Degaré*, *Sir Orfeo*, and *FranT*, displace "Celtic" otherworlds to Brittany and depict them as exotic, feminine, and supernatural—places of self-discovery that contrast with the domestic and familiar in the formation of the English character.

221. Ronquist, E. C. "The Franklin, Epicurus, and the Play of Values." In Robert Myles and David Williams, eds. *Chaucer and Language: Essays in Honour of Douglas Wurtele* (*SAC* 25 [2003], no. 123), pp. 44–60, 192–98. A variety of ethical systems—Christian, Boethian, Epicurean, Ciceronian, etc.—were available to Chaucer's audience, and he engages these systems in ways that enable the audience to observe and choose among them. Like commentators on Epicurean thought, Chaucer cites Epicurus (in the Franklin's description in *GP*) to provoke his audience to ethical consideration.

See also nos. 6, 16, 93, 111, 113, 135, 154, 164, 165.

CT—The Physician and His Tale

222. Bott, Robin. "'O, Keep Me from Their Worse than Killing Lust': Ideologies of Rape and Mutilation in Chaucer's *Physician's Tale* and Shakespeare's *Titus Andronicus*." In Elizabeth Robertson and Christine M. Rose, eds. *Representing Rape in Medieval and Early Modern Literature* (*SAC* 25 [2003], no. 130), pp. 189–211. Death is preferred to rape in both *PhyT* and *Titus Andronicus* because both works take for granted the notion that rape results in pollution or disease. In this way, the works contribute to negative views of women and their bodies in Western tradition.

223. Ishino, Harumi. "The Death of the Virgin in *The Physician's*

Tale." Shuryu (Doshisha University) 62 (2001): 1–24 (in Japanese). Ishino attempts to unravel enigmatic aspects of *PhyT*, especially the death of Virginia.

See also nos. 95, 144, 154, 164.

CT—The Pardoner and His Tale

224. Allen, Elizabeth. "The Pardoner in the 'Dogges Boure': Early Reception of the *Canterbury Tales." ChauR* 36 (2001): 91–127. The reception of the Pardoner can be more fully understood by examining medieval preachers' and orators' uses of examples, or stories that would "excite" an audience to behave virtuously. By "laying bare" his own selfish desires, the Pardoner elicits rage from the Host and the pilgrims, ironically making the audience desire morality. The Pardoner's reception can also be understood more effectively by analyzing manuscript variants and by seeking to understand why the audience responds to the Pardoner's challenge.

225. Bays, Terri Lynne. "Removable Feasts: Liturgical Inclusion in Late-Medieval English Literature." *DAI* 61 (2001): 3577A. The Sarum liturgy provokes powerful emotional response, as evident in *PardT* and in *Piers Plowman* (Passus 15; Passus 19).

226. Kelly, Henry Ansgar. "The Pardoner's Voice, Disjunctive Narrative, and Modes of Effemination." In R. F. Yeager and Charlotte C. Morse, eds. *Speaking Images: Essays in Honor of V. A. Kolve* (*SAC* 25 [2003], no. 147), pp. 411–44. Kelly re-considers the Pardoner's sexuality in light of biblical imagery, medieval medical lore, and fifteenth-century reception of *PardT*, arguing that implications of effeminacy in *GP* suggest neither homosexuality nor sterility but sexual insatiability.

227. Lynch, Kathryn L. "The Pardoner's Digestion: Eating Images in *The Canterbury Tales*." In R. F. Yeager and Charlotte C. Morse, eds. *Speaking Images: Essays in Honor of V. A. Kolve* (*SAC* 25 [2003], no. 147), pp. 393–409. The Pardoner's "misunderstanding" of gluttony as a sin "becomes emblematic of his inability to appreciate significance in general." Lynch discusses digestive imagery from medieval commentaries on memory and meditation to clarify the nature of the Pardoner's error, arguing that *PardT* directs its readers to proper understanding.

228. Patterson, Lee. "Chaucer's Pardoner on the Couch: Psyche and Clio in Medieval Literary Studies." *Speculum* 76 (2001): 638–80. A cri-

tique of psychoanalytic approaches to medieval literature—based on the "fatal flaws" of "Freudian methods of inquiry"—and a rejection of psychoanalytic approaches to Chaucer's Pardoner, including Patterson's previous work. Patterson suggests an approach that "interprets the symbolic structure by reference to discourses that are . . . contemporary to Chaucer," identifying the Pardoner's "sodomy" as "simony" and the Old Man as Despair, as well as an Oedipus figure. The article concludes with "some reflections on the place of theory . . . in medieval literary studies."

229. Schwebel, Lana. "Economy, Representation, and the Sale of Indulgences in Late-Medieval England." *DAI* 62 (2001): 1828A. In fourteenth-century England, the sale of indulgences was supported by orthodoxy and attacked by Wycliffites. Poetic fictions transcend this simple opposition, as seen in the artful deviousness of *PardT* and the revitalized idealism of *Piers Plowman*.

230. Williams, David. "'Lo How I Vanysshe': The Pardoner's War Against Signs." In Robert Myles and David Williams, eds. *Chaucer and Language: Essays in Honour of Douglas Wurtele* (*SAC* 25 [2003], no. 123), pp. 143–73, 218–21. Williams assesses the Pardoner's abuses of a wide range of signs, including words, relics, and the sacrament of the Eucharist, arguing that the Pardoner is "antisemiotic" and perverse in his privileging of signs over what they signify.

See also nos. 16, 93, 129, 154, 202, 203.

CT—The Shipman and His Tale

See nos. 6, 93, 163.

CT—The Prioress and Her Tale

231. Bauer, Kate. "'We Thurghoutly Hauen Cnawyng': Ideas of Learning and Knowing in Some Works of Chaucer, Gower, and the *Pearl*-Poet." In Nancy M. Reale and Ruth E. Sternglantz, eds. *Satura: Studies in Medieval Literature in Honour of Robert R. Raymo* (*SAC* 25 [2003], no. 128), pp. 205–26. Explores the figure of the *puer senex* (wise youth) in *Pearl*, Gower's *Confessio Amantis* ("Tale of Apollonius"), courtesy books, and *PrT*. Chaucer carefully presents an "ordinary world" in which the clergeon of *PrT* is educated through realistic educational prac-

tice; in contrast with the Prioress, however, the boy achieves transcendent knowledge.

232. Besserman, Lawrence L. "Ideology, Antisemitism, and Chaucer's *Prioress's Tale.*" *ChauR* 36 (2001): 48–72. Throughout the decades, Chaucer critics have argued their own biases in interpreting Chaucer's ideology—seeing Chaucer as a "Christian poet"; as a "poet first and foremost"; as an "atheist"; as a writer who was "politically incorrect." Eschewing close textual reading, modern theoretical critics provide "flawed and dangerous assumptions," often throwing critical scholarship "way off its true course."

233. Cox, Kenneth. "Geoffrey Chaucer: *The Prioress's Tale.*" In Kenneth Cox. *Collected Studies in the Use of English.* London: Agenda, 2001, pp. 43–62. Cox examines verse, style, and several cruces (textual and narrative) in *PrT* to clarify Chaucer's ironic technique and to argue that the "prioress's hold on reality is . . . weak and her language correspondingly lax, with a concern for decorum far in excess of its representational value."

234. Patterson, Lee. "'The Living Witnesses of Our Redemption': Martyrdom and Imitation in Chaucer's *Prioress's Tale.*" *JMEMSt* 31 (2001): 507–60. The narrator of *PrT* desires to transcend the particularities of language and history, echoing patterns of medieval Jewish martyrdom connected to the *kiddush ha-Shem*, which may have been known in Chaucer's England. Complex textual and historical intersections open the possibility of reading *PrT* not as an anti-Semitic tract but as a meditation on moral sophistication.

235. Rothwell, William. "Stratford atte Bowe Re-Visited." *ChauR* 36 (2001): 184–207. The Prioress's French of "Stratford atte Bowe" (as opposed to the French of Paris) has drawn considerable speculation, but it can be examined more effectively in light of "a wider background," including Chaucer's characterization of Madame Eglantine, the role of monasteries and convents in late fourteenth-century England, and the multilingual aspects of fourteenth-century English society.

236. Suzuki, Tetsuya. "Nuns in the *Canterbury Tales* and Medieval Lives of the Saints." *Bulletin of Kochi Women's University* (Faculty of Cultural Studies) 50 (2001): 43–50 (in Japanese). Compares and contrasts the images of medieval nuns as represented in Chaucer's Prioress and Second Nun.

See also nos. 115, 129, 152, 156, 163, 165.

CT—The Tale of Sir Thopas

See nos. 43, 111.

CT—The Tale of Melibee

237. Aers, David. "Chaucer's *Tale of Melibee*: Whose Virtues?" In David Aers, ed. *Medieval Literature and Historical Inquiry: Essays in Honor of Derek Pearsall* (*SAC* 25 [2003], no. 87), pp. 68–81. Challenges the notion that *Mel* asserts orthodox Christian sensibility. By privileging prudence over the theological virtues and by omitting "Christ, the Church [. . .], the Trinity" and sacramental forgiveness, *Mel* suggests heterodox views.

238. Burger, Glenn. "Mapping a History of Sexuality in *Melibee*." In Robert Myles and David Williams, eds. *Chaucer and Language: Essays in Honour of Douglas Wurtele* (*SAC* 25 [2003], no. 123), pp. 61–70, 198–203. Burger follows Gilles Deleuze and Féliz Guattari in associating "mapping" with modernity, resistance, and queerness and associating "tracing" with medieval times, hegemony, and heterosexuality. Explores how *Mel* can be seen to "map" Melibee's submission to Prudence as a process of feminization and a means to help its original audiences imagine ways to escape traditional categories and boundaries.

239. Jones, Christine. "Chaucer After the Linguistic Turn: Memory, History, and Fiction in the Link to *Melibee*." In Robert Myles and David Williams, eds. *Chaucer and Language: Essays in Honour of Douglas Wurtele* (*SAC* 25 [2003], no. 123), pp. 71–82, 203. Jones considers language and its ability to represent reality in *Th-MelL*, arguing that unlike poststructuralist thinkers (such as Richard Rorty), Chaucer retains the "traditional distinction between history and fiction" even while cognizant of their overlappings.

240. Pakkala-Weckström, Mari. "Prudence and the Power of Persuasion—Language and *Maistrie* in the *Tale of Melibee*." *ChauR* 35 (2001): 399–411. The debate between Prudence and Melibee is the struggle for *maistrie* between husband and wife. Learned and sophisticated, Prudence exhibits "feminine powers of persuasion." She changes from being "humble and respectful" to being "impatient," "authoritative," and even "angry," until she is clearly dominant and has attained her goal of persuading Melibee not to seek revenge.

See also nos. 111, 144.

CT—The Monk and His Tale

241. Norsworthy, Scott. "Hard Lords and Bad Food-Service in the *Monk's Tale." JEGP* 100 (2001): 313–32. In *MkP*, the Host associates the Monk with a sacristan or cellarer. Norsworthy surveys historical cellarers and the role of the cellarer according to the Rule of St. Benedict, connecting bad cellarers with *MkT*. The Monk's narratives pertain to tyrants and devourers who are supposed to be cared for (e.g., Nebuchadnezzar and Belshazzar), or they represent the sad plight of the victims of bad governors (e.g., Ugolino).

242. Treanor, Lucia. "Wings: A Comparative Study of Franciscan Characteristics in Boccaccio's 'Decameron,' Chaucer's 'Canterbury Tales,' and Marguerite de Navarre's 'Heptameron.'" *DAI* 61 (2001): 3553A. The traditions of patristic and Franciscan fourfold allegorical interpretation and radical puns are evident in Dante's letter to Can Grande and in Boccaccio, Chaucer (*MkT*), and Marguerite de Navarre.

See also nos. 36, 100, 135, 165.

CT—The Nun's Priest and His Tale

243. Alcázar, Jorge. "*The Nun's Priest's Tale* y sus fuentes a la luz de la sátira Menipea." *Acta Poetica* 21 (2000): 197–216. Examines various sources, intertextual relations, and the Bakhtinian dialogism of *NPT* as aspects of its relations with Menippean satire.

244. Bidard, Josseline. "L'Épilogue Renardien." In Leo Carruthers and Adrian Papahagi, eds. *Prologues et épilogues dans la littérature anglaise du Moyen Âge* (*SAC* 25 [2003], no. 98), pp. 155–69. Examines the use of prologues and epilogues in several narratives of the Reynard tradition (13th–15th centuries). *NPT* indicates Chaucer's preference for the prologue and the ambiguity of his assertions.

245. Federico, Sylvia. "The Imaginary Society: Women in 1381." *Journal of British Studies* 40 (2001): 159–81. Documents evidence of women's participation in the uprising of 1381, considering judicial records, chronicles by Henry Knighton and Thomas Walsingham, and poetic depictions by Chaucer and Gower. In the chase scene of *NPT*, Chaucer depicts women as "the justified, even sympathetic leaders of a community's protest against theft." In *Vox Clamantis*, Gower presents

Coppa the hen as a "discursively riotous woman" who is the "instigator of rebellious deeds."

246. Kane, George. "Language as Literature." In Christian J. Kay and Louise M. Sylvester, eds. *Lexis and Texts in Early English: Studies Presented to Jane Roberts*. Costerus New Series, no. 133. Amsterdam and Atlanta: Rodopi, 2001, pp. 161–71. Argues for "literary" rather than "historicist" analysis, examining the tone and rhetoric of the reference to the uprising of 1381 in *NPT* and arguing that Chaucer was "distancing" himself from the events.

See also nos. 89, 129.

CT—The Second Nun and Her Tale

247. Jankowski, Eileen S. "Chaucer's *Second Nun's Tale* and the Apocalyptic Imagination." *ChauR* 36 (2001): 128–48. Although *SNT* has been considered a straightforward account of St. Cecilia, apocalyptic techniques make it more complex. Engaging apocalyptic imagination, Chaucer focuses on "eschatology, renovation, and the collapse of time."

248. Winstead, Karen A., ed. and trans. "Saint Cecilia: Geoffrey Chaucer." In Karen A. Winstead. *Chaste Passions: Medieval English Virgin Martyr Legends*. Ithaca: Cornell University Press, 2000, pp. 49–60. A translation into Modern English of *SNT*, based on *The Riverside Chaucer* (3rd ed.). Includes a short introduction and select bibliography. See also no. 377.

See also nos. 86, 129, 154, 156, 165, 236.

CT—The Canon's Yeoman and His Tale

See nos. 93, 154, 156.

CT—The Manciple and His Tale

249. Kensak, Michael. "Apollo *Exterminans*: The God of Poetry in Chaucer's *Manciple's Tale*." *SP* 98 (2001): 143–57. Parallels between Chaucer's treatment of Phebus [Apollo] and the treatments in Dante's *Paradiso* and Alain de Lille suggest that *ManT* reflects the literary tradi-

tion of Apollonian ineptitude and prepares the way for the Parson's Christian reinvocation.

See also nos. 89, 113, 144.

CT—The Parson and His Tale

250. Carruthers, Leo. "Framing Doctrine." *Mediaevalia* 29 (2001): 119–27. Comments on literary framing structures in manuals of religious instruction and confession, from the *Somme le Roi* to *ParsT*. Briefly compares *ParsT* to *Jacob's Well*.

251. ———. "*Le Puits de Jacob*: À la rencontre d'un auteur anonyme." *La France latine: Revue d'études d'Oc*, n.s., 132, (2001): 145–79. Compares the anonymous author of *Jacob's Well* to a priest of the same type as Chaucer's Parson, or a canon such as John Mirk.

252. Little, Katherine. "Chaucer's Parson and the Specter of Wycliffism." *SAC* 23 (2001): 225–53. *ParsPT* and the *GP* description of the Parson reflect "concerns over the limits of late-medieval pastoral language." While the *GP* Parson suggests Wycliffite emphasis on Scripture, one finds a more orthodox view in *ParsPT*, with its focus on self-reformation through penance. The "disunity" of *ParsT*—an innovative vernacular articulation of contrition combined with a traditional catalog of sins—shows Chaucer exploring issues of language and lay instruction prompted by Wycliffite discourse.

See also nos. 25, 78, 86, 119, 144, 151, 154, 155.

CT—Chaucer's Retraction

253. Hallissy, Margaret. "The End of English Literature: The Case of Geoffrey Chaucer." *Confrontation* 70–71 (2000): 13–19. Explores Chaucer's play "with the very concepts of finished and unfinished" in *CT*, surveying the ends of several tales and *Ret*. Suggests that Chaucer's sense of an ending distinguishes him from modern sensibility.

See also nos. 151, 154, 268.

Anelida and Arcite

See nos. 90, 100.

A Treatise on the Astrolabe

254. Aloni, Gila, and Shirley Sharon-Zisser. "Geoffrey Chaucer's 'Lyne Oriental': Mediterranean and Oriental Languages in the *Treatise on the Astrolabe*." *Mediterranean Historical Review* 16.2 (2001): 69–77. Describes Chaucer's use of Arabic and Hebrew diction in *Astr* as "horizontal multilingualism," i.e., "not colonialist or Orientalist."

See also nos. 63, 91.

Boece

255. Malaczkov, Szilvia. "Geoffrey Chaucer's Translation Strategies." *Perspectives: Studies in Translatology* 9.1 (2001): 33–44. Malaczkov assesses Chaucer's techniques of translation in *Bo*, focusing on his glosses and arguing that Chaucer chose to translate for meaning or content rather than for form.

See also nos. 63, 83.

The Book of the Duchess

256. Bolens, Guillemette, and Paul Beekman Taylor. "Chess, Clocks, and Counsellors in Chaucer's *Book of the Duchess*." *ChauR* 35 (2001): 281–93. The *remedia* for the Black Knight's loss is achieved in two parts: the "reshaping" of the Black Knight's imaginative metaphor (chess representing the art of love) and the sounding of the castle bell, which awakens the poet and "ends both hunt and dream."

257. Howes, Laura L. "'The Slow Curve of the Footwalker': Narrative Time and Literary Landscapes in Middle English Poetry." *Soundings* 83 (2000): 161–83. Howes explains how walking through landscape ("pedestrian logic") helps to organize many medieval narratives, including *Sir Orfeo*, *Sir Gawain and the Green Knight*, and Chaucer's *BD*. She illuminates her explanations with comparisons to the layouts of medie-

val cathedrals and the late thirteenth-century pleasure garden, the Park of Hesdin.

258. Lassahn, Nicole. "Chaucer and Langland: Literary Representations of History in 14th Century England." *Essays in Medieval Studies* 17 (2001): 49–64. Compares Chaucer's use of history in *BD* with that of Langland in *Piers Plowman*, suggesting that focus on contemporary events is common to the poets and perhaps indicative of their common audience. Such commonalities and the habits of mind they reflect may enable us to define more clearly what is meant by "Ricardian" literature.

259. Watson, Robert A. "Dialogue and Invention in the *Book of the Duchess*." *MP* 98 (2001): 543–76. Watson coins the term "Ciceronian Platonism," defined as the "emphasis on the poetics of *sermo*," suggesting that the earliest evidence of Chaucer's interest in the notion appears in *BD*, a poem offering "a Socratic therapy as filtered through both Ciceronian and Christian experience."

See also nos. 117, 126, 140, 142, 144, 289.

The House of Fame

260. Amtower, Laurel. "Authorizing the Reader in Chaucer's *House of Fame*." *PQ* 79 (2000): 273–91. *HF* advocates an "ethics of reading" as the narrator struggles to accommodate contradictions found in literary texts. Book 1 ponders the legend and textual transmission of the Dido and Aeneas story. Book 2 learns about the suspect nature of language in its ability to relay "truth." Book 3 realizes the role of Fortune in canonizing literary texts and their subject matter. Because *HF* privileges reading over writing, subjective judgment prevails over *auctoritas*.

261. Davenport, Tony. "Chaucer's *House of Fame* 111–18: A Windsor Joke?" *N&Q* 246 (2001): 222–24. Argues that the pilgrimage of *HF* 116 was to the medieval hermitage of St. Leonard, two miles west of Windsor Castle; the associated weariness evokes the use of pilgrimages for amorous trysts.

262. Evans, Ruth. "Chaucer in Cyberspace: Medieval Technologies of Memory and *The House of Fame*." *SAC* 23 (2001): 43–69. *HF* provokes reflection on the "historical processes of memorialization." Such concepts as the brass tablet, apostrophe to Thought, inscribed ice block, and House of Rumor are analogous to conceptualizations of personal and cultural memory (history) by Bernard of Clairvaux (stained parch-

ment), Freud ("Mystic Pad"), and Derrida (the "archive"). Concern with gender, subjectivity, authority, and absence indicates the modernity of Chaucer's depictions of memory and encourages recognition of the paradoxical and constitutive relationships between past and present.

263. Hagiioannu, Michael. "Giotto's Bardi Chapel Frescoes and Chaucer's *House of Fame*: Influence, Evidence, and Interpretations." *ChauR* 36 (2001): 28–47. Chaucer's visit to Florence (December–May 1373) would have brought him into contact with Giotto's frescos. These, along with his exposure to Dante's works, led him to explore the implications and limitations of "individual perspective" in *HF*.

264. Wicher, Andrzej. "The Idea of Cultural Continuity in G. Chaucer's *House of Fame*." *SAP* 36 (2001): 289–301. In *HF,* the description of Fame's hall raises questions about the status of classical authors. The poem as a whole reflects "Chaucer's struggle to find some place . . . for his individual talent in the mainstream of the Western and Mediterranean tradition."

See also nos. 93, 113, 117, 140, 142.

The Legend of Good Women

265. Aloni, Gila. "A Curious Error? Geoffrey Chaucer's *Legend of Hypermnestra*." *ChauR* 36 (2001): 73–86. Chaucer's changes to the Ovidian version of Hypermnestra—exchanging the names of Danaus and Aegyptus and then reducing the number of daughters from fifty to one—in *LGW* were not an "error." Chaucer both indicates that men are not "stably positioned as agents and transactors" and "radically questions the very nature of the exchange of women."

266. Amsler, Mark. "Rape and Silence: Ovid's Mythography and Medieval Readers." In Elizabeth Robertson and Christine M. Rose, eds. *Representing Rape in Medieval and Early Modern Literature* (*SAC* 25 [2003], no. 130), pp. 61–96. Although "mythographers allegorized Ovid's rape narratives as stories of cosmological creation or spiritual desire," Christine de Pizan presents Apollo's assault on Daphne (*Épître d'Othéa*) as a disfigurement of the female body; in his tale of Philomela (*LGW*), Chaucer confronts the affective power of reading about sexual violence.

267. Boffey, Julia. " 'Twenty Thousand More': Some Fifteenth- and Sixteenth-Century Responses to *The Legend of Good Women*." In A. J.

Minnis, ed. *Middle English Poetry: Texts and Traditions. Essays in Honour of Derek Pearsall* (*SAC* 25 [2003], no. 121), pp. 279–97. Boffey summarizes the various numbers of legends included in *LGW* and in references to the work and assesses concern with these numbers. She considers *LGW* in light of the tradition of nine female Worthies in literature and the visual arts and in light of illustrated versions of Ovid's *Heroides*.

268. McNelis, James. "Parallel Manuscript Readings in the *CT* Retraction and Edward of Norwich's *Master of Game*." *ChauR* 36 (2001): 87–90. Not all manuscripts of *Ret* read *LGW* as "xxv" tales (other numbers are "xix" and "xx"). Edward of Norwich (ca. 1406) uses "xxv" and refers to the work as the "Goode Wymmen," not, as is more common, the book of "ladies." He may have read *Ret*, in which Chaucer uses the word "women"; family connections would account for his access to the works.

269. Sanok, Catherine. "Reading Hagiographically: *The Legend of Good Women* and Its Feminine Audience." *Exemplaria* 13 (2001): 323–54. Alceste's request for a "legend" of good women and reference to Queen Anne combine to establish the audience of *LGW*, raising questions about the gender ideology of saints' legends and resisting the "misogynist antiphrasis" recurrent in antifeminist literature. *LGW* enables misogynist readings but disables those readings through its implied audience. It thereby explores "the differences that an audience [. . .] makes" in understanding the "cultural status" of a text.

270. Schlosser, Donna. "Imagery, Rhetoric, and Imagination: Chaucer's Three-point Perspective on 'Trouthe-keeping' in *Legend of Good Women*." *InG* 22 (2001): 43–55. *LGW* illustrates the importance of fidelity to one's pledges. Chaucer shows that "act, speech, and writing, when captured by image, text, and imagination, preserve love beyond its transitory moment of existence" (50). The written experiences of the speakers transcend time and provide a continuing forum on "trouthe-keeping."

271. Woods, Marjorie Curry. "Boys Will Be Women: Musings on Classroom Nostalgia and the Chaucerian Audience(s)." In R. F. Yeager and Charlotte C. Morse, eds. *Speaking Images: Essays in Honor of V. A. Kolve* (*SAC* 25 [2003], no. 147), pp. 143–66. Woods hypothesizes how Chaucer and the male members of his audience may have been affected by their experiences in an "all-male medieval classroom" and how, in turn, their encounters with female literary characters and the rhetorical

exercises of abbreviation and amplification may be reflected in the writing and early reception of *LGW*.

See also nos. 37, 54, 88, 89, 91, 92, 113, 115, 117, 126, 140, 278.

The Parliament of Fowls

272. Harwood, Britton J. "Same-Sex Desire in the Unconscious of Chaucer's *Parliament of Fowls*." *Exemplaria* 13 (2001): 99–135. Psychoanalytic reading of *PF* that identifies a reversal of the "logical sequence of origin, wish, and desire." This reversal "represses consciousness" and disguises the presence of the "Chaucerian ego" of the poem that is recognizable in the narrator's identification with the formel eagle. The Freudian "dreamwork" of *PF* reflects repression of same-sex desire, sublimated in homosocial relations.

273. Kawasaki, Masatoshi. "'The Craft So Long to Lerne': 'Love' and 'Art' in *The Parliament of Fowls*." *Studies in British and American Literature* (Komazawa University) 36 (2001): 73–104 (in Japanese). Survey of love and art in *PF*.

274. Kiser, Lisa J. "Chaucer and the Politics of Nature." In Karla Armbruster and Kathleen R. Wallace, eds. *Beyond Nature Writing: Expanding the Boundaries of Ecocriticism*. Under the Sign of Nature: Explorations in Ecocriticism. Charlottesville and London: University of Virginia Press, 2001, pp. 41–56. Through the tree catalog and the "unassimilated voices of the lower birds" in *PF*, Chaucer records his awareness that distinctions between nature and culture and between human and nonhuman are "species-ist"—an awareness similar to modern environmental and ecological perspectives.

See also nos. 12, 37, 109, 113, 117, 126, 140, 142, 144.

Troilus and Criseyde

275. Besserman, Lawrence. "'Priest' and 'Pope,' 'Sire and Madame': Anachronistic Diction and Social Conflict in Chaucer's *Troilus*." *SAC* 23 (2001): 181–224. Various "titles, epithets, and images" in *TC* reflect Chaucer's "covert engagement" with political and religious contention. Pandarus and the narrator adopt priestly roles, Troilus is like an anti-Lollard zealot, and forms of address such as "madame" and "sire" carry

political overtones in *TC* and *CT*. In *TC*, the title "servant of servants" engages polemics of the Great Schism.

276. Dauby, Hélène. "Regards: Criseyde, Troilus, Chaucer." In Anne Berthelot, ed. *"Pur remembrance": Mélanges en mémoire de Wolfgang Spiewok.* WODAN, no. 79; Greifswalder Beiträge zum Mittelalter, no. 66. Greifswald: Reineke-Verlag, 2001, pp. 131–41. *TC* illustrates the mechanisms of perception, memory, and imagination as defined by fourteenth-century scientific theories. The two protagonists are enmeshed in a net of gazes—their own as well as those of others—and the narrative unfolds as viewed through a camera. The *mise-en-abyme* distances both the hero and the spectator-reader from this earth.

277. Evans, Trena Marie. "Late Medieval Meditations on Translating Subjects." *DAI* 62 (2002): 1008A. Late-medieval lay meditation extended the subject matter (previously the life of Christ) and the boundaries considered suitable for vernacular material. Evans treats Chaucer's *TC*, John Metham, Thomas Hoccleve, Nicholas Love, and anonymous works.

278. Goldstein, R. James. "Chaucer, Suicide, and the Agencies of Memory: Troilus and the Death Drive." In R. F. Yeager and Charlotte C. Morse, eds. *Speaking Images: Essays in Honor of V. A. Kolve* (*SAC* 25 [2003], no. 147), pp.185–204; 3 b&w figs. Goldstein assesses the "rhetoric of Troilus's suicidal death wish" in *TC* 1, 4, and 5, comparing passages with Boccaccio's version and challenging critical traditions that view Troilus's thoughts as merely rhetorical or absurd. Also evident in *LGW* and *MLP*, Chaucer's depictions of suicide or thoughts of suicide should be taken as earnest.

279. Hodges, Laura F. "Sartorial Signs in *Troilus and Criseyde*." *ChauR* 35 (2001): 223–58. Chaucer employs "costume signs" in *TC*, affecting plot and characterization. Signature costumes assigned to each character shed light on significant parts of the plot, as do the reversal and degeneration of costume patterns. Characterization through costume is one of Chaucer's artistic methods.

280. Kapera, Marta. "Traitor Calchas in Chaucer's and Shakespeare's Versions of the Troilus-Criseyde/Cressida Story." In Władysław Witalisz, ed. *"And Gladly Wolde He Lerne and Gladly Teche": Studies on Language and Literature in Honour of Professor Dr. Karl Heinz Göller* (*SAC* 25 [2003], no. 146), pp. 9–16. Chaucer presents Calchus as both a father in misery and a "sheer opportunist," enabling us to see Criseyde's decision as her

own. Shakespeare's Calchus is a manipulator; his Cressida, the object of manipulation.

281. Kikuchi, Shigeo. "Lose Heart, Gain Heaven: The False Reciprocity of Gain and Loss in Chaucer's *Troilus and Criseyde*." *NM* 102 (2001): 427–34. Dividing *TC* into eighteen episodes highlights a series of analogous and oppositional relations centering on "ethical debt"; in addition, the poem's action can be charted through four cycles. Similar patterns, in some instances less symmetrical, underlie *MilT*, *RvT*, and *WBT*.

282. Moore, Miriam Elizabeth. "Shapes of Desire: Representing the Body in 'Troilus and Criseyde' and 'Celestina.'" *DAI* 61 (2001): 3163A. Women in *TC* and Fernando de Rojas's *Celestina* seek to establish themselves and their fates through "control of language," but rhetorical control gives way as men eventually become subjects and women objects of physical desire.

283. Pugh, William White Tison. "Play and Game in *Sir Gawain and the Green Knight* and *Troilus and Criseyde*." *DAI* 61 (2001): 2705A. Play and game reveal to knightly protagonists human imperfection and divine truth. Pandarus is the "game-master" of *TC*, and Troilus achieves perspective through the game of courtly love.

284. Robertson, Elizabeth. "Public Bodies and Psychic Domains: Rape, Consent, and Female Subjectivity in Geoffrey Chaucer's *Troilus and Criseyde*." In Elizabeth Robertson and Christine M. Rose, eds. *Representing Rape in Medieval and Early Modern Literature* (*SAC* 25 [2003], no. 130), pp. 281–310. Examines "the role rape plays in the formation of Criseyde's character," contrasting Criseyde with Helen of Troy and Lucretia. Criseyde is a "choosing subject," and the language of rape helps to define the ambiguities of choice she faces.

285. Walls, Kathryn. "Chaucer's *Troilus and Criseyde* 1.540–875." *Expl* 59 (2001): 59–62. Neither Pandarus, Troilus, nor Chaucer is to be taken at face value in *TC* 1.540–875. All three are deceivers.

286. Warren, Victoria. "(Mis)Reading the 'Text' of Criseyde: Context and Identity in Chaucer's *Troilus and Criseyde*." *ChauR* 36 (2001): 1–15. Troilus cannot read the "text" of Criseyde's face because he is too self-absorbed. Thinking only of what she can do for him, he neglects her "context," fails to acknowledge her vulnerability, and thinks of her as an "image in stasis." Although critics have been willing to accept Troilus's critique, Chaucer expects the reader to go deeper.

287. Yang, Ming-Tsang. "The Poetics of Translation in Chaucer's

Troilus and Criseyde." Studies in Language and Literature (National Taiwan University) 10 (2001): 27–49. Yang considers several aspects of translation and the rhetoric of translation in *TC*: the narrator's "double role" as translator and author, Pandarus as translator, Diomede as a "force of the translation process," Criseyde as "text" that is translation and retranslated, and Troilus's rise to the sphere as Chaucer's translation of Boccaccio's *Filostrato* from a secular to a religious poem.

See also nos 2, 3, 15, 17, 40, 58, 65, 69, 70, 83, 91, 107, 136, 142, 144, 289.

Lyrics and Short Poems

288. Davenport, Tony. "Fifteenth-Century Complaints and Duke Humphrey's Wives." In Helen Cooney, ed. *Nation, Court and Culture: New Essays on Fifteenth-Century English Poetry* (*SAC* 25 [2003], no. 101), pp. 129–52. Examines two mid-fifteenth-century complaints that reflect public distrust of Humphrey, duke of Gloucester, arguing that these complaints are more Lydgatian than Chaucerian, since Chaucer's own complaints had little influence at the time. An appendix includes the two poems.

289. Kinch, Ashby McDalton. "Playing at Death: The Suspended Subject of Middle English Lyric." *DAI* 61 (2001): 3988A. Central to medieval love poetry is the figure of dying for love—found in works by Marcabru, Bernart de Ventadorn, Dante, Petrarch, Chaucer (*BD*, *TC*, complaints), and Alain Chartier, as well as in the Harley lyrics and the Findern manuscript. Donne provides an afterlife.

See also nos. 4, 65.

An ABC

290. Quinn, William A. "Chaucer's Problematic *Priere: An ABC* as Artifact and Critical Issue." *SAC* 23 (2001): 109–41. Explores *ABC* as a prayer, especially in its relations with Psalm 118 and 119 and the rosary, and in light of the possibility that it was presented to Duchess Blanche for inclusion in her devotional primer. Quinn confronts several formal features and rhetorical-theological cruces in *ABC*, showing that

they can be resolved as expressions of orthodox faith—valid as a heuristic method and as a form of historicism.

Chaucer's Wordes unto Adam, His Own Scriveyn

291. Mize, Britt. "Adam, and Chaucer's Words unto Him." *ChauR* 35 (2001): 351–77. *Adam* is a more complex work than generally thought, evoking Adam the "first father" and "the earthly instrument of chaos and capriciousness." The scribe's "long lokkes" link him to Chaucer's other prideful, foppish characters. The threatened "scabbes" would deface his hair and mirror the act of "rubbing and scraping the manuscript."

Truth

See no. 86.

Chaucerian Apocrypha

292. Forni, Kathleen. *The Chaucerian Apocrypha: A Counterfeit Canon*. Gainesville: University Press of Florida, 2001. xviii, 261 pp. Forni traces the complex relationship between Chaucer's canon and the apocrypha, with particular focus on the "Folio" canon, from Thynne's 1532 *Workes* edition to editions of the eighteenth century. The first part examines the formation of the Folio canon, considering the political, ideological, and commercial interests behind the various editions. Through case studies of spurious works, the second part assesses the impact of attribution and disattribution on Chaucer's reputation and lines of critical inquiry.

293. ———. "'Chaucer's Dreame': A Bibliographer's Nightmare." *HLQ* 64 (2001): 139–50. "The Isle of Ladies"—first published as "Chaucer's Dreame" with the "Fairest of the Fair" as "Additions" in Speght's 1598 edition—has been confused by both scribes and early editors with *BD* and Lydgate's *Temple of Glass*. This confused transmission illustrates the difference between pre-print culture, in which texts were part of a shared culture, and print culture, in which "the marketing of 'authority' is an important part of the revolution of 'print capitalism.'"

294. Landman, James H. "Pleading, Pragmatism, and Permissible Hypocrisy: The 'Colours' of Legal Discourse in Late Medieval England."

New Medieval Literatures 4 (2001): 139–70. Decried by detractors such as Gower and Langland, legal discourse was a way of bridging the growing gap between legal tradition and contemporary reality. Although it satirizes legal pragmatism, *The Tale of Beryn* reflects appreciation of such pragmatism, also evident in John Fortescue's *The Declaracion.*

295. Shippey, T. A. "*The Tale of Gamelyn*: Class Warfare and the Embarrassments of Genre." In Ad Putter and Jane Gilbert, eds. *The Spirit of Medieval English Popular Romance.* Longman Medieval and Renaissance Library. New York: Longman, 2000, pp. 78–96. Attributes the popularity of *Gamelyn*, in part, to its association with *CT*, arguing that Chaucer intended to adapt *Gamelyn* for telling by the Knight's Yeoman, even though Chaucer "did not like yeomen very much." Also assesses the tension between chivalric sentiment and the emphasis in *Gamelyn* on bourgeois ethos.

See also nos. 32, 48, 49, 172.

Book Reviews

296. Aers, David. *Faith, Ethics and Church: Writing in England, 1360–1409* (*SAC* 25 [2003], no. 86). Rev. Denise N. Baker, *YLS* 15 (2001): 227–30.

297. Amtower, Laurel. *Engaging Words: The Culture of Reading in the Later Middle Ages* (*SAC* 24 [2002], no. 131). Rev. Ralph Hanna, *Arthuriana* 11.4 (2001):124–25.

298. Andretta, Helen Ruth. *Chaucer's* Troilus and Criseyde*: A Poet's Response to Ockhamism* (*SAC* 21 [1999], no. 284). Rev. David Raybin, *Speculum* 76 (2001): 683–85.

299. Archibald, Elizabeth. *Incest and the Medieval Imagination* (*SAC* 25 [2003], no. 88). Rev. Helen Cooper, *TLS*, Oct. 26, 2001, p. 27.

300. Ashton, Gail. *The Generation of Identity in Late Medieval Hagiography: Speaking the Saint* (*SAC* 24 [2002], no. 132). Rev. Margaret Mary Dietz, *Speculum* 76 (2001): 994–95; Claire M. Waters, *SAC* 23 (2001): 521–23.

301. Astell, Ann W. *Chaucer and the Universe of Learning* (*SAC* 20 [1998], no. 112). Rev. Anne Schotter, *Arthuriana* 10.1 (2000): 131–32.

302. Beer, Jeanette, ed. *Translation Theory and Practice in the Middle Ages* (*SAC* 21 [1999], no. 83). Rev. Betsy Bowden, *Arthuriana* 10.3 (2000): 105–8.

303. Beidler, Peter G., and Elizabeth M. Biebel, eds. *Chaucer's* Wife of Bath's Prologue *and* Tale*: An Annotated Bibliography, 1900 to 1995* (*SAC* 24 [2002], no. 3). Rev. Leo Carruthers, *MA* 107 (2001): 152–53.

304. Bisson, Lillian M. *Chaucer and the Late Medieval World* (*SAC* 22 [2000], no. 99). Rev. E. C. Dunn, *ModA* 43 (2001): 268–71; Andrew Galloway, *Speculum* 76 (2001): 384–87; Rhiannon Purdie, *MÆ* 70 (2001): 333–34; M. J. Toswell, *CollL* 28.3 (2001): 155–62.

305. Blyth, Charles R., ed. *Thomas Hoccleve: The Regiment of Princes* (*SAC* 24 [2002], no. 16). Rev. Ethan Knapp, *Speculum* 76 (2002): 737–38.

306. Boenig, Robert, and Kathleen Davis, eds. *Manuscript, Narrative, Lexicon: Essays on Literary and Cultural Transmission in Honor of Whitney F. Bolton* (*SAC* 24 [2002], no. 138). Rev. Michiko Ogura, *N&Q* 246 (2001): 166–67.

307. Boffey, Julia, and A. S. G. Edwards, introd., with an appendix by B. C. Barker-Benfield. *Works of Geoffrey Chaucer and the* Kingis Quair: *A Facsimile of Bodleian Library, Oxford, MS Arch. Selden B. 24* (*SAC* 21 [1999], no. 9). Rev. Manfred Görlach, *Anglia* 119 (2001): 120–21.

308. Boitani, Piero, and Anna Torti, eds. *The Body and the Soul in Medieval Literature* (*SAC* 23 [2001], no. 75). Rev. Stephanie Trigg, *SAC* 23 (2001): 526–29.

309. Bradbury, Nancy Mason. *Writing Aloud: Storytelling in Late Medieval England* (*SAC* 22 [2000], no. 101). Rev. Velma Bourgeois Richmond, *Speculum* 76 (2001): 137–38.

310. Brewer, Derek. *A New Introduction to Chaucer* (*SAC* 22 [2000], no. 102). Rev. Matthew Giancarlo, *Speculum* 76 (2001): 138–40.

311. Brown, Peter, ed. *Reading Dreams: The Interpretation of Dreams from Chaucer to Shakespeare* (*SAC* 23 [2001], no. 78). Rev. L. S. Davidson, *Parergon* 18.3 (2001): 155–56; James A. Knapp, *SCJ* 32 (2001): 1201–3; Helen Phillips, *MLR* 96 (2001): 1043–45; Daniel Pinti, *SAC* 23 (2001): 524–26; J. Stephen Russell, *JEGP* 100 (2001): 131–33.

312. Brown, Sarah Annes. *The Metamorphosis of Ovid: From Chaucer to Ted Hughes* (*SAC* 23 [2001], no. 230). Rev. *Classical Review* 51 (2001): 209–10; *Critical Arts Journal* 15 (2001): 177–79.

313. Bullón-Fernández, María. *Fathers and Daughters in Gower's* Confessio Amantis*: Authority, Family, State, and Writing* (*SAC* 25 [2003], no. 95). Rev. Elizabeth Scala, *TMR*, May 8, 2001, n.p.

314. Burnley, David. *Courtliness and Literature in Medieval England*

(*SAC* 22 [2000], no. 103). Rev. Inge B. Milfull, *Anglia* 119 (2001): 279–84.

315. Burton, T. L., and Rosemary Greentree, eds. *Chaucer's* Miller's, Reeve's, *and* Cook's Tales (*SAC* 21 [1999], no. 3). Rev. *Manuscripta* 42.2 (1998): 130.

316. Cannon, Christopher. *The Making of Chaucer's English: A Study of Words* (*SAC* 23 [2001], no. 58). Rev. *FMLS* 37 (2001): 95; Francis Austin, *ES* 82 (2001): 272–73; Matthew Giancarlo, *MLQ* 62 (2001): 293–95; Seth Lerer, *JEGP* 100 (2001): 123–26; Jeremy J. Smith, *MLR* 96 (2001): 156–58.

317. Carlin, Martha, and Joel T. Rosenthal, eds. *Food and Eating in Medieval Europe* (*SAC* 22 [2000], no. 168). Rev. Barbara Harvey, *EHR* 115 (2000): 434.

318. Cohen, Jeffrey Jerome, ed. *The Postcolonial Middle Ages* (*SAC* 24 [2002], no. 145). Rev. Michael Calabrese, *TMR*, Oct. 16, 2001, n.p; Richard K. Emmerson, *Speculum* 76 (2001): 1014–16; Robert M. Stein, *SAC* 23 (2001): 538–43.

319. Cohen, Jeffrey Jerome. *Of Giants: Sex, Monsters, and the Middle Ages* (*SAC* 23 [2001], no. 199). Rev. John Friedman, *TMR*, May 3, 2001, n.p.

320. Condren, Edward I. *Chaucer and the Energy of Creation: The Design and the Organization of* The Canterbury Tales (*SAC* 23 [2001], no. 131). Rev. Laurel Amtower, *JEGP* 100 (2001): 435–37; Leo Carruthers, *SAC* 23 (2001): 543–47; Norman Klassen, *MÆ* 70 (2001): 139–41; Corinne Saunders, *L&T* 15 (2001): 302–6.

321. Connolly, Margaret. *John Shirley: Book Production and the Noble Household in Fifteenth-Century England* (*SAC* 22 [2000], no. 39). Rev. Nicholas Orme, *EHR* 115 (2000): 189–90.

322. Cox, Catherine S. *Gender and Language in Chaucer* (*SAC* 21 [1999], no. 97). Rev. Michael Uebel, *ANQ* 13.1 (2000): 67–68.

323. Craun, Edwin D. *Lies, Slander, and Obscenity in Medieval English Literature: Pastoral Rhetoric and the Deviant Speaker* (*SAC* 21 [1999], no. 98). Rev. Leo Carruthers, *ÉA* 54 (2001): 321–22.

324. Davenport, W. A. *Chaucer and His English Contemporaries: Prologue and Tale in* The Canterbury Tales (*SAC* 22 [2000], no. 53). Rev. Nicky Chatten, *English* 50 (2001): 73–75.

325. Davies, Martin, ed. *Incunabula: Studies in Fifteenth-Century Books Presented to Lotte Hellinga* (*SAC* 23 [2001], no. 17). Rev. Juliet Chadwick, *EHR* 115 (2000): 702–3.

326. De Weever, Jacqueline. *Chaucer Name Dictionary: A Guide to Astrological, Biblical, Historical, Literary, and Mythological Names in the Works of Geoffrey Chaucer* (*SAC* 11 [1989], no. 77). Rev. Sigmund Eisner, *JRMMRA* 18 (1997): 260–62.

327. Dean, James M. *The World Grown Old in Later Medieval Literature* (*SAC* 21 [1999], no. 100). Rev. Joerg O. Fichte, *Anglia* 119 (2001): 125–26.

328. Dinshaw, Carolyn. *Getting Medieval: Sexualities and Communities, Pre- and Postmodern* (*SAC* 23 [2001], no. 184). Rev. Dyan Elliott, *EHR* 115 (2000): 935–36; Ruth Evans, *SAC* 23 (2001): 547–51; Lara Farina, *Medieval Feminist Forum* 31 (2001): 54–56; Allen J. Frantzen, *Speculum* 76 (2001): 1027–29; Ruth Mazo Karras, *M&H* 28 (2001): 124–25; Steven F. Krueger, *CLIO* 31.1 (2001): 88–92.

329. Edwards, A. S. G., Vincent Gillespie, and Ralph Hanna, eds. *The English Medieval Book: Studies in Memory of Jeremy Griffiths* (*SAC* 24 [2002], no. 150). Rev. Susan Powell, *JEBS* 4 (2001): 288–91.

330. Ellis, Steve. *Chaucer at Large: The Poet in the Modern Imagination* (*SAC* 24 [2002], no. 75). Rev. Peter G. Christensen, *Arthuriana* 11.4 (2001): 129–31; Bernard O'Donoghue, *TLS*, Mar. 2, 2001, p. 25.

331. Fields, Peter John. *Craft and Anti-Craft in Chaucer's* Canterbury Tales (*SAC* 25 [2003], no. 156). Rev. David D. Joplin, *InG* 22 (2001): 91–106.

332. Frantzen, Allen J. *Before the Closet: Same-Sex Love from* Beowulf *to* Angels in America (*SAC* 22 [2000], no. 117). Rev. Renate Bauer, *Anglia* 119 (2001): 491–94.

333. Graver, Bruce E., ed. *Translations of Chaucer and Virgil by William Wordsworth* (*SAC* 22 [2000], no. 27). Rev. David Simpson, *Wordsworth Circle* 32.4 (2001): 175–77.

334. Green, Richard Firth. *A Crisis of Truth: Literature and Law in Ricardian England* (*SAC* 23 [2001], no. 92). Rev. Richard W. Kaeuper, *EHR* 115 (2000): 907–8.

335. Hanawalt, Barbara A., and David Wallace, eds. *Medieval Crime and Social Control* (*SAC* 23 [2001], no. 93). Rev. Emilia Jamroziak, *Bulletin of International Medieval Research* 7 (2001): 52–53; Maura B. Nolan, *SAC* 23 (2001): 551–55.

336. Heffernan, Carol Falvo. *The Melancholy Muse: Chaucer, Shakespeare, and Early Medicine* (*SAC* 19 [1997], no. 284). Rev. Howard Marchitell, *M&H* 28 (2001): 129–33.

337. Hellinga, Lotte, and J. B. Trapp, eds. *The Cambridge History of*

the Book in Britain. Volume 3: 1400–1557 (SAC 24 [2002], no. 50). Rev. Richard K. Emmerson, *Speculum* 76 (2001): 735–37.

338. Hill, John M., and Deborah M. Sinnreich-Levi, eds. *The Rhetorical Poetics of the Middle Ages: Reconstructive Polyphony. Essays in Honor of Robert O. Payne (SAC* 24 [2002], no. 163). Rev. R. Allen Shoaf, *SAC* 23 (2001): 555–59.

339. Hodges, Laura F. *Chaucer and Costume: The Secular Pilgrims in the General Prologue (SAC* 24 [2002], no. 229). Rev. Garrett Epp, *Arthuriana* 11.4 (2001): 132–33; C. M. Jackson-Houlston, *Textile History* 32 (2001): 125.

340. Howes, Laura L. *Chaucer's Gardens and the Language of Convention (SAC* 21 [1999], no. 112). Rev. *Manuscripta* 42.1 (1998): 64–65; Michael Uebel, *ANQ* 13.1 (2000): 67–68.

341. Knapp, Peggy A. *Time-Bound Words: Semantic and Social Economies from Chaucer's England to Shakespeare's (SAC* 24 [2002], no. 107). Rev. Mary Thomas Crane, *RenQ* 54 (2001): 976–78; Tim William Machan, *SAC* 23 (2001): 568–71.

342. Koff, Leonard Michael, and Brenda Deen Schildgen, eds. *The* Decameron *and the* Canterbury Tales*: New Essays on an Old Question (SAC* 24 [2002], no. 69). Rev. Warren Ginsberg, *SAC* 23 (2001): 571–76.

343. Krier, Theresa M., ed. *Refiguring Chaucer in the Renaissance (SAC* 22 [2000], no. 73). Rev. *Manuscripta* 42.3 (1998): 211; David Matthews, *SAC* 23 (2001): 576–79.

344. Lochrie, Karma. *Covert Operations: The Medieval Uses of Secrecy (SAC* 23 [2001], no. 100). Rev. Sheila Delany, *Speculum* 76 (2001): 489–90; Henrietta Leyser, *EHR* 115 (2000): 936–37.

345. Matthews, David, ed. *The Invention of Middle English: An Anthology of Primary Sources (SAC* 24 [2002], no. 173). Rev. Seth Lerer, *Envoi* 9.2 (2000): 181–93; Richard Utz, *SAQ* 66.3 (2001): 153–56.

346. Matthews, David. *The Making of Middle English, 1765–1910 (SAC* 23 [2001], no. 102). Rev. Christopher Cannon, *Speculum* 76 (2001): 197–99; Seth Lerer, *Envoi* 9.2 (2000): 181–93; Derek Pearsall, *SAC* 23 (2001): 579–81; Richard Utz, *SAQ* 66.4 (2001): 210–13.

347. McGavin, John J. *Chaucer and Dissimilarity: Literary Comparisons in Chaucer and Other Late-Medieval Writing (SAC* 24 [2002], no. 174). Rev. Jamie C. Fumo, *Envoi* 91 (2000): 45–55; J. Stephen Russell, *TMR*, Feb. 5, 2001, n.p.

348. McGerr, Rosemarie P. *Chaucer's Open Books: Resistance to Closure*

in Medieval Discourse (*SAC* 22 [2000], no. 137). Rev. *Manuscripta* 42.2 (1998): 134; R. W. Hanning, *Speculum* 76 (2001): 199–201.

349. McGillivray, Murray, ed. *Geoffrey Chaucer's* Book of the Duchess: *A Hypertext Edition* (*SAC* 22 [2000], no. 31). Rev. N. F. Blake, *ES* 82 (2001): 271–72.

350. Minnis, A. J., Charlotte C. Morse, and Thorlac Turville-Petre, eds. *Essays on Ricardian Literature: In Honour of J. A. Burrow* (*SAC* 21 [1999], no. 129). Rev. *Manuscripta* 42.2 (1998): 132–33.

351. Mullally, Evelyn, and John Thompson, eds. *The Court and Cultural Discourse: Selected Papers from the Eighth Triennial Congress of the International Courtly Literature Society, The Queen's University of Belfast, 26 July–1 August 1995* (*SAC* 21 [1999], no. 131). Rev. Inge B. Milfull, *Anglia* 119 (2001): 279–84.

352. Muscatine, Charles. *Medieval Literature, Style, and Culture: Essays by Charles Muscatine* (*SAC* 23 [2001], no. 106). Rev. John Bugge, *Arthuriana* 10.3 (2000): 114–16; Alfred David, *Speculum* 76 (2001): 766–68; Glending Olson, *JEGP* 100 (2001): 568–70; M. J. Toswell, *CollL* 28.3 (2001): 155–62.

353. Obst, Wolfgang, and Florian Schleburg. *Die Sprache Chaucers: Ein Lehrbuch des Mittelenglischen auf der Grundlage von* Troilus and Criseyde (*SAC* 24 [2002], no. 389). Rev. Klaus Bitterling, *ES* 82 (2001): 462–63; Muriel Kasper, *Anglia* 119 (2001): 117–20; Fritz Kemmler, *ZAA* 48 (2000): 374–76.

354. Palmer, R. Barton, ed. *Chaucer's French Contemporaries: The Poetry/Poetics of Self and Tradition* (*SAC* 23 [2001], no. 109). Rev. Barbara N. Sargent-Baur, *Speculum* 76 (2001): 218–21.

355. Parsons, John Carmi, and Bonnie Wheeler, eds. *Medieval Mothering* (*SAC* 22 [2000], no. 238). Rev. Raluca Radulescu, *Bulletin of International Medieval Research* 7 (2001): 10–21.

356. Paxson, James J., Lawrence M. Clopper, and Sylvia Tomasch, eds. *The Performance of Middle English Culture: Essays on Chaucer and the Drama in Honor of Martin Stevens* (*SAC* 22 [2000], no. 142). Rev. W. A. Davenport, *MLR* 96 (2001): 779–80.

357. Pearsall, Derek, ed. *Chaucer to Spenser: A Critical Reader* (*SAC* 23 [2001], no. 111). Rev. Kevin Gustafson, *Arthuriana* 10.1 (2000): 145–46.

358. Pearsall, Derek. *Chaucer to Spenser: An Anthology of Writings in English, 1375–1575* (*SAC* 23 [2001], no. 21). Rev. Kevin Gustafson, *Arthuriana* 10.1 (2000): 145–46.

359. Percival, Florence. *Chaucer's Legendary Good Women* (*SAC* 22 [2000], no. 301). Rev. Nicky Chatten, *English* 50 (2001): 75–77.

360. Phillips, Helen, and Nick Havely, eds. *Chaucer's Dream Poetry* (*SAC* 21 [1999], no. 15). Rev. Kathryn L. Lynch, *Speculum* 76 (2001): 410–12.

361. Phillips, Helen. *An Introduction to the* Canterbury Tales*: Reading, Fiction, Context* (*SAC* 24 [2002], no. 216). Rev. Candace Barrington, *TMR*, Dec. 3, 2000, n.p; Simon Horobin, *JEBS* 4 (2001): 309–10; Rhiannon Purdie, *MÆ* 70 (2001): 332–33.

362. Pinti, Daniel J., ed. *Writing After Chaucer: Essential Readings in Chaucer and the Fifteenth Century* (*SAC* 22 [2000], no. 77). Rev. Daniel W. Mosser, *Arthuriana* 10.1 (2000): 146–48.

363. Pratt, John H. *Chaucer and War* (*SAC* 24 [2002], no. 183). Rev. Denise N. Baker, *SAC* 23 (2001): 581–85; Alan Baragona, *Journal of Military History* 65 (2001): 170–71; Rhiannon Purdie, *MÆ* 70 (2001): 334–35; K. J. Thompson, *Albion* 33 (2001): 436–37.

364. Prendergast, Thomas A., and Barbara Kline, eds. *Rewriting Chaucer: Culture, Authority, and the Idea of the Authentic Text, 1400–1602* (*SAC* 23 [2001], no. 112). Rev. William Kuskin, *SAC* 23 (2001): 585–88.

365. Raybin, David, and Linda Tarte Holley, eds. *Closure in* The Canterbury Tales*: The Role of* The Parson's Tale (*SAC* 24 [2002], no. 337). Rev. David G. Allen, *TMR*, July 19, 2001, n.p.

366. Roberts, Anna. *Violence Against Women in Medieval Texts* (*SAC* 22 [2000], no. 147). Rev. Raluca Radulescu, *Bulletin of International Medieval Research* 7 (2001): 10–21.

367. Russell, J. Stephen. *Chaucer and the Trivium: The Mindsong of the* Canterbury Tales (*SAC* 22 [2000], no. 184). Rev. Martin Camargo, *JEGP* 100 (2001): 126–28; Edward I. Condren, *Speculum* 76 (2001): 1095–97; John M. Crafton, *C&L* 50 (2001): 729–31; Theresa M. Krier, *Arthuriana* 10.3 (2000): 119–20; Charlotte C. Morse, *N&Q* 246 (2001): 48–49.

368. Sinnreich-Levi, Deborah M., ed. *Eustache Deschamps, French Courtier-Poet: His Work and His World* (*SAC* 22 [2000], no. 151). Rev. Laura Kendrick, *SAC* 23 (2001): 588–92.

369. Stubbs, Estelle, ed. *The Hengwrt Chaucer Digital Facsimile* (*SAC* 25 [2003], no. 19). Rev. Sean Coughlan, *{London} Times Educational Supplement*, May 11, 2001, pp. 20–21.

370. Sturges, Robert S. *Chaucer's Pardoner and Gender Theory: Bodies of*

Discourse (*SAC* 24 [2002], no. 296). Rev. Glenn Burger, *SAC* 23 (2001): 595–98; Catherine S. Cox, *SAQ* 66 (2001): 168–70; Isabel Davis, *Medieval Feminist Forum* 31 (2001): 57–59; M. J. Toswell, *CollL* 28.3 (2001): 155–62.

371. Sweeney, Michelle. *Magic in Medieval Romance from Chrétien de Troyes to Geoffrey Chaucer* (*SAC* 24 [2002], no. 285). Rev. S. Echard, *Arthuriana* 11 (2001): 138–40.

372. Szarmach, Paul E., M. Teresa Tavormina, and Joel T. Rosenthal, eds. *Medieval England: An Encyclopedia* (*SAC* 22 [2000], no. 156). Rev. Julian Wasserman, *SAC* 23 (2001): 598–600.

373. Wallace, David, ed. *The Cambridge History of Medieval English Literature* (*SAC* 23 [2001], no. 124). Rev. Stanley Benfell, *Quidditas* 20 (1999): 261–65; J. A. Burrow, *Speculum* 76 (2001): 243–45; Christine Chism, Theresa Coletti, Anne Savage, Fiona Somerset, and Sarah Stanbury, "Colloquium," *SAC* 23 (2001): 471–519; Diane Watt, *English* 49 (2000): 179–81.

374. Wallace, David. *Chaucerian Polity: Absolutist Lineages and Associated Forms in England and Italy* (*SAC* 21 [1999], no. 155). Rev. Diane Watt, *English* 49 (2000): 177–79.

375. West, Richard. *Chaucer, 1340–1400: The Life and Times of the First English Poet* (*SAC* 24 [2002], no. 13). Rev. Bernard O'Donoghue, *TLS*, Jan. 26, 2001, p. 34.

376. Wheatley, Edward. *Mastering Aesop: Medieval Education, Chaucer, and His Followers* (*SAC* 24 [2002], no. 319). Rev. Jacqueline De Weever, *Arthuriana* 11 (2001): 132–33; John Hill, *Envoi* 9.1 (2000): 88–90; Margaret Connolly, *MÆ* 70 (2001): 335–36.

377. Winstead, Karen, ed. *Chaste Passions: Medieval English Virgin Martyr Legends* (*SAC* 25 [2003], no. 248). Rev. Jacqueline Jenkins, *Arthuriana* 11.2 (2001): 88–90.

378. Wogan-Browne, Jocelyn, Nicholas Watson, Andrew Taylor, and Ruth Evans, eds. *The Idea of the Vernacular: An Anthology of Middle English Literary Theory, 1280–1520* (*SAC* 23 [2001], no. 126). Rev. Kevin Gustafson, *Arthuriana* 11.3 (2001): 148–49; Robert Sturges, *JEGP* 100 (2001): 433–35.

379. Yamamoto, Dorothy. *The Boundaries of the Human in Medieval English Literature* (*SAC* 24 [2002], no. 197). Rev. Julia Boffey, *N&Q* 246 (2001): 171–72; Sally Mapstone, *TLS*, Aug. 4, 2000, p. 25; Lorraine K. Stock, *SAC* 23 (2001): 604–7.

380. Yeager, R. F., ed. *Re-Visioning Gower* (*SAC* 22 [2000], no. 164). Rev. Ann W. Astell, *Arthuriana* 10.2 (2000): 118–20.

Author Index—Bibliography

The New Chaucer Society
Thirteenth International Congress
July 18–21, 2002
University of Colorado at Boulder

THURSDAY, JULY 18

9:00   **Trustees' Meeting**
Center for British Studies

11:00–12:30   **Special Group Meetings**
- Chaucer Studio: Past, Present, Future (Tom Burton): *Koenig*
- NCS Bibliography (Mark Allen): *Koenig*
- Chaucer Encyclopedia (Dan Ransom, H. A. Kelly, Richard New-hauser): *Koenig*
- Langland in Boulder, NEH Group (Joan Baker, Louise Bishop, Thomas Goodman): *Center for British Studies*
- Sources and Analogues Project (Robert Correale): *Koenig*

1:30–2:30   **Opening Meeting** *Hale 270*
Welcome from University of Colorado Hosts; Introductory Remarks from Lisa Kiser, Chair of the Program Committee; Executive Director's Report from Susan Crane; President's Remarks from Helen Cooper

2:30–3:30   **Presidential Address** *Hale 270*
- Helen Cooper (University College, Oxford): "After Chaucer"

4:00–5:30   **Opening Plenary Session** *Hale 270* "Chaucer in the Twentieth Century" NCS Program Committee, Organizer; Derek Brewer, Emmanuel College, chair
- Musical Performance: "From The Prologue to the Canterbury Tales," by John Jeffrey Davis, translated by Anne Prescott; performed by The Rocky Mountain Chorale, Terry Crull, conductor; Chao-Pei Chen, accompanist
- Terry Jones (*Monty Python and the Holy Grail*; Author, *Chaucer's Knight*)
- Jonathan Myerson (Writer/Creator, *The Canterbury Tales*)

9:00–11:00   **Film** *Hale 270*
Screening of selections from Jonathan Myerson's *Canterbury Tales*, with discussion

FRIDAY, JULY 19

9:00–10:30   **Concurrent Sessions I**

Marriage in Chaucerian Fictions *Hale 230*
- Organizer and chair: Glenn Burger (Queens College and Graduate Center, CUNY)
- Emma Lipton (University of Missouri, Columbia): "Married Friendship in the *Franklin's Tale:* A Civic Ideology for Men"
- Kathleen Ashley (University of Southern Maine): "Ideologies of Marriage in Chaucer and Medieval Conduct Books"
- Kathleen Davis (Princeton University): "Warm Wax, Counterfeit Clykets, and Acrobatic Genre in the *Merchant's Tale*"

Chaucer and the English Language *Hale 240*
- Organizer: Marie Borroff (Yale University)
- Chair: Kellie Robertson (University of Pittsburgh)
- Karla Taylor (University of Michigan): "Chaucer the Sociolinguist"
- Elizabeth Allen (University of California, Irvine): "The 'stille wille' and the Unreliable Reader in Chaucer's *Clerk's Tale*"
- Marie Borroff (Yale University): "Verb Tense and Aspect and the Passage of Time in *Troilus and Criseyde*"

Chaucer and Lesser-Known Chaucerians *Humanities 125*
- Organizer: Jill Havens (Baylor University)
- Chair: David Raybin (Eastern Illinois University)
- Nancy Mason Bradbury (Smith College): "Thomas Usk, First Reader of *Troilus*"
- Marion Turner (St. Anne's College, Oxford): "Outdoing Chaucer or Overreaching Himself?: Thomas Usk and *Troilus and Criseyde*"
- Jill Havens (Baylor University): "Clanvowe's Courtly Anxiety: Chaucer's Influence on 'The Boke of Cupide'"

Chaucer and His Readers: Critics, Scholars, Poets *Humanities 1B70*
- Organizer: NCS Program Committee
- Chair: C. David Benson (University of Connecticut)
- Matthew Giancarlo (Yale University): "'Six Hundred Talking Asses': Representations of Parliament in Chaucer, Gower, and After"

- Geoff Gust (University of York): "'Persona' and Personalities: Chaucer the Man and His Critics"

Chaucer in Manuscript and Print *Humanities 1B80*
- Organizer and chair: Alexandra Gillespie (Corpus Christi College, Oxford)
- Satoko Tokunaga (Keio University): "A Typographical Analysis of Caxton's *Canterbury Tales* (c. 1476)"
- Matthew Boyd Goldie (Rider University): "Counseling Counselors: The *Clerk's Tale* in the Fifteenth Century"
- A. S. G. Edwards (University of Victoria, B.C.): "Bodleian Library MS Douce 45: A New Witness to the *Canterbury Tales*"

11:00–12:30   **Concurrent Sessions II**

The *Manciple's Tale* *Hale 240*
- Organizer and chair: Jim Rhodes (Southern Connecticut State University)
- Marianne Børch (University of Southern Denmark)
- John Hines (University of Cardiff)
- Eve Salisbury (Western Michigan University)
- Peter Travis (Dartmouth College)
- Stephanie Trigg (University of Melbourne)

Chaucer and the Natural World
Humanities 1B80
- Organizer and chair: Lisa J. Kiser (Ohio State University)
- Sarah Stanbury (College of the Holy Cross): "Metaphor and Chaucer's Ethics of Nature"
- Gillian Rudd (University of Liverpool): "'Erthe Toc of Erthe': Chaucer and the Revenge of Nature"
- Thomas Goodman (University of Miami): "'A forster was he': Chaucer and the Country of the Courtier"

Chaucer and the Langland Tradition *Hale 230*
- Organizer and chair: Fiona Somerset (University of Western Ontario)
- John M. Bowers (University of Nevada, Las Vegas): "Hoccleve's *Regement of Princes*: Chaucerian Poetry and Langlandian Themes"

- Andrew James Johnston (Freie University): "Chaucer, the *Piers Plowman* Tradition, and the Politics of Literary Ventriloquism"
- Wendy Scase (University of Birmingham): "Chaucer's Other"

Fifteenth-Century Genealogies *Humanities 125*
- Organizer and chair: Ethan Knapp (Ohio State University)
- Charles Blyth: "After Hoccleve"
- Julia Boffey (Queen Mary College, University of London): "Chaucer's Fortune in the 1530s"
- Catherine Sanok (University of Michigan): "English Legends: Fifteenth-Century Hagiography and the Boundaries of National and Christian Identity"

From Image to Illustration *Humanities 1B70*
- Organizers and chairs: Peter Brown (University of Kent, Canterbury) and Corinne Saunders (University of Durham)
- David Fuller (University of Durham): "Illustrations of Chaucer by Blake and Other Eighteenth-Century Artists"
- Deanna Mason (University of Western Ontario): "Beyond Nature: Burne-Jones's Depictions of Geoffrey Chaucer in the Kelmscott Chaucer"
- Elizabeth Scala (University of Texas): "Imag(in)ing the Nun's Priest and His Tale"

12:30–2:00   **Chaucer and Poetry Now** *Koenig*
Pick up your box lunch in Koenig and proceed to the lawn to hear Anselm Hollo, Anne Waldman, Reed Bye, Jeffrey Robinson, and Patrick Pritchett, poet-scholars associated with The Jack Kerouac School of Disembodied Poetics at Naropa University and the University of Colorado, engage in a lively session accounting for Chaucer's legacy to poetry in the twenty-first century.

2:00–4:00   **Concurrent Panels I**

"Swych love of frendes": The Fortunes of Friendship in Chaucer
Humanities 186
- Organizer and chair: Alcuin Blamires (Goldsmiths College, University of London)
- Lawrence Besserman (Hebrew University of Jerusalem)
- Louise Sylvester (King's College, University of London)

- Maria K. Greenwood (University of Paris, VII)
- Neil Cartlidge (University College, Dublin)
- Richard Zeikowitz (University of South Alabama)

Rethinking the *Legend of Good Women* Humanities 180
- Organizer and chair: Carolyn Collette (Mt. Holyoke College)
- Amy Goodwin (Randolph-Macon College)
- Betsy McCormick (Mount San Antonio College)
- Nicola McDonald (University of York)
- Simon Meecham-Jones (Cambridge University)

Teaching Chaucer *Hale 230*
- Organizers and chairs: Dee Dyas (Christianity and Culture, Centre for Medieval Studies, University of York) and Tom Hanks (Baylor University)
- Michael Cervas (Westminster School)
- Kate Crassons (Duke University)
- Julie Nelson Couch (Brown University)
- Michael Calabrese (California State University)
- Donna Dermond (Lewis and Clark College)
- Kurt Haas (Mesa State College)
- D. Thomas Hanks (Baylor University)
- Michelle Sweeney (University of Missouri, Rolla)
- Julian Wasserman (Loyola University)

Chaucerian Aesthetics: Theory, Practice, Pleasure *Hale 240*
- Organizers and chairs: Peggy Knapp (Carnegie-Mellon University) and Stephen Knight (University of Wales, Cardiff)
- John M. Hill (U.S. Naval Academy)
- Peggy Knapp (Carnegie Mellon University)
- Derrick Pitard (Slippery Rock University)
- Dana Symons (University of Rochester)
- Gregory Wilsbacher (University of South Carolina)

Chaucer's Short Poems *Hale 236*
- Organizers and chairs: Elizabeth Robertson (University of Colorado) and Al David (Indiana University)
- Jana Matthews (Duke University)
- Helen Phillips (University of Liverpool)

- Elizabeth Robertson (University of Colorado)
- Al David (Indiana University)
- Judith Kellogg (University of Hawaii)
- Jane Hilberry (Colorado College)
- Bruce Holsinger (University of Colorado)

4:30–6:00   Concurrent Sessions III

Shakespeare's Chaucer *Humanities 186*
- Organizer and chair: Kathryn Lynch (Wellesley College)
- Sherron E. Knopp (Williams College): "Magic and Art in the *Franklin's Tale* and *The Tempest*"
- Martha W. Driver (Pace University): "John Stow's Legacy: Reading Chaucer in Shakespeare's Early Plays"
- Kathryn Jacobs (Texas A&M University, Commerce): "Chaucer Figures on Shakespeare's Stage"

Discourses of Penance, Rhetorics of Confession in Late Medieval England *Hale 240*
- Organizer and chair: Robert Hanning (Columbia University)
- Henry Ansgar Kelly (UCLA): "Penitential Theology and Law in Chaucer's Time"
- Gregory Roper (University of Dallas): "Confessional Rhetoric in Chaucer's Last Tales: Fulfillment and Transformation"
- Elliot Kendall (Worcester College, Oxford): "The Politics of Penance and the Limits of Genius: Gower's Appropriation of Penitential Discourse in the *Confessio Amantis*"

Chaucer and the Restoration/18th Century *Hale 236*
- Organizer: Stefania D'Agata D'Ottavi (University of Macerata)
- Chair: Charlotte Sussman (University of Colorado)
- Betsy Bowden (Rutgers University, Camden): "The Leaders of the Pack: Stothard's Miller, Blake's Squire, and Their Respective Followers"
- Jean Jost (Bradley University): "The Marriage of Heaven and Hell"

Hoccleve and Lydgate *Hale 230*
- Organizer: Nicholas Perkins (Girton College, Cambridge)
- Chair: Jessica Brantley (Yale University)

- Nicholas Perkins (Girton College, Cambridge): "Hoccleve in Conversation with Chaucer"
- James Simpson (Girton College, Cambridge): "'For al my body . . . weieth nat an unce': Empty Poets and Rhetorical Weight in Lydgate's *Churl and the Bird*"
- Maura Nolan (University of Notre Dame): "Virtuous Prolongation: Lydgate's *Canacee*"

"In Forme of Text is Chaunge": Chaucer in the Age of E-Texts
Humanities 180
- Organizer and chair: Josephine Koster (Winthrop University)
- Alan Baragona (Virginia Military Institute)
- Geraldine S. Branca (Merrimack College)
- Barbara Bordelejo (De Montfort University and New York University)
- Thomas J. Farrell (Stetson University)

6:00–8:00 **Reception** *Norlin Library, 3ʳᵈ Floor, Special Collections,* accompanying the exhibit *Medieval Treasures: Books and Manuscripts from the 9ᵗʰ to the 15ᵗʰ Centuries*

9:00–11:00 **Film** *Hale 270* Screening of Powell/Pressburger, *A Canterbury Tale* (1944)

SATURDAY, JULY 20

9:00–10:30 **Concurrent Sessions IV**

Chaucer and Romanticism *Humanities 125*
- Organizer and chair: David Matthews (University of Newcastle)
- John Ganim (University of California, Riverside): "The Monster's Tale: Chaucer, *Frankenstein*, and the Family Romance"
- Robert J. Meyer-Lee (Rhodes College): "Wordsworth's Affective Piety"
- Michael Alexander (University of St. Andrews): "Chaucer chez Scott"

Tradition and the Individual Talent: Women's Writing After Chaucer *Hale 230*
- Organizer: Theresa Coletti (University of Maryland)
- Chair and respondent: Claire Waters (University of California, Davis)

- Ashby Kinch (Christopher Newport University): "'A Woman Can and Dar as Well as He': Chaucerian Imitation and the Female Voices of the Findern Lyrics"
- Theresa Coletti (University of Maryland): "Paths of Long Study: Reading Chaucer and Christine de Pizan in Tandem"
- Thomas Hahn (University of Rochester): "Chaucer's Sister: Gender, Language, and Literary Ambition in the Vernacular Culture of the Late Middle Ages"

Chaucer and the Dream Vision *Hale 240*
- Organizer and chair: Helen Phillips (University of Liverpool)
- Ruth Evans (Cardiff University): "Remembering White"
- Michael Sharp (SUNY-Binghamton): "The Post-Chaucerian Palinode: Visions of Tyranny in Early Modern Scotland"

Chaucer and the New Media *Humanities 1B80*
- Organizer and chair: Toshiyuki Takamiya (Keio University)
- Peter Robinson (De Montfort University): "The Canterbury Tales Project, Past, Present, Future"
- Graham Caie (University of Glasgow): "Digitization of the Romaunt of the Rose Manuscript"
- Mari Tomioka (Keio University): "Towards Digital Collation: The Case of the Gutenberg Bible"

11:00–12:30   **Concurrent Sessions V**

Chaucer and the Victorians *Humanities 1B80*
- Organizer: Lee Patterson (Yale University)
- Chair: Traugott Lawler (Yale University)
- Velma Bourgeois Richmond (Holy Names College): "Visual Representations of Chaucer in the Victorian Age"
- Judith L. Fisher (Trinity University) and Mark Allen (University of Texas, San Antonio): "Illustrating Chaucer Between Blake and the Kelmscott Chaucer"
- Vincent Lankewish (Pennsylvania State University): "Ruskin's Good Women"

Chaucer's Life and Afterlife *Humanities 125*
- Organizer and chair: Sarah Kelen (Nebraska Wesleyan University)
- Kellie Robertson (University of Pittsburgh): "Chaucer, Nineteenth-Century Anti-Capitalist?"

- Sarah Kelen: "Courting Chaucer"
- Miceál Vaughan (University of Washington): "Personal Politics and Gascoigne's Account of Chaucer's Death"

Advise and Consent: Marital and Theological Debate in Chaucer's Works *Hale 240*
- Organizer: NCS Program Committee
- Chair: Ann Dobyns (University of Denver)
- Susanna Fein (Kent State University): "Marriage with a Twist in the *Merchant's Tale*"
- R. James Goldstein (Auburn University): "Chaucer, Anti-Pelagianism, and the Theology of Christian Perfection"
- Louise Bishop (University of Oregon): " 'A lady's "verily" is as potent as a lord's': Counsel and Contraries in the *Tale of Melibee* and *The Winter's Tale*"

Translating Chaucer: Coghill and After *Humanities 1B70*
- Organizer and chair: Steve Ellis (University of Birmingham)
- Dolores Cullen (Claremont College): "A Devoted Reader Looks at Modern Chaucer"
- Susan Yager (Iowa State University): " 'I speke in prose': Lumiansky's Translation of Chaucer"
- Ebbe Klitgård (Roskilde University): "Chaucer in Modern English and Danish: Context, Reception, Comparison"

Religious Poetry After Chaucer: 15ᵗʰ–17ᵗʰ Centuries *Hale 230*
- Organizer and chair: Catherine Sanok (University of Michigan)
- Jennifer E. Bryan (Oberlin College): "(Female) Religious Subjectivity after Chaucer: Hoccleve's 'Complaint of the Virgin' "
- Seeta Chaganti (University of California, Davis): "Image, Bracelet, Crown: Politicizing Devotional Artifacts in Early Modern English Poetry"
- Fiona Somerset (University of Western Ontario): "Lydgate as Hagiographer, Again"

1:30–2:30 **Biennial Chaucer Lecture** Humanities 1B50
- Richard Firth Green (University of Western Ontario/Ohio State University): "Changing Chaucer"

557

SUNDAY, JULY 21

9:00–10:30   Concurrent Sessions VI

Chaucer's War *Hale 240*

- Organizer and chair: Andrew Lynch (University of Western Australia)
- Nancy Bradley Warren (Utah State University): "Women and War: The *Knight's Tale*, the *Legend of Good Women*, and Fourteenth-Century Politics"
- Patricia DeMarco (Ohio Wesleyan University): "'My shame for to venge': Private Warfare in the *Tale of Melibee*"

Chaucer and Spenser *Humanities 1B70*

- Organizer and chair: Craig Berry
- Judith H. Anderson (Indiana University): "Irony in Chaucer and Spenser"
- Glenn A. Steinberg (College of New Jersey): "Chaucer's Mute-ability in Spenser's *Mutabilitie Cantos*"
- Mark Rasmussen (Centre College): "Spenser, the *Franklin's Tale*, and Complaint"

Speaking in Tongues: Allegory, Language and the Marvelous in Chaucer—and After *Humanities 125*

- Organizer: NCS Program Committee
- Chair: Gila Aloni (Hunter College)
- Corinne Saunders (University of Durham): "Beyond Nature: Magic and Enchantment in Chaucer and After"
- Mark Sherman (Rhode Island School of Design): "Dante's Topazio, Chaucer's Thopas: Problems of Spenserian Genealogy"

Chaucerian Theologies *Hale 230*

- Organizer: Alastair Minnis (University of York)
- Chair: Alan J. Fletcher (University College, Dublin)
- Alastair Minnis (University of York): "Reclaiming the Pardoners"
- Nicholas Watson (Harvard University): "Chaucer's Churchmanship: High, Low, or Broad?"
- Alan J. Fletcher: "Chaucer the Heretic"

Chaucer and Modernism *Humanities 1B80*
- Organizer and chair: Stephanie Trigg (University of Melbourne)
- Andrew Cole (University of Georgia): "Make it Chaucer!: New Medievalism and New Modernity"
- Rebecca Beal (University of Scranton): "Reading Chaucer's Endings: A Modernist Lens?"
- Thomas A. Prendergast (College of Wooster): "Genius, Pathology, and the Disembodiment of Chaucer"

10:45–12:00   Brunch and Closing Plenary Session *Hale 270*
- Chair: Helen Cooper (University College, Oxford)
- Derek Pearsall (Harvard University): "Chaucer and After"

INDEX